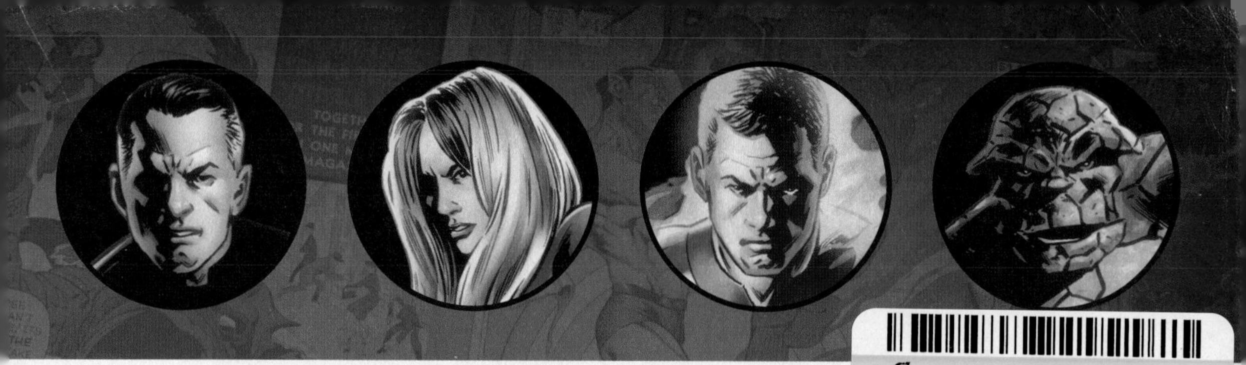

"MY ENEMY, MY SON!"
FROM *Fantastic Four #384*
(JANUARY 1994)
WRITER: **Tom DeFalco & Paul Ryan**
PENCILER: **Paul Ryan**
INKER: **Danny Bulanadi**
COLORS: **Gina Going**
LETTERER: **Richard Starkings & Jason Levine**
EDITOR: **Ralph Macchio**

"A CLEAR & PRESENT DANGER"
FROM *Fantastic Four #42*
(JUNE 2001)
PLOT: **Carlos Pacheco & Rafael Marin**
SCRIPT: **Jeph Loeb**
PENCILER: **Stuart Immonen**
INKER: **Wade Von Grawbadger**
COLORS: **Liquid! Graphics**
LETTERER: **David Sharpe**
EDITOR: **Bobbie Chase**

"RECONSTRUCTION: CHAPTER ONE – FROM THE RIDICULOUS TO THE SUBLIME"
FROM *Fantastic Four #544*
(MARCH 2007)
WRITER: **Dwayne McDuffie**
PENCILER: **Paul Pelletier**
INKER: **Rick Magyar**
COLORS: **Paul Mounts**
LETTERER: **Rus Wooton**
EDITOR: **Tom Brevoort**

FRONT COVER ART:
Steve Epting & Paul Mounts
BACK COVER ART: **Michael Turner & Peter Steigerwald**

COLLECTION EDITOR:
Mark D. Beazley
EDITORIAL ASSISTANTS:
James Emmett & Joe Hochstein
ASSISTANT EDITORS:
Nelson Ribeiro & Alex Starbuck
EDITOR, SPECIAL PROJECTS:
Jennifer Grünwald
SENIOR EDITOR, SPECIAL PROJECTS:
Jeff Youngquist
SENIOR VICE PRESIDENT OF SALES:
David Gabriel

RESEARCH:
Jeph York
PRODUCTION:
Ryan Devall
BOOK DESIGNER:
Rodolfo Muraguchi

EDITOR IN CHIEF:
Axel Alonso
CHIEF CREATIVE OFFICER:
Joe Quesada
PUBLISHER:
Dan Buckley
EXECUTIVE PRODUCER:
Alan Fine

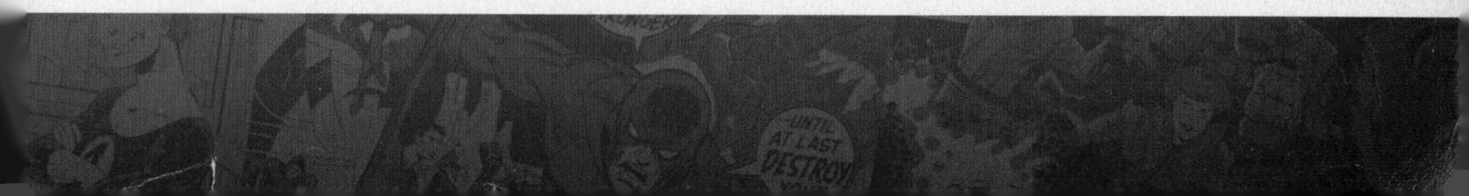

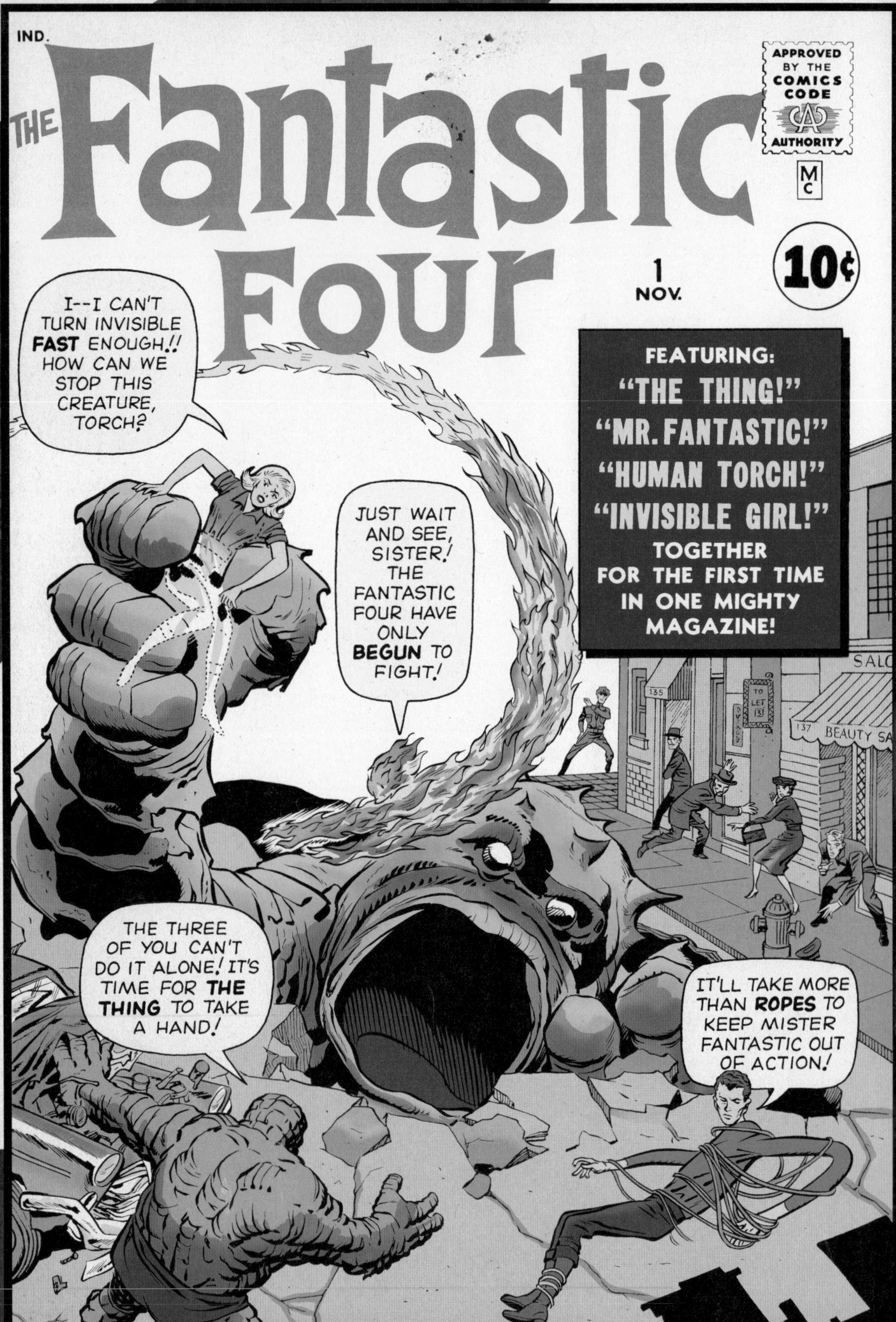

IND.
THE Fantastic FOUR
APPROVED BY THE COMICS CODE AUTHORITY
MC
1 NOV.
10¢
I--I CAN'T TURN INVISIBLE FAST ENOUGH!! HOW CAN WE STOP THIS CREATURE, TORCH?
FEATURING: "THE THING!" "MR. FANTASTIC!" "HUMAN TORCH!" "INVISIBLE GIRL!" TOGETHER FOR THE FIRST TIME IN ONE MIGHTY MAGAZINE!
JUST WAIT AND SEE, SISTER! THE FANTASTIC FOUR HAVE ONLY BEGUN TO FIGHT!
135
TO LET
137 BEAUTY SA
THE THREE OF YOU CAN'T DO IT ALONE! IT'S TIME FOR THE THING TO TAKE A HAND!
IT'LL TAKE MORE THAN ROPES TO KEEP MISTER FANTASTIC OUT OF ACTION!

FANTASTIC FOUR

EXTENDED FAMILY

FANTASTIC FOUR
EXTENDED FAMILY

"THE FANTASTIC FOUR!"
FROM *Fantastic Four #1*
(NOVEMBER 1961)
WRITER: **Stan Lee**
PENCILER: **Jack Kirby**
LETTERER: **Art Simek**

"ENTER — THE EXQUISITE ELEMENTAL"
FROM *Fantastic Four #81*
(DECEMBER 1968)
WRITER: **Stan Lee**
PENCILER: **Jack Kirby**
INKER: **Joe Sinnott**
LETTERER: **Art Simek**

"OMEGA THE ULTIMATE ENEMY"
FROM *Fantastic Four #132*
(MARCH 1973)
WRITER: **Roy Thomas**
PENCILER: **John Buscema**
INKER: **Joe Sinnott**
COLORS: **Petra Goldberg**
LETTERER: **John Costanza**

"WHERE HAVE ALL THE POWERS GONE?"
FROM *Fantastic Four #168*
(MARCH 1976)
WRITER: **Roy Thomas**
BREAKDOWNS: **Rich Buckler**
FINISHED ART: **Joe Sinnott**
COLORS: **Phil Rachelson**
LETTERER: **Joe Rosen**

"THE HOUSE THAT REED BUILT"
FROM *Fantastic Four #265*
(APRIL 1984)
WRITER & ARTIST: **John Byrne**
COLORS: **Glynis Wein**
LETTERER: **Michael Higgins**
EDITOR: **Bob Budiansky**

"HOME ARE THE HEROES"
FROM *Fantastic Four #265*
(APRIL 1984)
WRITER & ARTIST: **John Byrne**
COLORS: **Glynis Wein**
LETTERER: **Michael Higgins**
EDITOR: **Bob Budiansky**

"GOOD-BYE!"
FROM *Fantastic Four #307*
(OCTOBER 1987)
WRITER: **Steve Englehart**
LAYOUTS: **John Buscema**
FINISHED ART: **Joe Sinnott**
COLORS: **George Roussos**
LETTERER: **John Workman**
EDITOR: **Ralph Macchio**

"BIG TROUBLE ON LITTLE EARTH!"
FROM *Fantastic Four #347*
(DECEMBER 1990)
WRITER: **Walter Simonson**
PENCILER: **Arthur Adams**
INKER: **Art Thibert**
COLORS: **Steve Buccellato**
LETTERER: **Bill Oakley**
EDITOR: **Ralph Macchio**

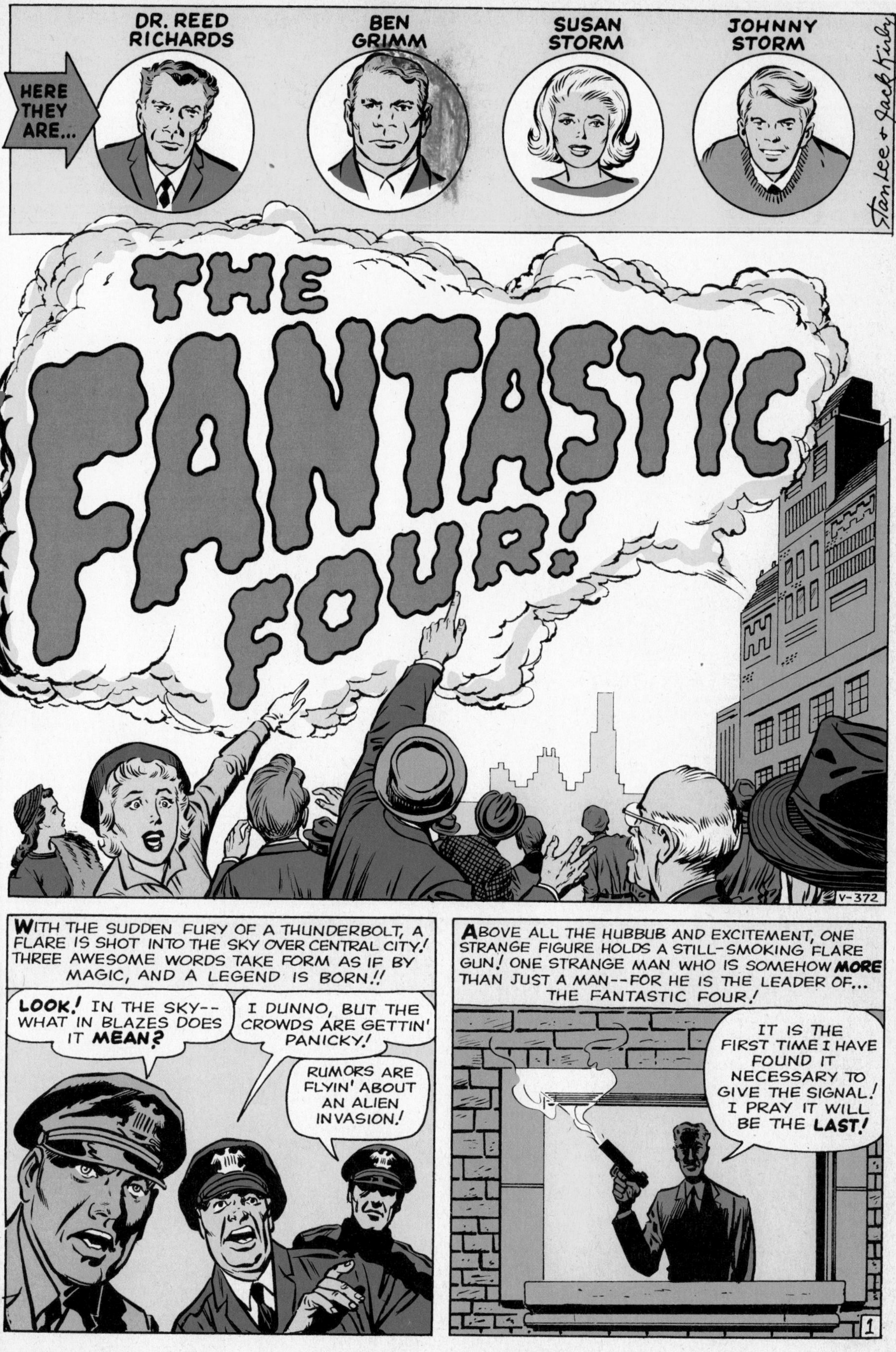
HERE THEY ARE...
DR. REED RICHARDS
BEN GRIMM
SUSAN STORM
JOHNNY STORM
Stan Lee + Jack Kirby
THE FANTASTIC FOUR!
V-372
WITH THE SUDDEN FURY OF A THUNDERBOLT, A FLARE IS SHOT INTO THE SKY OVER CENTRAL CITY! THREE AWESOME WORDS TAKE FORM AS IF BY MAGIC, AND A LEGEND IS BORN!!
LOOK! IN THE SKY-- WHAT IN BLAZES DOES IT MEAN?
I DUNNO, BUT THE CROWDS ARE GETTIN' PANICKY!
RUMORS ARE FLYIN' ABOUT AN ALIEN INVASION!
ABOVE ALL THE HUBBUB AND EXCITEMENT, ONE STRANGE FIGURE HOLDS A STILL-SMOKING FLARE GUN! ONE STRANGE MAN WHO IS SOMEHOW MORE THAN JUST A MAN--FOR HE IS THE LEADER OF... THE FANTASTIC FOUR!
IT IS THE FIRST TIME I HAVE FOUND IT NECESSARY TO GIVE THE SIGNAL! I PRAY IT WILL BE THE LAST!
1

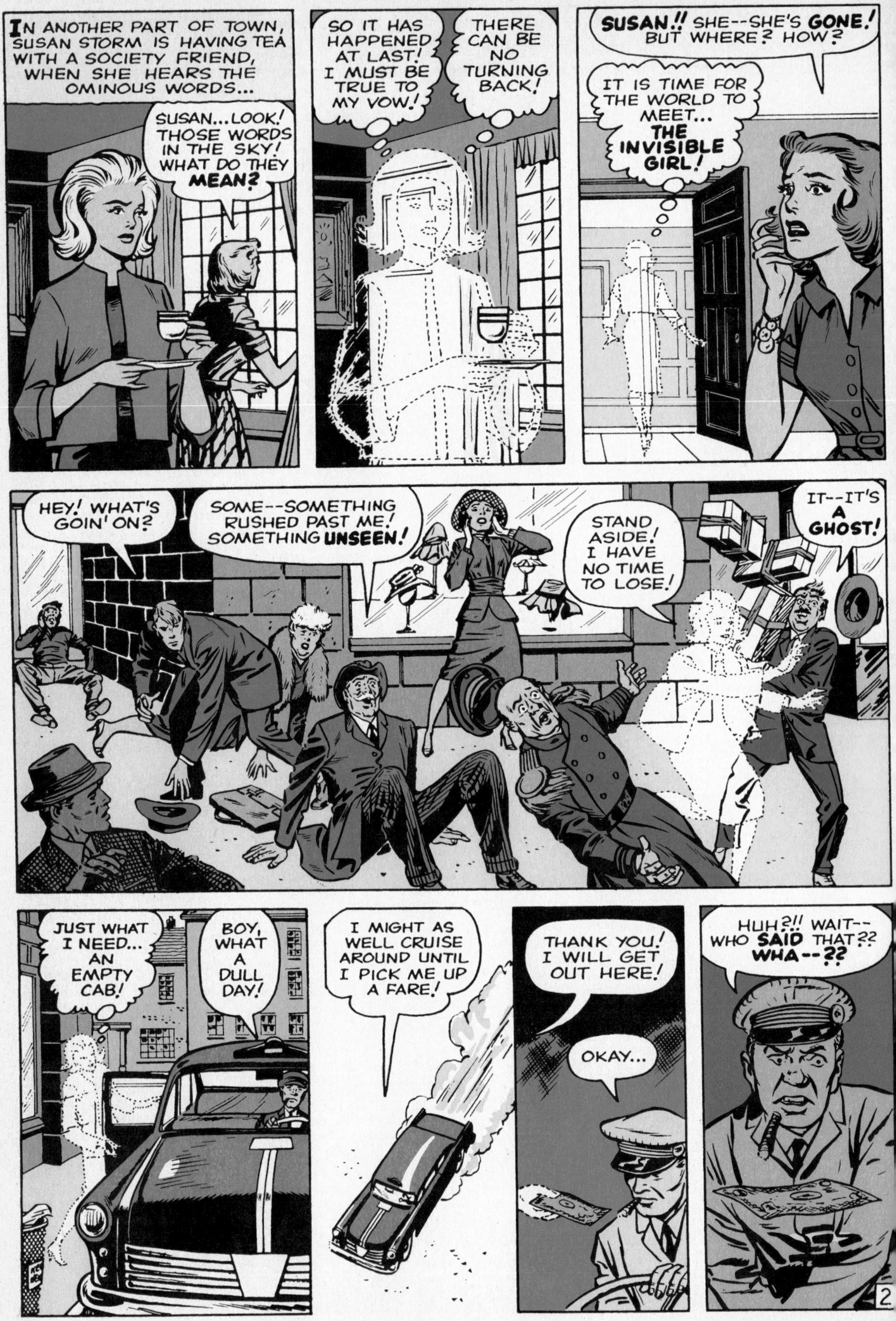
IN ANOTHER PART OF TOWN, SUSAN STORM IS HAVING TEA WITH A SOCIETY FRIEND, WHEN SHE HEARS THE OMINOUS WORDS...
SUSAN...LOOK! THOSE WORDS IN THE SKY! WHAT DO THEY **MEAN?**
SO IT HAS HAPPENED AT LAST! I MUST BE TRUE TO MY VOW!
THERE CAN BE NO TURNING BACK!
SUSAN!! SHE--SHE'S **GONE!** BUT WHERE? HOW?
IT IS TIME FOR THE WORLD TO MEET... **THE INVISIBLE GIRL!**
HEY! WHAT'S GOIN' ON?
SOME--SOMETHING RUSHED PAST ME! SOMETHING **UNSEEN!**
STAND ASIDE! I HAVE NO TIME TO LOSE!
IT--IT'S **A GHOST!**
JUST WHAT I NEED... AN EMPTY CAB!
BOY, WHAT A DULL DAY!
I MIGHT AS WELL CRUISE AROUND UNTIL I PICK ME UP A FARE!
THANK YOU! I WILL GET OUT HERE!
OKAY...
HUH?!! WAIT-- WHO **SAID** THAT?? **WHA--??**
2

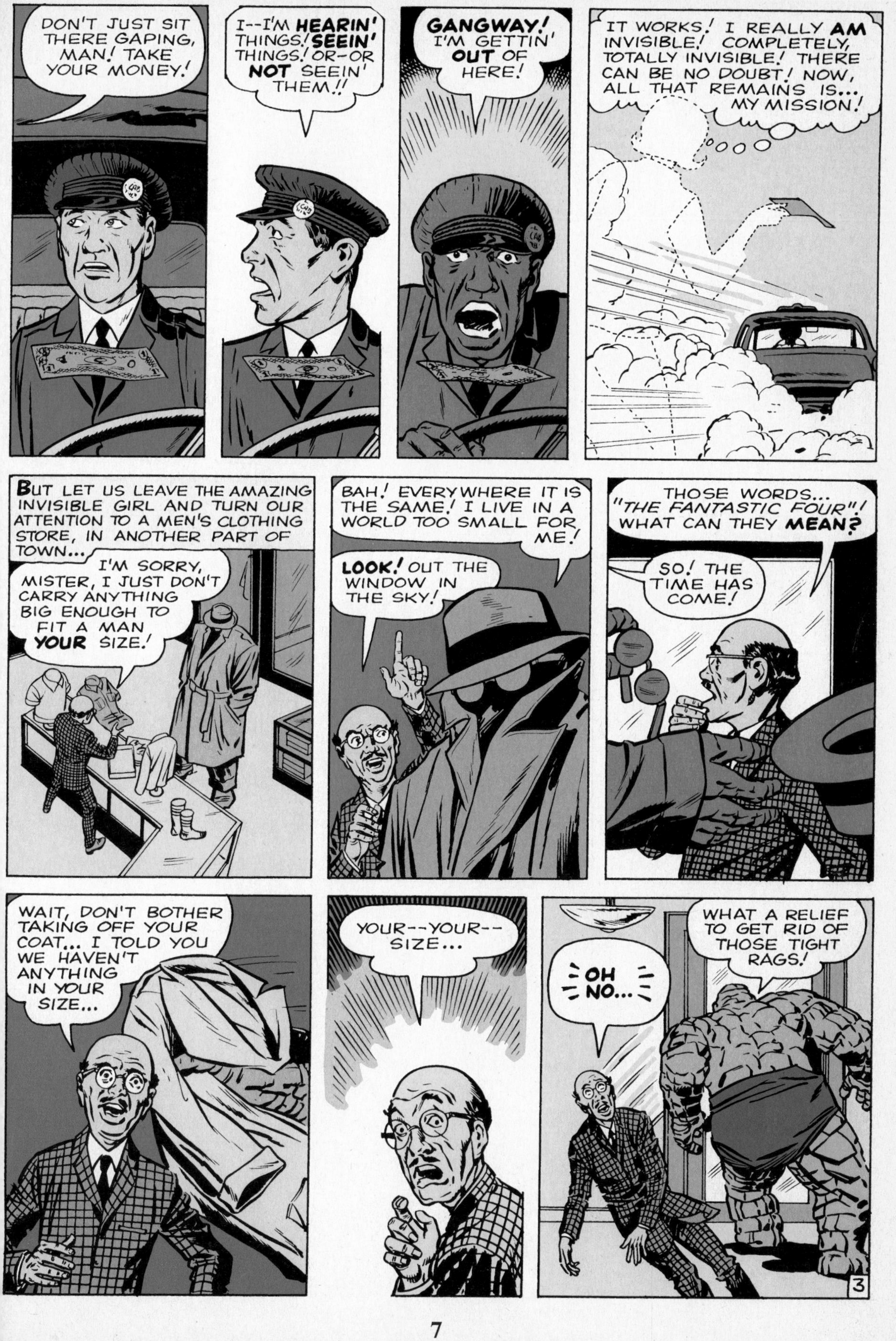
DON'T JUST SIT THERE GAPING, MAN! TAKE YOUR MONEY!
I--I'M HEARIN' THINGS! SEEIN' THINGS! OR--OR NOT SEEIN' THEM!!
GANGWAY! I'M GETTIN' OUT OF HERE!
IT WORKS! I REALLY AM INVISIBLE! COMPLETELY, TOTALLY INVISIBLE! THERE CAN BE NO DOUBT! NOW, ALL THAT REMAINS IS... MY MISSION!
BUT LET US LEAVE THE AMAZING INVISIBLE GIRL AND TURN OUR ATTENTION TO A MEN'S CLOTHING STORE, IN ANOTHER PART OF TOWN...
I'M SORRY, MISTER, I JUST DON'T CARRY ANYTHING BIG ENOUGH TO FIT A MAN YOUR SIZE!
BAH! EVERYWHERE IT IS THE SAME! I LIVE IN A WORLD TOO SMALL FOR ME!
LOOK! OUT THE WINDOW IN THE SKY!
THOSE WORDS... "THE FANTASTIC FOUR"! WHAT CAN THEY MEAN?
SO! THE TIME HAS COME!
WAIT, DON'T BOTHER TAKING OFF YOUR COAT... I TOLD YOU WE HAVEN'T ANYTHING IN YOUR SIZE...
YOUR--YOUR-- SIZE...
WHAT A RELIEF TO GET RID OF THOSE TIGHT RAGS!
OH NO...
3

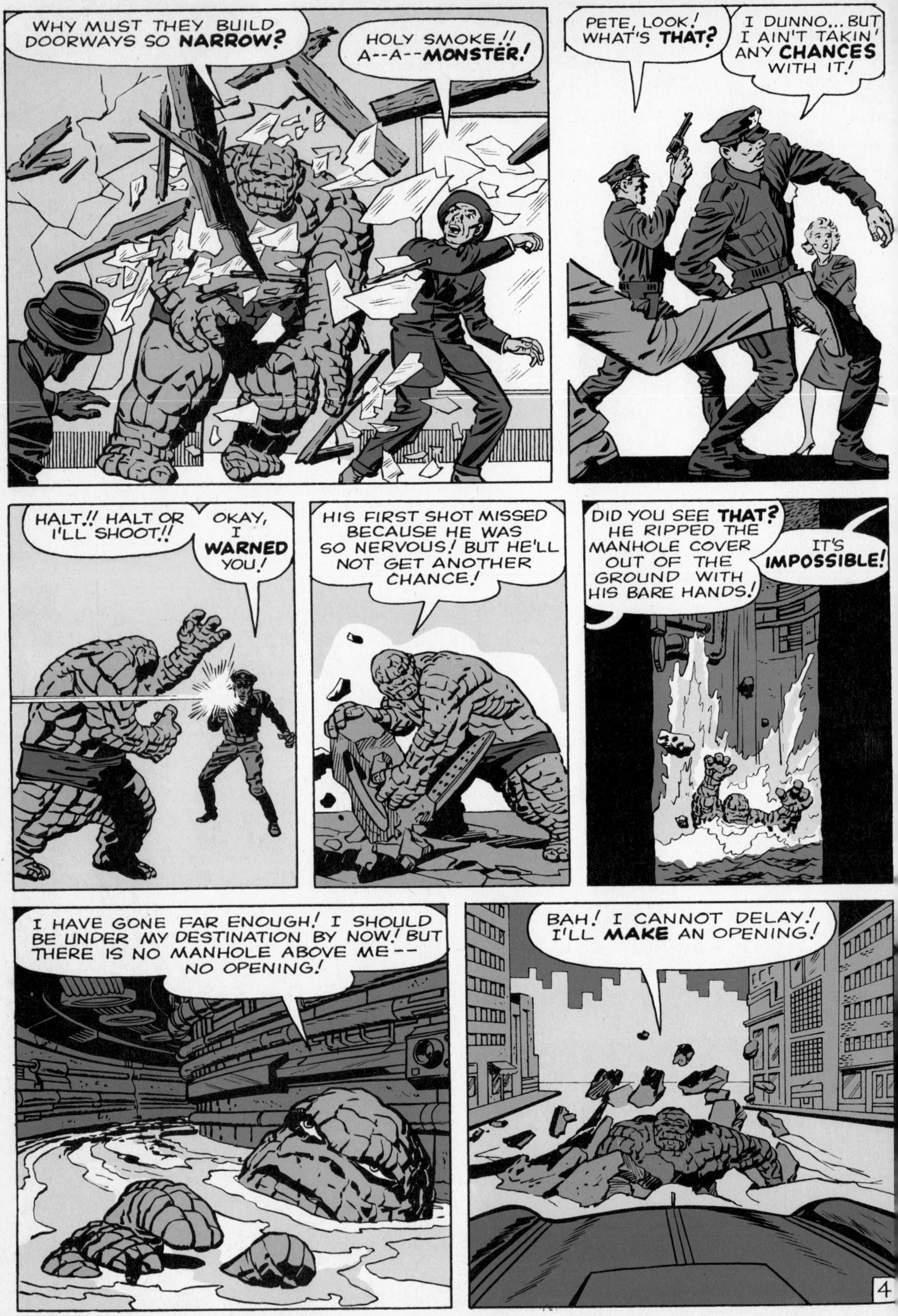
WHY MUST THEY BUILD DOORWAYS SO NARROW?
HOLY SMOKE!! A--A--MONSTER!
PETE, LOOK! WHAT'S THAT?
I DUNNO... BUT I AIN'T TAKIN' ANY CHANCES WITH IT!
HALT!! HALT OR I'LL SHOOT!!
OKAY, I WARNED YOU!
HIS FIRST SHOT MISSED BECAUSE HE WAS SO NERVOUS! BUT HE'LL NOT GET ANOTHER CHANCE!
DID YOU SEE THAT? HE RIPPED THE MANHOLE COVER OUT OF THE GROUND WITH HIS BARE HANDS!
IT'S IMPOSSIBLE!
I HAVE GONE FAR ENOUGH! I SHOULD BE UNDER MY DESTINATION BY NOW! BUT THERE IS NO MANHOLE ABOVE ME -- NO OPENING!
BAH! I CANNOT DELAY! I'LL MAKE AN OPENING!
4

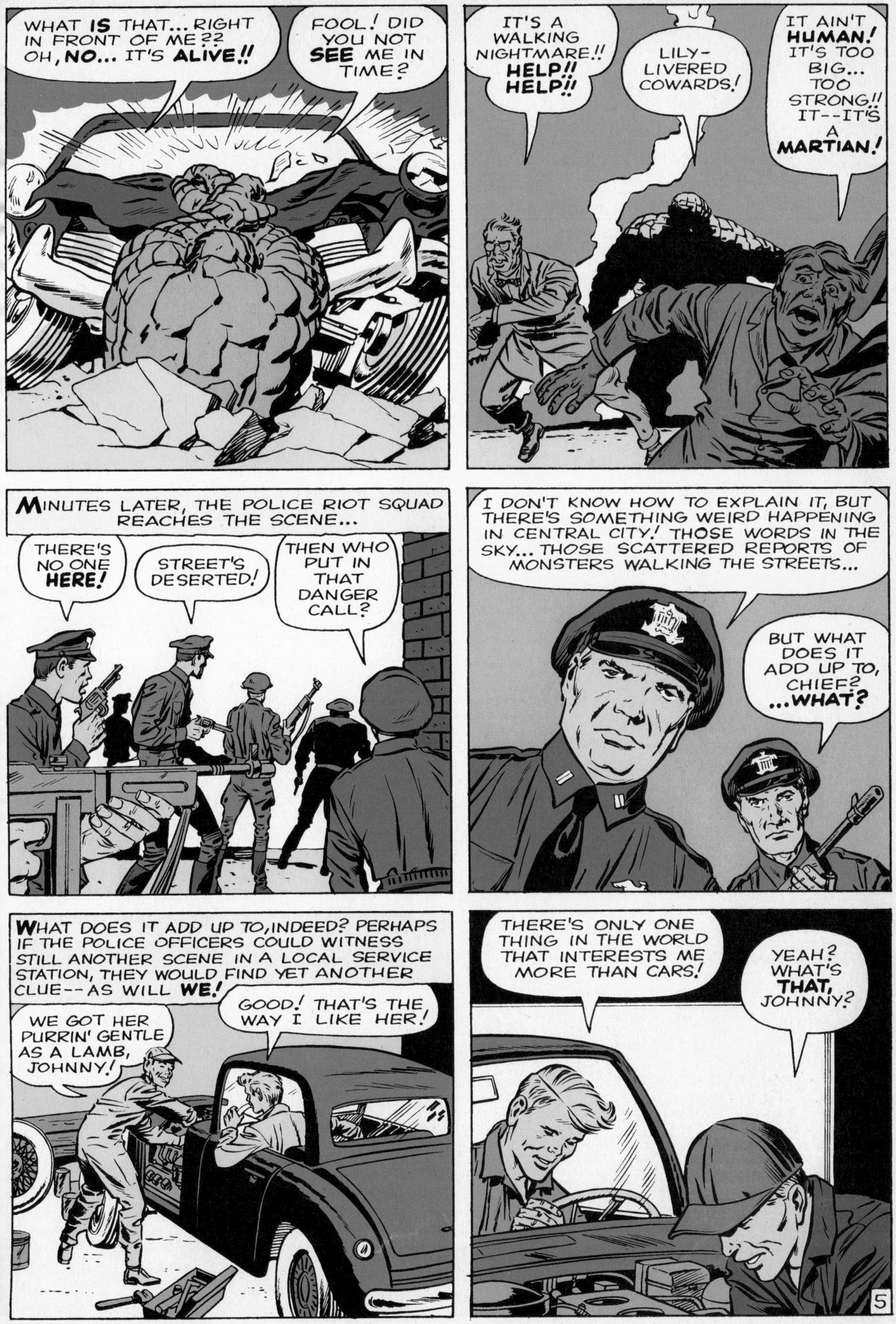
WHAT IS THAT... RIGHT IN FRONT OF ME?? OH, NO... IT'S ALIVE!!
FOOL! DID YOU NOT SEE ME IN TIME?
IT'S A WALKING NIGHTMARE!! HELP!! HELP!!
LILY-LIVERED COWARDS!
IT AIN'T HUMAN! IT'S TOO BIG... TOO STRONG!! IT--IT'S A MARTIAN!
MINUTES LATER, THE POLICE RIOT SQUAD REACHES THE SCENE...
THERE'S NO ONE HERE!
STREET'S DESERTED!
THEN WHO PUT IN THAT DANGER CALL?
I DON'T KNOW HOW TO EXPLAIN IT, BUT THERE'S SOMETHING WEIRD HAPPENING IN CENTRAL CITY! THOSE WORDS IN THE SKY... THOSE SCATTERED REPORTS OF MONSTERS WALKING THE STREETS...
BUT WHAT DOES IT ADD UP TO, CHIEF? ...WHAT?
WHAT DOES IT ADD UP TO, INDEED? PERHAPS IF THE POLICE OFFICERS COULD WITNESS STILL ANOTHER SCENE IN A LOCAL SERVICE STATION, THEY WOULD FIND YET ANOTHER CLUE--AS WILL WE!
WE GOT HER PURRIN' GENTLE AS A LAMB, JOHNNY!
GOOD! THAT'S THE WAY I LIKE HER!
THERE'S ONLY ONE THING IN THE WORLD THAT INTERESTS ME MORE THAN CARS!
YEAH? WHAT'S THAT, JOHNNY?
5

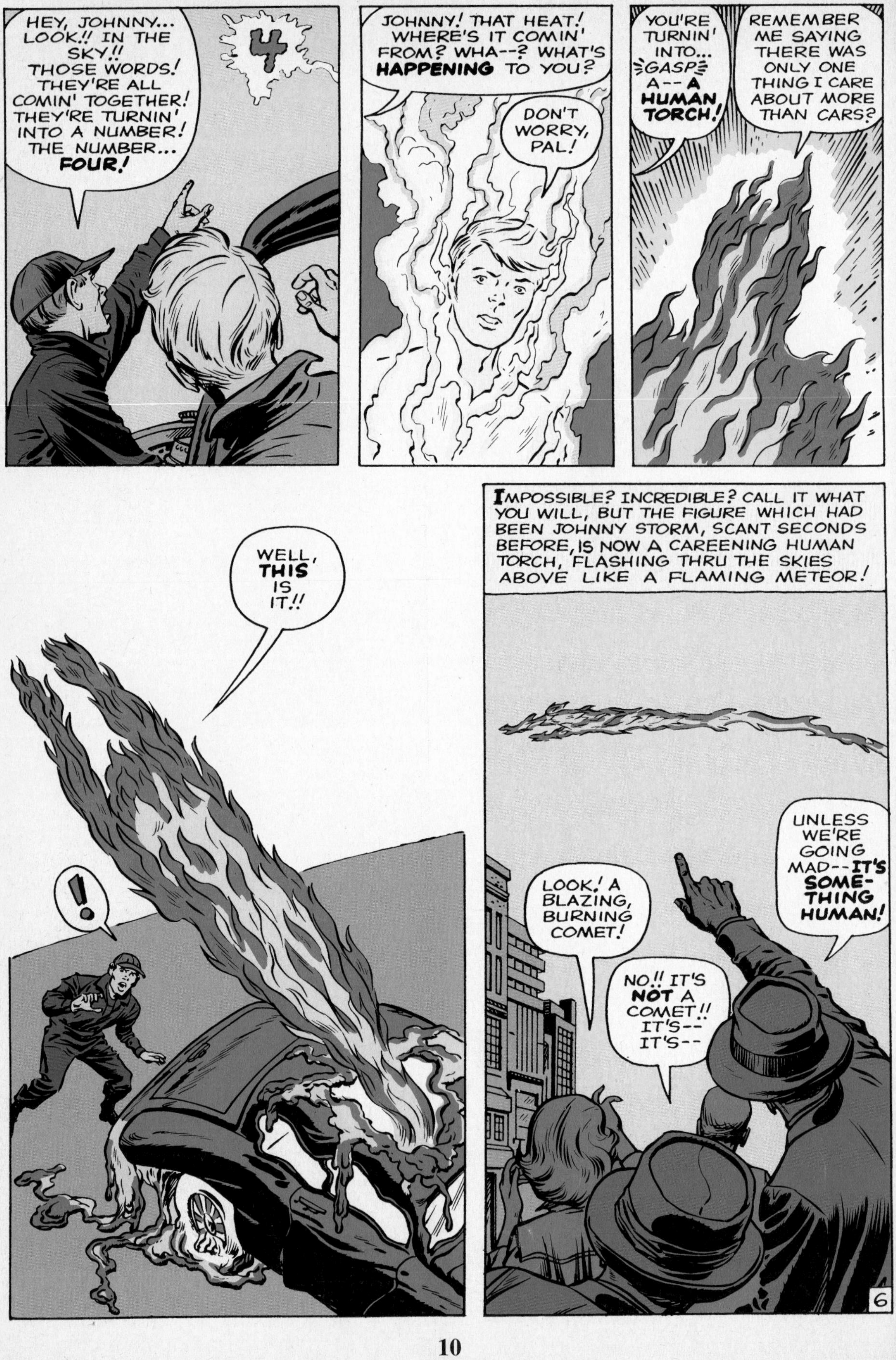
HEY, JOHNNY... LOOK!! IN THE SKY!! THOSE WORDS! THEY'RE ALL COMIN' TOGETHER! THEY'RE TURNIN' INTO A NUMBER! THE NUMBER... **FOUR!**
4
JOHNNY! THAT HEAT! WHERE'S IT COMIN' FROM? WHA--? WHAT'S **HAPPENING** TO YOU?
DON'T WORRY, PAL!
YOU'RE TURNIN' INTO... GASP A-- **A HUMAN TORCH!**
REMEMBER ME SAYING THERE WAS ONLY ONE THING I CARE ABOUT MORE THAN CARS?
WELL, **THIS** IS IT!!
!
IMPOSSIBLE? INCREDIBLE? CALL IT WHAT YOU WILL, BUT THE FIGURE WHICH HAD BEEN JOHNNY STORM, SCANT SECONDS BEFORE, IS NOW A CAREENING HUMAN TORCH, FLASHING THRU THE SKIES ABOVE LIKE A FLAMING METEOR!
LOOK! A BLAZING, BURNING COMET!
NO!! IT'S **NOT** A COMET!! IT'S-- IT'S--
UNLESS WE'RE GOING MAD--**IT'S SOME-THING HUMAN!**
6

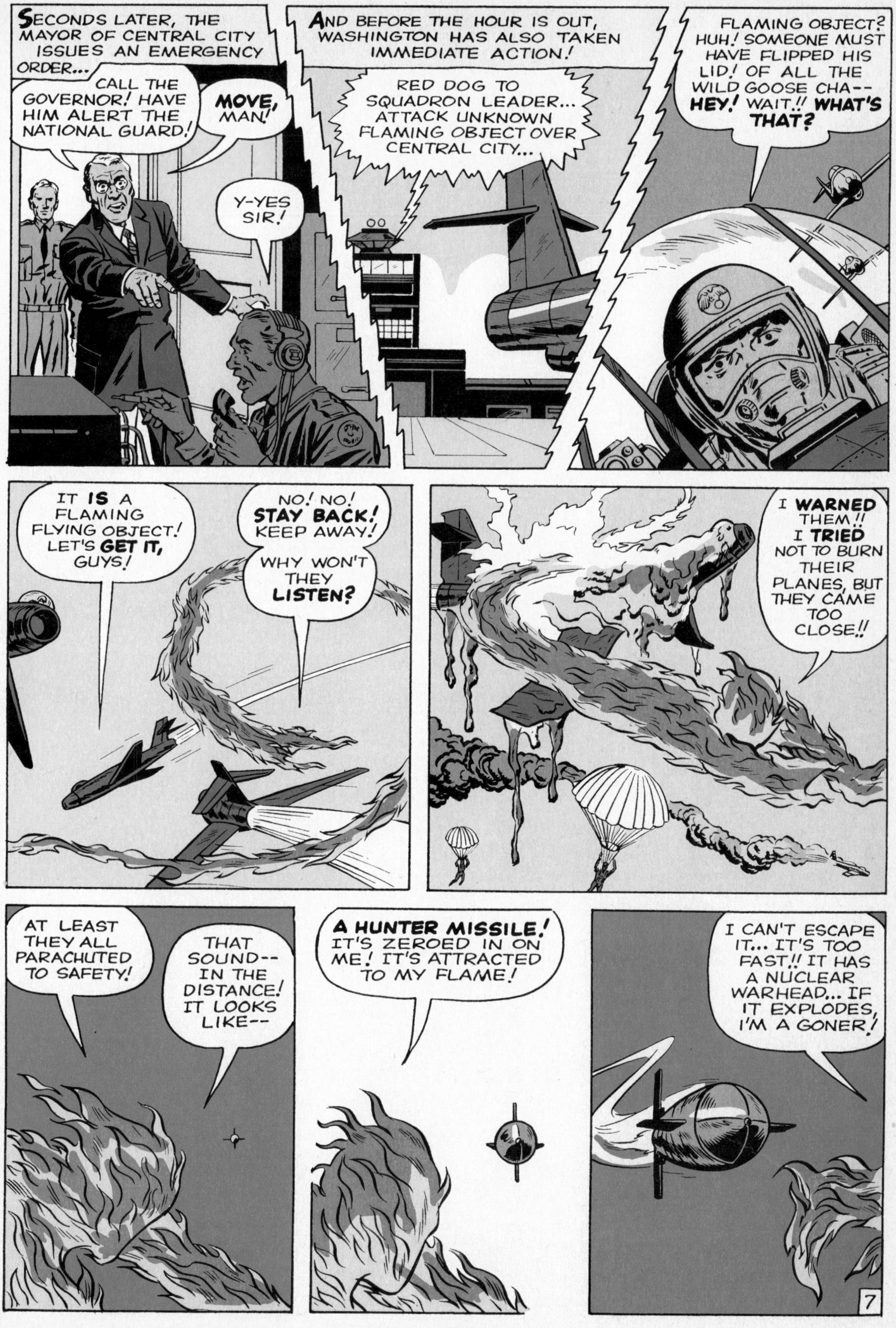
SECONDS LATER, THE MAYOR OF CENTRAL CITY ISSUES AN EMERGENCY ORDER...
CALL THE GOVERNOR! HAVE HIM ALERT THE NATIONAL GUARD!
MOVE, MAN!
Y-YES SIR!
AND BEFORE THE HOUR IS OUT, WASHINGTON HAS ALSO TAKEN IMMEDIATE ACTION!
RED DOG TO SQUADRON LEADER... ATTACK UNKNOWN FLAMING OBJECT OVER CENTRAL CITY...
FLAMING OBJECT? HUH! SOMEONE MUST HAVE FLIPPED HIS LID! OF ALL THE WILD GOOSE CHA-- HEY! WAIT!! WHAT'S THAT?
IT IS A FLAMING FLYING OBJECT! LET'S GET IT, GUYS!
NO! NO! STAY BACK! KEEP AWAY!
WHY WON'T THEY LISTEN?
I WARNED THEM!! I TRIED NOT TO BURN THEIR PLANES, BUT THEY CAME TOO CLOSE!!
AT LEAST THEY ALL PARACHUTED TO SAFETY!
THAT SOUND-- IN THE DISTANCE! IT LOOKS LIKE--
A HUNTER MISSILE! IT'S ZEROED IN ON ME! IT'S ATTRACTED TO MY FLAME!
I CAN'T ESCAPE IT... IT'S TOO FAST!! IT HAS A NUCLEAR WARHEAD... IF IT EXPLODES, I'M A GONER!
7

SUDDENLY, THE HUMAN TORCH'S FLAME BEGINS TO DIMINISH... AND, AS THE MISSILE IS ABOUT TO STRIKE HIM, TWO IMPOSSIBLY LONG ARMS REACH ABOVE THE ROOF-TOPS, AND...

GOT IT!!

MOVING WITH DAZZLING SPEED, ONE OF THE IN-CREDIBLE ARMS HURLS THE MIGHTY MISSILE FAR FROM SHORE, WHERE IT EXPLODES HARMLESSLY OVER THE SEA!

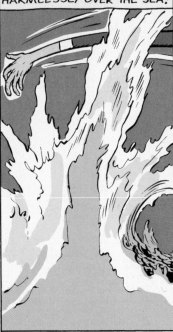

BUT, AS THE FLYING BOY'S FLAME FLICKERS OUT ALTOGETHER, HE BEGINS TO PLUMMET TOWARD EARTH... TOWARD A CERTAIN DOOM!

GRAB ME, JOHNNY BOY!! THAT'S IT.!!

WHO IS THIS UNBELIEVABLE STRANGER WHO HAS SAVED THE HUMAN TORCH?

YOU'RE SAFE NOW, LAD! YOU'RE SAFE.!

IN FACT, WHO ARE ALL FOUR OF THESE STRANGE AND ASTONISHING HUMANS? HOW DID THEY BECOME WHAT THEY ARE? WHAT MYSTIC QUIRK OF FATE BROUGHT THEM TOGETHER, TO FORM THE AWE-INSPIRING GROUP KNOWN AS THE FANTASTIC FOUR??

YOU ALL HEEDED MY SUMMONS.!! GOOD.!! THERE IS A TASK THAT AWAITS US... A FEARFUL TASK!

8

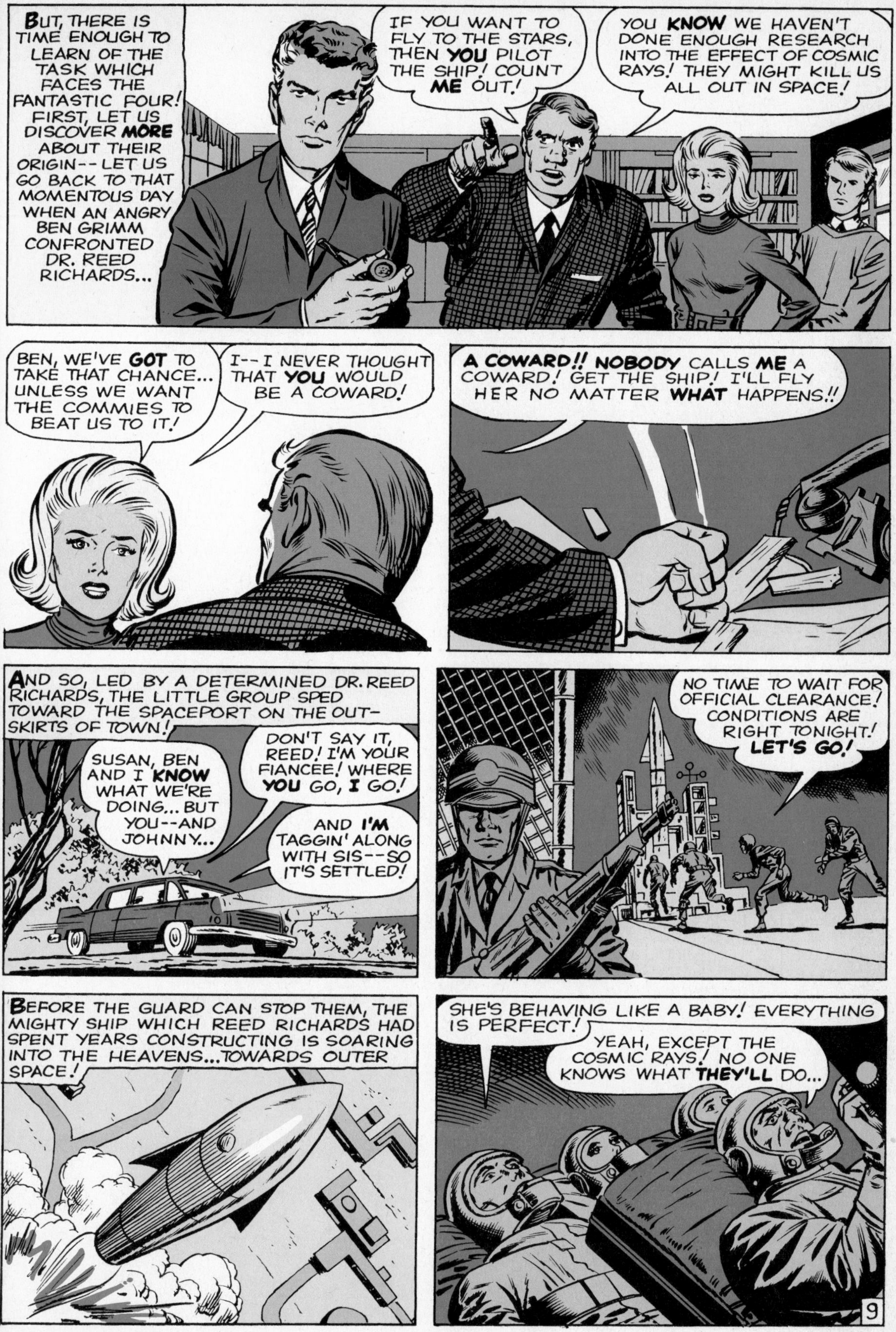
BUT, THERE IS TIME ENOUGH TO LEARN OF THE TASK WHICH FACES THE FANTASTIC FOUR! FIRST, LET US DISCOVER MORE ABOUT THEIR ORIGIN-- LET US GO BACK TO THAT MOMENTOUS DAY WHEN AN ANGRY BEN GRIMM CONFRONTED DR. REED RICHARDS...
IF YOU WANT TO FLY TO THE STARS, THEN YOU PILOT THE SHIP! COUNT ME OUT!
YOU KNOW WE HAVEN'T DONE ENOUGH RESEARCH INTO THE EFFECT OF COSMIC RAYS! THEY MIGHT KILL US ALL OUT IN SPACE!
BEN, WE'VE GOT TO TAKE THAT CHANCE... UNLESS WE WANT THE COMMIES TO BEAT US TO IT!
I-- I NEVER THOUGHT THAT YOU WOULD BE A COWARD!
A COWARD!! NOBODY CALLS ME A COWARD! GET THE SHIP! I'LL FLY HER NO MATTER WHAT HAPPENS!!
AND SO, LED BY A DETERMINED DR. REED RICHARDS, THE LITTLE GROUP SPED TOWARD THE SPACEPORT ON THE OUT-SKIRTS OF TOWN!
SUSAN, BEN AND I KNOW WHAT WE'RE DOING... BUT YOU--AND JOHNNY...
DON'T SAY IT, REED! I'M YOUR FIANCEE! WHERE YOU GO, I GO!
AND I'M TAGGIN' ALONG WITH SIS--SO IT'S SETTLED!
NO TIME TO WAIT FOR OFFICIAL CLEARANCE! CONDITIONS ARE RIGHT TONIGHT! LET'S GO!
BEFORE THE GUARD CAN STOP THEM, THE MIGHTY SHIP WHICH REED RICHARDS HAD SPENT YEARS CONSTRUCTING IS SOARING INTO THE HEAVENS... TOWARDS OUTER SPACE!
SHE'S BEHAVING LIKE A BABY! EVERYTHING IS PERFECT!
YEAH, EXCEPT THE COSMIC RAYS! NO ONE KNOWS WHAT THEY'LL DO...
9

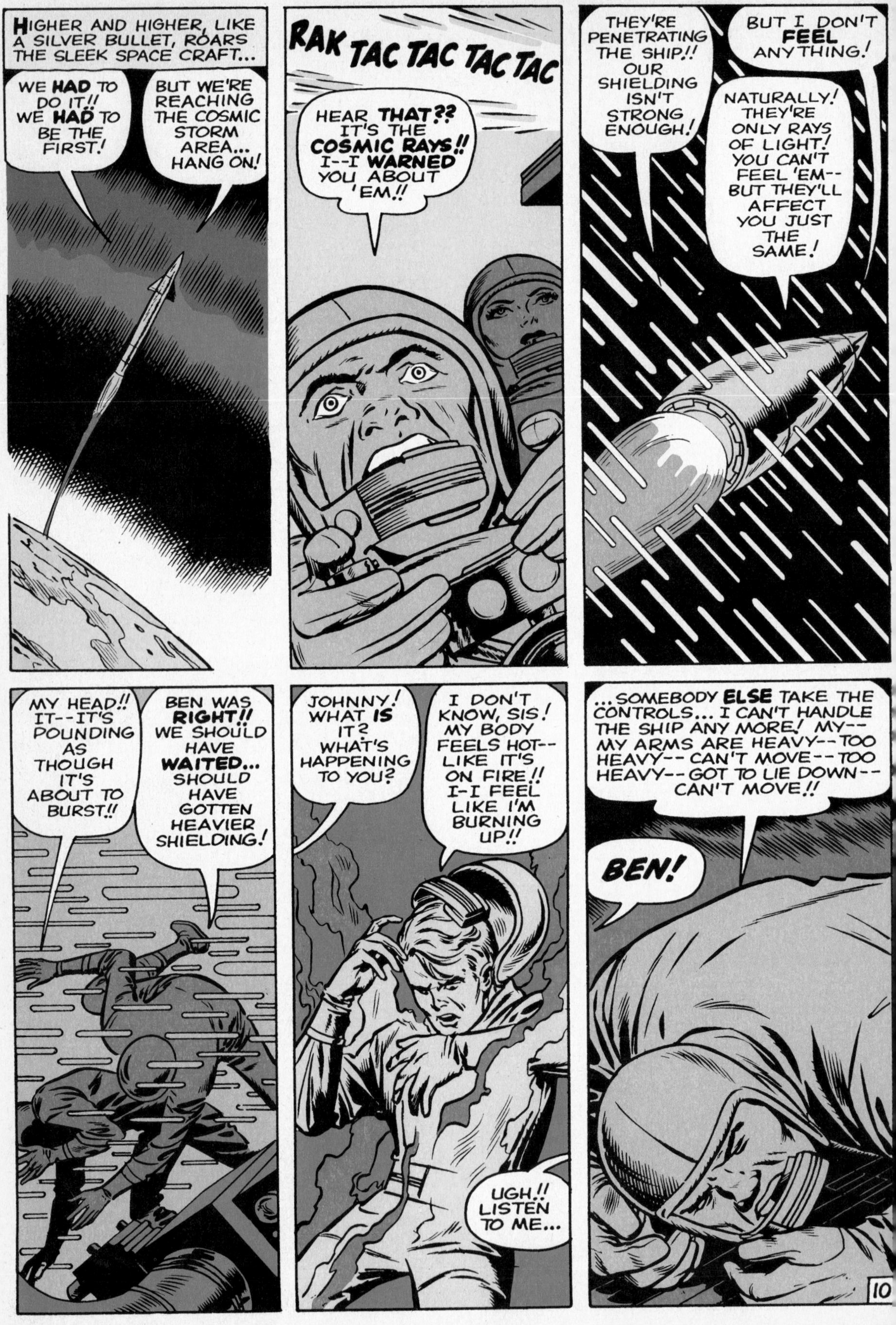
HIGHER AND HIGHER, LIKE A SILVER BULLET, ROARS THE SLEEK SPACE CRAFT...
WE HAD TO DO IT!! WE HAD TO BE THE FIRST!
BUT WE'RE REACHING THE COSMIC STORM AREA... HANG ON!
RAK TAC TAC TAC TAC TAC
HEAR THAT?? IT'S THE COSMIC RAYS!! I--I WARNED YOU ABOUT 'EM!!
THEY'RE PENETRATING THE SHIP!! OUR SHIELDING ISN'T STRONG ENOUGH!
BUT I DON'T FEEL ANYTHING!
NATURALLY! THEY'RE ONLY RAYS OF LIGHT! YOU CAN'T FEEL 'EM-- BUT THEY'LL AFFECT YOU JUST THE SAME!
MY HEAD!! IT--IT'S POUNDING AS THOUGH IT'S ABOUT TO BURST!!
BEN WAS RIGHT!! WE SHOULD HAVE WAITED... SHOULD HAVE GOTTEN HEAVIER SHIELDING!
JOHNNY! WHAT IS IT? WHAT'S HAPPENING TO YOU?
I DON'T KNOW, SIS! MY BODY FEELS HOT-- LIKE IT'S ON FIRE!! I-I FEEL LIKE I'M BURNING UP!!
UGH!! LISTEN TO ME...
...SOMEBODY ELSE TAKE THE CONTROLS... I CAN'T HANDLE THE SHIP ANY MORE! MY-- MY ARMS ARE HEAVY--TOO HEAVY-- CAN'T MOVE--TOO HEAVY--GOT TO LIE DOWN-- CAN'T MOVE!!
BEN!
10

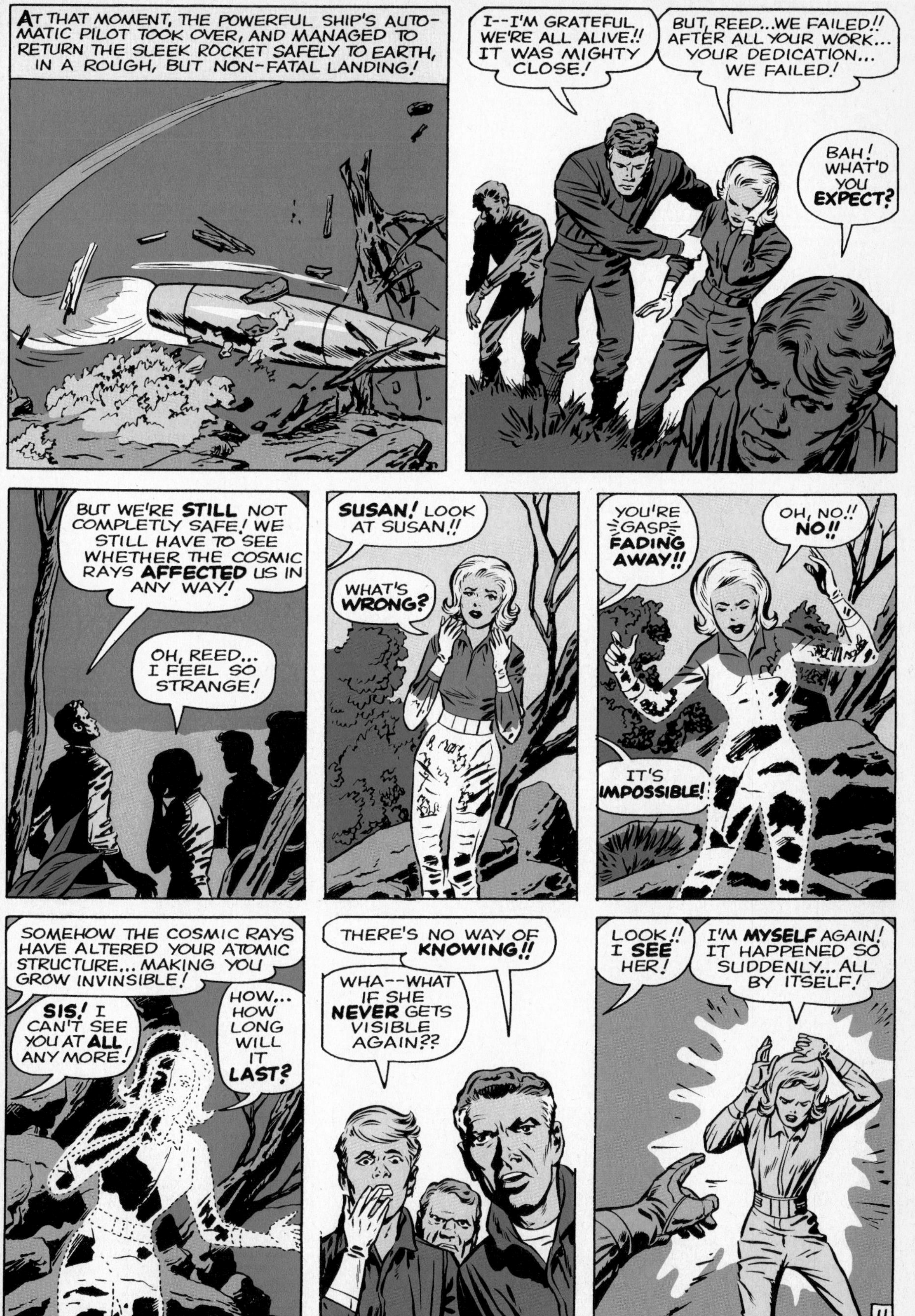
AT THAT MOMENT, THE POWERFUL SHIP'S AUTOMATIC PILOT TOOK OVER, AND MANAGED TO RETURN THE SLEEK ROCKET SAFELY TO EARTH, IN A ROUGH, BUT NON-FATAL LANDING!
I--I'M GRATEFUL WE'RE ALL ALIVE!! IT WAS MIGHTY CLOSE!
BUT, REED...WE FAILED!! AFTER ALL YOUR WORK... YOUR DEDICATION... WE FAILED!
BAH! WHAT'D YOU EXPECT?
BUT WE'RE STILL NOT COMPLETLY SAFE! WE STILL HAVE TO SEE WHETHER THE COSMIC RAYS AFFECTED US IN ANY WAY!
OH, REED... I FEEL SO STRANGE!
SUSAN! LOOK AT SUSAN!!
WHAT'S WRONG?
YOU'RE GASP FADING AWAY!!
OH, NO!! NO!!
IT'S IMPOSSIBLE!
SOMEHOW THE COSMIC RAYS HAVE ALTERED YOUR ATOMIC STRUCTURE...MAKING YOU GROW INVINSIBLE!
SIS! I CAN'T SEE YOU AT ALL ANY MORE!
HOW... HOW LONG WILL IT LAST?
THERE'S NO WAY OF KNOWING!!
WHA--WHAT IF SHE NEVER GETS VISIBLE AGAIN??
LOOK!! I SEE HER!
I'M MYSELF AGAIN! IT HAPPENED SO SUDDENLY...ALL BY ITSELF!
11

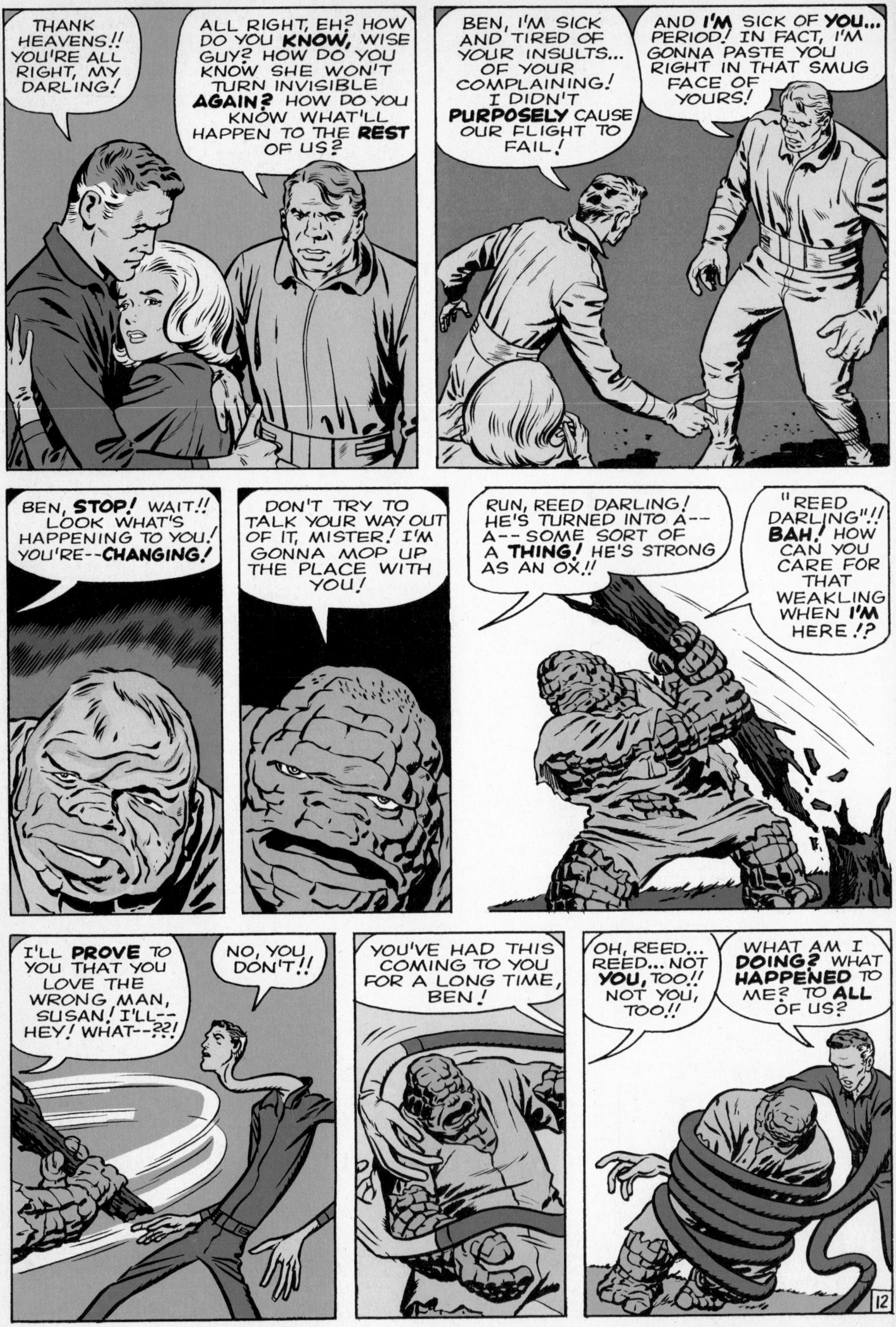
THANK HEAVENS!! YOU'RE ALL RIGHT, MY DARLING!
ALL RIGHT, EH? HOW DO YOU KNOW, WISE GUY? HOW DO YOU KNOW SHE WON'T TURN INVISIBLE AGAIN? HOW DO YOU KNOW WHAT'LL HAPPEN TO THE REST OF US?
BEN, I'M SICK AND TIRED OF YOUR INSULTS... OF YOUR COMPLAINING! I DIDN'T PURPOSELY CAUSE OUR FLIGHT TO FAIL!
AND I'M SICK OF YOU... PERIOD! IN FACT, I'M GONNA PASTE YOU RIGHT IN THAT SMUG FACE OF YOURS!
BEN, STOP! WAIT!! LOOK WHAT'S HAPPENING TO YOU! YOU'RE--CHANGING!
DON'T TRY TO TALK YOUR WAY OUT OF IT, MISTER! I'M GONNA MOP UP THE PLACE WITH YOU!
RUN, REED DARLING! HE'S TURNED INTO A-- A--SOME SORT OF A THING! HE'S STRONG AS AN OX!!
"REED DARLING"!! BAH! HOW CAN YOU CARE FOR THAT WEAKLING WHEN I'M HERE!?
I'LL PROVE TO YOU THAT YOU LOVE THE WRONG MAN, SUSAN! I'LL-- HEY! WHAT--??!
NO, YOU DON'T!!
YOU'VE HAD THIS COMING TO YOU FOR A LONG TIME, BEN!
OH, REED... REED... NOT YOU, TOO!! NOT YOU, TOO!!
WHAT AM I DOING? WHAT HAPPENED TO ME? TO ALL OF US?
12

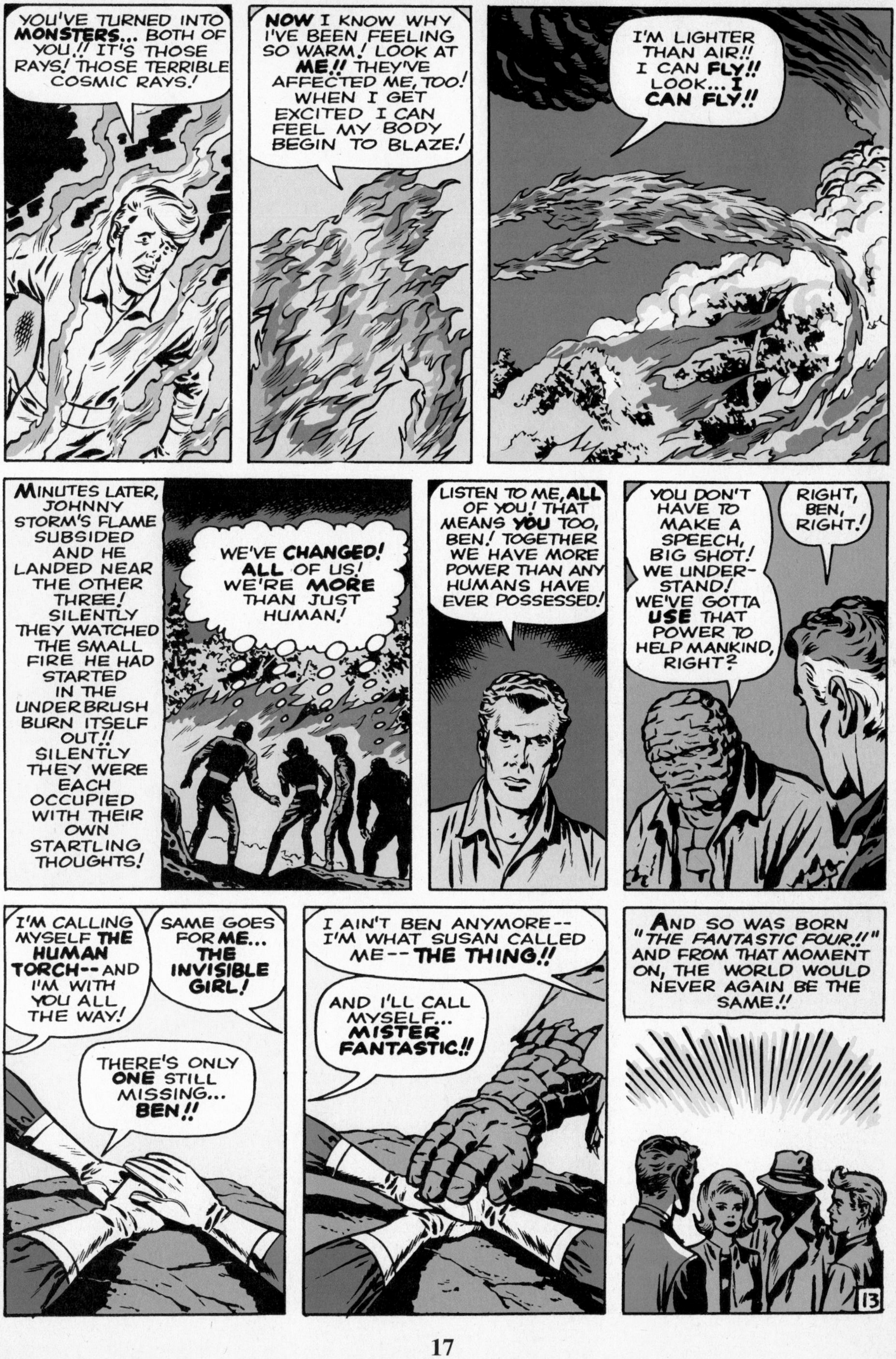
YOU'VE TURNED INTO MONSTERS... BOTH OF YOU!! IT'S THOSE RAYS! THOSE TERRIBLE COSMIC RAYS!
NOW I KNOW WHY I'VE BEEN FEELING SO WARM! LOOK AT ME!! THEY'VE AFFECTED ME, TOO! WHEN I GET EXCITED I CAN FEEL MY BODY BEGIN TO BLAZE!
I'M LIGHTER THAN AIR!! I CAN FLY!! LOOK... I CAN FLY!!
MINUTES LATER, JOHNNY STORM'S FLAME SUBSIDED AND HE LANDED NEAR THE OTHER THREE! SILENTLY THEY WATCHED THE SMALL FIRE HE HAD STARTED IN THE UNDERBRUSH BURN ITSELF OUT!! SILENTLY THEY WERE EACH OCCUPIED WITH THEIR OWN STARTLING THOUGHTS!
WE'VE CHANGED! ALL OF US! WE'RE MORE THAN JUST HUMAN!
LISTEN TO ME, ALL OF YOU! THAT MEANS YOU TOO, BEN! TOGETHER WE HAVE MORE POWER THAN ANY HUMANS HAVE EVER POSSESSED!
YOU DON'T HAVE TO MAKE A SPEECH, BIG SHOT! WE UNDERSTAND! WE'VE GOTTA USE THAT POWER TO HELP MANKIND, RIGHT?
RIGHT, BEN, RIGHT!
I'M CALLING MYSELF THE HUMAN TORCH-- AND I'M WITH YOU ALL THE WAY!
SAME GOES FOR ME... THE INVISIBLE GIRL!
THERE'S ONLY ONE STILL MISSING... BEN!!
I AIN'T BEN ANYMORE-- I'M WHAT SUSAN CALLED ME-- THE THING!!
AND I'LL CALL MYSELF... MISTER FANTASTIC!!
AND SO WAS BORN "THE FANTASTIC FOUR!!" AND FROM THAT MOMENT ON, THE WORLD WOULD NEVER AGAIN BE THE SAME!!
13

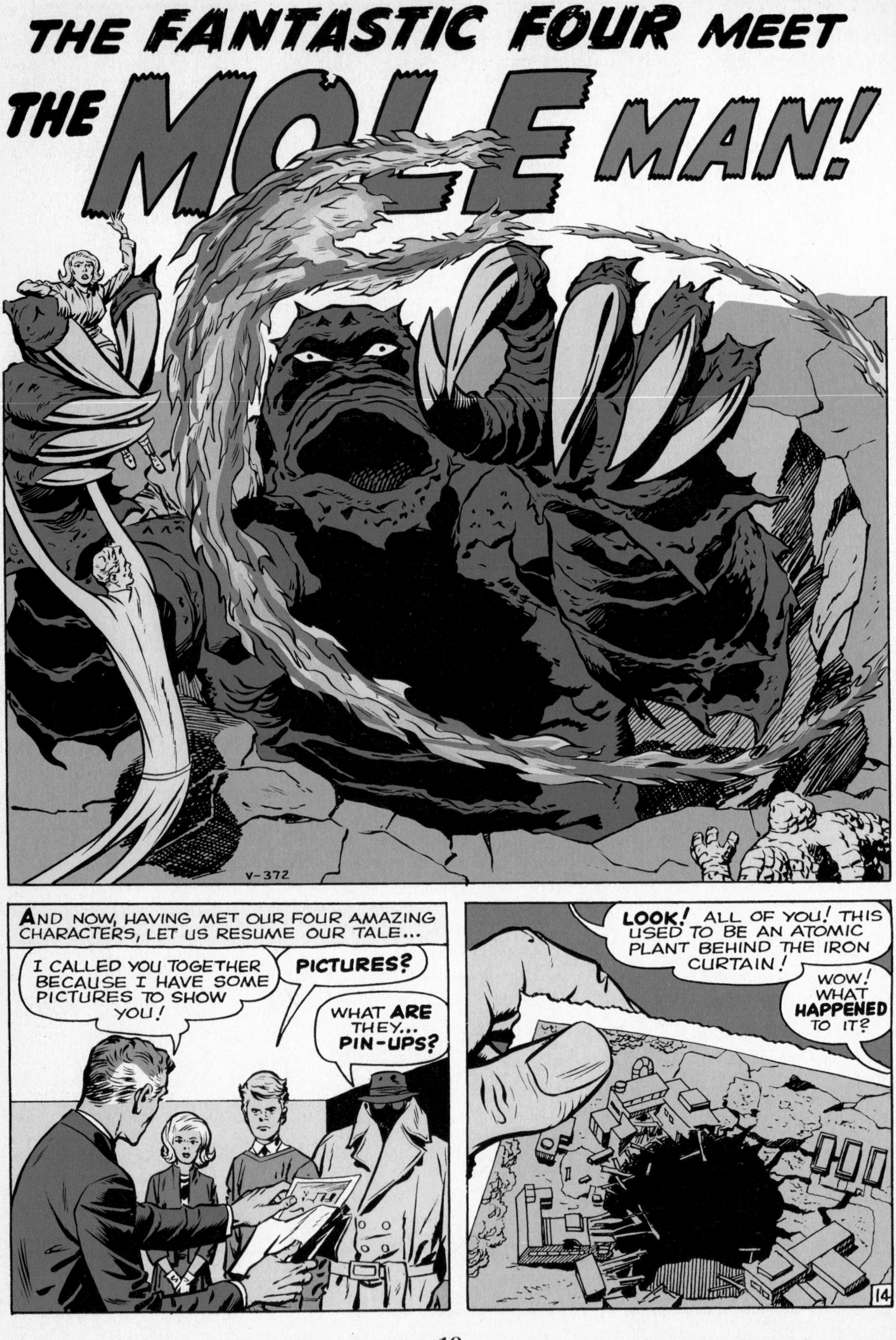
THE FANTASTIC FOUR MEET
THE MOLE MAN!
V-372
AND NOW, HAVING MET OUR FOUR AMAZING CHARACTERS, LET US RESUME OUR TALE...
I CALLED YOU TOGETHER BECAUSE I HAVE SOME PICTURES TO SHOW YOU!
PICTURES?
WHAT ARE THEY... PIN-UPS?
LOOK! ALL OF YOU! THIS USED TO BE AN ATOMIC PLANT BEHIND THE IRON CURTAIN!
WOW! WHAT HAPPENED TO IT?
14

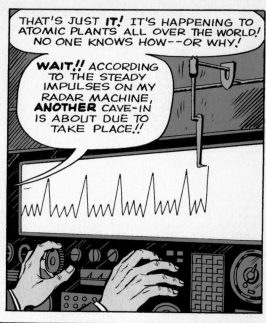

THE SAME THING THAT HAPPENED TO THE **OTHER** ATOMIC PLANTS ON THOSE PHOTOS!

THIS ONE IS IN **AUSTRALIA!**

AND **THIS** IS IN SOUTH AMERICA!

THAT'S JUST **IT!** IT'S HAPPENING TO ATOMIC PLANTS ALL OVER THE WORLD! NO ONE KNOWS HOW--OR WHY!

WAIT!! ACCORDING TO THE STEADY IMPULSES ON MY RADAR MACHINE, **ANOTHER** CAVE-IN IS ABOUT DUE TO TAKE PLACE!!

AND, EVEN AS REED RICHARDS SPEAKS, HALF-WAY AROUND THE WORLD, IN FRENCH AFRICA, THE FOLLOWING SCENE IS TAKING PLACE...

WHAT IS WRONG, PIERRE?

I DO NOT KNOW! IT SOUNDS IN-SANE, BUT THE SAND BENEATH MY FEET SEEMS TO BE **THROBBING!**

...ALMOST AS IF SOMETHING IS **MOVING** BELOW US! ALMOST AS IF... **LISTEN!** DON'T YOU FEEL IT??

RUMBLE RUMBLE

HELP!!

RUMBLE ROAR

IT IS AN **EARTHQUAKE!** BUT HERE IN THE DESERT?? **IMPOSSIBLE!!**

IMPOSSIBLE OR NOT, PIERRÉ ALMOST FELL TO HIS **DOOM!**

WAIT!! THE GROUND IS TREMBLING AGAIN!! WHAT CAN IT BE??

SACRE BLEU!! THE EARTH IS GOING **MAD!!**

ROOOOOMM

15

19

THE ENTIRE INSTALLATION..!! IT--IT IS **CAVING IN!**

RRROOMM

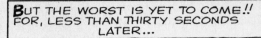

BUT THE WORST IS YET TO COME!! FOR, LESS THAN THIRTY SECONDS LATER...

IN THE NAME OF HEAVEN..!!

WHAT IS **THAT?**

WHAT INDEED?? IT IS A GIGANTIC PAIR OF CLAWS, THE LIKE OF WHICH HAVE NEVER BEEN SEEN ON EARTH, OR ON ANY PLANET IN THE UNIVERSE!! IT IS UNBELIEVABLE... MIND STAGGERING... BUT **REAL!**

ARTILLERY!! BRING THE ARTILLERY!! HURRY! **HURRY!**

ARTILLERY! OF WHAT USE IS ARTILLERY AGAINST A CREATURE WHOSE HIDE IS POWERFUL ENOUGH TO DIG ITS WAY UP THRU COUTLESS TONS OF ROCK-HARD EARTH??

ARTILLERY! OF WHAT USE IS ARTILLERY AGAINST A MONSTER WHO CAN CRUSH A HEAVY TANK WITH ONE HAND??

BUT, JUST AS IT SEEMS THAT NOTHING IN THE WORLD WILL HALT THE NIGHTMARE MENACE, THE SHRILL SOUND OF A COMMANDING VOICE IS HEARD... AND THE GOLIATH STOPS IN ITS TRACKS!

ENOUGH! RETURN TO EARTH'S CORE! OUR MISSION HERE IS FINISHED! **GO!!**

FOR EVEN SUCH A MONSTER HEEDS ITS MASTER! A MASTER KNOWN AS... **THE MOLEMAN!!**

16

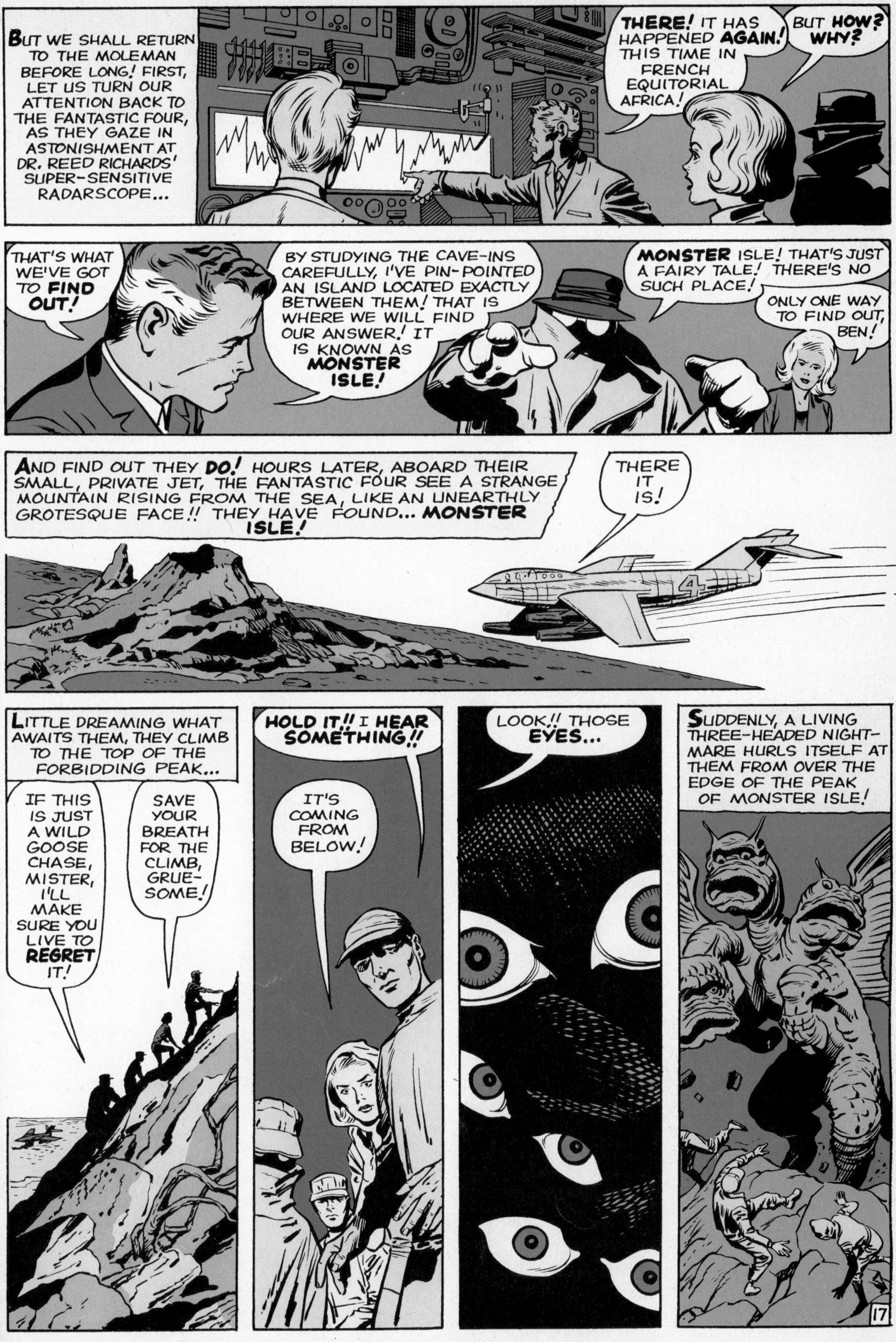
BUT WE SHALL RETURN TO THE MOLEMAN BEFORE LONG! FIRST, LET US TURN OUR ATTENTION BACK TO THE FANTASTIC FOUR, AS THEY GAZE IN ASTONISHMENT AT DR. REED RICHARDS' SUPER-SENSITIVE RADARSCOPE...
THERE! IT HAS HAPPENED AGAIN! THIS TIME IN FRENCH EQUITORIAL AFRICA!
BUT HOW? WHY?
THAT'S WHAT WE'VE GOT TO FIND OUT!
BY STUDYING THE CAVE-INS CAREFULLY, I'VE PIN-POINTED AN ISLAND LOCATED EXACTLY BETWEEN THEM! THAT IS WHERE WE WILL FIND OUR ANSWER! IT IS KNOWN AS MONSTER ISLE!
MONSTER ISLE! THAT'S JUST A FAIRY TALE! THERE'S NO SUCH PLACE!
ONLY ONE WAY TO FIND OUT, BEN!
AND FIND OUT THEY DO! HOURS LATER, ABOARD THEIR SMALL, PRIVATE JET, THE FANTASTIC FOUR SEE A STRANGE MOUNTAIN RISING FROM THE SEA, LIKE AN UNEARTHLY GROTESQUE FACE!! THEY HAVE FOUND... MONSTER ISLE!
THERE IT IS!
4
LITTLE DREAMING WHAT AWAITS THEM, THEY CLIMB TO THE TOP OF THE FORBIDDING PEAK...
IF THIS IS JUST A WILD GOOSE CHASE, MISTER, I'LL MAKE SURE YOU LIVE TO REGRET IT!
SAVE YOUR BREATH FOR THE CLIMB, GRUESOME!
HOLD IT!! I HEAR SOMETHING!!
IT'S COMING FROM BELOW!
LOOK!! THOSE EYES...
SUDDENLY, A LIVING THREE-HEADED NIGHTMARE HURLS ITSELF AT THEM FROM OVER THE EDGE OF THE PEAK OF MONSTER ISLE!
17

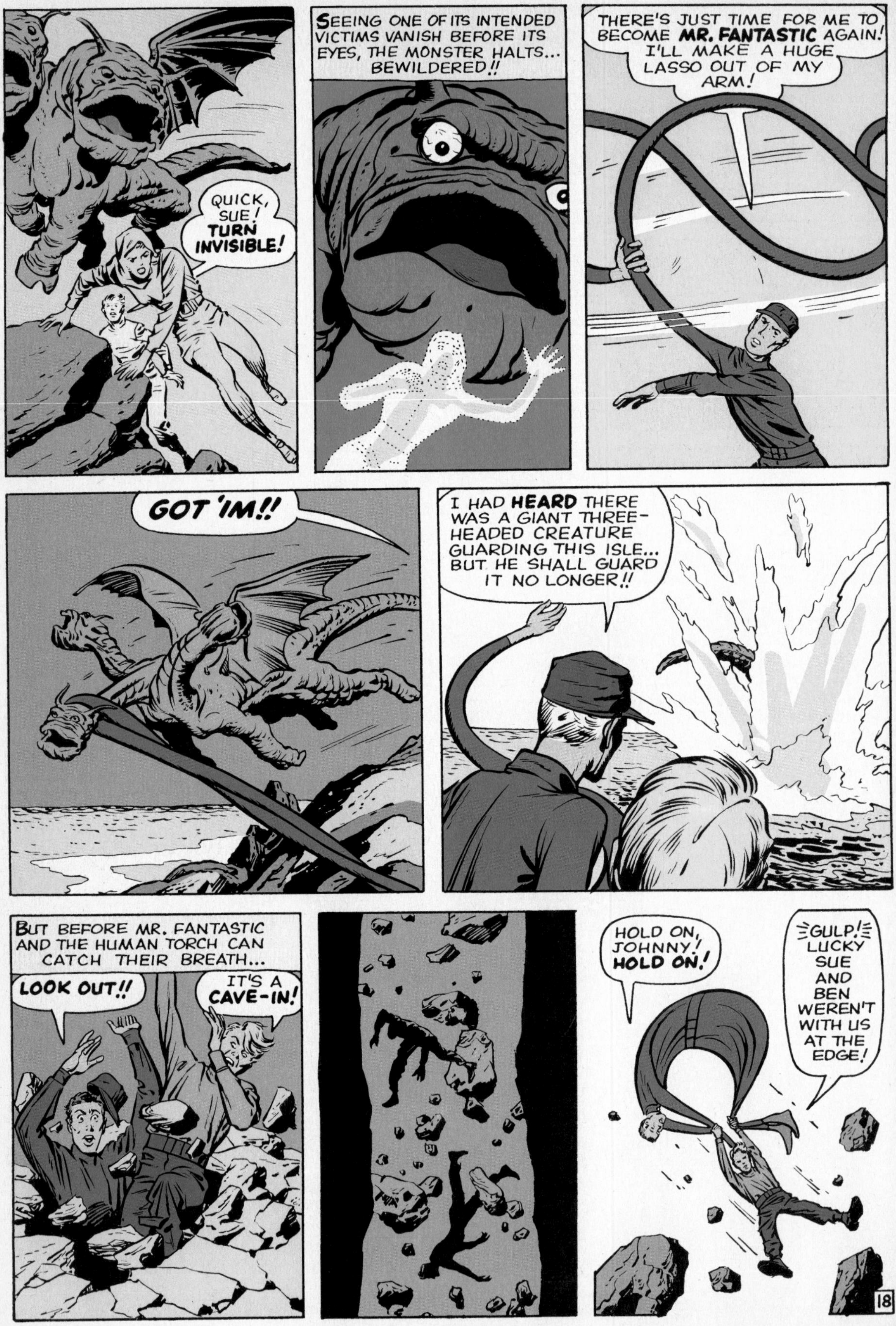
QUICK, SUE! TURN INVISIBLE!
SEEING ONE OF ITS INTENDED VICTIMS VANISH BEFORE ITS EYES, THE MONSTER HALTS... BEWILDERED!!
THERE'S JUST TIME FOR ME TO BECOME MR. FANTASTIC AGAIN! I'LL MAKE A HUGE LASSO OUT OF MY ARM!
GOT 'IM!!
I HAD HEARD THERE WAS A GIANT THREE-HEADED CREATURE GUARDING THIS ISLE... BUT HE SHALL GUARD IT NO LONGER!!
BUT BEFORE MR. FANTASTIC AND THE HUMAN TORCH CAN CATCH THEIR BREATH...
LOOK OUT!!
IT'S A CAVE-IN!
HOLD ON, JOHNNY! HOLD ON!
GULP! LUCKY SUE AND BEN WEREN'T WITH US AT THE EDGE!
18

FINALLY, THE AMAZING DUO FLOAT DOWN TO THE BOTTOM OF THE PIT...

IT'S PITCH DARK.!! WHAT SORT OF PLACE CAN IT BE?

REED! I FEEL SOMETHING!

IT'S A TRAP DOOR IN THE WALL!

IT'S MOVING!

THAT LIGHT!! WHERE DID IT COME FROM!

IT'S BLINDING! I CAN'T SEE!

I-I'M BLACKING OUT!

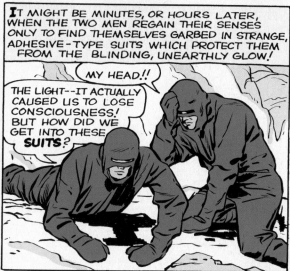

IT MIGHT BE MINUTES, OR HOURS LATER, WHEN THE TWO MEN REGAIN THEIR SENSES ONLY TO FIND THEMSELVES GARBED IN STRANGE, ADHESIVE-TYPE SUITS WHICH PROTECT THEM FROM THE BLINDING, UNEARTHLY GLOW!

MY HEAD.!!

THE LIGHT--IT ACTUALLY CAUSED US TO LOSE CONSCIOUSNESS! BUT HOW DID WE GET INTO THESE SUITS?

SO, YOU HAVE RECOVERED, HAVE YOU !! IT IS ABOUT TIME !!

WHO--WHO ARE YOU? I CAN'T SEE...

AND WHERE ARE WE?

THE REASON YOU CANNOT SEE IS... YOU ARE BLINDED BY THE GLARE FROM-- THE VALLEY OF DIAMONDS !!

--AND AS FOR ME-- I AM THE MOLEMAN !!

19

23

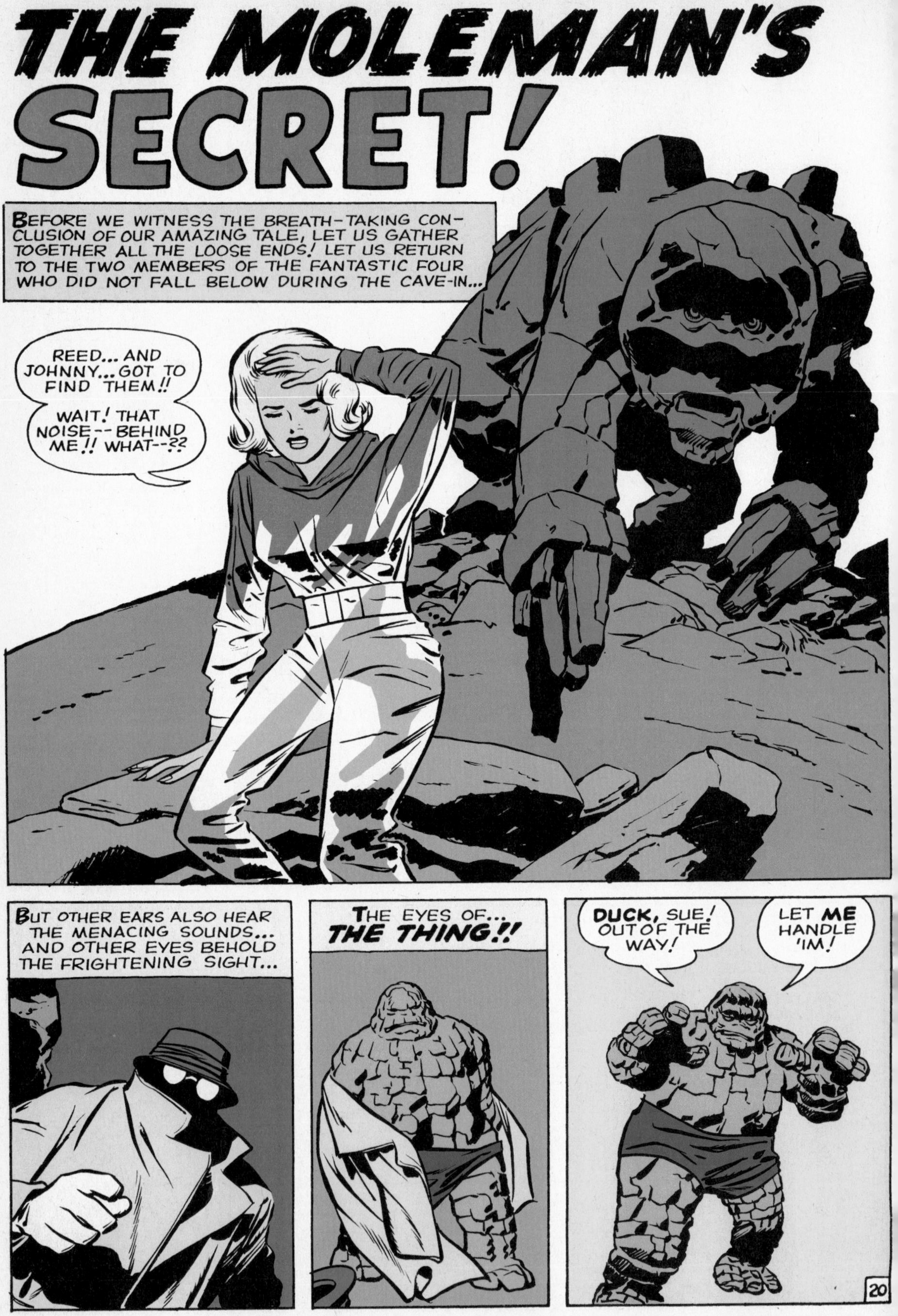
THE MOLEMAN'S SECRET!
BEFORE WE WITNESS THE BREATH-TAKING CONCLUSION OF OUR AMAZING TALE, LET US GATHER TOGETHER ALL THE LOOSE ENDS! LET US RETURN TO THE TWO MEMBERS OF THE FANTASTIC FOUR WHO DID NOT FALL BELOW DURING THE CAVE-IN...
REED... AND JOHNNY... GOT TO FIND THEM!!
WAIT! THAT NOISE--BEHIND ME!! WHAT--??
BUT OTHER EARS ALSO HEAR THE MENACING SOUNDS... AND OTHER EYES BEHOLD THE FRIGHTENING SIGHT...
THE EYES OF... THE THING!!
DUCK, SUE! OUT OF THE WAY!
LET ME HANDLE 'IM!
20

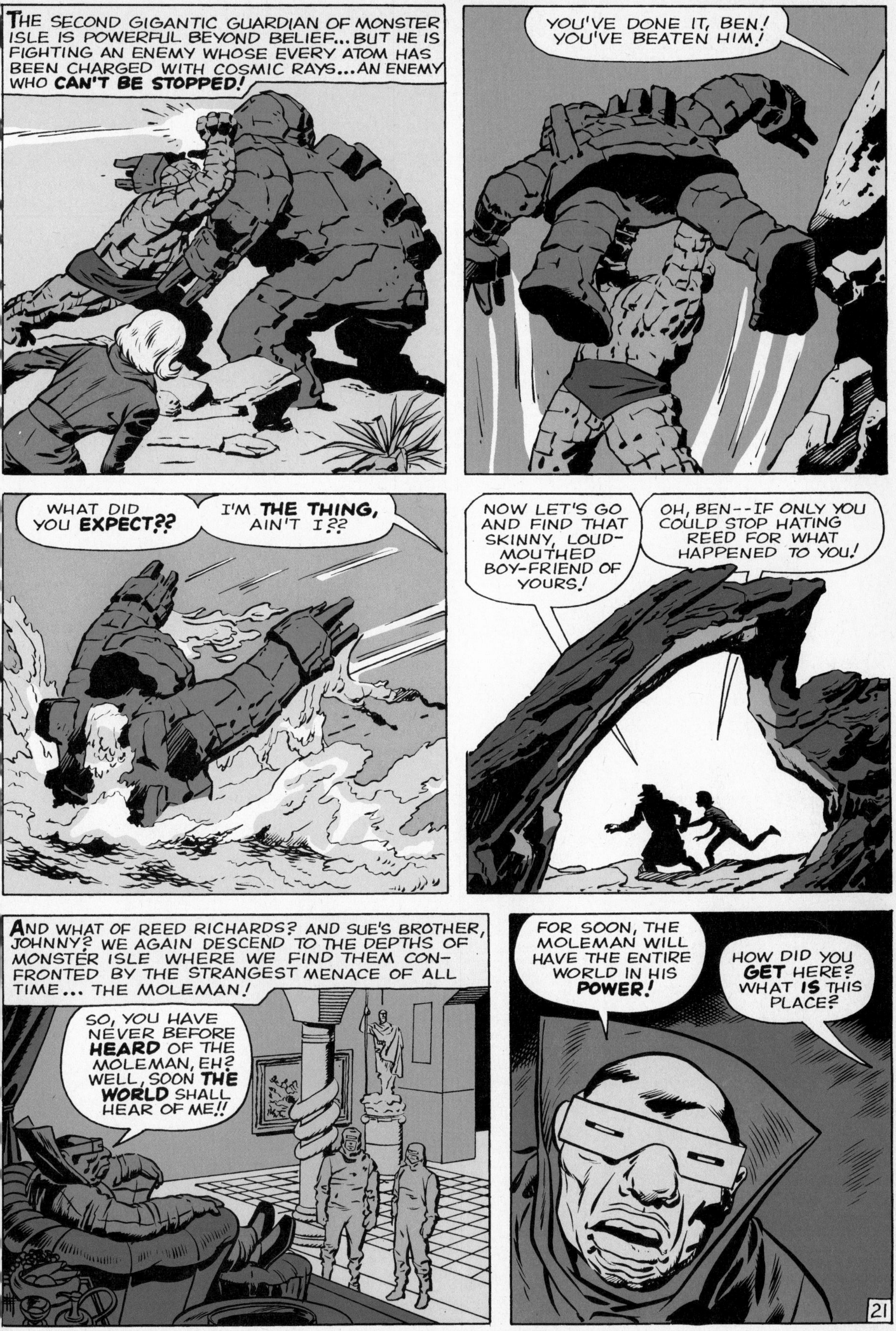
THE SECOND GIGANTIC GUARDIAN OF MONSTER ISLE IS POWERFUL BEYOND BELIEF... BUT HE IS FIGHTING AN ENEMY WHOSE EVERY ATOM HAS BEEN CHARGED WITH COSMIC RAYS... AN ENEMY WHO CAN'T BE STOPPED!
YOU'VE DONE IT, BEN! YOU'VE BEATEN HIM!
WHAT DID YOU EXPECT??
I'M THE THING, AIN'T I??
NOW LET'S GO AND FIND THAT SKINNY, LOUD-MOUTHED BOY-FRIEND OF YOURS!
OH, BEN--IF ONLY YOU COULD STOP HATING REED FOR WHAT HAPPENED TO YOU!
AND WHAT OF REED RICHARDS? AND SUE'S BROTHER, JOHNNY? WE AGAIN DESCEND TO THE DEPTHS OF MONSTER ISLE WHERE WE FIND THEM CONFRONTED BY THE STRANGEST MENACE OF ALL TIME... THE MOLEMAN!
SO, YOU HAVE NEVER BEFORE HEARD OF THE MOLEMAN, EH? WELL, SOON THE WORLD SHALL HEAR OF ME!!
FOR SOON, THE MOLEMAN WILL HAVE THE ENTIRE WORLD IN HIS POWER!
HOW DID YOU GET HERE? WHAT IS THIS PLACE?
21

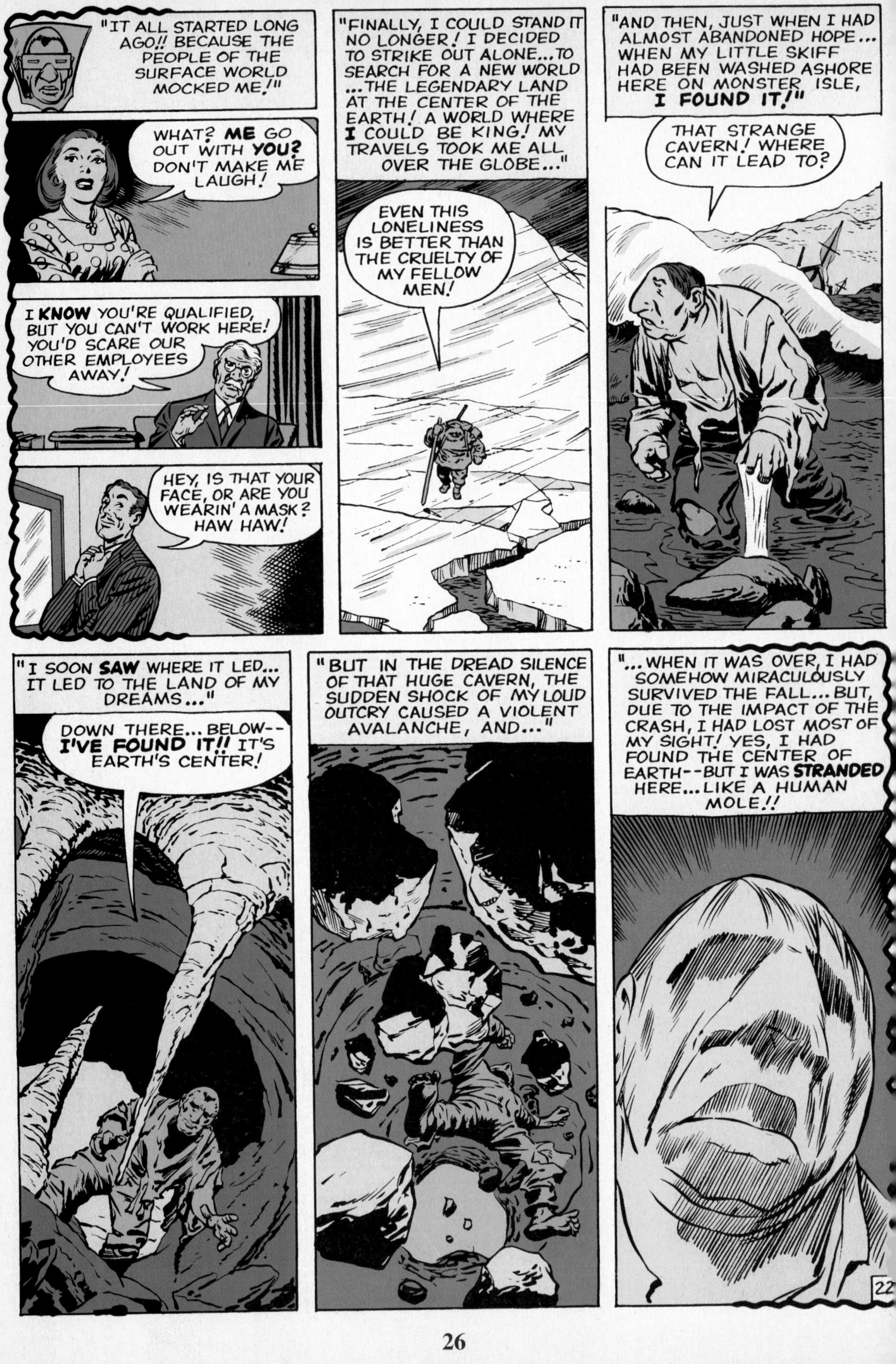
"IT ALL STARTED LONG AGO!! BECAUSE THE PEOPLE OF THE SURFACE WORLD MOCKED ME!"
WHAT? ME GO OUT WITH YOU? DON'T MAKE ME LAUGH!
I KNOW YOU'RE QUALIFIED, BUT YOU CAN'T WORK HERE! YOU'D SCARE OUR OTHER EMPLOYEES AWAY!
HEY, IS THAT YOUR FACE, OR ARE YOU WEARIN' A MASK? HAW HAW!
"FINALLY, I COULD STAND IT NO LONGER! I DECIDED TO STRIKE OUT ALONE...TO SEARCH FOR A NEW WORLD ...THE LEGENDARY LAND AT THE CENTER OF THE EARTH! A WORLD WHERE I COULD BE KING! MY TRAVELS TOOK ME ALL OVER THE GLOBE..."
EVEN THIS LONELINESS IS BETTER THAN THE CRUELTY OF MY FELLOW MEN!
"AND THEN, JUST WHEN I HAD ALMOST ABANDONED HOPE... WHEN MY LITTLE SKIFF HAD BEEN WASHED ASHORE HERE ON MONSTER ISLE, I FOUND IT!"
THAT STRANGE CAVERN! WHERE CAN IT LEAD TO?
"I SOON SAW WHERE IT LED... IT LED TO THE LAND OF MY DREAMS..."
DOWN THERE... BELOW-- I'VE FOUND IT!! IT'S EARTH'S CENTER!
"BUT IN THE DREAD SILENCE OF THAT HUGE CAVERN, THE SUDDEN SHOCK OF MY LOUD OUTCRY CAUSED A VIOLENT AVALANCHE, AND..."
"...WHEN IT WAS OVER, I HAD SOMEHOW MIRACULOUSLY SURVIVED THE FALL... BUT, DUE TO THE IMPACT OF THE CRASH, I HAD LOST MOST OF MY SIGHT! YES, I HAD FOUND THE CENTER OF EARTH--BUT I WAS STRANDED HERE...LIKE A HUMAN MOLE!!
22

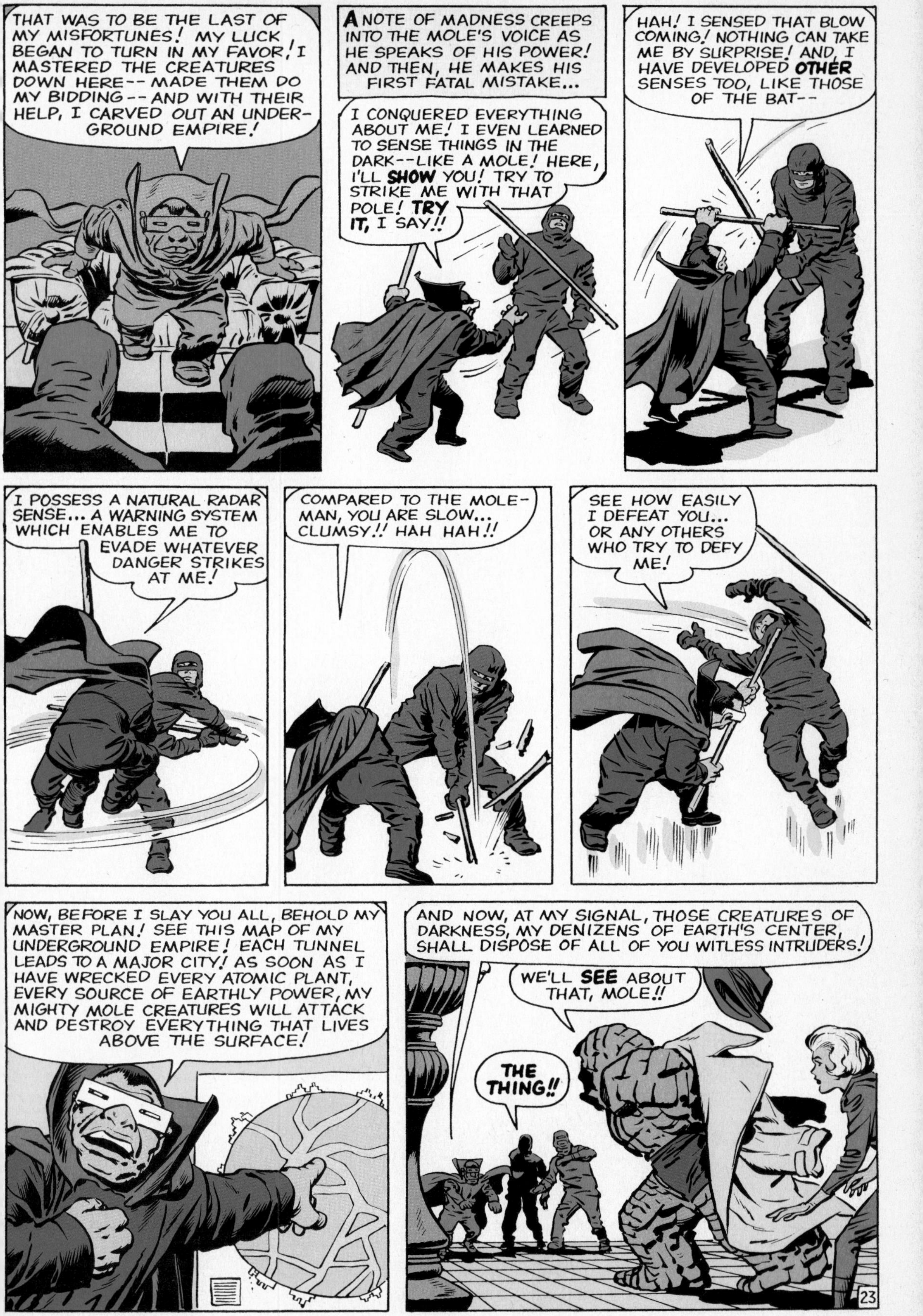
THAT WAS TO BE THE LAST OF MY MISFORTUNES! MY LUCK BEGAN TO TURN IN MY FAVOR! I MASTERED THE CREATURES DOWN HERE-- MADE THEM DO MY BIDDING-- AND WITH THEIR HELP, I CARVED OUT AN UNDER-GROUND EMPIRE!
A NOTE OF MADNESS CREEPS INTO THE MOLE'S VOICE AS HE SPEAKS OF HIS POWER! AND THEN, HE MAKES HIS FIRST FATAL MISTAKE...
I CONQUERED EVERYTHING ABOUT ME! I EVEN LEARNED TO SENSE THINGS IN THE DARK--LIKE A MOLE! HERE, I'LL SHOW YOU! TRY TO STRIKE ME WITH THAT POLE! TRY IT, I SAY!!
HAH! I SENSED THAT BLOW COMING! NOTHING CAN TAKE ME BY SURPRISE! AND, I HAVE DEVELOPED OTHER SENSES TOO, LIKE THOSE OF THE BAT--
I POSSESS A NATURAL RADAR SENSE... A WARNING SYSTEM WHICH ENABLES ME TO EVADE WHATEVER DANGER STRIKES AT ME!
COMPARED TO THE MOLE-MAN, YOU ARE SLOW... CLUMSY!! HAH HAH!!
SEE HOW EASILY I DEFEAT YOU... OR ANY OTHERS WHO TRY TO DEFY ME!
NOW, BEFORE I SLAY YOU ALL, BEHOLD MY MASTER PLAN! SEE THIS MAP OF MY UNDERGROUND EMPIRE! EACH TUNNEL LEADS TO A MAJOR CITY! AS SOON AS I HAVE WRECKED EVERY ATOMIC PLANT, EVERY SOURCE OF EARTHLY POWER, MY MIGHTY MOLE CREATURES WILL ATTACK AND DESTROY EVERYTHING THAT LIVES ABOVE THE SURFACE!
AND NOW, AT MY SIGNAL, THOSE CREATURES OF DARKNESS, MY DENIZENS OF EARTH'S CENTER, SHALL DISPOSE OF ALL OF YOU WITLESS INTRUDERS!
WE'LL SEE ABOUT THAT, MOLE!!
THE THING!!
23

TOO LATE, FOOL! THE DIE IS CAST! THERE IS NO TURNING BACK.!!

THING!! LOOK OUT... BEHIND YOU!

BONG! BONG!

HEARING THE MOLE'S SIGNAL, THE LARGEST AND MOST DEADLY OF HIS UNDERGROUND CREATURES PONDEROUSLY RAISES ITSELF INTO THE ROOM... ITS BRAINLESS RAGE DIRECTED AT THE FOUR ASTONISHED HUMANS!

AND THEN, THE FANTASTIC FOUR FLY INTO BLAZING ACTION...

LOOK OUT, REED! I'M GONNA BURN MY WAY OUTTA THIS MONKEY SUIT!

GOOD BOY, TORCH!

STAND ASIDE, GANG! IT'S GONNA GET MIGHTY WARM AROUND HERE!

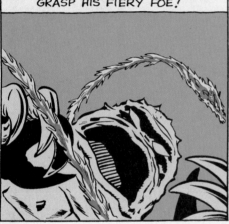

BACK AND FORTH, BUZZING AROUND THE MONSTER'S HEAD LIKE A HORNET, FLIES THE HUMAN TORCH, AS THE GIGANTIC CREATURE VAINLY TRIES TO GRASP HIS FIERY FOE!

REED! THE MOLEMAN! HE'S ESCAPING!

NOT IF I CAN HELP IT, SUE!

AND HELP IT I CAN!

24

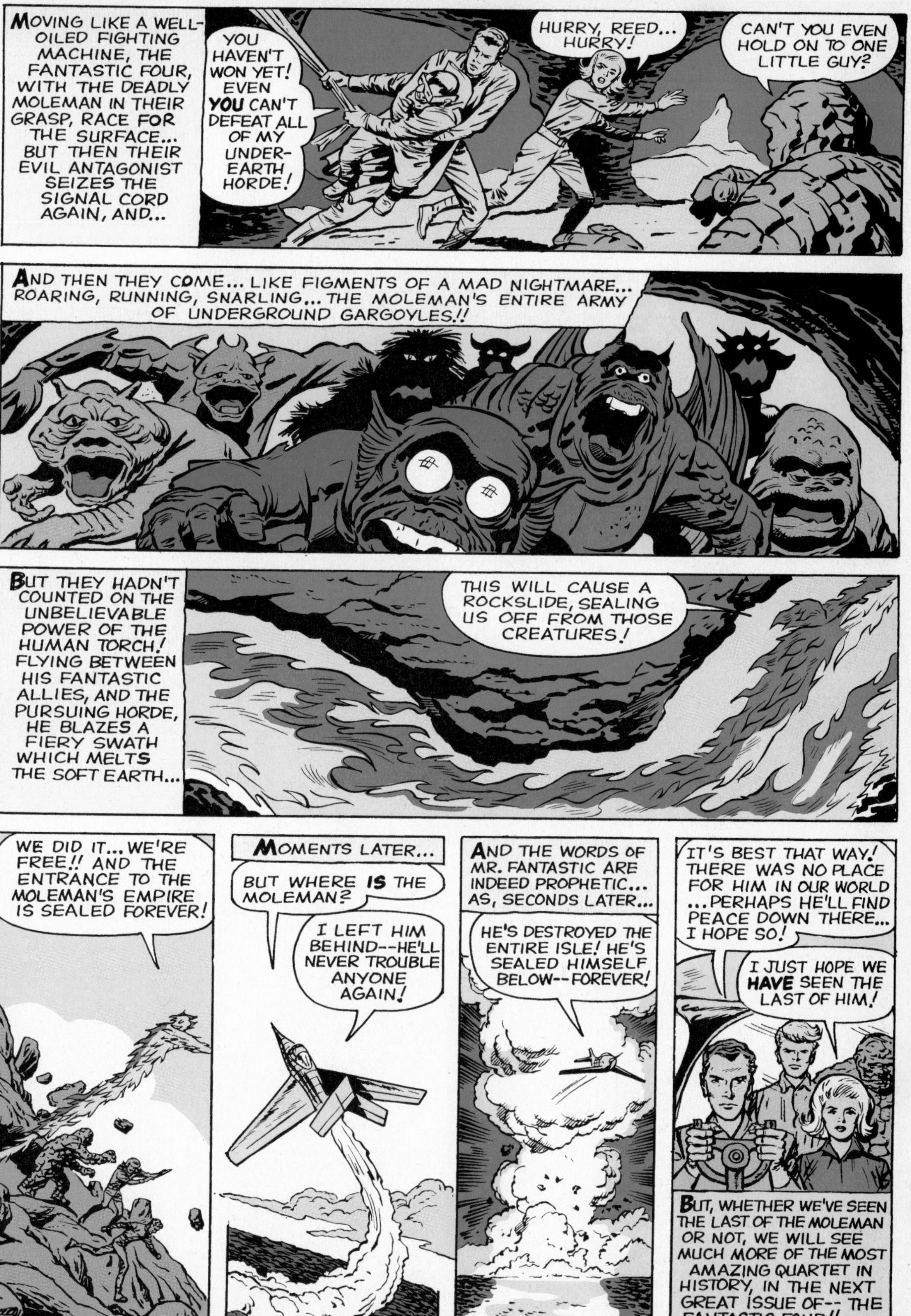
MOVING LIKE A WELL-OILED FIGHTING MACHINE, THE FANTASTIC FOUR, WITH THE DEADLY MOLEMAN IN THEIR GRASP, RACE FOR THE SURFACE... BUT THEN THEIR EVIL ANTAGONIST SEIZES THE SIGNAL CORD AGAIN, AND...
YOU HAVEN'T WON YET! EVEN YOU CAN'T DEFEAT ALL OF MY UNDER-EARTH HORDE!
HURRY, REED... HURRY!
CAN'T YOU EVEN HOLD ON TO ONE LITTLE GUY?
AND THEN THEY COME... LIKE FIGMENTS OF A MAD NIGHTMARE... ROARING, RUNNING, SNARLING... THE MOLEMAN'S ENTIRE ARMY OF UNDERGROUND GARGOYLES!!
BUT THEY HADN'T COUNTED ON THE UNBELIEVABLE POWER OF THE HUMAN TORCH! FLYING BETWEEN HIS FANTASTIC ALLIES, AND THE PURSUING HORDE, HE BLAZES A FIERY SWATH WHICH MELTS THE SOFT EARTH...
THIS WILL CAUSE A ROCKSLIDE, SEALING US OFF FROM THOSE CREATURES!
WE DID IT... WE'RE FREE!! AND THE ENTRANCE TO THE MOLEMAN'S EMPIRE IS SEALED FOREVER!
25
MOMENTS LATER...
BUT WHERE IS THE MOLEMAN?
I LEFT HIM BEHIND--HE'LL NEVER TROUBLE ANYONE AGAIN!
AND THE WORDS OF MR. FANTASTIC ARE INDEED PROPHETIC... AS, SECONDS LATER...
HE'S DESTROYED THE ENTIRE ISLE! HE'S SEALED HIMSELF BELOW--FOREVER!
IT'S BEST THAT WAY! THERE WAS NO PLACE FOR HIM IN OUR WORLD ...PERHAPS HE'LL FIND PEACE DOWN THERE... I HOPE SO!
I JUST HOPE WE HAVE SEEN THE LAST OF HIM!
BUT, WHETHER WE'VE SEEN THE LAST OF THE MOLEMAN OR NOT, WE WILL SEE MUCH MORE OF THE MOST AMAZING QUARTET IN HISTORY, IN THE NEXT GREAT ISSUE OF-- THE FANTASTIC FOUR!! DON'T MISS IT!!
THE END

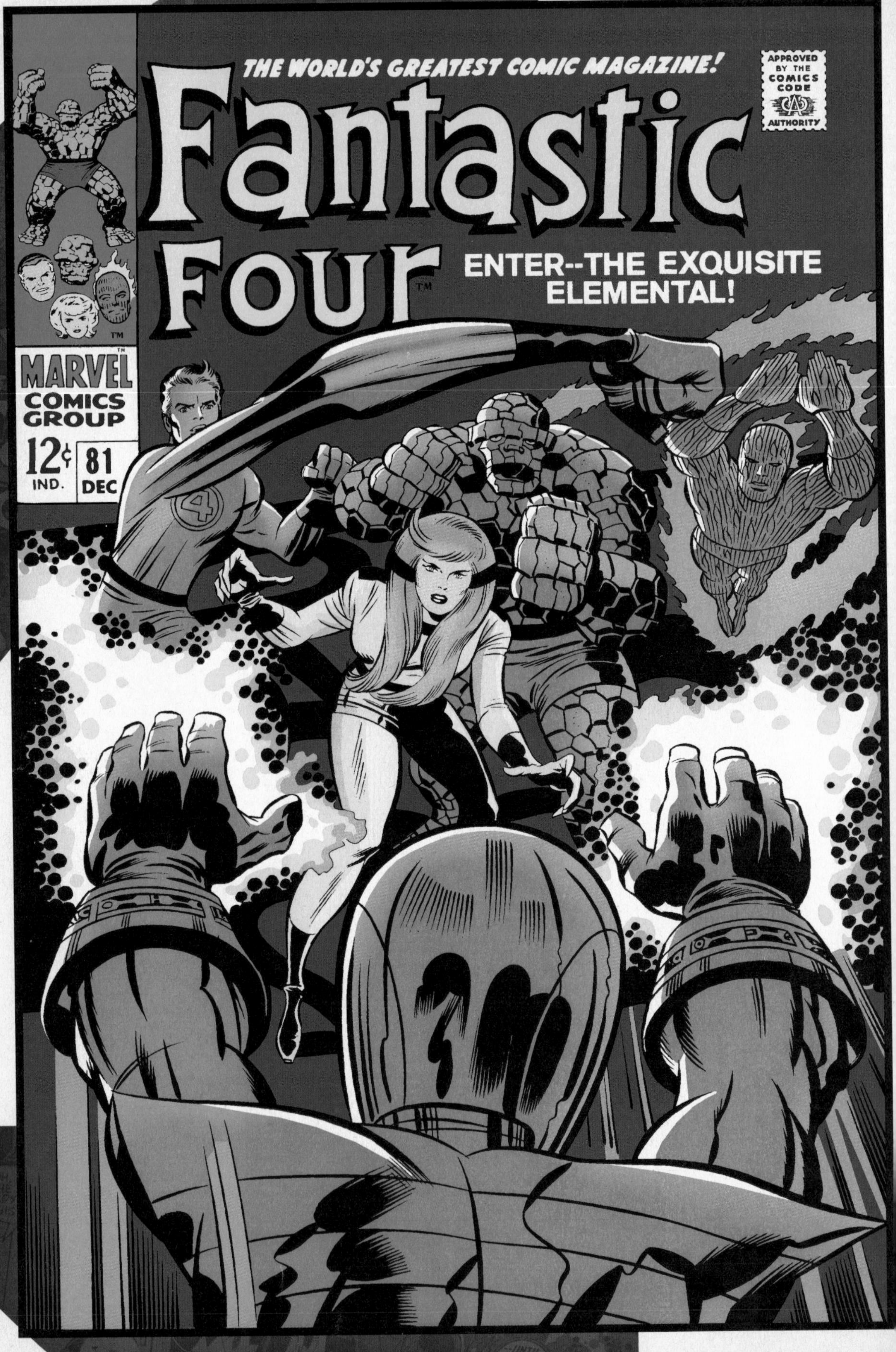
THE WORLD'S GREATEST COMIC MAGAZINE!
APPROVED BY THE COMICS CODE AUTHORITY
Fantastic Four™
ENTER--THE EXQUISITE ELEMENTAL!
MARVEL COMICS GROUP
12¢ IND.
81 DEC

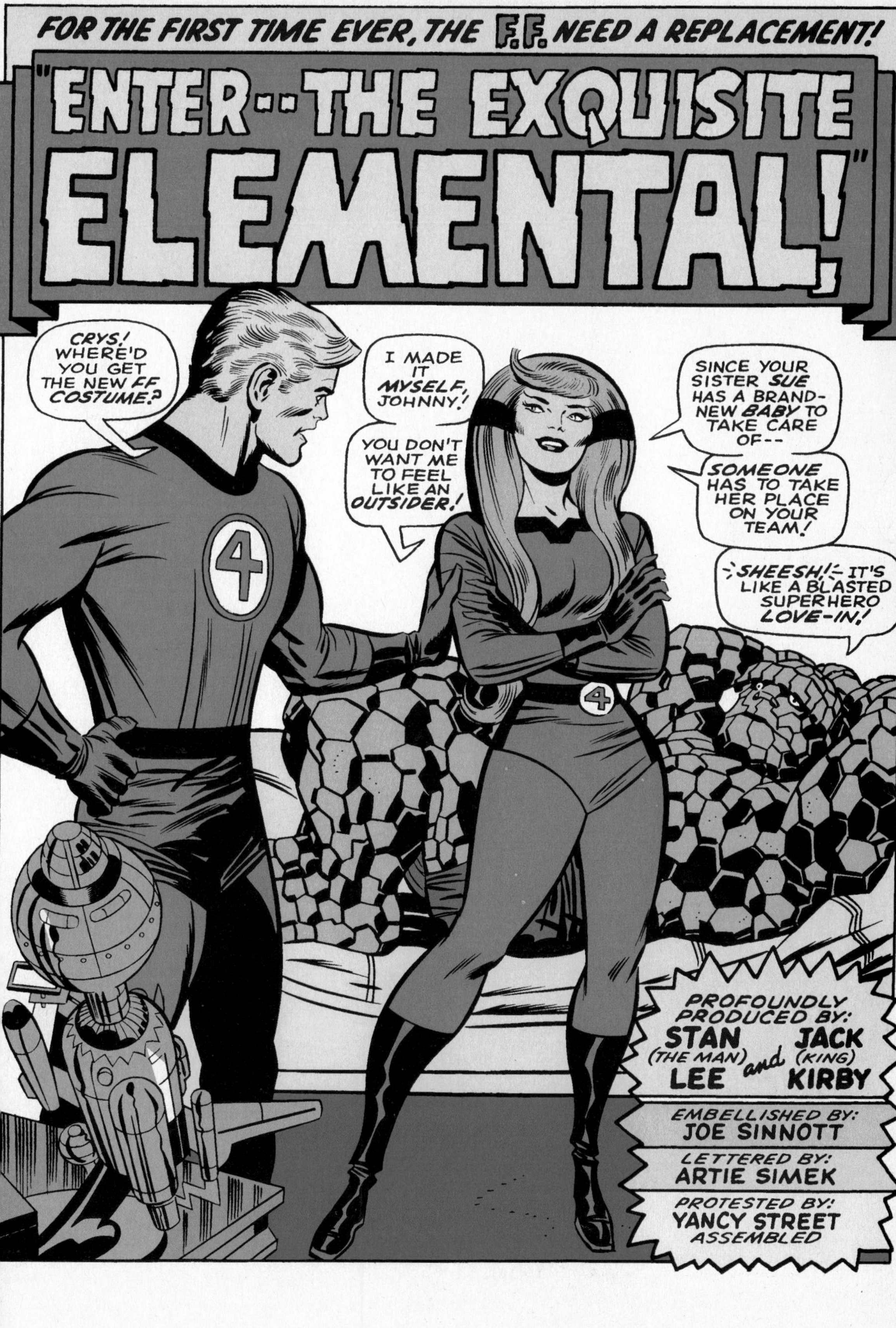
FOR THE FIRST TIME EVER, THE F.F. NEED A REPLACEMENT!
"ENTER--THE EXQUISITE ELEMENTAL!"
CRYS! WHERE'D YOU GET THE NEW FF COSTUME?
I MADE IT MYSELF, JOHNNY!
YOU DON'T WANT ME TO FEEL LIKE AN OUTSIDER!
SINCE YOUR SISTER SUE HAS A BRAND-NEW BABY TO TAKE CARE OF--
SOMEONE HAS TO TAKE HER PLACE ON YOUR TEAM!
SHEESH! IT'S LIKE A BLASTED SUPERHERO LOVE-IN!
PROFOUNDLY PRODUCED BY: STAN (THE MAN) LEE and JACK (KING) KIRBY
EMBELLISHED BY: JOE SINNOTT
LETTERED BY: ARTIE SIMEK
PROTESTED BY: YANCY STREET ASSEMBLED

BUT, IT'S NOT THAT *EASY*, HONEY! YOU CAN'T JUST *DECIDE* YOU'LL BECOME AN *FF* MEMBER!

I'VE *LIVED* WITH DANGER ALL MY *LIFE*, JOHNNY!

BESIDES, THINK OF THE *DANGER*, CRYS!

IT'S FAR *BETTER* --THAN TRYING TO LIVE--WITHOUT *YOU*!

YECHH! DO I *HAVE TA* LISTEN TO THAT ON A *EMPTY STOMACH?*

ADMIT IT, MR. STORM--YOU *KNOW* I'M THE PERFECT *REPLACEMENT* FOR SUE RICHARDS!

YOU'D BE PERFECT FOR *ANYTHING*, LOVELY LADY!

BUT YOU *STILL* CAN'T JOIN THE *FF* AS EASY AS ALL *THAT!*

FIRST, YOU'VE GOT TO *PROVE* YOURSELF! AND THEN--

AWW, WHY WASTE TIME *TALKING--?*

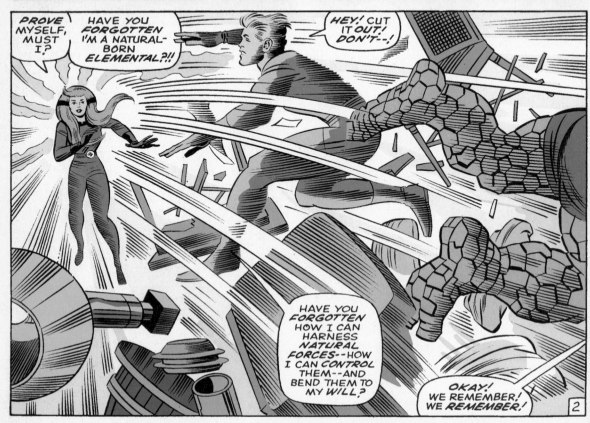

PROVE MYSELF, MUST I?

HAVE YOU *FORGOTTEN* I'M A NATURAL-BORN *ELEMENTAL?!!*

HEY! CUT IT *OUT!* DON'T--!

HAVE YOU *FORGOTTEN* HOW I CAN HARNESS *NATURAL FORCES*--HOW I CAN *CONTROL* THEM--AND BEND THEM TO MY *WILL?*

OKAY! WE REMEMBER! WE *REMEMBER!*

2

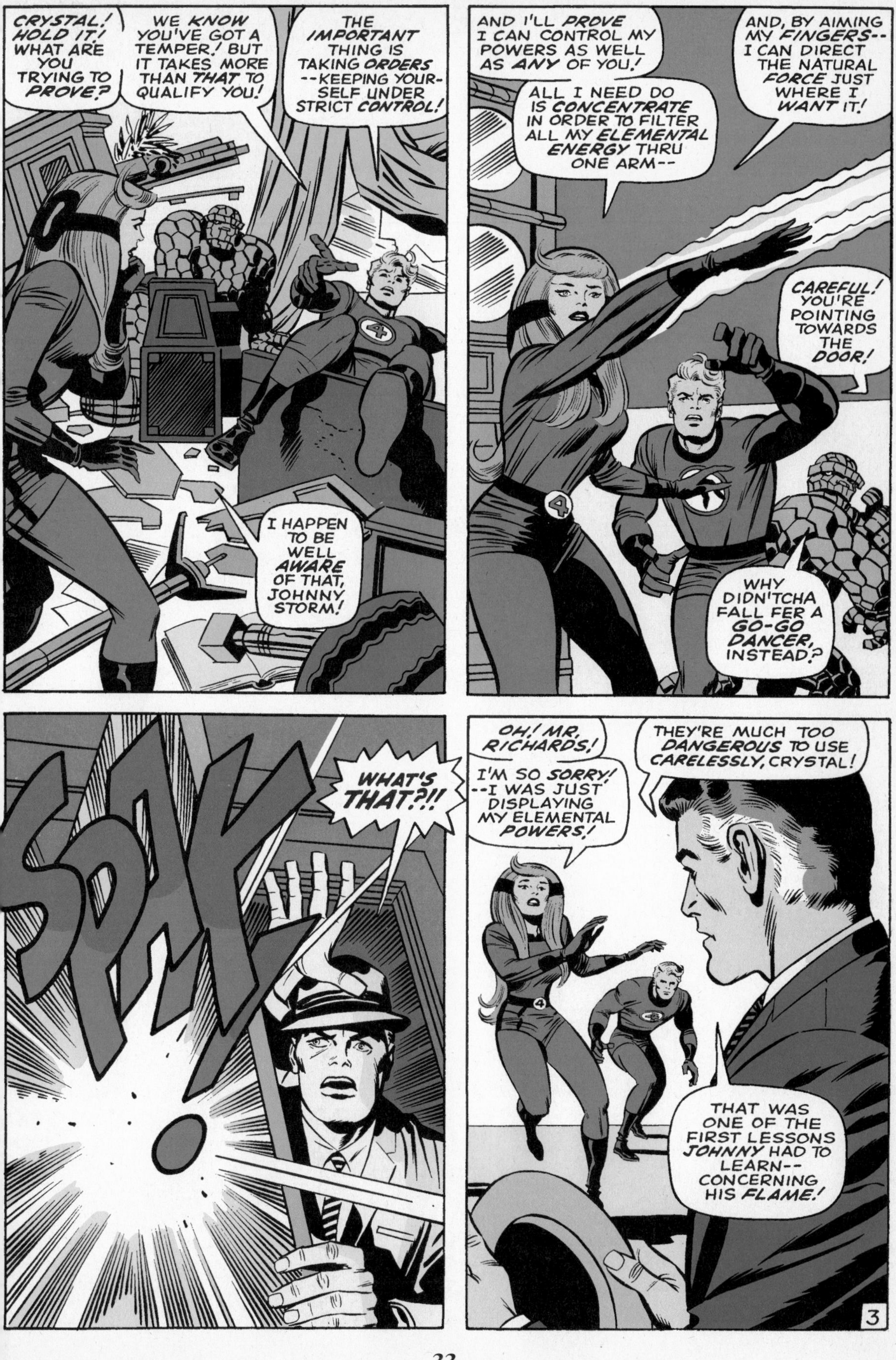
CRYSTAL! HOLD IT! WHAT ARE YOU TRYING TO PROVE?
WE KNOW YOU'VE GOT A TEMPER! BUT IT TAKES MORE THAN THAT TO QUALIFY YOU!
THE IMPORTANT THING IS TAKING ORDERS --KEEPING YOURSELF UNDER STRICT CONTROL!
I HAPPEN TO BE WELL AWARE OF THAT, JOHNNY STORM!
AND I'LL PROVE I CAN CONTROL MY POWERS AS WELL AS ANY OF YOU!
ALL I NEED DO IS CONCENTRATE IN ORDER TO FILTER ALL MY ELEMENTAL ENERGY THRU ONE ARM--
AND, BY AIMING MY FINGERS-- I CAN DIRECT THE NATURAL FORCE JUST WHERE I WANT IT!
CAREFUL! YOU'RE POINTING TOWARDS THE DOOR!
WHY DIDN'TCHA FALL FER A GO-GO DANCER, INSTEAD?
SPAK
WHAT'S THAT?!!
OH! MR. RICHARDS!
I'M SO SORRY! --I WAS JUST DISPLAYING MY ELEMENTAL POWERS!
THEY'RE MUCH TOO DANGEROUS TO USE CARELESSLY, CRYSTAL!
THAT WAS ONE OF THE FIRST LESSONS JOHNNY HAD TO LEARN-- CONCERNING HIS FLAME!
3

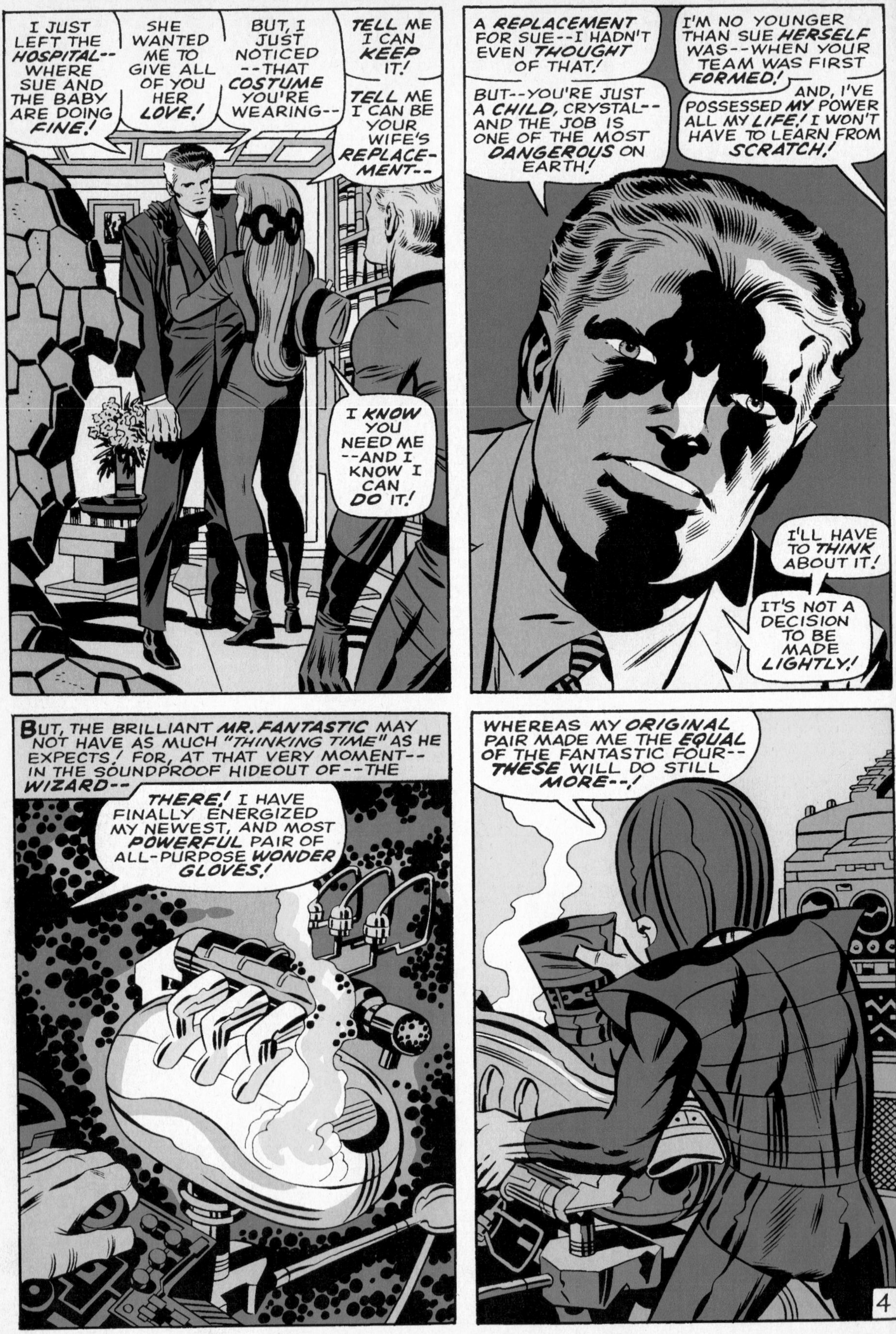
I JUST LEFT THE HOSPITAL-- WHERE SUE AND THE BABY ARE DOING FINE!
SHE WANTED ME TO GIVE ALL OF YOU HER LOVE!
BUT, I JUST NOTICED --THAT COSTUME YOU'RE WEARING--
TELL ME I CAN KEEP IT!
TELL ME I CAN BE YOUR WIFE'S REPLACEMENT--
I KNOW YOU NEED ME --AND I KNOW I CAN DO IT!
A REPLACEMENT FOR SUE--I HADN'T EVEN THOUGHT OF THAT!
BUT--YOU'RE JUST A CHILD, CRYSTAL-- AND THE JOB IS ONE OF THE MOST DANGEROUS ON EARTH!
I'M NO YOUNGER THAN SUE HERSELF WAS--WHEN YOUR TEAM WAS FIRST FORMED!
AND, I'VE POSSESSED MY POWER ALL MY LIFE! I WON'T HAVE TO LEARN FROM SCRATCH!
I'LL HAVE TO THINK ABOUT IT!
IT'S NOT A DECISION TO BE MADE LIGHTLY!
BUT, THE BRILLIANT MR. FANTASTIC MAY NOT HAVE AS MUCH "THINKING TIME" AS HE EXPECTS! FOR, AT THAT VERY MOMENT-- IN THE SOUNDPROOF HIDEOUT OF--THE WIZARD--
THERE! I HAVE FINALLY ENERGIZED MY NEWEST, AND MOST POWERFUL PAIR OF ALL-PURPOSE WONDER GLOVES!
WHEREAS MY ORIGINAL PAIR MADE ME THE EQUAL OF THE FANTASTIC FOUR-- THESE WILL DO STILL MORE--!
4

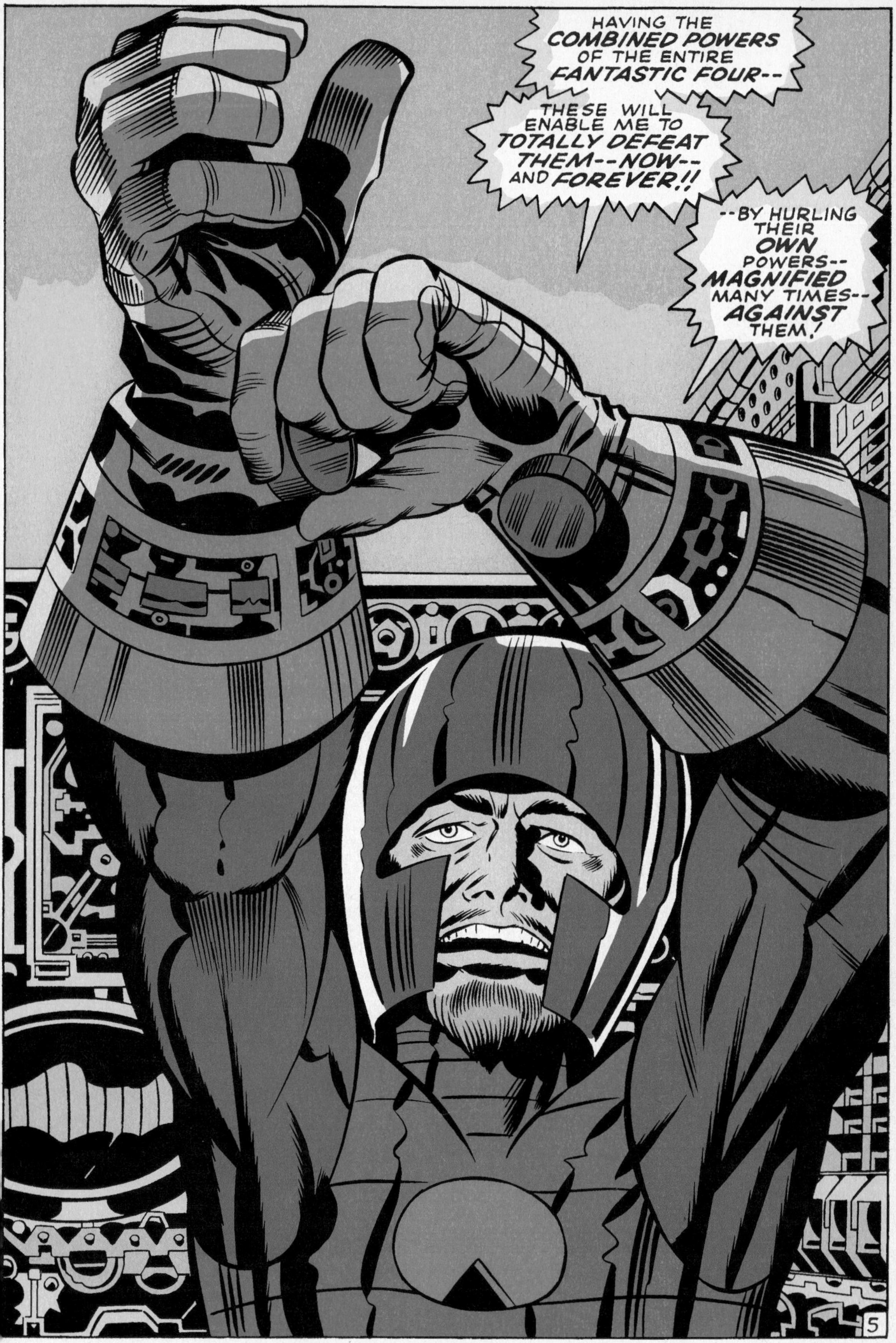
HAVING THE COMBINED POWERS OF THE ENTIRE FANTASTIC FOUR--
THESE WILL ENABLE ME TO TOTALLY DEFEAT THEM--NOW--AND FOREVER!!
--BY HURLING THEIR OWN POWERS--MAGNIFIED MANY TIMES--AGAINST THEM!
5

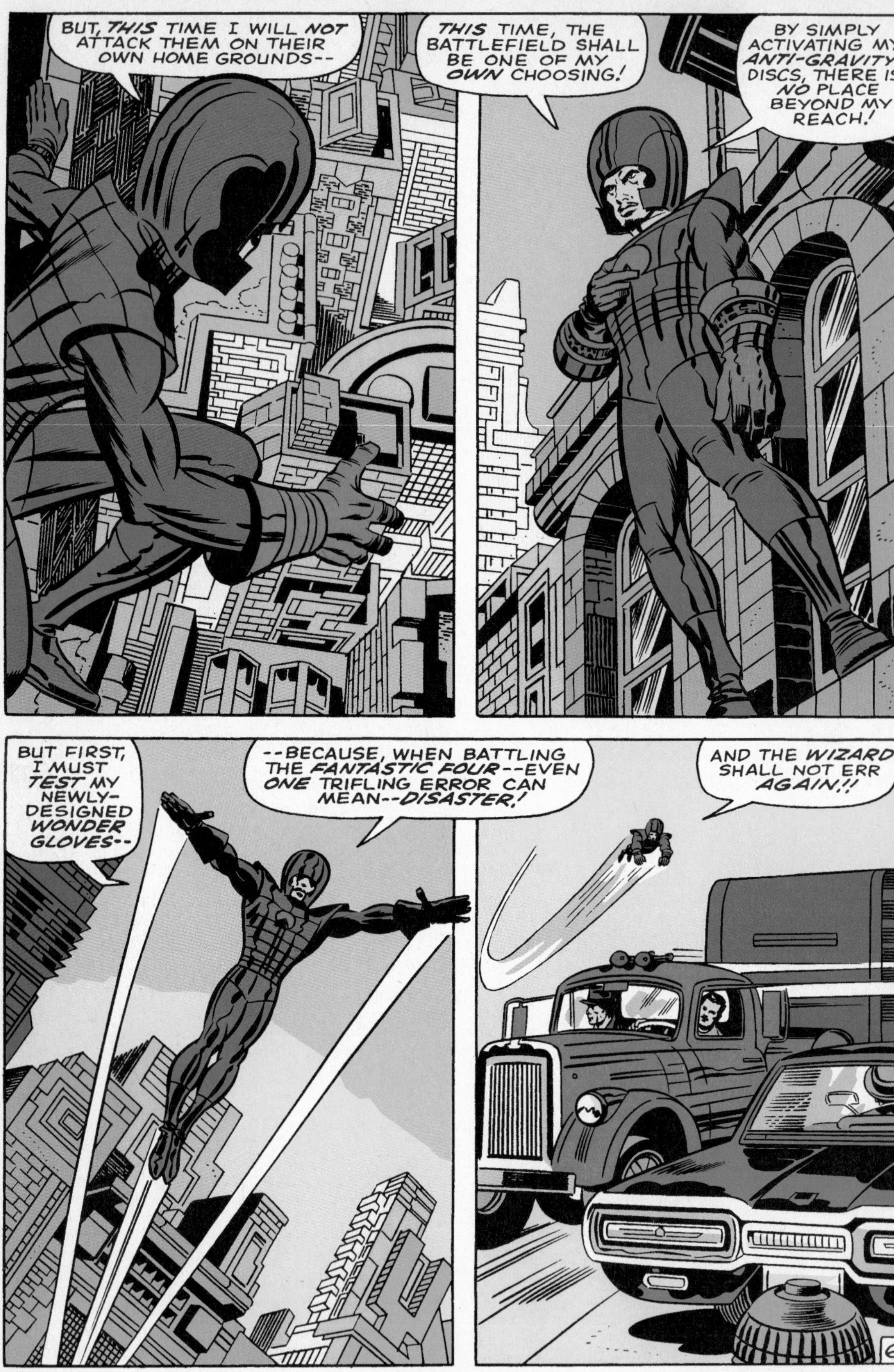
BUT, THIS TIME I WILL NOT ATTACK THEM ON THEIR OWN HOME GROUNDS--
THIS TIME, THE BATTLEFIELD SHALL BE ONE OF MY OWN CHOOSING!
BY SIMPLY ACTIVATING MY ANTI-GRAVITY DISCS, THERE IS NO PLACE BEYOND MY REACH!
BUT FIRST, I MUST TEST MY NEWLY-DESIGNED WONDER GLOVES--
--BECAUSE, WHEN BATTLING THE FANTASTIC FOUR--EVEN ONE TRIFLING ERROR CAN MEAN--DISASTER!
AND THE WIZARD SHALL NOT ERR AGAIN!!
6

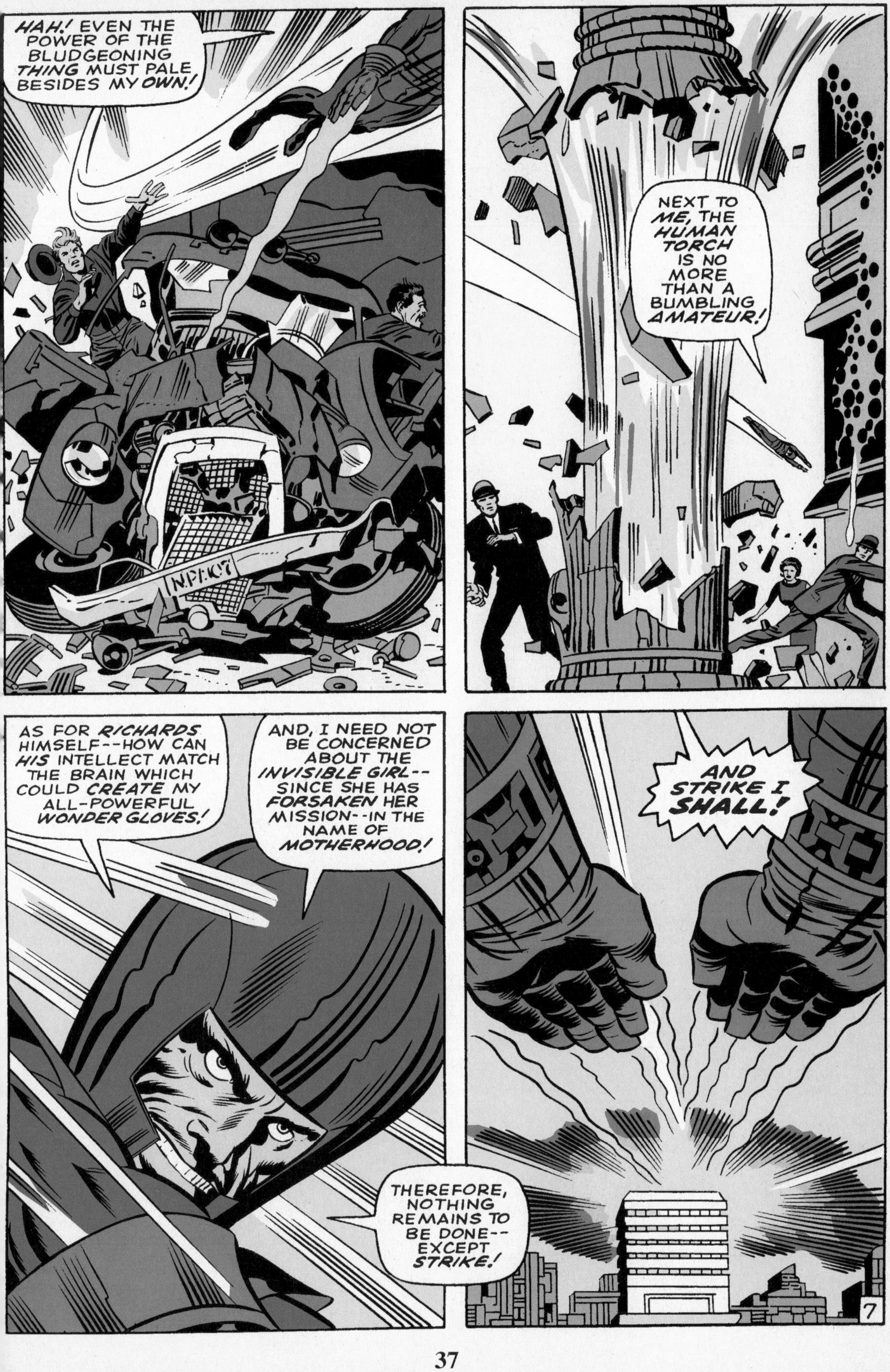
HAH! EVEN THE POWER OF THE BLUDGEONING THING MUST PALE BESIDES MY OWN!
N.P.A.07
NEXT TO ME, THE HUMAN TORCH IS NO MORE THAN A BUMBLING AMATEUR!
AS FOR RICHARDS HIMSELF--HOW CAN HIS INTELLECT MATCH THE BRAIN WHICH COULD CREATE MY ALL-POWERFUL WONDER GLOVES!
AND, I NEED NOT BE CONCERNED ABOUT THE INVISIBLE GIRL--SINCE SHE HAS FORSAKEN HER MISSION--IN THE NAME OF MOTHERHOOD!
AND STRIKE I SHALL!
THEREFORE, NOTHING REMAINS TO BE DONE--EXCEPT STRIKE!
7

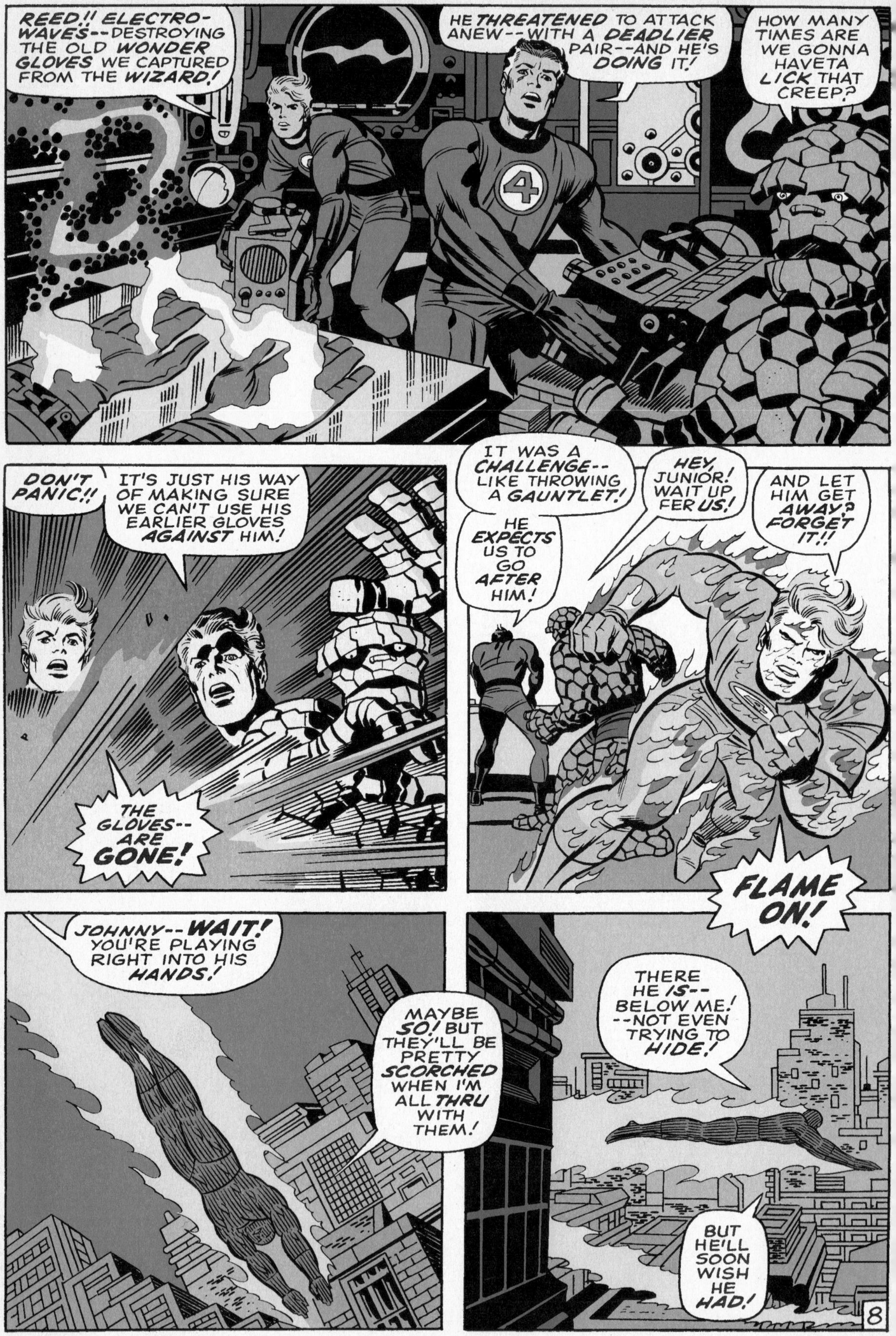
REED!! ELECTRO-WAVES--DESTROYING THE OLD WONDER GLOVES WE CAPTURED FROM THE WIZARD!
HE THREATENED TO ATTACK ANEW--WITH A DEADLIER PAIR--AND HE'S DOING IT!
HOW MANY TIMES ARE WE GONNA HAVETA LICK THAT CREEP?
DON'T PANIC!!
IT'S JUST HIS WAY OF MAKING SURE WE CAN'T USE HIS EARLIER GLOVES AGAINST HIM!
THE GLOVES--ARE GONE!
IT WAS A CHALLENGE--LIKE THROWING A GAUNTLET!
HE EXPECTS US TO GO AFTER HIM!
HEY, JUNIOR! WAIT UP FER US!
AND LET HIM GET AWAY? FORGET IT!!
FLAME ON!
JOHNNY--WAIT! YOU'RE PLAYING RIGHT INTO HIS HANDS!
MAYBE SO! BUT THEY'LL BE PRETTY SCORCHED WHEN I'M ALL THRU WITH THEM!
THERE HE IS--BELOW ME! --NOT EVEN TRYING TO HIDE!
BUT HE'LL SOON WISH HE HAD!
8

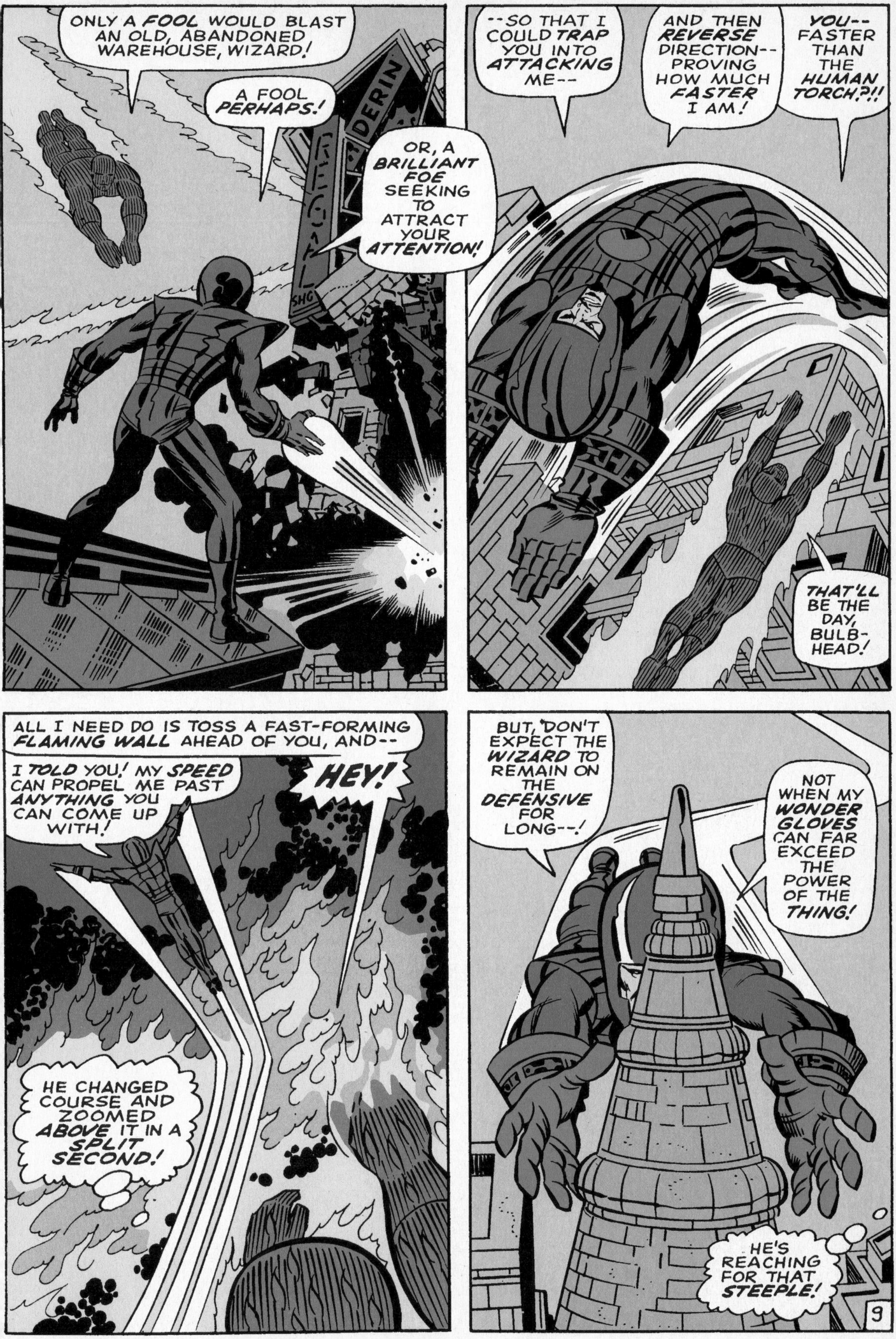
ONLY A FOOL WOULD BLAST AN OLD, ABANDONED WAREHOUSE, WIZARD!
A FOOL PERHAPS!
OR, A BRILLIANT FOE SEEKING TO ATTRACT YOUR ATTENTION!
--SO THAT I COULD TRAP YOU INTO ATTACKING ME--
AND THEN REVERSE DIRECTION--PROVING HOW MUCH FASTER I AM!
YOU--FASTER THAN THE HUMAN TORCH?!!
THAT'LL BE THE DAY, BULB-HEAD!
ALL I NEED DO IS TOSS A FAST-FORMING FLAMING WALL AHEAD OF YOU, AND--
I TOLD YOU! MY SPEED CAN PROPEL ME PAST ANYTHING YOU CAN COME UP WITH!
HEY!
HE CHANGED COURSE AND ZOOMED ABOVE IT IN A SPLIT SECOND!
BUT, DON'T EXPECT THE WIZARD TO REMAIN ON THE DEFENSIVE FOR LONG--!
NOT WHEN MY WONDER GLOVES CAN FAR EXCEED THE POWER OF THE THING!
HE'S REACHING FOR THAT STEEPLE!
9

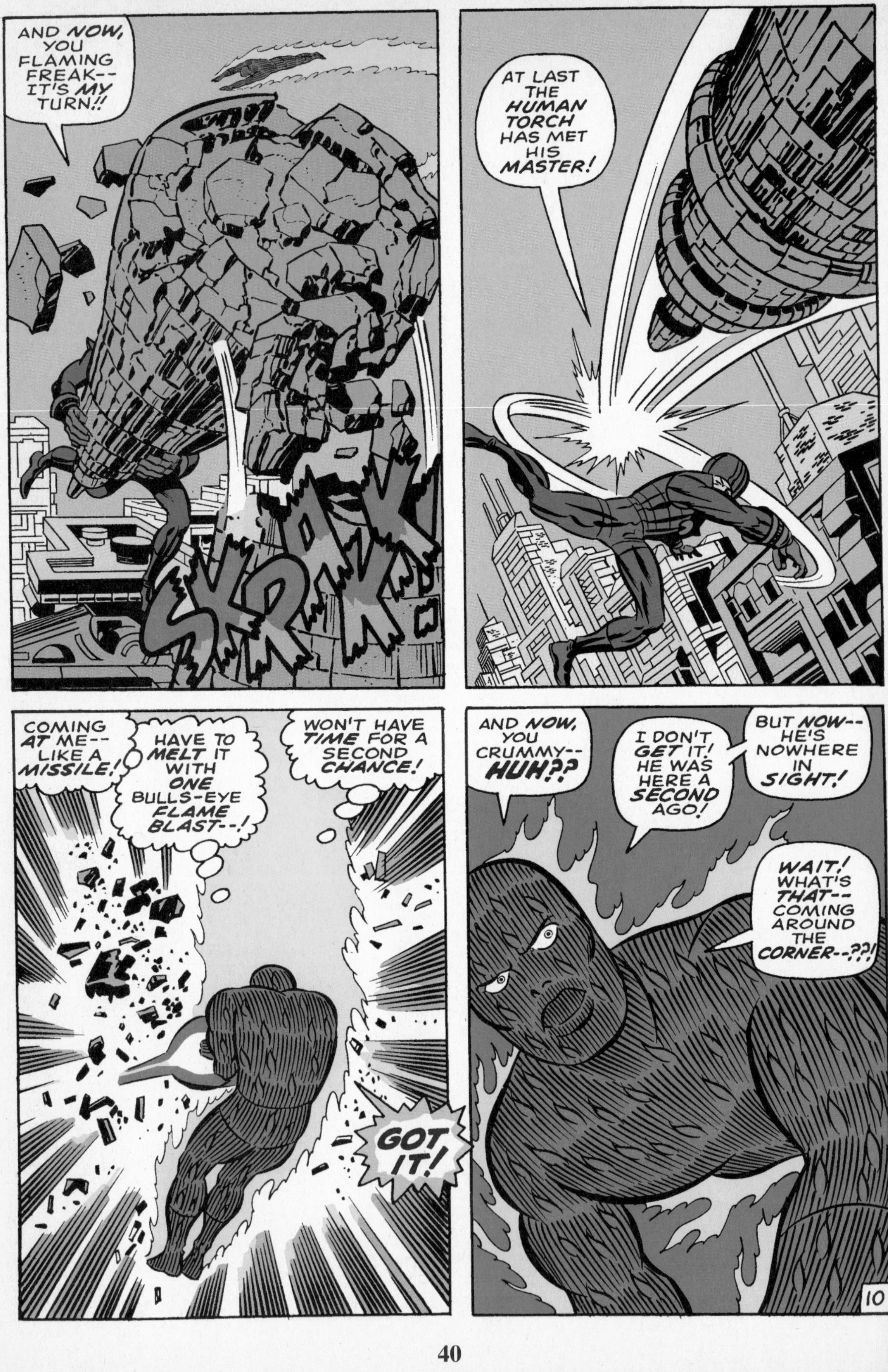
AND NOW, YOU FLAMING FREAK-- IT'S MY TURN!!
SKRAKK
AT LAST THE HUMAN TORCH HAS MET HIS MASTER!
COMING AT ME-- LIKE A MISSILE!
HAVE TO MELT IT WITH ONE BULLS-EYE FLAME BLAST--!
WON'T HAVE TIME FOR A SECOND CHANCE!
GOT IT!
AND NOW, YOU CRUMMY-- HUH??
I DON'T GET IT! HE WAS HERE A SECOND AGO!
BUT NOW-- HE'S NOWHERE IN SIGHT!
WAIT! WHAT'S THAT-- COMING AROUND THE CORNER--??!
10

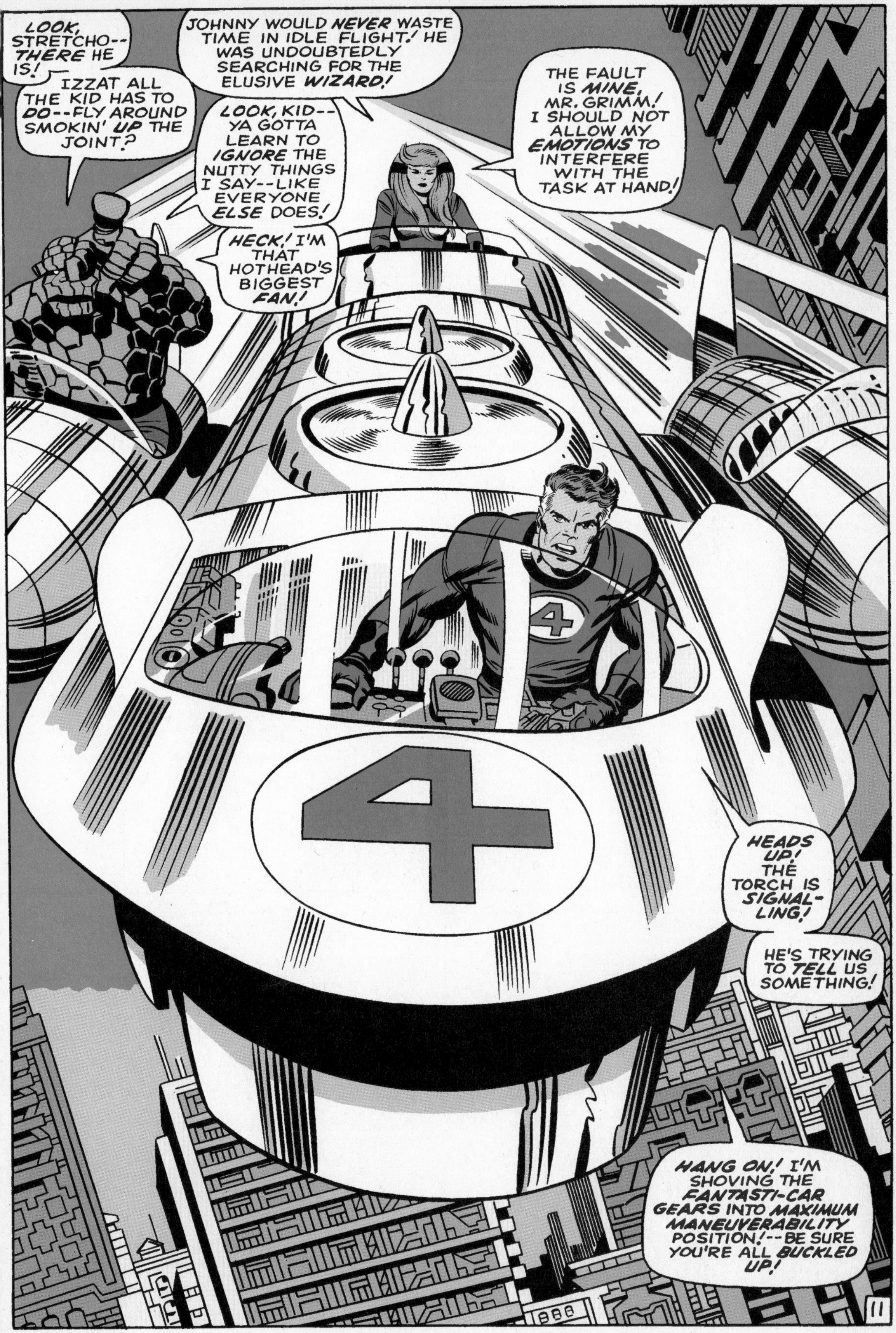
LOOK, STRETCHO-- THERE HE IS!
IZZAT ALL THE KID HAS TO DO--FLY AROUND SMOKIN' UP THE JOINT?
JOHNNY WOULD NEVER WASTE TIME IN IDLE FLIGHT! HE WAS UNDOUBTEDLY SEARCHING FOR THE ELUSIVE WIZARD!
LOOK, KID-- YA GOTTA LEARN TO IGNORE THE NUTTY THINGS I SAY--LIKE EVERYONE ELSE DOES!
HECK! I'M THAT HOTHEAD'S BIGGEST FAN!
THE FAULT IS MINE, MR. GRIMM! I SHOULD NOT ALLOW MY EMOTIONS TO INTERFERE WITH THE TASK AT HAND!
HEADS UP! THE TORCH IS SIGNAL-LING!
HE'S TRYING TO TELL US SOMETHING!
HANG ON! I'M SHOVING THE FANTASTI-CAR GEARS INTO MAXIMUM MANEUVERABILITY POSITION!--BE SURE YOU'RE ALL BUCKLED UP!
11

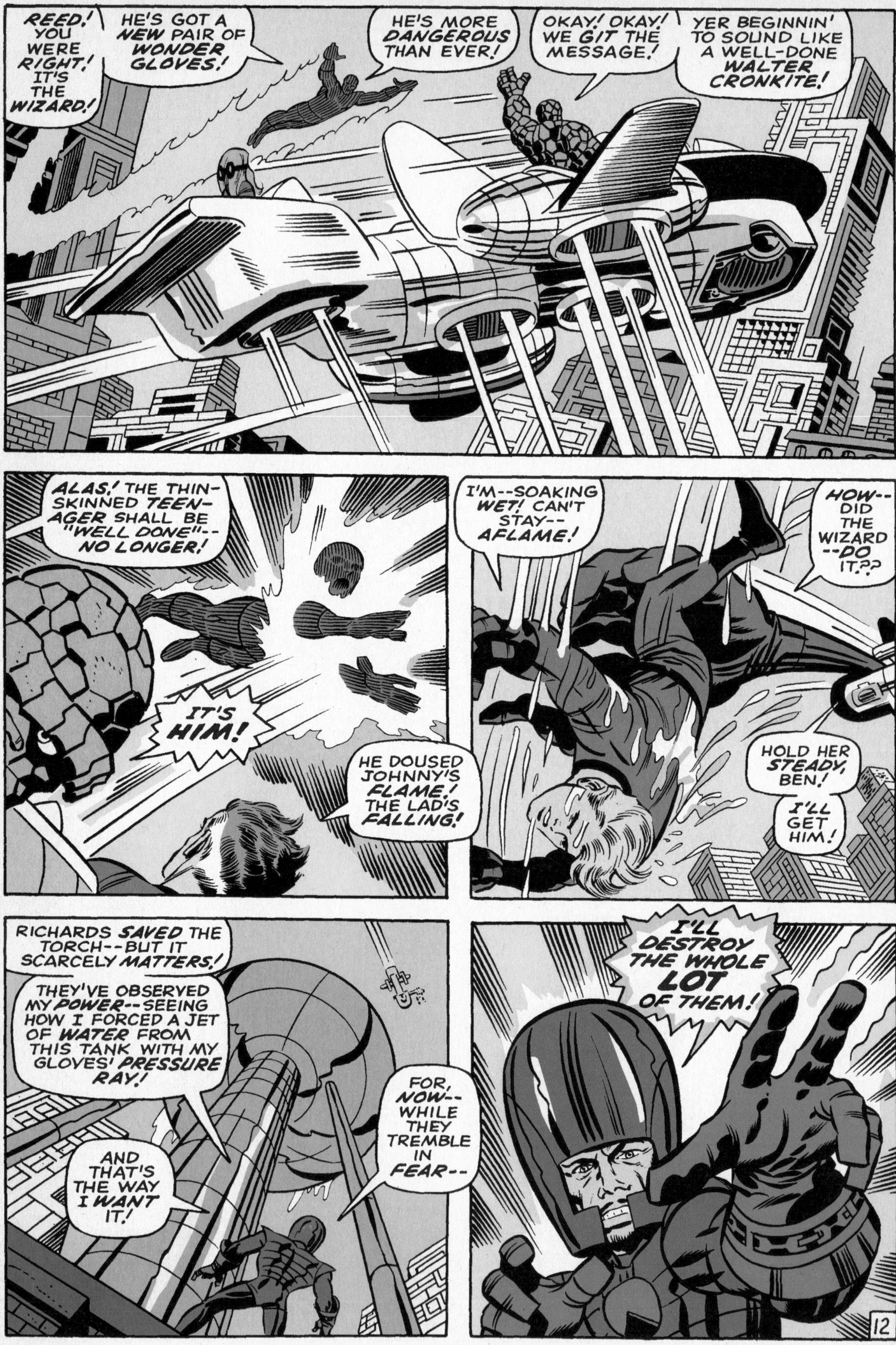
REED! YOU WERE RIGHT! IT'S THE WIZARD!
HE'S GOT A NEW PAIR OF WONDER GLOVES!
HE'S MORE DANGEROUS THAN EVER!
OKAY! OKAY! WE GIT THE MESSAGE!
YER BEGINNIN' TO SOUND LIKE A WELL-DONE WALTER CRONKITE!
ALAS! THE THIN-SKINNED TEEN-AGER SHALL BE "WELL DONE"--NO LONGER!
IT'S HIM!
HE DOUSED JOHNNY'S FLAME! THE LAD'S FALLING!
I'M--SOAKING WET! CAN'T STAY--AFLAME!
HOW--DID THE WIZARD--DO IT??
HOLD HER STEADY, BEN!
I'LL GET HIM!
RICHARDS SAVED THE TORCH--BUT IT SCARCELY MATTERS!
THEY'VE OBSERVED MY POWER--SEEING HOW I FORCED A JET OF WATER FROM THIS TANK WITH MY GLOVES' PRESSURE RAY!
AND THAT'S THE WAY I WANT IT!
FOR, NOW--WHILE THEY TREMBLE IN FEAR--
I'LL DESTROY THE WHOLE LOT OF THEM!
12

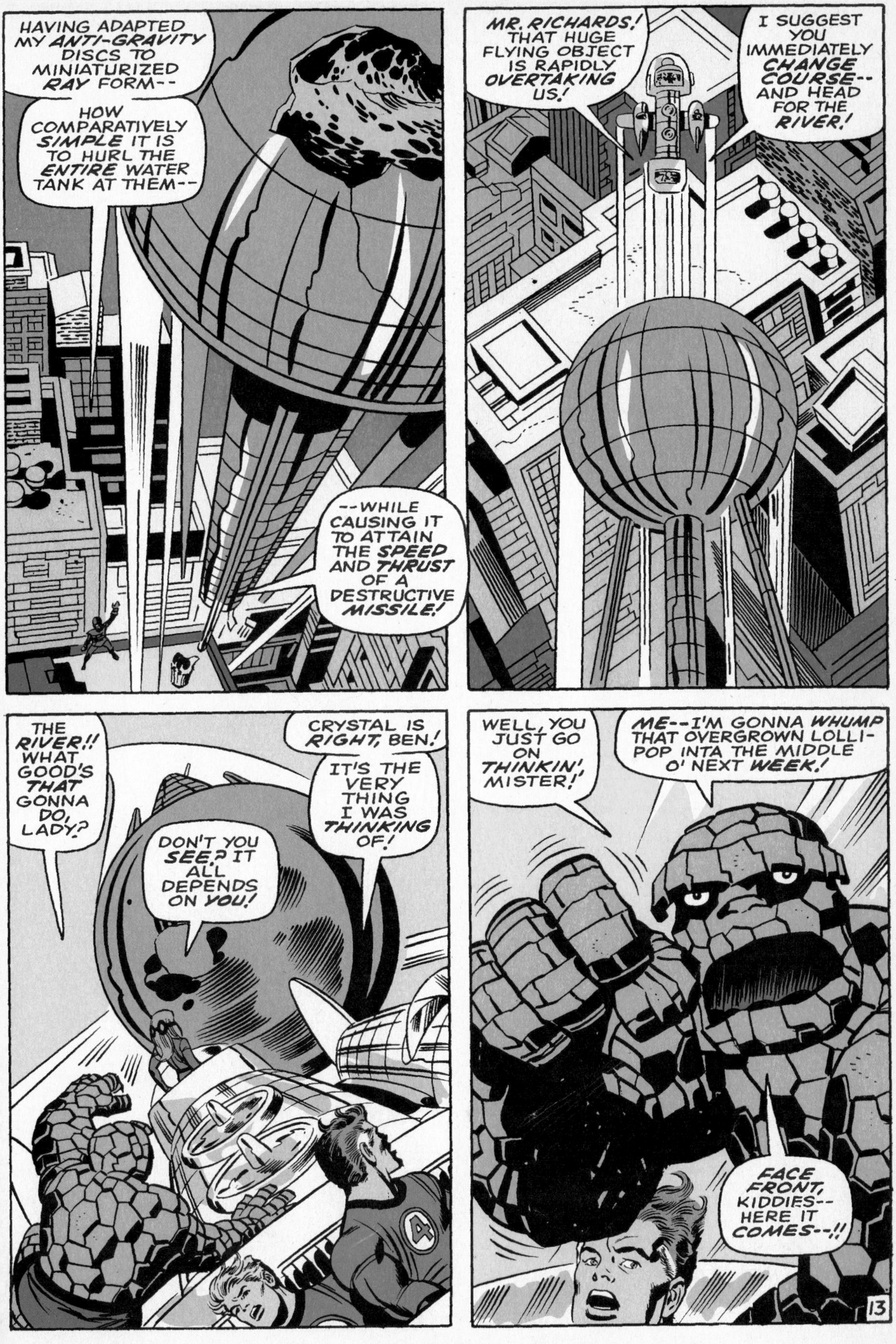
HAVING ADAPTED MY ANTI-GRAVITY DISCS TO MINIATURIZED RAY FORM--
HOW COMPARATIVELY SIMPLE IT IS TO HURL THE ENTIRE WATER TANK AT THEM--
--WHILE CAUSING IT TO ATTAIN THE SPEED AND THRUST OF A DESTRUCTIVE MISSILE!
MR. RICHARDS! THAT HUGE FLYING OBJECT IS RAPIDLY OVERTAKING US!
I SUGGEST YOU IMMEDIATELY CHANGE COURSE-- AND HEAD FOR THE RIVER!
THE RIVER!! WHAT GOOD'S THAT GONNA DO, LADY?
DON'T YOU SEE? IT ALL DEPENDS ON YOU!
CRYSTAL IS RIGHT, BEN!
IT'S THE VERY THING I WAS THINKING OF!
WELL, YOU JUST GO ON THINKIN', MISTER!
ME--I'M GONNA WHUMP THAT OVERGROWN LOLLI-POP INTA THE MIDDLE O' NEXT WEEK!
FACE FRONT, KIDDIES-- HERE IT COMES--!!
13

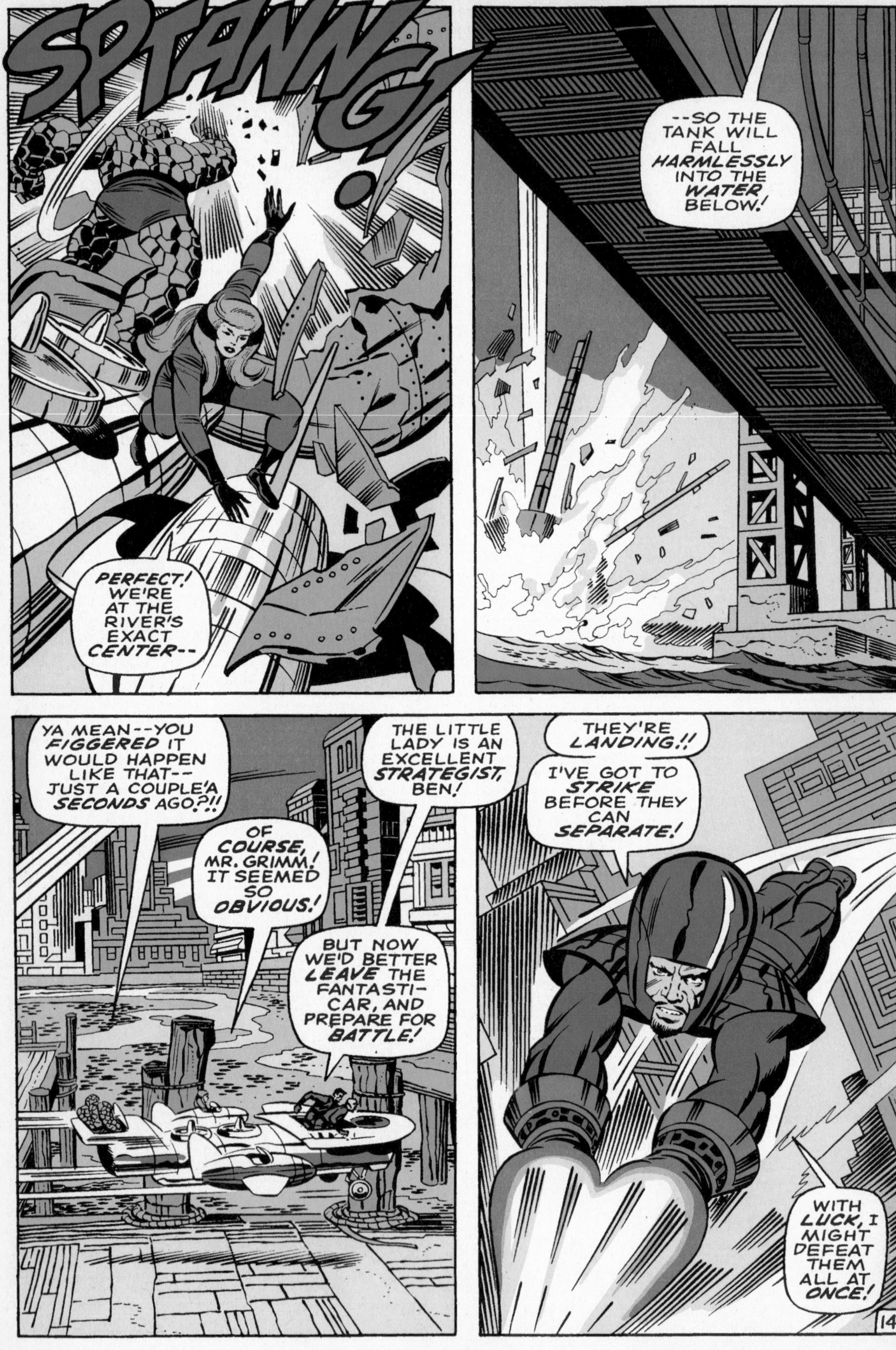
SPTANNG!
PERFECT! WE'RE AT THE RIVER'S EXACT CENTER--
--SO THE TANK WILL FALL HARMLESSLY INTO THE WATER BELOW!
YA MEAN--YOU FIGGERED IT WOULD HAPPEN LIKE THAT-- JUST A COUPLE'A SECONDS AGO?!!
OF COURSE, MR. GRIMM! IT SEEMED SO OBVIOUS!
THE LITTLE LADY IS AN EXCELLENT STRATEGIST, BEN!
BUT NOW WE'D BETTER LEAVE THE FANTASTI-CAR, AND PREPARE FOR BATTLE!
THEY'RE LANDING!!
I'VE GOT TO STRIKE BEFORE THEY CAN SEPARATE!
WITH LUCK, I MIGHT DEFEAT THEM ALL AT ONCE!
14

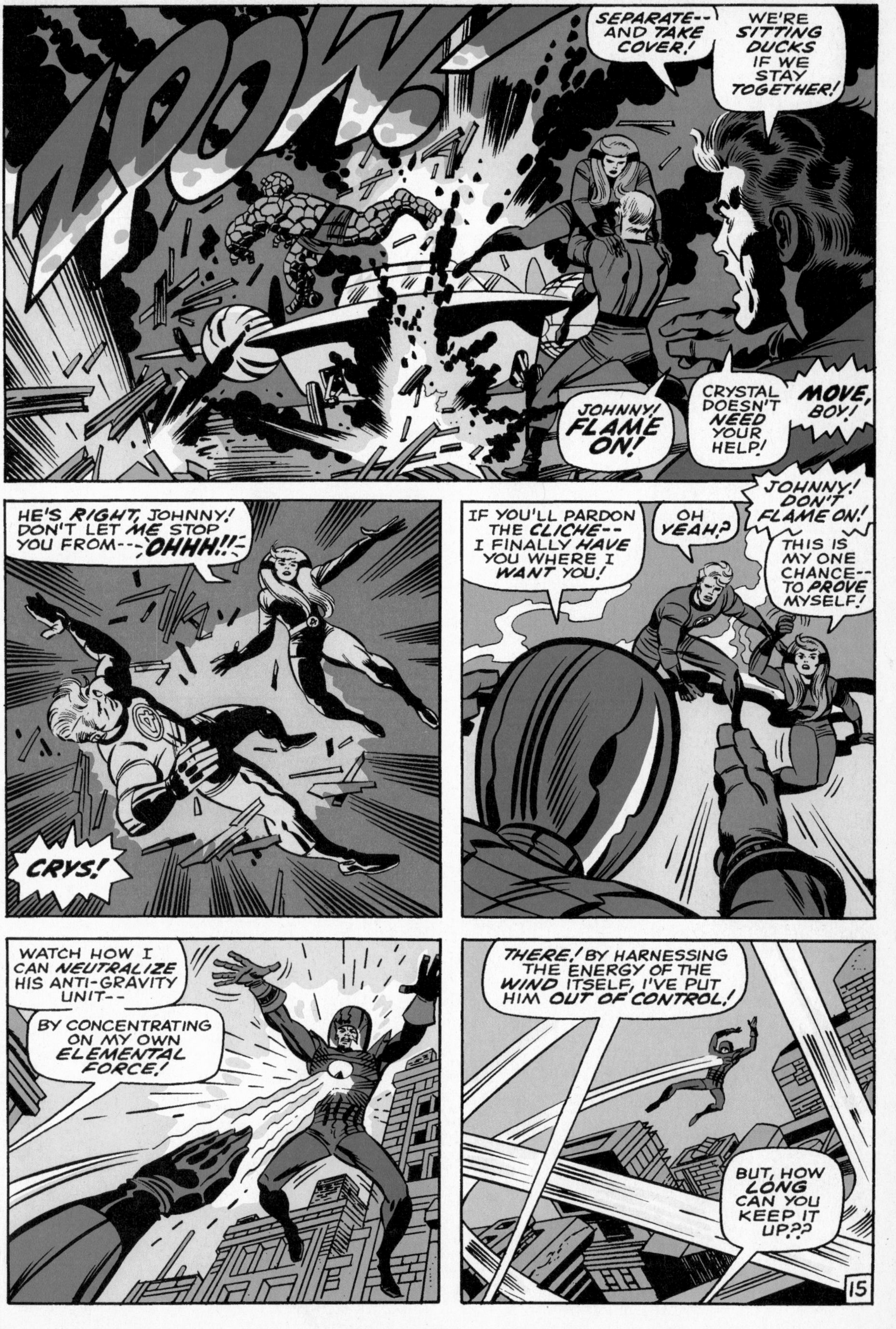
ZOOW!
SEPARATE-- AND TAKE COVER!
WE'RE SITTING DUCKS IF WE STAY TOGETHER!
JOHNNY! FLAME ON!
CRYSTAL DOESN'T NEED YOUR HELP!
MOVE, BOY!
HE'S RIGHT, JOHNNY! DON'T LET ME STOP YOU FROM---OHHH!!
CRYS!
IF YOU'LL PARDON THE CLICHE-- I FINALLY HAVE YOU WHERE I WANT YOU!
OH YEAH?
JOHNNY! DON'T FLAME ON!
THIS IS MY ONE CHANCE-- TO PROVE MYSELF!
WATCH HOW I CAN NEUTRALIZE HIS ANTI-GRAVITY UNIT--
BY CONCENTRATING ON MY OWN ELEMENTAL FORCE!
THERE! BY HARNESSING THE ENERGY OF THE WIND ITSELF, I'VE PUT HIM OUT OF CONTROL!
BUT, HOW LONG CAN YOU KEEP IT UP??
15

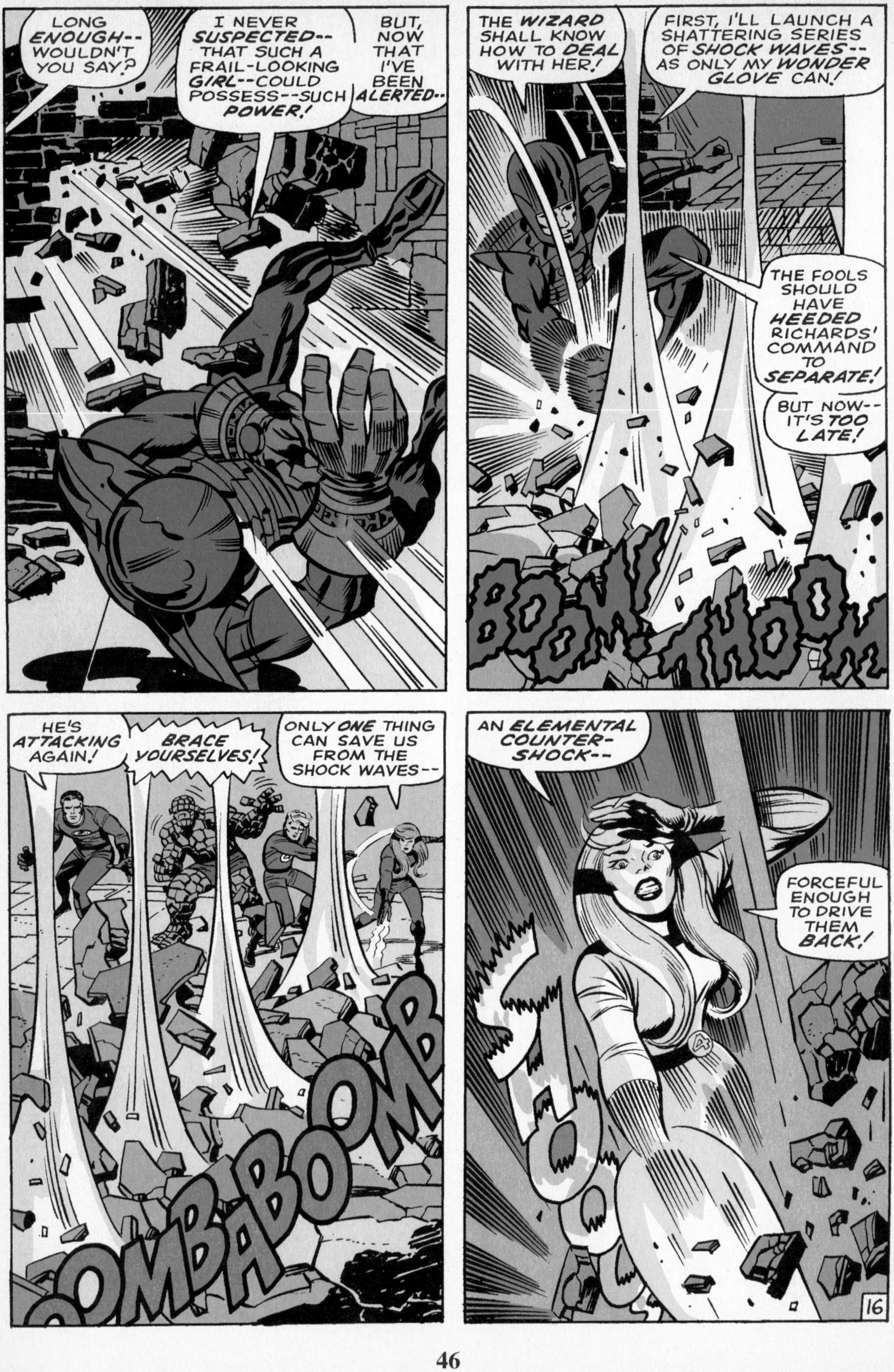
LONG ENOUGH-- WOULDN'T YOU SAY?
I NEVER SUSPECTED-- THAT SUCH A FRAIL-LOOKING GIRL--COULD POSSESS--SUCH POWER!
BUT, NOW THAT I'VE BEEN ALERTED--
THE WIZARD SHALL KNOW HOW TO DEAL WITH HER!
FIRST, I'LL LAUNCH A SHATTERING SERIES OF SHOCK WAVES-- AS ONLY MY WONDER GLOVE CAN!
THE FOOLS SHOULD HAVE HEEDED RICHARDS' COMMAND TO SEPARATE!
BUT NOW-- IT'S TOO LATE!
BOOM! THOOM
HE'S ATTACKING AGAIN!
BRACE YOURSELVES!
ONLY ONE THING CAN SAVE US FROM THE SHOCK WAVES--
OOMBABOOMB
AN ELEMENTAL COUNTER-SHOCK--
FORCEFUL ENOUGH TO DRIVE THEM BACK!
16

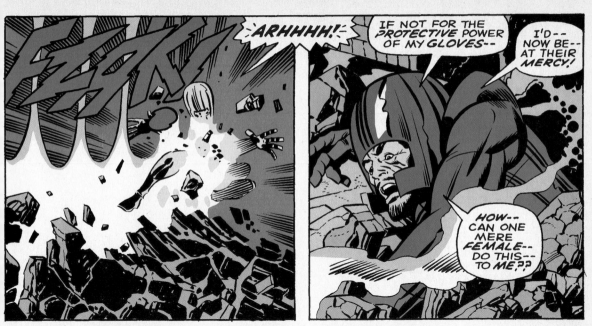

ARHHHH!

IF NOT FOR THE *PROTECTIVE* POWER OF MY *GLOVES*--

I'D-- NOW BE-- AT THEIR *MERCY!*

HOW-- CAN ONE MERE *FEMALE*-- DO THIS-- TO *ME*??

BUT, *THIS* TIME--SHE HAS TRULY GONE *TOO FAR!*

FOR *THIS* TIME --I'LL SET MY GLOVE CONTROLS --TO *HIGHEST INTENSITY!*

NOW YOU WILL LEARN THE FATAL *FOLLY* OF TAMPERING WITH FORCES BEYOND YOUR YOUTHFUL *KEN*--!

YOU CANNOT THREATEN *ME!!*

YOU CANNOT THREATEN ONE WHO IS THE *SISTER* OF *MEDUSA*--

ONE WHO HAS DWELLED AMONG THE INCOMPARABLE *INHUMANS*--

AND FACED *PERILS* WITHOUT NUMBER AT THE SIDE OF MIGHTY *BLACK BOLT!*

BUT *MOST* OF ALL--YOU CANNOT THREATEN-- A BORN *ELEMENTAL!*

17

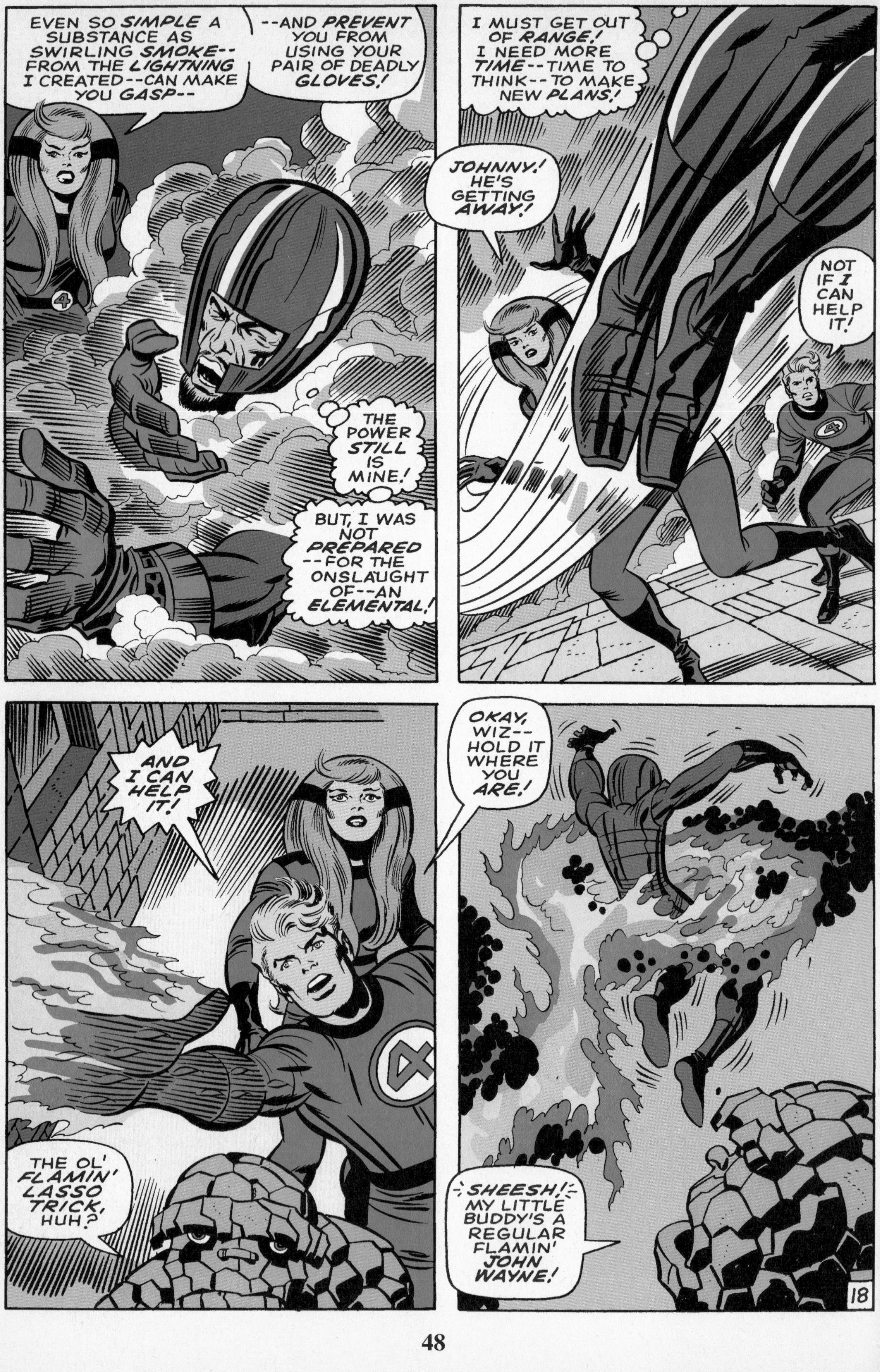
EVEN SO SIMPLE A SUBSTANCE AS SWIRLING SMOKE-- FROM THE LIGHTNING I CREATED--CAN MAKE YOU GASP--
--AND PREVENT YOU FROM USING YOUR PAIR OF DEADLY GLOVES!
THE POWER STILL IS MINE!
BUT, I WAS NOT PREPARED --FOR THE ONSLAUGHT OF--AN ELEMENTAL!
I MUST GET OUT OF RANGE! I NEED MORE TIME--TIME TO THINK--TO MAKE NEW PLANS!
JOHNNY! HE'S GETTING AWAY!
NOT IF I CAN HELP IT!
AND I CAN HELP IT!
THE OL' FLAMIN' LASSO TRICK, HUH?
OKAY, WIZ-- HOLD IT WHERE YOU ARE!
SHEESH! MY LITTLE BUDDY'S A REGULAR FLAMIN' JOHN WAYNE!
18

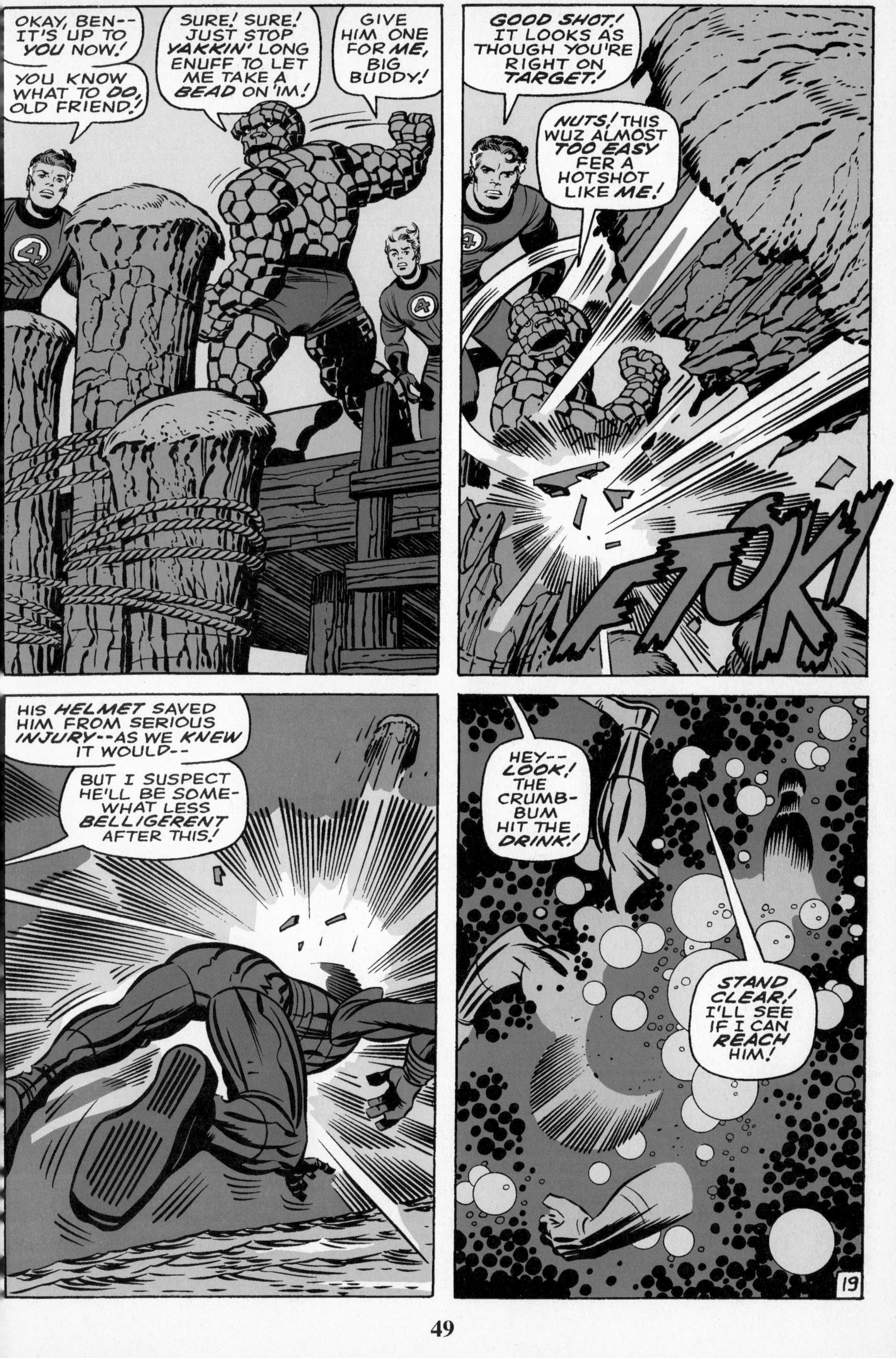
OKAY, BEN-- IT'S UP TO YOU NOW!
YOU KNOW WHAT TO DO, OLD FRIEND!
SURE! SURE! JUST STOP YAKKIN' LONG ENUFF TO LET ME TAKE A BEAD ON 'IM!
GIVE HIM ONE FOR ME, BIG BUDDY!
GOOD SHOT! IT LOOKS AS THOUGH YOU'RE RIGHT ON TARGET!
NUTS! THIS WUZ ALMOST TOO EASY FER A HOTSHOT LIKE ME!
FTOK!
HIS HELMET SAVED HIM FROM SERIOUS INJURY--AS WE KNEW IT WOULD--
BUT I SUSPECT HE'LL BE SOMEWHAT LESS BELLIGERENT AFTER THIS!
HEY--LOOK! THE CRUMB-BUM HIT THE DRINK!
STAND CLEAR! I'LL SEE IF I CAN REACH HIM!
19

I'M IN *LUCK!* THE WATER *REVIVED* ME--JUST IN *TIME!*

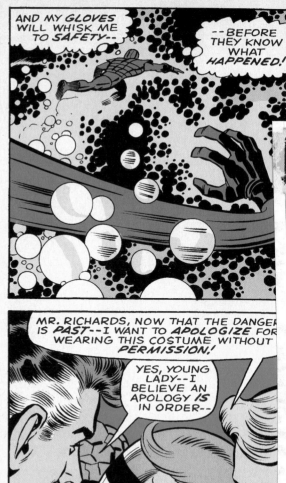

AND MY *GLOVES* WILL WHISK ME TO *SAFETY*--

--BEFORE THEY KNOW WHAT *HAPPENED!*

THERE'S NO *SIGN* OF HIM DOWN THERE!

I DON'T *GET* IT!

HIS BLASTED *HELMET* WOULD'A KEPT 'IM FROM *DROWNIN'!*

HE *DIDN'T* DROWN! HE MANAGED TO *ESCAPE!*

AND I *FEAR* THAT MEANS--WE HAVEN'T HEARD THE *LAST* OF HIM!

MR. RICHARDS, NOW THAT THE DANGER IS *PAST*--I WANT TO *APOLOGIZE* FOR WEARING THIS COSTUME WITHOUT *PERMISSION!*

YES, YOUNG LADY--I BELIEVE AN APOLOGY *IS* IN ORDER--

--FROM *ME*--FOR EVER EVEN *DOUBTING* YOU!

AND NOW, BY THE *AUTHORITY* VESTED IN ME--BY NOBODY IN PARTICULAR--

I MOST WARMLY *WELCOME* YOU TO THE ROLLICKING RANKS OF THE FABULOUS FREE-WHEELING *FANTASTIC FOUR!*

IF ANYONE MESSES WITH *US*, SHE'LL WHUMP 'EM WITH A *POWDER PUFF!*

MAN! FROM NOW ON, THE *SUPER-HERO* BIZ IS GONNA BE A *BLAST!*

--AND YOU BETTER *BELIEVE* IT!

20

FANTASTIC FOUR
MARVEL COMICS GROUP
APPROVED BY THE COMICS CODE AUTHORITY
20¢ 132 MAR 02462
THE WORLD'S GREATEST COMIC MAGAZINE!
FANTASTIC FOUR
FIGHT ME! RESIST ME! YOU'LL BUT MAKE ME STRONGER-- EVER STRONGER!
--UNTIL AT LAST DESTROY YOU!!
OMEGA! THE ULTIMATE ASSASSIN!

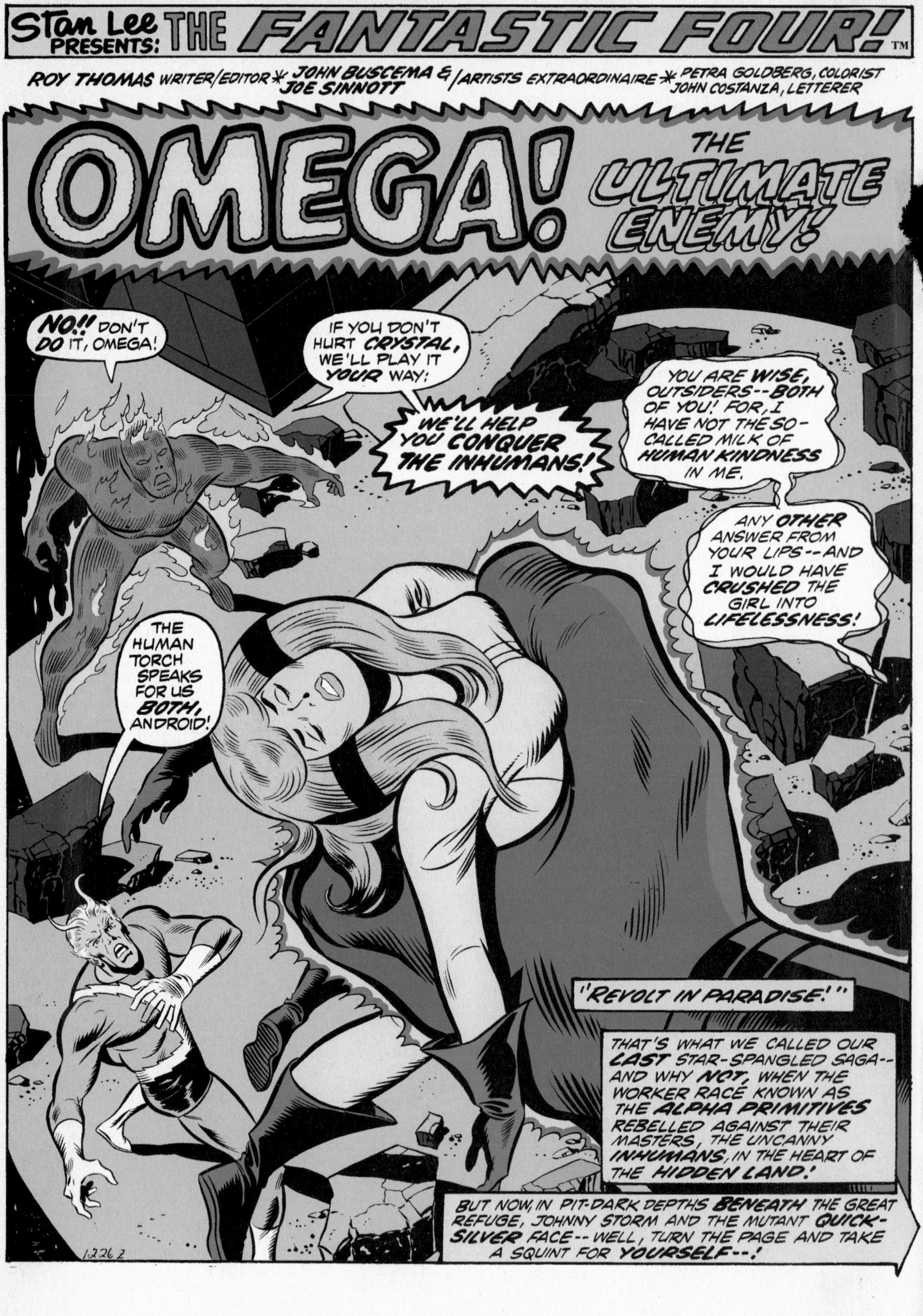
Stan Lee PRESENTS: THE FANTASTIC FOUR! TM
ROY THOMAS WRITER/EDITOR * JOHN BUSCEMA & JOE SINNOTT / ARTISTS EXTRAORDINAIRE * PETRA GOLDBERG, COLORIST JOHN COSTANZA, LETTERER
OMEGA! THE ULTIMATE ENEMY!
NO!! DON'T DO IT, OMEGA!
IF YOU DON'T HURT CRYSTAL, WE'LL PLAY IT YOUR WAY:
WE'LL HELP YOU CONQUER THE INHUMANS!
YOU ARE WISE, OUTSIDERS--BOTH OF YOU! FOR, I HAVE NOT THE SO-CALLED MILK OF HUMAN KINDNESS IN ME.
ANY OTHER ANSWER FROM YOUR LIPS--AND I WOULD HAVE CRUSHED THE GIRL INTO LIFELESSNESS!
THE HUMAN TORCH SPEAKS FOR US BOTH, ANDROID!
"REVOLT IN PARADISE!"
THAT'S WHAT WE CALLED OUR LAST STAR-SPANGLED SAGA--AND WHY NOT, WHEN THE WORKER RACE KNOWN AS THE ALPHA PRIMITIVES REBELLED AGAINST THEIR MASTERS, THE UNCANNY INHUMANS, IN THE HEART OF THE HIDDEN LAND!
BUT NOW, IN PIT-DARK DEPTHS BENEATH THE GREAT REFUGE, JOHNNY STORM AND THE MUTANT QUICK-SILVER FACE-- WELL, TURN THE PAGE AND TAKE A SQUINT FOR YOURSELF--!

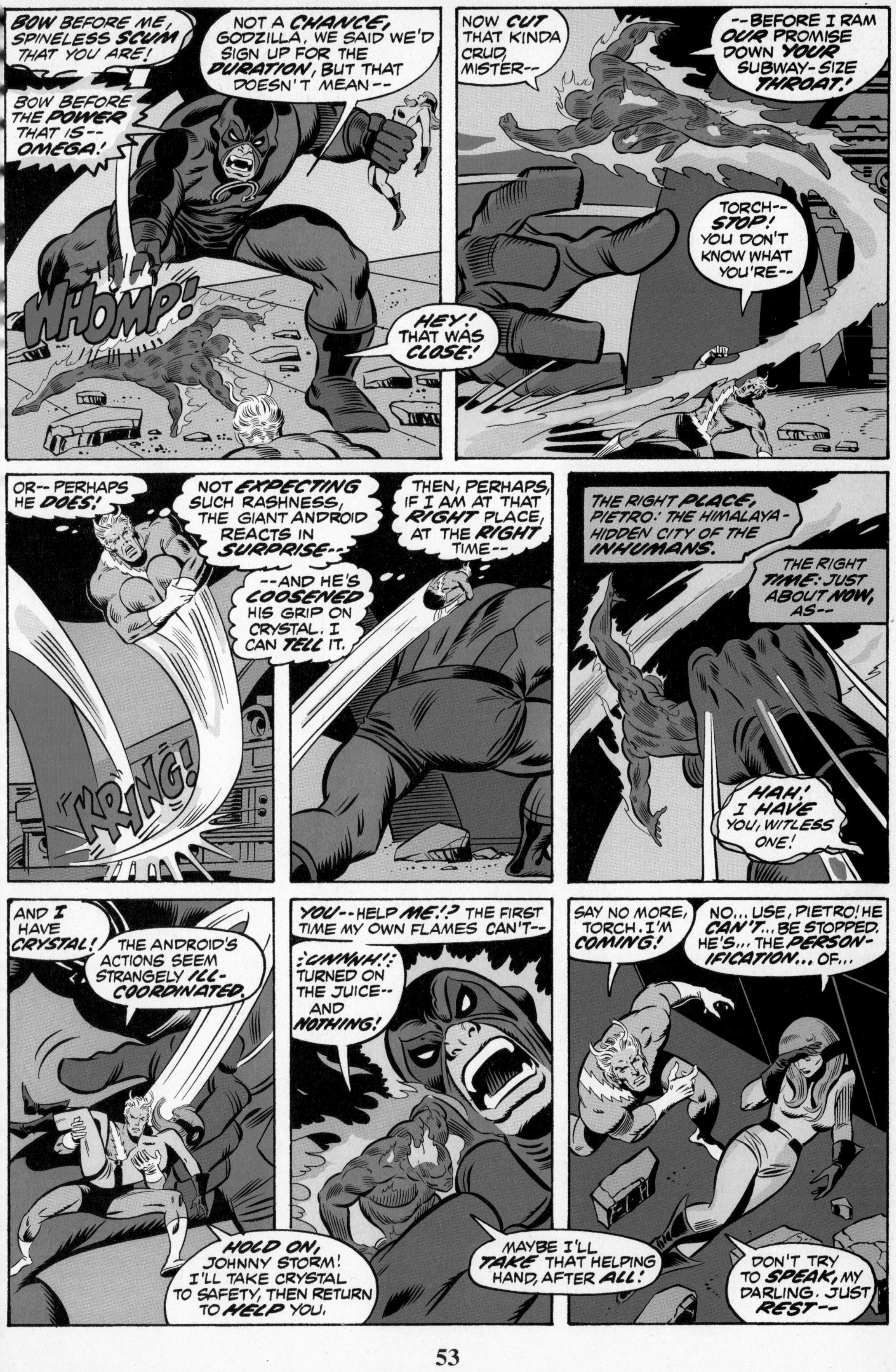
BOW BEFORE ME, SPINELESS SCUM THAT YOU ARE!
BOW BEFORE THE POWER THAT IS-- OMEGA!
NOT A CHANCE, GODZILLA, WE SAID WE'D SIGN UP FOR THE DURATION, BUT THAT DOESN'T MEAN--
WHOMP!
HEY! THAT WAS CLOSE!
NOW CUT THAT KINDA CRUD, MISTER--
--BEFORE I RAM OUR PROMISE DOWN YOUR SUBWAY-SIZE THROAT!
TORCH-- STOP! YOU DON'T KNOW WHAT YOU'RE--
OR--PERHAPS HE DOES!
NOT EXPECTING SUCH RASHNESS, THE GIANT ANDROID REACTS IN SURPRISE--
--AND HE'S LOOSENED HIS GRIP ON CRYSTAL. I CAN TELL IT.
KRING!
THEN, PERHAPS, IF I AM AT THAT RIGHT PLACE, AT THE RIGHT TIME--
THE RIGHT PLACE, PIETRO: THE HIMALAYA-HIDDEN CITY OF THE INHUMANS.
THE RIGHT TIME: JUST ABOUT NOW, AS--
HAH! I HAVE YOU, WITLESS ONE!
AND I HAVE CRYSTAL!
THE ANDROID'S ACTIONS SEEM STRANGELY ILL-COORDINATED.
HOLD ON, JOHNNY STORM! I'LL TAKE CRYSTAL TO SAFETY, THEN RETURN TO HELP YOU.
YOU--HELP ME!? THE FIRST TIME MY OWN FLAMES CAN'T--
UNNNH! TURNED ON THE JUICE-- AND NOTHING!
MAYBE I'LL TAKE THAT HELPING HAND, AFTER ALL!
SAY NO MORE, TORCH. I'M COMING!
NO... USE, PIETRO! HE CAN'T... BE STOPPED. HE'S... THE PERSON-IFICATION... OF...
DON'T TRY TO SPEAK, MY DARLING. JUST REST--

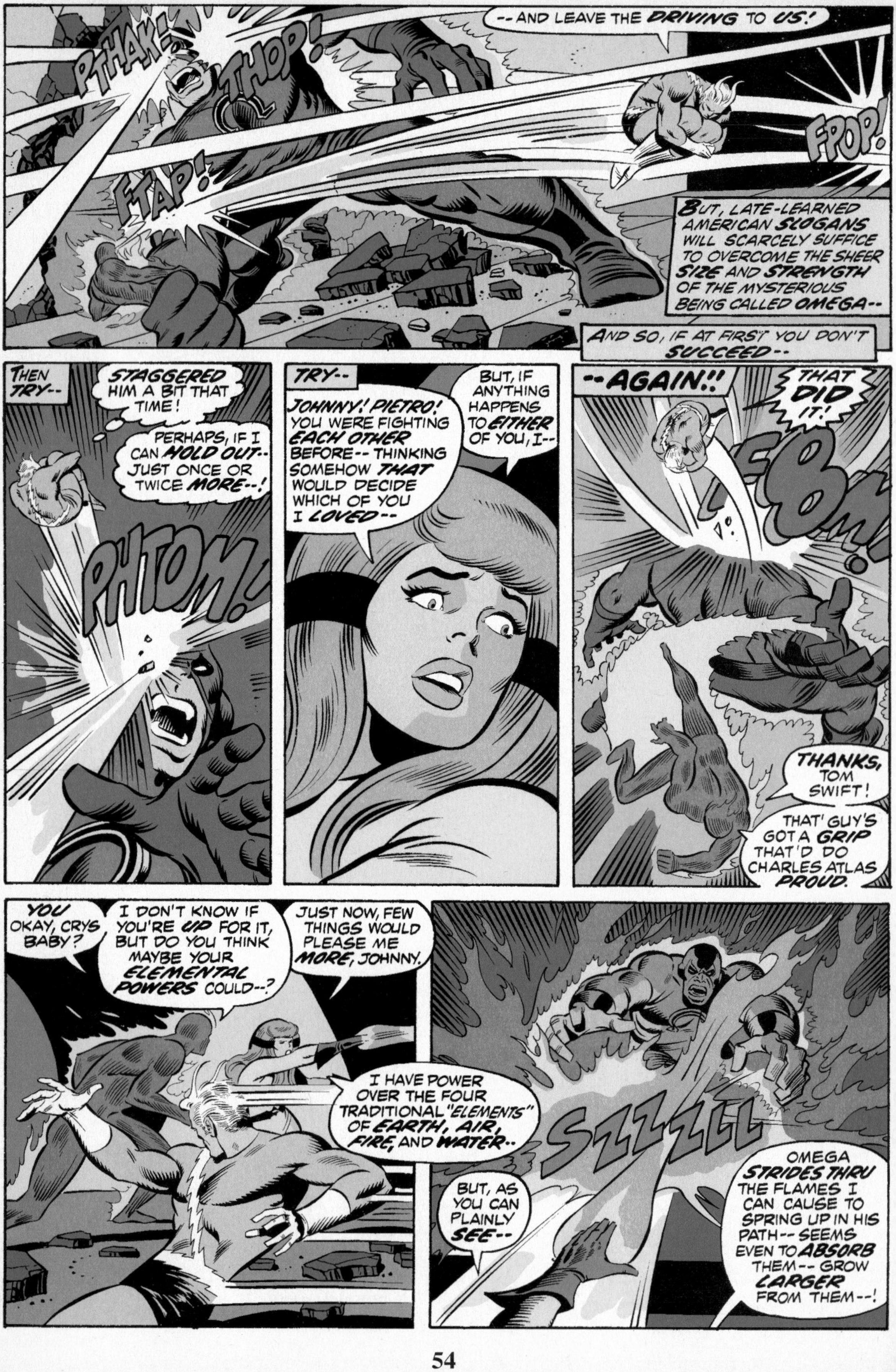

PTHAK!
THOP!
--AND LEAVE THE DRIVING TO US!
FPOP!
FTAP!
BUT, LATE-LEARNED AMERICAN SLOGANS WILL SCARCELY SUFFICE TO OVERCOME THE SHEER SIZE AND STRENGTH OF THE MYSTERIOUS BEING CALLED OMEGA--
AND SO, IF AT FIRST YOU DON'T SUCCEED--
THEN TRY--
STAGGERED HIM A BIT THAT TIME!
PERHAPS, IF I CAN HOLD OUT-- JUST ONCE OR TWICE MORE--!
PHTOM!
TRY--
JOHNNY! PIETRO! YOU WERE FIGHTING EACH OTHER BEFORE-- THINKING SOMEHOW THAT WOULD DECIDE WHICH OF YOU I LOVED--
BUT, IF ANYTHING HAPPENS TO EITHER OF YOU, I--
--AGAIN!!
THAT DID IT!
THANKS, TOM SWIFT!
THAT' GUY'S GOT A GRIP THAT'D DO CHARLES ATLAS PROUD.
YOU OKAY, CRYS BABY?
I DON'T KNOW IF YOU'RE UP FOR IT, BUT DO YOU THINK MAYBE YOUR ELEMENTAL POWERS COULD--?
JUST NOW, FEW THINGS WOULD PLEASE ME MORE, JOHNNY.
I HAVE POWER OVER THE FOUR TRADITIONAL "ELEMENTS" OF EARTH, AIR, FIRE, AND WATER..
SZZZLL
BUT, AS YOU CAN PLAINLY SEE--
OMEGA STRIDES THRU THE FLAMES I CAN CAUSE TO SPRING UP IN HIS PATH-- SEEMS EVEN TO ABSORB THEM-- GROW LARGER FROM THEM--!

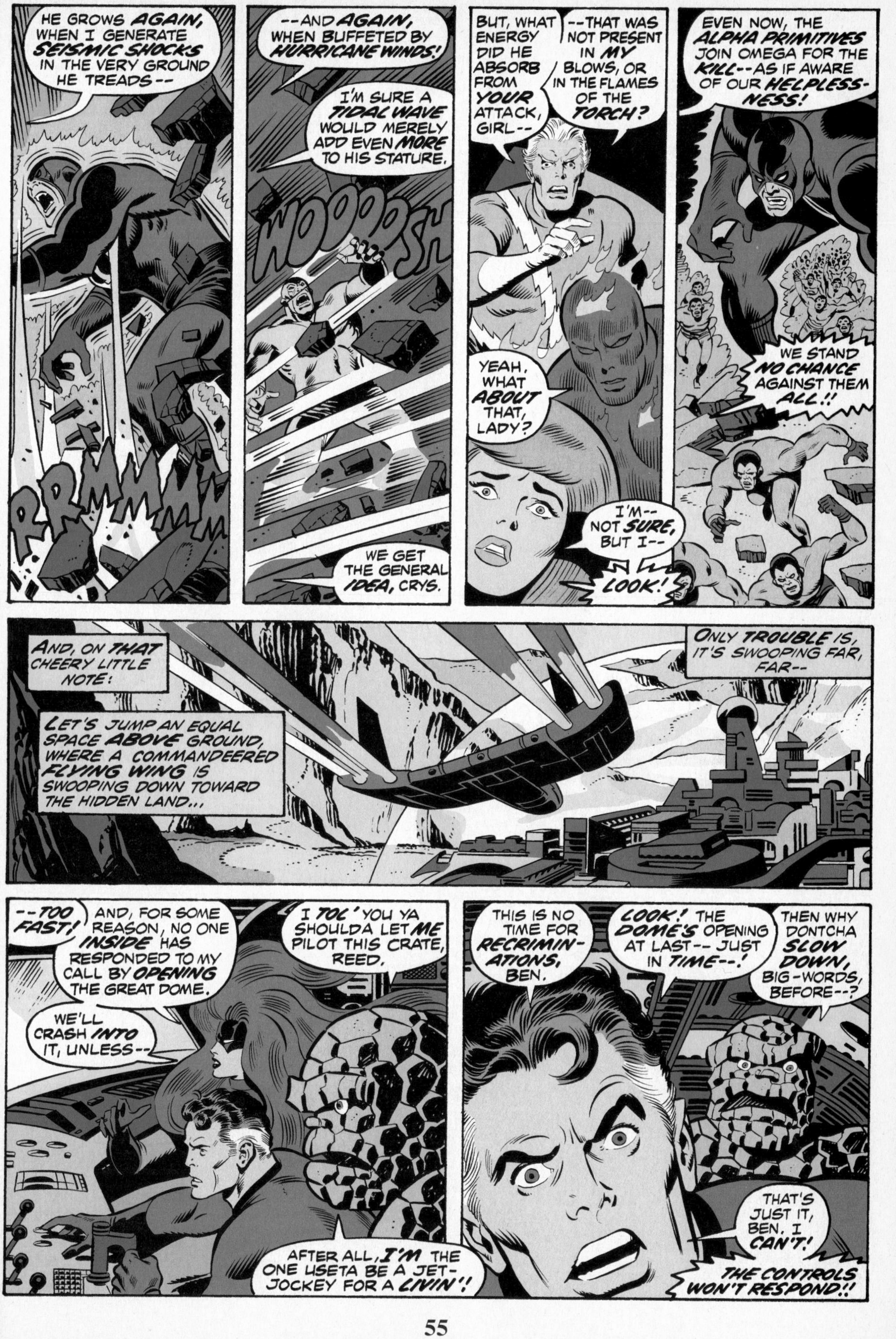
HE GROWS AGAIN, WHEN I GENERATE SEISMIC SHOCKS IN THE VERY GROUND HE TREADS--
RRRMMMM
--AND AGAIN, WHEN BUFFETED BY HURRICANE WINDS!
I'M SURE A TIDAL WAVE WOULD MERELY ADD EVEN MORE TO HIS STATURE.
WOOOOSH
WE GET THE GENERAL IDEA, CRYS.
BUT, WHAT ENERGY DID HE ABSORB FROM YOUR ATTACK, GIRL--
--THAT WAS NOT PRESENT IN MY BLOWS, OR IN THE FLAMES OF THE TORCH?
YEAH, WHAT ABOUT THAT, LADY?
I'M-- NOT SURE, BUT I--
LOOK!
EVEN NOW, THE ALPHA PRIMITIVES JOIN OMEGA FOR THE KILL--AS IF AWARE OF OUR HELPLESSNESS!
WE STAND NO CHANCE AGAINST THEM ALL!!
AND, ON THAT CHEERY LITTLE NOTE:
LET'S JUMP AN EQUAL SPACE ABOVE GROUND, WHERE A COMMANDEERED FLYING WING IS SWOOPING DOWN TOWARD THE HIDDEN LAND...
ONLY TROUBLE IS, IT'S SWOOPING FAR, FAR--
--TOO FAST!
AND, FOR SOME REASON, NO ONE INSIDE HAS RESPONDED TO MY CALL BY OPENING THE GREAT DOME.
WE'LL CRASH INTO IT, UNLESS--
I TOL' YOU YA SHOULDA LET ME PILOT THIS CRATE, REED.
AFTER ALL, I'M THE ONE USETA BE A JET-JOCKEY FOR A LIVIN'!
THIS IS NO TIME FOR RECRIMINATIONS, BEN.
LOOK! THE DOME'S OPENING AT LAST-- JUST IN TIME--!
THEN WHY DONTCHA SLOW DOWN, BIG-WORDS, BEFORE--?
THAT'S JUST IT, BEN. I CAN'T!
THE CONTROLS WON'T RESPOND!!

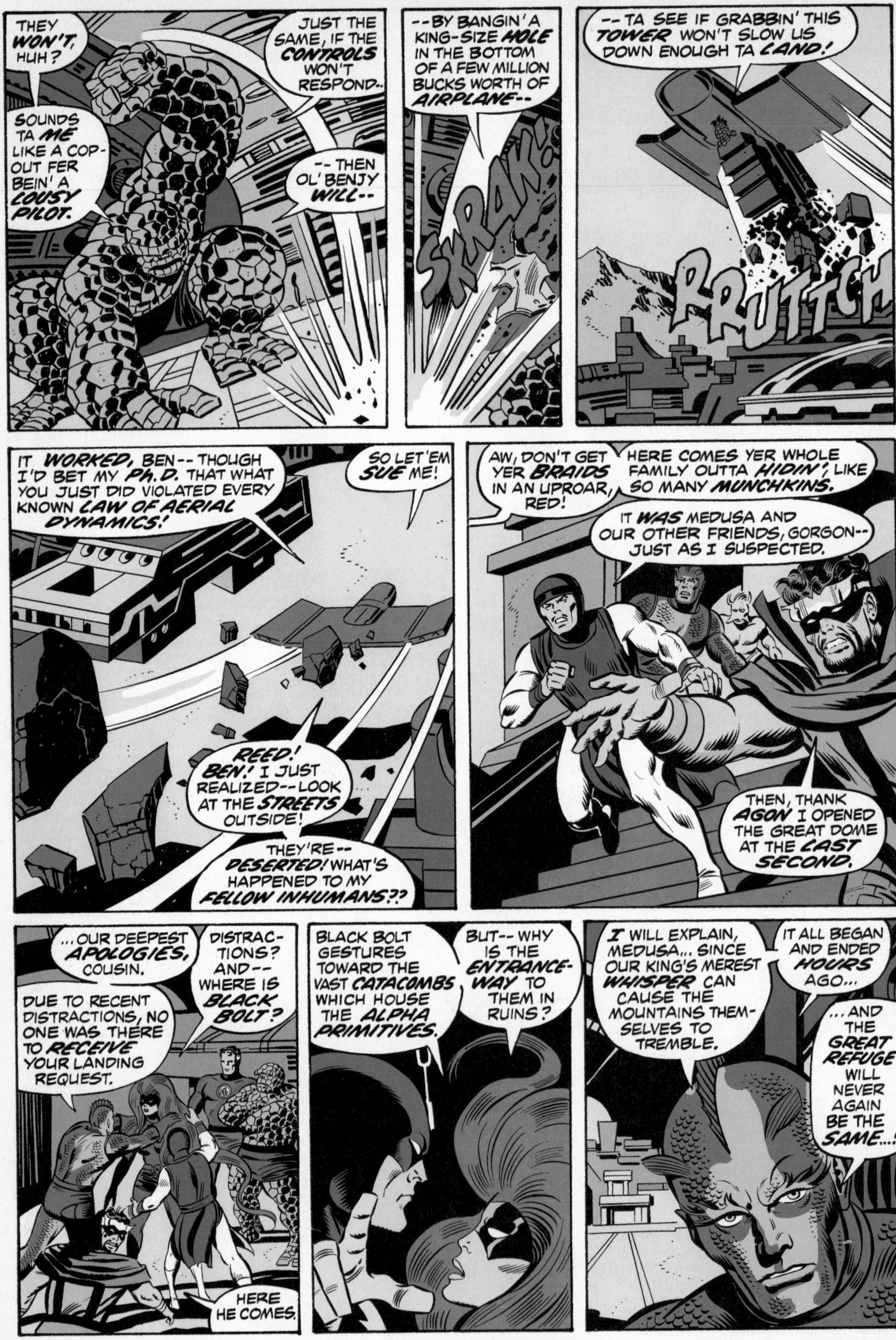
THEY WON'T, HUH?
SOUNDS TA ME LIKE A COP-OUT FER BEIN' A LOUSY PILOT.
JUST THE SAME, IF THE CONTROLS WON'T RESPOND..
--THEN OL' BENJY WILL--
--BY BANGIN' A KING-SIZE HOLE IN THE BOTTOM OF A FEW MILLION BUCKS WORTH OF AIRPLANE--
SKRAK!
--TA SEE IF GRABBIN' THIS TOWER WON'T SLOW US DOWN ENOUGH TA LAND!
RRUTTCH
IT WORKED, BEN-- THOUGH I'D BET MY Ph.D. THAT WHAT YOU JUST DID VIOLATED EVERY KNOWN LAW OF AERIAL DYNAMICS!
SO LET'EM SUE ME!
REED! BEN! I JUST REALIZED--LOOK AT THE STREETS OUTSIDE!
THEY'RE-- DESERTED! WHAT'S HAPPENED TO MY FELLOW INHUMANS??
AW, DON'T GET YER BRAIDS IN AN UPROAR, RED!
HERE COMES YER WHOLE FAMILY OUTTA HIDIN', LIKE SO MANY MUNCHKINS.
IT WAS MEDUSA AND OUR OTHER FRIENDS, GORGON-- JUST AS I SUSPECTED.
THEN, THANK AGON I OPENED THE GREAT DOME AT THE LAST SECOND.
...OUR DEEPEST APOLOGIES, COUSIN.
DUE TO RECENT DISTRACTIONS, NO ONE WAS THERE TO RECEIVE YOUR LANDING REQUEST.
DISTRACTIONS? AND-- WHERE IS BLACK BOLT?
HERE HE COMES.
BLACK BOLT GESTURES TOWARD THE VAST CATACOMBS WHICH HOUSE THE ALPHA PRIMITIVES.
BUT-- WHY IS THE ENTRANCE-WAY TO THEM IN RUINS?
I WILL EXPLAIN, MEDUSA... SINCE OUR KING'S MEREST WHISPER CAN CAUSE THE MOUNTAINS THEM-SELVES TO TREMBLE.
IT ALL BEGAN AND ENDED HOURS AGO...
...AND THE GREAT REFUGE WILL NEVER AGAIN BE THE SAME...!

"FROM DOCILE *WORKERS*, BORN AND BRED FOR MILLENNIA TO THEIR SIMPLE LIVES AND MENIALS TASKS--"

"-- THE *ALPHA PRIMITIVES* SUDDENLY BECAME A FIERCE PRIDE OF RAMPAGING *LIONS*--"

"NO-- *WORSE* THAN THAT: THEY BECAME AN ARMY OF RELENTLESS *ANTS*, WITH NO THOUGHT FOR INDIVIDUAL SAFETY, NO RELUCTANCE TO *SACRIFICE* INFINITE NUMBERS --"

"--TO *DESTROY* THEIR MASTERS, AND TAKE COMMAND OF THE *HIDDEN LAND!*"

"FORTUNATELY, WE *DEFEATED* THEM--DROVE THEM BACK, THEN IMPRISONED THEM IN THEIR SUBTERRANEAN *LABYRINTH*.

"YET, WHEN IT WAS LEARNED THAT *CRYSTAL* HAD BEEN TAKEN BY THEM, *JOHNNY STORM* AND *QUICKSILVER* RECKLESSLY PURSUED THEM --"

"--AIDED BY THE TELEPORTATIONAL PROWESS OF *LOCKJAW*--"

"-- AND SUSTAINED BY THE *LOVE* WHICH EACH BEARS FOR OUR FAIR COUSIN!"

"FOR OURSELVES, WE SOUGHT SOME *CLUE* TO THE UPRISING, EVEN VISITED THE CELL OF OUR SOVEREIGN'S BROTHER, *MAXIMUS THE MAD* --"

"BUT HE DOES *NAUGHT* THESE DAYS, SAVE TINKER WITH A HARMLESS ATTEMPT AT A *PERPETUAL MOTION* DEVICE..."

"...AND PROCLAIMED, FOR ONCE, A RARE AND UNACCUSTOMED *INNOCENCE!*"

AND *NOW*, TRITON?

AND NOW WE *WAIT*, MEDUSA-- WAIT AND DO *NOTHING*--

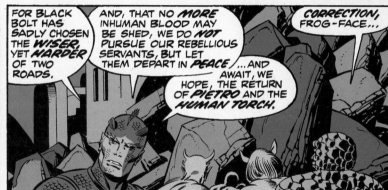

FOR BLACK BOLT HAS SADLY CHOSEN THE *WISER*, YET *HARDER* OF TWO ROADS.

AND, THAT NO *MORE* INHUMAN BLOOD MAY BE SHED, WE DO *NOT* PURSUE OUR REBELLIOUS SERVANTS, BUT LET THEM DEPART IN *PEACE* ...AND AWAIT, WE HOPE, THE RETURN OF *PIETRO* AND THE *HUMAN TORCH.*

CORRECTION, FROG-FACE...,

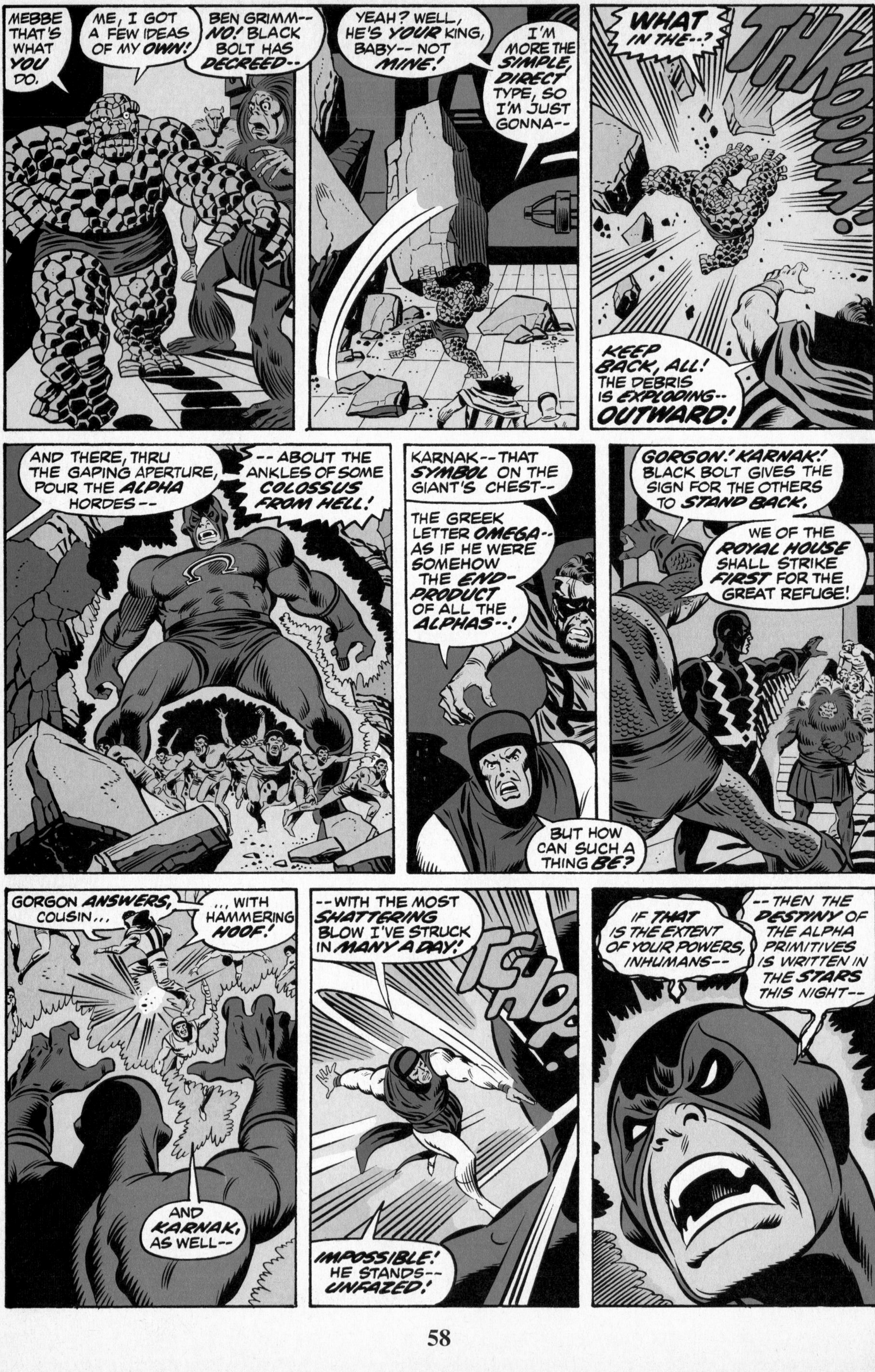
MEBBE THAT'S WHAT YOU DO.
ME, I GOT A FEW IDEAS OF MY OWN!
BEN GRIMM-- NO! BLACK BOLT HAS DECREED--
YEAH? WELL, HE'S YOUR KING, BABY-- NOT MINE!
I'M MORE THE SIMPLE, DIRECT TYPE, SO I'M JUST GONNA--
WHAT IN THE--?
THHOOOOM!
KEEP BACK, ALL! THE DEBRIS IS EXPLODING-- OUTWARD!
AND THERE, THRU THE GAPING APERTURE, POUR THE ALPHA HORDES--
--ABOUT THE ANKLES OF SOME COLOSSUS FROM HELL!
KARNAK--THAT SYMBOL ON THE GIANT'S CHEST--
THE GREEK LETTER OMEGA-- AS IF HE WERE SOMEHOW THE END-PRODUCT OF ALL THE ALPHAS--!
BUT HOW CAN SUCH A THING BE?
GORGON! KARNAK! BLACK BOLT GIVES THE SIGN FOR THE OTHERS TO STAND BACK.
WE OF THE ROYAL HOUSE SHALL STRIKE FIRST FOR THE GREAT REFUGE!
GORGON ANSWERS, COUSIN...
..., WITH HAMMERING HOOF!
AND KARNAK, AS WELL--
--WITH THE MOST SHATTERING BLOW I'VE STRUCK IN MANY A DAY!
TCHOK!
IMPOSSIBLE! HE STANDS-- UNFAZED!
IF THAT IS THE EXTENT OF YOUR POWERS, INHUMANS--
--THEN THE DESTINY OF THE ALPHA PRIMITIVES IS WRITTEN IN THE STARS THIS NIGHT--

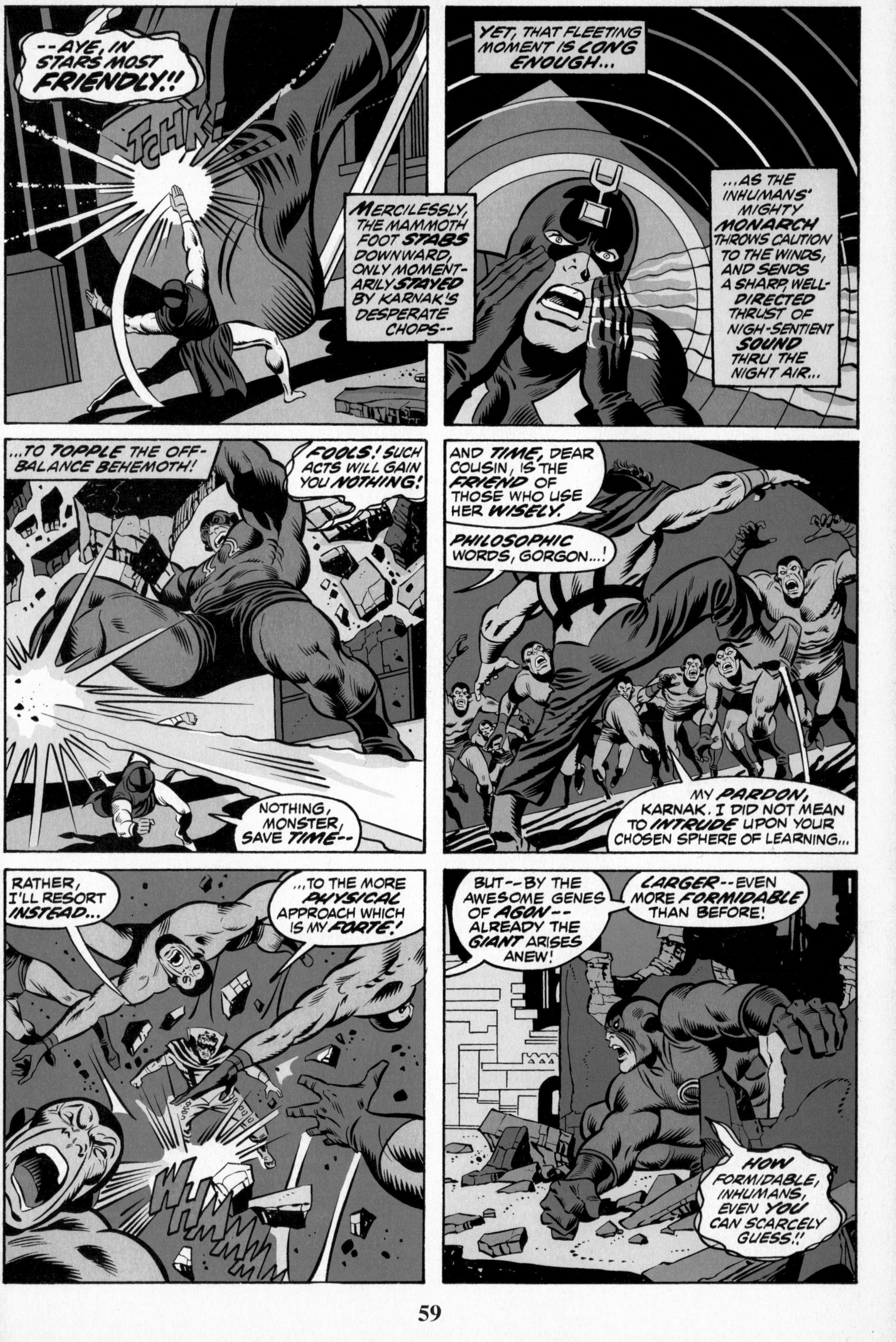
--AYE, IN STARS MOST FRIENDLY!!
TCHK!
MERCILESSLY, THE MAMMOTH FOOT STABS DOWNWARD, ONLY MOMENTARILY STAYED BY KARNAK'S DESPERATE CHOPS--
YET, THAT FLEETING MOMENT IS LONG ENOUGH...
...AS THE INHUMANS' MIGHTY MONARCH THROWS CAUTION TO THE WINDS, AND SENDS A SHARP, WELL-DIRECTED THRUST OF NIGH-SENTIENT SOUND THRU THE NIGHT AIR...
...TO TOPPLE THE OFF-BALANCE BEHEMOTH!
FOOLS! SUCH ACTS WILL GAIN YOU NOTHING!
NOTHING, MONSTER, SAVE TIME--
AND TIME, DEAR COUSIN, IS THE FRIEND OF THOSE WHO USE HER WISELY.
PHILOSOPHIC WORDS, GORGON...!
MY PARDON, KARNAK. I DID NOT MEAN TO INTRUDE UPON YOUR CHOSEN SPHERE OF LEARNING...
RATHER, I'LL RESORT INSTEAD...
...TO THE MORE PHYSICAL APPROACH WHICH IS MY FORTE!
WHAM
BUT--BY THE AWESOME GENES OF AGON--ALREADY THE GIANT ARISES ANEW!
LARGER--EVEN MORE FORMIDABLE THAN BEFORE!
HOW FORMIDABLE, INHUMANS, EVEN YOU CAN SCARCELY GUESS!!

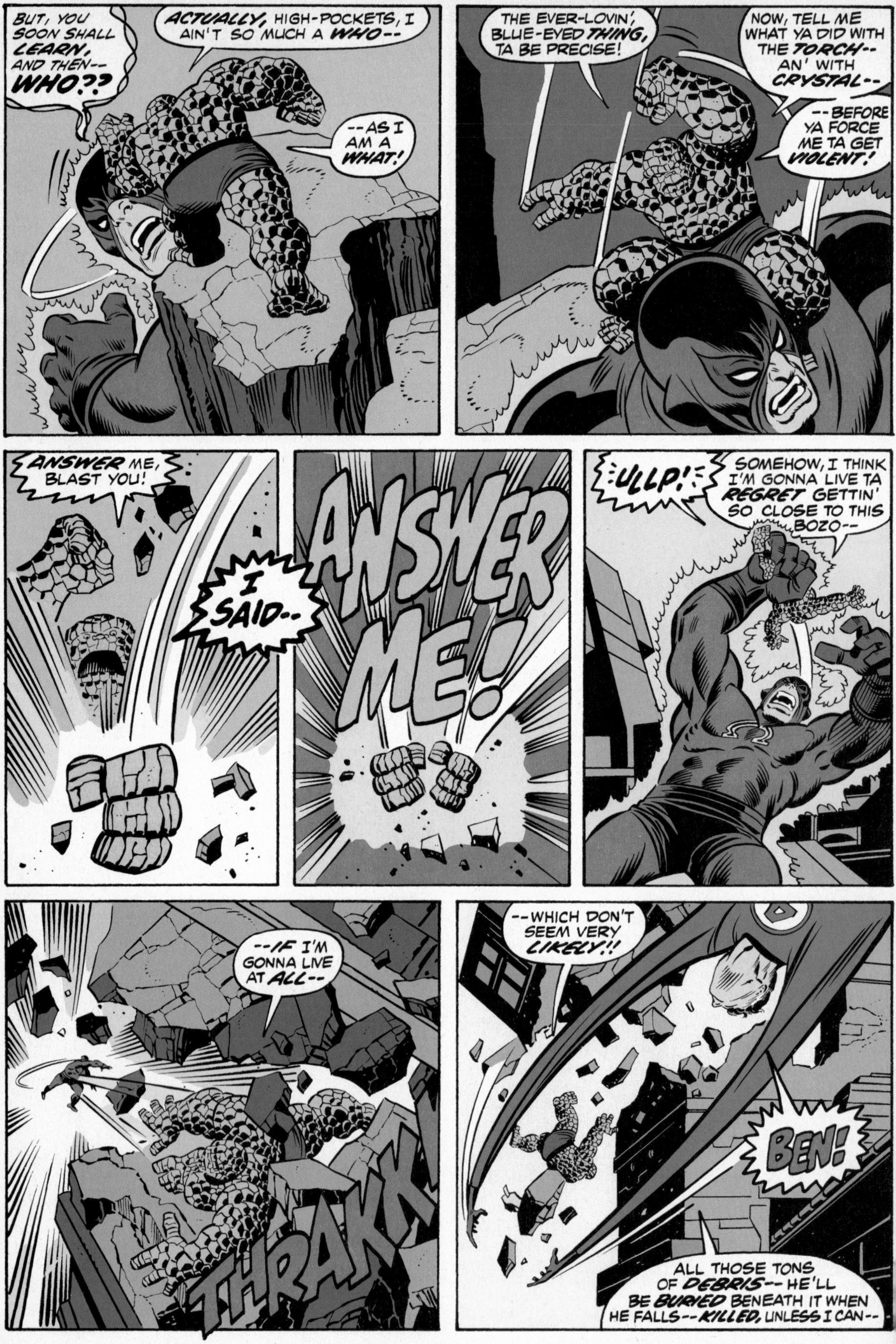
BUT, YOU SOON SHALL LEARN, AND THEN-- WHO??
ACTUALLY, HIGH-POCKETS, I AIN'T SO MUCH A WHO--
--AS I AM A WHAT!
THE EVER-LOVIN', BLUE-EYED THING, TA BE PRECISE!
NOW, TELL ME WHAT YA DID WITH THE TORCH-- AN' WITH CRYSTAL--
--BEFORE YA FORCE ME TA GET VIOLENT!
ANSWER ME, BLAST YOU!
I SAID--
ANSWER ME!
ULLP!
SOMEHOW, I THINK I'M GONNA LIVE TA REGRET GETTIN' SO CLOSE TO THIS BOZO--
--IF I'M GONNA LIVE AT ALL--
THRAKK
--WHICH DON'T SEEM VERY LIKELY!!
BEN!
ALL THOSE TONS OF DEBRIS-- HE'LL BE BURIED BENEATH IT WHEN HE FALLS--KILLED, UNLESS I CAN--

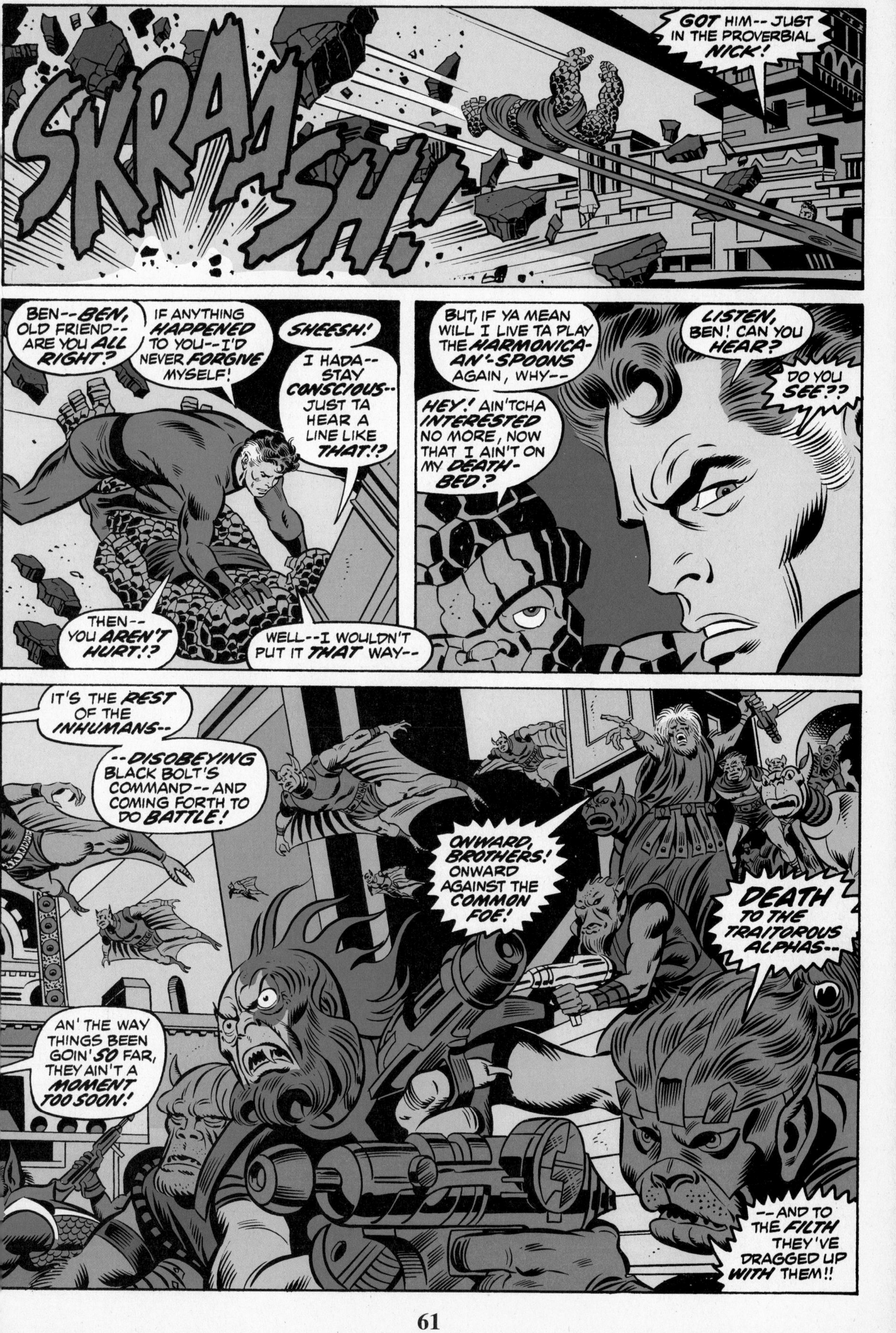
SKRAASH!
GOT HIM-- JUST IN THE PROVERBIAL NICK!
BEN--BEN, OLD FRIEND-- ARE YOU ALL RIGHT?
IF ANYTHING HAPPENED TO YOU--I'D NEVER FORGIVE MYSELF!
SHEESH!
I HADA-- STAY CONSCIOUS-- JUST TA HEAR A LINE LIKE THAT!?
THEN-- YOU AREN'T HURT!?
WELL--I WOULDN'T PUT IT THAT WAY--
BUT, IF YA MEAN WILL I LIVE TA PLAY THE HARMONICA-AN'-SPOONS AGAIN, WHY--
HEY! AIN'TCHA INTERESTED NO MORE, NOW THAT I AIN'T ON MY DEATH-BED?
LISTEN, BEN! CAN YOU HEAR?
DO YOU SEE??
IT'S THE REST OF THE INHUMANS--
--DISOBEYING BLACK BOLT'S COMMAND--AND COMING FORTH TO DO BATTLE!
ONWARD, BROTHERS! ONWARD AGAINST THE COMMON FOE!
DEATH TO THE TRAITOROUS ALPHAS--
AN' THE WAY THINGS BEEN GOIN' SO FAR, THEY AIN'T A MOMENT TOO SOON!
--AND TO THE FILTH THEY'VE DRAGGED UP WITH THEM!!

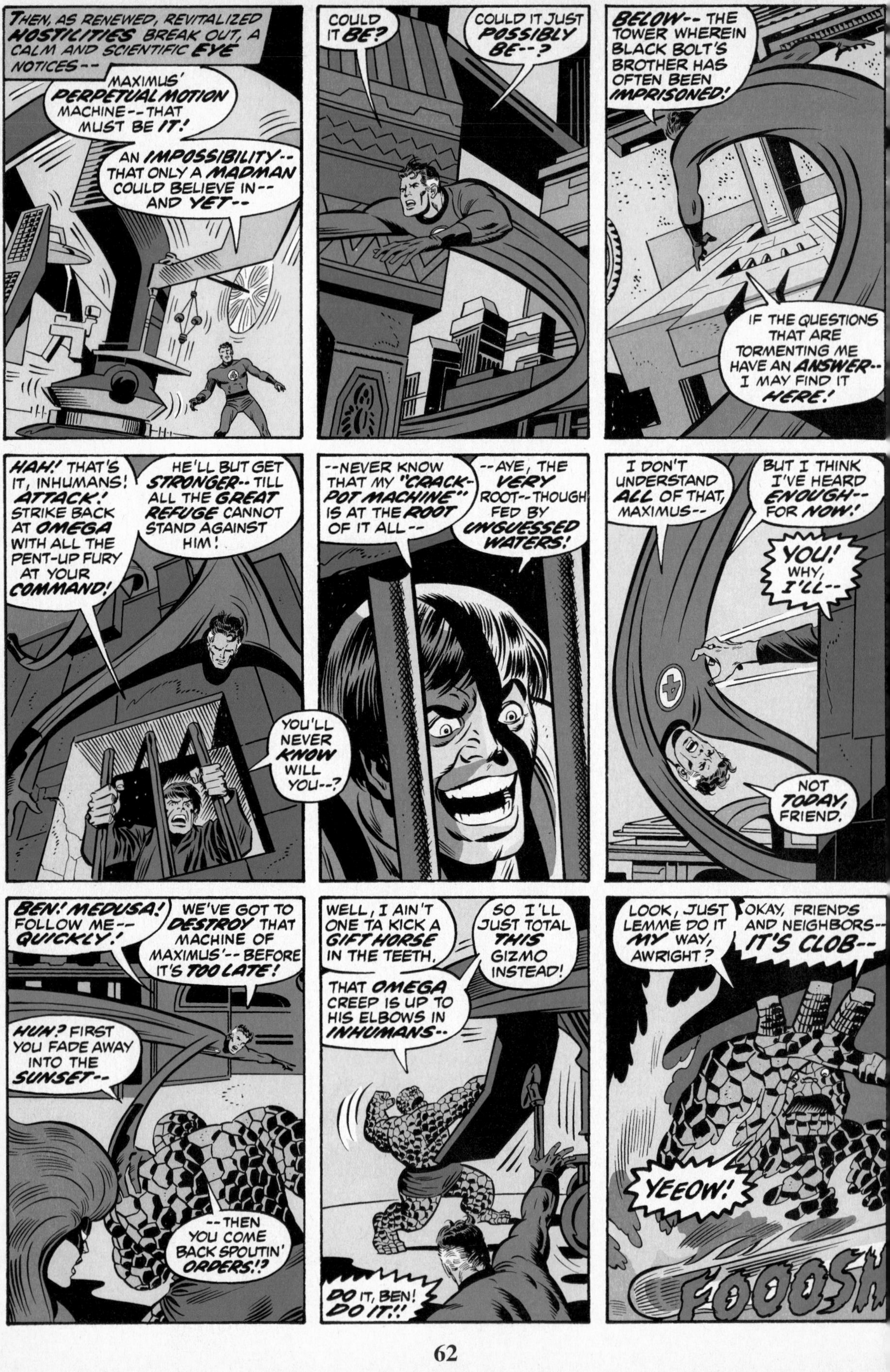
THEN, AS RENEWED, REVITALIZED HOSTILITIES BREAK OUT, A CALM AND SCIENTIFIC EYE NOTICES--
MAXIMUS' PERPETUAL MOTION MACHINE--THAT MUST BE IT!
AN IMPOSSIBILITY--THAT ONLY A MADMAN COULD BELIEVE IN--AND YET--
COULD IT BE?
COULD IT JUST POSSIBLY BE--?
BELOW--THE TOWER WHEREIN BLACK BOLT'S BROTHER HAS OFTEN BEEN IMPRISONED!
IF THE QUESTIONS THAT ARE TORMENTING ME HAVE AN ANSWER--I MAY FIND IT HERE!
HAH! THAT'S IT, INHUMANS! ATTACK! STRIKE BACK AT OMEGA WITH ALL THE PENT-UP FURY AT YOUR COMMAND!
HE'LL BUT GET STRONGER--TILL ALL THE GREAT REFUGE CANNOT STAND AGAINST HIM!
YOU'LL NEVER KNOW WILL YOU--?
--NEVER KNOW THAT MY "CRACK-POT MACHINE" IS AT THE ROOT OF IT ALL--
--AYE, THE VERY ROOT--THOUGH FED BY UNGUESSED WATERS!
I DON'T UNDERSTAND ALL OF THAT, MAXIMUS--
BUT I THINK I'VE HEARD ENOUGH--FOR NOW!
YOU! WHY, I'LL--
NOT TODAY, FRIEND.
BEN! MEDUSA! FOLLOW ME--QUICKLY!
WE'VE GOT TO DESTROY THAT MACHINE OF MAXIMUS'--BEFORE IT'S TOO LATE!
HUH? FIRST YOU FADE AWAY INTO THE SUNSET--
--THEN YOU COME BACK SPOUTIN' ORDERS!?
WELL, I AIN'T ONE TA KICK A GIFT HORSE IN THE TEETH.
THAT OMEGA CREEP IS UP TO HIS ELBOWS IN INHUMANS--
SO I'LL JUST TOTAL THIS GIZMO INSTEAD!
DO IT, BEN! DO IT!!
LOOK, JUST LEMME DO IT MY WAY, AWRIGHT?
OKAY, FRIENDS AND NEIGHBORS--IT'S CLOB--
YEEOW!
FOOSH

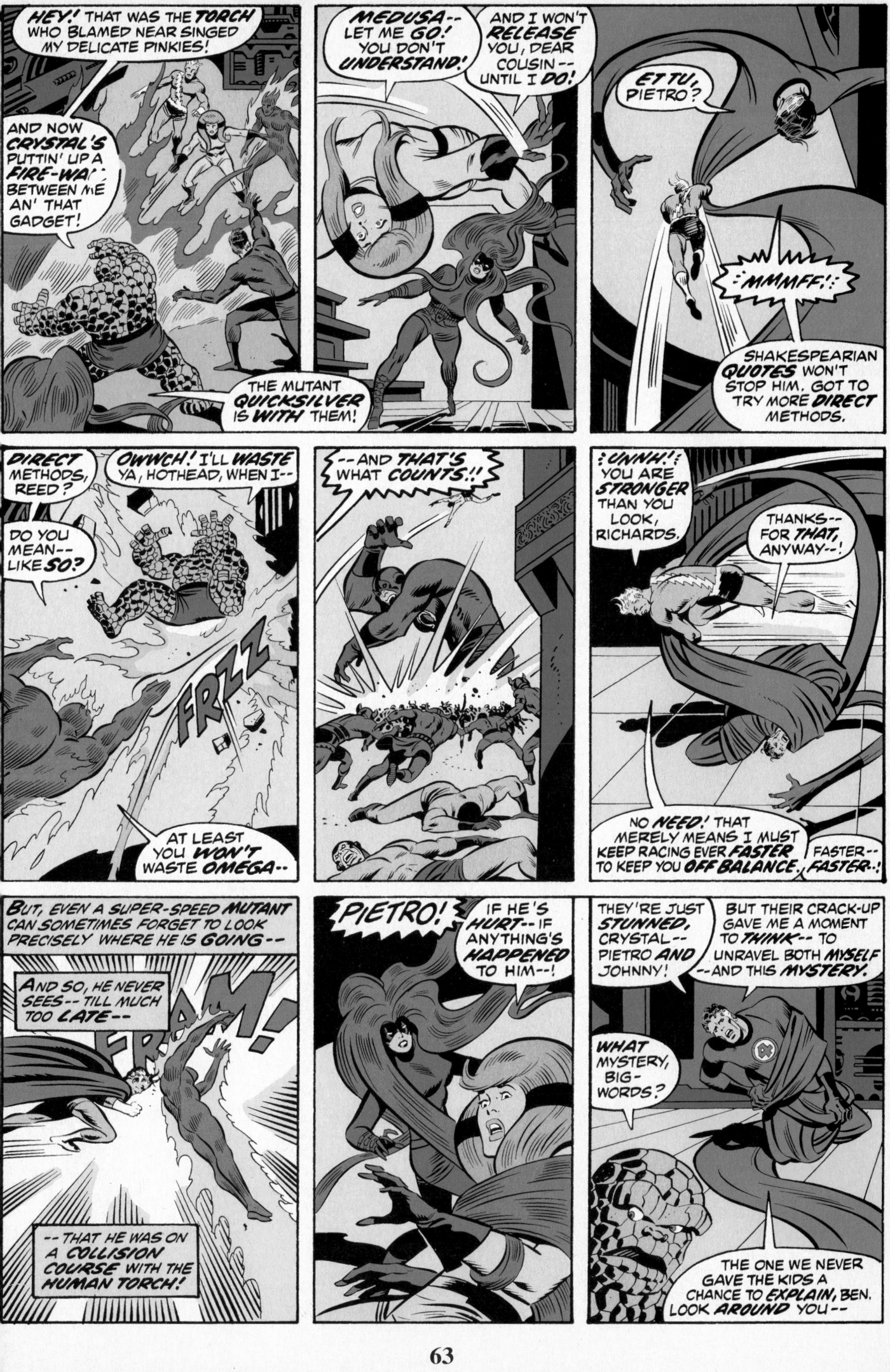
HEY! THAT WAS THE TORCH WHO BLAMED NEAR SINGED MY DELICATE PINKIES!
AND NOW CRYSTAL'S PUTTIN' UP A FIRE-WALL BETWEEN ME AN' THAT GADGET!
THE MUTANT QUICKSILVER IS WITH THEM!
MEDUSA-- LET ME GO! YOU DON'T UNDERSTAND!
AND I WON'T RELEASE YOU, DEAR COUSIN-- UNTIL I DO!
ET TU, PIETRO?
MMMFF!
SHAKESPEARIAN QUOTES WON'T STOP HIM. GOT TO TRY MORE DIRECT METHODS.
DIRECT METHODS, REED?
OWWCH! I'LL WASTE YA, HOTHEAD, WHEN I--
DO YOU MEAN-- LIKE SO?
FRZZ
AT LEAST YOU WON'T WASTE OMEGA--
--AND THAT'S WHAT COUNTS!!
UNNH!! YOU ARE STRONGER THAN YOU LOOK, RICHARDS.
THANKS-- FOR THAT, ANYWAY--!
NO NEED! THAT MERELY MEANS I MUST KEEP RACING EVER FASTER TO KEEP YOU OFF BALANCE.
FASTER-- FASTER--!
BUT, EVEN A SUPER-SPEED MUTANT CAN SOMETIMES FORGET TO LOOK PRECISELY WHERE HE IS GOING--
AND SO, HE NEVER SEES-- TILL MUCH TOO LATE--
FRAM!
--THAT HE WAS ON A COLLISION COURSE WITH THE HUMAN TORCH!
PIETRO!
IF HE'S HURT-- IF ANYTHING'S HAPPENED TO HIM--!
THEY'RE JUST STUNNED, CRYSTAL-- PIETRO AND JOHNNY!
BUT THEIR CRACK-UP GAVE ME A MOMENT TO THINK-- TO UNRAVEL BOTH MYSELF --AND THIS MYSTERY.
WHAT MYSTERY, BIG-WORDS?
THE ONE WE NEVER GAVE THE KIDS A CHANCE TO EXPLAIN, BEN. LOOK AROUND YOU--

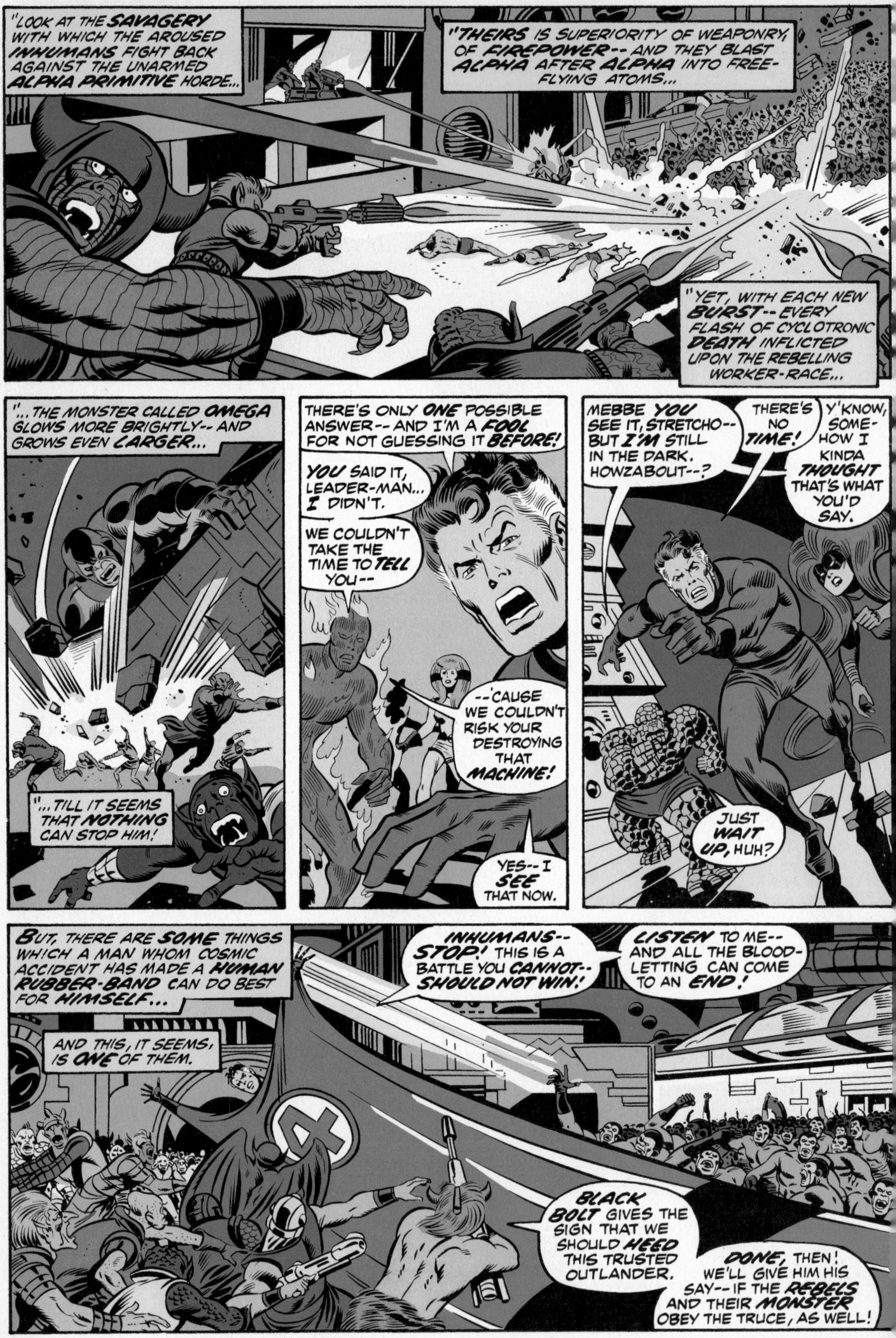
"LOOK AT THE SAVAGERY WITH WHICH THE AROUSED INHUMANS FIGHT BACK AGAINST THE UNARMED ALPHA PRIMITIVE HORDE...
"THEIRS IS SUPERIORITY OF WEAPONRY, OF FIREPOWER-- AND THEY BLAST ALPHA AFTER ALPHA INTO FREE-FLYING ATOMS...
"YET, WITH EACH NEW BURST-- EVERY FLASH OF CYCLOTRONIC DEATH INFLICTED UPON THE REBELLING WORKER-RACE...
"...THE MONSTER CALLED OMEGA GLOWS MORE BRIGHTLY-- AND GROWS EVEN LARGER...
"...TILL IT SEEMS THAT NOTHING CAN STOP HIM!
THERE'S ONLY ONE POSSIBLE ANSWER-- AND I'M A FOOL FOR NOT GUESSING IT BEFORE!
YOU SAID IT, LEADER-MAN... I DIDN'T.
WE COULDN'T TAKE THE TIME TO TELL YOU--
--'CAUSE WE COULDN'T RISK YOUR DESTROYING THAT MACHINE!
YES-- I SEE THAT NOW.
MEBBE YOU SEE IT, STRETCHO-- BUT I'M STILL IN THE DARK. HOWZABOUT--?
THERE'S NO TIME!
Y'KNOW, SOME-HOW I KINDA THOUGHT THAT'S WHAT YOU'D SAY.
JUST WAIT UP, HUH?
BUT, THERE ARE SOME THINGS WHICH A MAN WHOM COSMIC ACCIDENT HAS MADE A HUMAN RUBBER-BAND CAN DO BEST FOR HIMSELF...
AND THIS, IT SEEMS, IS ONE OF THEM.
INHUMANS-- STOP! THIS IS A BATTLE YOU CANNOT-- SHOULD NOT WIN!
LISTEN TO ME-- AND ALL THE BLOOD-LETTING CAN COME TO AN END!
BLACK BOLT GIVES THE SIGN THAT WE SHOULD HEED THIS TRUSTED OUTLANDER.
DONE, THEN! WE'LL GIVE HIM HIS SAY-- IF THE REBELS AND THEIR MONSTER OBEY THE TRUCE, AS WELL!

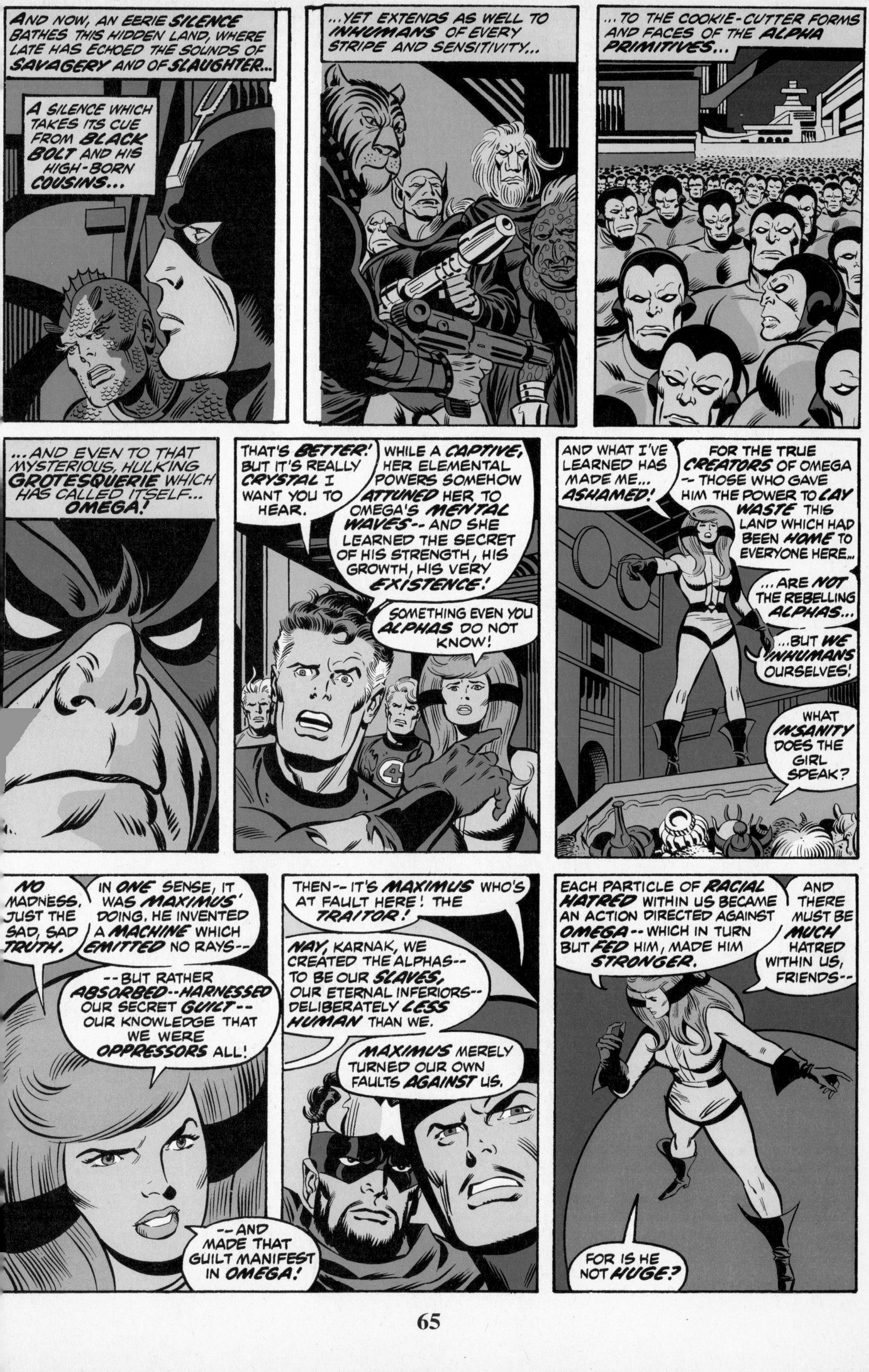
AND NOW, AN EERIE SILENCE BATHES THIS HIDDEN LAND, WHERE LATE HAS ECHOED THE SOUNDS OF SAVAGERY AND OF SLAUGHTER...
A SILENCE WHICH TAKES ITS CUE FROM BLACK BOLT AND HIS HIGH-BORN COUSINS...
...YET EXTENDS AS WELL TO INHUMANS OF EVERY STRIPE AND SENSITIVITY...
...TO THE COOKIE-CUTTER FORMS AND FACES OF THE ALPHA PRIMITIVES...
...AND EVEN TO THAT MYSTERIOUS, HULKING GROTESQUERIE WHICH HAS CALLED ITSELF... OMEGA!
THAT'S BETTER! BUT IT'S REALLY CRYSTAL I WANT YOU TO HEAR.
WHILE A CAPTIVE, HER ELEMENTAL POWERS SOMEHOW ATTUNED HER TO OMEGA'S MENTAL WAVES-- AND SHE LEARNED THE SECRET OF HIS STRENGTH, HIS GROWTH, HIS VERY EXISTENCE!
SOMETHING EVEN YOU ALPHAS DO NOT KNOW!
AND WHAT I'VE LEARNED HAS MADE ME... ASHAMED!
FOR THE TRUE CREATORS OF OMEGA -- THOSE WHO GAVE HIM THE POWER TO LAY WASTE THIS LAND WHICH HAD BEEN HOME TO EVERYONE HERE...
...ARE NOT THE REBELLING ALPHAS...
...BUT WE INHUMANS OURSELVES!
WHAT INSANITY DOES THE GIRL SPEAK?
NO MADNESS. JUST THE SAD, SAD TRUTH.
IN ONE SENSE, IT WAS MAXIMUS' DOING. HE INVENTED A MACHINE WHICH EMITTED NO RAYS--
--BUT RATHER ABSORBED--HARNESSED OUR SECRET GUILT-- OUR KNOWLEDGE THAT WE WERE OPPRESSORS ALL!
--AND MADE THAT GUILT MANIFEST IN OMEGA!
THEN-- IT'S MAXIMUS WHO'S AT FAULT HERE! THE TRAITOR!
NAY, KARNAK, WE CREATED THE ALPHAS-- TO BE OUR SLAVES, OUR ETERNAL INFERIORS-- DELIBERATELY LESS HUMAN THAN WE.
MAXIMUS MERELY TURNED OUR OWN FAULTS AGAINST US.
EACH PARTICLE OF RACIAL HATRED WITHIN US BECAME AN ACTION DIRECTED AGAINST OMEGA -- WHICH IN TURN BUT FED HIM, MADE HIM STRONGER.
AND THERE MUST BE MUCH HATRED WITHIN US, FRIENDS--
FOR IS HE NOT HUGE?

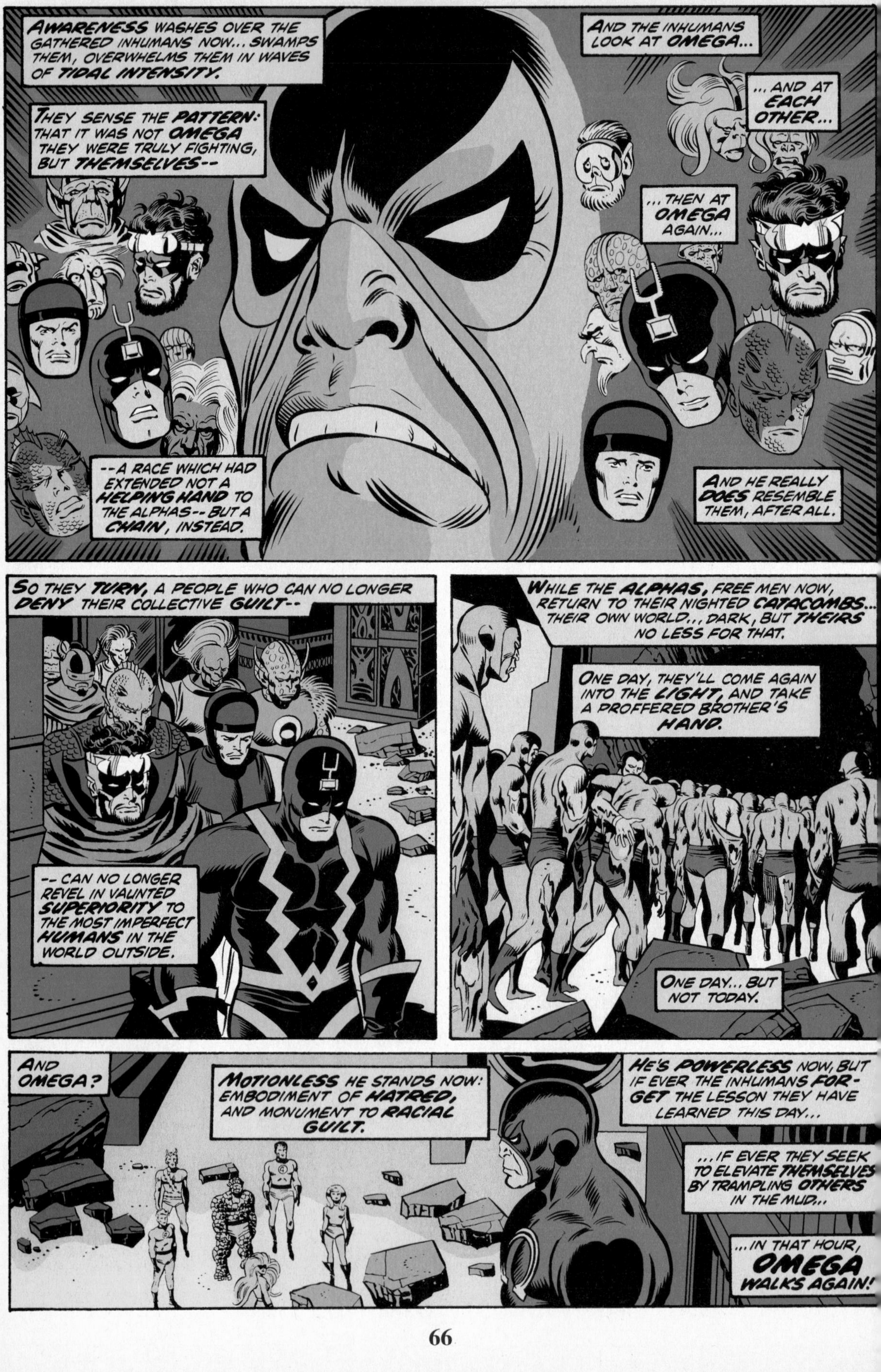
AWARENESS WASHES OVER THE GATHERED INHUMANS NOW... SWAMPS THEM, OVERWHELMS THEM IN WAVES OF TIDAL INTENSITY.
THEY SENSE THE PATTERN: THAT IT WAS NOT OMEGA THEY WERE TRULY FIGHTING, BUT THEMSELVES--
--A RACE WHICH HAD EXTENDED NOT A HELPING HAND TO THE ALPHAS--BUT A CHAIN, INSTEAD.
AND THE INHUMANS LOOK AT OMEGA...
...AND AT EACH OTHER...
...THEN AT OMEGA AGAIN...
AND HE REALLY DOES RESEMBLE THEM, AFTER ALL.
SO THEY TURN, A PEOPLE WHO CAN NO LONGER DENY THEIR COLLECTIVE GUILT--
--CAN NO LONGER REVEL IN VAUNTED SUPERIORITY TO THE MOST IMPERFECT HUMANS IN THE WORLD OUTSIDE.
WHILE THE ALPHAS, FREE MEN NOW, RETURN TO THEIR NIGHTED CATACOMBS... THEIR OWN WORLD.., DARK, BUT THEIRS NO LESS FOR THAT.
ONE DAY, THEY'LL COME AGAIN INTO THE LIGHT, AND TAKE A PROFFERED BROTHER'S HAND.
ONE DAY... BUT NOT TODAY.
AND OMEGA?
MOTIONLESS HE STANDS NOW: EMBODIMENT OF HATRED, AND MONUMENT TO RACIAL GUILT.
HE'S POWERLESS NOW, BUT IF EVER THE INHUMANS FORGET THE LESSON THEY HAVE LEARNED THIS DAY...
...IF EVER THEY SEEK TO ELEVATE THEMSELVES BY TRAMPLING OTHERS IN THE MUD...
...IN THAT HOUR, OMEGA WALKS AGAIN!

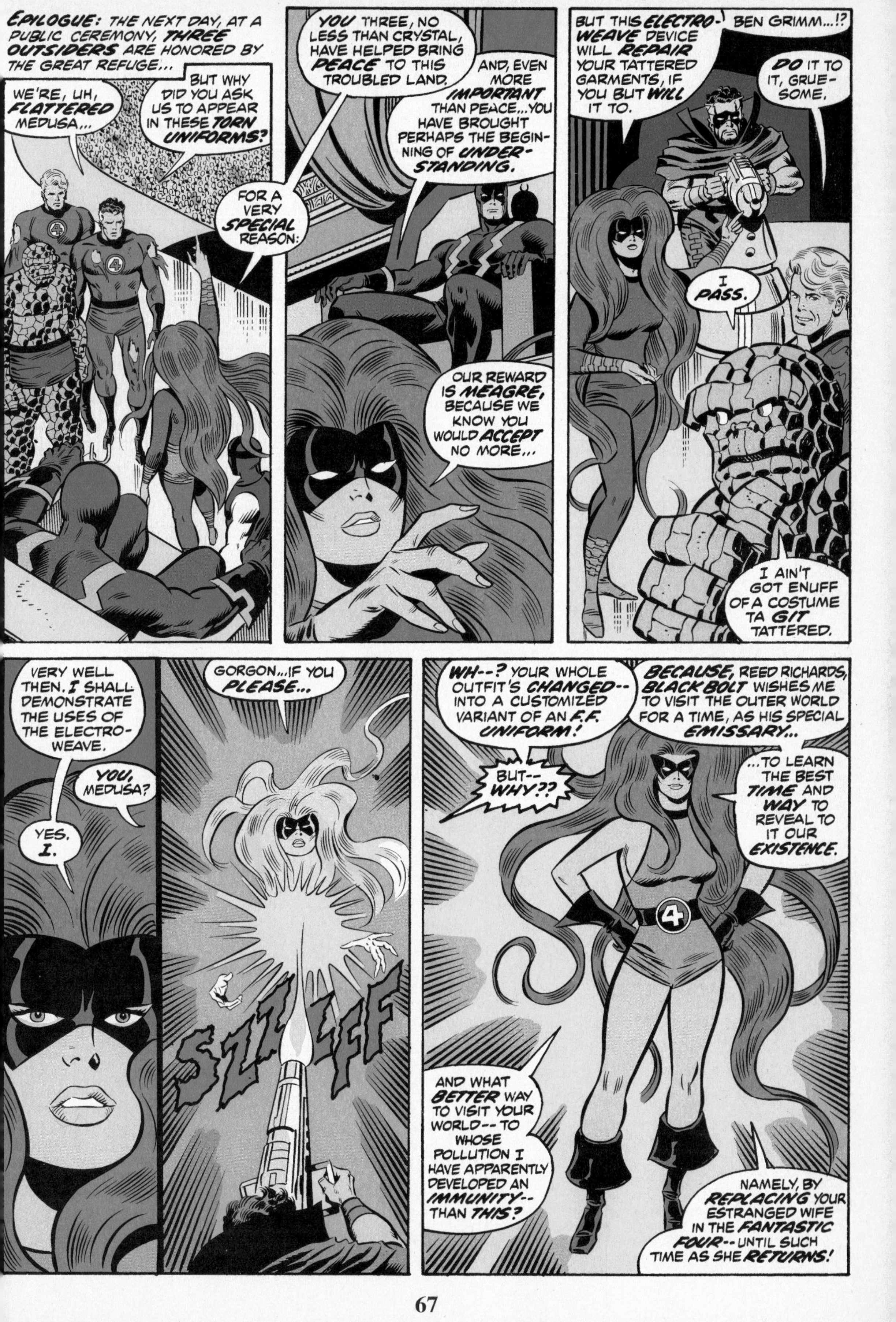
EPILOGUE: THE NEXT DAY, AT A PUBLIC CEREMONY, THREE OUTSIDERS ARE HONORED BY THE GREAT REFUGE...
WE'RE, UH, FLATTERED MEDUSA...
BUT WHY DID YOU ASK US TO APPEAR IN THESE TORN UNIFORMS?
FOR A VERY SPECIAL REASON:
YOU THREE, NO LESS THAN CRYSTAL, HAVE HELPED BRING PEACE TO THIS TROUBLED LAND.
AND, EVEN MORE IMPORTANT THAN PEACE...YOU HAVE BROUGHT PERHAPS THE BEGINNING OF UNDERSTANDING.
OUR REWARD IS MEAGRE, BECAUSE WE KNOW YOU WOULD ACCEPT NO MORE...
BUT THIS ELECTRO-WEAVE DEVICE WILL REPAIR YOUR TATTERED GARMENTS, IF YOU BUT WILL IT TO.
BEN GRIMM...!?
DO IT TO IT, GRUESOME.
I PASS.
I AIN'T GOT ENUFF OF A COSTUME TA GIT TATTERED.
VERY WELL THEN. I SHALL DEMONSTRATE THE USES OF THE ELECTRO-WEAVE.
YOU, MEDUSA?
YES. I.
GORGON...IF YOU PLEASE...
SZZZAFF
WH--? YOUR WHOLE OUTFIT'S CHANGED--INTO A CUSTOMIZED VARIANT OF AN F.F. UNIFORM!
BUT--WHY??
BECAUSE, REED RICHARDS, BLACK BOLT WISHES ME TO VISIT THE OUTER WORLD FOR A TIME, AS HIS SPECIAL EMISSARY...
...TO LEARN THE BEST TIME AND WAY TO REVEAL TO IT OUR EXISTENCE.
AND WHAT BETTER WAY TO VISIT YOUR WORLD-- TO WHOSE POLLUTION I HAVE APPARENTLY DEVELOPED AN IMMUNITY--THAN THIS?
NAMELY, BY REPLACING YOUR ESTRANGED WIFE IN THE FANTASTIC FOUR--UNTIL SUCH TIME AS SHE RETURNS!

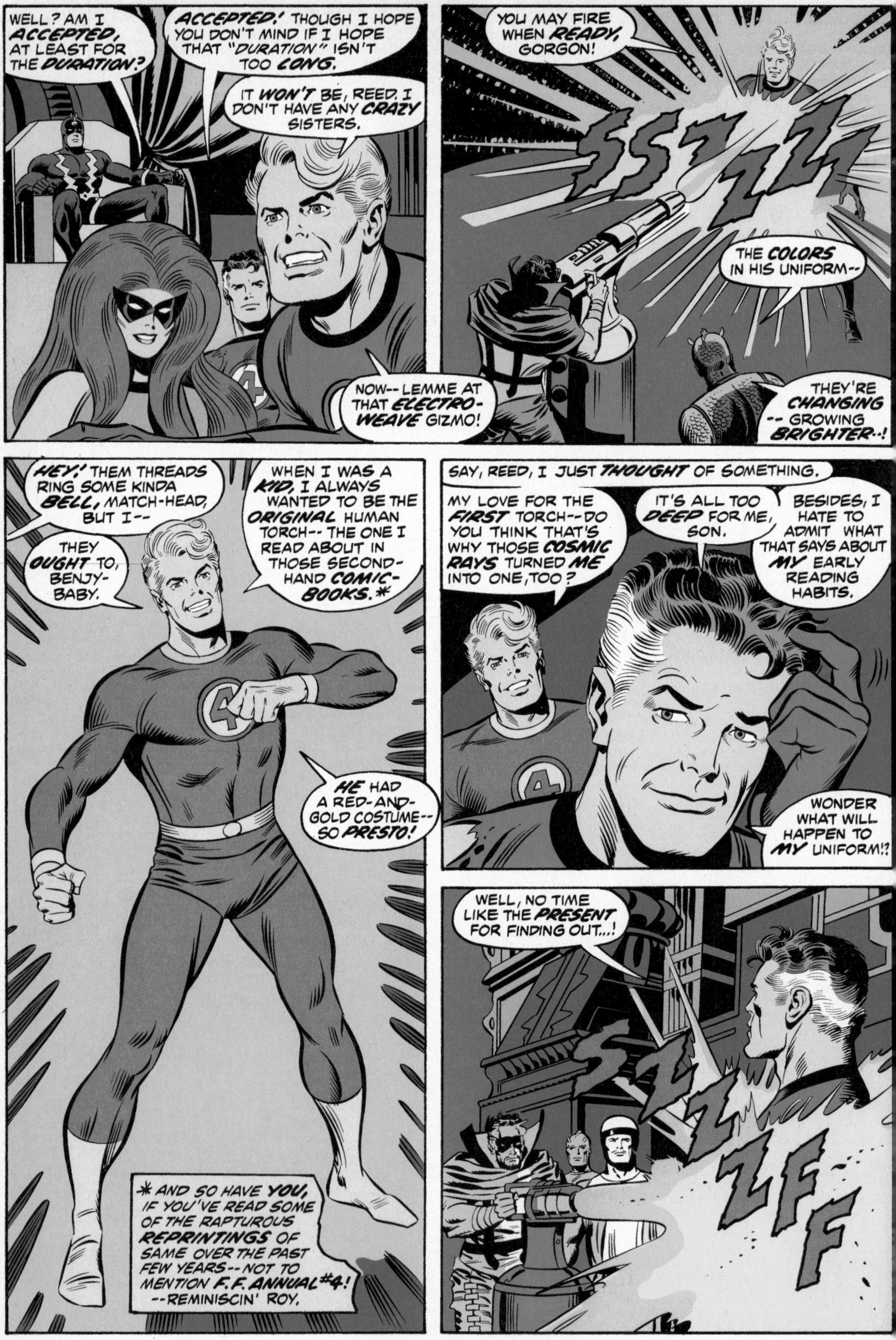
WELL? AM I ACCEPTED, AT LEAST FOR THE DURATION?
ACCEPTED! THOUGH I HOPE YOU DON'T MIND IF I HOPE THAT "DURATION" ISN'T TOO LONG.
IT WON'T BE, REED. I DON'T HAVE ANY CRAZY SISTERS.
NOW-- LEMME AT THAT ELECTRO-WEAVE GIZMO!
YOU MAY FIRE WHEN READY, GORGON!
SSZZZZT
THE COLORS IN HIS UNIFORM--
THEY'RE CHANGING -- GROWING BRIGHTER--!
HEY! THEM THREADS RING SOME KINDA BELL, MATCH-HEAD, BUT I--
THEY OUGHT TO, BENJY-BABY.
WHEN I WAS A KID, I ALWAYS WANTED TO BE THE ORIGINAL HUMAN TORCH-- THE ONE I READ ABOUT IN THOSE SECOND-HAND COMIC-BOOKS.*
HE HAD A RED-AND-GOLD COSTUME-- SO PRESTO!
* AND SO HAVE YOU, IF YOU'VE READ SOME OF THE RAPTUROUS REPRINTINGS OF SAME OVER THE PAST FEW YEARS--NOT TO MENTION F.F. ANNUAL #4! --REMINISCIN' ROY.
SAY, REED, I JUST THOUGHT OF SOMETHING.
MY LOVE FOR THE FIRST TORCH--DO YOU THINK THAT'S WHY THOSE COSMIC RAYS TURNED ME INTO ONE, TOO?
IT'S ALL TOO DEEP FOR ME, SON.
BESIDES, I HATE TO ADMIT WHAT THAT SAYS ABOUT MY EARLY READING HABITS.
WONDER WHAT WILL HAPPEN TO MY UNIFORM!?
WELL, NO TIME LIKE THE PRESENT FOR FINDING OUT...!
SZZZFF

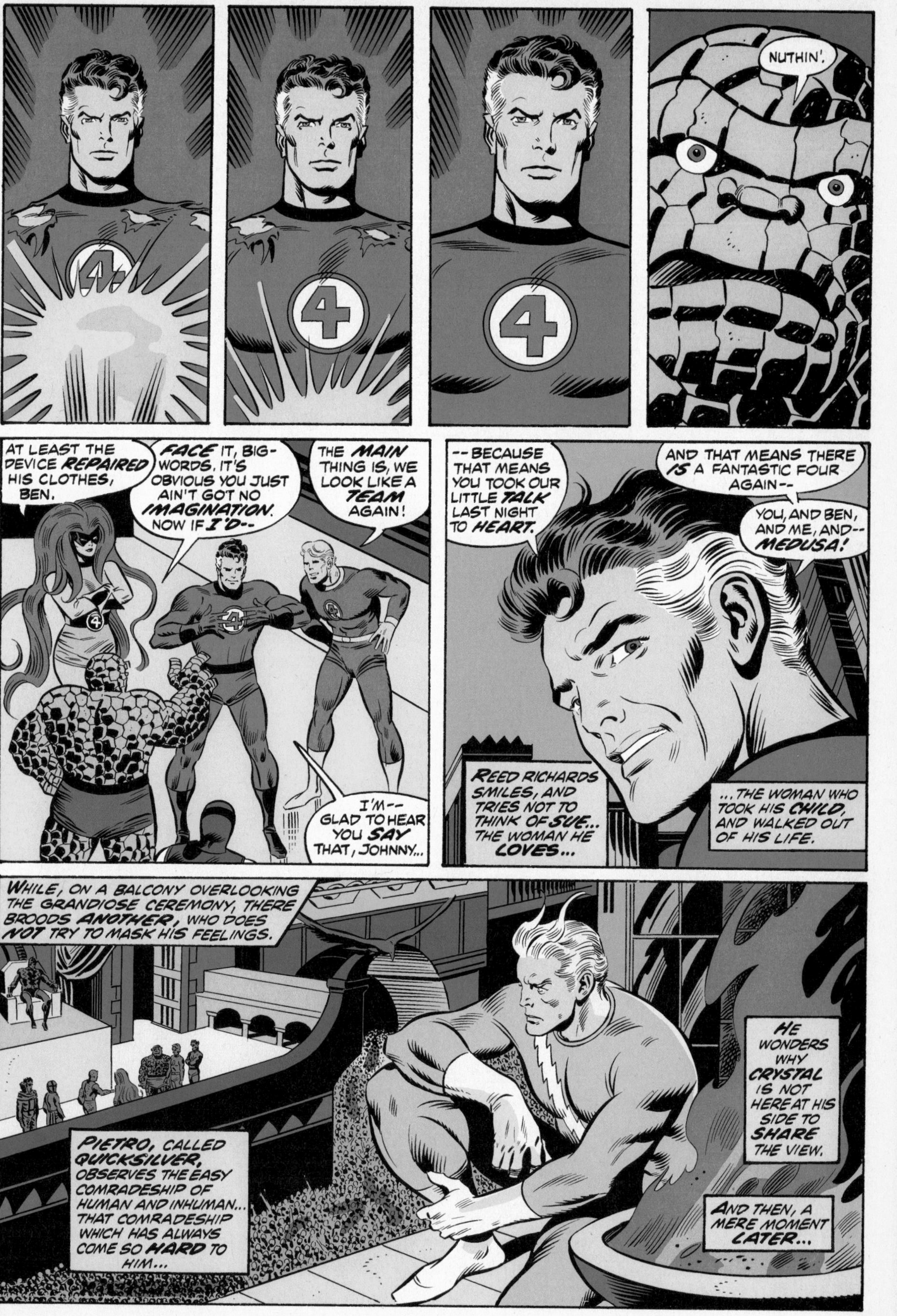
NUTHIN'.
AT LEAST THE DEVICE REPAIRED HIS CLOTHES, BEN.
FACE IT, BIG-WORDS. IT'S OBVIOUS YOU JUST AIN'T GOT NO IMAGINATION. NOW IF I'D--
THE MAIN THING IS, WE LOOK LIKE A TEAM AGAIN!
I'M-- GLAD TO HEAR YOU SAY THAT, JOHNNY...
--BECAUSE THAT MEANS YOU TOOK OUR LITTLE TALK LAST NIGHT TO HEART.
AND THAT MEANS THERE IS A FANTASTIC FOUR AGAIN--
YOU, AND BEN, AND ME, AND-- MEDUSA!
REED RICHARDS SMILES, AND TRIES NOT TO THINK OF SUE... THE WOMAN HE LOVES...
...THE WOMAN WHO TOOK HIS CHILD, AND WALKED OUT OF HIS LIFE.
WHILE, ON A BALCONY OVERLOOKING THE GRANDIOSE CEREMONY, THERE BROODS ANOTHER, WHO DOES NOT TRY TO MASK HIS FEELINGS.
PIETRO, CALLED QUICKSILVER, OBSERVES THE EASY COMRADESHIP OF HUMAN AND INHUMAN... THAT COMRADESHIP WHICH HAS ALWAYS COME SO HARD TO HIM...
HE WONDERS WHY CRYSTAL IS NOT HERE AT HIS SIDE TO SHARE THE VIEW.
AND THEN, A MERE MOMENT LATER...

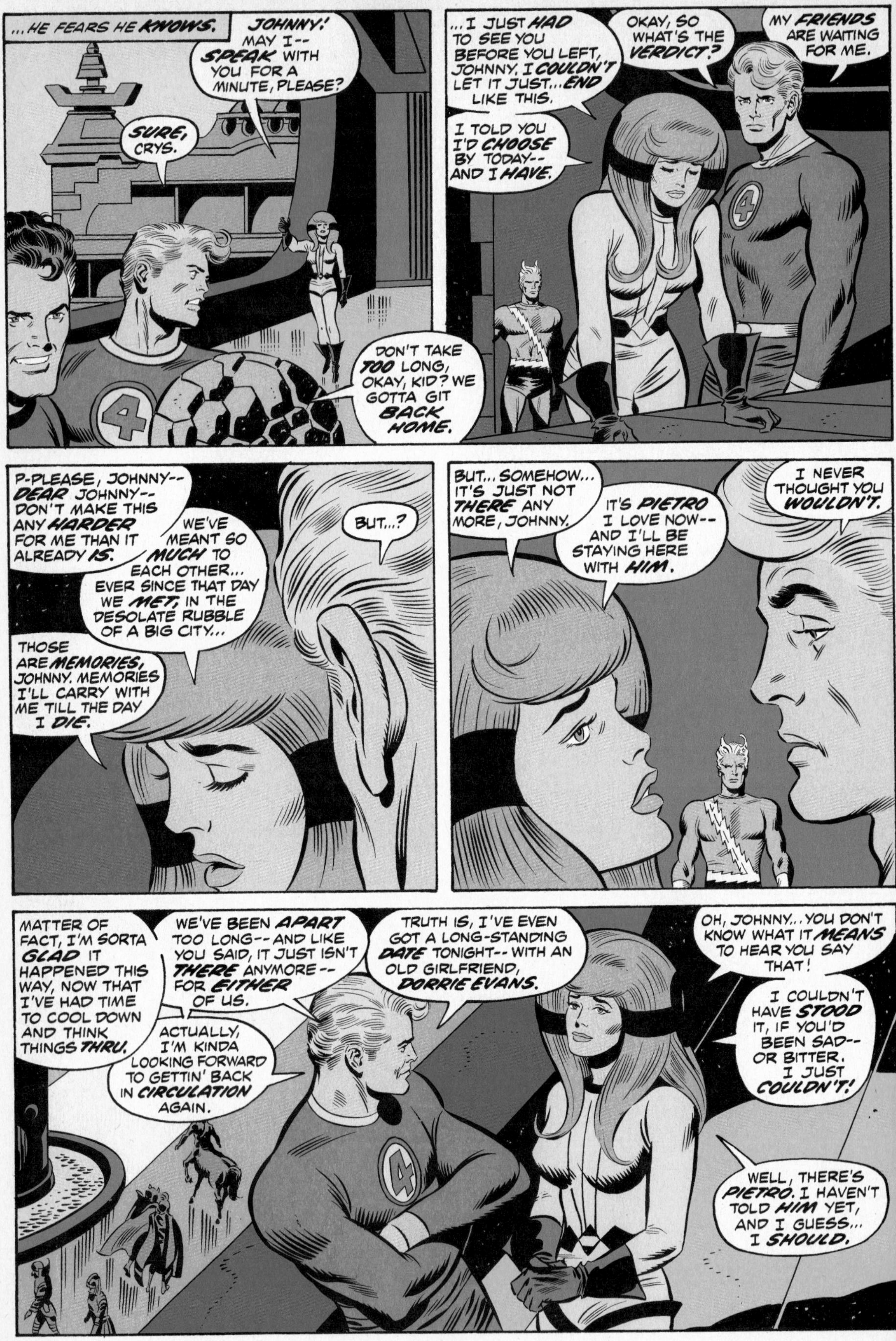
...HE FEARS HE KNOWS.
JOHNNY! MAY I-- SPEAK WITH YOU FOR A MINUTE, PLEASE?
SURE, CRYS.
DON'T TAKE TOO LONG, OKAY, KID? WE GOTTA GIT BACK HOME.
...I JUST HAD TO SEE YOU BEFORE YOU LEFT, JOHNNY. I COULDN'T LET IT JUST...END LIKE THIS.
OKAY, SO WHAT'S THE VERDICT?
MY FRIENDS ARE WAITING FOR ME.
I TOLD YOU I'D CHOOSE BY TODAY-- AND I HAVE.
P-PLEASE, JOHNNY-- DEAR JOHNNY-- DON'T MAKE THIS ANY HARDER FOR ME THAN IT ALREADY IS.
WE'VE MEANT SO MUCH TO EACH OTHER... EVER SINCE THAT DAY WE MET, IN THE DESOLATE RUBBLE OF A BIG CITY...
THOSE ARE MEMORIES, JOHNNY. MEMORIES I'LL CARRY WITH ME TILL THE DAY I DIE.
BUT...?
BUT... SOMEHOW... IT'S JUST NOT THERE ANY MORE, JOHNNY.
IT'S PIETRO I LOVE NOW-- AND I'LL BE STAYING HERE WITH HIM.
I NEVER THOUGHT YOU WOULDN'T.
MATTER OF FACT, I'M SORTA GLAD IT HAPPENED THIS WAY, NOW THAT I'VE HAD TIME TO COOL DOWN AND THINK THINGS THRU.
WE'VE BEEN APART TOO LONG-- AND LIKE YOU SAID, IT JUST ISN'T THERE ANYMORE-- FOR EITHER OF US.
ACTUALLY, I'M KINDA LOOKING FORWARD TO GETTIN' BACK IN CIRCULATION AGAIN.
TRUTH IS, I'VE EVEN GOT A LONG-STANDING DATE TONIGHT-- WITH AN OLD GIRLFRIEND, DORRIE EVANS.
OH, JOHNNY... YOU DON'T KNOW WHAT IT MEANS TO HEAR YOU SAY THAT!
I COULDN'T HAVE STOOD IT, IF YOU'D BEEN SAD-- OR BITTER. I JUST COULDN'T!
WELL, THERE'S PIETRO. I HAVEN'T TOLD HIM YET, AND I GUESS... I SHOULD.

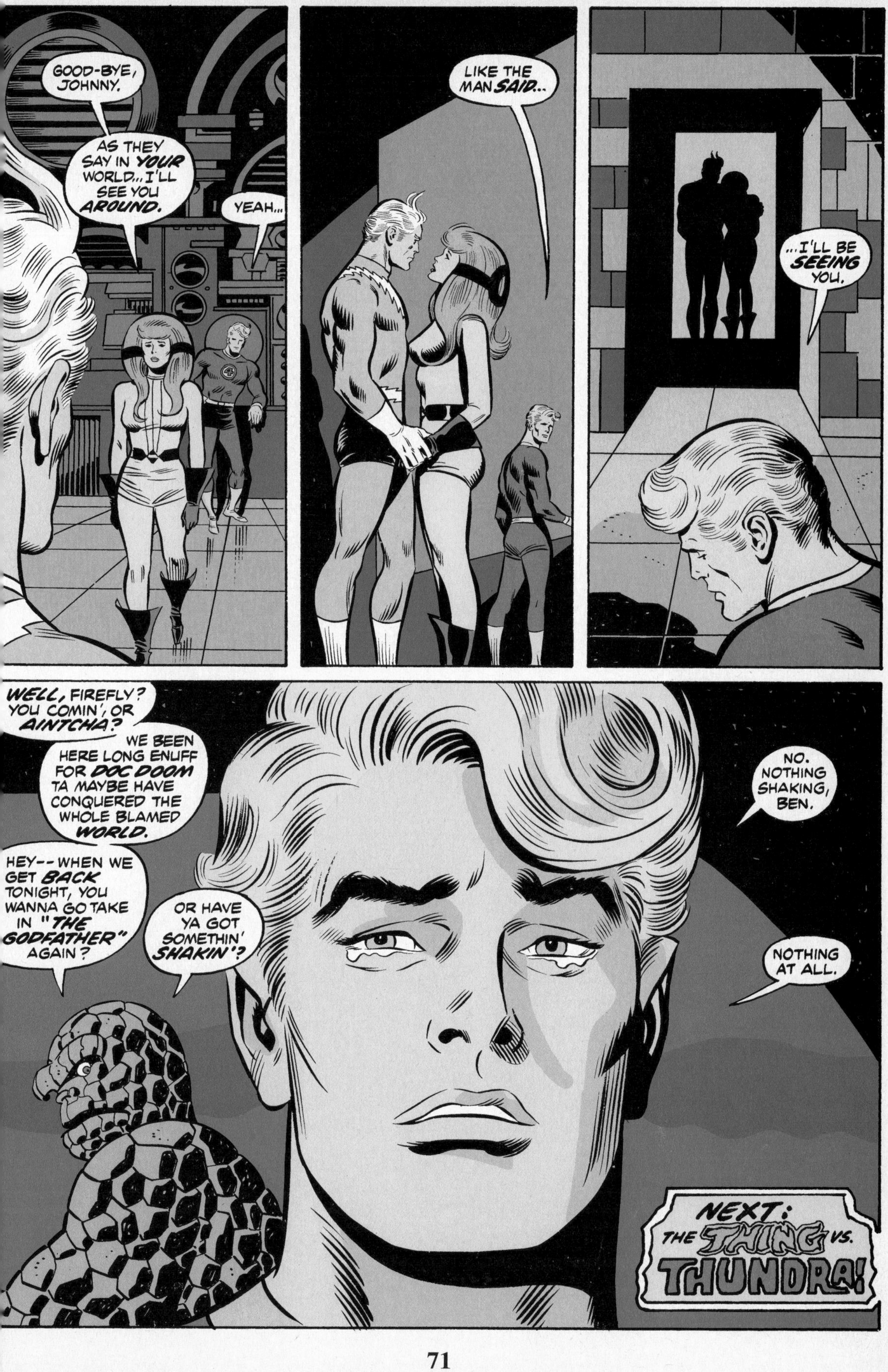
GOOD-BYE, JOHNNY.
AS THEY SAY IN YOUR WORLD... I'LL SEE YOU AROUND.
YEAH...
LIKE THE MAN SAID...
...I'LL BE SEEING YOU.
WELL, FIREFLY? YOU COMIN', OR AINTCHA?
WE BEEN HERE LONG ENUFF FOR DOC DOOM TA MAYBE HAVE CONQUERED THE WHOLE BLAMED WORLD.
HEY-- WHEN WE GET BACK TONIGHT, YOU WANNA GO TAKE IN "THE GODFATHER" AGAIN?
OR HAVE YA GOT SOMETHIN' SHAKIN'?
NO. NOTHING SHAKING, BEN.
NOTHING AT ALL.
NEXT: THE THING VS. THUNDRA!

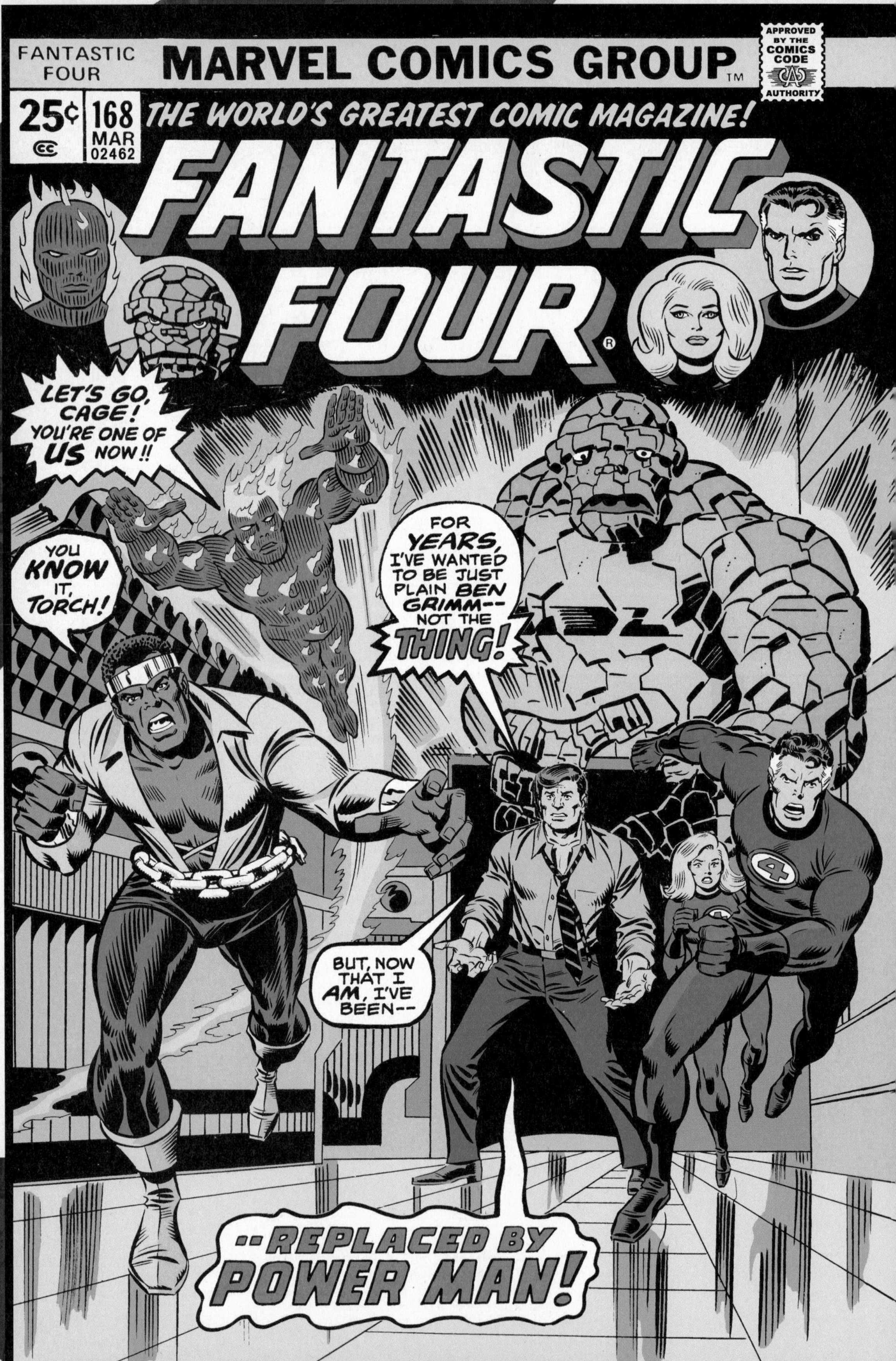

FANTASTIC FOUR
MARVEL COMICS GROUP
APPROVED BY THE COMICS CODE AUTHORITY
25¢
168 MAR 02462
THE WORLD'S GREATEST COMIC MAGAZINE!
FANTASTIC FOUR
LET'S GO, CAGE! YOU'RE ONE OF US NOW!!
YOU KNOW IT, TORCH!
FOR YEARS, I'VE WANTED TO BE JUST PLAIN BEN GRIMM-- NOT THE THING!
BUT, NOW THAT I AM, I'VE BEEN--
--REPLACED BY POWER MAN!

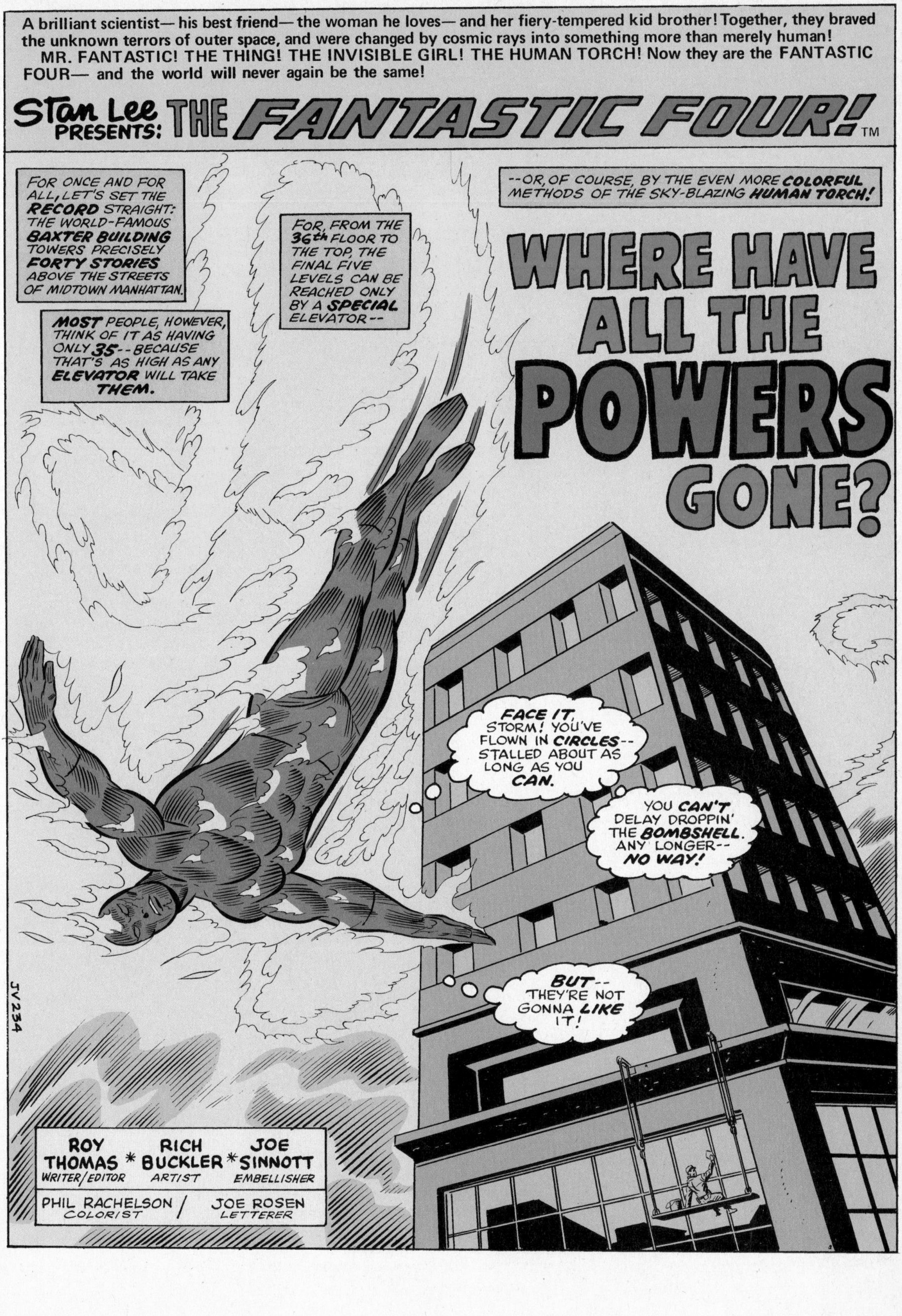

A brilliant scientist— his best friend— the woman he loves— and her fiery-tempered kid brother! Together, they braved the unknown terrors of outer space, and were changed by cosmic rays into something more than merely human!
MR. FANTASTIC! THE THING! THE INVISIBLE GIRL! THE HUMAN TORCH! Now they are the FANTASTIC FOUR— and the world will never again be the same!
Stan Lee PRESENTS: THE FANTASTIC FOUR! TM
FOR ONCE AND FOR ALL, LET'S SET THE RECORD STRAIGHT: THE WORLD-FAMOUS BAXTER BUILDING TOWERS PRECISELY FORTY STORIES ABOVE THE STREETS OF MIDTOWN MANHATTAN.
MOST PEOPLE, HOWEVER, THINK OF IT AS HAVING ONLY 35--BECAUSE THAT'S AS HIGH AS ANY ELEVATOR WILL TAKE THEM.
FOR, FROM THE 36th FLOOR TO THE TOP, THE FINAL FIVE LEVELS CAN BE REACHED ONLY BY A SPECIAL ELEVATOR--
--OR, OF COURSE, BY THE EVEN MORE COLORFUL METHODS OF THE SKY-BLAZING HUMAN TORCH!
WHERE HAVE ALL THE POWERS GONE?
FACE IT, STORM! YOU'VE FLOWN IN CIRCLES--STALLED ABOUT AS LONG AS YOU CAN.
YOU CAN'T DELAY DROPPIN' THE BOMBSHELL ANY LONGER--NO WAY!
BUT--THEY'RE NOT GONNA LIKE IT!
JV234
ROY THOMAS WRITER/EDITOR * RICH BUCKLER ARTIST * JOE SINNOTT EMBELLISHER
PHIL RACHELSON COLORIST / JOE ROSEN LETTERER

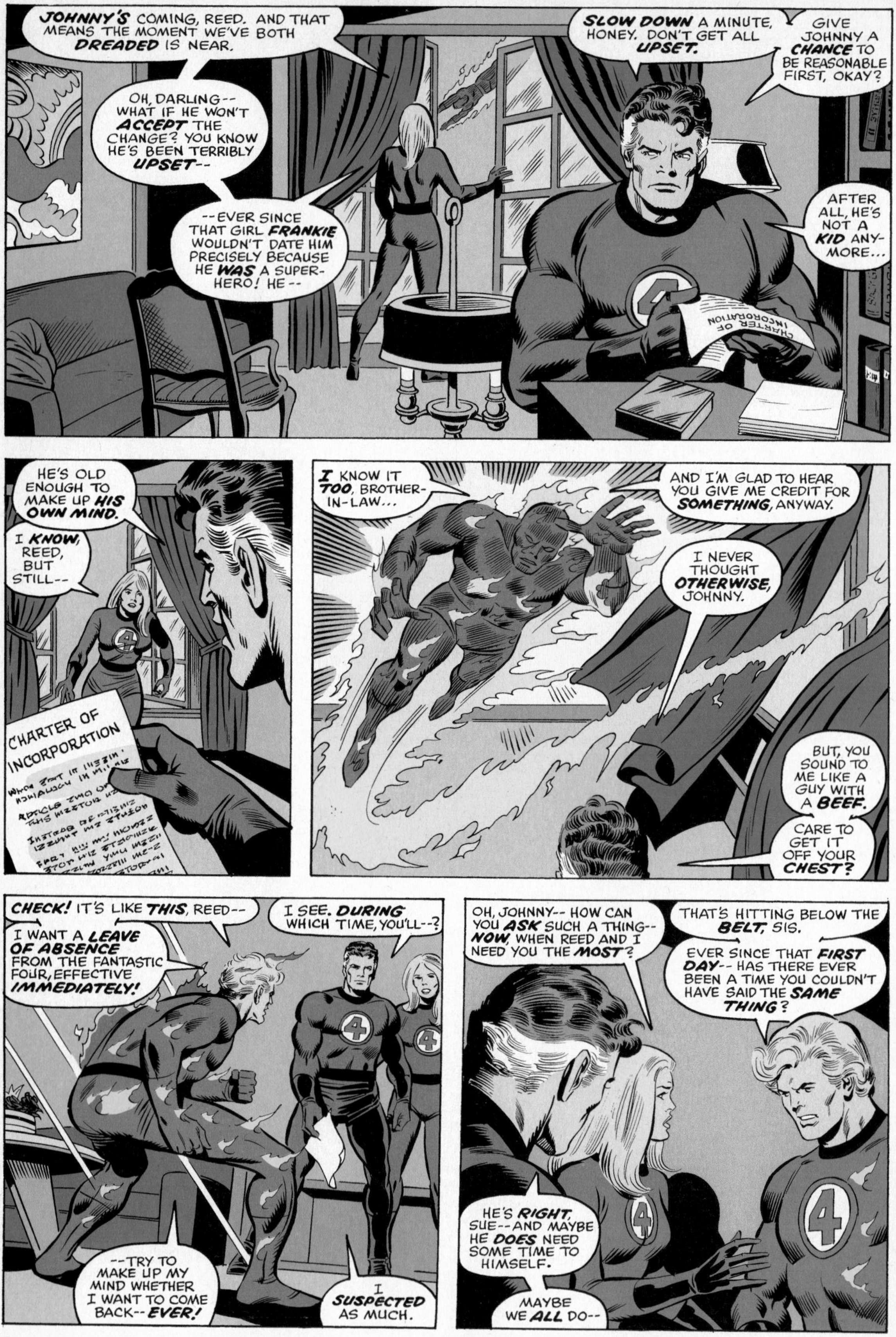
JOHNNY'S COMING, REED. AND THAT MEANS THE MOMENT WE'VE BOTH DREADED IS NEAR.
OH, DARLING-- WHAT IF HE WON'T ACCEPT THE CHANGE? YOU KNOW HE'S BEEN TERRIBLY UPSET--
--EVER SINCE THAT GIRL FRANKIE WOULDN'T DATE HIM PRECISELY BECAUSE HE WAS A SUPER-HERO! HE--
SLOW DOWN A MINUTE, HONEY. DON'T GET ALL UPSET.
GIVE JOHNNY A CHANCE TO BE REASONABLE FIRST, OKAY?
AFTER ALL, HE'S NOT A KID ANY-MORE...
CHARTER OF INCORPORATION
HE'S OLD ENOUGH TO MAKE UP HIS OWN MIND.
I KNOW, REED, BUT STILL--
CHARTER OF INCORPORATION
I KNOW IT TOO, BROTHER-IN-LAW...
AND I'M GLAD TO HEAR YOU GIVE ME CREDIT FOR SOMETHING, ANYWAY.
I NEVER THOUGHT OTHERWISE, JOHNNY.
BUT, YOU SOUND TO ME LIKE A GUY WITH A BEEF.
CARE TO GET IT OFF YOUR CHEST?
CHECK! IT'S LIKE THIS, REED--
I WANT A LEAVE OF ABSENCE FROM THE FANTASTIC FOUR, EFFECTIVE IMMEDIATELY!
I SEE. DURING WHICH TIME, YOU'LL--?
--TRY TO MAKE UP MY MIND WHETHER I WANT TO COME BACK--EVER!
I SUSPECTED AS MUCH.
OH, JOHNNY-- HOW CAN YOU ASK SUCH A THING-- NOW, WHEN REED AND I NEED YOU THE MOST?
THAT'S HITTING BELOW THE BELT, SIS.
EVER SINCE THAT FIRST DAY-- HAS THERE EVER BEEN A TIME YOU COULDN'T HAVE SAID THE SAME THING?
HE'S RIGHT, SUE--AND MAYBE HE DOES NEED SOME TIME TO HIMSELF.
MAYBE WE ALL DO--

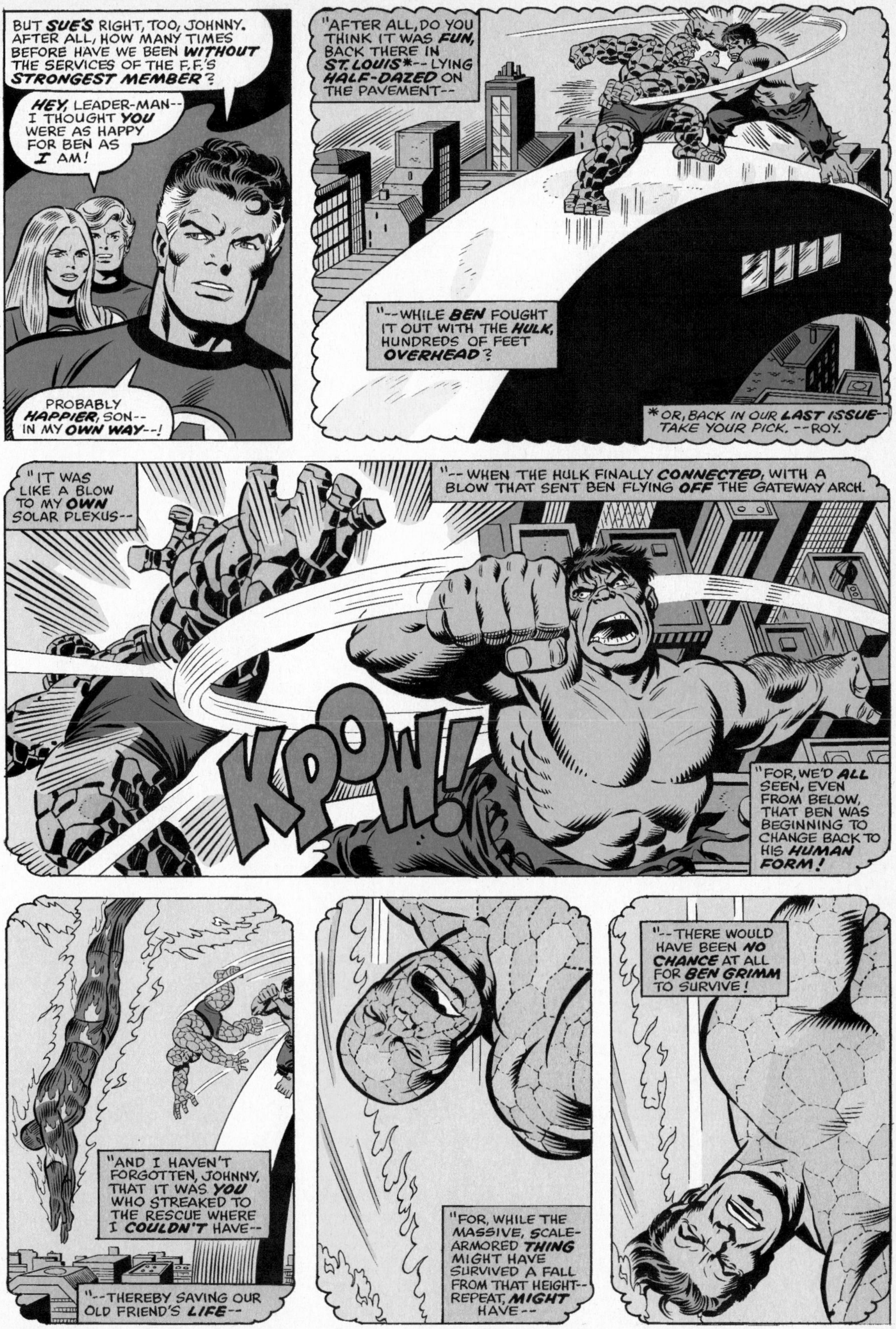
BUT SUE'S RIGHT, TOO, JOHNNY. AFTER ALL, HOW MANY TIMES BEFORE HAVE WE BEEN WITHOUT THE SERVICES OF THE F.F.'S STRONGEST MEMBER?
HEY, LEADER-MAN-- I THOUGHT YOU WERE AS HAPPY FOR BEN AS I AM!
PROBABLY HAPPIER, SON-- IN MY OWN WAY--!
"AFTER ALL, DO YOU THINK IT WAS FUN, BACK THERE IN ST. LOUIS*-- LYING HALF-DAZED ON THE PAVEMENT--
"--WHILE BEN FOUGHT IT OUT WITH THE HULK, HUNDREDS OF FEET OVERHEAD?
*OR, BACK IN OUR LAST ISSUE-- TAKE YOUR PICK. --ROY.
"IT WAS LIKE A BLOW TO MY OWN SOLAR PLEXUS--
"-- WHEN THE HULK FINALLY CONNECTED, WITH A BLOW THAT SENT BEN FLYING OFF THE GATEWAY ARCH.
KPOOW!
"FOR, WE'D ALL SEEN, EVEN FROM BELOW, THAT BEN WAS BEGINNING TO CHANGE BACK TO HIS HUMAN FORM!
"AND I HAVEN'T FORGOTTEN, JOHNNY, THAT IT WAS YOU WHO STREAKED TO THE RESCUE WHERE I COULDN'T HAVE--
"--THEREBY SAVING OUR OLD FRIEND'S LIFE--
"FOR, WHILE THE MASSIVE, SCALE-ARMORED THING MIGHT HAVE SURVIVED A FALL FROM THAT HEIGHT-- REPEAT, MIGHT HAVE--
"--THERE WOULD HAVE BEEN NO CHANCE AT ALL FOR BEN GRIMM TO SURVIVE!

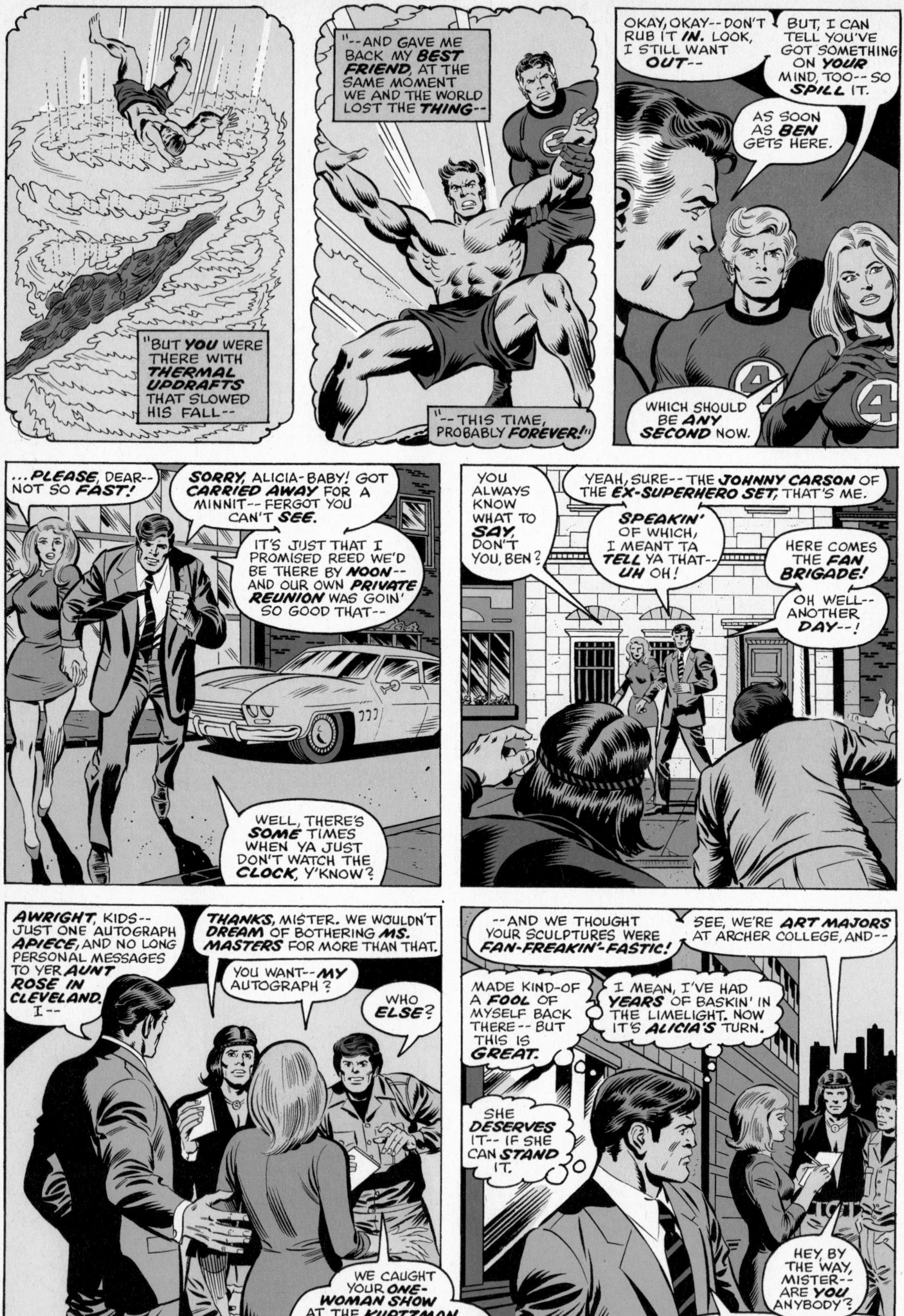
"BUT YOU WERE THERE WITH THERMAL UPDRAFTS THAT SLOWED HIS FALL--
"--AND GAVE ME BACK MY BEST FRIEND, AT THE SAME MOMENT WE AND THE WORLD LOST THE THING--
"--THIS TIME, PROBABLY FOREVER!"
OKAY, OKAY--DON'T RUB IT IN. LOOK, I STILL WANT OUT--
BUT, I CAN TELL YOU'VE GOT SOMETHING ON YOUR MIND, TOO--SO SPILL IT.
AS SOON AS BEN GETS HERE.
WHICH SHOULD BE ANY SECOND NOW.
...PLEASE, DEAR--NOT SO FAST!
SORRY, ALICIA-BABY! GOT CARRIED AWAY FOR A MINNIT--FERGOT YOU CAN'T SEE.
IT'S JUST THAT I PROMISED REED WE'D BE THERE BY NOON--AND OUR OWN PRIVATE REUNION WAS GOIN' SO GOOD THAT--
WELL, THERE'S SOME TIMES WHEN YA JUST DON'T WATCH THE CLOCK, Y'KNOW?
YOU ALWAYS KNOW WHAT TO SAY, DON'T YOU, BEN?
YEAH, SURE--THE JOHNNY CARSON OF THE EX-SUPERHERO SET, THAT'S ME.
SPEAKIN' OF WHICH, I MEANT TA TELL YA THAT--UH OH!
HERE COMES THE FAN BRIGADE!
OH WELL--ANOTHER DAY--!
AWRIGHT, KIDS--JUST ONE AUTOGRAPH APIECE, AND NO LONG PERSONAL MESSAGES TO YER AUNT ROSE IN CLEVELAND. I--
THANKS, MISTER. WE WOULDN'T DREAM OF BOTHERING MS. MASTERS FOR MORE THAN THAT.
YOU WANT--MY AUTOGRAPH?
WHO ELSE?
WE CAUGHT YOUR ONE-WOMAN SHOW AT THE KURTZMAN ART GALLERY LAST WEEK--
--AND WE THOUGHT YOUR SCULPTURES WERE FAN-FREAKIN'-FASTIC!
SEE, WE'RE ART MAJORS AT ARCHER COLLEGE, AND--
MADE KIND-OF A FOOL OF MYSELF BACK THERE--BUT THIS IS GREAT.
I MEAN, I'VE HAD YEARS OF BASKIN' IN THE LIMELIGHT. NOW IT'S ALICIA'S TURN.
SHE DESERVES IT--IF SHE CAN STAND IT.
HEY, BY THE WAY, MISTER--ARE YOU ANYBODY?
NOPE, KID...NOT ANY MORE.

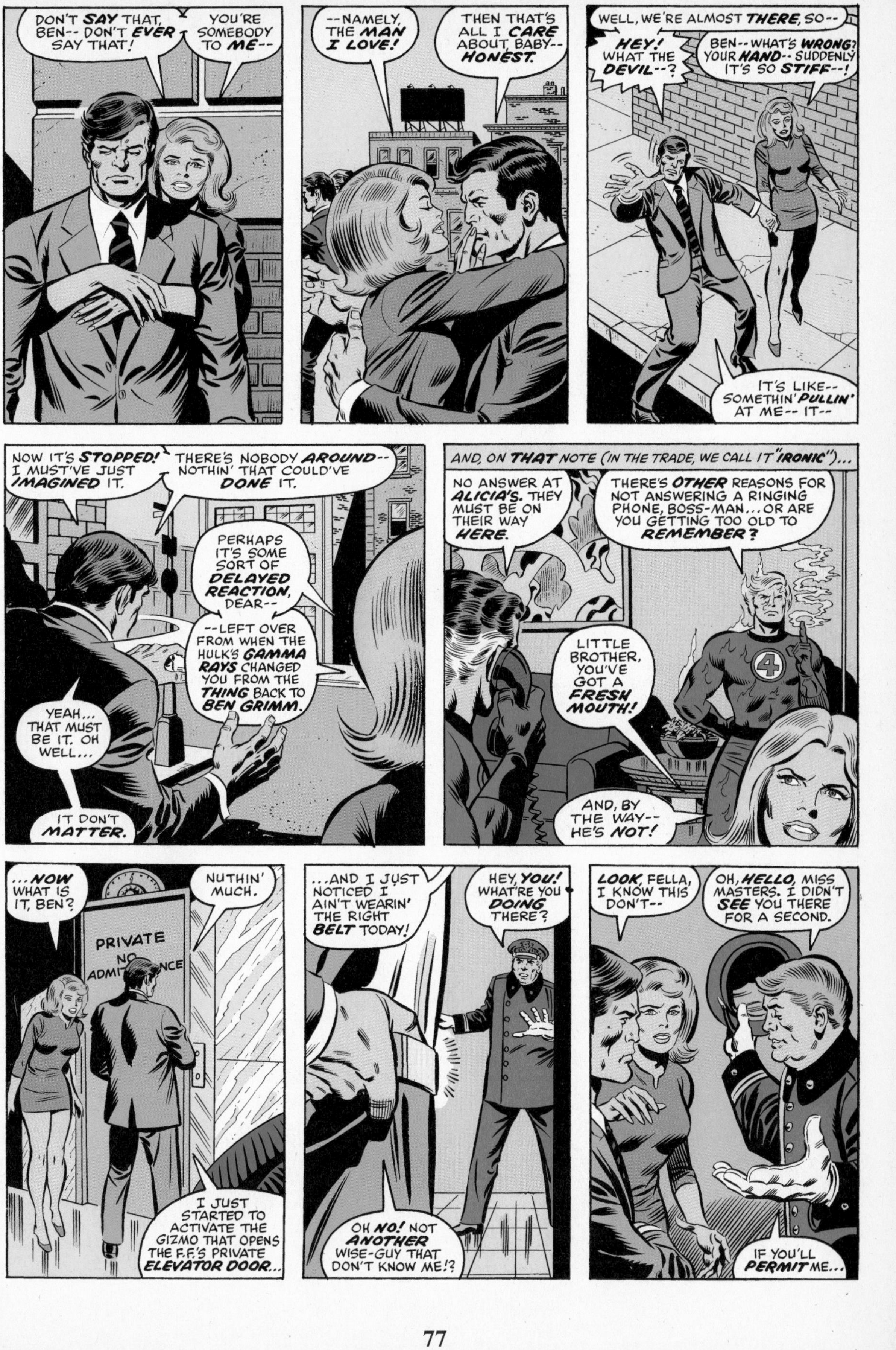
DON'T SAY THAT, BEN-- DON'T EVER SAY THAT!
YOU'RE SOMEBODY TO ME--
--NAMELY, THE MAN I LOVE!
THEN THAT'S ALL I CARE ABOUT, BABY-- HONEST.
WELL, WE'RE ALMOST THERE, SO--
HEY! WHAT THE DEVIL--?
BEN--WHAT'S WRONG? YOUR HAND-- SUDDENLY IT'S SO STIFF--!
IT'S LIKE-- SOMETHIN' PULLIN' AT ME-- IT--
NOW IT'S STOPPED! I MUST'VE JUST IMAGINED IT.
THERE'S NOBODY AROUND-- NOTHIN' THAT COULD'VE DONE IT.
PERHAPS IT'S SOME SORT OF DELAYED REACTION, DEAR--
--LEFT OVER FROM WHEN THE HULK'S GAMMA RAYS CHANGED YOU FROM THE THING BACK TO BEN GRIMM.
YEAH... THAT MUST BE IT. OH WELL...
IT DON'T MATTER.
AND, ON THAT NOTE (IN THE TRADE, WE CALL IT "IRONIC")...
NO ANSWER AT ALICIA'S. THEY MUST BE ON THEIR WAY HERE.
THERE'S OTHER REASONS FOR NOT ANSWERING A RINGING PHONE, BOSS-MAN... OR ARE YOU GETTING TOO OLD TO REMEMBER?
LITTLE BROTHER, YOU'VE GOT A FRESH MOUTH!
AND, BY THE WAY-- HE'S NOT!
...NOW WHAT IS IT, BEN?
NUTHIN' MUCH.
PRIVATE
NO ADMI NCE
I JUST STARTED TO ACTIVATE THE GIZMO THAT OPENS THE F.F.'S PRIVATE ELEVATOR DOOR...
...AND I JUST NOTICED I AIN'T WEARIN' THE RIGHT BELT TODAY!
HEY, YOU! WHAT'RE YOU DOING THERE?
OH NO! NOT ANOTHER WISE-GUY THAT DON'T KNOW ME!?
LOOK, FELLA, I KNOW THIS DON'T--
OH, HELLO, MISS MASTERS. I DIDN'T SEE YOU THERE FOR A SECOND.
IF YOU'LL PERMIT ME...

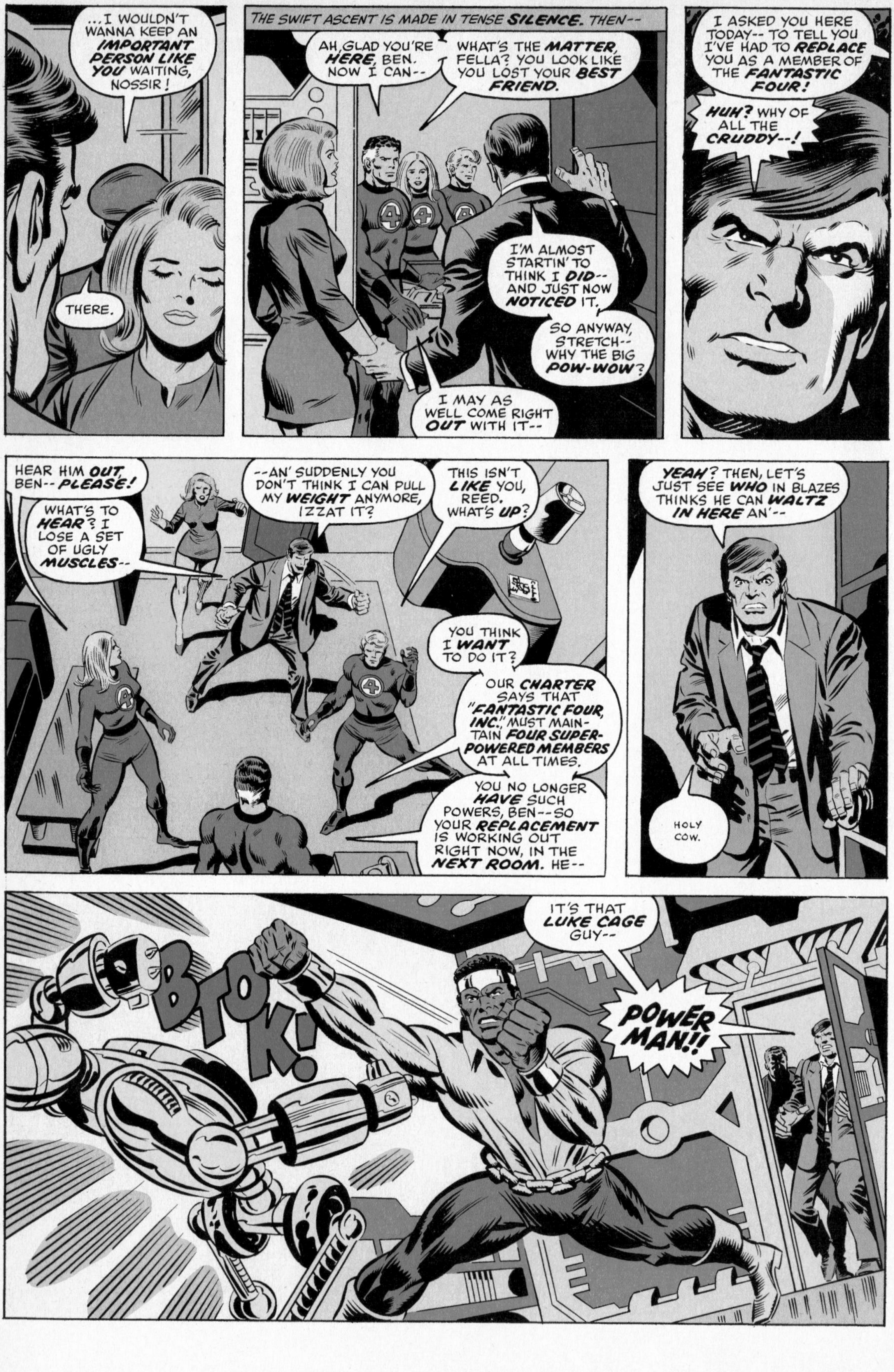
...I WOULDN'T WANNA KEEP AN IMPORTANT PERSON LIKE YOU WAITING, NOSSIR!
THERE.
THE SWIFT ASCENT IS MADE IN TENSE SILENCE. THEN--
AH, GLAD YOU'RE HERE, BEN. NOW I CAN--
WHAT'S THE MATTER, FELLA? YOU LOOK LIKE YOU LOST YOUR BEST FRIEND.
I'M ALMOST STARTIN' TO THINK I DID-- AND JUST NOW NOTICED IT.
SO ANYWAY, STRETCH-- WHY THE BIG POW-WOW?
I MAY AS WELL COME RIGHT OUT WITH IT--
I ASKED YOU HERE TODAY-- TO TELL YOU I'VE HAD TO REPLACE YOU AS A MEMBER OF THE FANTASTIC FOUR!
HUH? WHY OF ALL THE CRUDDY--!
HEAR HIM OUT, BEN-- PLEASE!
WHAT'S TO HEAR? I LOSE A SET OF UGLY MUSCLES--
--AN' SUDDENLY YOU DON'T THINK I CAN PULL MY WEIGHT ANYMORE, IZZAT IT?
THIS ISN'T LIKE YOU, REED. WHAT'S UP?
YOU THINK I WANT TO DO IT?
OUR CHARTER SAYS THAT "FANTASTIC FOUR, INC." MUST MAINTAIN FOUR SUPER-POWERED MEMBERS AT ALL TIMES.
YOU NO LONGER HAVE SUCH POWERS, BEN--SO YOUR REPLACEMENT IS WORKING OUT RIGHT NOW, IN THE NEXT ROOM. HE--
YEAH? THEN, LET'S JUST SEE WHO IN BLAZES THINKS HE CAN WALTZ IN HERE AN'--
HOLY COW.
IT'S THAT LUKE CAGE GUY--
POWER MAN!!
BTOK!

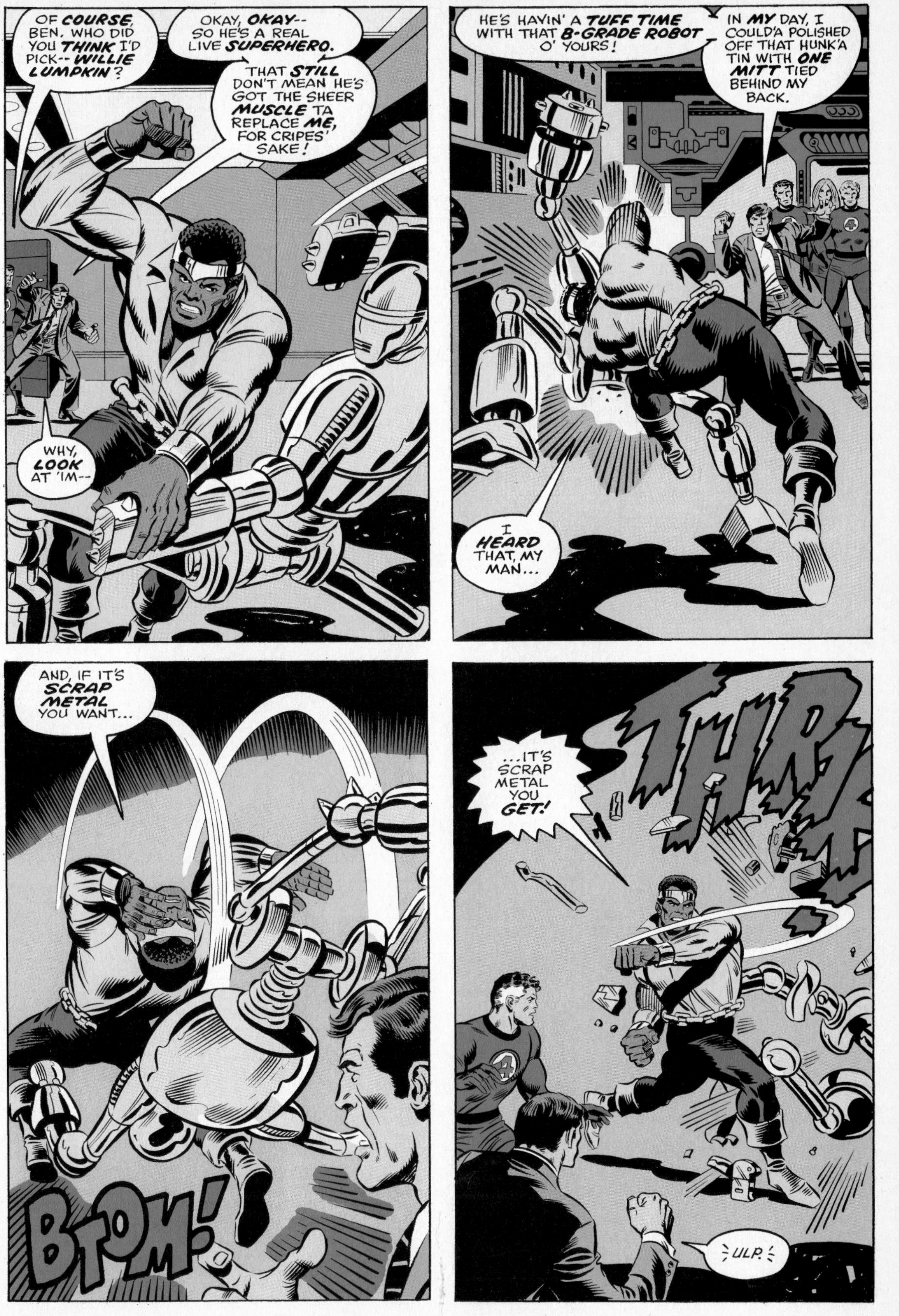
OF COURSE, BEN. WHO DID YOU THINK I'D PICK-- WILLIE LUMPKIN?
OKAY, OKAY-- SO HE'S A REAL LIVE SUPERHERO.
THAT STILL DON'T MEAN HE'S GOT THE SHEER MUSCLE TA REPLACE ME, FOR CRIPES' SAKE!
WHY, LOOK AT 'IM--
HE'S HAVIN' A TUFF TIME WITH THAT B-GRADE ROBOT O' YOURS!
IN MY DAY, I COULD'A POLISHED OFF THAT HUNK'A TIN WITH ONE MITT TIED BEHIND MY BACK.
I HEARD THAT, MY MAN...
AND, IF IT'S SCRAP METAL YOU WANT...
BTOM!
...IT'S SCRAP METAL YOU GET!
THR
ULP.

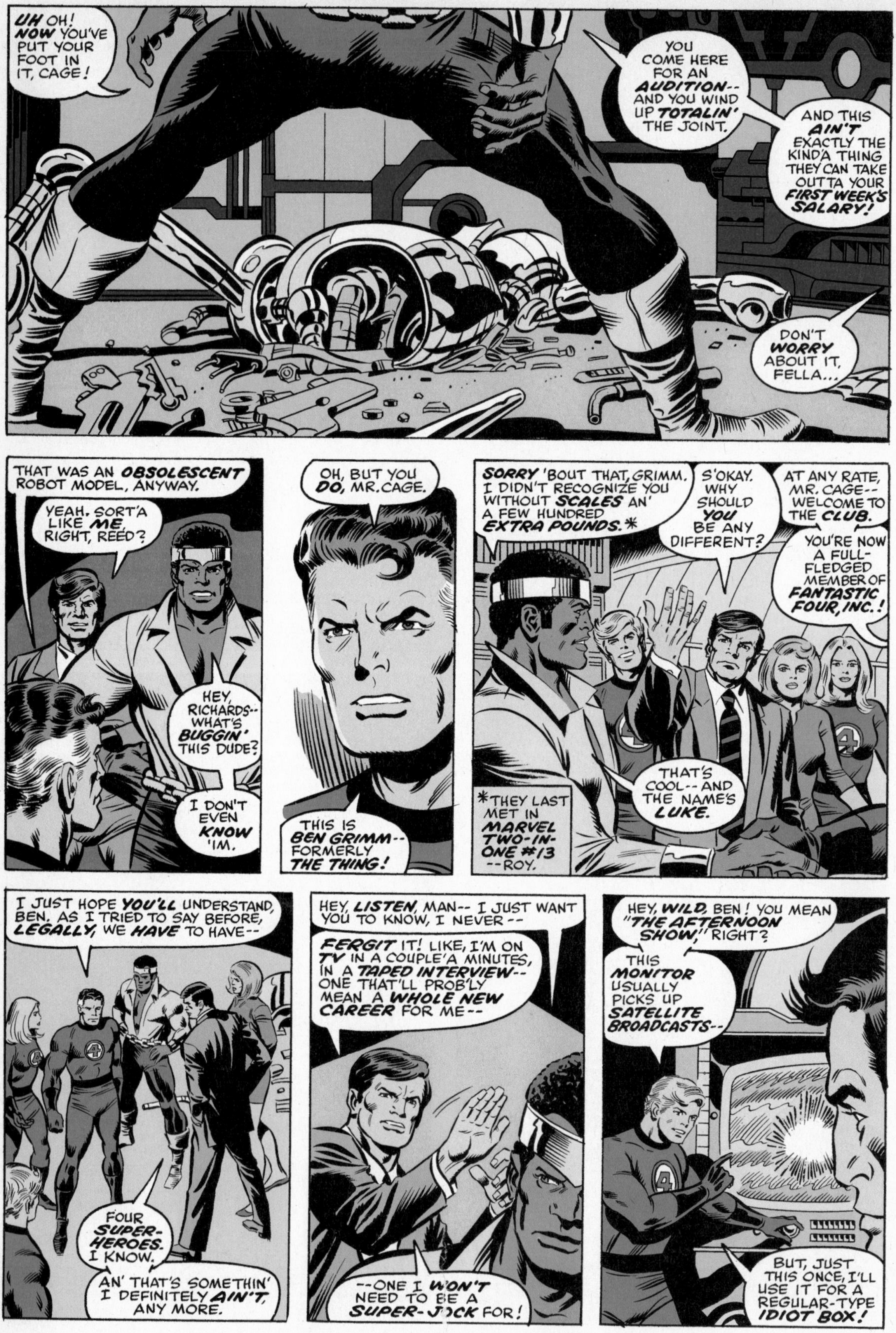
UH OH! NOW YOU'VE PUT YOUR FOOT IN IT, CAGE!
YOU COME HERE FOR AN AUDITION-- AND YOU WIND UP TOTALIN' THE JOINT.
AND THIS AIN'T EXACTLY THE KIND'A THING THEY CAN TAKE OUTTA YOUR FIRST WEEK'S SALARY!
DON'T WORRY ABOUT IT, FELLA...
THAT WAS AN OBSOLESCENT ROBOT MODEL, ANYWAY.
YEAH. SORT'A LIKE ME. RIGHT, REED?
HEY, RICHARDS-- WHAT'S BUGGIN' THIS DUDE?
I DON'T EVEN KNOW 'IM.
OH, BUT YOU DO, MR. CAGE.
THIS IS BEN GRIMM-- FORMERLY THE THING!
SORRY 'BOUT THAT, GRIMM. I DIDN'T RECOGNIZE YOU WITHOUT SCALES AN' A FEW HUNDRED EXTRA POUNDS.*
S'OKAY. WHY SHOULD YOU BE ANY DIFFERENT?
AT ANY RATE, MR. CAGE-- WELCOME TO THE CLUB.
YOU'RE NOW A FULL-FLEDGED MEMBER OF FANTASTIC FOUR, INC.!
THAT'S COOL-- AND THE NAME'S LUKE.
*THEY LAST MET IN MARVEL TWO-IN-ONE #13 --ROY.
I JUST HOPE YOU'LL UNDERSTAND, BEN. AS I TRIED TO SAY BEFORE, LEGALLY, WE HAVE TO HAVE--
FOUR SUPER-HEROES. I KNOW.
AN' THAT'S SOMETHIN' I DEFINITELY AIN'T, ANY MORE.
HEY, LISTEN, MAN-- I JUST WANT YOU TO KNOW, I NEVER--
FERGIT IT! LIKE, I'M ON TV IN A COUPLE'A MINUTES, IN A TAPED INTERVIEW-- ONE THAT'LL PROB'LY MEAN A WHOLE NEW CAREER FOR ME--
--ONE I WON'T NEED TO BE A SUPER-JOCK FOR!
HEY, WILD, BEN! YOU MEAN "THE AFTERNOON SHOW," RIGHT?
THIS MONITOR USUALLY PICKS UP SATELLITE BROADCASTS--
BUT, JUST THIS ONCE, I'LL USE IT FOR A REGULAR-TYPE IDIOT BOX!

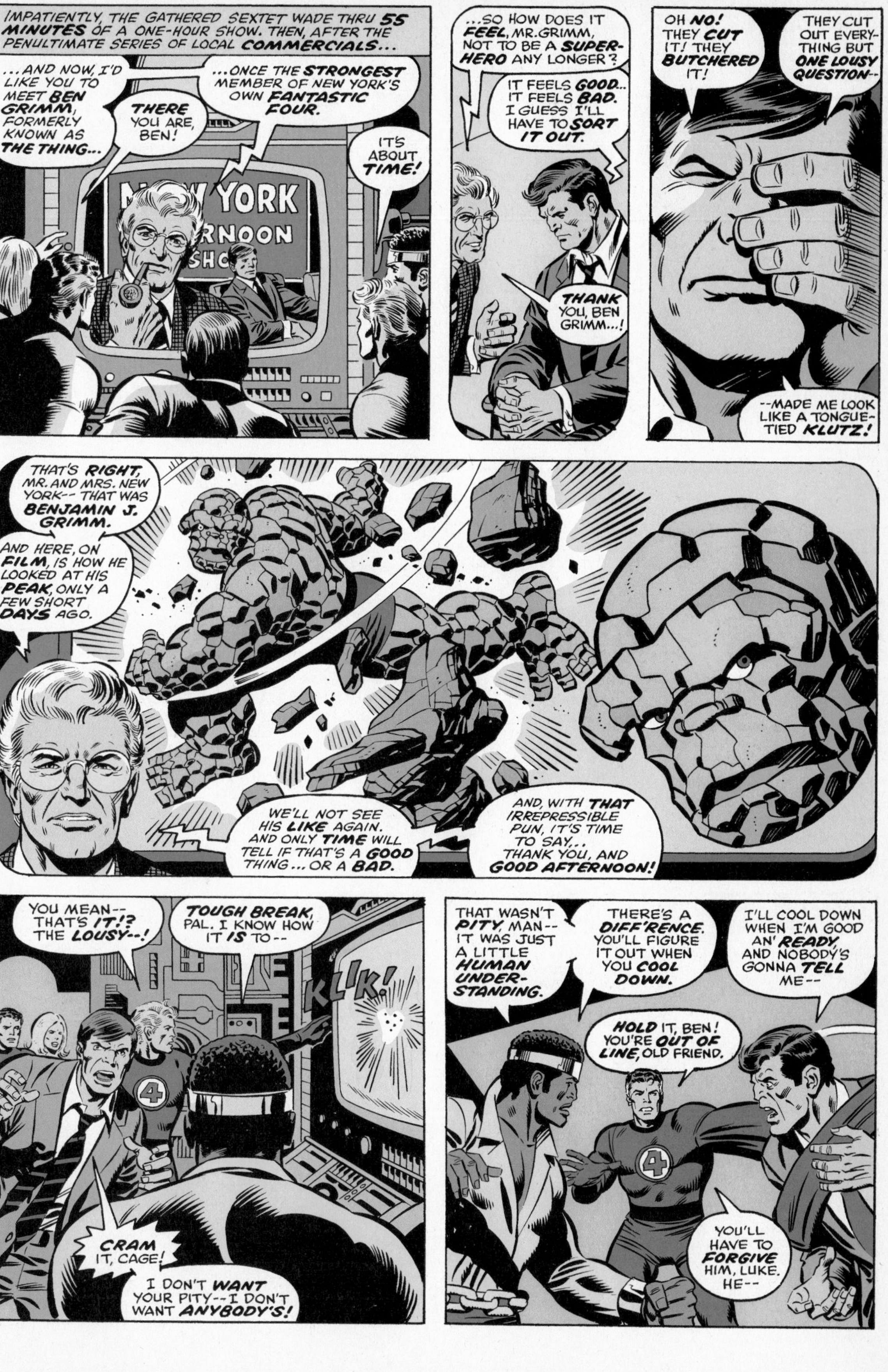
IMPATIENTLY, THE GATHERED SEXTET WADE THRU 55 MINUTES OF A ONE-HOUR SHOW. THEN, AFTER THE PENULTIMATE SERIES OF LOCAL COMMERCIALS...
...AND NOW, I'D LIKE YOU TO MEET BEN GRIMM, FORMERLY KNOWN AS THE THING...
...ONCE THE STRONGEST MEMBER OF NEW YORK'S OWN FANTASTIC FOUR.
THERE YOU ARE, BEN!
IT'S ABOUT TIME!
NEW YORK
RNOON
...SO HOW DOES IT FEEL, MR. GRIMM, NOT TO BE A SUPER-HERO ANY LONGER?
IT FEELS GOOD... IT FEELS BAD. I GUESS I'LL HAVE TO SORT IT OUT.
THANK YOU, BEN GRIMM...!
OH NO! THEY CUT IT! THEY BUTCHERED IT!
THEY CUT OUT EVERY-THING BUT ONE LOUSY QUESTION--
--MADE ME LOOK LIKE A TONGUE-TIED KLUTZ!
THAT'S RIGHT, MR. AND MRS. NEW YORK-- THAT WAS BENJAMIN J. GRIMM.
AND HERE, ON FILM, IS HOW HE LOOKED AT HIS PEAK, ONLY A FEW SHORT DAYS AGO.
WE'LL NOT SEE HIS LIKE AGAIN. AND ONLY TIME WILL TELL IF THAT'S A GOOD THING... OR A BAD.
AND, WITH THAT IRREPRESSIBLE PUN, IT'S TIME TO SAY... THANK YOU, AND GOOD AFTERNOON!
YOU MEAN-- THAT'S IT!? THE LOUSY--!
TOUGH BREAK, PAL. I KNOW HOW IT IS TO--
KLIK!
CRAM IT, CAGE!
I DON'T WANT YOUR PITY--I DON'T WANT ANYBODY'S!
THAT WASN'T PITY, MAN-- IT WAS JUST A LITTLE HUMAN UNDER-STANDING.
THERE'S A DIFF'RENCE. YOU'LL FIGURE IT OUT WHEN YOU COOL DOWN.
I'LL COOL DOWN WHEN I'M GOOD AN' READY, AND NOBODY'S GONNA TELL ME--
HOLD IT, BEN! YOU'RE OUT OF LINE, OLD FRIEND.
YOU'LL HAVE TO FORGIVE HIM, LUKE. HE--

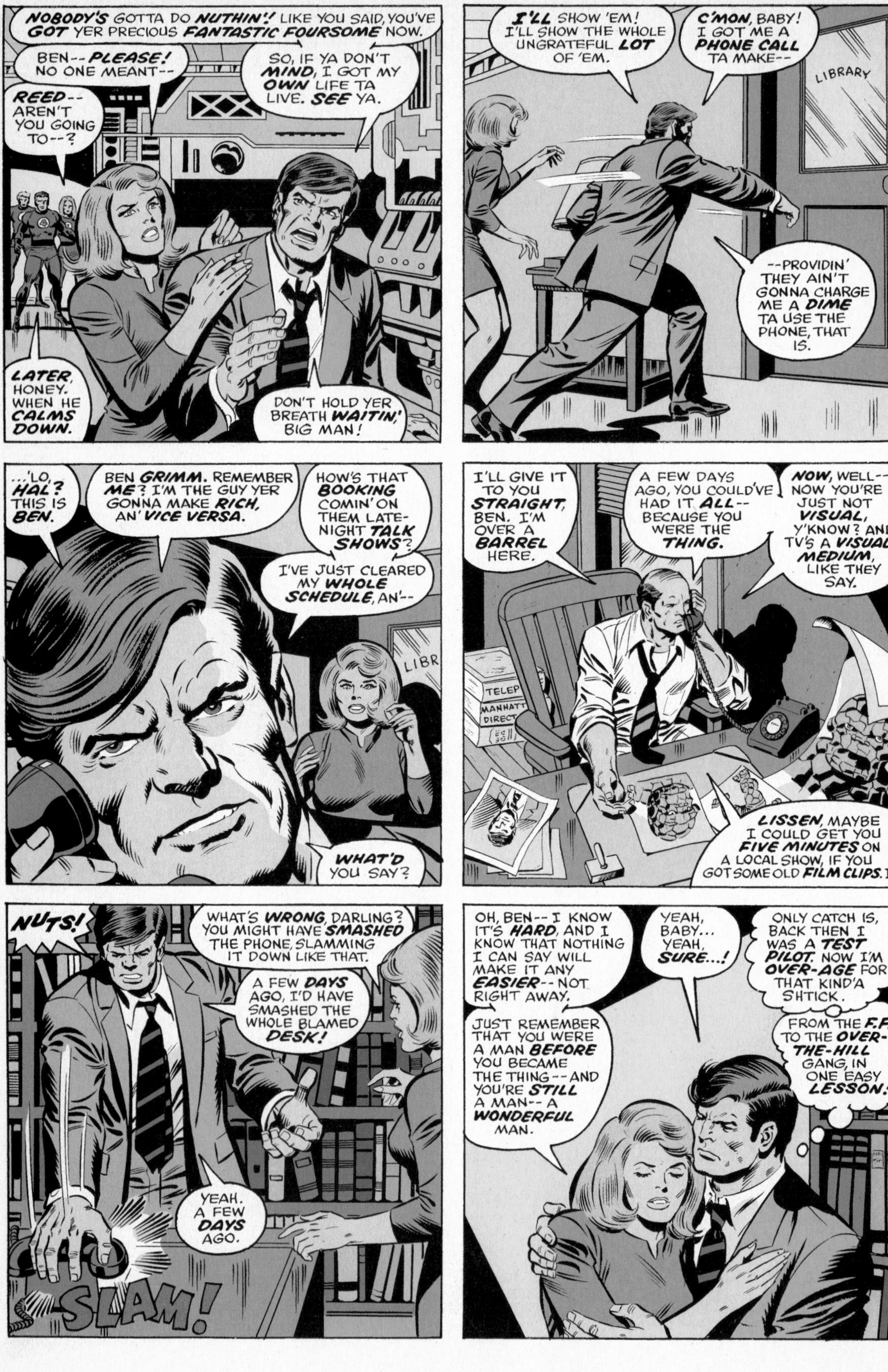
NOBODY'S GOTTA DO NUTHIN'! LIKE YOU SAID, YOU'VE GOT YER PRECIOUS FANTASTIC FOURSOME NOW.
BEN-- PLEASE! NO ONE MEANT--
SO, IF YA DON'T MIND, I GOT MY OWN LIFE TA LIVE. SEE YA.
REED-- AREN'T YOU GOING TO--?
LATER, HONEY. WHEN HE CALMS DOWN.
DON'T HOLD YER BREATH WAITIN', BIG MAN!
I'LL SHOW 'EM! I'LL SHOW THE WHOLE UNGRATEFUL LOT OF 'EM.
C'MON, BABY! I GOT ME A PHONE CALL TA MAKE--
LIBRARY
--PROVIDIN' THEY AIN'T GONNA CHARGE ME A DIME TA USE THE PHONE, THAT IS.
...'LO, HAL? THIS IS BEN.
BEN GRIMM. REMEMBER ME? I'M THE GUY YER GONNA MAKE RICH, AN' VICE VERSA.
HOW'S THAT BOOKING COMIN' ON THEM LATE-NIGHT TALK SHOWS?
I'VE JUST CLEARED MY WHOLE SCHEDULE, AN'--
LIBR
WHAT'D YOU SAY?
I'LL GIVE IT TO YOU STRAIGHT, BEN. I'M OVER A BARREL HERE.
A FEW DAYS AGO, YOU COULD'VE HAD IT ALL-- BECAUSE YOU WERE THE THING.
NOW, WELL-- NOW YOU'RE JUST NOT VISUAL, Y'KNOW? AND TV'S A VISUAL MEDIUM, LIKE THEY SAY.
TELEP
MANHATT
DIRECT
LISSEN, MAYBE I COULD GET YOU FIVE MINUTES ON A LOCAL SHOW, IF YOU GOT SOME OLD FILM CLIPS. I--
NUTS!
WHAT'S WRONG, DARLING? YOU MIGHT HAVE SMASHED THE PHONE, SLAMMING IT DOWN LIKE THAT.
A FEW DAYS AGO, I'D HAVE SMASHED THE WHOLE BLAMED DESK!
YEAH. A FEW DAYS AGO.
SLAM!
OH, BEN-- I KNOW IT'S HARD, AND I KNOW THAT NOTHING I CAN SAY WILL MAKE IT ANY EASIER-- NOT RIGHT AWAY.
YEAH, BABY... YEAH, SURE...!
ONLY CATCH IS, BACK THEN I WAS A TEST PILOT. NOW I'M OVER-AGE FOR THAT KIND'A SHTICK.
JUST REMEMBER THAT YOU WERE A MAN BEFORE YOU BECAME THE THING--AND YOU'RE STILL A MAN-- A WONDERFUL MAN.
FROM THE F.F. TO THE OVER-THE-HILL GANG, IN ONE EASY LESSON!

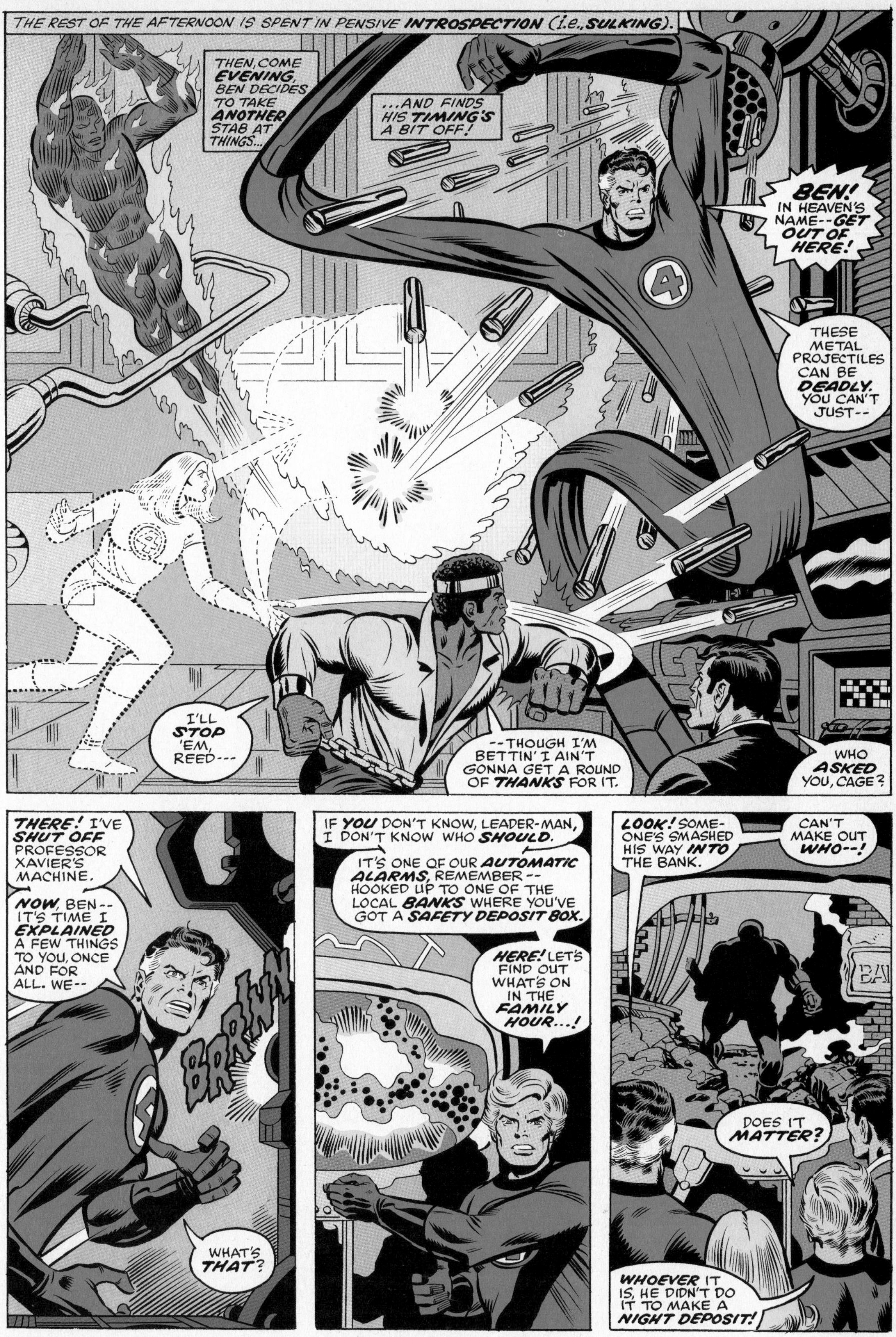

THE REST OF THE AFTERNOON IS SPENT IN PENSIVE INTROSPECTION (i.e., SULKING).
THEN, COME EVENING, BEN DECIDES TO TAKE ANOTHER STAB AT THINGS...
...AND FINDS HIS TIMING'S A BIT OFF!
BEN! IN HEAVEN'S NAME--GET OUT OF HERE!
THESE METAL PROJECTILES CAN BE DEADLY. YOU CAN'T JUST--
I'LL STOP 'EM, REED---
--THOUGH I'M BETTIN' I AIN'T GONNA GET A ROUND OF THANKS FOR IT.
WHO ASKED YOU, CAGE?
THERE! I'VE SHUT OFF PROFESSOR XAVIER'S MACHINE.
NOW, BEN-- IT'S TIME I EXPLAINED A FEW THINGS TO YOU, ONCE AND FOR ALL. WE--
WHAT'S THAT?
IF YOU DON'T KNOW, LEADER-MAN, I DON'T KNOW WHO SHOULD.
IT'S ONE OF OUR AUTOMATIC ALARMS, REMEMBER-- HOOKED UP TO ONE OF THE LOCAL BANKS WHERE YOU'VE GOT A SAFETY DEPOSIT BOX.
HERE! LET'S FIND OUT WHAT'S ON IN THE FAMILY HOUR...!
LOOK! SOME-ONE'S SMASHED HIS WAY INTO THE BANK.
CAN'T MAKE OUT WHO--!
DOES IT MATTER?
WHOEVER IT IS, HE DIDN'T DO IT TO MAKE A NIGHT DEPOSIT!

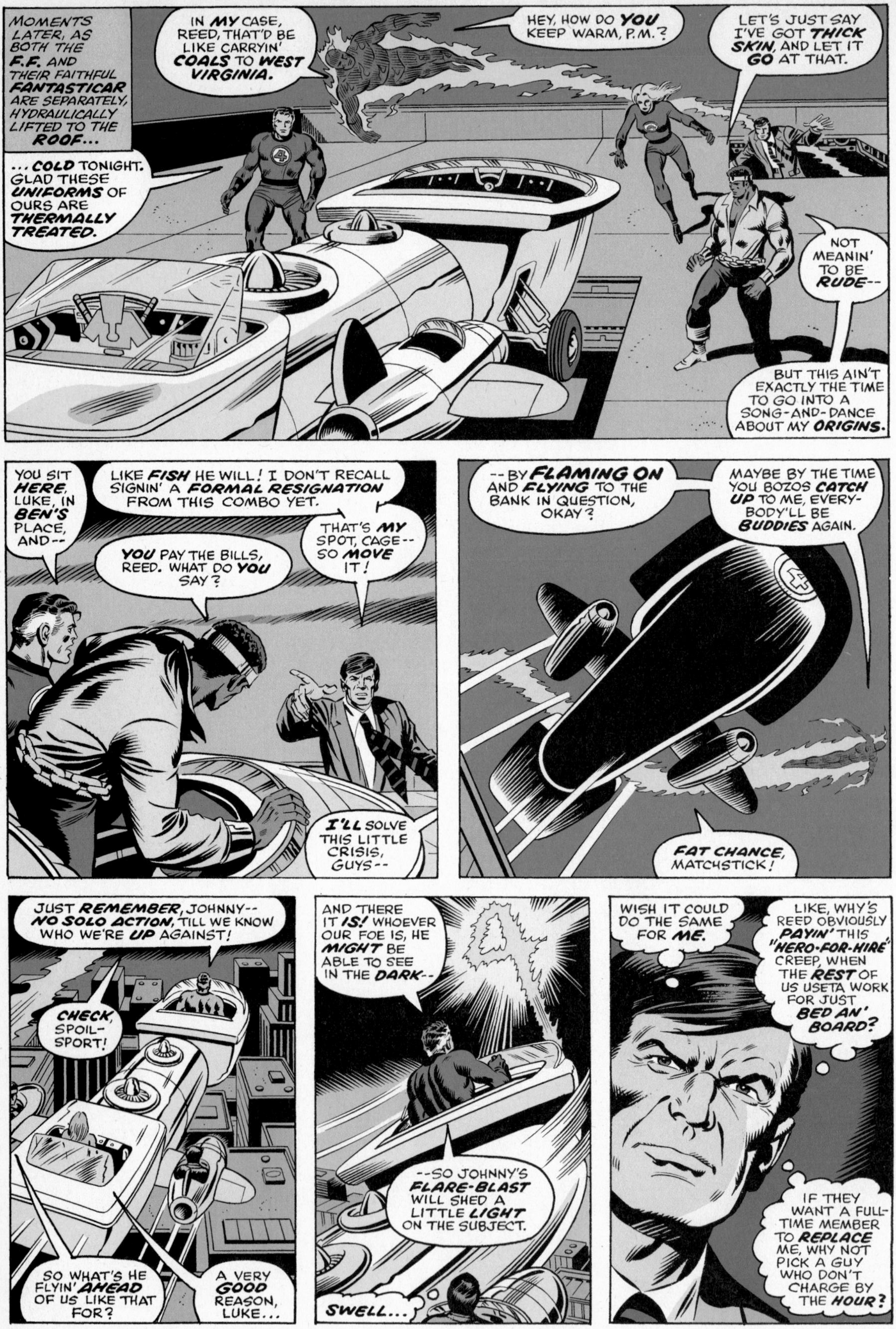
MOMENTS LATER, AS BOTH THE F.F. AND THEIR FAITHFUL FANTASTICAR ARE SEPARATELY, HYDRAULICALLY LIFTED TO THE ROOF...
IN MY CASE, REED, THAT'D BE LIKE CARRYIN' COALS TO WEST VIRGINIA.
HEY, HOW DO YOU KEEP WARM, P.M.?
LET'S JUST SAY I'VE GOT THICK SKIN, AND LET IT GO AT THAT.
...COLD TONIGHT. GLAD THESE UNIFORMS OF OURS ARE THERMALLY TREATED.
NOT MEANIN' TO BE RUDE--
BUT THIS AIN'T EXACTLY THE TIME TO GO INTO A SONG-AND-DANCE ABOUT MY ORIGINS.
YOU SIT HERE, LUKE, IN BEN'S PLACE, AND--
LIKE FISH HE WILL! I DON'T RECALL SIGNIN' A FORMAL RESIGNATION FROM THIS COMBO YET.
YOU PAY THE BILLS, REED. WHAT DO YOU SAY?
THAT'S MY SPOT, CAGE-- SO MOVE IT!
I'LL SOLVE THIS LITTLE CRISIS, GUYS--
--BY FLAMING ON AND FLYING TO THE BANK IN QUESTION, OKAY?
MAYBE BY THE TIME YOU BOZOS CATCH UP TO ME, EVERY-BODY'LL BE BUDDIES AGAIN.
FAT CHANCE, MATCHSTICK!
JUST REMEMBER, JOHNNY-- NO SOLO ACTION, TILL WE KNOW WHO WE'RE UP AGAINST!
CHECK, SPOIL-SPORT!
SO WHAT'S HE FLYIN' AHEAD OF US LIKE THAT FOR?
A VERY GOOD REASON, LUKE...
AND THERE IT IS! WHOEVER OUR FOE IS, HE MIGHT BE ABLE TO SEE IN THE DARK--
--SO JOHNNY'S FLARE-BLAST WILL SHED A LITTLE LIGHT ON THE SUBJECT.
SWELL...
WISH IT COULD DO THE SAME FOR ME.
LIKE, WHY'S REED OBVIOUSLY PAYIN' THIS "HERO-FOR-HIRE" CREEP, WHEN THE REST OF US USETA WORK FOR JUST BED AN' BOARD?
IF THEY WANT A FULL-TIME MEMBER TO REPLACE ME, WHY NOT PICK A GUY WHO DON'T CHARGE BY THE HOUR?

NUTS AND DOUBLE-NUTS!

I AIN'T GONNA LEARN ANY ANSWERS STICKIN' AROUND *HERE*, LIKE THE ORIGINAL *FIFTH WHEEL*, SO-- *GERONIMO!*

BEN! WHAT THE *DEVIL*--?

SEE YOU DOWN *BELOW*, PEOPLE.

HERE'S WHERE I LEARN IF *BEN GRIMM'S* STILL GOT WHAT IT *TAKES!*

THE TORCH'S *4-FLARE'S* STILL LIGHTING UP THE SKY, SO I CAN *SEE* JUST WHO--

HEY! THAT *GUY* DOWN THERE-- I RECOGNIZE HIM FROM HIS *MUG SHOTS!* IT'S--

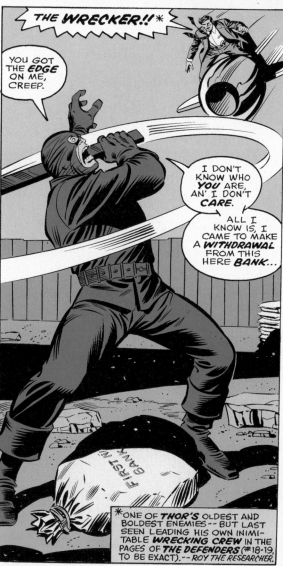

THE *WRECKER!!* *

YOU GOT THE *EDGE* ON ME, CREEP.

I DON'T KNOW WHO *YOU* ARE, AN' I DON'T *CARE.*

ALL I KNOW IS, I CAME TO MAKE A *WITHDRAWAL* FROM THIS HERE *BANK...*

*ONE OF *THOR'S* OLDEST AND BOLDEST ENEMIES-- BUT LAST SEEN LEADING HIS OWN INIMITABLE *WRECKING CREW* IN THE PAGES OF *THE DEFENDERS* (#18-19, TO BE EXACT). --ROY THE RESEARCHER.

...AND NOBODY IN A *TOY PLANE* STRAIGHT OUTTA *CONEY ISLAND* IS GONNA *STOP* ME!

SMASH!

HOLY JOE! THAT *CROWBAR* OF HIS SMASHED MY CRATE TO *SMITHEREENS!*

JUMPED OUT JUST IN *TIME*--

--OR DID I??

UNNNH--!

HECK, I DON'T *NEED* MY CROWBAR TO TAKE CARE OF A PUNK LIKE *YOU.*

BOK!

MORE FUN WITH MY *FISTS*, ANY OLD DAY!

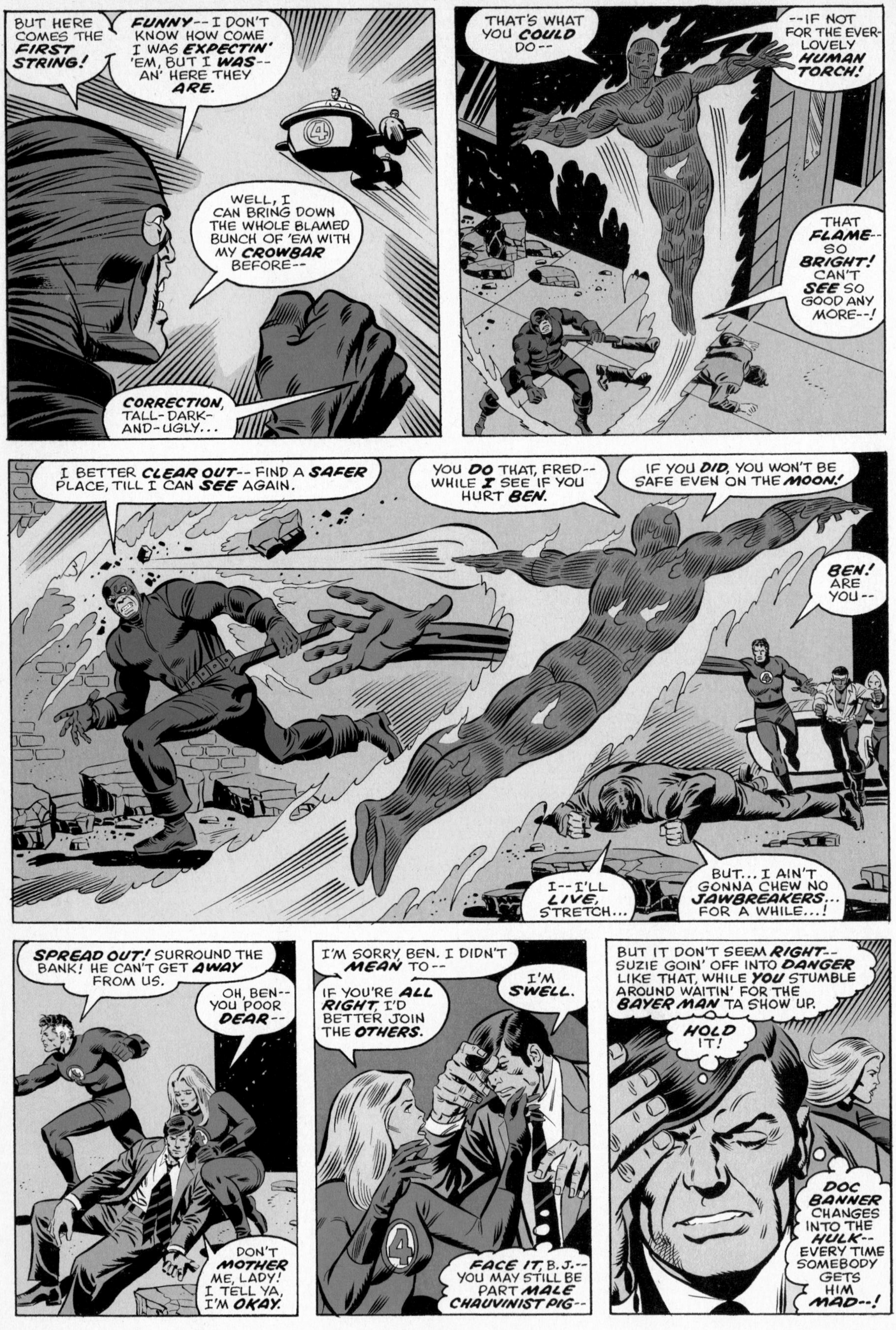
BUT HERE COMES THE FIRST STRING!
FUNNY-- I DON'T KNOW HOW COME I WAS EXPECTIN' 'EM, BUT I WAS-- AN' HERE THEY ARE.
WELL, I CAN BRING DOWN THE WHOLE BLAMED BUNCH OF 'EM WITH MY CROWBAR BEFORE--
CORRECTION, TALL-DARK-AND-UGLY...
THAT'S WHAT YOU COULD DO--
--IF NOT FOR THE EVER-LOVELY HUMAN TORCH!
THAT FLAME-- SO BRIGHT! CAN'T SEE SO GOOD ANY MORE--!
I BETTER CLEAR OUT-- FIND A SAFER PLACE, TILL I CAN SEE AGAIN.
YOU DO THAT, FRED-- WHILE I SEE IF YOU HURT BEN.
IF YOU DID, YOU WON'T BE SAFE EVEN ON THE MOON!
BEN! ARE YOU--
I--I'LL LIVE, STRETCH...
BUT... I AIN'T GONNA CHEW NO JAWBREAKERS... FOR A WHILE...!
SPREAD OUT! SURROUND THE BANK! HE CAN'T GET AWAY FROM US.
OH, BEN-- YOU POOR DEAR--
DON'T MOTHER ME, LADY! I TELL YA, I'M OKAY.
I'M SORRY, BEN. I DIDN'T MEAN TO--
IF YOU'RE ALL RIGHT, I'D BETTER JOIN THE OTHERS.
I'M SWELL.
FACE IT, B.J.-- YOU MAY STILL BE PART MALE CHAUVINIST PIG--
BUT IT DON'T SEEM RIGHT-- SUZIE GOIN' OFF INTO DANGER LIKE THAT, WHILE YOU STUMBLE AROUND WAITIN' FOR THE BAYER MAN TA SHOW UP.
HOLD IT!
DOC BANNER CHANGES INTO THE HULK-- EVERY TIME SOMEBODY GETS HIM MAD--!

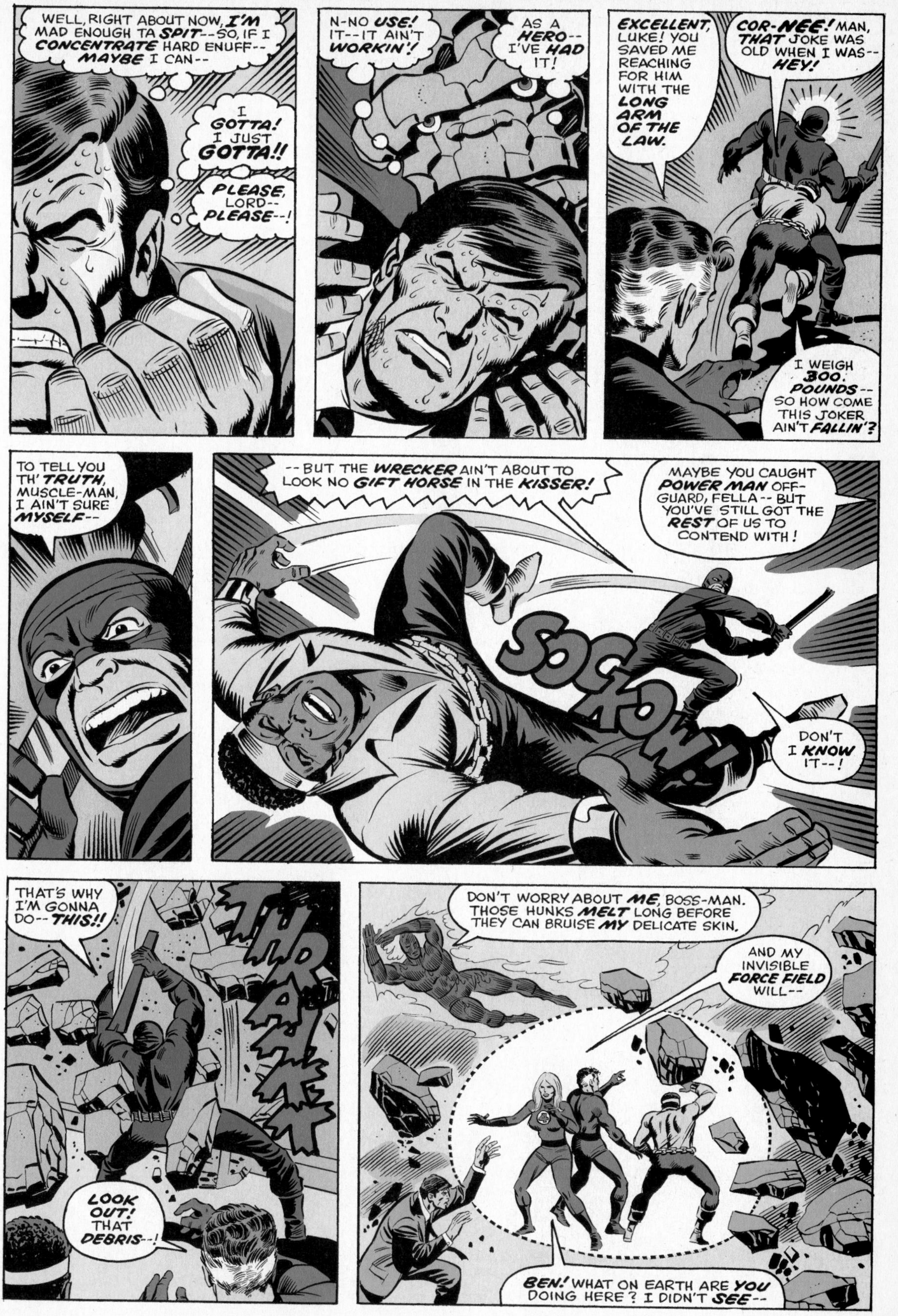

WELL, RIGHT ABOUT NOW, I'M MAD ENOUGH TA SPIT--SO, IF I CONCENTRATE HARD ENUFF-- MAYBE I CAN--
I GOTTA! I JUST GOTTA!!
PLEASE, LORD-- PLEASE--!
N-NO USE! IT--IT AIN'T WORKIN'!
AS A HERO-- I'VE HAD IT!
EXCELLENT, LUKE! YOU SAVED ME REACHING FOR HIM WITH THE LONG ARM OF THE LAW.
COR-NEE! MAN, THAT JOKE WAS OLD WHEN I WAS-- HEY!
I WEIGH 800 POUNDS-- SO HOW COME THIS JOKER AIN'T FALLIN'?
TO TELL YOU TH' TRUTH, MUSCLE-MAN, I AIN'T SURE MYSELF--
--BUT THE WRECKER AIN'T ABOUT TO LOOK NO GIFT HORSE IN THE KISSER!
MAYBE YOU CAUGHT POWER MAN OFF-GUARD, FELLA-- BUT YOU'VE STILL GOT THE REST OF US TO CONTEND WITH!
SOCKOW!
DON'T I KNOW IT--!
THAT'S WHY I'M GONNA DO--THIS!!
THRAKK
LOOK OUT! THAT DEBRIS--!
DON'T WORRY ABOUT ME, BOSS-MAN. THOSE HUNKS MELT LONG BEFORE THEY CAN BRUISE MY DELICATE SKIN.
AND MY INVISIBLE FORCE FIELD WILL--
BEN! WHAT ON EARTH ARE YOU DOING HERE? I DIDN'T SEE--

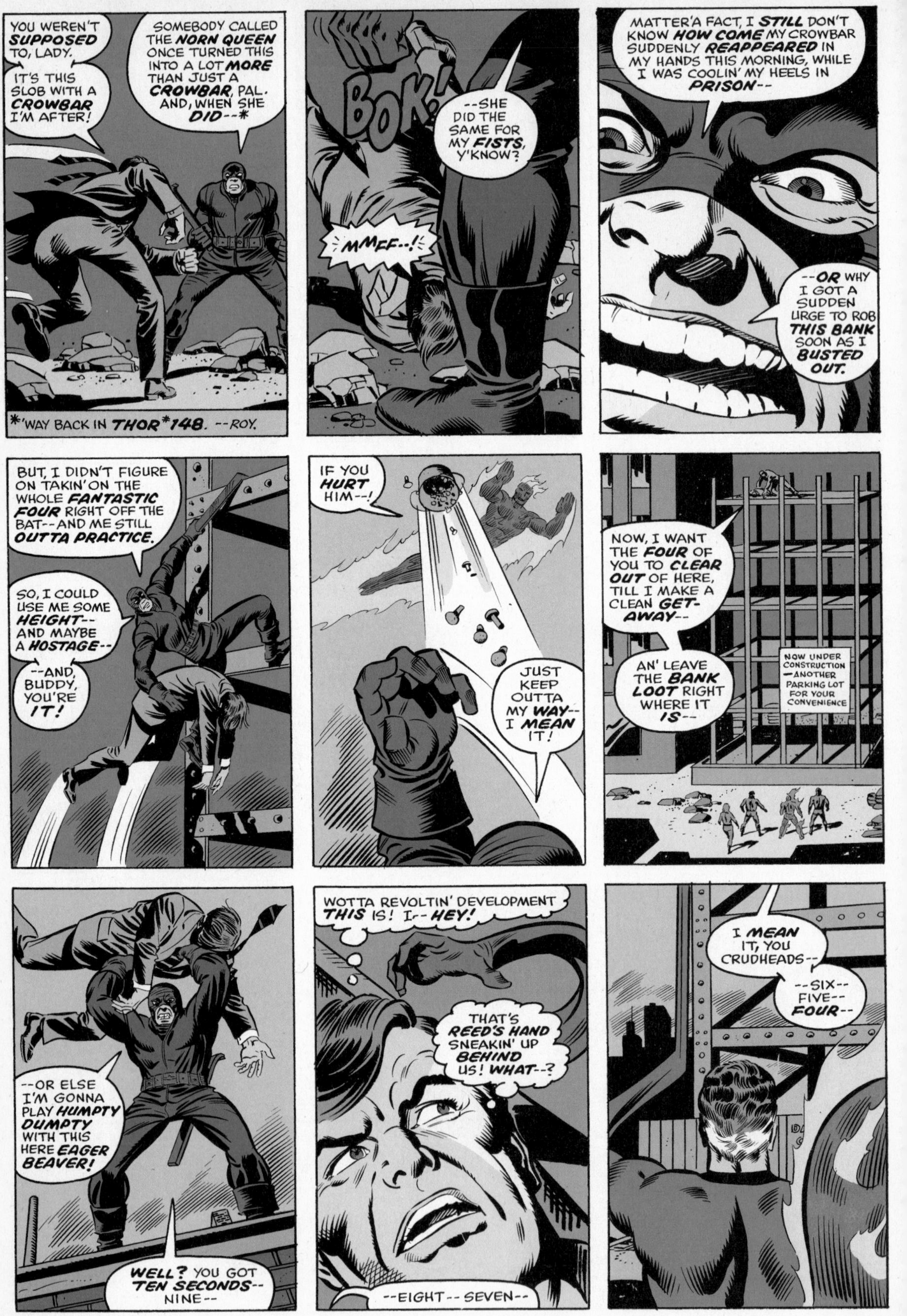
YOU WEREN'T SUPPOSED TO, LADY.
IT'S THIS SLOB WITH A CROWBAR I'M AFTER!
SOMEBODY CALLED THE NORN QUEEN ONCE TURNED THIS INTO A LOT MORE THAN JUST A CROWBAR, PAL. AND, WHEN SHE DID--*
*'WAY BACK IN THOR*148. --ROY.
BOK!
--SHE DID THE SAME FOR MY FISTS, Y'KNOW?
MMFF--!
MATTER'A FACT, I STILL DON'T KNOW HOW COME MY CROWBAR SUDDENLY REAPPEARED IN MY HANDS THIS MORNING, WHILE I WAS COOLIN' MY HEELS IN PRISON--
--OR WHY I GOT A SUDDEN URGE TO ROB THIS BANK SOON AS I BUSTED OUT.
BUT, I DIDN'T FIGURE ON TAKIN' ON THE WHOLE FANTASTIC FOUR RIGHT OFF THE BAT--AND ME STILL OUTTA PRACTICE.
SO, I COULD USE ME SOME HEIGHT--AND MAYBE A HOSTAGE--
--AND, BUDDY, YOU'RE IT!
IF YOU HURT HIM--!
JUST KEEP OUTTA MY WAY--I MEAN IT!
NOW, I WANT THE FOUR OF YOU TO CLEAR OUT OF HERE, TILL I MAKE A CLEAN GET-AWAY--
AN' LEAVE THE BANK LOOT RIGHT WHERE IT IS--
NOW UNDER CONSTRUCTION —ANOTHER PARKING LOT FOR YOUR CONVENIENCE
--OR ELSE I'M GONNA PLAY HUMPTY DUMPTY WITH THIS HERE EAGER BEAVER!
WELL? YOU GOT TEN SECONDS--NINE--
WOTTA REVOLTIN' DEVELOPMENT THIS IS! I--HEY!
THAT'S REED'S HAND SNEAKIN' UP BEHIND US! WHAT--?
--EIGHT--SEVEN--
I MEAN IT, YOU CRUDHEADS--
--SIX-FIVE--FOUR--

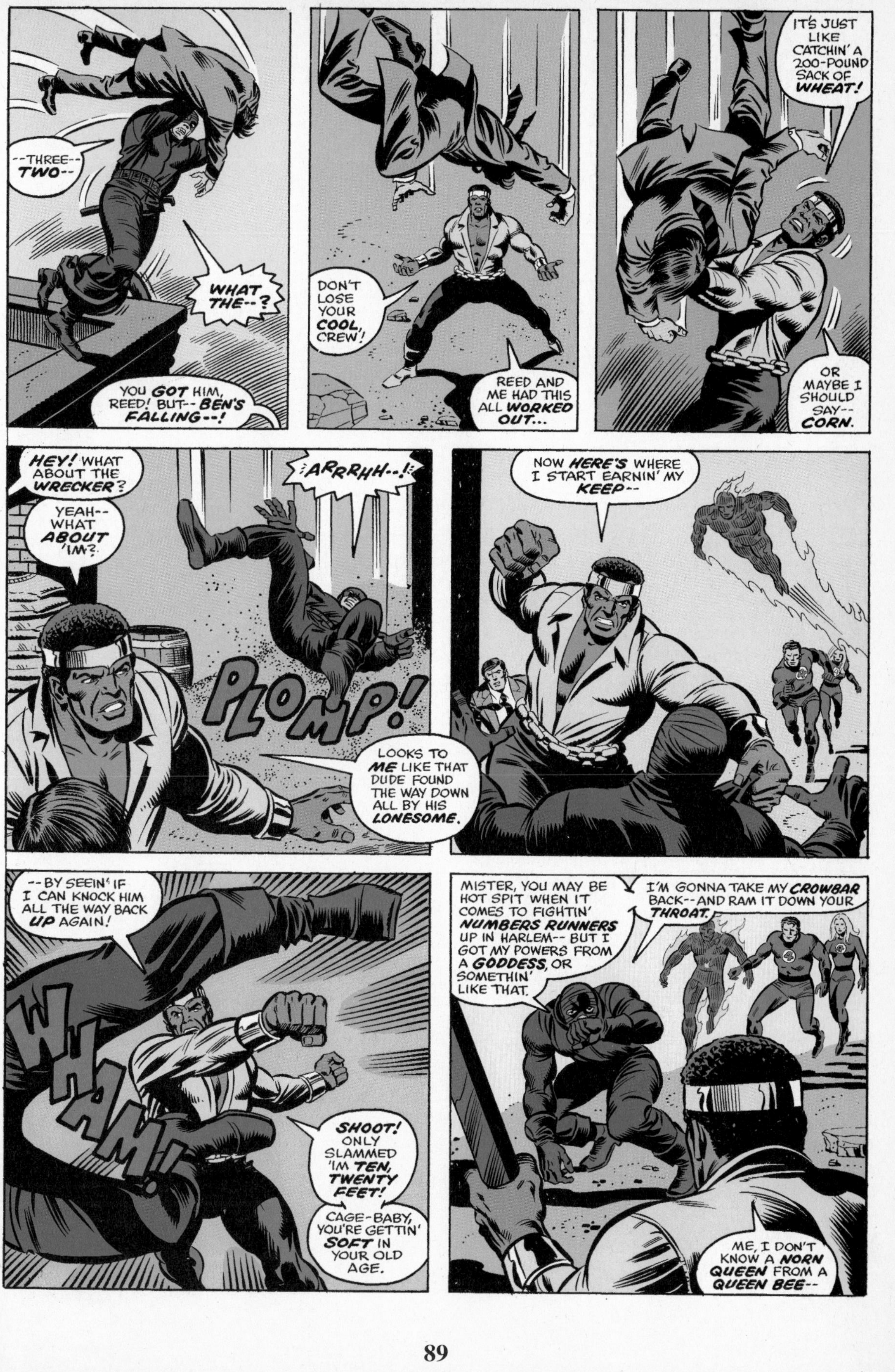
--THREE--
TWO--
WHAT THE--?
YOU GOT HIM, REED! BUT-- BEN'S FALLING--!
DON'T LOSE YOUR COOL, CREW!
REED AND ME HAD THIS ALL WORKED OUT...
IT'S JUST LIKE CATCHIN' A 200-POUND SACK OF WHEAT!
OR MAYBE I SHOULD SAY-- CORN.
HEY! WHAT ABOUT THE WRECKER?
YEAH-- WHAT ABOUT 'IM?
ARRRHH--!
PLOMP!
LOOKS TO ME LIKE THAT DUDE FOUND THE WAY DOWN ALL BY HIS LONESOME.
NOW HERE'S WHERE I START EARNIN' MY KEEP--
--BY SEEIN' IF I CAN KNOCK HIM ALL THE WAY BACK UP AGAIN!
WHAM!
SHOOT! ONLY SLAMMED 'IM TEN, TWENTY FEET!
CAGE-BABY, YOU'RE GETTIN' SOFT IN YOUR OLD AGE.
MISTER, YOU MAY BE HOT SPIT WHEN IT COMES TO FIGHTIN' NUMBERS RUNNERS UP IN HARLEM-- BUT I GOT MY POWERS FROM A GODDESS, OR SOMETHIN' LIKE THAT.
I'M GONNA TAKE MY CROWBAR BACK--AND RAM IT DOWN YOUR THROAT.
ME, I DON'T KNOW A NORN QUEEN FROM A QUEEN BEE--

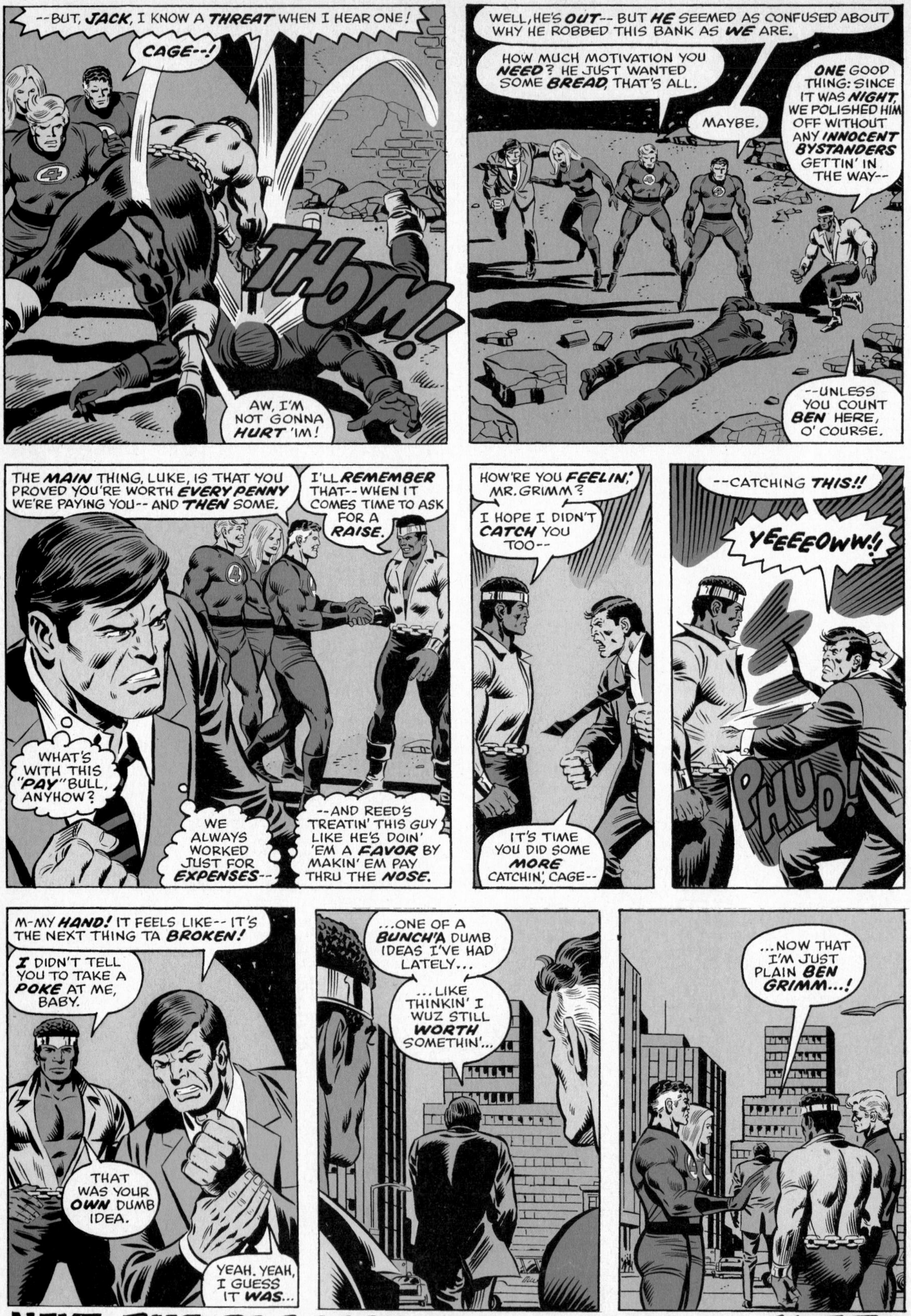
--BUT, JACK, I KNOW A THREAT WHEN I HEAR ONE!
CAGE--!
THOM!
AW, I'M NOT GONNA HURT 'IM!
WELL, HE'S OUT-- BUT HE SEEMED AS CONFUSED ABOUT WHY HE ROBBED THIS BANK AS WE ARE.
HOW MUCH MOTIVATION YOU NEED? HE JUST WANTED SOME BREAD, THAT'S ALL.
MAYBE.
ONE GOOD THING: SINCE IT WAS NIGHT, WE POLISHED HIM OFF WITHOUT ANY INNOCENT BYSTANDERS GETTIN' IN THE WAY--
--UNLESS YOU COUNT BEN HERE, O' COURSE.
THE MAIN THING, LUKE, IS THAT YOU PROVED YOU'RE WORTH EVERY PENNY WE'RE PAYING YOU-- AND THEN SOME.
I'LL REMEMBER THAT-- WHEN IT COMES TIME TO ASK FOR A RAISE.
WHAT'S WITH THIS "PAY" BULL, ANYHOW?
WE ALWAYS WORKED JUST FOR EXPENSES--
--AND REED'S TREATIN' THIS GUY LIKE HE'S DOIN' 'EM A FAVOR BY MAKIN' EM PAY THRU THE NOSE.
HOW'RE YOU FEELIN', MR. GRIMM?
I HOPE I DIDN'T CATCH YOU TOO--
IT'S TIME YOU DID SOME MORE CATCHIN', CAGE--
--CATCHING THIS!!
YEEEEOWW!!
PHUD!
M-MY HAND! IT FEELS LIKE-- IT'S THE NEXT THING TA BROKEN!
I DIDN'T TELL YOU TO TAKE A POKE AT ME, BABY.
THAT WAS YOUR OWN DUMB IDEA.
YEAH. YEAH, I GUESS IT WAS...
...ONE OF A BUNCH'A DUMB IDEAS I'VE HAD LATELY...
...LIKE THINKIN' I WUZ STILL WORTH SOMETHIN'...
...NOW THAT I'M JUST PLAIN BEN GRIMM...!
NEXT: THE BIGGEST SHOCK-ENDING YET!!

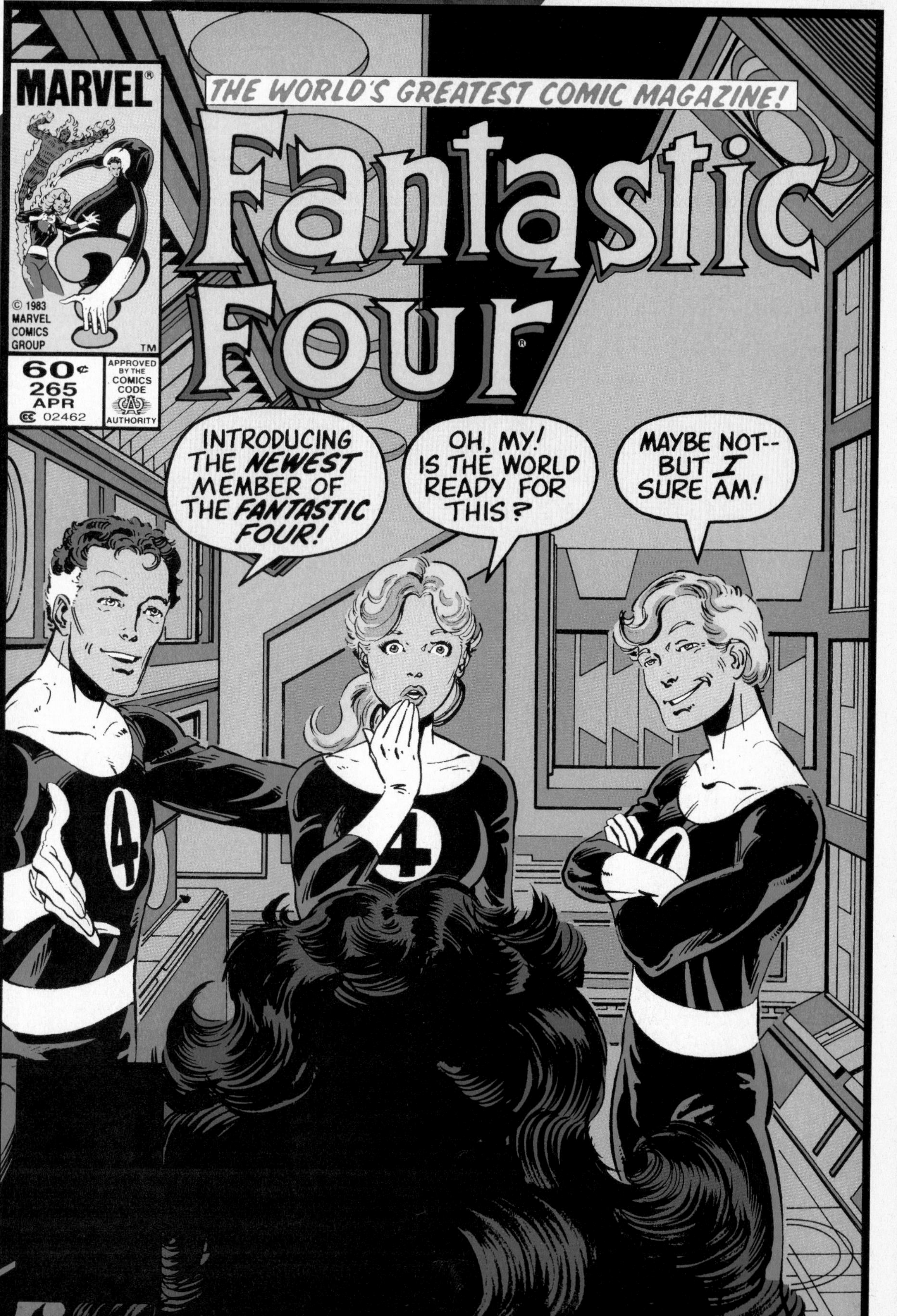
MARVEL®
© 1983 MARVEL COMICS GROUP
TM
60¢
265
APR
02462
APPROVED BY THE COMICS CODE AUTHORITY
THE WORLD'S GREATEST COMIC MAGAZINE!
Fantastic Four®
INTRODUCING THE NEWEST MEMBER OF THE FANTASTIC FOUR!
OH, MY! IS THE WORLD READY FOR THIS?
MAYBE NOT-- BUT I SURE AM!

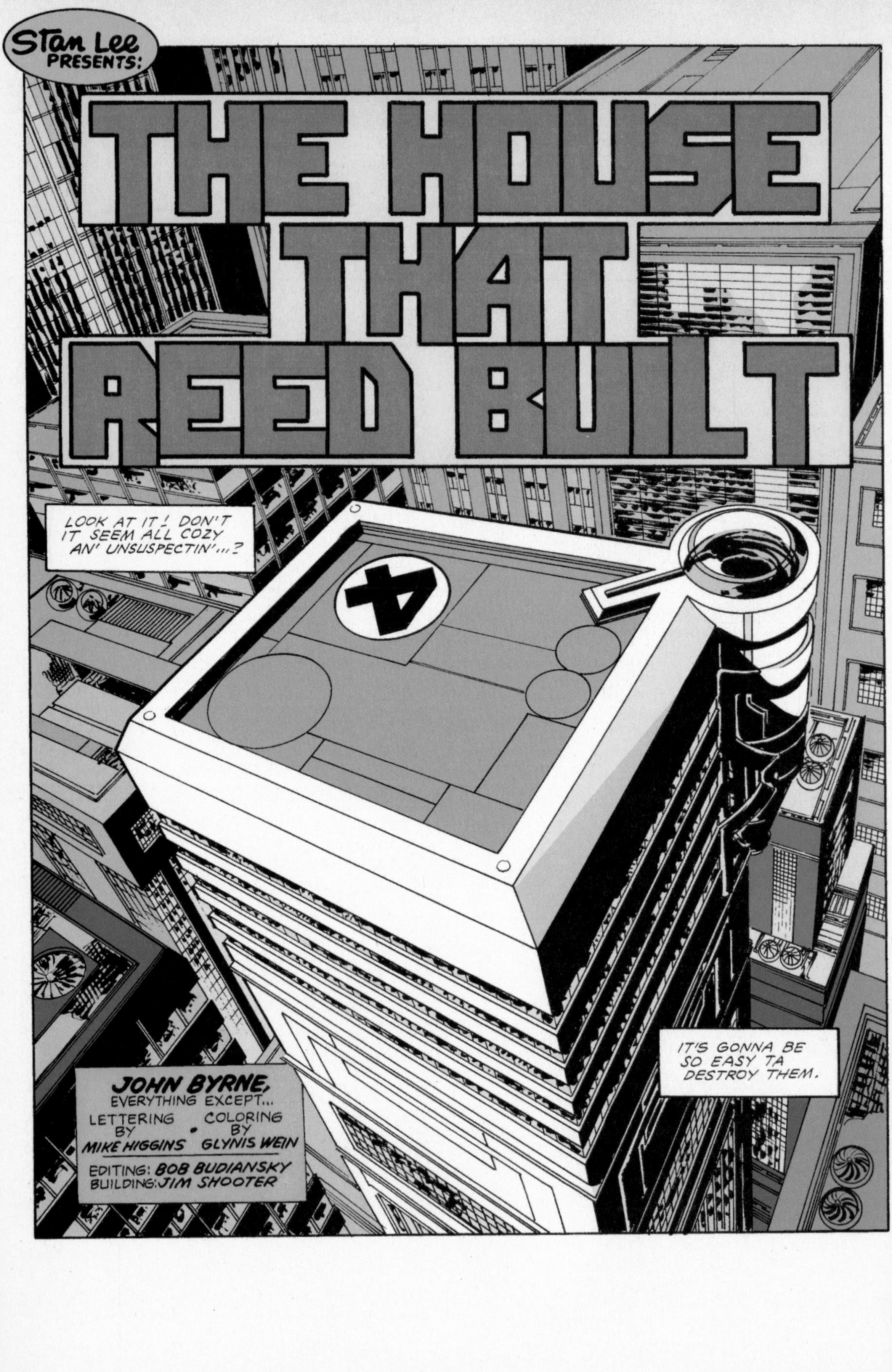

Stan Lee PRESENTS:
THE HOUSE THAT REED BUILT
LOOK AT IT! DON'T IT SEEM ALL COZY AN' UNSUSPECTIN'...?
IT'S GONNA BE SO EASY TA DESTROY THEM.
JOHN BYRNE, EVERYTHING EXCEPT...
LETTERING BY MIKE HIGGINS • COLORING BY GLYNIS WEIN
EDITING: BOB BUDIANSKY
BUILDING: JIM SHOOTER

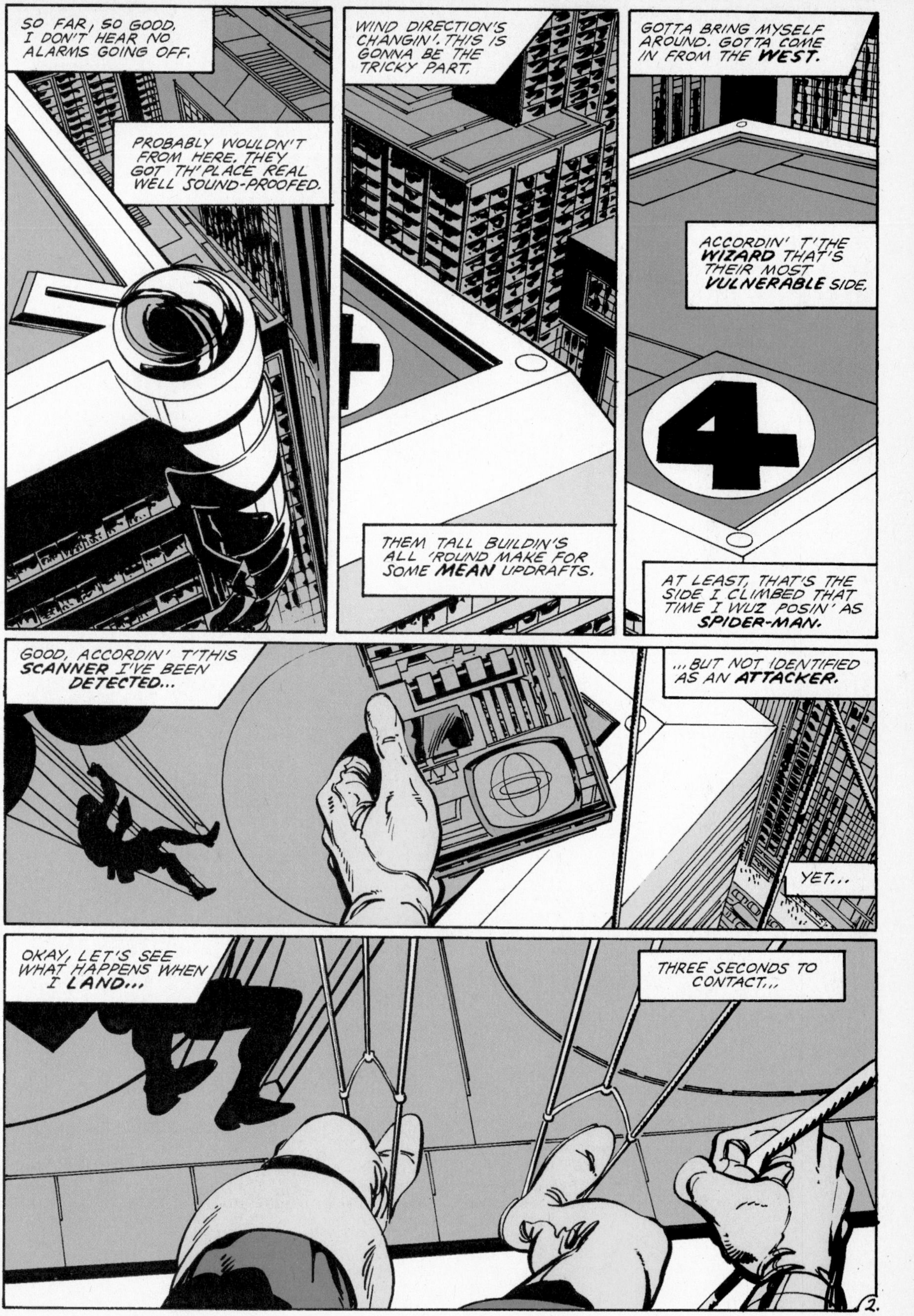
SO FAR, SO GOOD. I DON'T HEAR NO ALARMS GOING OFF.
PROBABLY WOULDN'T FROM HERE. THEY GOT TH' PLACE REAL WELL SOUND-PROOFED.
WIND DIRECTION'S CHANGIN'. THIS IS GONNA BE THE TRICKY PART.
THEM TALL BUILDIN'S ALL 'ROUND MAKE FOR SOME MEAN UPDRAFTS.
GOTTA BRING MYSELF AROUND. GOTTA COME IN FROM THE WEST.
ACCORDIN' T'THE WIZARD THAT'S THEIR MOST VULNERABLE SIDE.
4
AT LEAST, THAT'S THE SIDE I CLIMBED THAT TIME I WUZ POSIN' AS SPIDER-MAN.
GOOD, ACCORDIN' T'THIS SCANNER I'VE BEEN DETECTED...
...BUT NOT IDENTIFIED AS AN ATTACKER.
YET...
OKAY, LET'S SEE WHAT HAPPENS WHEN I LAND...
THREE SECONDS TO CONTACT...
2.

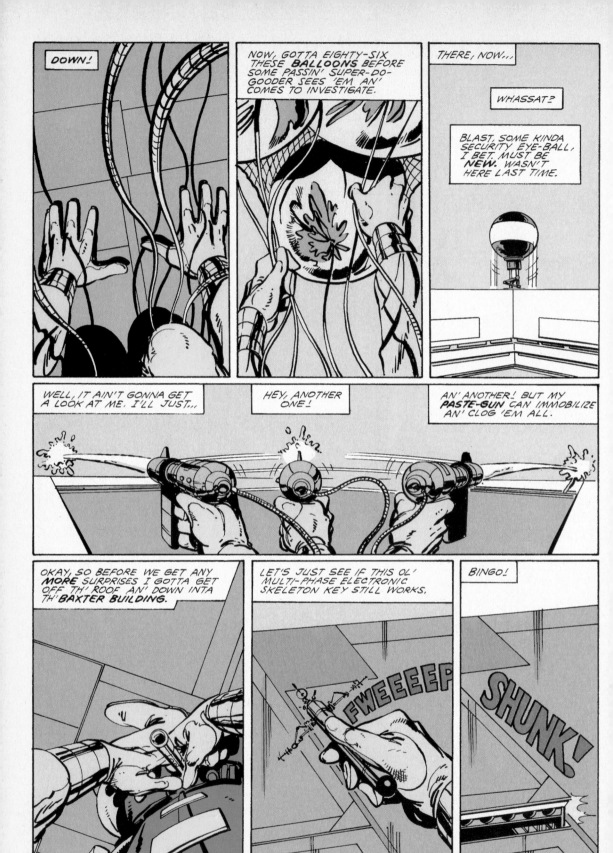

DOWN!

NOW, GOTTA EIGHTY-SIX THESE **BALLOONS** BEFORE SOME PASSIN' SUPER-DO-GOODER SEES 'EM AN' COMES TO INVESTIGATE.

THERE, NOW....

WHASSAT?

BLAST, SOME KINDA SECURITY EYE-BALL, I BET. MUST BE **NEW.** WASN'T HERE LAST TIME.

WELL, IT AIN'T GONNA GET A LOOK AT ME. I'LL JUST....

HEY, ANOTHER ONE!

AN' ANOTHER! BUT MY **PASTE-GUN** CAN IMMOBILIZE AN' CLOG 'EM ALL.

OKAY, SO BEFORE WE GET ANY **MORE** SURPRISES I GOTTA GET OFF TH' **ROOF** AN' DOWN INTA TH' **BAXTER BUILDING.**

LET'S JUST SEE IF THIS OL' MULTI-PHASE ELECTRONIC SKELETON KEY STILL WORKS,

BINGO!

FWEEEEP

SHUNK!

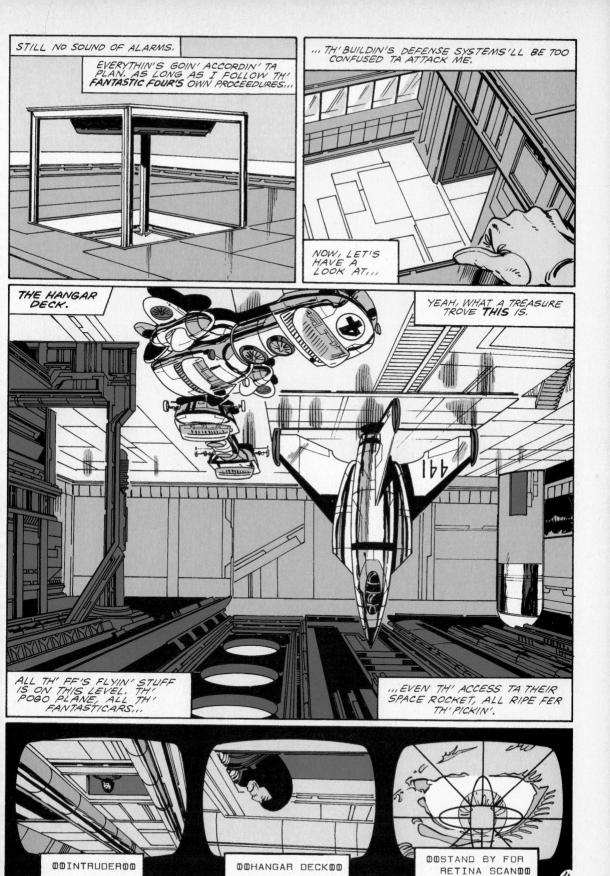

STILL NO SOUND OF ALARMS,

EVERYTHIN'S GOIN' ACCORDIN' TA PLAN. AS LONG AS I FOLLOW TH' *FANTASTIC FOUR'S* OWN PROCEEDURES...

... TH' BUILDIN'S DEFENSE SYSTEMS'LL BE TOO CONFUSED TA ATTACK ME.

NOW, LET'S HAVE A LOOK AT...

THE HANGAR DECK.

YEAH, WHAT A TREASURE TROVE *THIS* IS.

ALL TH' FF'S FLYIN' STUFF IS ON THIS LEVEL. TH' POGO PLANE, ALL TH' FANTASTICARS...

...EVEN TH' ACCESS TA THEIR SPACE ROCKET, ALL RIPE FER TH' PICKIN'.

⊞⊞INTRUDER⊞⊞

⊞⊞HANGAR DECK⊞⊞

⊞⊞STAND BY FOR RETINA SCAN⊞⊞

4.

95

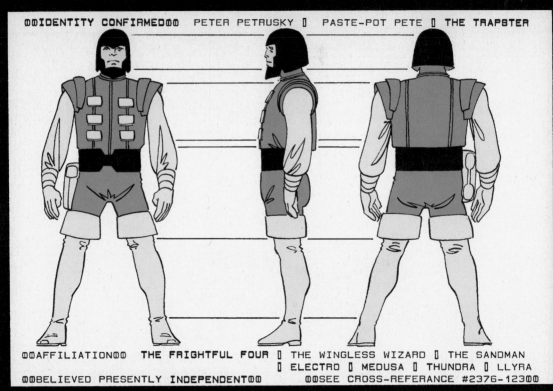

OOIDENTITY CONFIRMEDOO   PETER PETRUSKY O   PASTE-POT PETE O   **THE TRAPSTER**

OOAFFILIATIONOO **THE FRIGHTFUL FOUR** O THE WINGLESS WIZARD O THE SANDMAN
                                        O ELECTRO O MEDUSA O THUNDRA O LLYRA
OOBELIEVED PRESENTLY INDEPENDENTOO   OOSEE CROSS-REFERANCE #2376-123OO

OOINTRUDER HAS ENTERED HANGAR DECK O MAINTAIN SCANNING MODEOO

THERE'S NOTHIN' TA STOP ME FROM RIGGIN' THIS FANTASTI-CAR TA **BLOW UP** TH' NEXT TIME TH'FF USE IT...

BUT THAT'D TAKE TIME, AN' TH' BERTH FOR THEIR SHORT RANGE CAR IS EMPTY...

ONE OF 'EM MUST HAVE TH' OL' FLYIN' BATHTUB OUT T'DAY.

AN' THAT MEANS HE CO'ILD BE BACK ANY TIME AN' CATCH ME BEFORE I REACH THE OTHERS. BETTER GET MOVING...

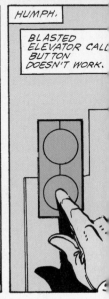

HUMPH.

BLASTED ELEVATOR CALL BUTTON DOESN'T WORK.

⊙⊙RECORDED: ATTEMPTED IMPROPER USE OF SOL-ENOID ELEVATOR LOCK⊙⊙

⊙⊙SCAN CONTINUING⊙⊙

⊙⊙SUBJECT ATTEMPTING HANGAR DECK EXIT⊙⊙

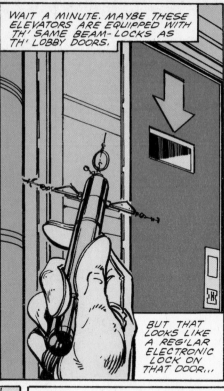

WAIT A MINUTE. MAYBE THESE ELEVATORS ARE EQUIPPED WITH TH' SAME BEAM-LOCKS AS TH' LOBBY DOORS.

BUT THAT LOOKS LIKE A REG'LAR ELECTRONIC LOCK ON THAT DOOR...

I WUZ RIGHT.

GREAT! A STAIR-WELL. I FIGGERED THERE'D BE SOME OTHER WAY BE-TWEEN FLOORS IN CASE TH' POWER FAILED.

NOW, IF I REMEMBER RIGHT, THE NEXT LEVEL DOWN SHOULD BE TH' ASTRO-SCIENCE...

AW.. CRUD! THIS PLACE IS STARTIN' TA SPOOK ME.

WHO'S THAT?!?

I'LL BE JUMPIN' AT MY OWN SHADOW NEXT.

6.

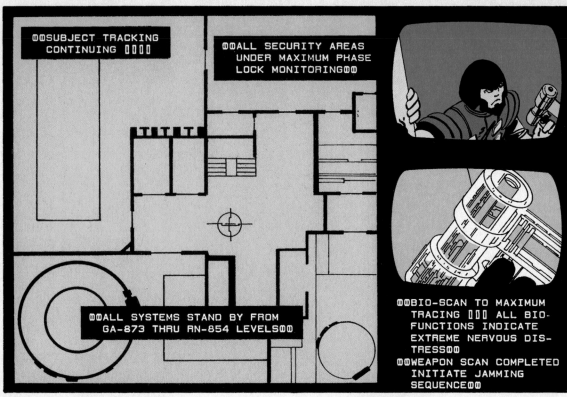

‖‖SUBJECT TRACKING CONTINUING ‖‖‖‖

‖‖ALL SECURITY AREAS UNDER MAXIMUM PHASE LOCK MONITORING‖‖

‖‖ALL SYSTEMS STAND BY FROM GA-873 THRU RN-854 LEVELS‖‖

‖‖BIO-SCAN TO MAXIMUM TRACING ‖‖‖ ALL BIO-FUNCTIONS INDICATE EXTREME NERVOUS DIS-TRESS‖‖

‖‖WEAPON SCAN COMPLETED INITIATE JAMMING SEQUENCE‖‖

DOWN WE GO ANOTHER LEVEL.

THIS SHOULD BE THEIR PHYSICS LAB AN' LIKE THAT.

AN' TH' SCANNER SHOWS A BIG ENERGY SOURCE OVER TA TH' RIGHT SOMEWHERES.

THAT LOOKS PRO-MISIN'. THE DOOR IS HEAVILY SHIELDED.

A REG'LAR ENERGY SENSOR PROBABLY WOULDN'T HAVE DETECTED ANY-THING THROUGH ALL THAT METAL.

LUCKY THIS SCANNER WUZ MADE BY TH' WIZARD, HE'S ALMOST AS BRAINY AS MISTER FANTASTIC.

HMM. THAT'S ONE MOTHER OF A LOCK, THEY SURE DON'T WANT ANYONE...

7.

YEOW!

BLAST! SOME KINDA ELECTRO-SHOCK DEFENSE SYSTEM. TH' SCANNER DIDN'T PICK IT UP.

BUT I CAN FIX IT REAL QUICK WITH MY PASTE-GUN...

JUST A QUICK ZAP OF TH' LIQUID EMULSION WITHOUT TH' ADHESIVE AN TH' LOCK SHOULD SHORT...

WHAT TH',...?

THE GUN'S JAMMED!

⑩⑩CONFIRMATION OF WEAPON DEACT-IVATION ⑪⑪⑪ SCAN CONTINUING⑩⑩

⑩⑩SUBJECT PROCEEDING TO STAIRS⑩⑩

⑩⑩SWITCHING TO LATERAL SCAN⑩⑩

⑩⑩SUBJECT APPROACHING
RESIDENTIAL LEVEL ⑪⑪

⑩⑩DEFENSE ALERT TO ALL
FIRST LEVEL SYSTEMS⑩⑩

⑩⑩DEFEN-MODE KL8-0037
SCAN FOR SUBJECT'S
PRIME VULNERABILITIES
AND COMMENCE CAPTURE
SEQUENCE⑩⑩

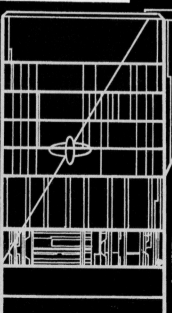

⑩⑩LATERAL SCAN ACTIVATED
SUBJECT LOCATED⑩⑩

8.

WHERE TH' HECK IS EVERYBODY?

THE WHOLE BLASTED TOWER COMPLEX IS **DESERTED!**

IT AIN'T **FAIR!** I CAME TA PROVE I'M NOT TH' **LOSER** EVERYONE THINKS I AM...

...TA PROVE I COULD BEAT TH' **FF** WITHOUT TH' REST OF TH' **FRIGHTFUL FOUR.**

MEEP!

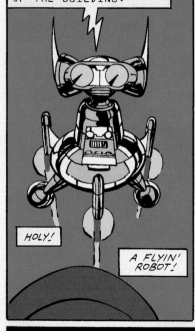

EXCUSE ME, SIR, BUT YOU ARE NOT AUTHORIZED TO BE IN THIS PART OF THE BUILDING.

HOLY!

A FLYIN' ROBOT!

I KNEW IT WAS TOO GOOD TO BE TRUE!

TH' SECURITY SYSTEM MUSTA BIN TRACKIN' ME ALL ALONG.

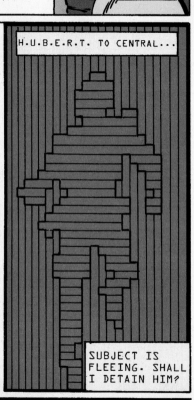

H.U.B.E.R.T. TO CENTRAL...

SUBJECT IS FLEEING. SHALL I DETAIN HIM?

⊡⊡NEGATIVE⊡⊡

⊡⊡SUBJECT IS ABOUT

‖ TO DETAIN HIMSELF⊡⊡

9.

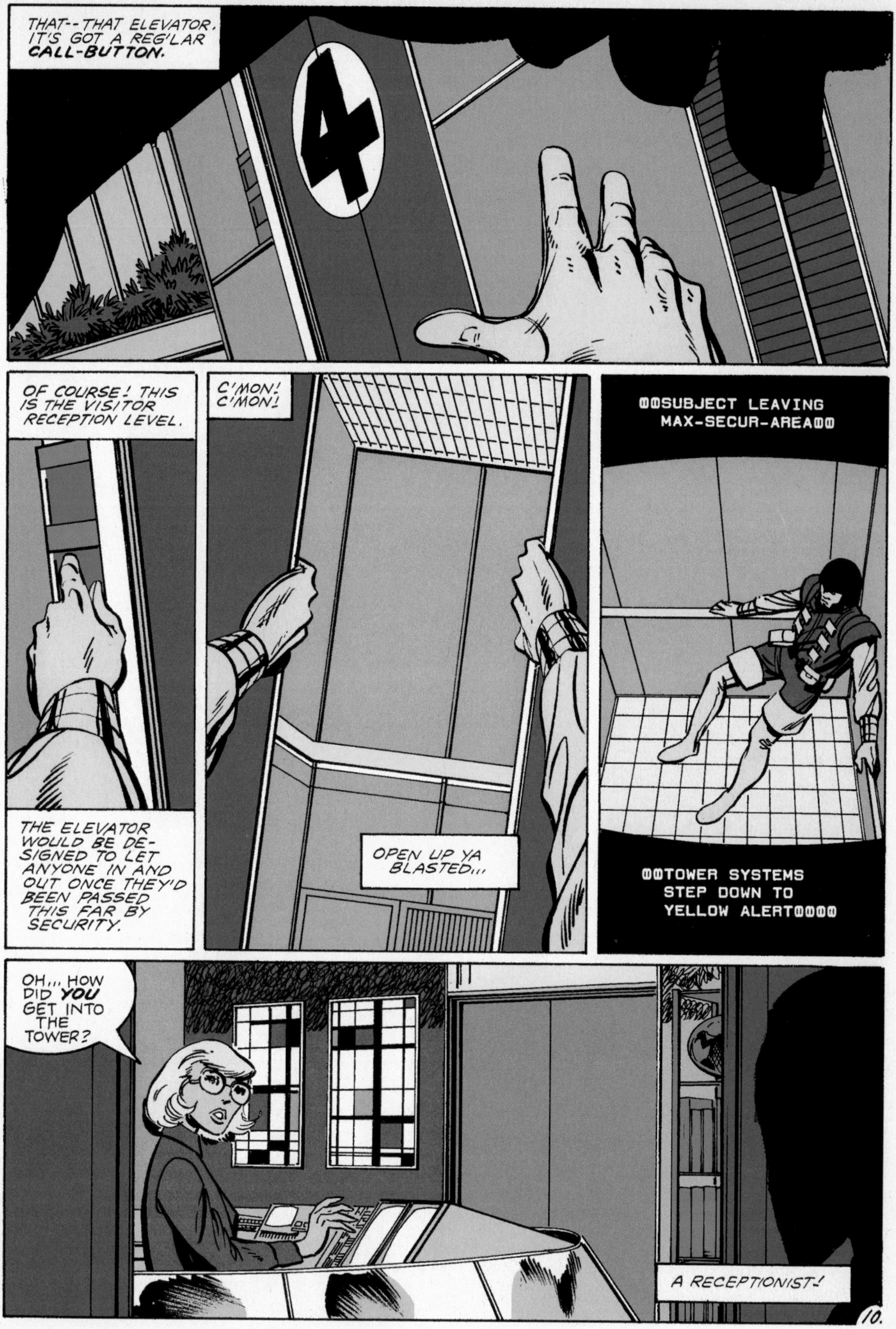
THAT--THAT ELEVATOR. IT'S GOT A REG'LAR CALL-BUTTON.
OF COURSE! THIS IS THE VISITOR RECEPTION LEVEL.
THE ELEVATOR WOULD BE DE-SIGNED TO LET ANYONE IN AND OUT ONCE THEY'D BEEN PASSED THIS FAR BY SECURITY.
C'MON! C'MON!
OPEN UP YA BLASTED...
SUBJECT LEAVING MAX-SECUR-AREA
TOWER SYSTEMS STEP DOWN TO YELLOW ALERT
OH... HOW DID YOU GET INTO THE TOWER?
A RECEPTIONIST!
10.

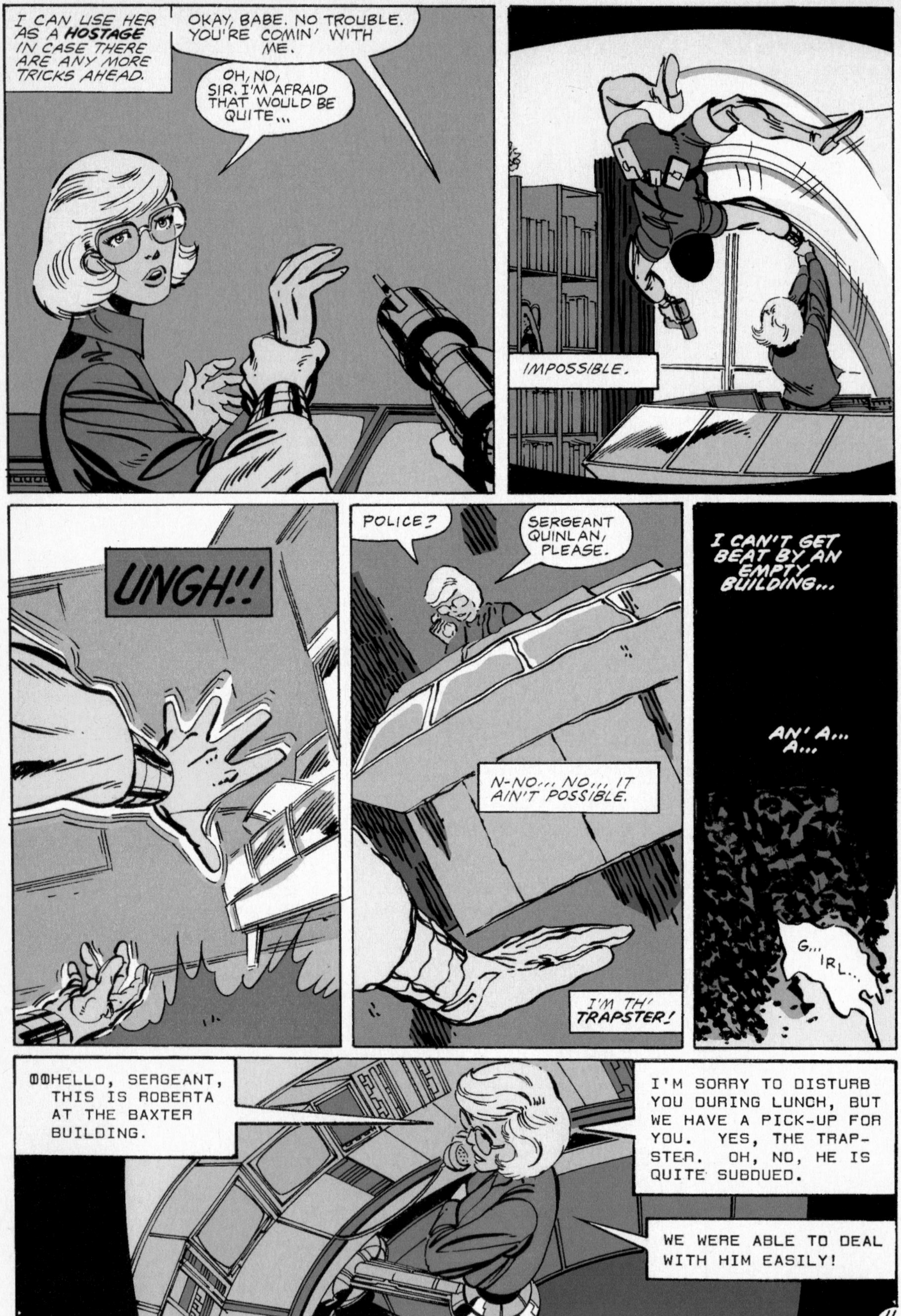

I CAN USE HER AS A **HOSTAGE** IN CASE THERE ARE ANY MORE TRICKS AHEAD.
OKAY, BABE. NO TROUBLE. YOU'RE COMIN' WITH ME.
OH, NO, SIR. I'M AFRAID THAT WOULD BE QUITE...
IMPOSSIBLE.
UNGH!!
POLICE?
SERGEANT QUINLAN, PLEASE.
N-NO... NO... IT AIN'T POSSIBLE.
I'M TH' **TRAPSTER!**
I CAN'T GET BEAT BY AN EMPTY BUILDING...
AN' A... A...
G... IRL...
HELLO, SERGEANT, THIS IS ROBERTA AT THE BAXTER BUILDING.
I'M SORRY TO DISTURB YOU DURING LUNCH, BUT WE HAVE A PICK-UP FOR YOU. YES, THE TRAPSTER. OH, NO, HE IS QUITE SUBDUED.
WE WERE ABLE TO DEAL WITH HIM EASILY!
11.

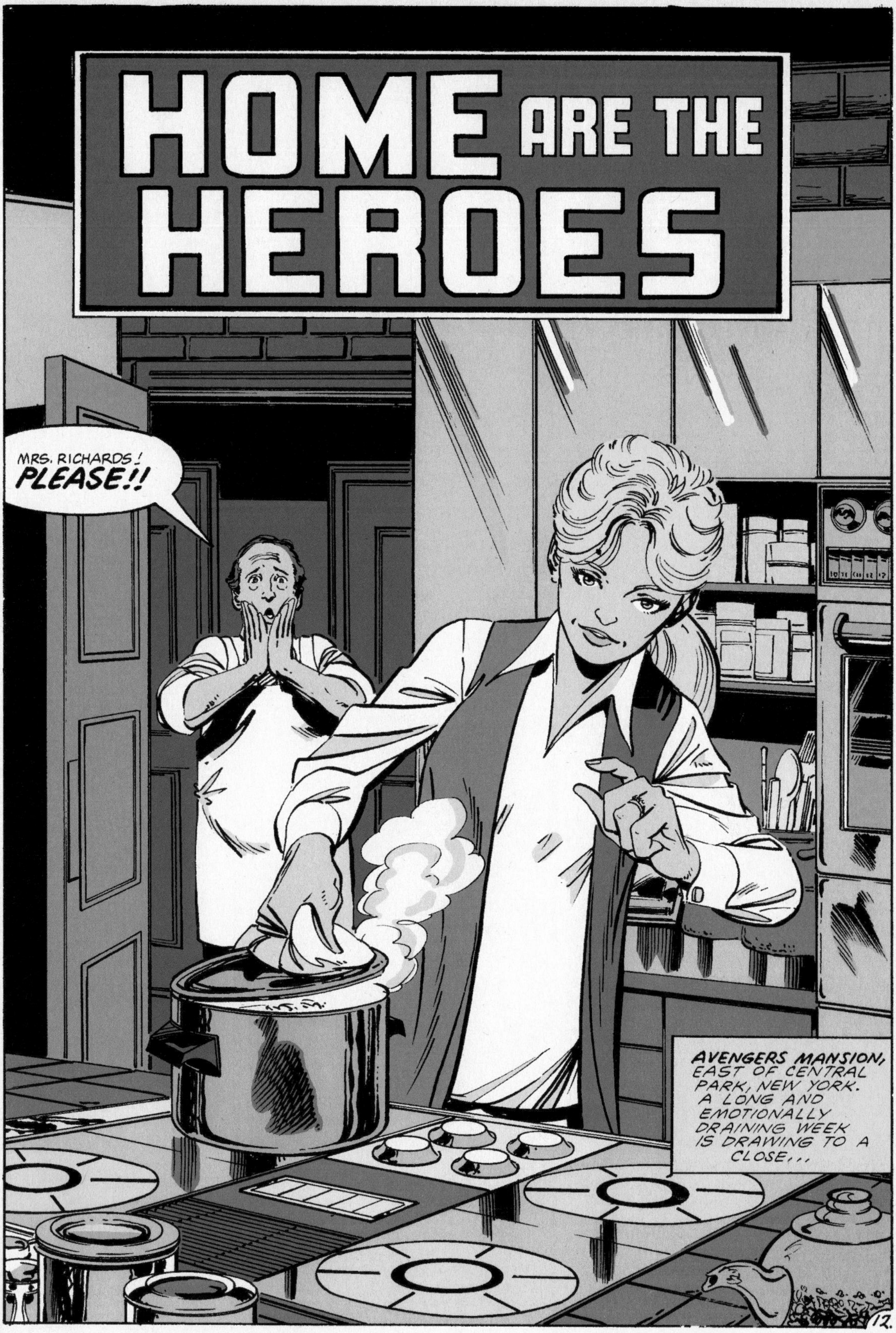
HOME ARE THE HEROES
MRS. RICHARDS! PLEASE!!
AVENGERS MANSION, EAST OF CENTRAL PARK, NEW YORK. A LONG AND EMOTIONALLY DRAINING WEEK IS DRAWING TO A CLOSE...
12.

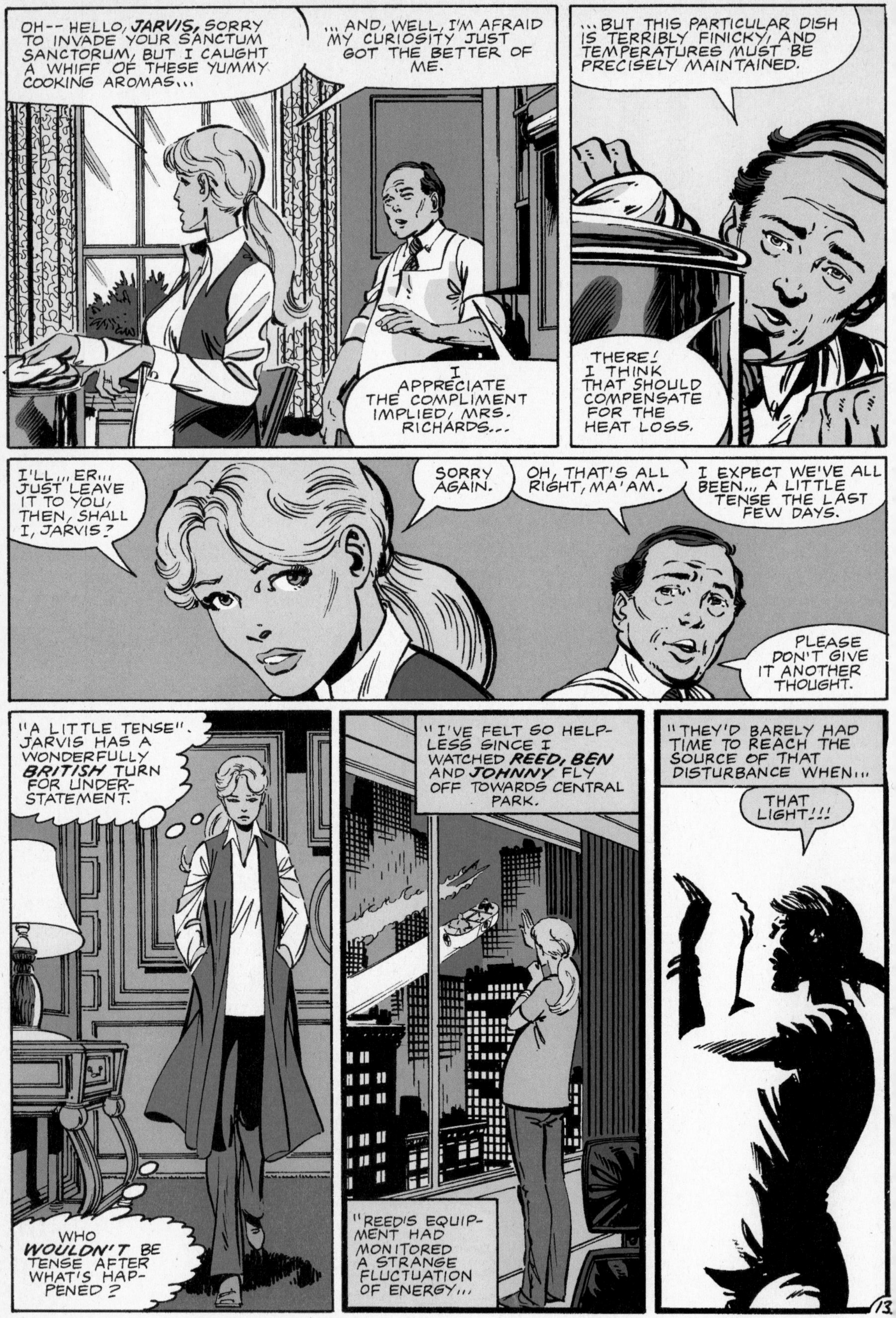
OH-- HELLO, JARVIS, SORRY TO INVADE YOUR SANCTUM SANCTORUM, BUT I CAUGHT A WHIFF OF THESE YUMMY COOKING AROMAS...
... AND, WELL, I'M AFRAID MY CURIOSITY JUST GOT THE BETTER OF ME.
I APPRECIATE THE COMPLIMENT IMPLIED, MRS. RICHARDS...
...BUT THIS PARTICULAR DISH IS TERRIBLY FINICKY, AND TEMPERATURES MUST BE PRECISELY MAINTAINED.
THERE! I THINK THAT SHOULD COMPENSATE FOR THE HEAT LOSS.
I'LL... ER... JUST LEAVE IT TO YOU, THEN, SHALL I, JARVIS?
SORRY AGAIN.
OH, THAT'S ALL RIGHT, MA'AM.
I EXPECT WE'VE ALL BEEN... A LITTLE TENSE THE LAST FEW DAYS.
PLEASE DON'T GIVE IT ANOTHER THOUGHT.
"A LITTLE TENSE". JARVIS HAS A WONDERFULLY BRITISH TURN FOR UNDER-STATEMENT.
WHO WOULDN'T BE TENSE AFTER WHAT'S HAP-PENED?
"I'VE FELT SO HELP-LESS SINCE I WATCHED REED, BEN AND JOHNNY FLY OFF TOWARDS CENTRAL PARK.
"REED'S EQUIP-MENT HAD MONITORED A STRANGE FLUCTUATION OF ENERGY...
"THEY'D BARELY HAD TIME TO REACH THE SOURCE OF THAT DISTURBANCE WHEN...
THAT LIGHT!!!
13

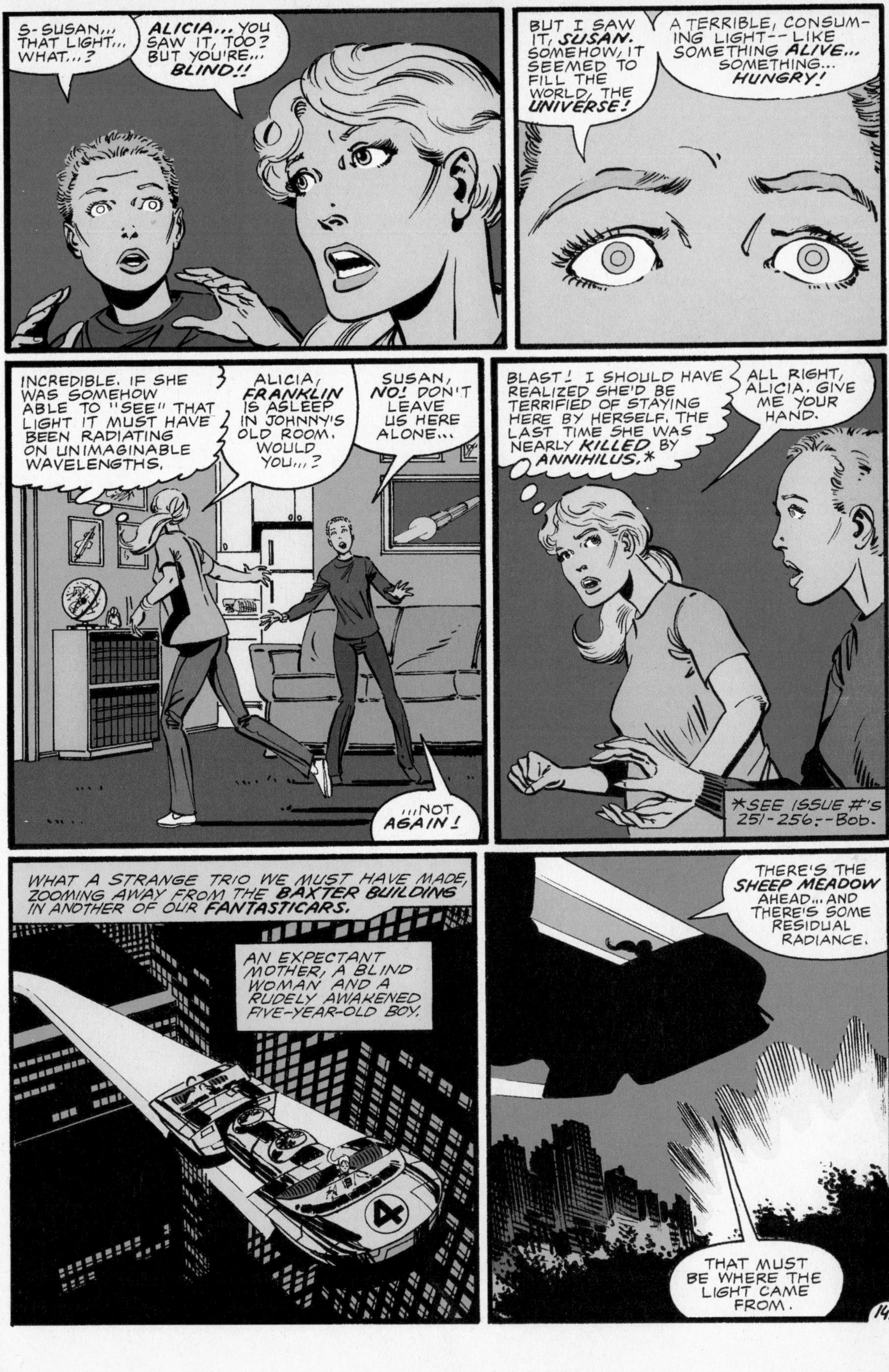
S-SUSAN... THAT LIGHT... WHAT...?
ALICIA... YOU SAW IT, TOO? BUT YOU'RE... BLIND!!
BUT I SAW IT, SUSAN. SOMEHOW, IT SEEMED TO FILL THE WORLD, THE UNIVERSE!
A TERRIBLE, CONSUMING LIGHT--LIKE SOMETHING ALIVE... SOMETHING... HUNGRY!
INCREDIBLE. IF SHE WAS SOMEHOW ABLE TO "SEE" THAT LIGHT IT MUST HAVE BEEN RADIATING ON UNIMAGINABLE WAVELENGTHS.
ALICIA, FRANKLIN IS ASLEEP IN JOHNNY'S OLD ROOM. WOULD YOU...?
SUSAN, NO! DON'T LEAVE US HERE ALONE...
...NOT AGAIN!
BLAST! I SHOULD HAVE REALIZED SHE'D BE TERRIFIED OF STAYING HERE BY HERSELF. THE LAST TIME SHE WAS NEARLY KILLED BY ANNIHILUS.*
ALL RIGHT, ALICIA. GIVE ME YOUR HAND.
*SEE ISSUE #'s 251-256.--Bob.
WHAT A STRANGE TRIO WE MUST HAVE MADE, ZOOMING AWAY FROM THE BAXTER BUILDING IN ANOTHER OF OUR FANTASTICARS.
AN EXPECTANT MOTHER, A BLIND WOMAN AND A RUDELY AWAKENED FIVE-YEAR-OLD BOY.
THERE'S THE SHEEP MEADOW AHEAD... AND THERE'S SOME RESIDUAL RADIANCE.
THAT MUST BE WHERE THE LIGHT CAME FROM.
14.

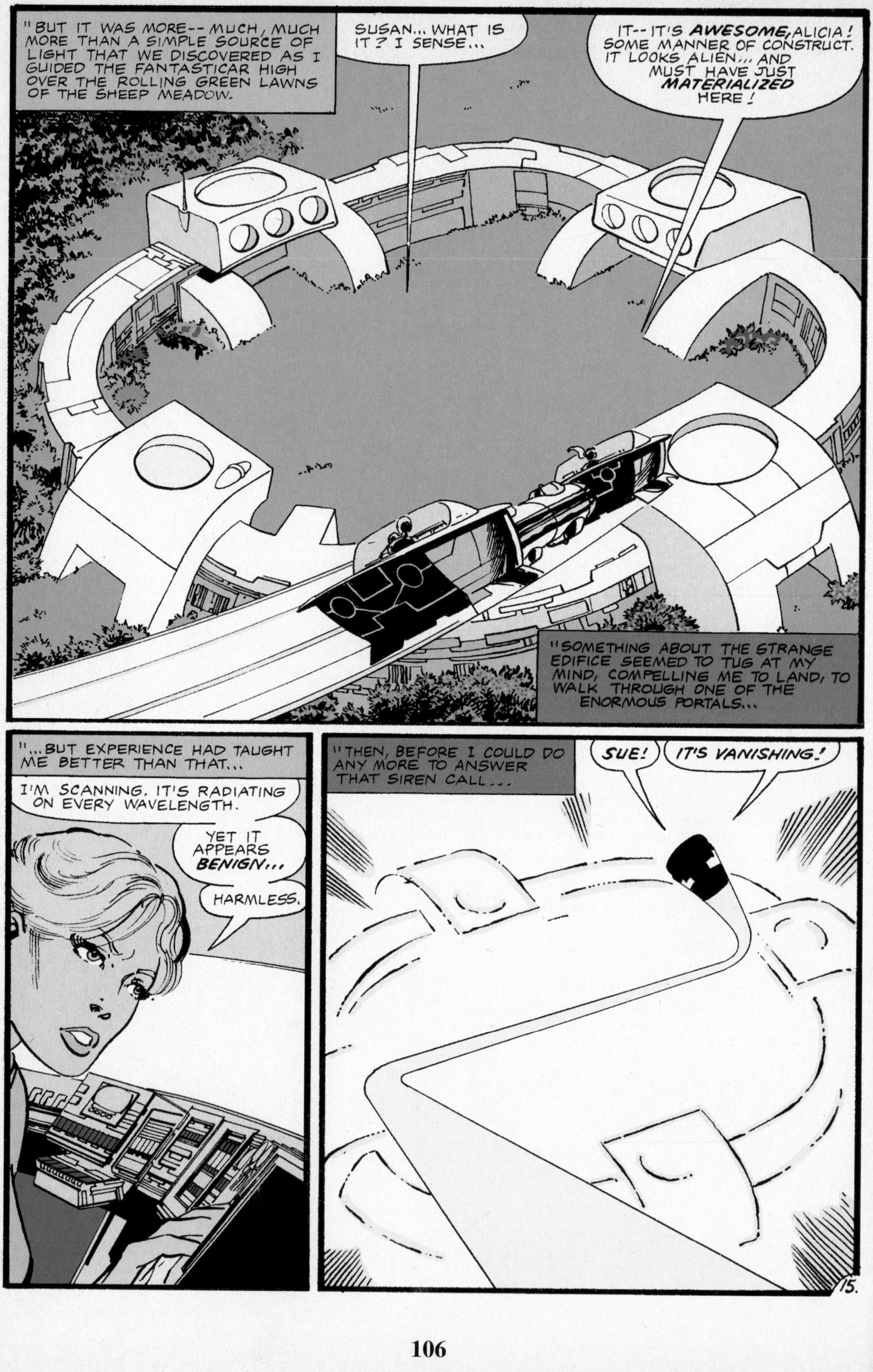
"BUT IT WAS MORE-- MUCH, MUCH MORE THAN A SIMPLE SOURCE OF LIGHT THAT WE DISCOVERED AS I GUIDED THE FANTASTICAR HIGH OVER THE ROLLING GREEN LAWNS OF THE SHEEP MEADOW.
SUSAN... WHAT IS IT? I SENSE...
IT-- IT'S AWESOME, ALICIA! SOME MANNER OF CONSTRUCT. IT LOOKS ALIEN... AND MUST HAVE JUST MATERIALIZED HERE!
"SOMETHING ABOUT THE STRANGE EDIFICE SEEMED TO TUG AT MY MIND, COMPELLING ME TO LAND, TO WALK THROUGH ONE OF THE ENORMOUS PORTALS...
"...BUT EXPERIENCE HAD TAUGHT ME BETTER THAN THAT...
I'M SCANNING. IT'S RADIATING ON EVERY WAVELENGTH.
YET IT APPEARS BENIGN...
HARMLESS.
"THEN, BEFORE I COULD DO ANY MORE TO ANSWER THAT SIREN CALL...
SUE!
IT'S VANISHING!
15.

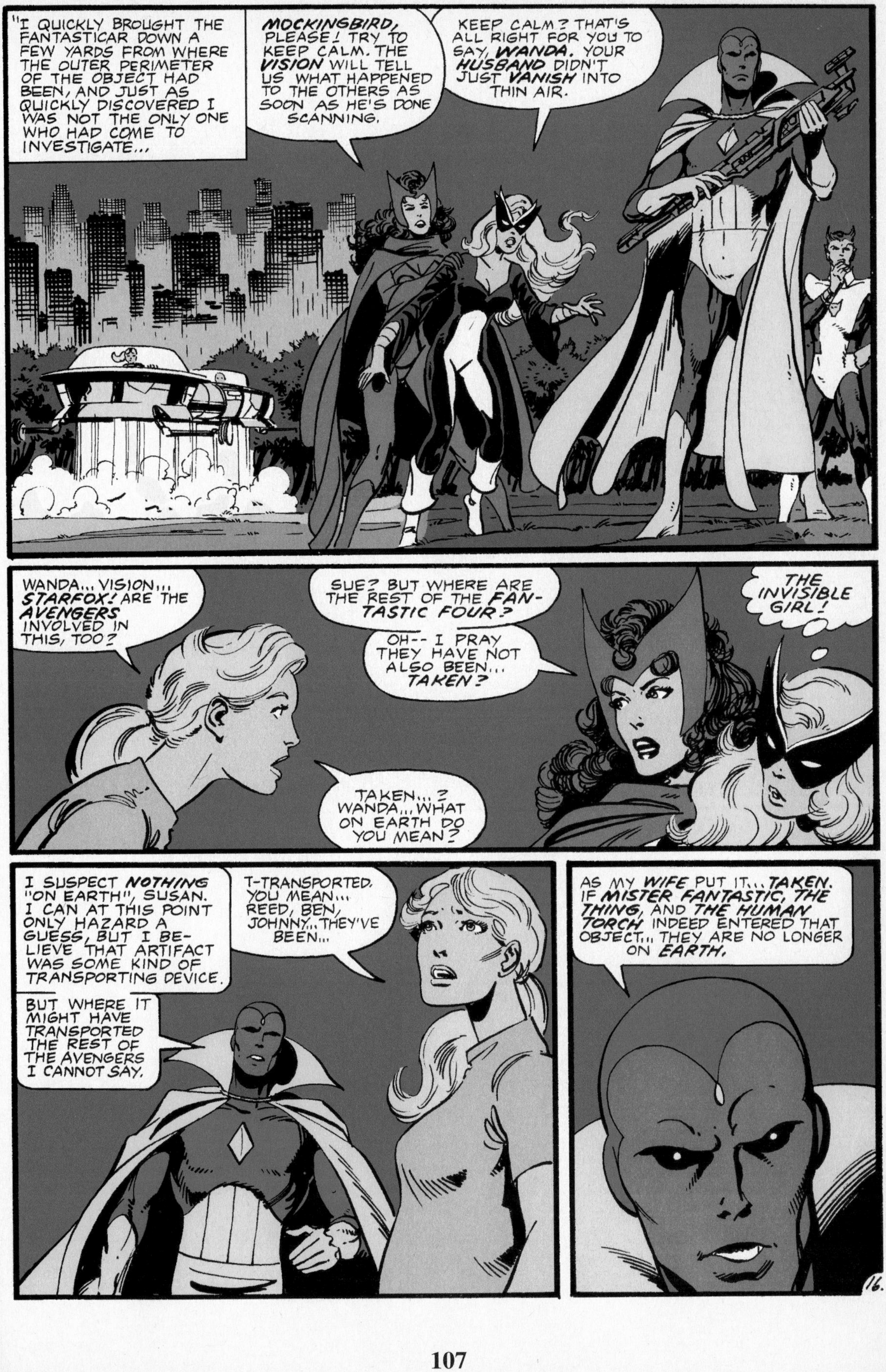
"I QUICKLY BROUGHT THE FANTASTICAR DOWN A FEW YARDS FROM WHERE THE OUTER PERIMETER OF THE OBJECT HAD BEEN, AND JUST AS QUICKLY DISCOVERED I WAS NOT THE ONLY ONE WHO HAD COME TO INVESTIGATE...
MOCKINGBIRD, PLEASE! TRY TO KEEP CALM. THE VISION WILL TELL US WHAT HAPPENED TO THE OTHERS AS SOON AS HE'S DONE SCANNING.
KEEP CALM? THAT'S ALL RIGHT FOR YOU TO SAY, WANDA. YOUR HUSBAND DIDN'T JUST VANISH INTO THIN AIR.
WANDA... VISION... STARFOX! ARE THE AVENGERS INVOLVED IN THIS, TOO?
SUE? BUT WHERE ARE THE REST OF THE FANTASTIC FOUR?
OH-- I PRAY THEY HAVE NOT ALSO BEEN... TAKEN?
THE INVISIBLE GIRL!
TAKEN...? WANDA... WHAT ON EARTH DO YOU MEAN?
I SUSPECT NOTHING "ON EARTH", SUSAN. I CAN AT THIS POINT ONLY HAZARD A GUESS, BUT I BELIEVE THAT ARTIFACT WAS SOME KIND OF TRANSPORTING DEVICE.
T-TRANSPORTED. YOU MEAN... REED, BEN, JOHNNY... THEY'VE BEEN...
BUT WHERE IT MIGHT HAVE TRANSPORTED THE REST OF THE AVENGERS I CANNOT SAY.
AS MY WIFE PUT IT... TAKEN. IF MISTER FANTASTIC, THE THING, AND THE HUMAN TORCH INDEED ENTERED THAT OBJECT... THEY ARE NO LONGER ON EARTH.
16.

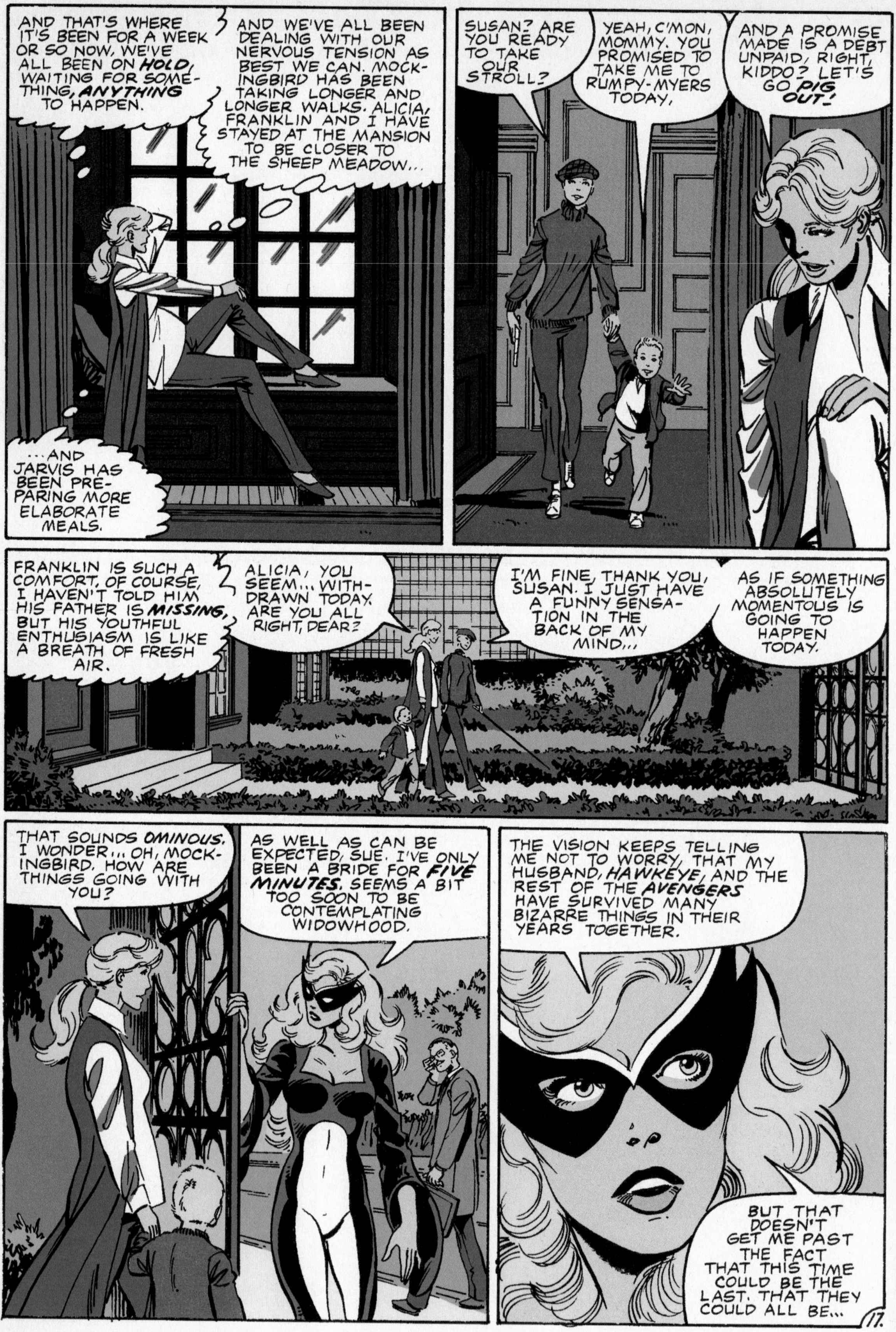
AND THAT'S WHERE IT'S BEEN FOR A WEEK OR SO NOW. WE'VE ALL BEEN ON HOLD, WAITING FOR SOMETHING, ANYTHING TO HAPPEN.
AND WE'VE ALL BEEN DEALING WITH OUR NERVOUS TENSION AS BEST WE CAN. MOCKINGBIRD HAS BEEN TAKING LONGER AND LONGER WALKS. ALICIA, FRANKLIN AND I HAVE STAYED AT THE MANSION TO BE CLOSER TO THE SHEEP MEADOW...
...AND JARVIS HAS BEEN PREPARING MORE ELABORATE MEALS.
SUSAN? ARE YOU READY TO TAKE OUR STROLL?
YEAH, C'MON, MOMMY. YOU PROMISED TO TAKE ME TO RUMPY-MYERS TODAY.
AND A PROMISE MADE IS A DEBT UNPAID, RIGHT, KIDDO? LET'S GO PIG OUT!
FRANKLIN IS SUCH A COMFORT, OF COURSE, I HAVEN'T TOLD HIM HIS FATHER IS MISSING, BUT HIS YOUTHFUL ENTHUSIASM IS LIKE A BREATH OF FRESH AIR.
ALICIA, YOU SEEM... WITHDRAWN TODAY. ARE YOU ALL RIGHT, DEAR?
I'M FINE, THANK YOU, SUSAN. I JUST HAVE A FUNNY SENSATION IN THE BACK OF MY MIND...
AS IF SOMETHING ABSOLUTELY MOMENTOUS IS GOING TO HAPPEN TODAY.
THAT SOUNDS OMINOUS. I WONDER... OH, MOCKINGBIRD. HOW ARE THINGS GOING WITH YOU?
AS WELL AS CAN BE EXPECTED, SUE. I'VE ONLY BEEN A BRIDE FOR FIVE MINUTES. SEEMS A BIT TOO SOON TO BE CONTEMPLATING WIDOWHOOD.
THE VISION KEEPS TELLING ME NOT TO WORRY, THAT MY HUSBAND, HAWKEYE, AND THE REST OF THE AVENGERS HAVE SURVIVED MANY BIZARRE THINGS IN THEIR YEARS TOGETHER.
BUT THAT DOESN'T GET ME PAST THE FACT THAT THIS TIME COULD BE THE LAST. THAT THEY COULD ALL BE...
17.

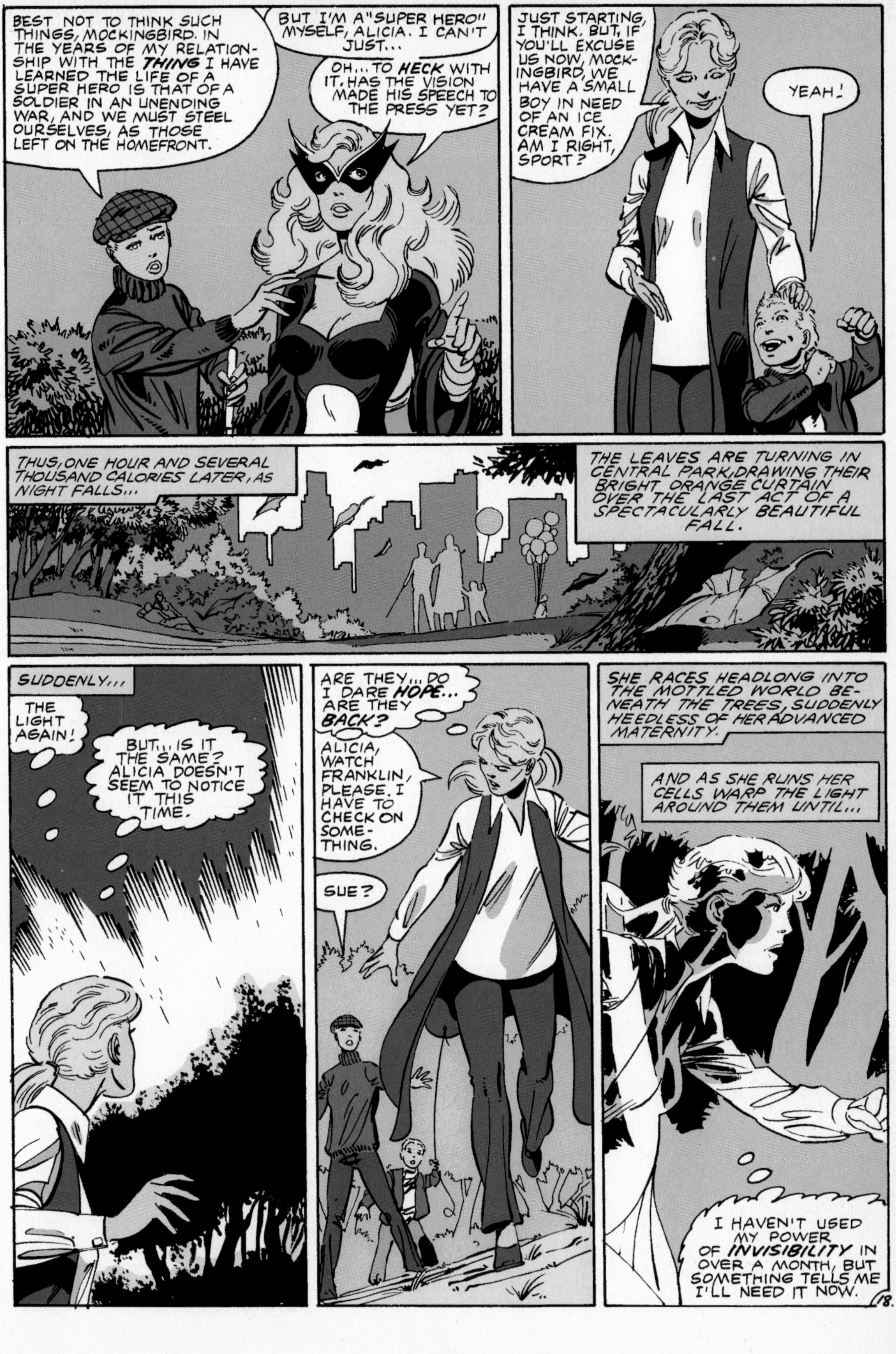
BEST NOT TO THINK SUCH THINGS, MOCKINGBIRD. IN THE YEARS OF MY RELATIONSHIP WITH THE THING I HAVE LEARNED THE LIFE OF A SUPER HERO IS THAT OF A SOLDIER IN AN UNENDING WAR, AND WE MUST STEEL OURSELVES, AS THOSE LEFT ON THE HOMEFRONT.
BUT I'M A "SUPER HERO" MYSELF, ALICIA. I CAN'T JUST...
OH... TO HECK WITH IT. HAS THE VISION MADE HIS SPEECH TO THE PRESS YET?
JUST STARTING, I THINK. BUT, IF YOU'LL EXCUSE US NOW, MOCKINGBIRD, WE HAVE A SMALL BOY IN NEED OF AN ICE CREAM FIX. AM I RIGHT, SPORT?
YEAH!
THUS, ONE HOUR AND SEVERAL THOUSAND CALORIES LATER, AS NIGHT FALLS...
THE LEAVES ARE TURNING IN CENTRAL PARK, DRAWING THEIR BRIGHT ORANGE CURTAIN OVER THE LAST ACT OF A SPECTACULARLY BEAUTIFUL FALL.
SUDDENLY...
THE LIGHT AGAIN!
BUT... IS IT THE SAME? ALICIA DOESN'T SEEM TO NOTICE IT THIS TIME.
ARE THEY... DO I DARE HOPE... ARE THEY BACK?
ALICIA, WATCH FRANKLIN, PLEASE. I HAVE TO CHECK ON SOMETHING.
SUE?
SHE RACES HEADLONG INTO THE MOTTLED WORLD BENEATH THE TREES, SUDDENLY HEEDLESS OF HER ADVANCED MATERNITY.
AND AS SHE RUNS HER CELLS WARP THE LIGHT AROUND THEM UNTIL...
I HAVEN'T USED MY POWER OF INVISIBILITY IN OVER A MONTH, BUT SOMETHING TELLS ME I'LL NEED IT NOW.
18.

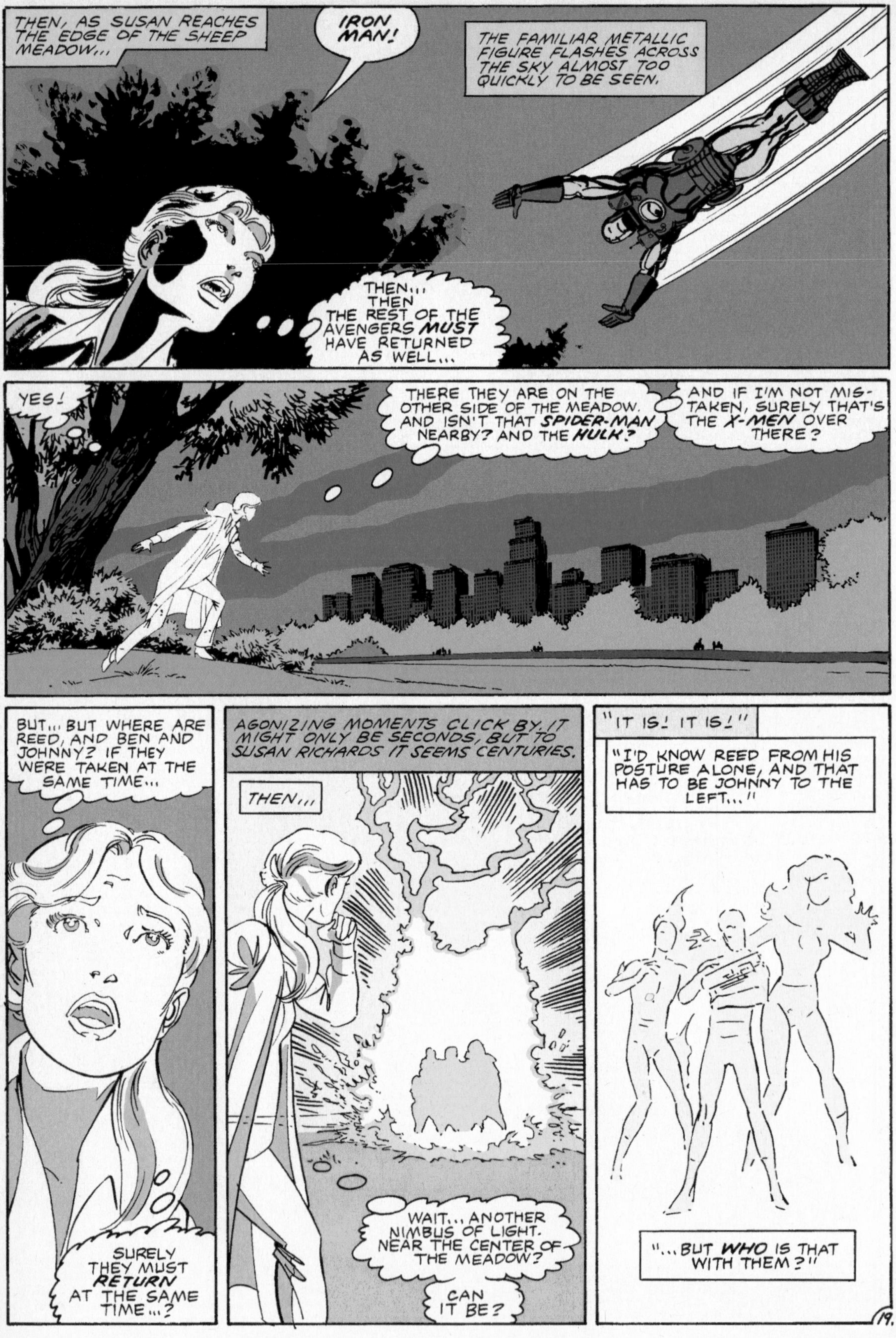

THEN, AS SUSAN REACHES THE EDGE OF THE SHEEP MEADOW...
IRON MAN!
THE FAMILIAR METALLIC FIGURE FLASHES ACROSS THE SKY ALMOST TOO QUICKLY TO BE SEEN.
THEN... THEN THE REST OF THE AVENGERS MUST HAVE RETURNED AS WELL...
YES!
THERE THEY ARE ON THE OTHER SIDE OF THE MEADOW. AND ISN'T THAT SPIDER-MAN NEARBY? AND THE HULK?
AND IF I'M NOT MIS-TAKEN, SURELY THAT'S THE X-MEN OVER THERE?
BUT... BUT WHERE ARE REED, AND BEN AND JOHNNY? IF THEY WERE TAKEN AT THE SAME TIME...
SURELY THEY MUST RETURN AT THE SAME TIME...?
AGONIZING MOMENTS CLICK BY. IT MIGHT ONLY BE SECONDS, BUT TO SUSAN RICHARDS IT SEEMS CENTURIES.
THEN...
WAIT... ANOTHER NIMBUS OF LIGHT. NEAR THE CENTER OF THE MEADOW?
CAN IT BE?
"IT IS! IT IS!"
"I'D KNOW REED FROM HIS POSTURE ALONE, AND THAT HAS TO BE JOHNNY TO THE LEFT..."
"...BUT WHO IS THAT WITH THEM?"
19.

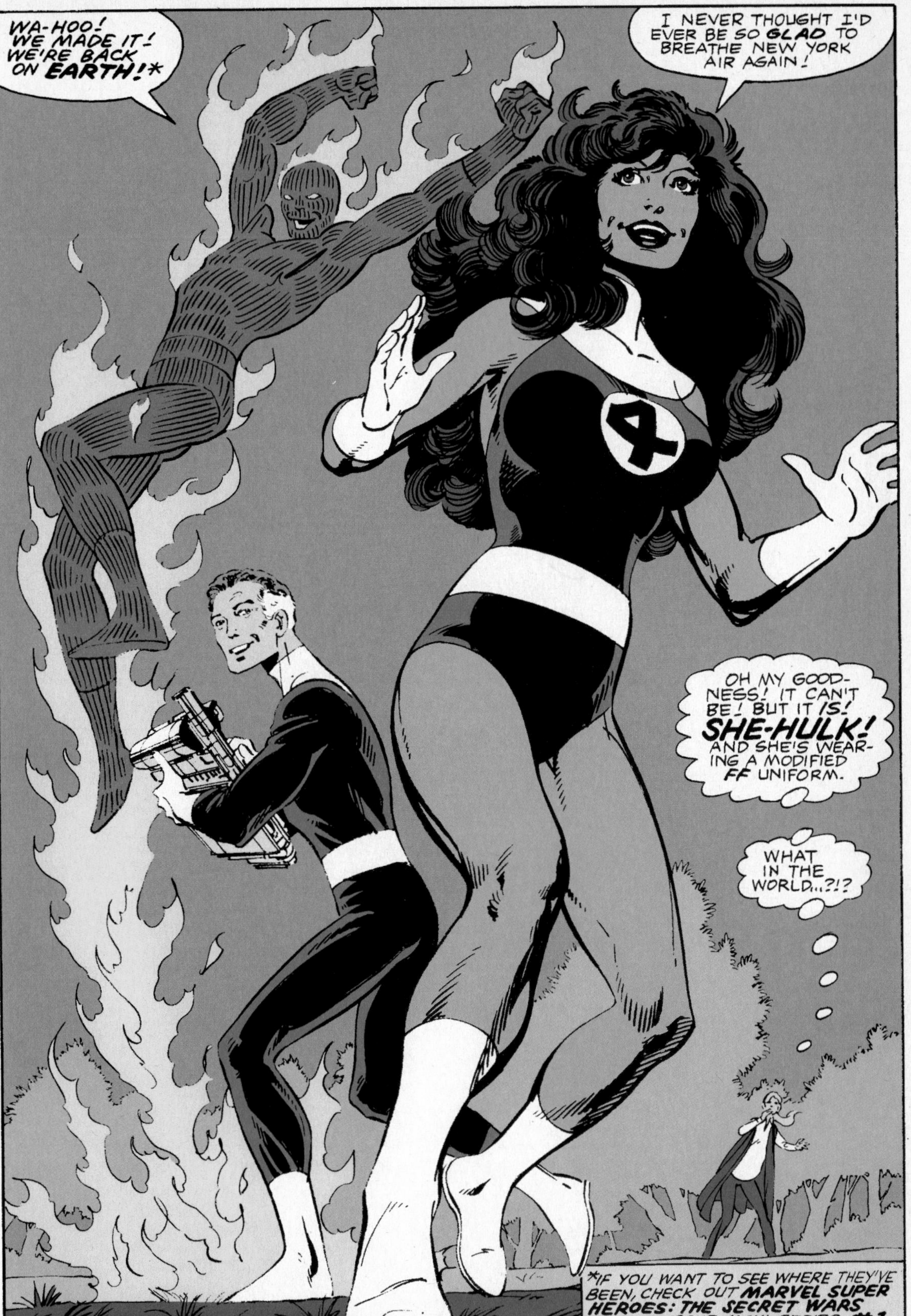
WA-HOO! WE MADE IT! WE'RE BACK ON EARTH!*
I NEVER THOUGHT I'D EVER BE SO GLAD TO BREATHE NEW YORK AIR AGAIN!
OH MY GOODNESS! IT CAN'T BE! BUT IT IS! SHE-HULK! AND SHE'S WEARING A MODIFIED FF UNIFORM.
WHAT IN THE WORLD...?!?
*IF YOU WANT TO SEE WHERE THEY'VE BEEN, CHECK OUT MARVEL SUPER HEROES: THE SECRET WARS TWELVE-ISSUE MAXI-SERIES, #1 ON SALE NEXT MONTH! --Bob
20.

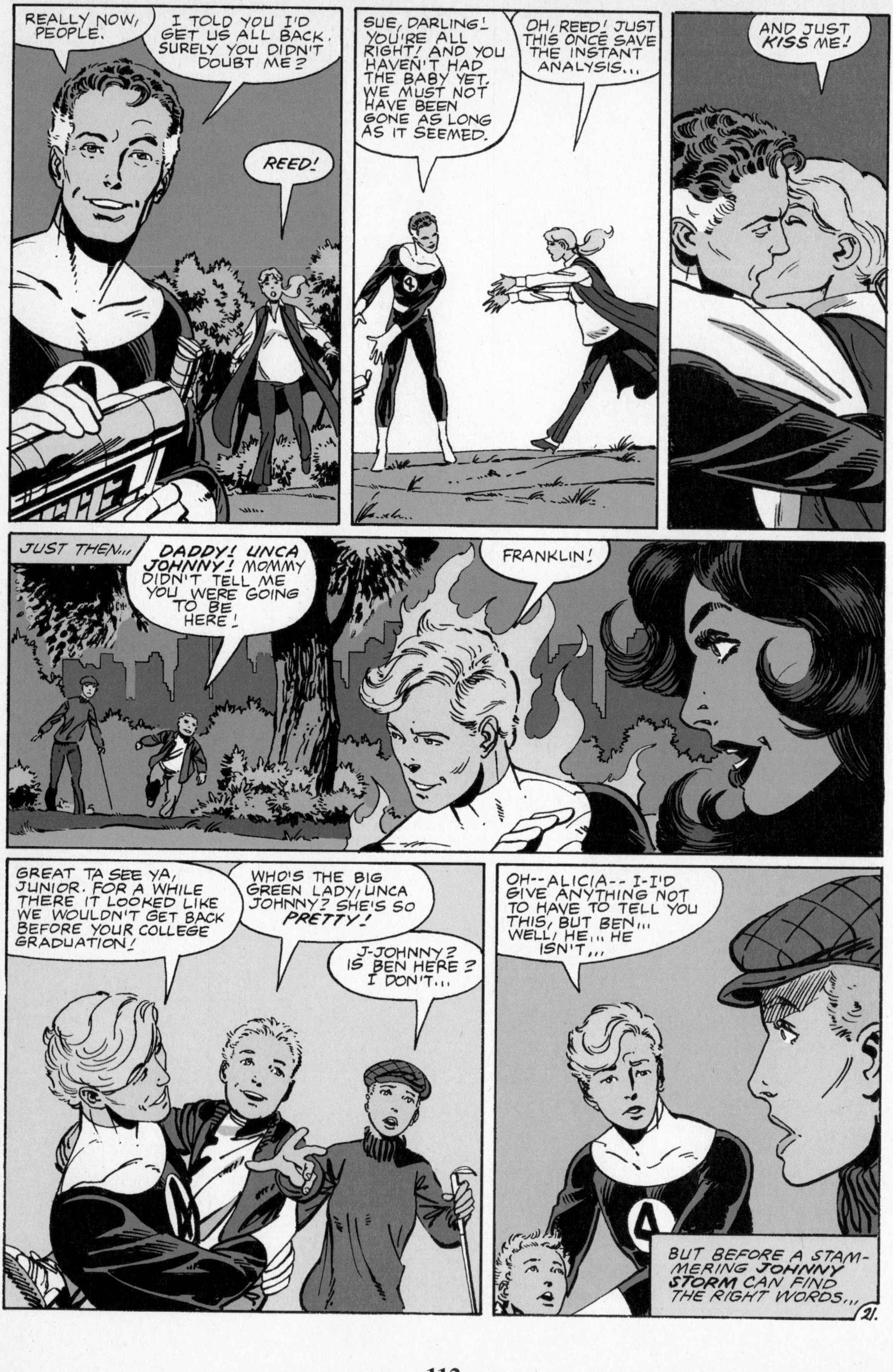
REALLY NOW, PEOPLE.
I TOLD YOU I'D GET US ALL BACK. SURELY YOU DIDN'T DOUBT ME?
REED!
SUE, DARLING! YOU'RE ALL RIGHT! AND YOU HAVEN'T HAD THE BABY YET. WE MUST NOT HAVE BEEN GONE AS LONG AS IT SEEMED.
OH, REED! JUST THIS ONCE SAVE THE INSTANT ANALYSIS...
AND JUST KISS ME!
JUST THEN...
DADDY! UNCA JOHNNY! MOMMY DIDN'T TELL ME YOU WERE GOING TO BE HERE!
FRANKLIN!
GREAT TA SEE YA, JUNIOR. FOR A WHILE THERE IT LOOKED LIKE WE WOULDN'T GET BACK BEFORE YOUR COLLEGE GRADUATION!
WHO'S THE BIG GREEN LADY, UNCA JOHNNY? SHE'S SO PRETTY!
J-JOHNNY? IS BEN HERE? I DON'T...
OH--ALICIA-- I-I'D GIVE ANYTHING NOT TO HAVE TO TELL YOU THIS, BUT BEN... WELL, HE... HE ISN'T...
BUT BEFORE A STAMMERING JOHNNY STORM CAN FIND THE RIGHT WORDS...
21.

SUE!

ARRGH!

TH-THAT WAS *HARD RADIATION!* A SUDDEN, ALMOST EXPLOSIVE BURST.

SUE, DARLING, CAN YOU *SPEAK?* ARE YOU... ARE YOU...?

R-REED...

REED... IT WAS THE *BABY!*

I FELT IT! I FELT IT MOVE... FELT IT *LASH OUT!*

H-HELP... ME...

GOT TO GET HER TO A HOSPITAL IMMEDIATELY... EVEN THOUGH I RISK ANOTHER RADIATION BURST...

DON'T BE A FOOL, REED, MY TOLERANCE TO RADIOACTIVITY IS FAR *GREATER* THAN YOURS...

...AND NO ONE'S GOING TO WASTE MY TIME ASKING FOR FORMS TO BE FILLED OUT. I'LL GET SUE TO A HOSPITAL...

JOHNNY, FLY AHEAD TO *MERCY GENERAL.* LET 'EM KNOW WE'RE COMING.

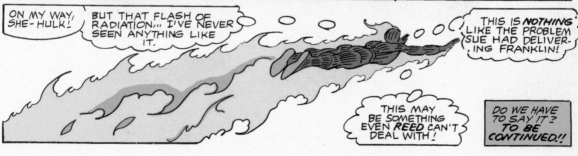

ON MY WAY, SHE-HULK!

BUT THAT FLASH OF RADIATION... I'VE NEVER SEEN ANYTHING LIKE IT.

THIS IS *NOTHING* LIKE THE PROBLEM SUE HAD DELIVERING FRANKLIN!

THIS MAY BE SOMETHING EVEN *REED* CAN'T DEAL WITH!

DO WE HAVE TO SAY IT? *TO BE CONTINUED!!*

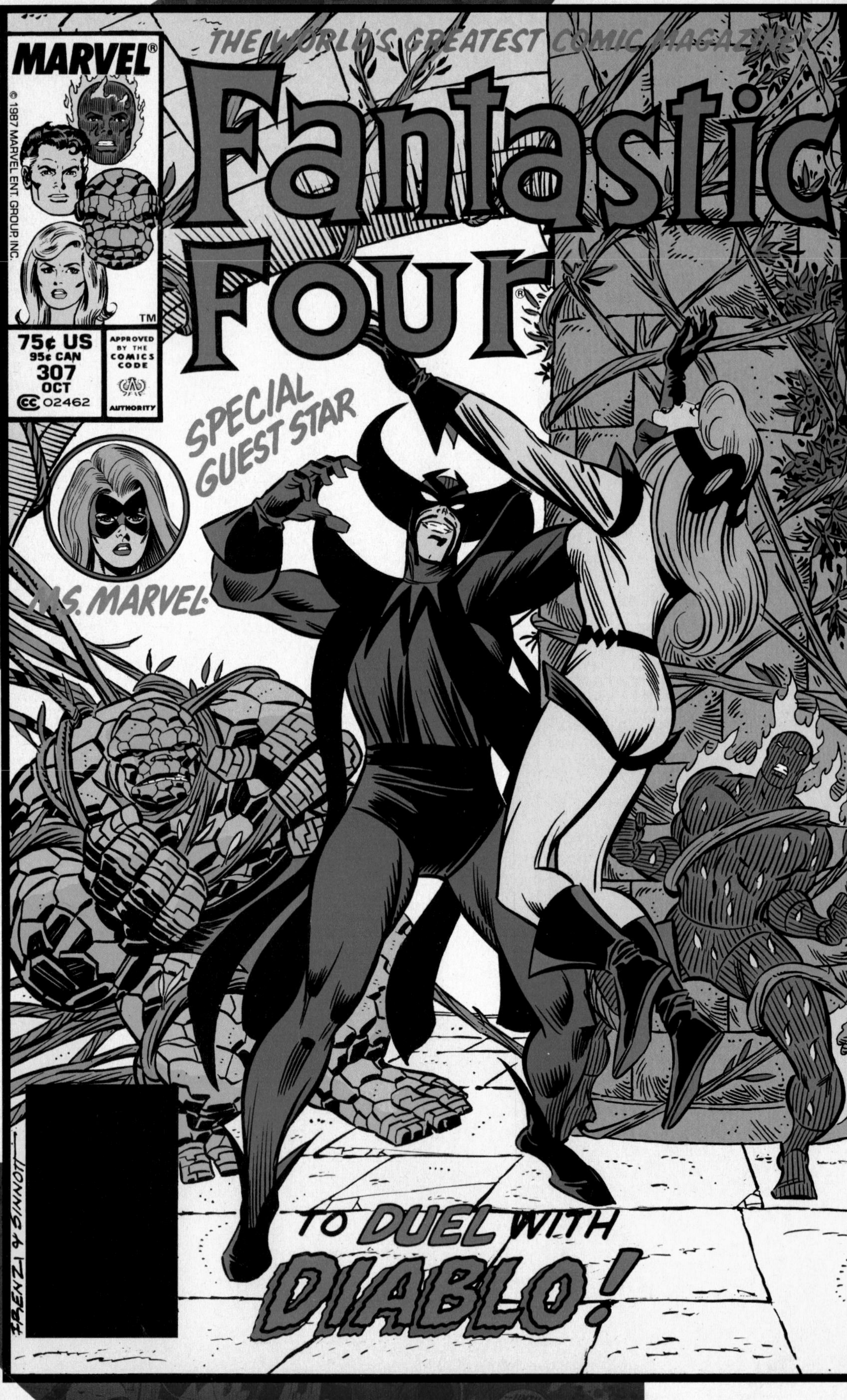
THE WORLD'S GREATEST COMIC MAGAZINE!
MARVEL
© 1987 MARVEL ENT. GROUP INC.
Fantastic Four
75¢ US
95¢ CAN
307
OCT
CC 02462
APPROVED BY THE COMICS CODE AUTHORITY
SPECIAL GUEST STAR
MS. MARVEL
TO DUEL WITH
DIABLO!

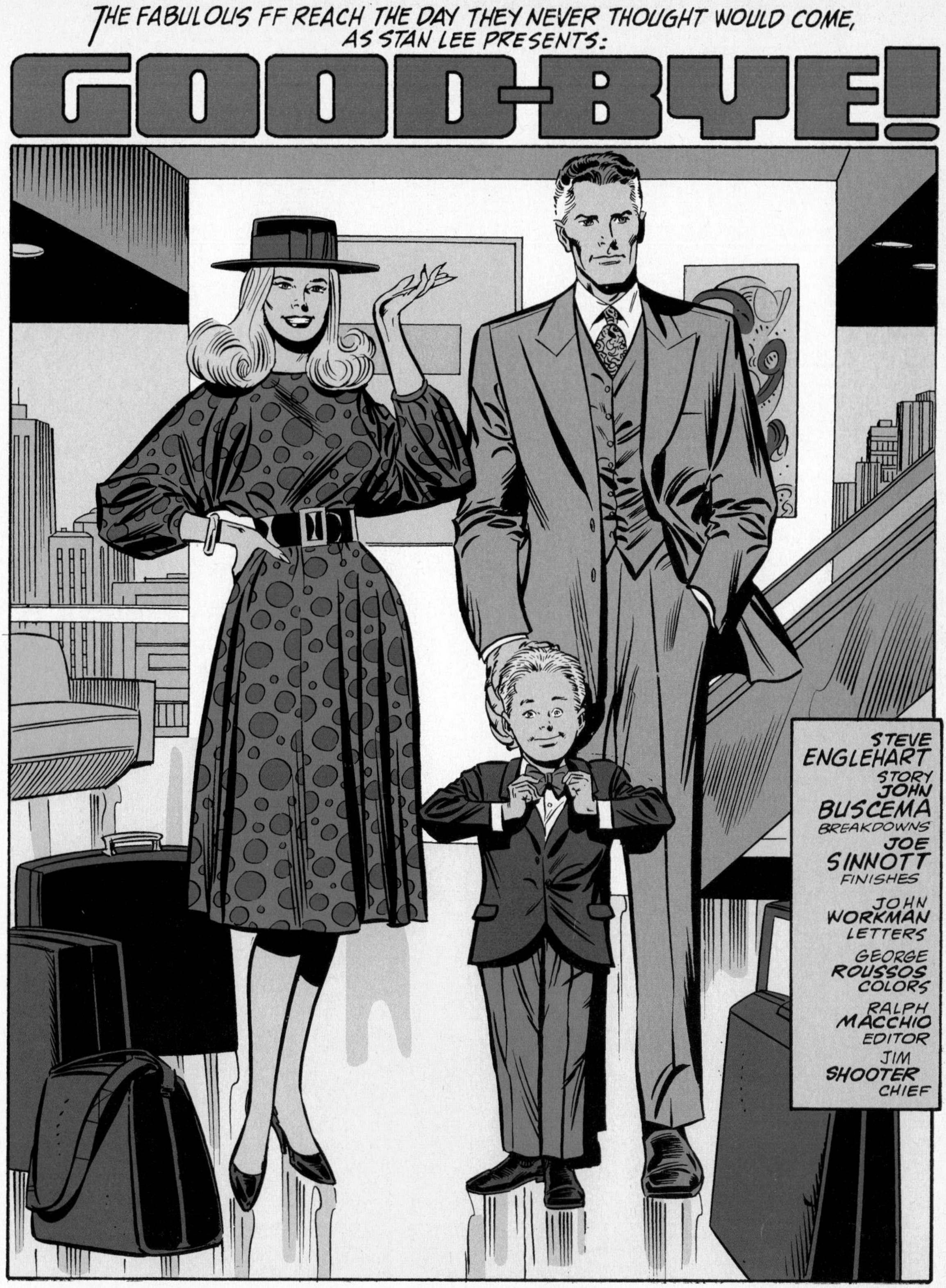
THE FABULOUS FF REACH THE DAY THEY NEVER THOUGHT WOULD COME, AS STAN LEE PRESENTS:
GOOD-BYE!
STEVE ENGLEHART STORY
JOHN BUSCEMA BREAKDOWNS
JOE SINNOTT FINISHES
JOHN WORKMAN LETTERS
GEORGE ROUSSOS COLORS
RALPH MACCHIO EDITOR
JIM SHOOTER CHIEF

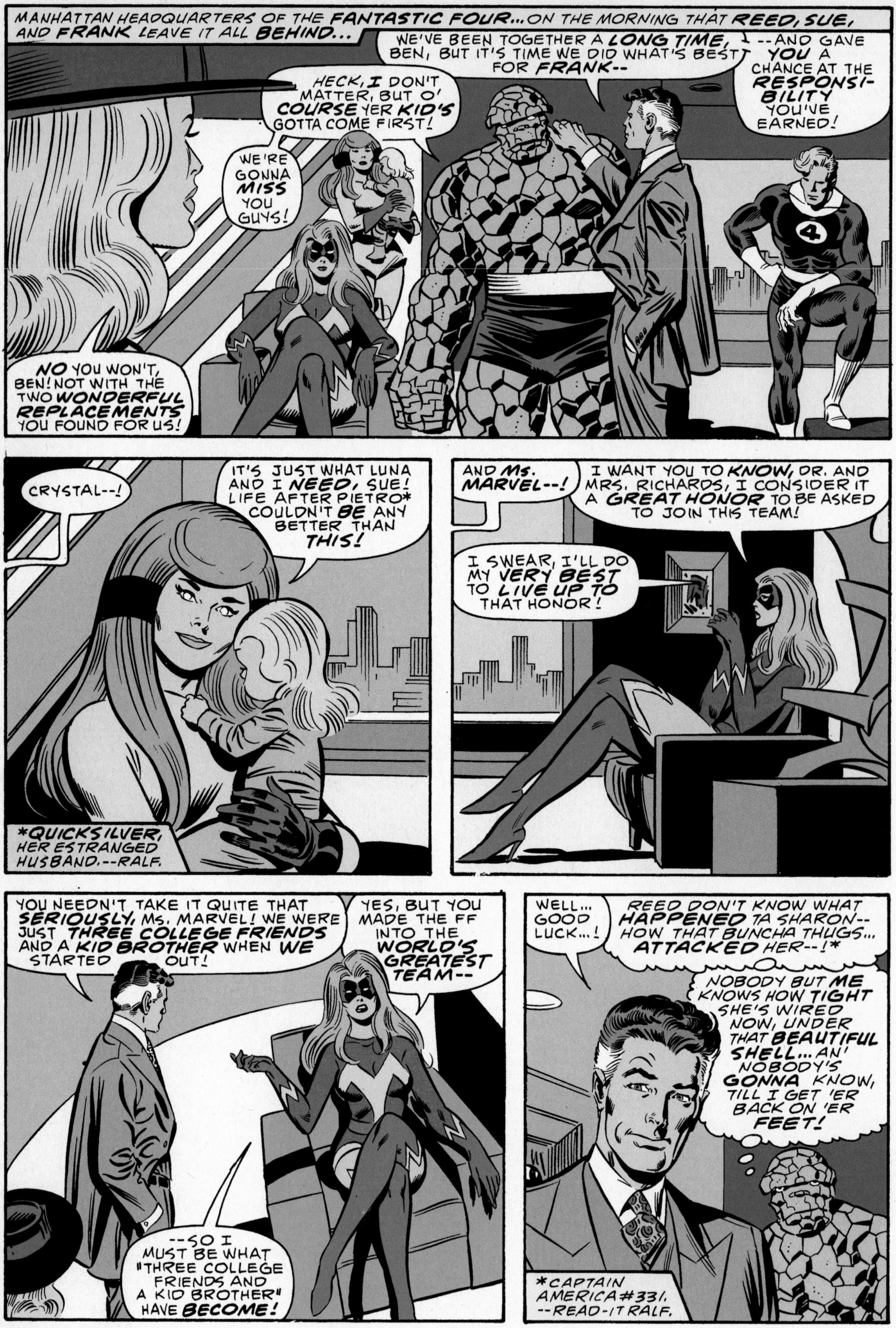

MANHATTAN HEADQUARTERS OF THE FANTASTIC FOUR... ON THE MORNING THAT REED, SUE, AND FRANK LEAVE IT ALL BEHIND...
WE'VE BEEN TOGETHER A LONG TIME, BEN, BUT IT'S TIME WE DID WHAT'S BEST FOR FRANK--
--AND GAVE YOU A CHANCE AT THE RESPONSIBILITY YOU'VE EARNED!
HECK, I DON'T MATTER, BUT O' COURSE YER KID'S GOTTA COME FIRST!
WE'RE GONNA MISS YOU GUYS!
NO YOU WON'T, BEN! NOT WITH THE TWO WONDERFUL REPLACEMENTS YOU FOUND FOR US!
CRYSTAL--!
IT'S JUST WHAT LUNA AND I NEED, SUE! LIFE AFTER PIETRO* COULDN'T BE ANY BETTER THAN THIS!
*QUICKSILVER, HER ESTRANGED HUSBAND. --RALF.
AND Ms. MARVEL--!
I WANT YOU TO KNOW, DR. AND MRS. RICHARDS, I CONSIDER IT A GREAT HONOR TO BE ASKED TO JOIN THIS TEAM!
I SWEAR, I'LL DO MY VERY BEST TO LIVE UP TO THAT HONOR!
YOU NEEDN'T TAKE IT QUITE THAT SERIOUSLY, Ms. MARVEL! WE WERE JUST THREE COLLEGE FRIENDS AND A KID BROTHER WHEN WE STARTED OUT!
YES, BUT YOU MADE THE FF INTO THE WORLD'S GREATEST TEAM--
--SO I MUST BE WHAT "THREE COLLEGE FRIENDS AND A KID BROTHER" HAVE BECOME!
WELL... GOOD LUCK...!
REED DON'T KNOW WHAT HAPPENED TA SHARON-- HOW THAT BUNCHA THUGS... ATTACKED HER--!*
NOBODY BUT ME KNOWS HOW TIGHT SHE'S WIRED NOW, UNDER THAT BEAUTIFUL SHELL... AN' NOBODY'S GONNA KNOW, TILL I GET 'ER BACK ON 'ER FEET!
*CAPTAIN AMERICA #331. --READ-IT RALF.

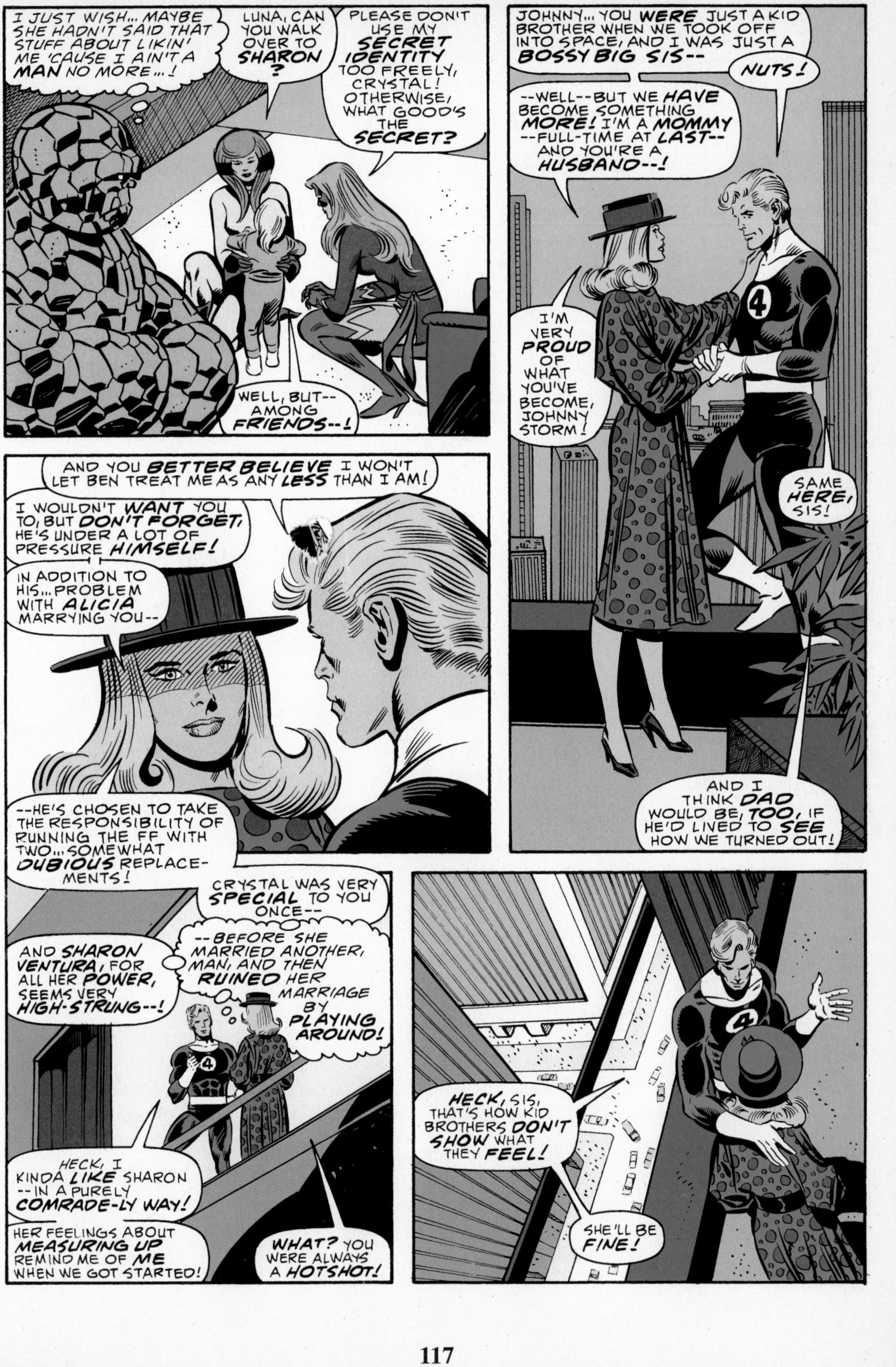
I JUST WISH... MAYBE SHE HADN'T SAID THAT STUFF ABOUT LIKIN' ME 'CAUSE I AIN'T A MAN NO MORE...!
LUNA, CAN YOU WALK OVER TO SHARON?
PLEASE DON'T USE MY SECRET IDENTITY TOO FREELY, CRYSTAL! OTHERWISE, WHAT GOOD'S THE SECRET?
WELL, BUT-- AMONG FRIENDS--!
JOHNNY... YOU WERE JUST A KID BROTHER WHEN WE TOOK OFF INTO SPACE, AND I WAS JUST A BOSSY BIG SIS--
NUTS!
--WELL--BUT WE HAVE BECOME SOMETHING MORE! I'M A MOMMY --FULL-TIME AT LAST-- AND YOU'RE A HUSBAND--!
I'M VERY PROUD OF WHAT YOU'VE BECOME, JOHNNY STORM!
SAME HERE, SIS!
AND I THINK DAD WOULD BE, TOO, IF HE'D LIVED TO SEE HOW WE TURNED OUT!
AND YOU BETTER BELIEVE I WON'T LET BEN TREAT ME AS ANY LESS THAN I AM!
I WOULDN'T WANT YOU TO, BUT DON'T FORGET, HE'S UNDER A LOT OF PRESSURE HIMSELF!
IN ADDITION TO HIS... PROBLEM WITH ALICIA MARRYING YOU--
--HE'S CHOSEN TO TAKE THE RESPONSIBILITY OF RUNNING THE FF WITH TWO... SOMEWHAT DUBIOUS REPLACEMENTS!
CRYSTAL WAS VERY SPECIAL TO YOU ONCE--
AND SHARON VENTURA, FOR ALL HER POWER, SEEMS VERY HIGH-STRUNG--!
--BEFORE SHE MARRIED ANOTHER, MAN, AND THEN RUINED HER MARRIAGE BY PLAYING AROUND!
HECK, I KINDA LIKE SHARON --IN A PURELY COMRADE-LY WAY!
HER FEELINGS ABOUT MEASURING UP REMIND ME OF ME WHEN WE GOT STARTED!
WHAT? YOU WERE ALWAYS A HOTSHOT!
HECK, SIS, THAT'S HOW KID BROTHERS DON'T SHOW WHAT THEY FEEL!
SHE'LL BE FINE!

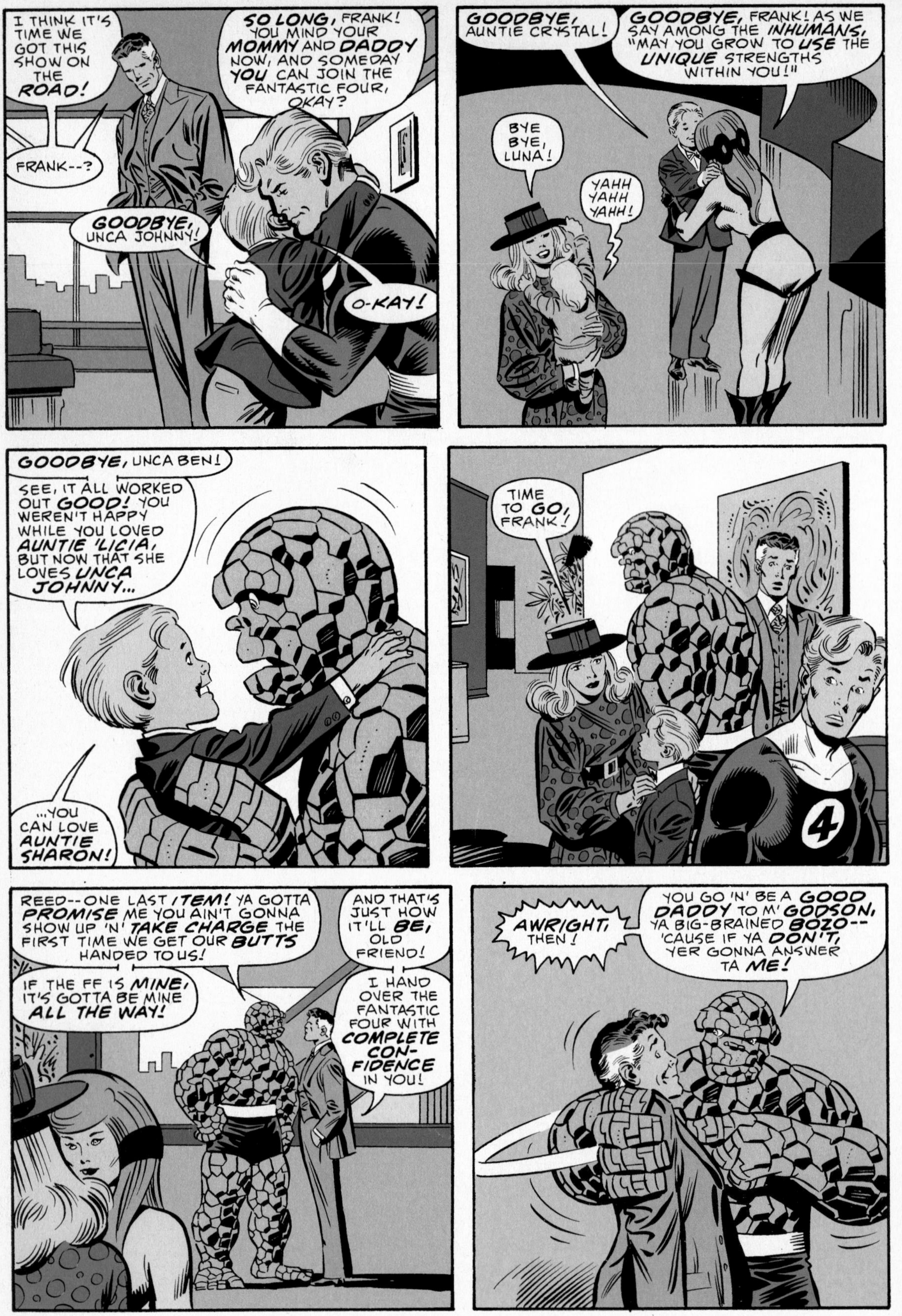
I THINK IT'S TIME WE GOT THIS SHOW ON THE ROAD!
FRANK--?
SO LONG, FRANK! YOU MIND YOUR MOMMY AND DADDY NOW, AND SOMEDAY YOU CAN JOIN THE FANTASTIC FOUR, OKAY?
GOODBYE, UNCA JOHNNY!
O-KAY!
GOODBYE, AUNTIE CRYSTAL!
GOODBYE, FRANK! AS WE SAY AMONG THE INHUMANS, "MAY YOU GROW TO USE THE UNIQUE STRENGTHS WITHIN YOU!"
BYE BYE, LUNA!
YAHH YAHH YAHH!
GOODBYE, UNCA BEN!
SEE, IT ALL WORKED OUT GOOD! YOU WEREN'T HAPPY WHILE YOU LOVED AUNTIE 'LICIA, BUT NOW THAT SHE LOVES UNCA JOHNNY...
...YOU CAN LOVE AUNTIE SHARON!
TIME TO GO, FRANK!
REED--ONE LAST ITEM! YA GOTTA PROMISE ME YOU AIN'T GONNA SHOW UP 'N' TAKE CHARGE THE FIRST TIME WE GET OUR BUTTS HANDED TO US!
IF THE FF IS MINE, IT'S GOTTA BE MINE ALL THE WAY!
AND THAT'S JUST HOW IT'LL BE, OLD FRIEND!
I HAND OVER THE FANTASTIC FOUR WITH COMPLETE CON-FIDENCE IN YOU!
AWRIGHT, THEN!
YOU GO 'N' BE A GOOD DADDY TO M' GODSON, YA BIG-BRAINED BOZO-- 'CAUSE IF YA DON'T, YER GONNA ANSWER TA ME!

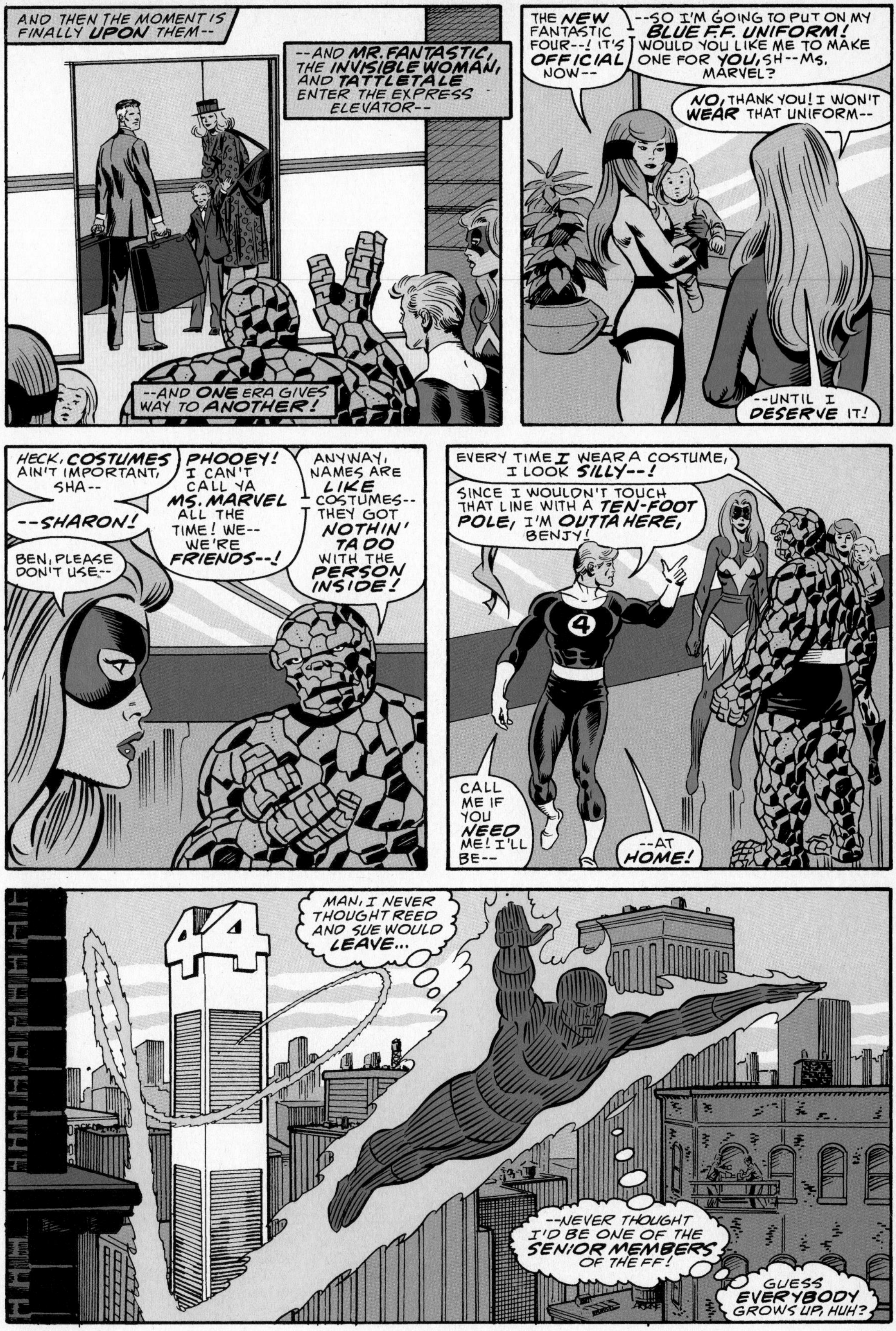
AND THEN THE MOMENT IS FINALLY UPON THEM--
--AND MR. FANTASTIC, THE INVISIBLE WOMAN, AND TATTLETALE ENTER THE EXPRESS ELEVATOR--
--AND ONE ERA GIVES WAY TO ANOTHER!
THE NEW FANTASTIC FOUR--! IT'S OFFICIAL NOW--
--SO I'M GOING TO PUT ON MY BLUE F.F. UNIFORM! WOULD YOU LIKE ME TO MAKE ONE FOR YOU, SH--Ms. MARVEL?
NO, THANK YOU! I WON'T WEAR THAT UNIFORM--
--UNTIL I DESERVE IT!
HECK, COSTUMES AIN'T IMPORTANT, SHA--
--SHARON!
BEN, PLEASE DON'T USE--
PHOOEY! I CAN'T CALL YA MS. MARVEL ALL THE TIME! WE--WE'RE FRIENDS--!
ANYWAY, NAMES ARE LIKE COSTUMES-- THEY GOT NOTHIN' TA DO WITH THE PERSON INSIDE!
EVERY TIME I WEAR A COSTUME, I LOOK SILLY--!
SINCE I WOULDN'T TOUCH THAT LINE WITH A TEN-FOOT POLE, I'M OUTTA HERE, BENJY!
CALL ME IF YOU NEED ME! I'LL BE--
--AT HOME!
MAN, I NEVER THOUGHT REED AND SUE WOULD LEAVE...
--NEVER THOUGHT I'D BE ONE OF THE SENIOR MEMBERS OF THE FF!
GUESS EVERYBODY GROWS UP, HUH?

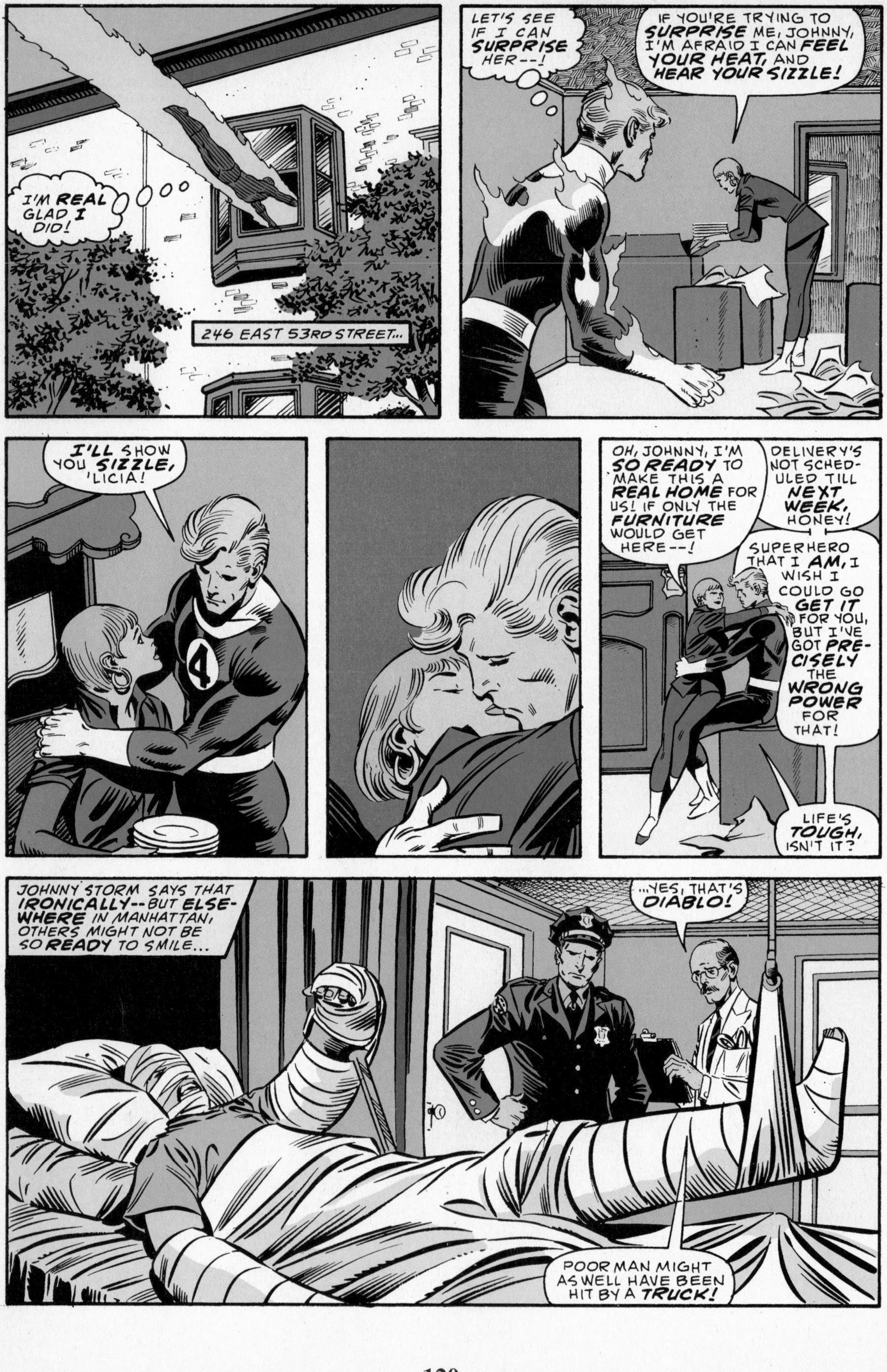
I'M REAL GLAD I DID!
246 EAST 53RD STREET...
LET'S SEE IF I CAN SURPRISE HER--!
IF YOU'RE TRYING TO SURPRISE ME, JOHNNY, I'M AFRAID I CAN FEEL YOUR HEAT, AND HEAR YOUR SIZZLE!
I'LL SHOW YOU SIZZLE, 'LICIA!
OH, JOHNNY, I'M SO READY TO MAKE THIS A REAL HOME FOR US! IF ONLY THE FURNITURE WOULD GET HERE--!
DELIVERY'S NOT SCHEDULED TILL NEXT WEEK, HONEY!
SUPERHERO THAT I AM, I WISH I COULD GO GET IT FOR YOU, BUT I'VE GOT PRECISELY THE WRONG POWER FOR THAT!
LIFE'S TOUGH, ISN'T IT?
JOHNNY STORM SAYS THAT IRONICALLY--BUT ELSEWHERE IN MANHATTAN, OTHERS MIGHT NOT BE SO READY TO SMILE...
...YES, THAT'S DIABLO!
POOR MAN MIGHT AS WELL HAVE BEEN HIT BY A TRUCK!

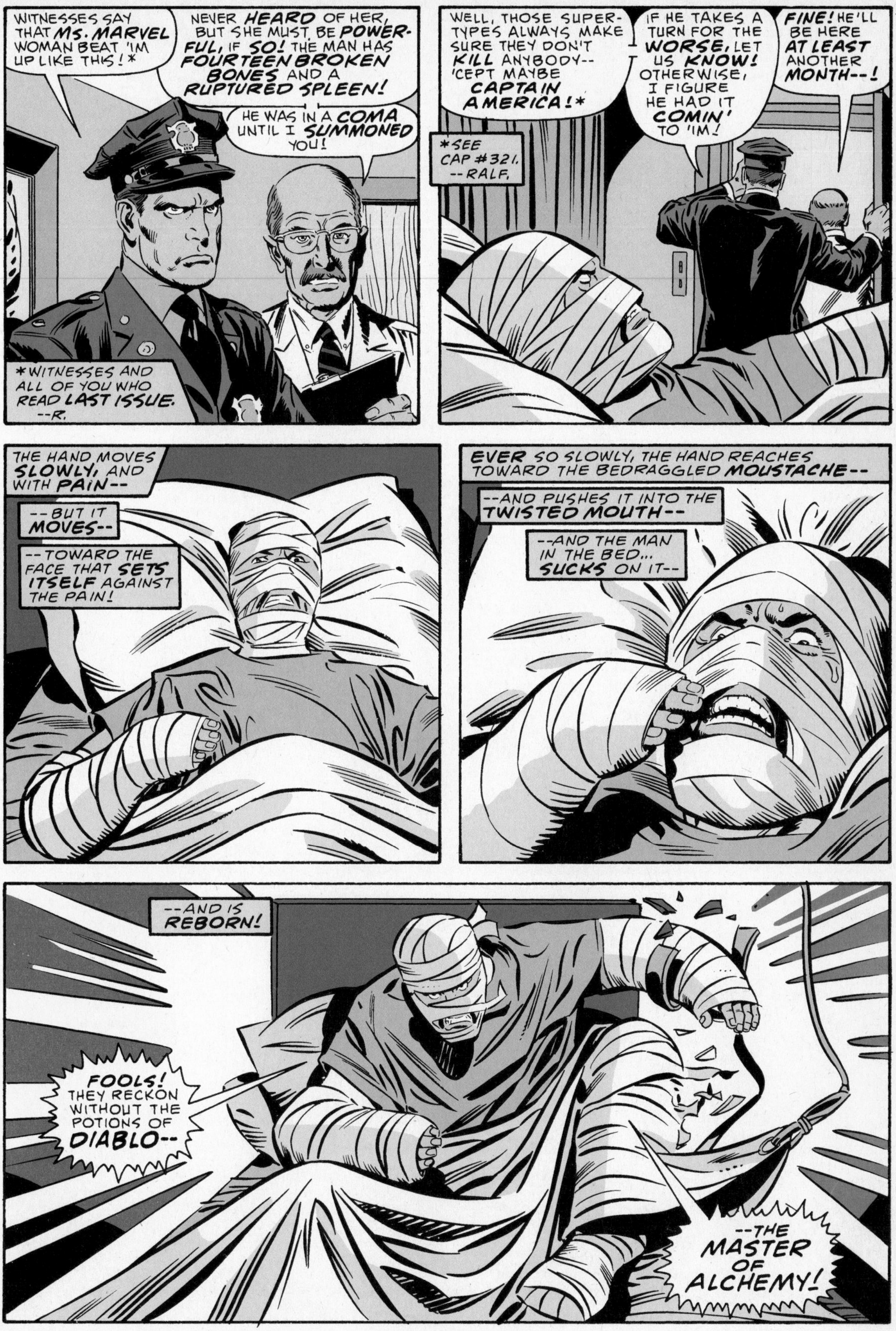
WITNESSES SAY THAT MS. MARVEL WOMAN BEAT 'IM UP LIKE THIS! *
NEVER HEARD OF HER, BUT SHE MUST BE POWERFUL, IF SO! THE MAN HAS FOURTEEN BROKEN BONES AND A RUPTURED SPLEEN!
HE WAS IN A COMA UNTIL I SUMMONED YOU!
*WITNESSES AND ALL OF YOU WHO READ LAST ISSUE. --R.
WELL, THOSE SUPER-TYPES ALWAYS MAKE SURE THEY DON'T KILL ANYBODY-- 'CEPT MAYBE CAPTAIN AMERICA! *
IF HE TAKES A TURN FOR THE WORSE, LET US KNOW! OTHERWISE, I FIGURE HE HAD IT COMIN' TO 'IM!
FINE! HE'LL BE HERE AT LEAST ANOTHER MONTH--!
*SEE CAP #321. --RALF.
THE HAND MOVES SLOWLY, AND WITH PAIN--
--BUT IT MOVES--
--TOWARD THE FACE THAT SETS ITSELF AGAINST THE PAIN!
EVER SO SLOWLY, THE HAND REACHES TOWARD THE BEDRAGGLED MOUSTACHE--
--AND PUSHES IT INTO THE TWISTED MOUTH--
--AND THE MAN IN THE BED... SUCKS ON IT--
--AND IS REBORN!
FOOLS! THEY RECKON WITHOUT THE POTIONS OF DIABLO--
--THE MASTER OF ALCHEMY!

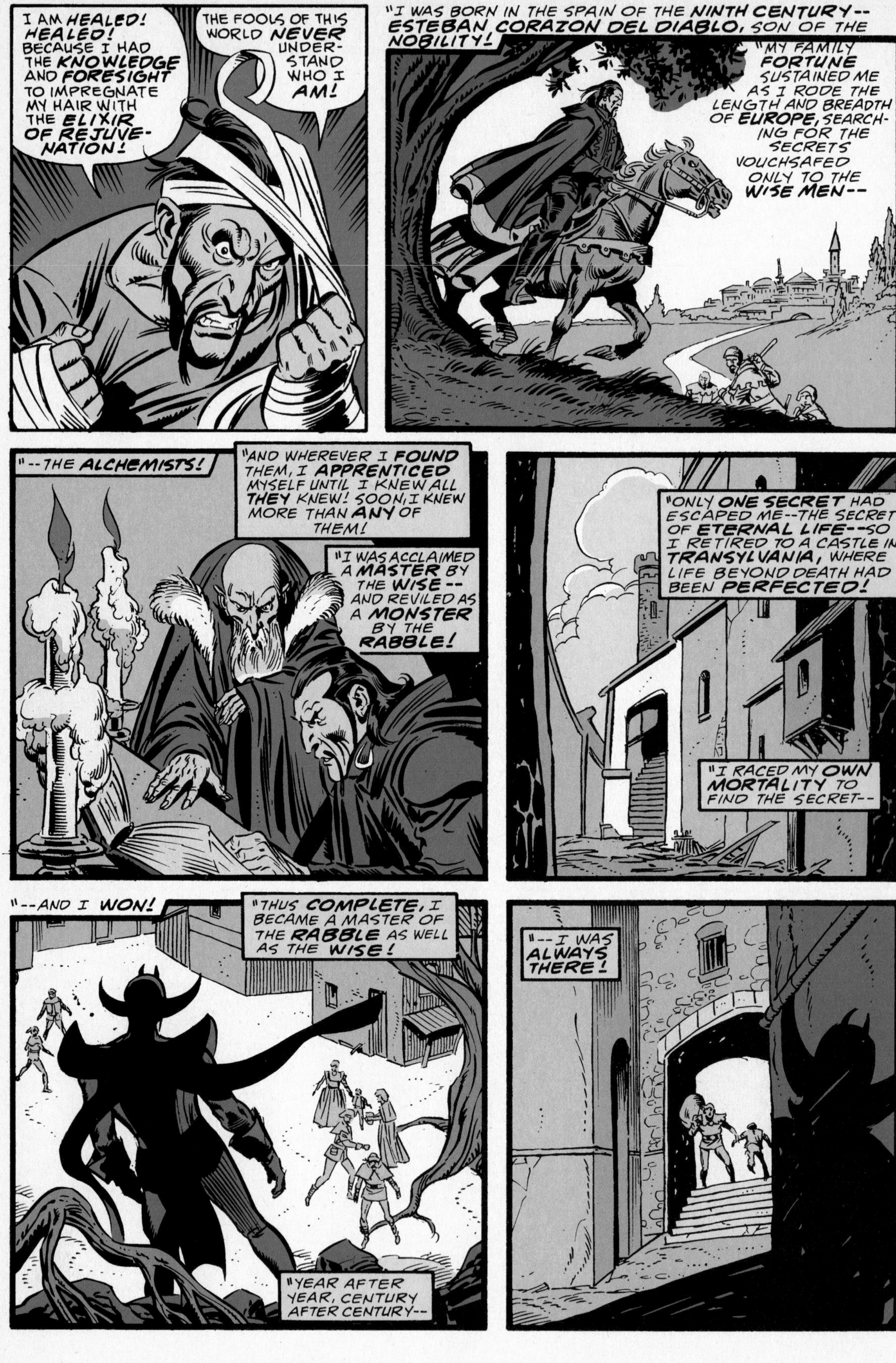
I AM HEALED! HEALED! BECAUSE I HAD THE KNOWLEDGE AND FORESIGHT TO IMPREGNATE MY HAIR WITH THE ELIXIR OF REJUVENATION!
THE FOOLS OF THIS WORLD NEVER UNDERSTAND WHO I AM!
"I WAS BORN IN THE SPAIN OF THE NINTH CENTURY-- ESTEBAN CORAZON DEL DIABLO, SON OF THE NOBILITY!
"MY FAMILY FORTUNE SUSTAINED ME AS I RODE THE LENGTH AND BREADTH OF EUROPE, SEARCHING FOR THE SECRETS VOUCHSAFED ONLY TO THE WISE MEN--
"--THE ALCHEMISTS!
"AND WHEREVER I FOUND THEM, I APPRENTICED MYSELF UNTIL I KNEW ALL THEY KNEW! SOON, I KNEW MORE THAN ANY OF THEM!
"I WAS ACCLAIMED A MASTER BY THE WISE-- AND REVILED AS A MONSTER BY THE RABBLE!
"ONLY ONE SECRET HAD ESCAPED ME--THE SECRET OF ETERNAL LIFE--SO I RETIRED TO A CASTLE IN TRANSYLVANIA, WHERE LIFE BEYOND DEATH HAD BEEN PERFECTED!
"I RACED MY OWN MORTALITY TO FIND THE SECRET--
"--AND I WON!
"THUS COMPLETE, I BECAME A MASTER OF THE RABBLE AS WELL AS THE WISE!
"YEAR AFTER YEAR, CENTURY AFTER CENTURY--
"--I WAS ALWAYS THERE!

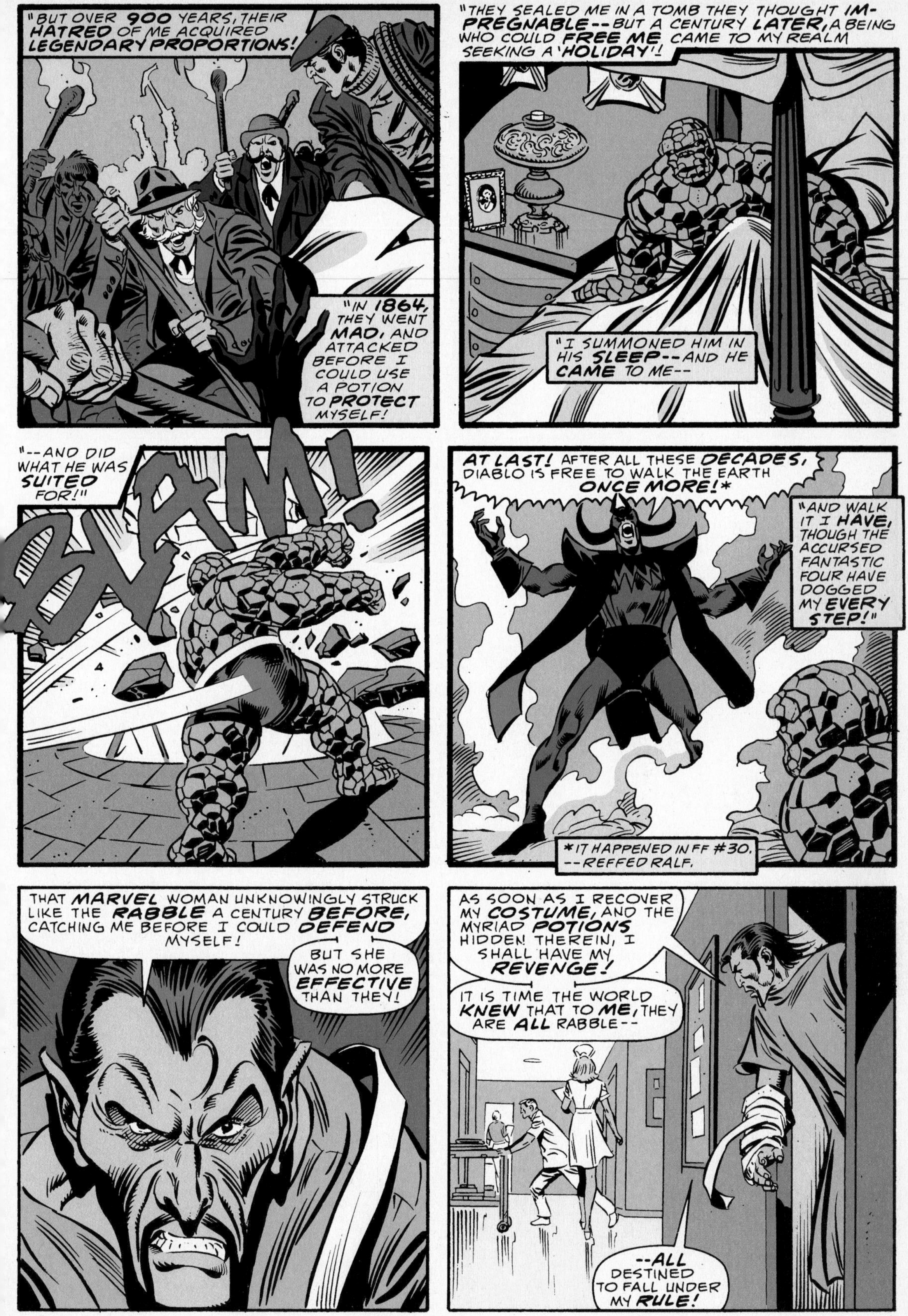
"BUT OVER 900 YEARS, THEIR HATRED OF ME ACQUIRED LEGENDARY PROPORTIONS!
"IN 1864, THEY WENT MAD, AND ATTACKED BEFORE I COULD USE A POTION TO PROTECT MYSELF!
"THEY SEALED ME IN A TOMB THEY THOUGHT IMPREGNABLE-- BUT A CENTURY LATER, A BEING WHO COULD FREE ME CAME TO MY REALM SEEKING A 'HOLIDAY'!
"I SUMMONED HIM IN HIS SLEEP--AND HE CAME TO ME--
"--AND DID WHAT HE WAS SUITED FOR!"
BLAM!
AT LAST! AFTER ALL THESE DECADES, DIABLO IS FREE TO WALK THE EARTH ONCE MORE!*
"AND WALK IT I HAVE, THOUGH THE ACCURSED FANTASTIC FOUR HAVE DOGGED MY EVERY STEP!"
*IT HAPPENED IN FF #30. --REFFED RALF.
THAT MARVEL WOMAN UNKNOWINGLY STRUCK LIKE THE RABBLE A CENTURY BEFORE, CATCHING ME BEFORE I COULD DEFEND MYSELF!
BUT SHE WAS NO MORE EFFECTIVE THAN THEY!
AS SOON AS I RECOVER MY COSTUME, AND THE MYRIAD POTIONS HIDDEN THEREIN, I SHALL HAVE MY REVENGE!
IT IS TIME THE WORLD KNEW THAT TO ME, THEY ARE ALL RABBLE--
--ALL DESTINED TO FALL UNDER MY RULE!

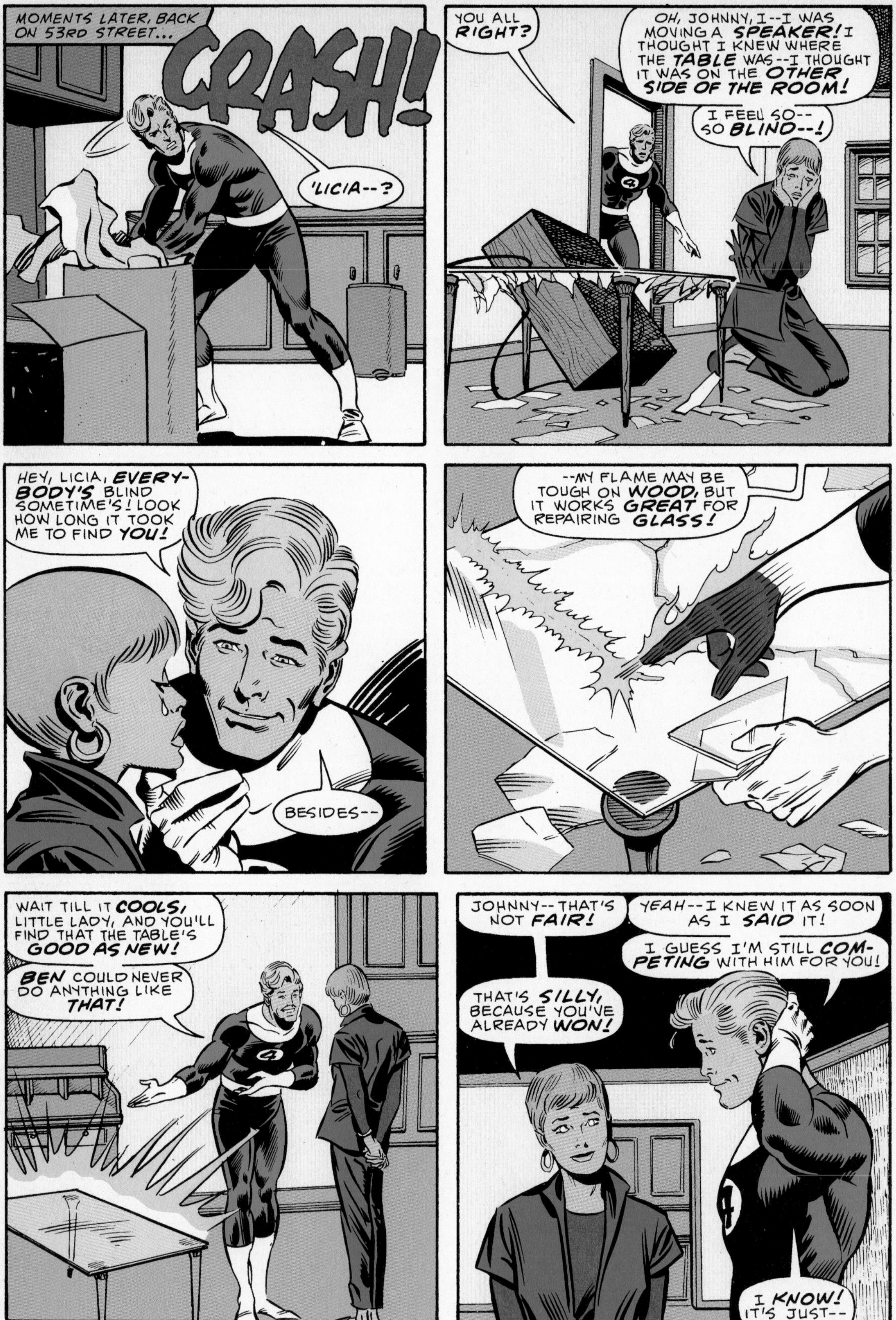
MOMENTS LATER, BACK ON 53RD STREET...
CRASH!
'LICIA--?
YOU ALL RIGHT?
OH, JOHNNY, I--I WAS MOVING A SPEAKER! I THOUGHT I KNEW WHERE THE TABLE WAS--I THOUGHT IT WAS ON THE OTHER SIDE OF THE ROOM!
I FEEL SO-- SO BLIND--!
HEY, LICIA, EVERYBODY'S BLIND SOMETIME'S! LOOK HOW LONG IT TOOK ME TO FIND YOU!
BESIDES--
--MY FLAME MAY BE TOUGH ON WOOD, BUT IT WORKS GREAT FOR REPAIRING GLASS!
WAIT TILL IT COOLS, LITTLE LADY, AND YOU'LL FIND THAT THE TABLE'S GOOD AS NEW!
BEN COULD NEVER DO ANYTHING LIKE THAT!
JOHNNY-- THAT'S NOT FAIR!
YEAH--I KNEW IT AS SOON AS I SAID IT!
I GUESS I'M STILL COMPETING WITH HIM FOR YOU!
THAT'S SILLY, BECAUSE YOU'VE ALREADY WON!
I KNOW! IT'S JUST--

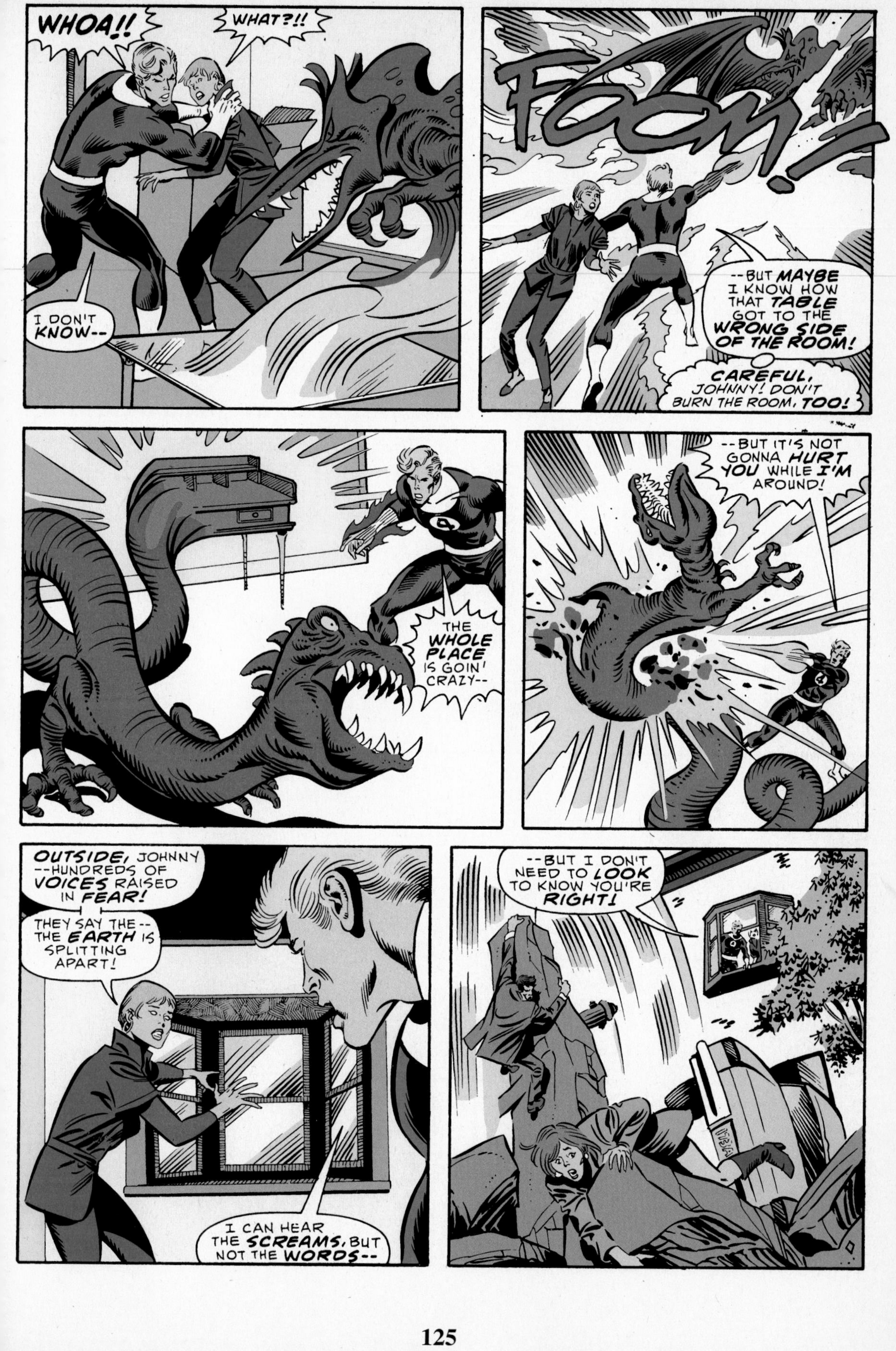
WHOA!!
WHAT?!!
I DON'T KNOW--
FOOM!
--BUT MAYBE I KNOW HOW THAT TABLE GOT TO THE WRONG SIDE OF THE ROOM!
CAREFUL, JOHNNY! DON'T BURN THE ROOM, TOO!
THE WHOLE PLACE IS GOIN' CRAZY--
--BUT IT'S NOT GONNA HURT YOU WHILE I'M AROUND!
OUTSIDE, JOHNNY --HUNDREDS OF VOICES RAISED IN FEAR!
THEY SAY THE-- THE EARTH IS SPLITTING APART!
I CAN HEAR THE SCREAMS, BUT NOT THE WORDS--
--BUT I DON'T NEED TO LOOK TO KNOW YOU'RE RIGHT!

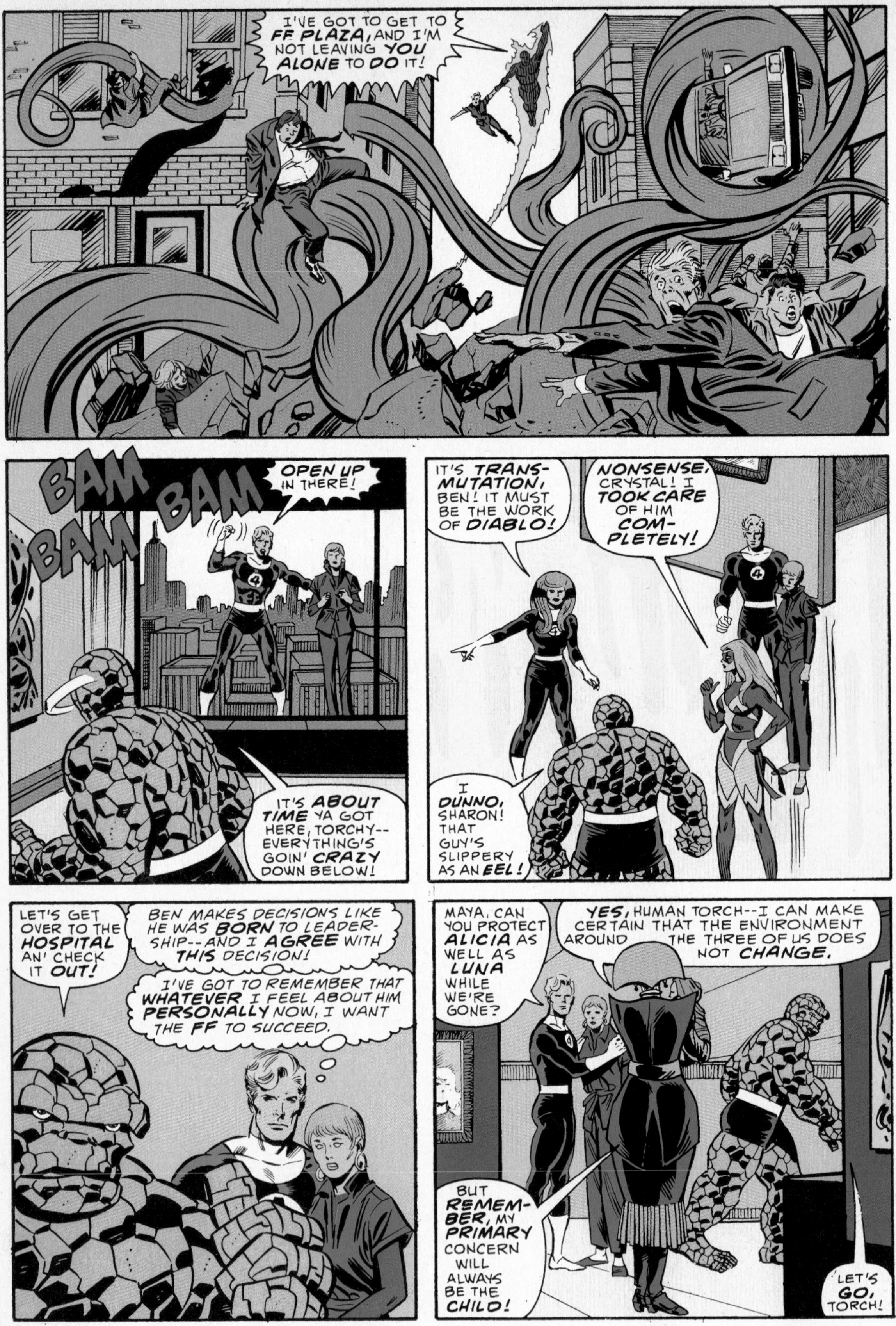
I'VE GOT TO GET TO FF PLAZA, AND I'M NOT LEAVING YOU ALONE TO DO IT!
BAM BAM BAM
OPEN UP IN THERE!
IT'S ABOUT TIME YA GOT HERE, TORCHY-- EVERYTHING'S GOIN' CRAZY DOWN BELOW!
IT'S TRANS-MUTATION, BEN! IT MUST BE THE WORK OF DIABLO!
NONSENSE, CRYSTAL! I TOOK CARE OF HIM COM-PLETELY!
I DUNNO, SHARON! THAT GUY'S SLIPPERY AS AN EEL!
LET'S GET OVER TO THE HOSPITAL AN' CHECK IT OUT!
BEN MAKES DECISIONS LIKE HE WAS BORN TO LEADER-SHIP--AND I AGREE WITH THIS DECISION!
I'VE GOT TO REMEMBER THAT WHATEVER I FEEL ABOUT HIM PERSONALLY NOW, I WANT THE FF TO SUCCEED.
MAYA, CAN YOU PROTECT ALICIA AS WELL AS LUNA WHILE WE'RE GONE?
YES, HUMAN TORCH--I CAN MAKE CERTAIN THAT THE ENVIRONMENT AROUND THE THREE OF US DOES NOT CHANGE.
BUT REMEM-BER, MY PRIMARY CONCERN WILL ALWAYS BE THE CHILD!
LET'S GO, TORCH!

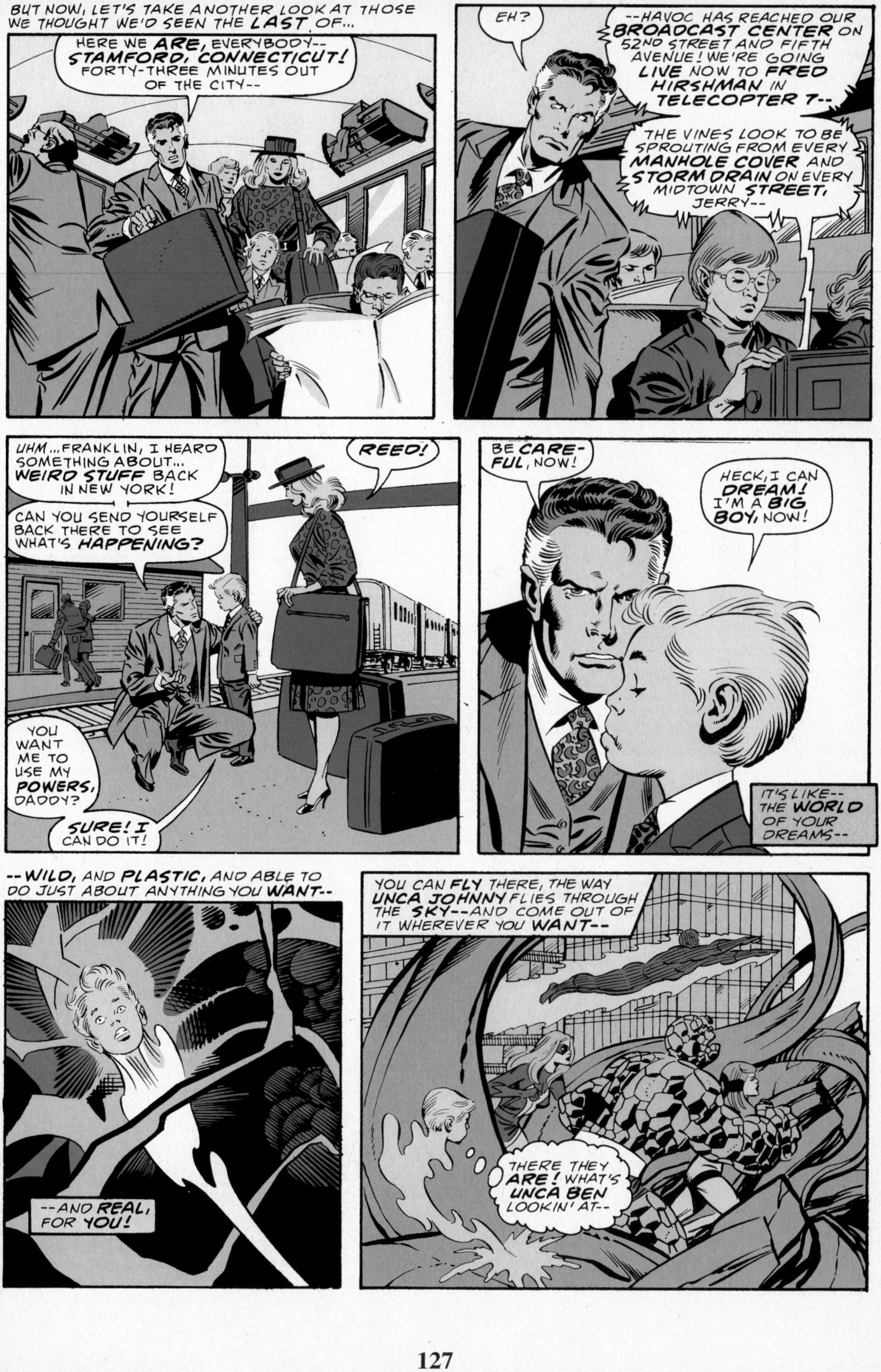
BUT NOW, LET'S TAKE ANOTHER LOOK AT THOSE WE THOUGHT WE'D SEEN THE LAST OF...
HERE WE ARE, EVERYBODY-- STAMFORD, CONNECTICUT! FORTY-THREE MINUTES OUT OF THE CITY--
EH?
--HAVOC HAS REACHED OUR BROADCAST CENTER ON 52ND STREET AND FIFTH AVENUE! WE'RE GOING LIVE NOW TO FRED HIRSHMAN IN TELECOPTER 7--
THE VINES LOOK TO BE SPROUTING FROM EVERY MANHOLE COVER AND STORM DRAIN ON EVERY MIDTOWN STREET, JERRY--
UHM... FRANKLIN, I HEARD SOMETHING ABOUT... WEIRD STUFF BACK IN NEW YORK!
CAN YOU SEND YOURSELF BACK THERE TO SEE WHAT'S HAPPENING?
REED!
YOU WANT ME TO USE MY POWERS, DADDY?
SURE! I CAN DO IT!
BE CARE-FUL, NOW!
HECK, I CAN DREAM! I'M A BIG BOY, NOW!
IT'S LIKE-- THE WORLD OF YOUR DREAMS--
--WILD, AND PLASTIC, AND ABLE TO DO JUST ABOUT ANYTHING YOU WANT--
--AND REAL, FOR YOU!
YOU CAN FLY THERE, THE WAY UNCA JOHNNY FLIES THROUGH THE SKY--AND COME OUT OF IT WHEREVER YOU WANT--
THERE THEY ARE! WHAT'S UNCA BEN LOOKIN' AT--

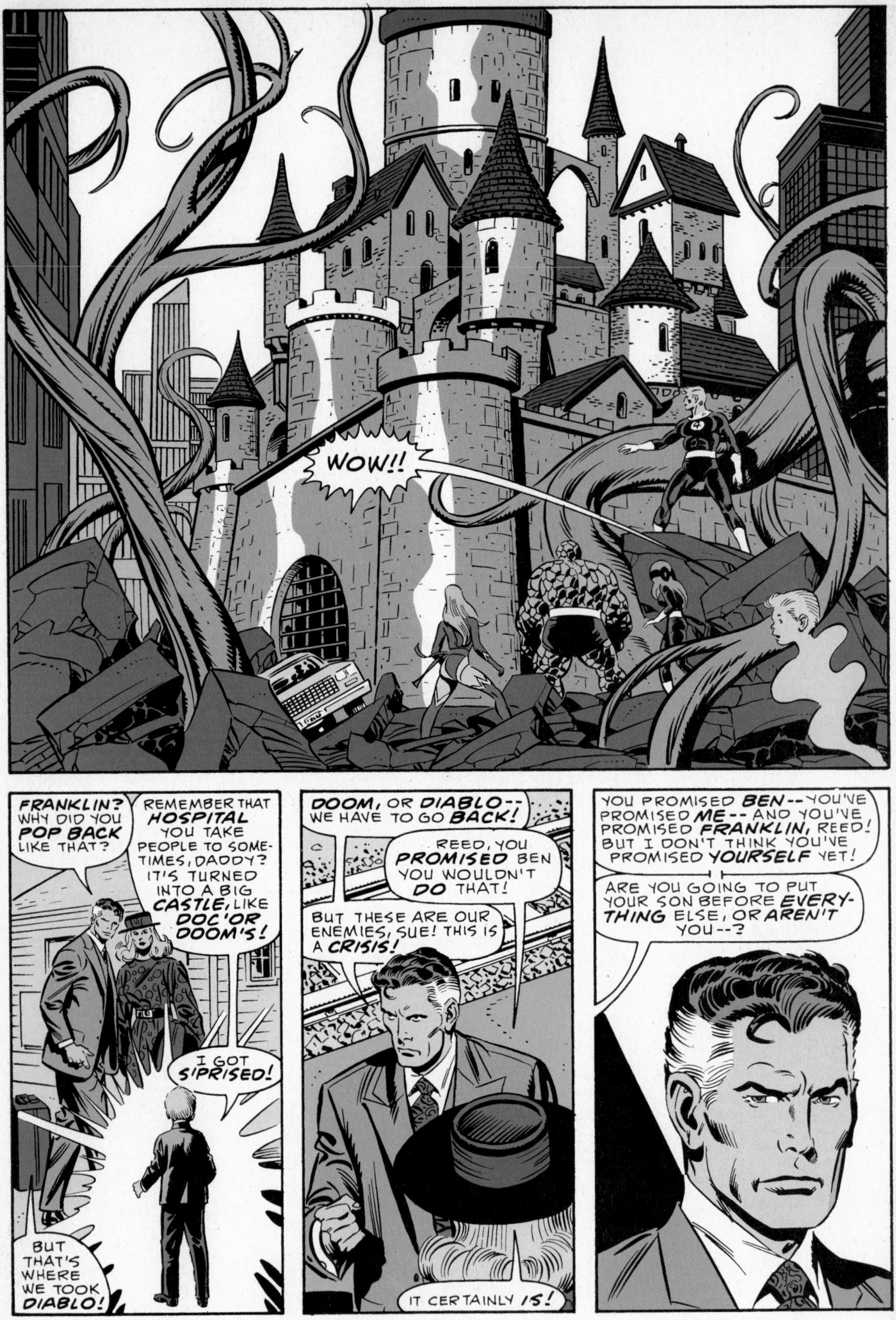
WOW!!
FRANKLIN? WHY DID YOU POP BACK LIKE THAT?
REMEMBER THAT HOSPITAL YOU TAKE PEOPLE TO SOME-TIMES, DADDY? IT'S TURNED INTO A BIG CASTLE, LIKE DOC 'OR DOOM'S!
I GOT S'PRISED!
BUT THAT'S WHERE WE TOOK DIABLO!
DOOM, OR DIABLO-- WE HAVE TO GO BACK!
REED, YOU PROMISED BEN YOU WOULDN'T DO THAT!
BUT THESE ARE OUR ENEMIES, SUE! THIS IS A CRISIS!
IT CERTAINLY IS!
YOU PROMISED BEN--YOU'VE PROMISED ME--AND YOU'VE PROMISED FRANKLIN, REED! BUT I DON'T THINK YOU'VE PROMISED YOURSELF YET!
ARE YOU GOING TO PUT YOUR SON BEFORE EVERY-THING ELSE, OR AREN'T YOU--?

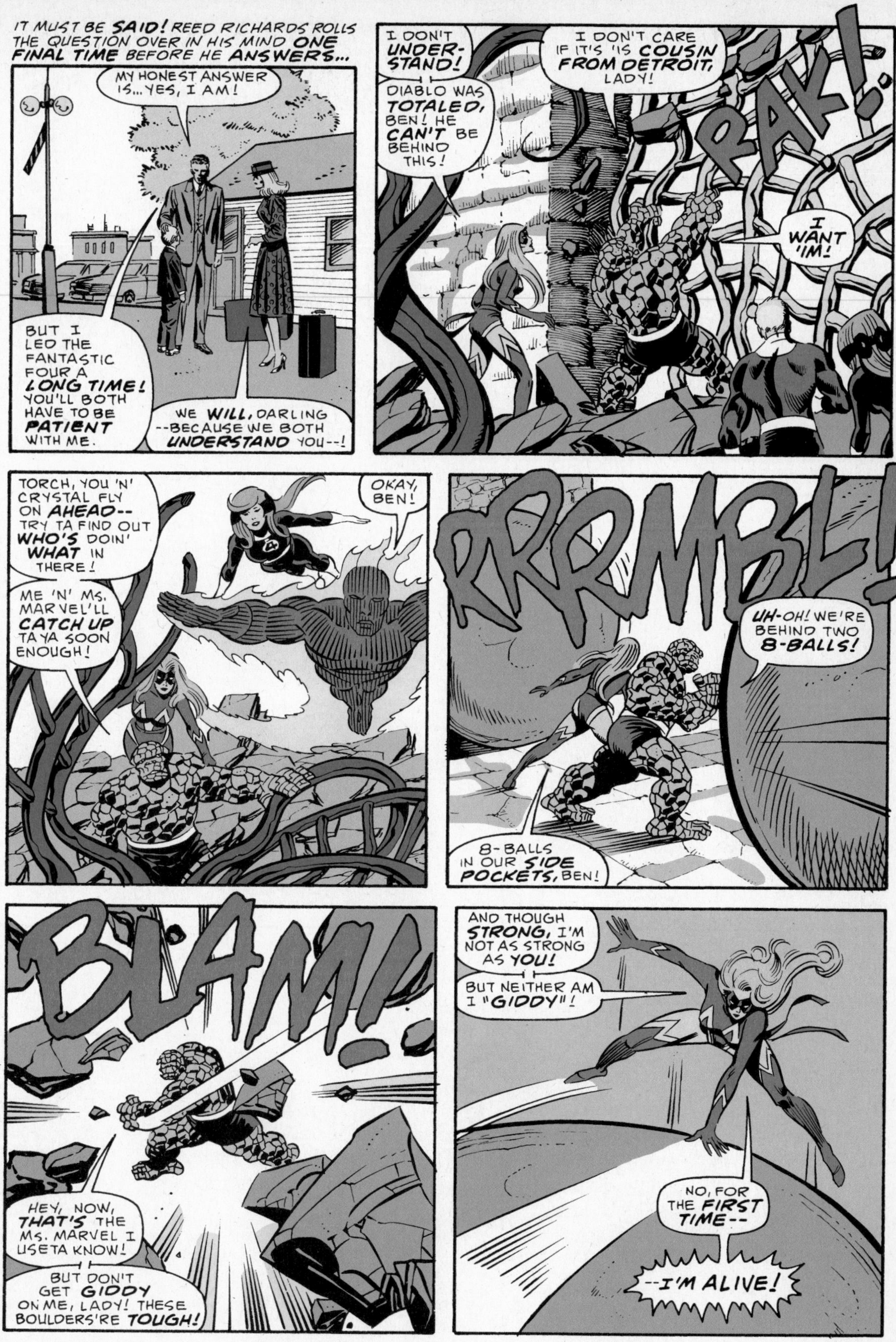
IT MUST BE SAID! REED RICHARDS ROLLS THE QUESTION OVER IN HIS MIND ONE FINAL TIME BEFORE HE ANSWERS...
MY HONEST ANSWER IS... YES, I AM!
BUT I LED THE FANTASTIC FOUR A LONG TIME! YOU'LL BOTH HAVE TO BE PATIENT WITH ME.
WE WILL, DARLING --BECAUSE WE BOTH UNDERSTAND YOU--!
I DON'T UNDERSTAND!
DIABLO WAS TOTALED, BEN! HE CAN'T BE BEHIND THIS!
I DON'T CARE IF IT'S 'IS COUSIN FROM DETROIT, LADY!
RAK!
I WANT 'IM!
TORCH, YOU 'N' CRYSTAL FLY ON AHEAD-- TRY TA FIND OUT WHO'S DOIN' WHAT IN THERE!
ME 'N' MS. MARVEL'LL CATCH UP TA YA SOON ENOUGH!
OKAY, BEN!
RRRMBL!
UH-OH! WE'RE BEHIND TWO 8-BALLS!
8-BALLS IN OUR SIDE POCKETS, BEN!
BLAM!
HEY, NOW, THAT'S THE MS. MARVEL I USETA KNOW!
BUT DON'T GET GIDDY ON ME, LADY! THESE BOULDERS'RE TOUGH!
AND THOUGH STRONG, I'M NOT AS STRONG AS YOU!
BUT NEITHER AM I "GIDDY"!
NO, FOR THE FIRST TIME--
--I'M ALIVE!

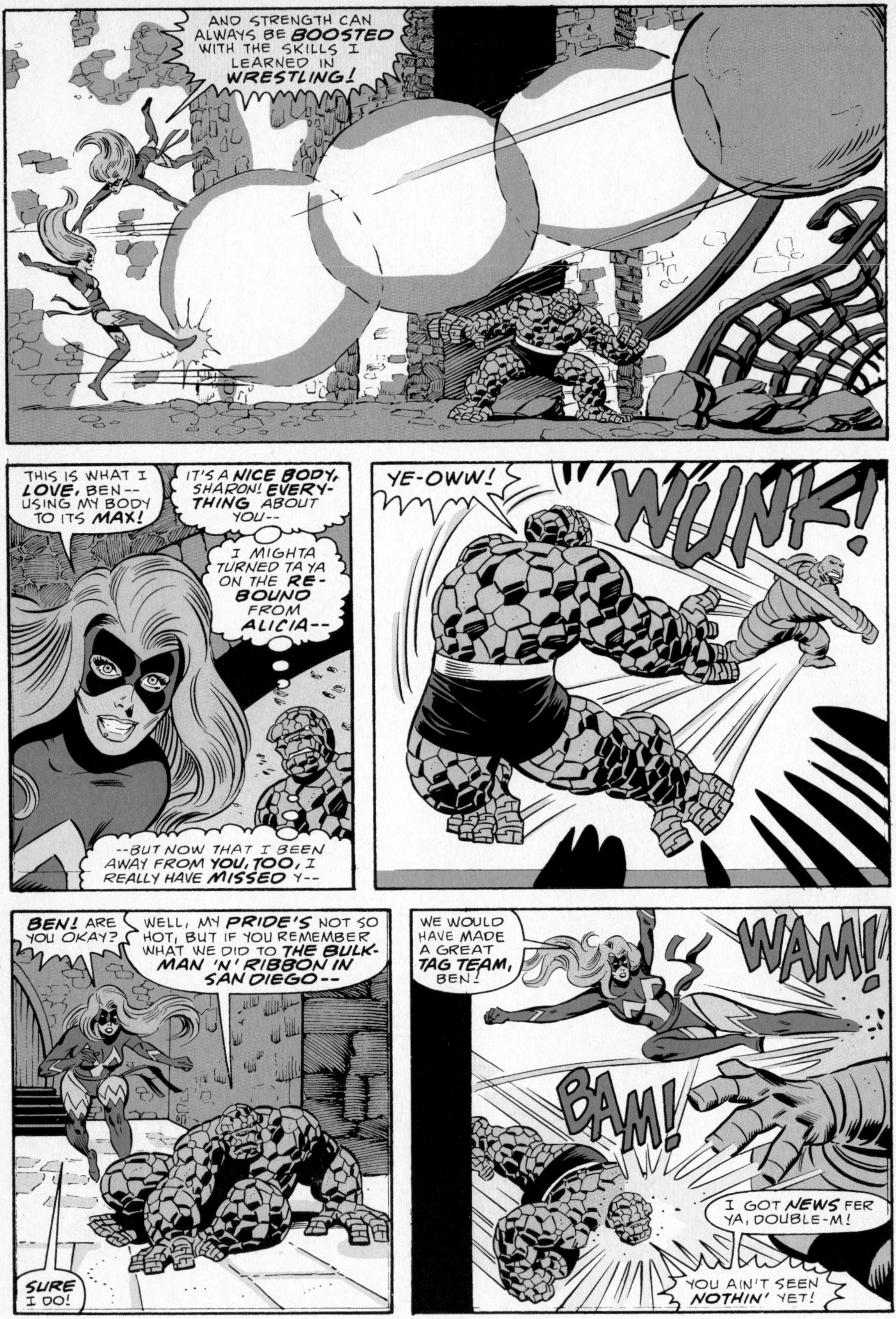
AND STRENGTH CAN ALWAYS BE BOOSTED WITH THE SKILLS I LEARNED IN WRESTLING!
THIS IS WHAT I LOVE, BEN-- USING MY BODY TO ITS MAX!
IT'S A NICE BODY, SHARON! EVERYTHING ABOUT YOU--
I MIGHTA TURNED TA YA ON THE REBOUND FROM ALICIA--
--BUT NOW THAT I BEEN AWAY FROM YOU, TOO, I REALLY HAVE MISSED Y--
YE-OWW!
WUNK!
BEN! ARE YOU OKAY?
WELL, MY PRIDE'S NOT SO HOT, BUT IF YOU REMEMBER WHAT WE DID TO THE BULKMAN 'N' RIBBON IN SAN DIEGO--
SURE I DO!
WE WOULD HAVE MADE A GREAT TAG TEAM, BEN!
WAM!
BAM!
I GOT NEWS FER YA, DOUBLE-M!
YOU AIN'T SEEN NOTHIN' YET!

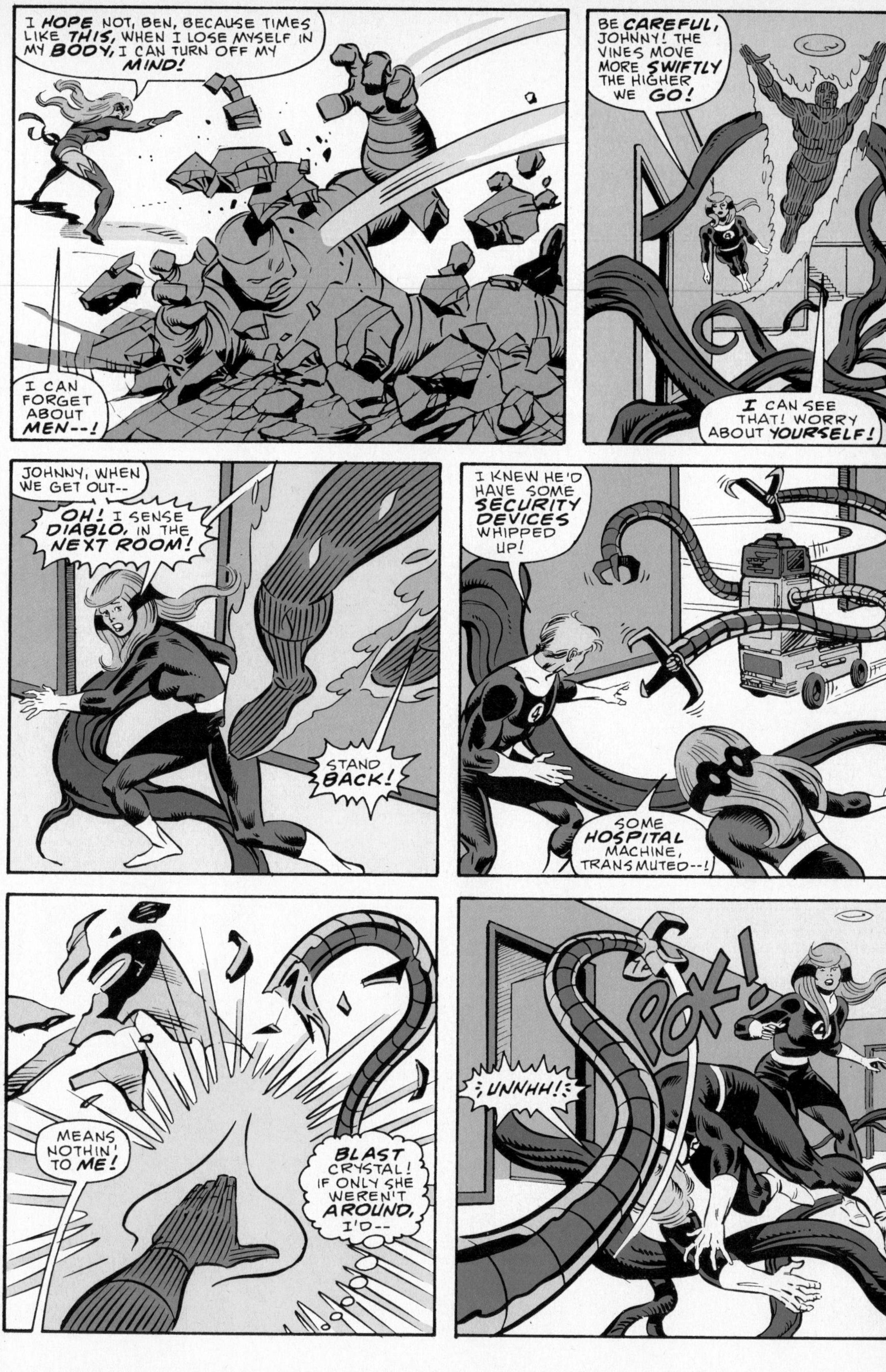
I HOPE NOT, BEN, BECAUSE TIMES LIKE THIS, WHEN I LOSE MYSELF IN MY BODY, I CAN TURN OFF MY MIND!
I CAN FORGET ABOUT MEN--!
BE CAREFUL, JOHNNY! THE VINES MOVE MORE SWIFTLY THE HIGHER WE GO!
I CAN SEE THAT! WORRY ABOUT YOURSELF!
JOHNNY, WHEN WE GET OUT--
OH! I SENSE DIABLO, IN THE NEXT ROOM!
STAND BACK!
I KNEW HE'D HAVE SOME SECURITY DEVICES WHIPPED UP!
SOME HOSPITAL MACHINE, TRANSMUTED--!
MEANS NOTHIN' TO ME!
BLAST CRYSTAL! IF ONLY SHE WEREN'T AROUND, I'D--
UNNHH!
POK!

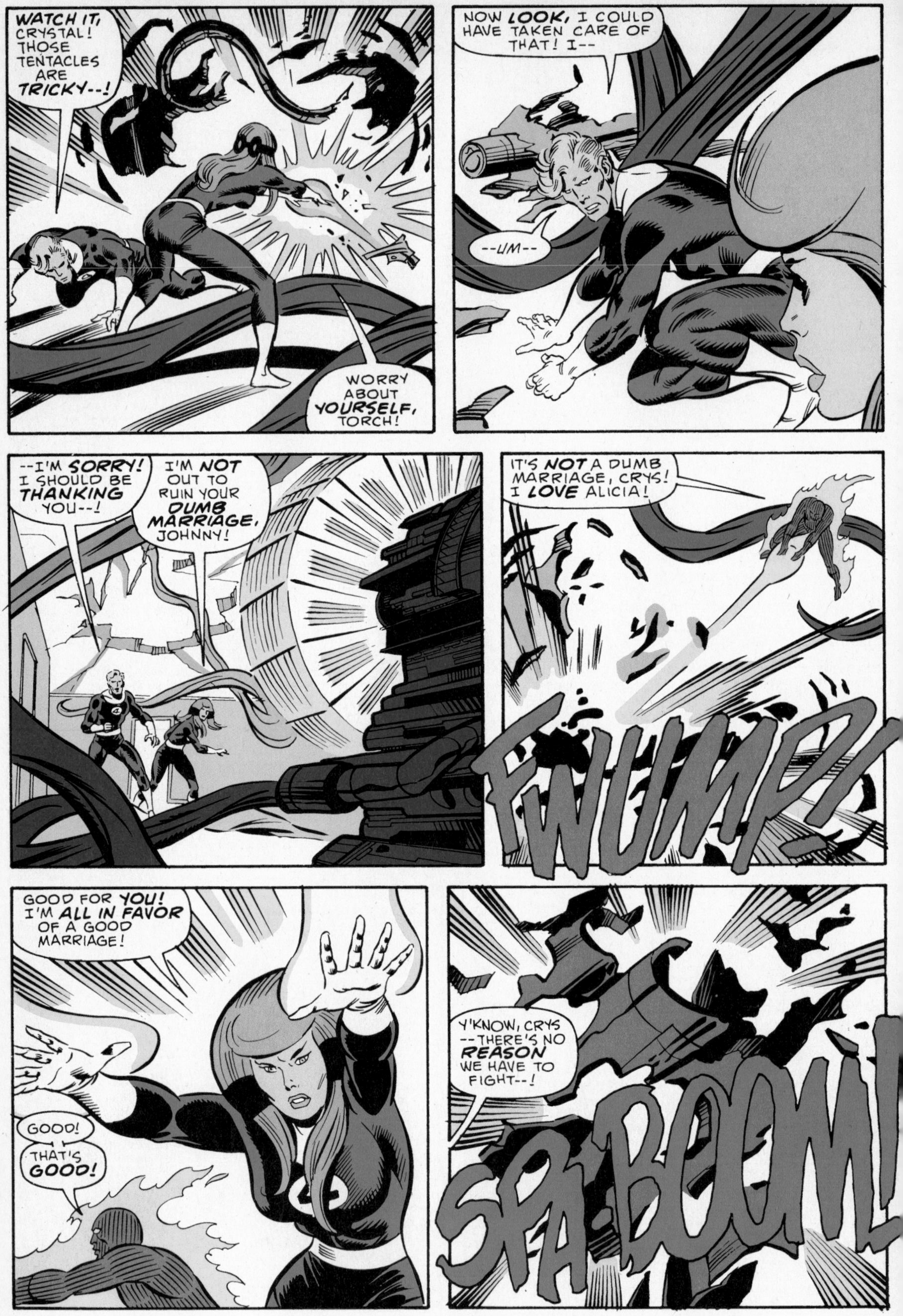
WATCH IT, CRYSTAL! THOSE TENTACLES ARE TRICKY--!
WORRY ABOUT YOURSELF, TORCH!
NOW LOOK, I COULD HAVE TAKEN CARE OF THAT! I--
--UM--
--I'M SORRY! I SHOULD BE THANKING YOU--!
I'M NOT OUT TO RUIN YOUR DUMB MARRIAGE, JOHNNY!
IT'S NOT A DUMB MARRIAGE, CRYS! I LOVE ALICIA!
FWUMP!
GOOD FOR YOU! I'M ALL IN FAVOR OF A GOOD MARRIAGE!
GOOD! THAT'S GOOD!
Y'KNOW, CRYS --THERE'S NO REASON WE HAVE TO FIGHT--!
SPA-BOOM!

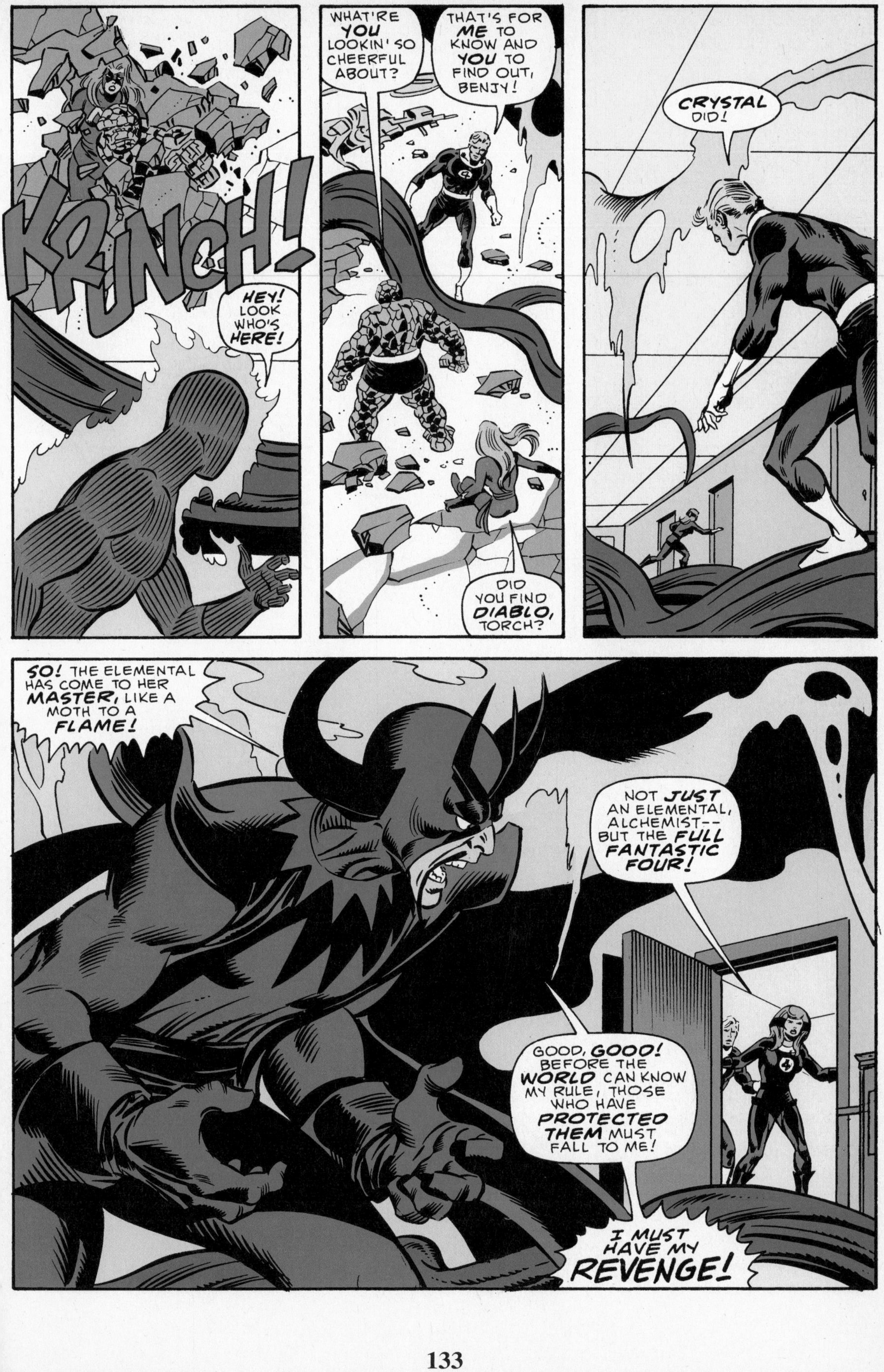
KRUNCH!
HEY! LOOK WHO'S HERE!
WHAT'RE YOU LOOKIN' SO CHEERFUL ABOUT?
THAT'S FOR ME TO KNOW AND YOU TO FIND OUT, BENJY!
DID YOU FIND DIABLO, TORCH?
CRYSTAL DID!
SO! THE ELEMENTAL HAS COME TO HER MASTER, LIKE A MOTH TO A FLAME!
NOT JUST AN ELEMENTAL, ALCHEMIST-- BUT THE FULL FANTASTIC FOUR!
GOOD, GOOD! BEFORE THE WORLD CAN KNOW MY RULE, THOSE WHO HAVE PROTECTED THEM MUST FALL TO ME!
I MUST HAVE MY REVENGE!

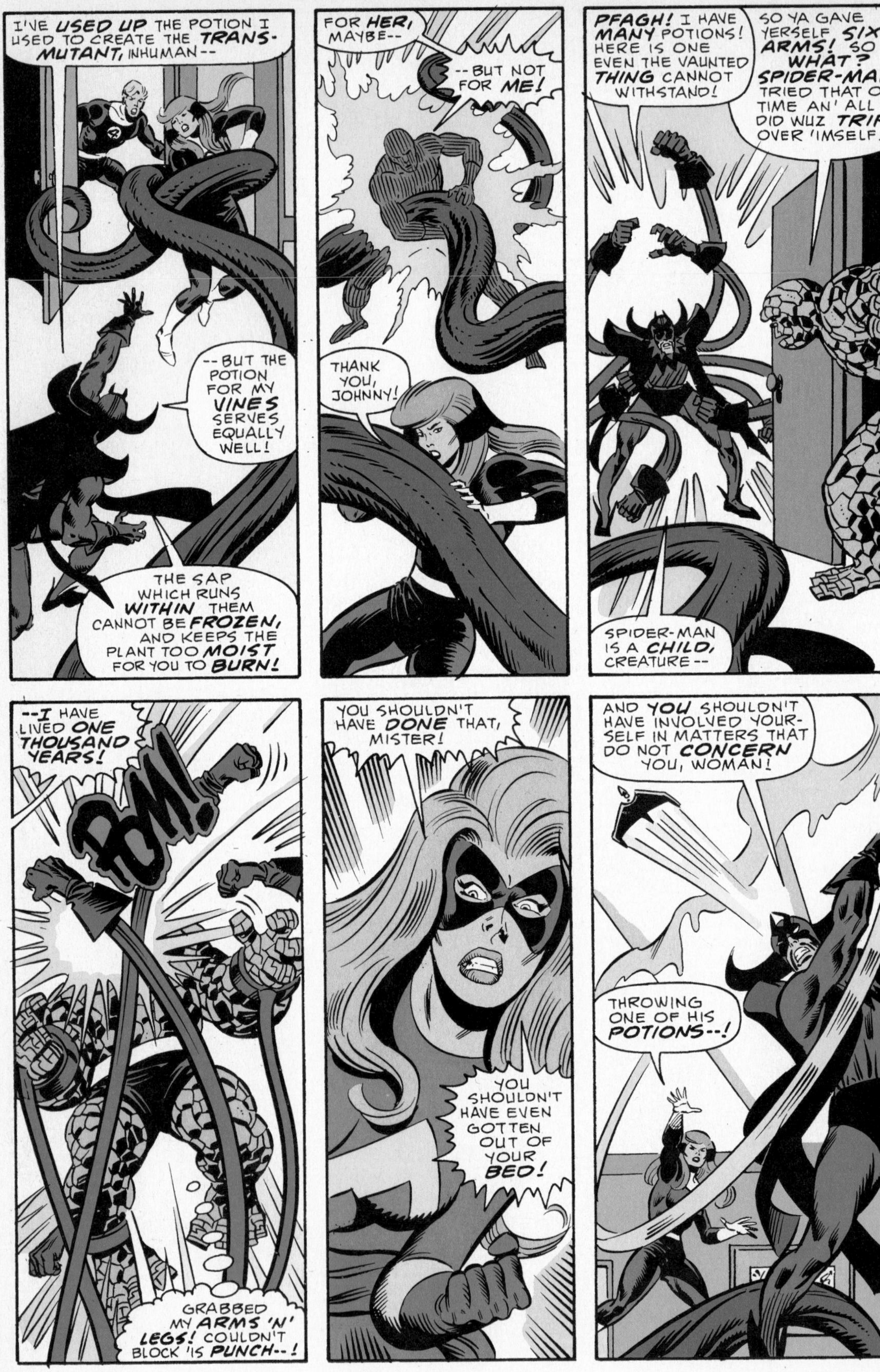
I'VE USED UP THE POTION I USED TO CREATE THE TRANS-MUTANT, INHUMAN--
--BUT THE POTION FOR MY VINES SERVES EQUALLY WELL!
THE SAP WHICH RUNS WITHIN THEM CANNOT BE FROZEN, AND KEEPS THE PLANT TOO MOIST FOR YOU TO BURN!
FOR HER, MAYBE--
--BUT NOT FOR ME!
THANK YOU, JOHNNY!
PFAGH! I HAVE MANY POTIONS! HERE IS ONE EVEN THE VAUNTED THING CANNOT WITHSTAND!
SO YA GAVE YERSELF SIX ARMS! SO WHAT? SPIDER-MAN TRIED THAT ONE TIME AN' ALL HE DID WUZ TRIP OVER 'IMSELF!
SPIDER-MAN IS A CHILD, CREATURE--
--I HAVE LIVED ONE THOUSAND YEARS!
POM!
GRABBED MY ARMS 'N' LEGS! COULDN'T BLOCK 'IS PUNCH--!
YOU SHOULDN'T HAVE DONE THAT, MISTER!
YOU SHOULDN'T HAVE EVEN GOTTEN OUT OF YOUR BED!
AND YOU SHOULDN'T HAVE INVOLVED YOUR-SELF IN MATTERS THAT DO NOT CONCERN YOU, WOMAN!
THROWING ONE OF HIS POTIONS--!

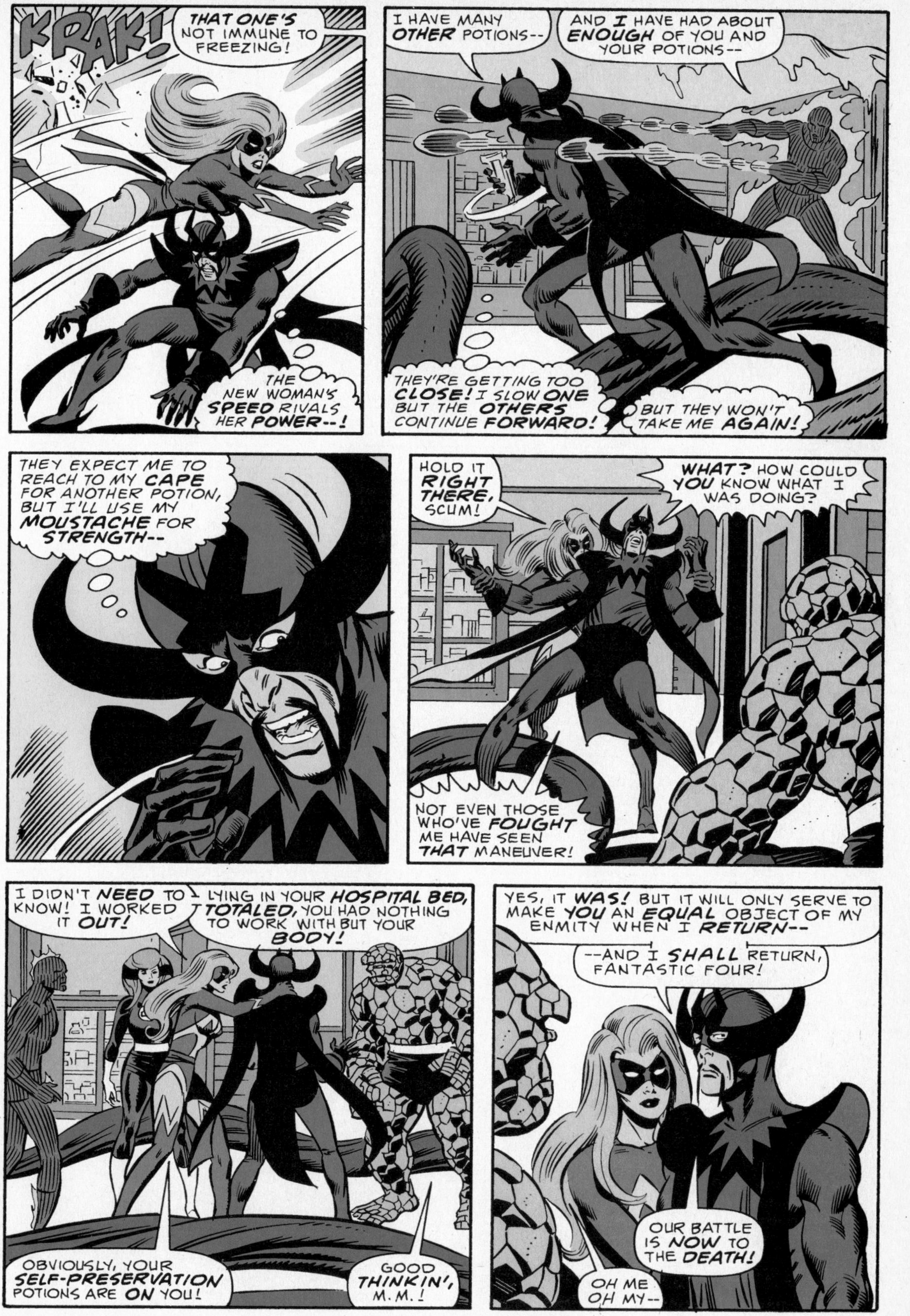
KRAK!
THAT ONE'S NOT IMMUNE TO FREEZING!
THE NEW WOMAN'S SPEED RIVALS HER POWER--!
I HAVE MANY OTHER POTIONS--
AND I HAVE HAD ABOUT ENOUGH OF YOU AND YOUR POTIONS--
THEY'RE GETTING TOO CLOSE! I SLOW ONE BUT THE OTHERS CONTINUE FORWARD!
BUT THEY WON'T TAKE ME AGAIN!
THEY EXPECT ME TO REACH TO MY CAPE FOR ANOTHER POTION, BUT I'LL USE MY MOUSTACHE FOR STRENGTH--
HOLD IT RIGHT THERE, SCUM!
WHAT? HOW COULD YOU KNOW WHAT I WAS DOING?
NOT EVEN THOSE WHO'VE FOUGHT ME HAVE SEEN THAT MANEUVER!
I DIDN'T NEED TO KNOW! I WORKED IT OUT!
LYING IN YOUR HOSPITAL BED, TOTALED, YOU HAD NOTHING TO WORK WITH BUT YOUR BODY!
OBVIOUSLY, YOUR SELF-PRESERVATION POTIONS ARE ON YOU!
GOOD THINKIN', M.M.!
YES, IT WAS! BUT IT WILL ONLY SERVE TO MAKE YOU AN EQUAL OBJECT OF MY ENMITY WHEN I RETURN--
--AND I SHALL RETURN, FANTASTIC FOUR!
OUR BATTLE IS NOW TO THE DEATH!
OH ME OH MY--

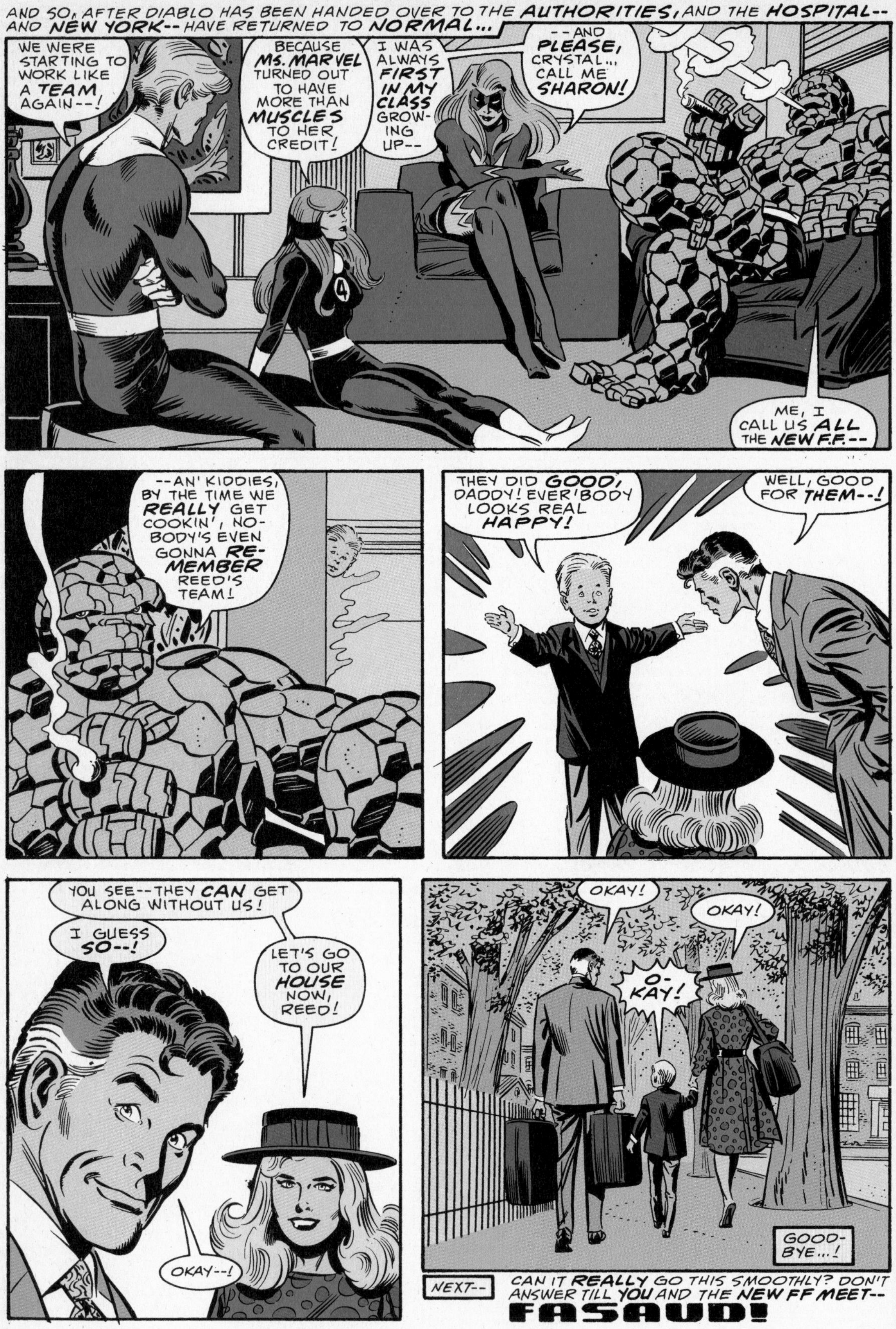
AND SO, AFTER DIABLO HAS BEEN HANDED OVER TO THE AUTHORITIES, AND THE HOSPITAL-- AND NEW YORK--HAVE RETURNED TO NORMAL...
WE WERE STARTING TO WORK LIKE A TEAM AGAIN--!
BECAUSE MS. MARVEL TURNED OUT TO HAVE MORE THAN MUSCLES TO HER CREDIT!
I WAS ALWAYS FIRST IN MY CLASS GROWING UP--
--AND PLEASE, CRYSTAL... CALL ME SHARON!
ME, I CALL US ALL THE NEW F.F.--
--AN' KIDDIES, BY THE TIME WE REALLY GET COOKIN', NOBODY'S EVEN GONNA REMEMBER REED'S TEAM!
THEY DID GOOD, DADDY! EVER'BODY LOOKS REAL HAPPY!
WELL, GOOD FOR THEM--!
YOU SEE--THEY CAN GET ALONG WITHOUT US!
I GUESS SO--!
LET'S GO TO OUR HOUSE NOW, REED!
OKAY--!
OKAY!
OKAY!
O-KAY!
GOOD-BYE...!
NEXT--
CAN IT REALLY GO THIS SMOOTHLY? DON'T ANSWER TILL YOU AND THE NEW FF MEET--
FASAUD!

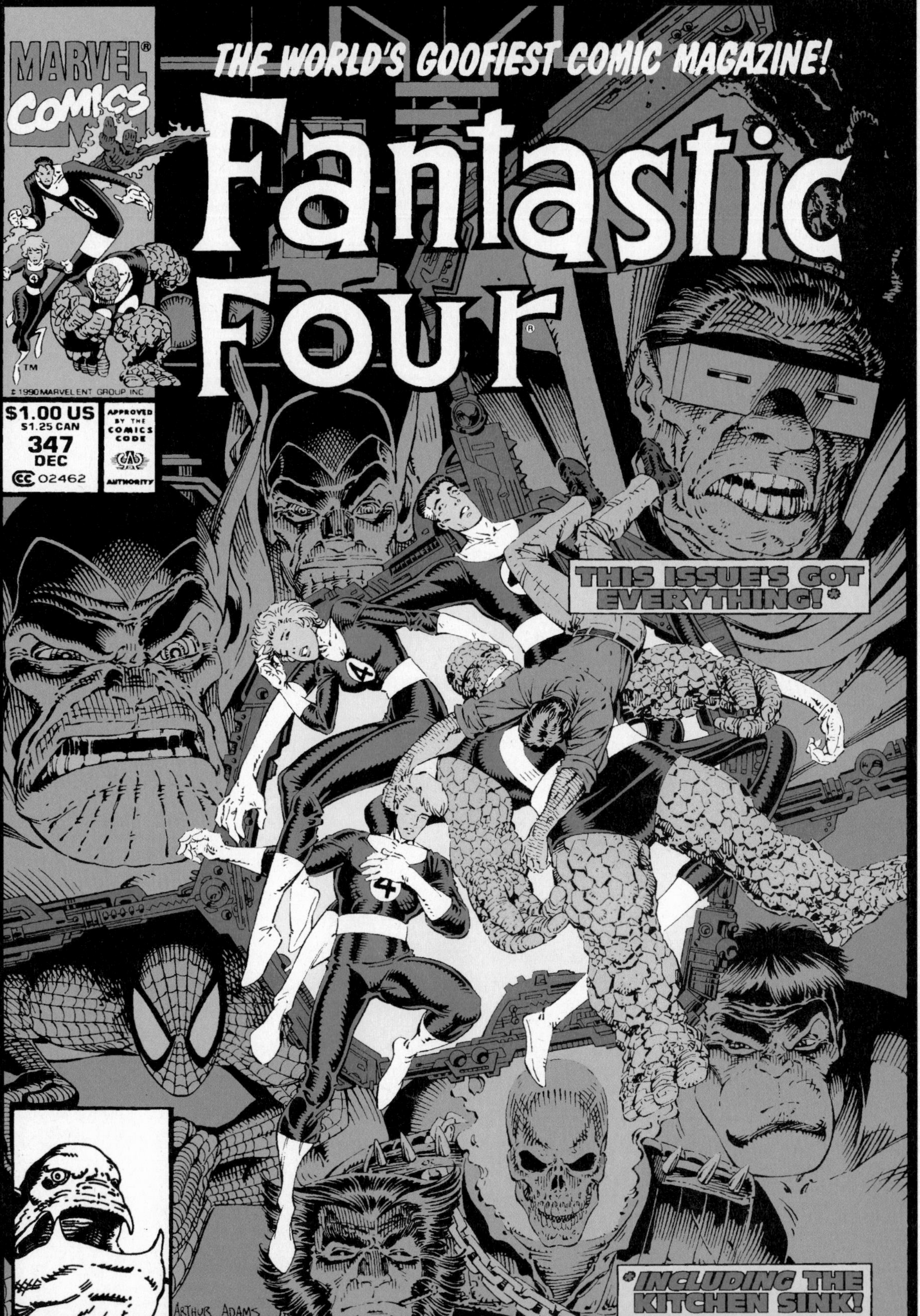
MARVEL COMICS
THE WORLD'S GOOFIEST COMIC MAGAZINE!
Fantastic Four
© 1990 MARVEL ENT GROUP INC
$1.00 US
$1.25 CAN
347
DEC
02462
APPROVED BY THE COMICS CODE AUTHORITY
THIS ISSUE'S GOT EVERYTHING!*
*INCLUDING THE KITCHEN SINK!
ARTHUR ADAMS 9-90
ART THIBERT

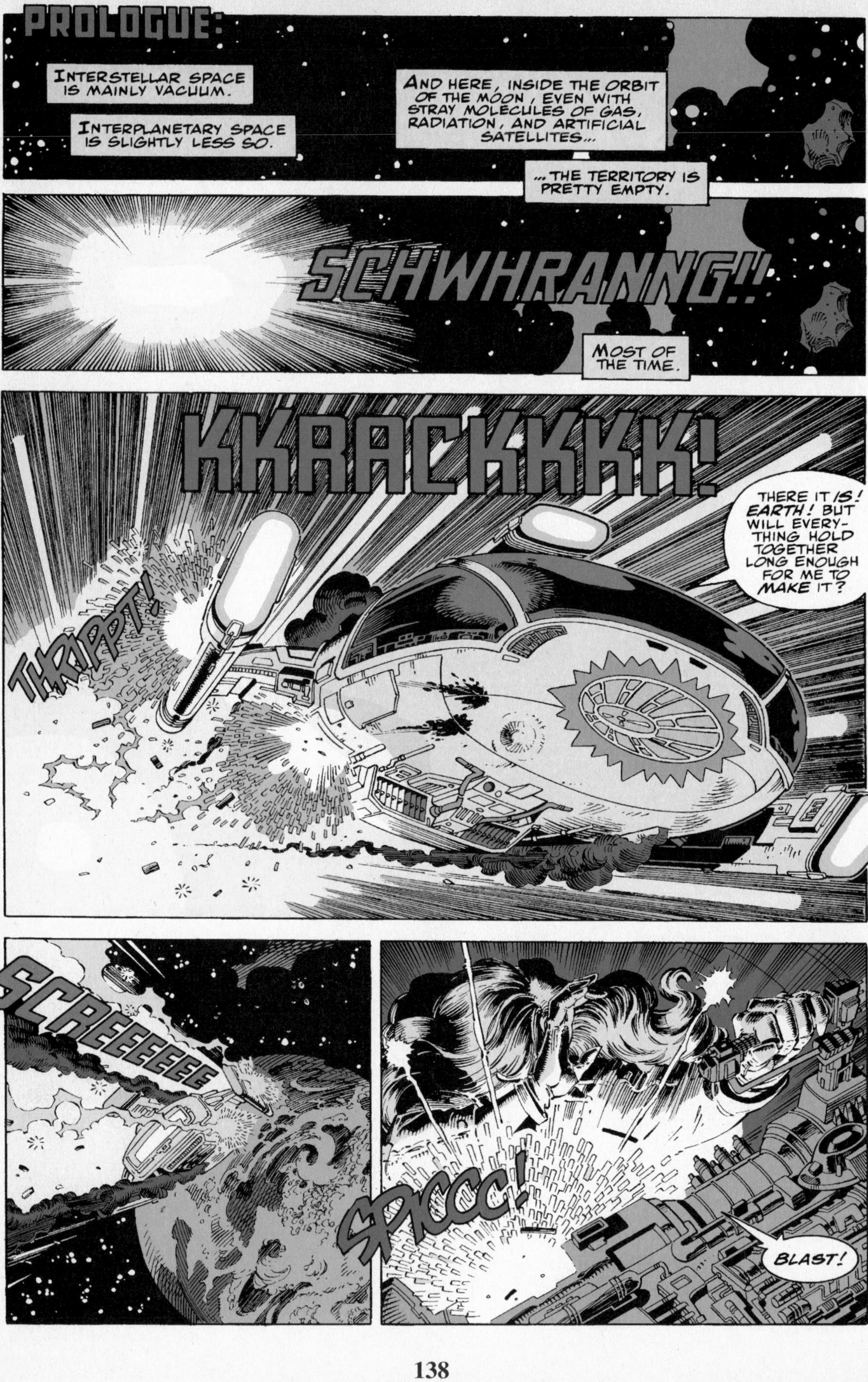
PROLOGUE:
INTERSTELLAR SPACE IS MAINLY VACUUM.
INTERPLANETARY SPACE IS SLIGHTLY LESS SO.
AND HERE, INSIDE THE ORBIT OF THE MOON, EVEN WITH STRAY MOLECULES OF GAS, RADIATION, AND ARTIFICIAL SATELLITES...
...THE TERRITORY IS PRETTY EMPTY.
SCHWHRANNG!!
MOST OF THE TIME.
KKRACKKKK!
THERE IT IS! EARTH! BUT WILL EVERYTHING HOLD TOGETHER LONG ENOUGH FOR ME TO MAKE IT?
THRIPPT!
SCREEEEEEE
SPICCC!
BLAST!

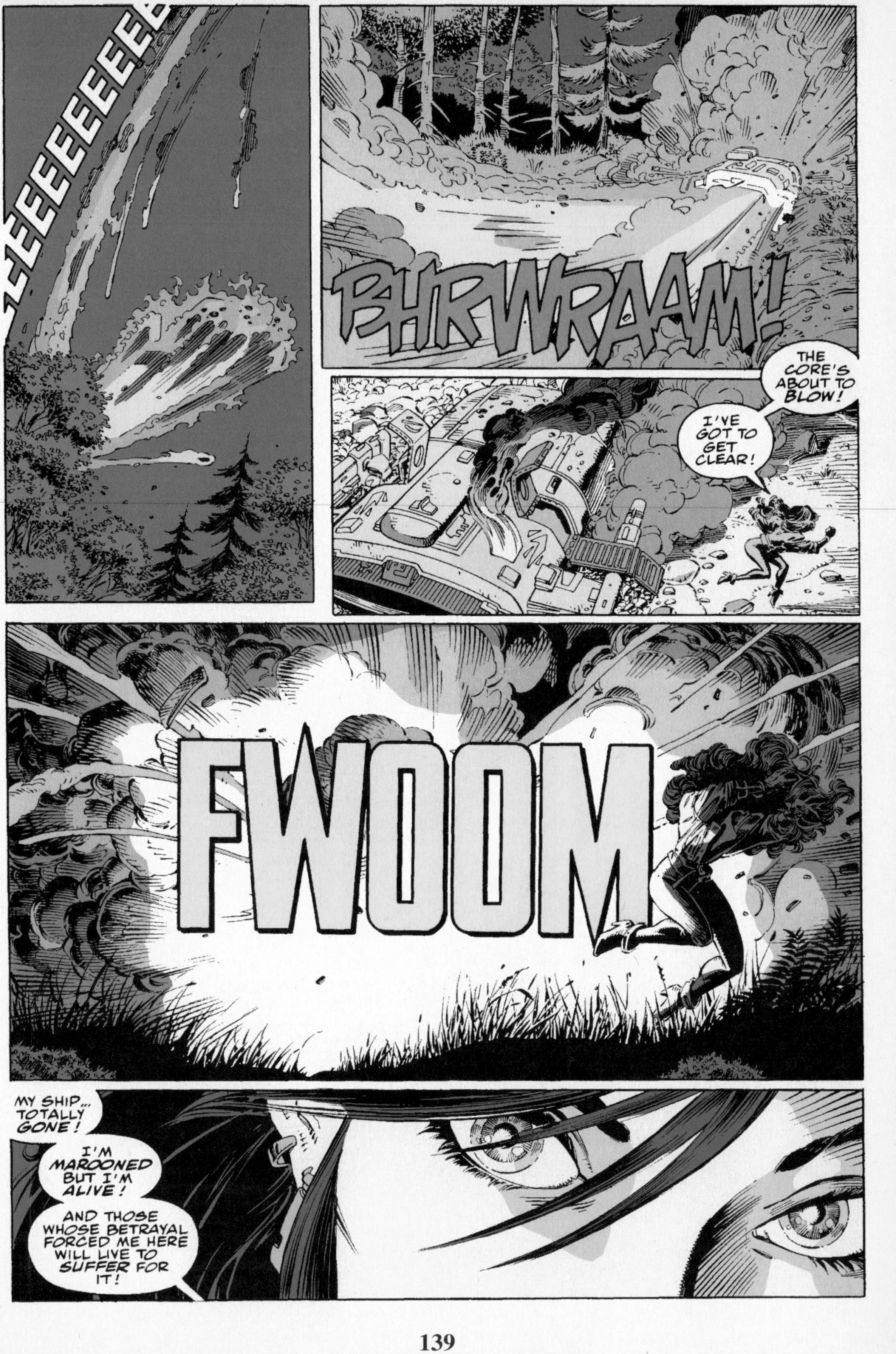
EEEEEEEEEEE
BHRWRAAM!
THE CORE'S ABOUT TO BLOW!
I'VE GOT TO GET CLEAR!
FWOOM
MY SHIP... TOTALLY GONE!
I'M MAROONED BUT I'M ALIVE!
AND THOSE WHOSE BETRAYAL FORCED ME HERE WILL LIVE TO SUFFER FOR IT!

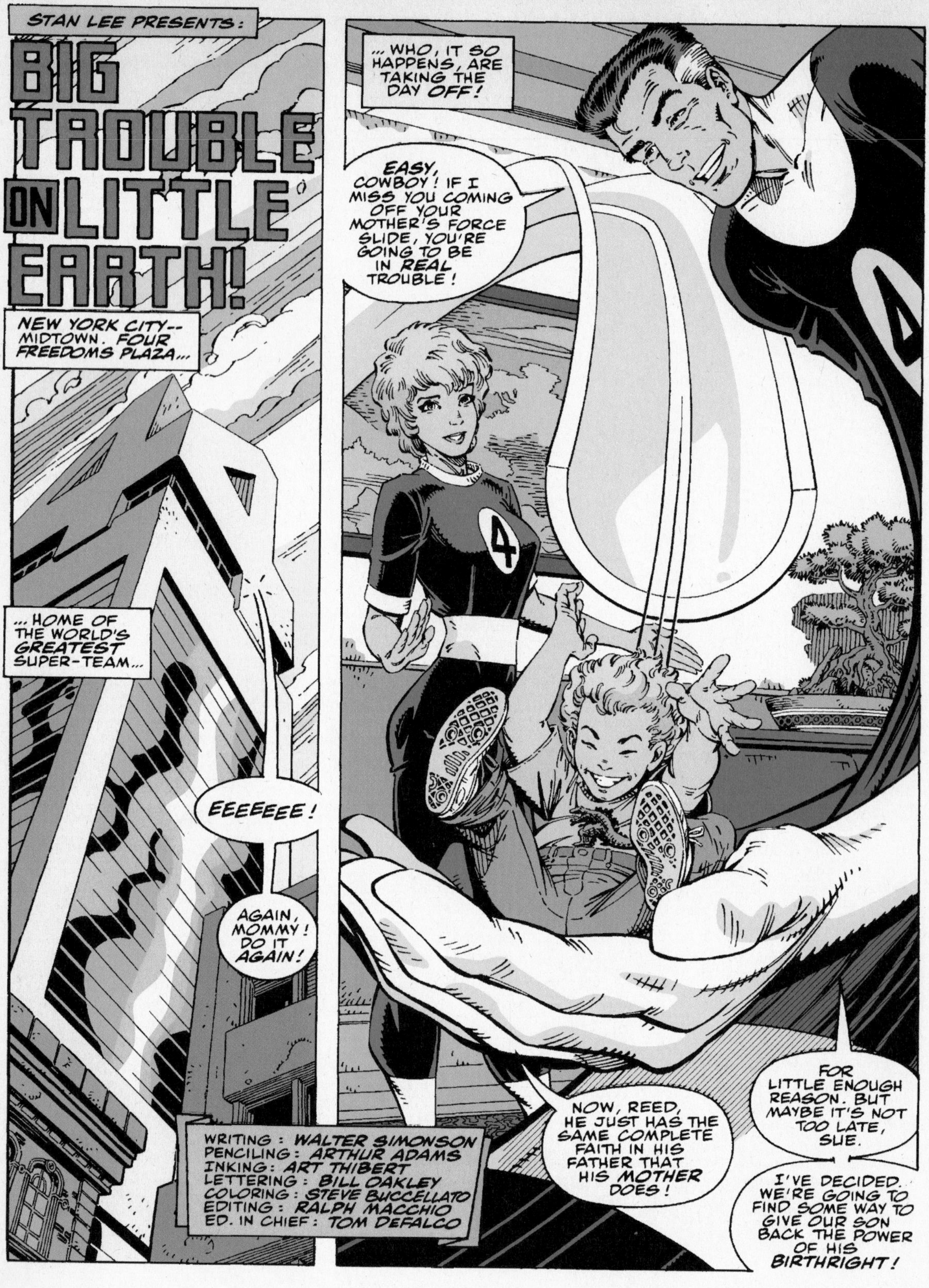
STAN LEE PRESENTS:
BIG TROUBLE ON LITTLE EARTH!
NEW YORK CITY-- MIDTOWN. FOUR FREEDOMS PLAZA...
...HOME OF THE WORLD'S GREATEST SUPER-TEAM...
EEEEEEE!
AGAIN, MOMMY! DO IT AGAIN!
...WHO, IT SO HAPPENS, ARE TAKING THE DAY OFF!
EASY, COWBOY! IF I MISS YOU COMING OFF YOUR MOTHER'S FORCE SLIDE, YOU'RE GOING TO BE IN REAL TROUBLE!
WRITING: WALTER SIMONSON PENCILING: ARTHUR ADAMS INKING: ART THIBERT LETTERING: BILL OAKLEY COLORING: STEVE BUCCELLATO EDITING: RALPH MACCHIO ED. IN CHIEF: TOM DEFALCO
NOW, REED, HE JUST HAS THE SAME COMPLETE FAITH IN HIS FATHER THAT HIS MOTHER DOES!
FOR LITTLE ENOUGH REASON. BUT MAYBE IT'S NOT TOO LATE, SUE.
I'VE DECIDED. WE'RE GOING TO FIND SOME WAY TO GIVE OUR SON BACK THE POWER OF HIS BIRTHRIGHT!

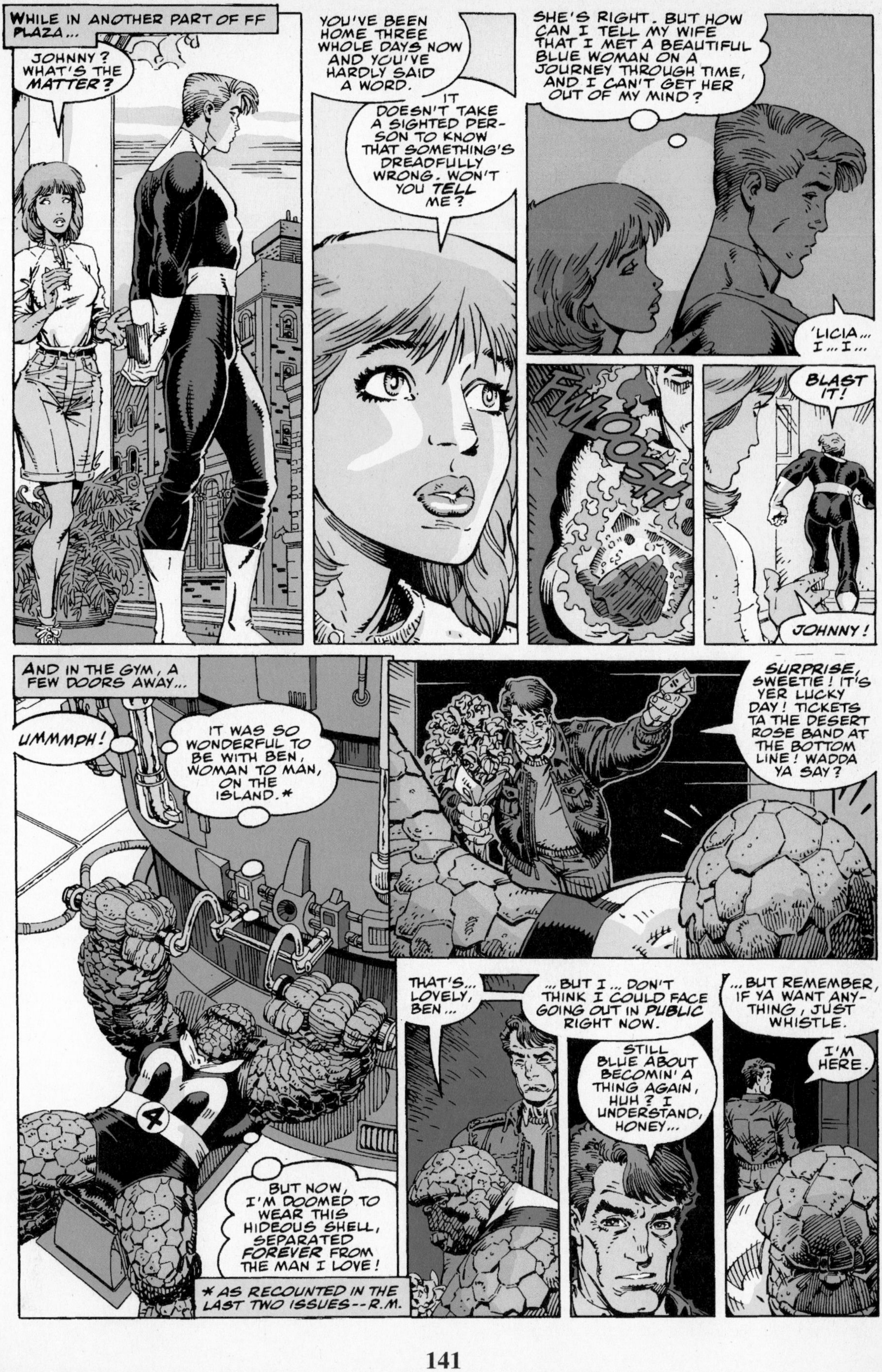
WHILE IN ANOTHER PART OF FF PLAZA...
JOHNNY? WHAT'S THE MATTER?
YOU'VE BEEN HOME THREE WHOLE DAYS NOW AND YOU'VE HARDLY SAID A WORD.
IT DOESN'T TAKE A SIGHTED PERSON TO KNOW THAT SOMETHING'S DREADFULLY WRONG. WON'T YOU TELL ME?
SHE'S RIGHT. BUT HOW CAN I TELL MY WIFE THAT I MET A BEAUTIFUL BLUE WOMAN ON A JOURNEY THROUGH TIME, AND I CAN'T GET HER OUT OF MY MIND?
'LICIA... I... I...
FWOOSH
BLAST IT!
JOHNNY!
AND IN THE GYM, A FEW DOORS AWAY...
UMMMPH!
IT WAS SO WONDERFUL TO BE WITH BEN, WOMAN TO MAN, ON THE ISLAND.*
BUT NOW, I'M DOOMED TO WEAR THIS HIDEOUS SHELL, SEPARATED FOREVER FROM THE MAN I LOVE!
*AS RECOUNTED IN THE LAST TWO ISSUES--R.M.
SURPRISE, SWEETIE! IT'S YER LUCKY DAY! TICKETS TA THE DESERT ROSE BAND AT THE BOTTOM LINE! WADDA YA SAY?
THAT'S... LOVELY, BEN...
...BUT I... DON'T THINK I COULD FACE GOING OUT IN PUBLIC RIGHT NOW.
STILL BLUE ABOUT BECOMIN' A THING AGAIN, HUH? I UNDERSTAND, HONEY...
...BUT REMEMBER, IF YA WANT ANYTHING, JUST WHISTLE.
I'M HERE.

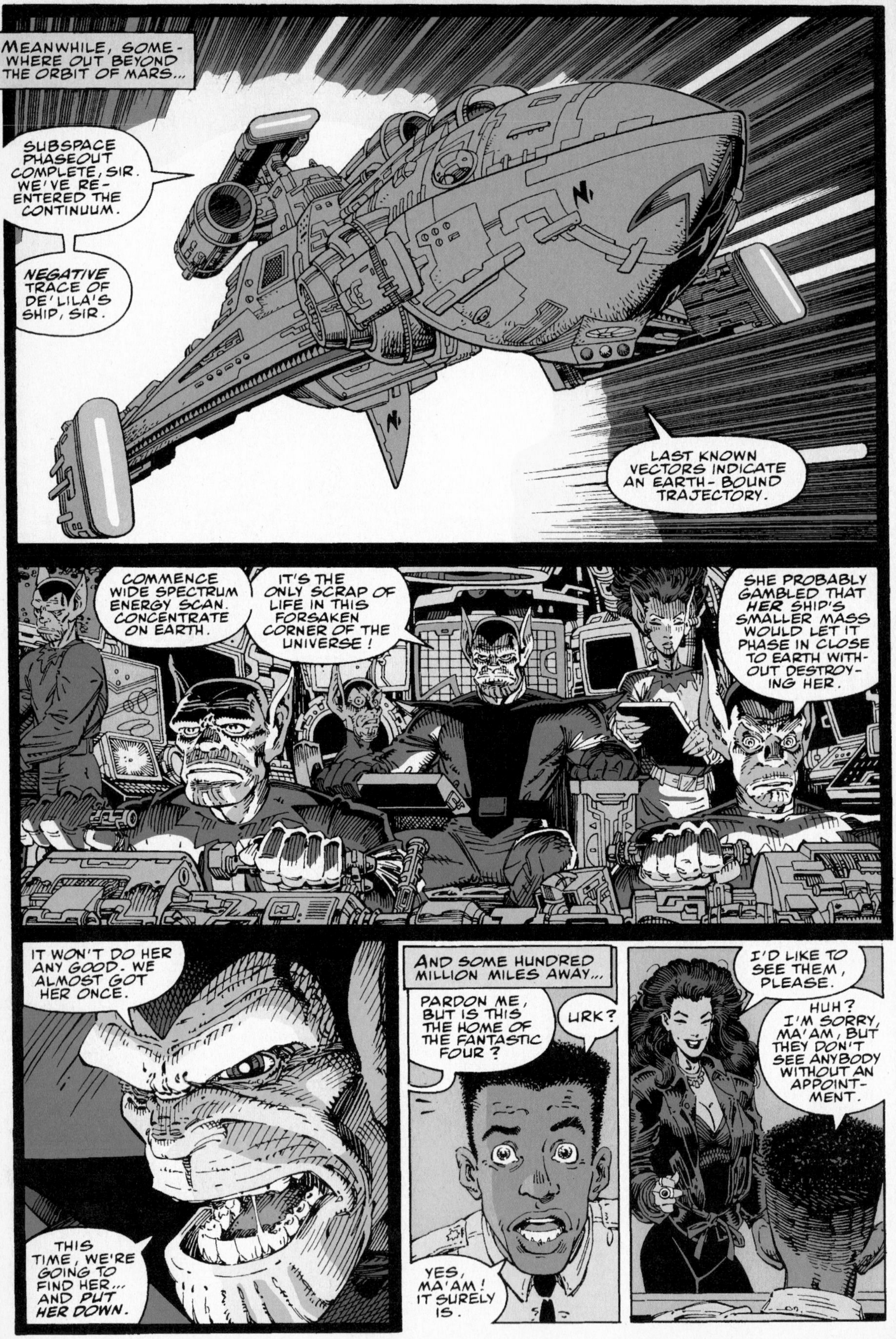
MEANWHILE, SOMEWHERE OUT BEYOND THE ORBIT OF MARS...
SUBSPACE PHASEOUT COMPLETE, SIR. WE'VE RE-ENTERED THE CONTINUUM.
NEGATIVE TRACE OF DE'LILA'S SHIP, SIR.
LAST KNOWN VECTORS INDICATE AN EARTH-BOUND TRAJECTORY.
COMMENCE WIDE SPECTRUM ENERGY SCAN. CONCENTRATE ON EARTH.
IT'S THE ONLY SCRAP OF LIFE IN THIS FORSAKEN CORNER OF THE UNIVERSE!
SHE PROBABLY GAMBLED THAT HER SHIP'S SMALLER MASS WOULD LET IT PHASE IN CLOSE TO EARTH WITHOUT DESTROYING HER.
IT WON'T DO HER ANY GOOD. WE ALMOST GOT HER ONCE.
THIS TIME, WE'RE GOING TO FIND HER... AND PUT HER DOWN.
AND SOME HUNDRED MILLION MILES AWAY...
PARDON ME, BUT IS THIS THE HOME OF THE FANTASTIC FOUR?
URK?
YES, MA'AM! IT SURELY IS.
I'D LIKE TO SEE THEM, PLEASE.
HUH? I'M SORRY, MA'AM, BUT THEY DON'T SEE ANYBODY WITHOUT AN APPOINTMENT.

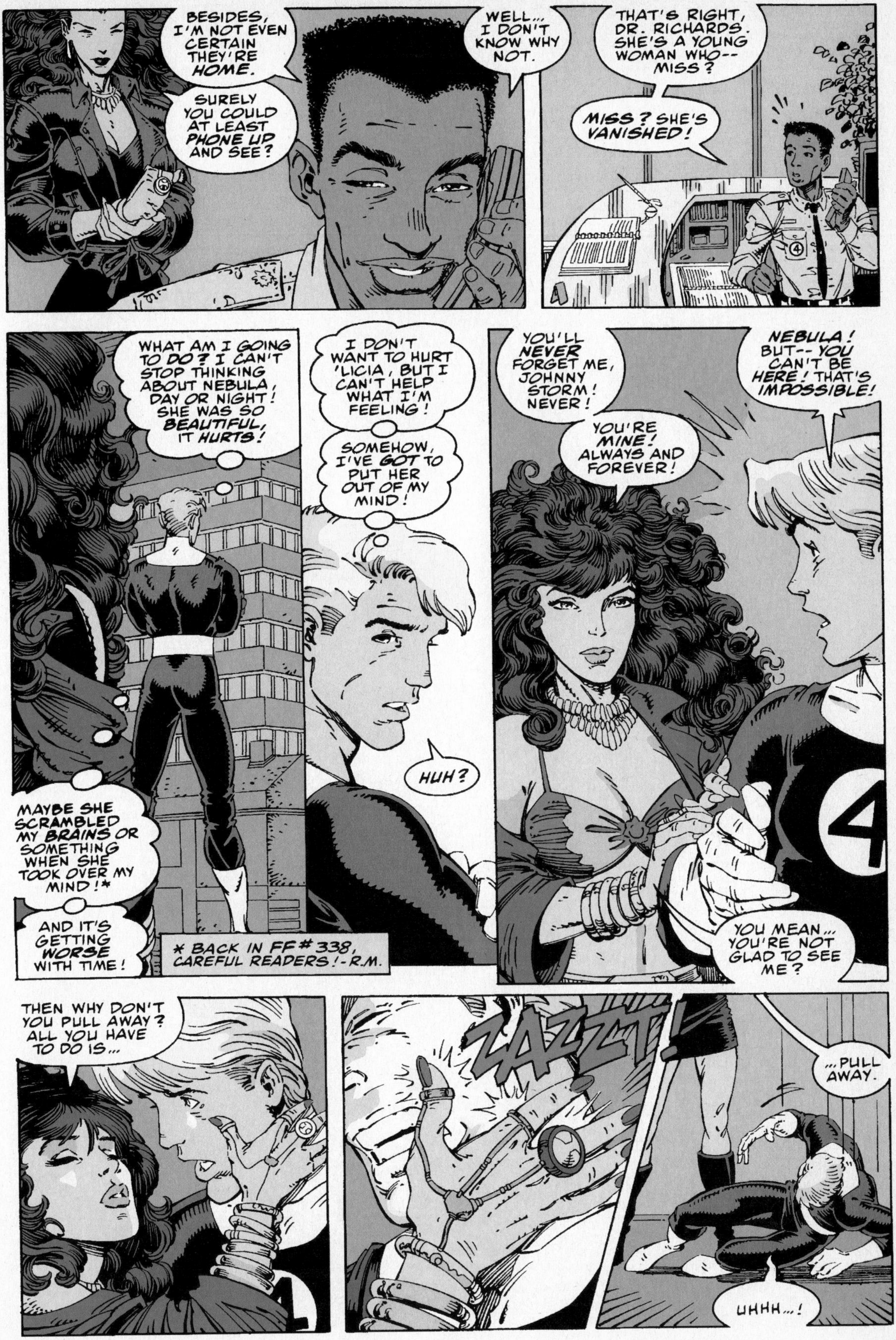
BESIDES, I'M NOT EVEN CERTAIN THEY'RE HOME.
SURELY YOU COULD AT LEAST PHONE UP AND SEE?
WELL... I DON'T KNOW WHY NOT.
THAT'S RIGHT, DR. RICHARDS. SHE'S A YOUNG WOMAN WHO-- MISS?
MISS? SHE'S VANISHED!
WHAT AM I GOING TO DO? I CAN'T STOP THINKING ABOUT NEBULA, DAY OR NIGHT! SHE WAS SO BEAUTIFUL, IT HURTS!
MAYBE SHE SCRAMBLED MY BRAINS OR SOMETHING WHEN SHE TOOK OVER MY MIND!*
AND IT'S GETTING WORSE WITH TIME!
I DON'T WANT TO HURT 'LICIA, BUT I CAN'T HELP WHAT I'M FEELING!
SOMEHOW, I'VE GOT TO PUT HER OUT OF MY MIND!
HUH?
* BACK IN FF #338, CAREFUL READERS! -R.M.
YOU'LL NEVER FORGET ME, JOHNNY STORM! NEVER!
YOU'RE MINE! ALWAYS AND FOREVER!
NEBULA! BUT-- YOU CAN'T BE HERE! THAT'S IMPOSSIBLE!
YOU MEAN... YOU'RE NOT GLAD TO SEE ME?
THEN WHY DON'T YOU PULL AWAY? ALL YOU HAVE TO DO IS...
ZAZZT!
...PULL AWAY.
UHHH...!

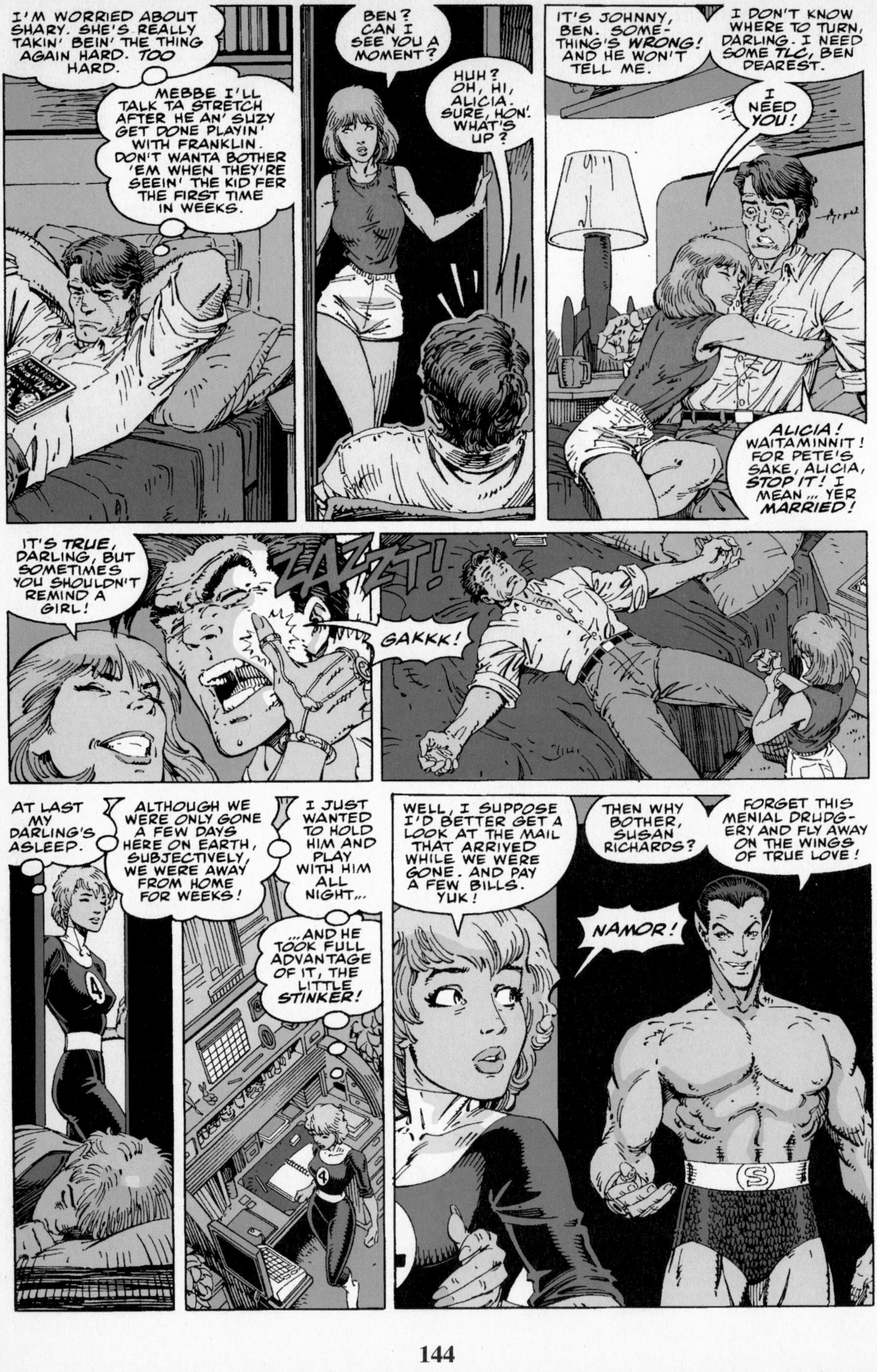
I'M WORRIED ABOUT SHARY. SHE'S REALLY TAKIN' BEIN' THE THING AGAIN HARD. TOO HARD.
MEBBE I'LL TALK TA STRETCH AFTER HE AN' SUZY GET DONE PLAYIN' WITH FRANKLIN. DON'T WANTA BOTHER 'EM WHEN THEY'RE SEEIN' THE KID FER THE FIRST TIME IN WEEKS.
BEN? CAN I SEE YOU A MOMENT?
HUH? OH, HI, ALICIA. SURE, HON'. WHAT'S UP?
IT'S JOHNNY, BEN. SOMETHING'S WRONG! AND HE WON'T TELL ME.
I DON'T KNOW WHERE TO TURN, DARLING. I NEED SOME TLC, BEN DEAREST.
I NEED YOU!
ALICIA! WAITAMINNIT! FOR PETE'S SAKE, ALICIA, STOP IT! I MEAN... YER MARRIED!
IT'S TRUE, DARLING, BUT SOMETIMES YOU SHOULDN'T REMIND A GIRL!
ZAZZT!
GAKKK!
AT LAST MY DARLING'S ASLEEP.
ALTHOUGH WE WERE ONLY GONE A FEW DAYS HERE ON EARTH, SUBJECTIVELY, WE WERE AWAY FROM HOME FOR WEEKS!
I JUST WANTED TO HOLD HIM AND PLAY WITH HIM ALL NIGHT...
...AND HE TOOK FULL ADVANTAGE OF IT, THE LITTLE STINKER!
WELL, I SUPPOSE I'D BETTER GET A LOOK AT THE MAIL THAT ARRIVED WHILE WE WERE GONE. AND PAY A FEW BILLS. YUK!
THEN WHY BOTHER, SUSAN RICHARDS?
FORGET THIS MENIAL DRUDGERY AND FLY AWAY ON THE WINGS OF TRUE LOVE!
NAMOR!

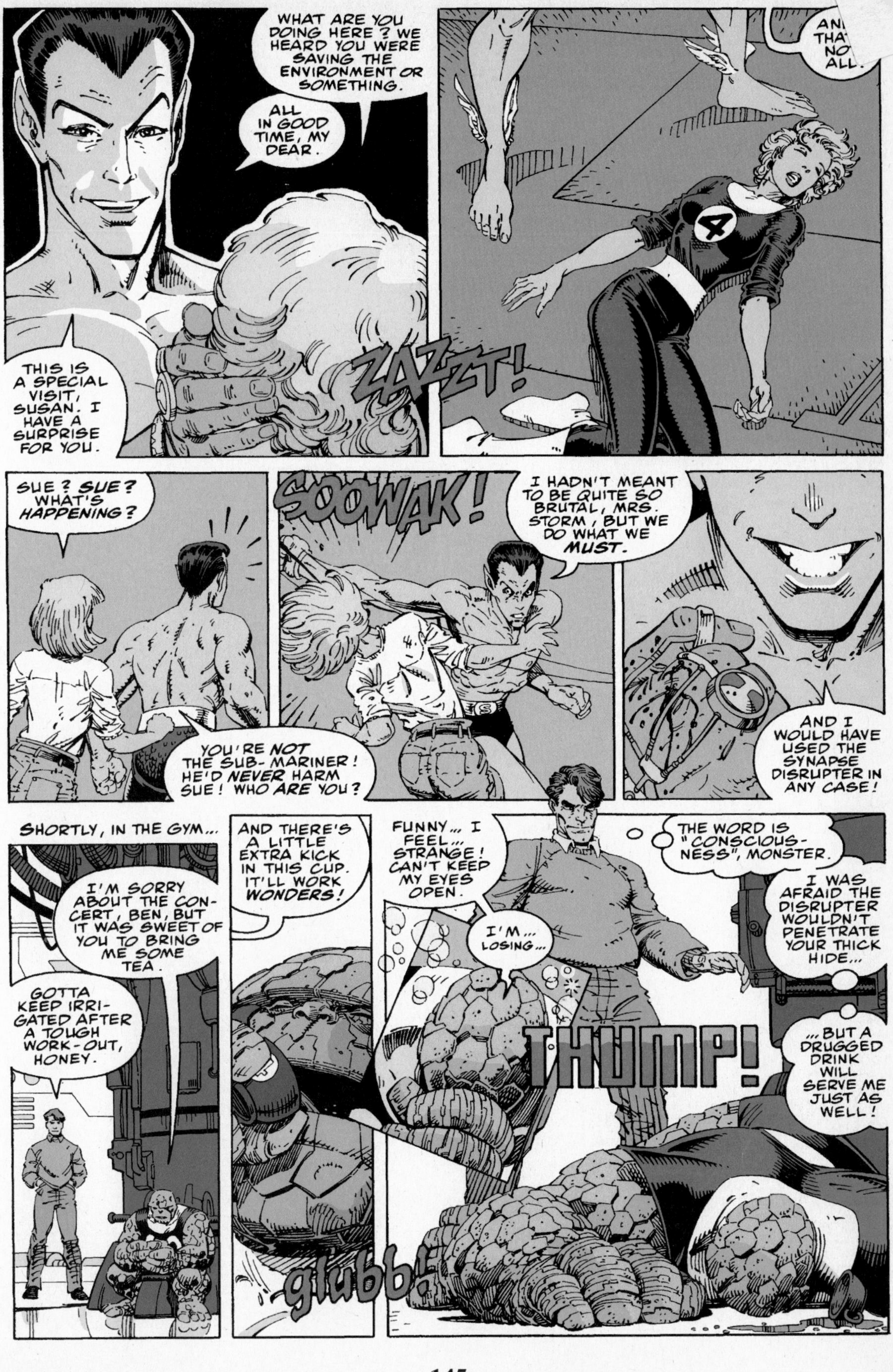
WHAT ARE YOU DOING HERE ? WE HEARD YOU WERE SAVING THE ENVIRONMENT OR SOMETHING.
ALL IN GOOD TIME, MY DEAR.
THIS IS A SPECIAL VISIT, SUSAN. I HAVE A SURPRISE FOR YOU.
ZAZZT!
SUE ? SUE ? WHAT'S HAPPENING ?
YOU'RE NOT THE SUB-MARINER ! HE'D NEVER HARM SUE ! WHO ARE YOU ?
SOOWAK !
I HADN'T MEANT TO BE QUITE SO BRUTAL, MRS. STORM , BUT WE DO WHAT WE MUST.
AND I WOULD HAVE USED THE SYNAPSE DISRUPTER IN ANY CASE !
SHORTLY, IN THE GYM...
I'M SORRY ABOUT THE CONCERT, BEN, BUT IT WAS SWEET OF YOU TO BRING ME SOME TEA.
GOTTA KEEP IRRIGATED AFTER A TOUGH WORK-OUT, HONEY.
AND THERE'S A LITTLE EXTRA KICK IN THIS CUP. IT'LL WORK WONDERS !
FUNNY... I FEEL... STRANGE ! CAN'T KEEP MY EYES OPEN.
glubb!
I'M... LOSING...
THE WORD IS "CONSCIOUSNESS", MONSTER.
I WAS AFRAID THE DISRUPTER WOULDN'T PENETRATE YOUR THICK HIDE...
THUMP!
...BUT A DRUGGED DRINK WILL SERVE ME JUST AS WELL !

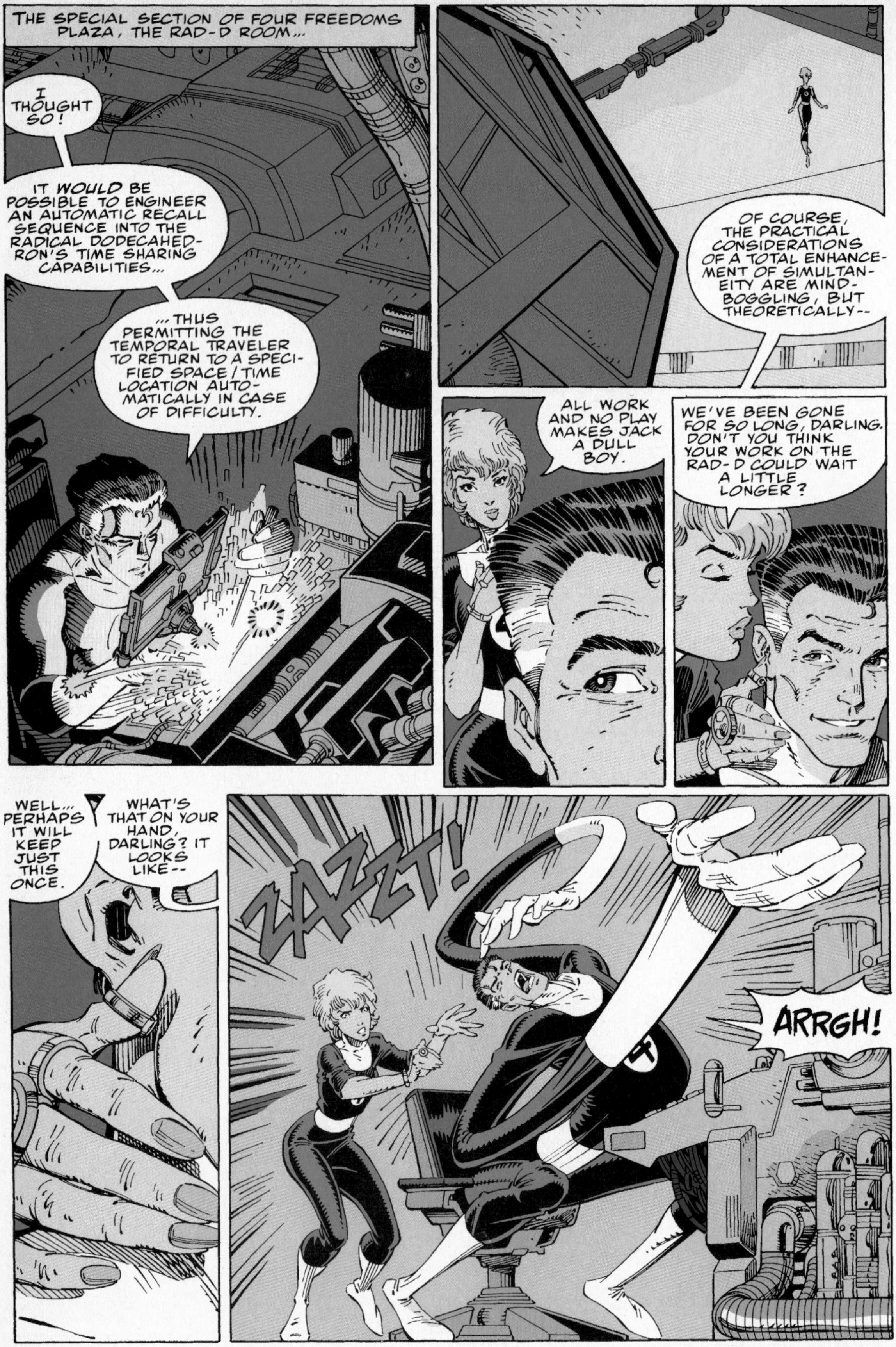
THE SPECIAL SECTION OF FOUR FREEDOMS PLAZA, THE RAD-D ROOM...
I THOUGHT SO!
IT WOULD BE POSSIBLE TO ENGINEER AN AUTOMATIC RECALL SEQUENCE INTO THE RADICAL DODECAHEDRON'S TIME SHARING CAPABILITIES...
...THUS PERMITTING THE TEMPORAL TRAVELER TO RETURN TO A SPECIFIED SPACE/TIME LOCATION AUTOMATICALLY IN CASE OF DIFFICULTY.
OF COURSE, THE PRACTICAL CONSIDERATIONS OF A TOTAL ENHANCEMENT OF SIMULTANEITY ARE MIND-BOGGLING, BUT THEORETICALLY--
ALL WORK AND NO PLAY MAKES JACK A DULL BOY.
WE'VE BEEN GONE FOR SO LONG, DARLING. DON'T YOU THINK YOUR WORK ON THE RAD-D COULD WAIT A LITTLE LONGER?
WELL... PERHAPS IT WILL KEEP JUST THIS ONCE.
WHAT'S THAT ON YOUR HAND, DARLING? IT LOOKS LIKE--
ZAZZT!
ARRGH!

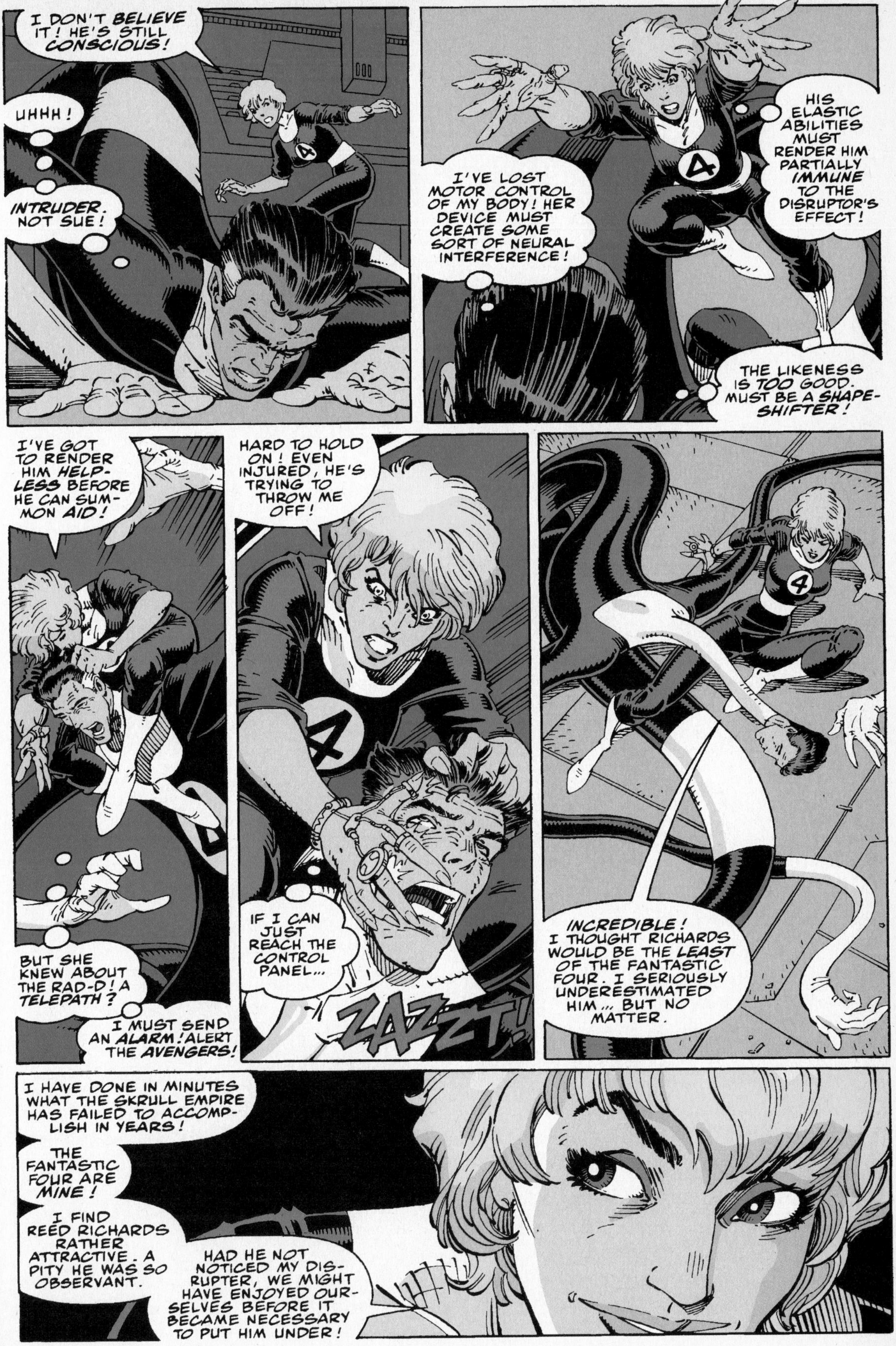
I DON'T BELIEVE IT! HE'S STILL CONSCIOUS!
UHHH!
INTRUDER. NOT SUE!
I'VE LOST MOTOR CONTROL OF MY BODY! HER DEVICE MUST CREATE SOME SORT OF NEURAL INTERFERENCE!
HIS ELASTIC ABILITIES MUST RENDER HIM PARTIALLY IMMUNE TO THE DISRUPTOR'S EFFECT!
THE LIKENESS IS TOO GOOD. MUST BE A SHAPE-SHIFTER!
I'VE GOT TO RENDER HIM HELP-LESS BEFORE HE CAN SUM-MON AID!
BUT SHE KNEW ABOUT THE RAD-D! A TELEPATH?
I MUST SEND AN ALARM! ALERT THE AVENGERS!
HARD TO HOLD ON! EVEN INJURED, HE'S TRYING TO THROW ME OFF!
IF I CAN JUST REACH THE CONTROL PANEL...
ZAZZT!
INCREDIBLE! I THOUGHT RICHARDS WOULD BE THE LEAST OF THE FANTASTIC FOUR. I SERIOUSLY UNDERESTIMATED HIM... BUT NO MATTER.
I HAVE DONE IN MINUTES WHAT THE SKRULL EMPIRE HAS FAILED TO ACCOMP-LISH IN YEARS!
THE FANTASTIC FOUR ARE MINE!
I FIND REED RICHARDS RATHER ATTRACTIVE. A PITY HE WAS SO OBSERVANT.
HAD HE NOT NOTICED MY DIS-RUPTER, WE MIGHT HAVE ENJOYED OUR-SELVES BEFORE IT BECAME NECESSARY TO PUT HIM UNDER!

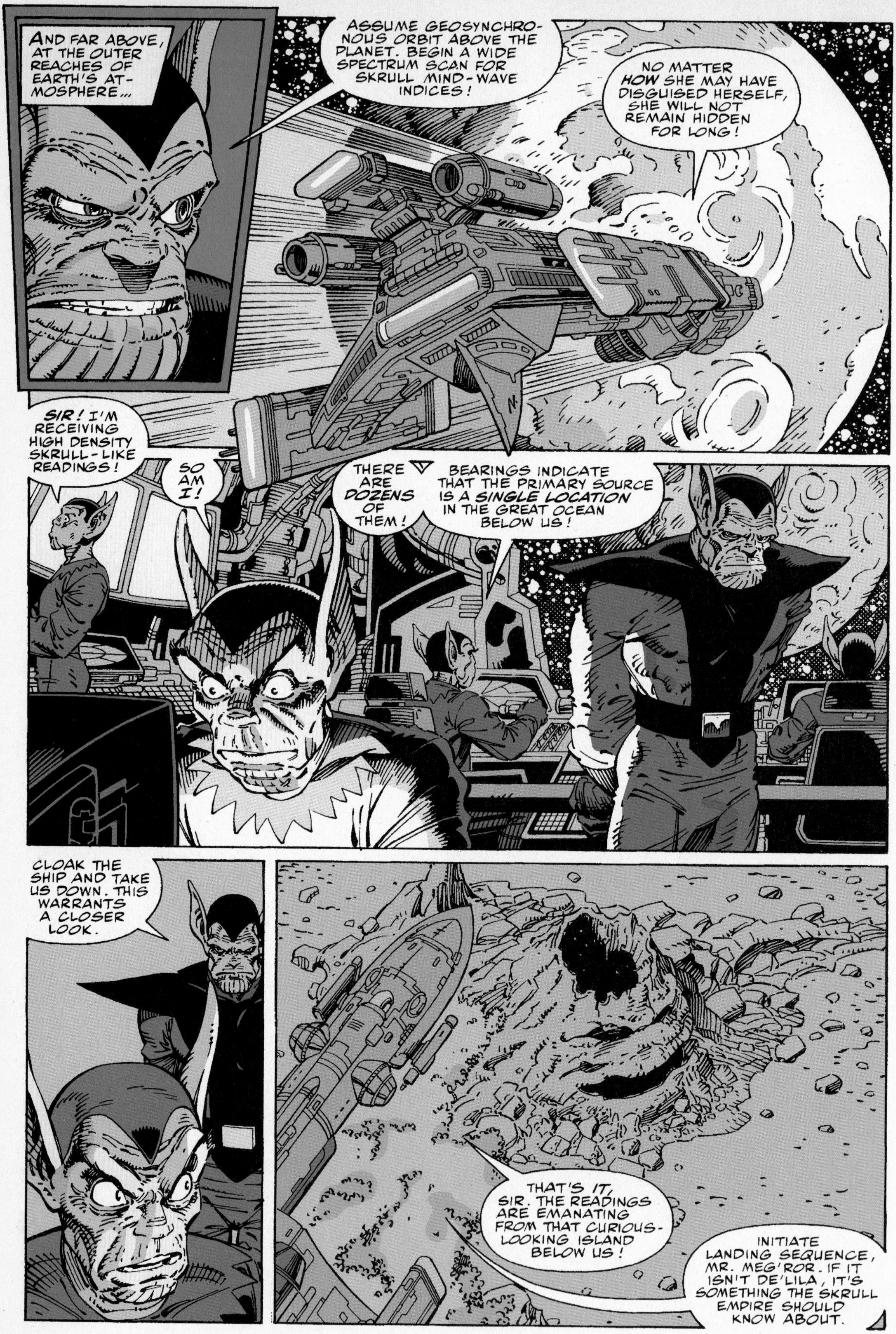
AND FAR ABOVE, AT THE OUTER REACHES OF EARTH'S AT-MOSPHERE...
ASSUME GEOSYNCHRO-NOUS ORBIT ABOVE THE PLANET. BEGIN A WIDE SPECTRUM SCAN FOR SKRULL MIND-WAVE INDICES!
NO MATTER HOW SHE MAY HAVE DISGUISED HERSELF, SHE WILL NOT REMAIN HIDDEN FOR LONG!
SIR! I'M RECEIVING HIGH DENSITY SKRULL-LIKE READINGS!
SO AM I!
THERE ARE DOZENS OF THEM!
BEARINGS INDICATE THAT THE PRIMARY SOURCE IS A SINGLE LOCATION IN THE GREAT OCEAN BELOW US!
CLOAK THE SHIP AND TAKE US DOWN. THIS WARRANTS A CLOSER LOOK.
THAT'S IT, SIR. THE READINGS ARE EMANATING FROM THAT CURIOUS-LOOKING ISLAND BELOW US!
INITIATE LANDING SEQUENCE, MR. MEG'ROR. IF IT ISN'T DE'LILA, IT'S SOMETHING THE SKRULL EMPIRE SHOULD KNOW ABOUT.

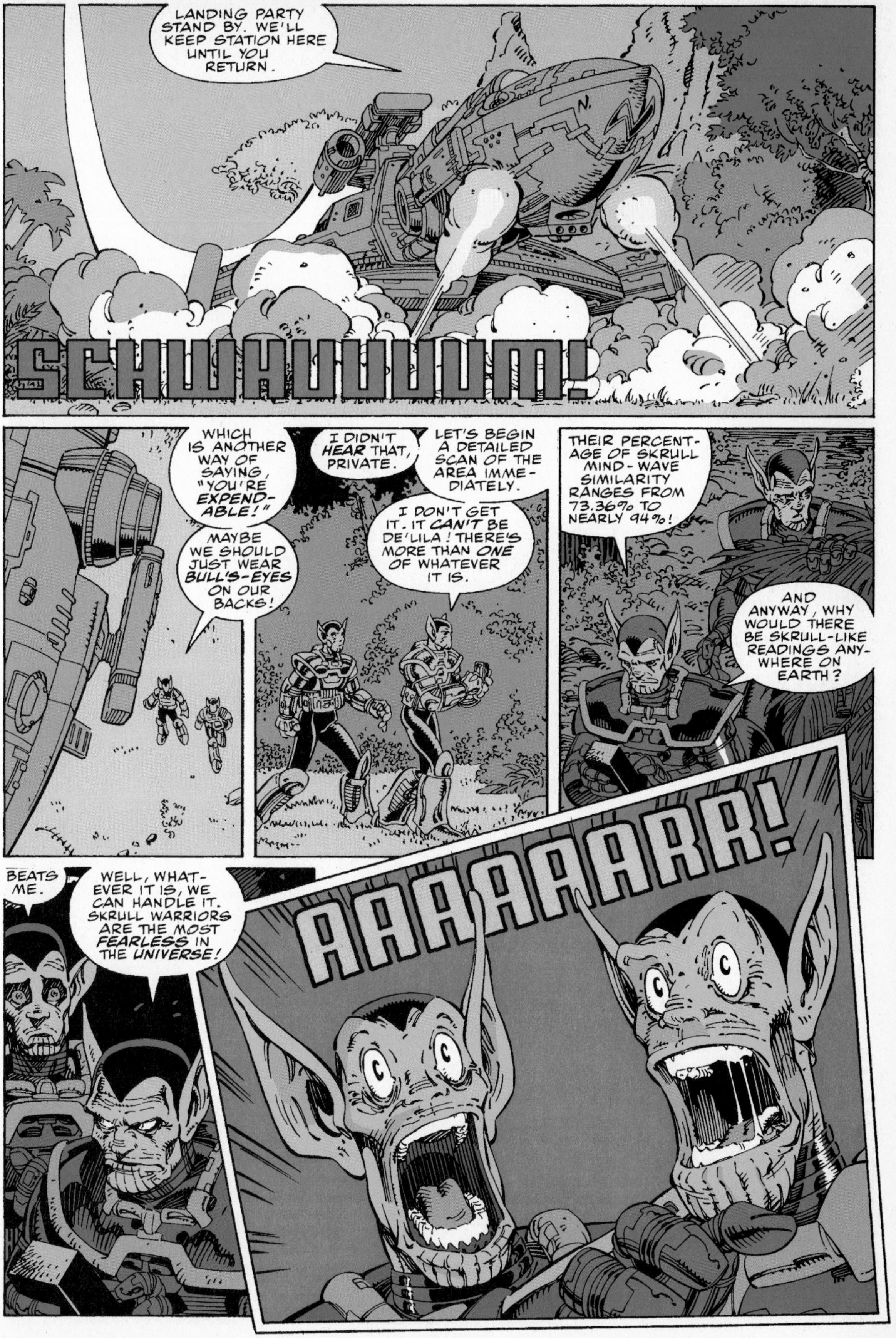
LANDING PARTY STAND BY. WE'LL KEEP STATION HERE UNTIL YOU RETURN.
SCHWHUUUUUM!
WHICH IS ANOTHER WAY OF SAYING, "YOU'RE EXPENDABLE!"
MAYBE WE SHOULD JUST WEAR BULL'S-EYES ON OUR BACKS!
I DIDN'T HEAR THAT, PRIVATE.
LET'S BEGIN A DETAILED SCAN OF THE AREA IMMEDIATELY.
I DON'T GET IT. IT CAN'T BE DE'LILA! THERE'S MORE THAN ONE OF WHATEVER IT IS.
THEIR PERCENTAGE OF SKRULL MIND-WAVE SIMILARITY RANGES FROM 73.36% TO NEARLY 94%!
AND ANYWAY, WHY WOULD THERE BE SKRULL-LIKE READINGS ANYWHERE ON EARTH?
BEATS ME.
WELL, WHATEVER IT IS, WE CAN HANDLE IT. SKRULL WARRIORS ARE THE MOST FEARLESS IN THE UNIVERSE!
AAAAAAARR!

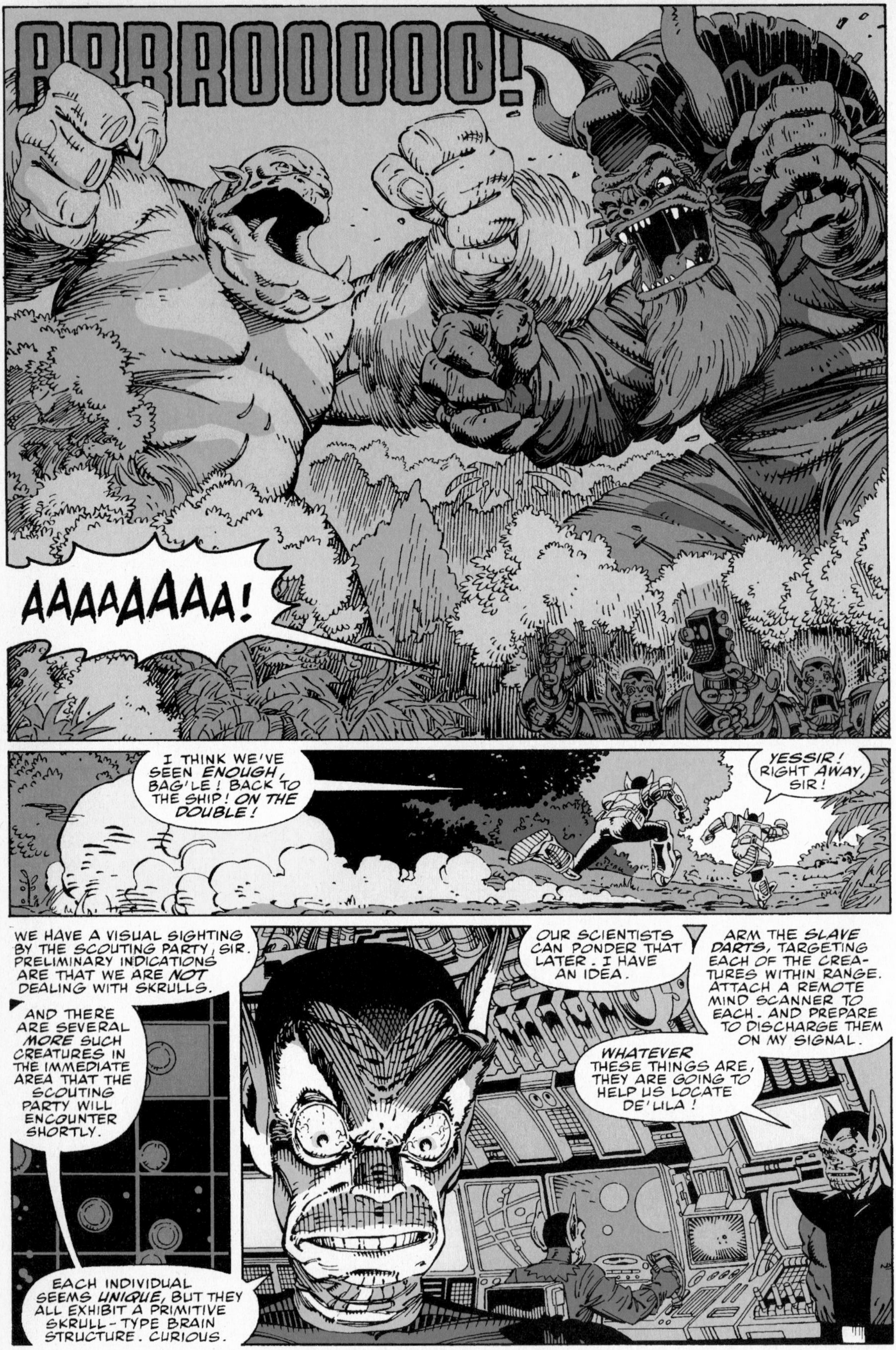
ARRROOOOOO!
AAAAAAAA!
I THINK WE'VE SEEN ENOUGH, BAG'LE! BACK TO THE SHIP! ON THE DOUBLE!
YESSIR! RIGHT AWAY, SIR!
WE HAVE A VISUAL SIGHTING BY THE SCOUTING PARTY, SIR. PRELIMINARY INDICATIONS ARE THAT WE ARE NOT DEALING WITH SKRULLS.
AND THERE ARE SEVERAL MORE SUCH CREATURES IN THE IMMEDIATE AREA THAT THE SCOUTING PARTY WILL ENCOUNTER SHORTLY.
EACH INDIVIDUAL SEEMS UNIQUE, BUT THEY ALL EXHIBIT A PRIMITIVE SKRULL-TYPE BRAIN STRUCTURE. CURIOUS.
OUR SCIENTISTS CAN PONDER THAT LATER. I HAVE AN IDEA.
ARM THE SLAVE DARTS, TARGETING EACH OF THE CREATURES WITHIN RANGE. ATTACH A REMOTE MIND SCANNER TO EACH. AND PREPARE TO DISCHARGE THEM ON MY SIGNAL.
WHATEVER THESE THINGS ARE, THEY ARE GOING TO HELP US LOCATE DE'LILA!

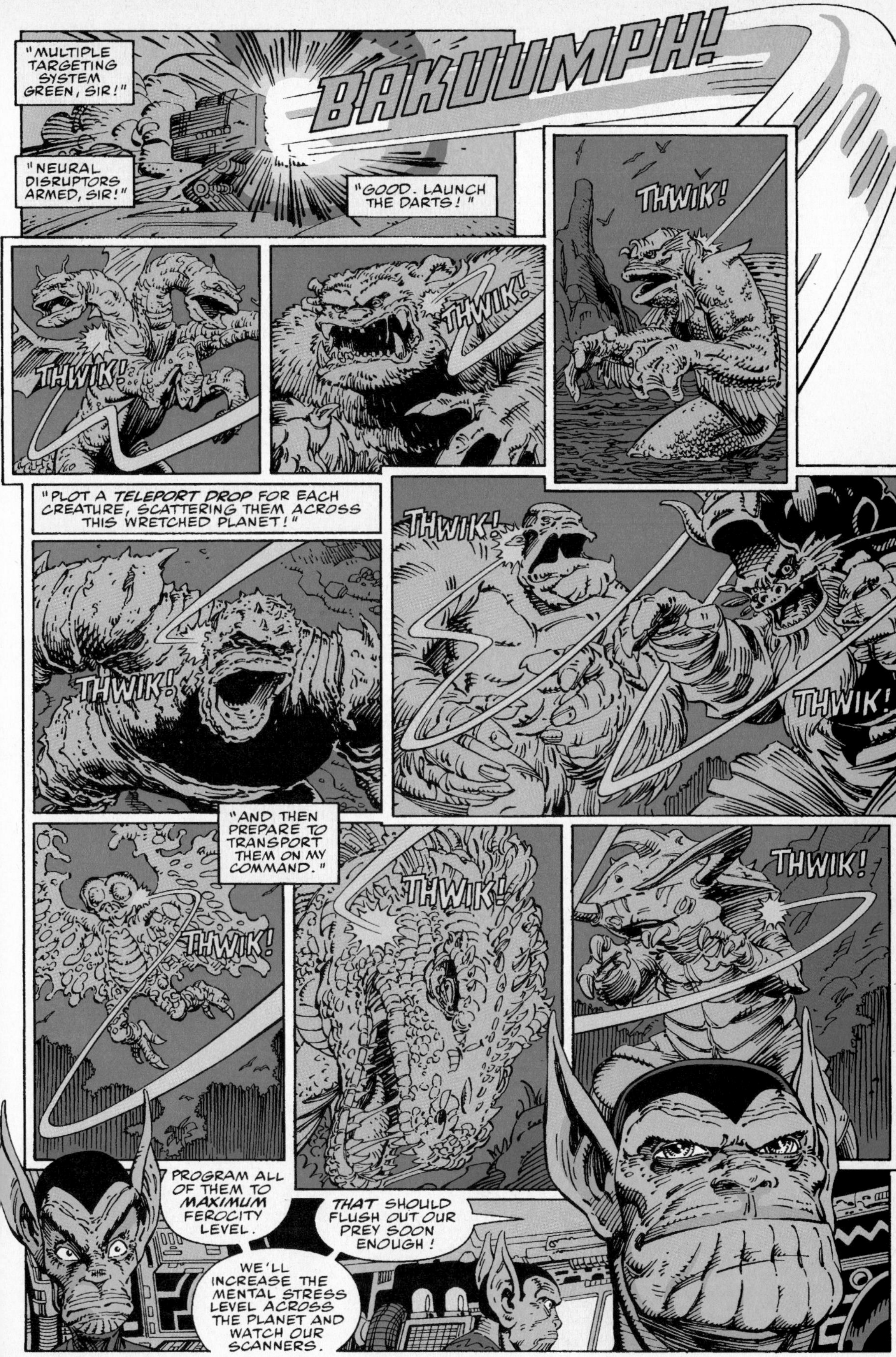
"MULTIPLE TARGETING SYSTEM GREEN, SIR!"
"NEURAL DISRUPTORS ARMED, SIR!"
BAKUUMPH!
"GOOD. LAUNCH THE DARTS!"
THWIK!
THWIK!
THWIK!
"PLOT A TELEPORT DROP FOR EACH CREATURE, SCATTERING THEM ACROSS THIS WRETCHED PLANET!"
THWIK!
THWIK!
THWIK!
"AND THEN PREPARE TO TRANSPORT THEM ON MY COMMAND."
THWIK!
THWIK!
THWIK!
PROGRAM ALL OF THEM TO MAXIMUM FEROCITY LEVEL.
WE'LL INCREASE THE MENTAL STRESS LEVEL ACROSS THE PLANET AND WATCH OUR SCANNERS.
THAT SHOULD FLUSH OUT OUR PREY SOON ENOUGH!

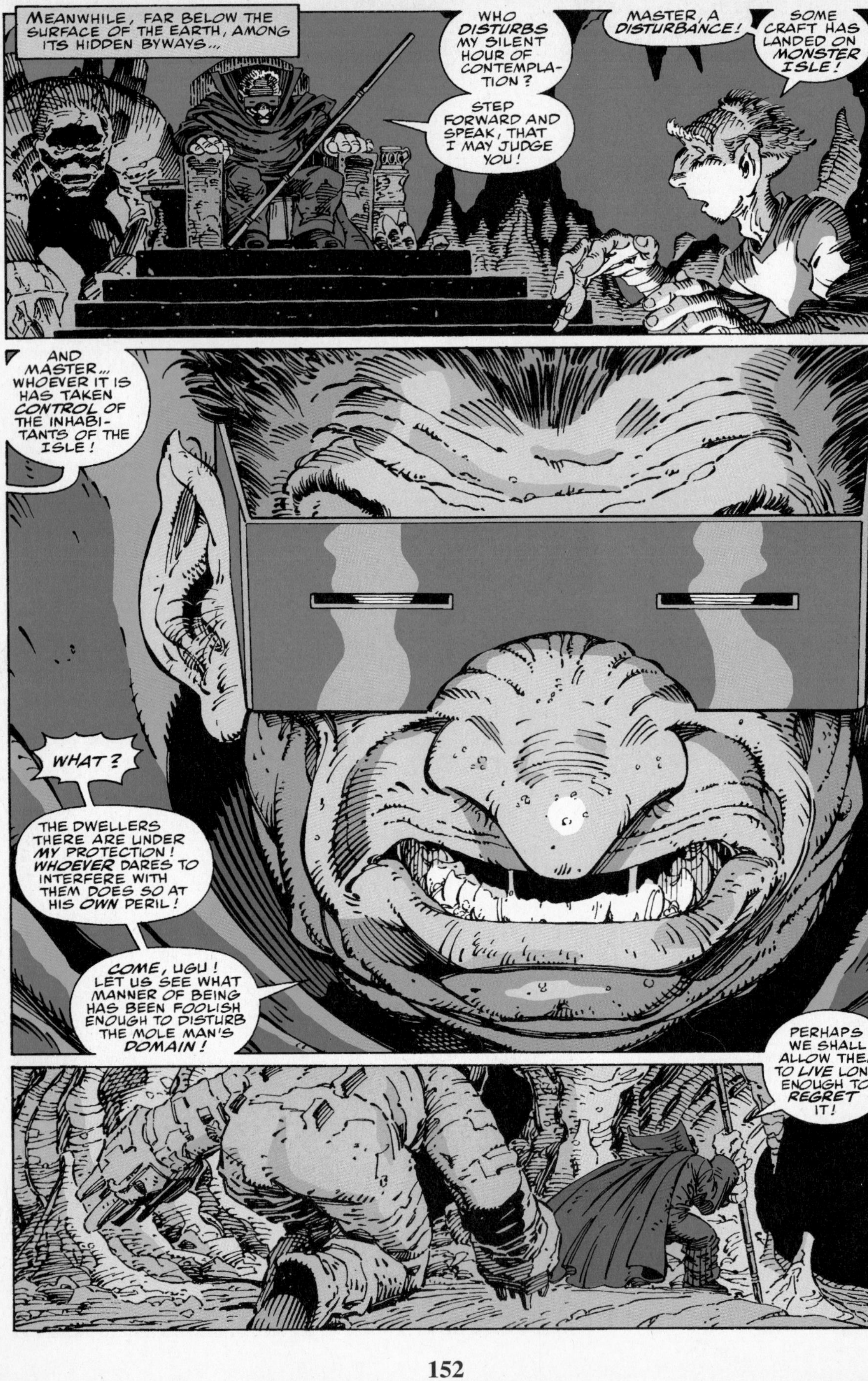
MEANWHILE, FAR BELOW THE SURFACE OF THE EARTH, AMONG ITS HIDDEN BYWAYS...
WHO DISTURBS MY SILENT HOUR OF CONTEMPLATION?
STEP FORWARD AND SPEAK, THAT I MAY JUDGE YOU!
MASTER, A DISTURBANCE!
SOME CRAFT HAS LANDED ON MONSTER ISLE!
AND MASTER... WHOEVER IT IS HAS TAKEN CONTROL OF THE INHABITANTS OF THE ISLE!
WHAT?
THE DWELLERS THERE ARE UNDER MY PROTECTION! WHOEVER DARES TO INTERFERE WITH THEM DOES SO AT HIS OWN PERIL!
COME, UGU! LET US SEE WHAT MANNER OF BEING HAS BEEN FOOLISH ENOUGH TO DISTURB THE MOLE MAN'S DOMAIN!
PERHAPS WE SHALL ALLOW THEM TO LIVE LONG ENOUGH TO REGRET IT!

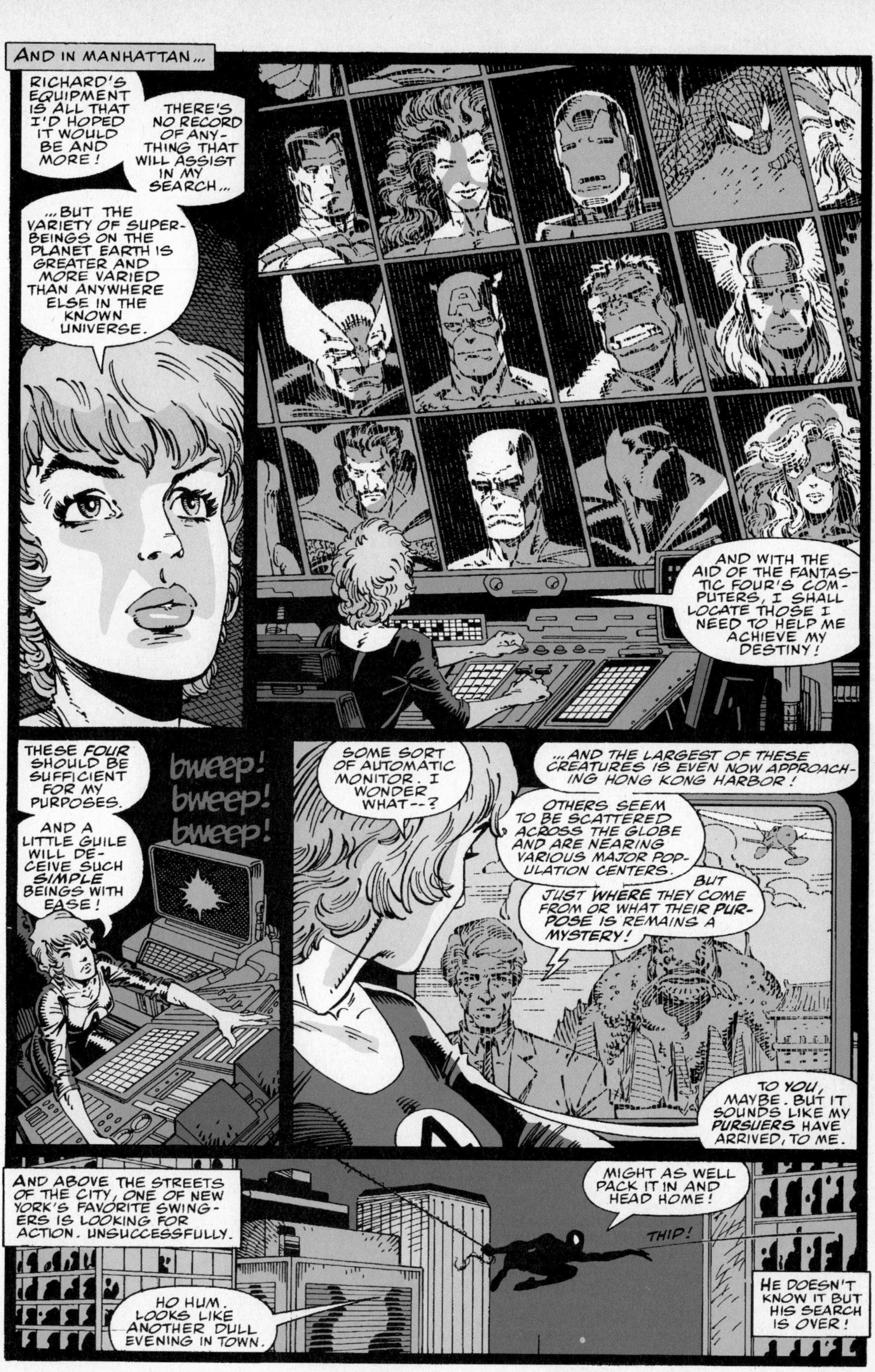
AND IN MANHATTAN...
RICHARD'S EQUIPMENT IS ALL THAT I'D HOPED IT WOULD BE AND MORE!
THERE'S NO RECORD OF ANYTHING THAT WILL ASSIST IN MY SEARCH...
...BUT THE VARIETY OF SUPER-BEINGS ON THE PLANET EARTH IS GREATER AND MORE VARIED THAN ANYWHERE ELSE IN THE KNOWN UNIVERSE.
AND WITH THE AID OF THE FANTASTIC FOUR'S COMPUTERS, I SHALL LOCATE THOSE I NEED TO HELP ME ACHIEVE MY DESTINY!
THESE FOUR SHOULD BE SUFFICIENT FOR MY PURPOSES.
AND A LITTLE GUILE WILL DECEIVE SUCH SIMPLE BEINGS WITH EASE!
bweep! bweep! bweep!
SOME SORT OF AUTOMATIC MONITOR. I WONDER WHAT--?
...AND THE LARGEST OF THESE CREATURES IS EVEN NOW APPROACHING HONG KONG HARBOR!
OTHERS SEEM TO BE SCATTERED ACROSS THE GLOBE AND ARE NEARING VARIOUS MAJOR POPULATION CENTERS.
BUT JUST WHERE THEY COME FROM OR WHAT THEIR PURPOSE IS REMAINS A MYSTERY!
TO YOU, MAYBE. BUT IT SOUNDS LIKE MY PURSUERS HAVE ARRIVED, TO ME.
AND ABOVE THE STREETS OF THE CITY, ONE OF NEW YORK'S FAVORITE SWINGERS IS LOOKING FOR ACTION. UNSUCCESSFULLY.
MIGHT AS WELL PACK IT IN AND HEAD HOME!
THIP!
HO HUM. LOOKS LIKE ANOTHER DULL EVENING IN TOWN.
HE DOESN'T KNOW IT BUT HIS SEARCH IS OVER!

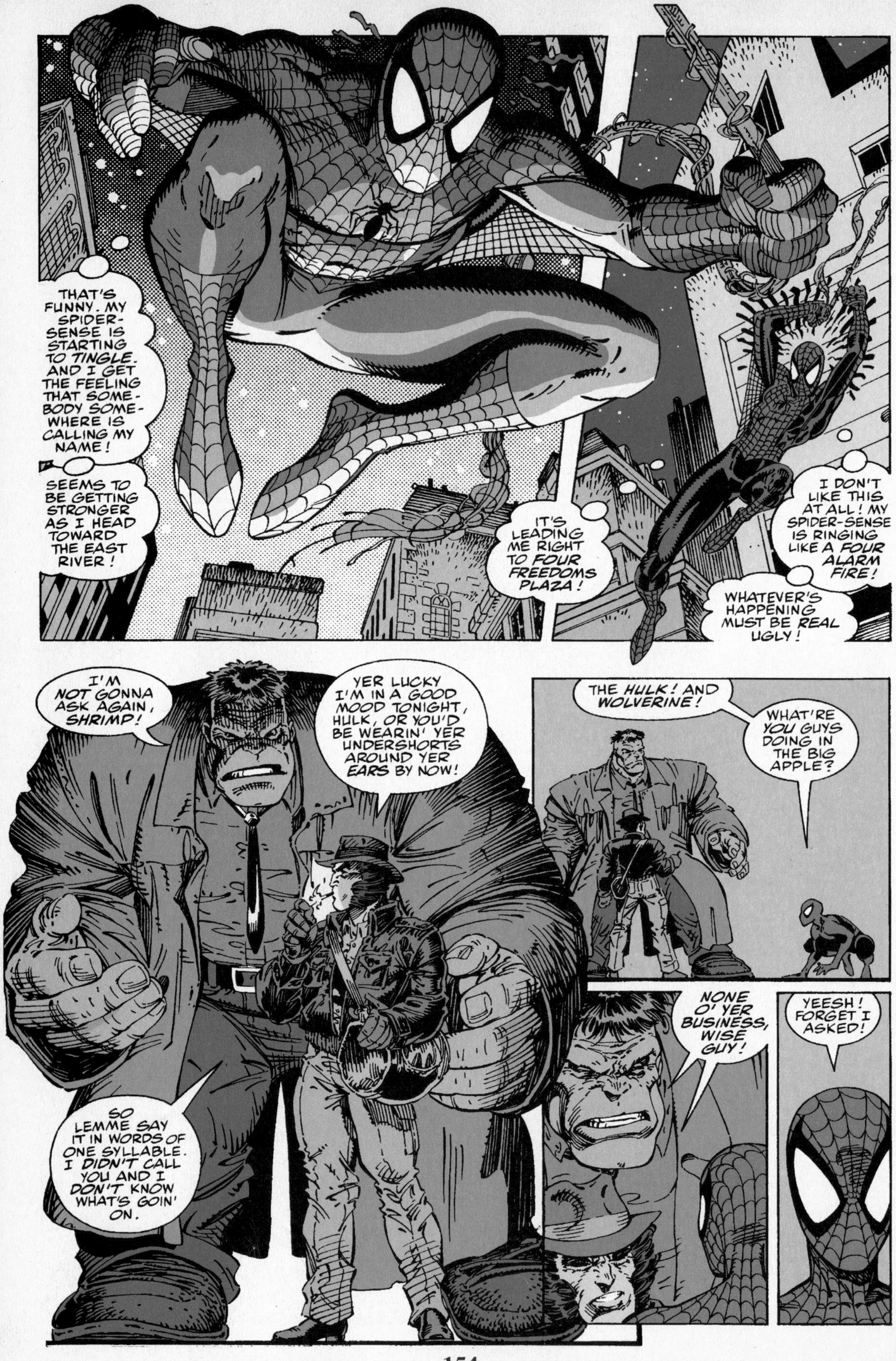

THAT'S FUNNY. MY SPIDER-SENSE IS STARTING TO TINGLE. AND I GET THE FEELING THAT SOMEBODY SOMEWHERE IS CALLING MY NAME!
SEEMS TO BE GETTING STRONGER AS I HEAD TOWARD THE EAST RIVER!
IT'S LEADING ME RIGHT TO FOUR FREEDOMS PLAZA!
I DON'T LIKE THIS AT ALL! MY SPIDER-SENSE IS RINGING LIKE A FOUR ALARM FIRE!
WHATEVER'S HAPPENING MUST BE REAL UGLY!
I'M NOT GONNA ASK AGAIN, SHRIMP!
YER LUCKY I'M IN A GOOD MOOD TONIGHT, HULK, OR YOU'D BE WEARIN' YER UNDERSHORTS AROUND YER EARS BY NOW!
SO LEMME SAY IT IN WORDS OF ONE SYLLABLE. I DIDN'T CALL YOU AND I DON'T KNOW WHAT'S GOIN' ON.
THE HULK! AND WOLVERINE!
WHAT'RE YOU GUYS DOING IN THE BIG APPLE?
NONE O' YER BUSINESS, WISE GUY!
YEESH! FORGET I ASKED!

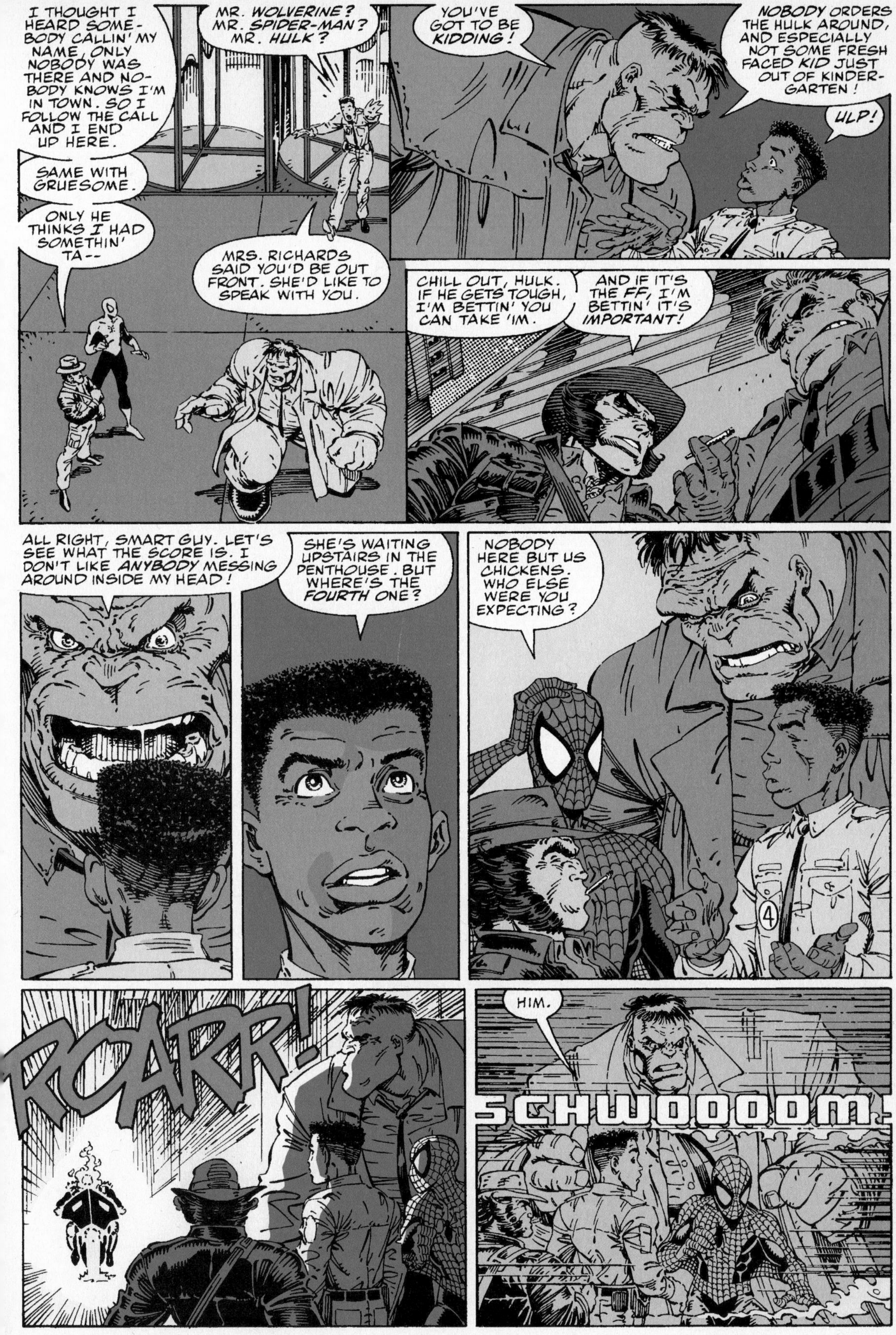
I THOUGHT I HEARD SOMEBODY CALLIN' MY NAME, ONLY NOBODY WAS THERE AND NOBODY KNOWS I'M IN TOWN. SO I FOLLOW THE CALL AND I END UP HERE.
SAME WITH GRUESOME.
ONLY HE THINKS I HAD SOMETHIN' TA--
MR. WOLVERINE? MR. SPIDER-MAN? MR. HULK?
MRS. RICHARDS SAID YOU'D BE OUT FRONT. SHE'D LIKE TO SPEAK WITH YOU.
YOU'VE GOT TO BE KIDDING!
NOBODY ORDERS THE HULK AROUND, AND ESPECIALLY NOT SOME FRESH FACED KID JUST OUT OF KINDERGARTEN!
ULP!
CHILL OUT, HULK. IF HE GETS TOUGH, I'M BETTIN' YOU CAN TAKE 'IM.
AND IF IT'S THE FF, I'M BETTIN' IT'S IMPORTANT!
ALL RIGHT, SMART GUY. LET'S SEE WHAT THE SCORE IS. I DON'T LIKE ANYBODY MESSING AROUND INSIDE MY HEAD!
SHE'S WAITING UPSTAIRS IN THE PENTHOUSE. BUT WHERE'S THE FOURTH ONE?
NOBODY HERE BUT US CHICKENS. WHO ELSE WERE YOU EXPECTING?
4
RCARR!
HIM.
SCHWOOOOOM!

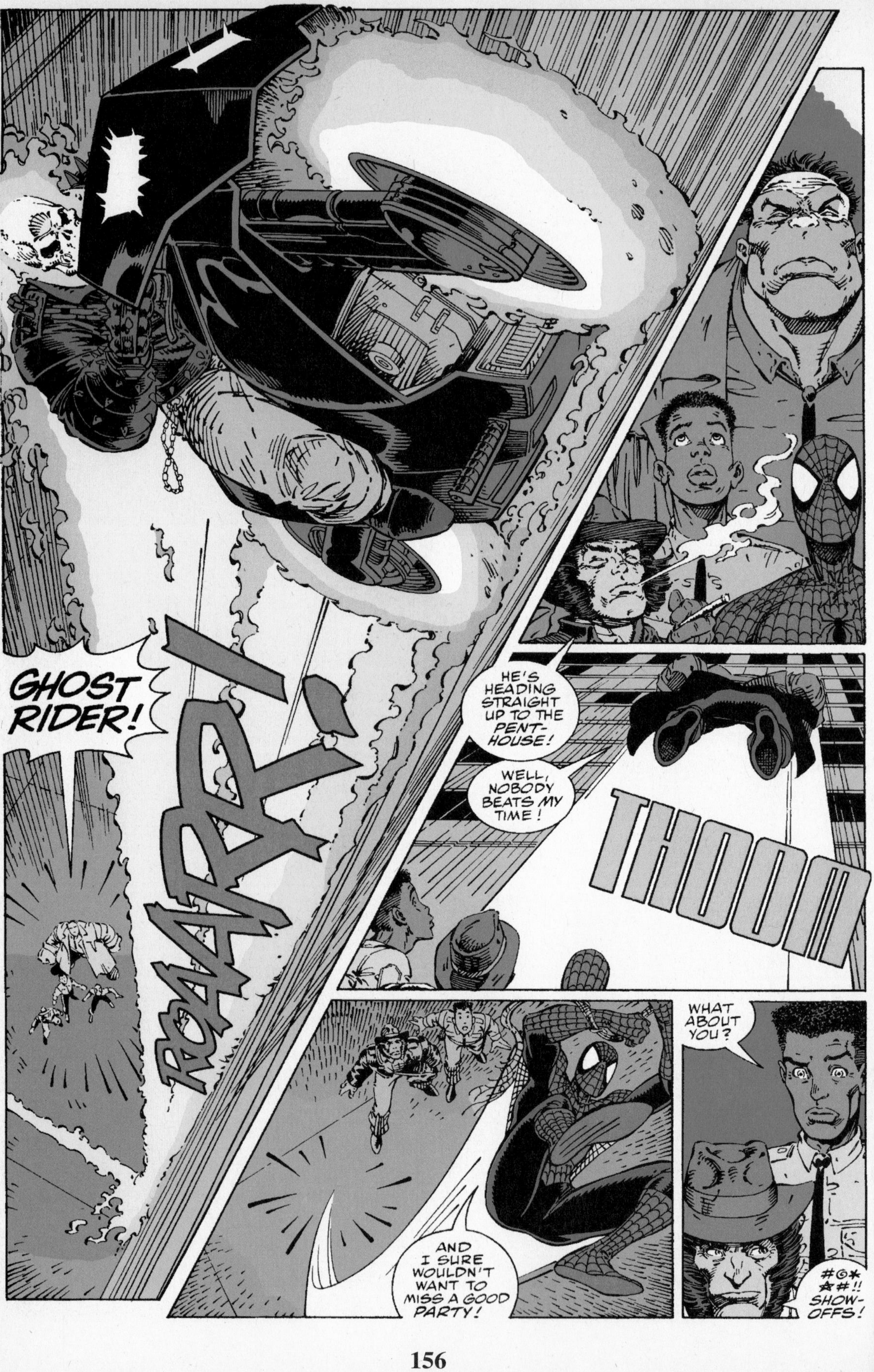
GHOST RIDER!
ROAAARR!
HE'S HEADING STRAIGHT UP TO THE PENT-HOUSE!
WELL, NOBODY BEATS MY TIME!
THOOM
AND I SURE WOULDN'T WANT TO MISS A GOOD PARTY!
WHAT ABOUT YOU?
#@*☆#!! SHOW-OFFS!

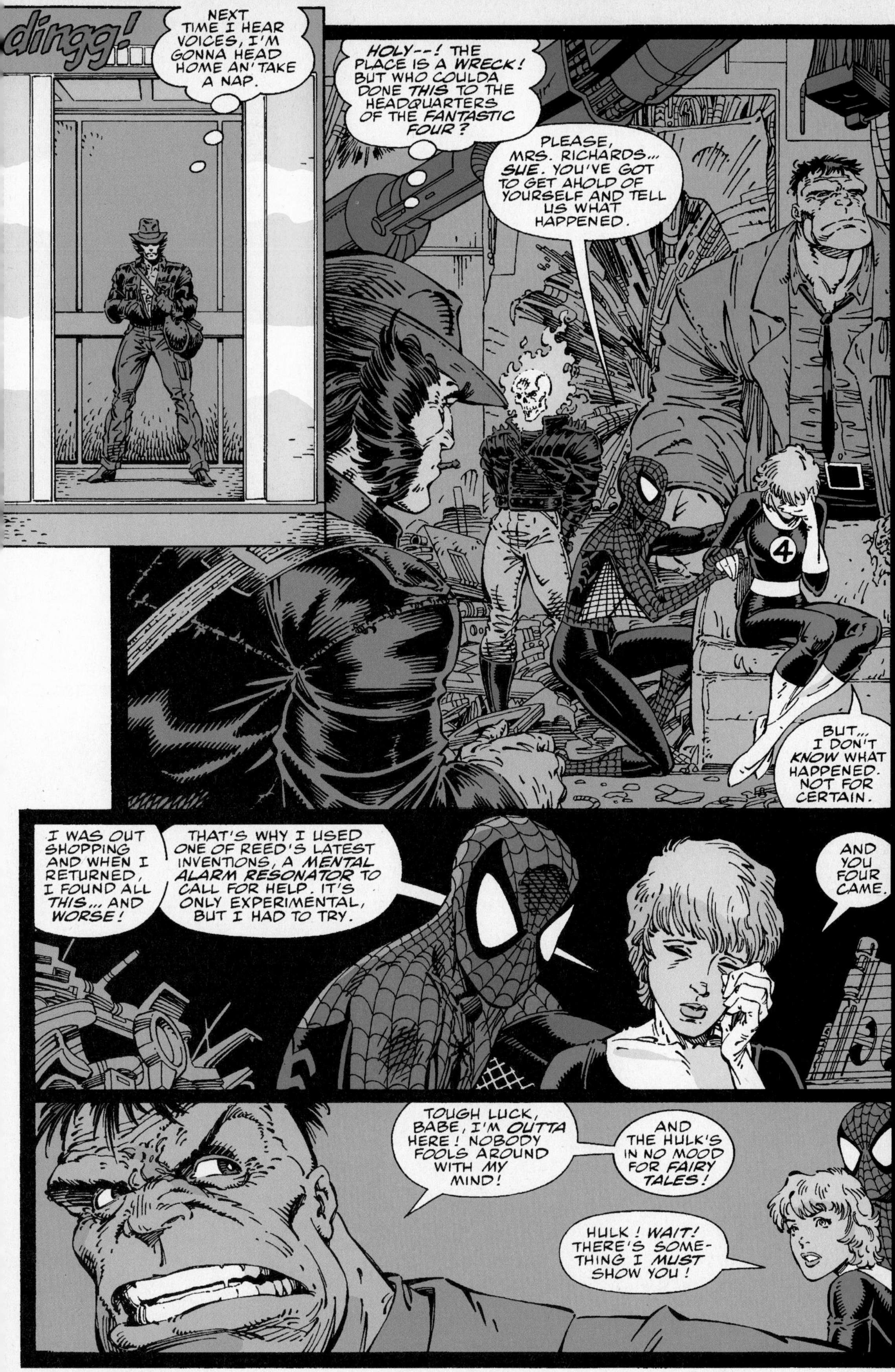
dingg!
NEXT TIME I HEAR VOICES, I'M GONNA HEAD HOME AN' TAKE A NAP.
HOLY--! THE PLACE IS A WRECK! BUT WHO COULDA DONE THIS TO THE HEADQUARTERS OF THE FANTASTIC FOUR?
PLEASE, MRS. RICHARDS... SUE. YOU'VE GOT TO GET AHOLD OF YOURSELF AND TELL US WHAT HAPPENED.
BUT... I DON'T KNOW WHAT HAPPENED. NOT FOR CERTAIN.
I WAS OUT SHOPPING AND WHEN I RETURNED, I FOUND ALL THIS... AND WORSE!
THAT'S WHY I USED ONE OF REED'S LATEST INVENTIONS, A MENTAL ALARM RESONATOR TO CALL FOR HELP. IT'S ONLY EXPERIMENTAL, BUT I HAD TO TRY.
AND YOU FOUR CAME.
TOUGH LUCK, BABE, I'M OUTTA HERE! NOBODY FOOLS AROUND WITH MY MIND!
AND THE HULK'S IN NO MOOD FOR FAIRY TALES!
HULK! WAIT! THERE'S SOME-THING I MUST SHOW YOU!

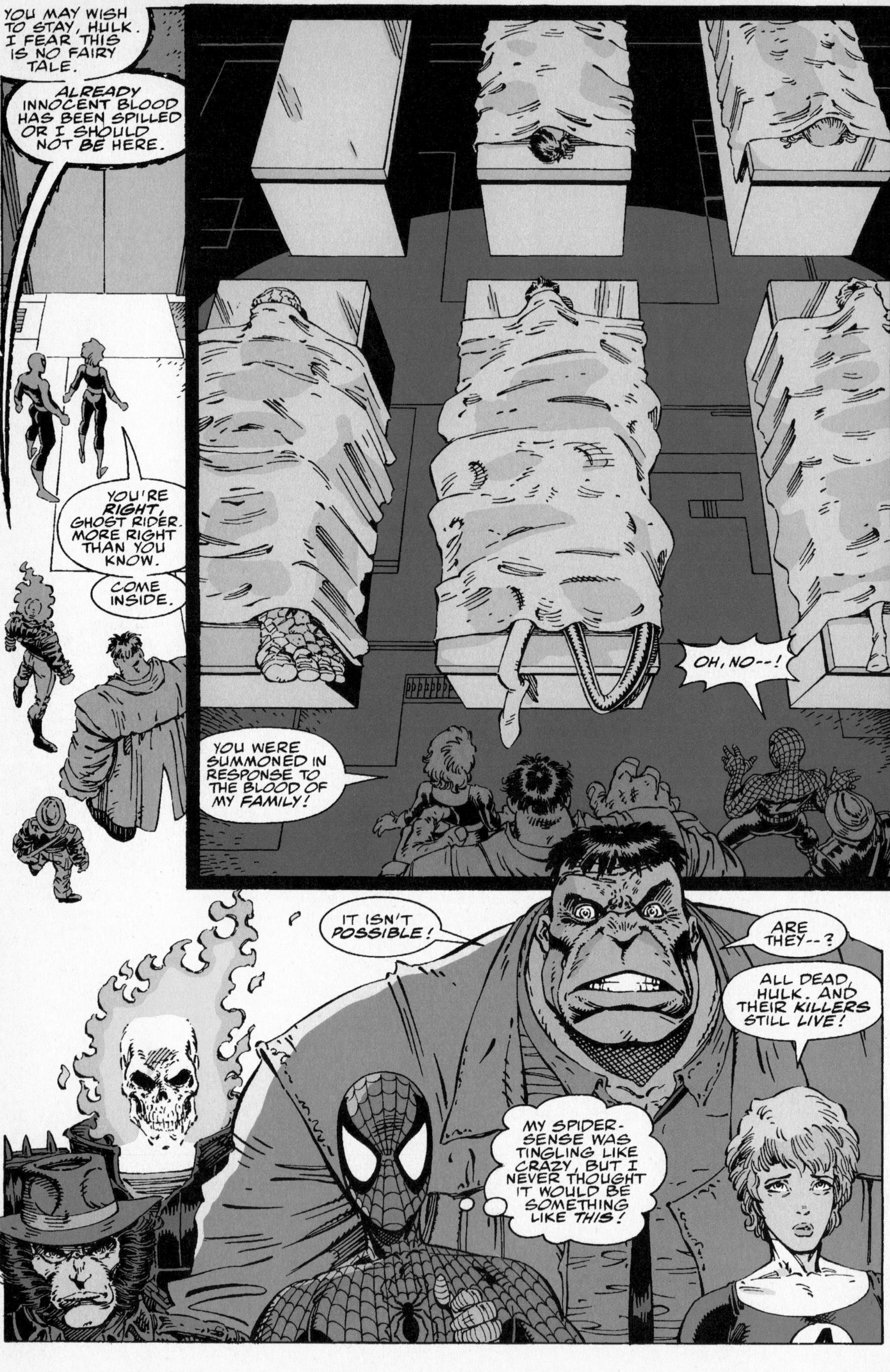

YOU MAY WISH TO STAY, HULK. I FEAR THIS IS NO FAIRY TALE.
ALREADY INNOCENT BLOOD HAS BEEN SPILLED OR I SHOULD NOT BE HERE.
YOU'RE RIGHT, GHOST RIDER. MORE RIGHT THAN YOU KNOW.
COME INSIDE.
YOU WERE SUMMONED IN RESPONSE TO THE BLOOD OF MY FAMILY!
OH, NO--!
IT ISN'T POSSIBLE!
ARE THEY--?
ALL DEAD, HULK. AND THEIR KILLERS STILL LIVE!
MY SPIDER-SENSE WAS TINGLING LIKE CRAZY, BUT I NEVER THOUGHT IT WOULD BE SOMETHING LIKE THIS!

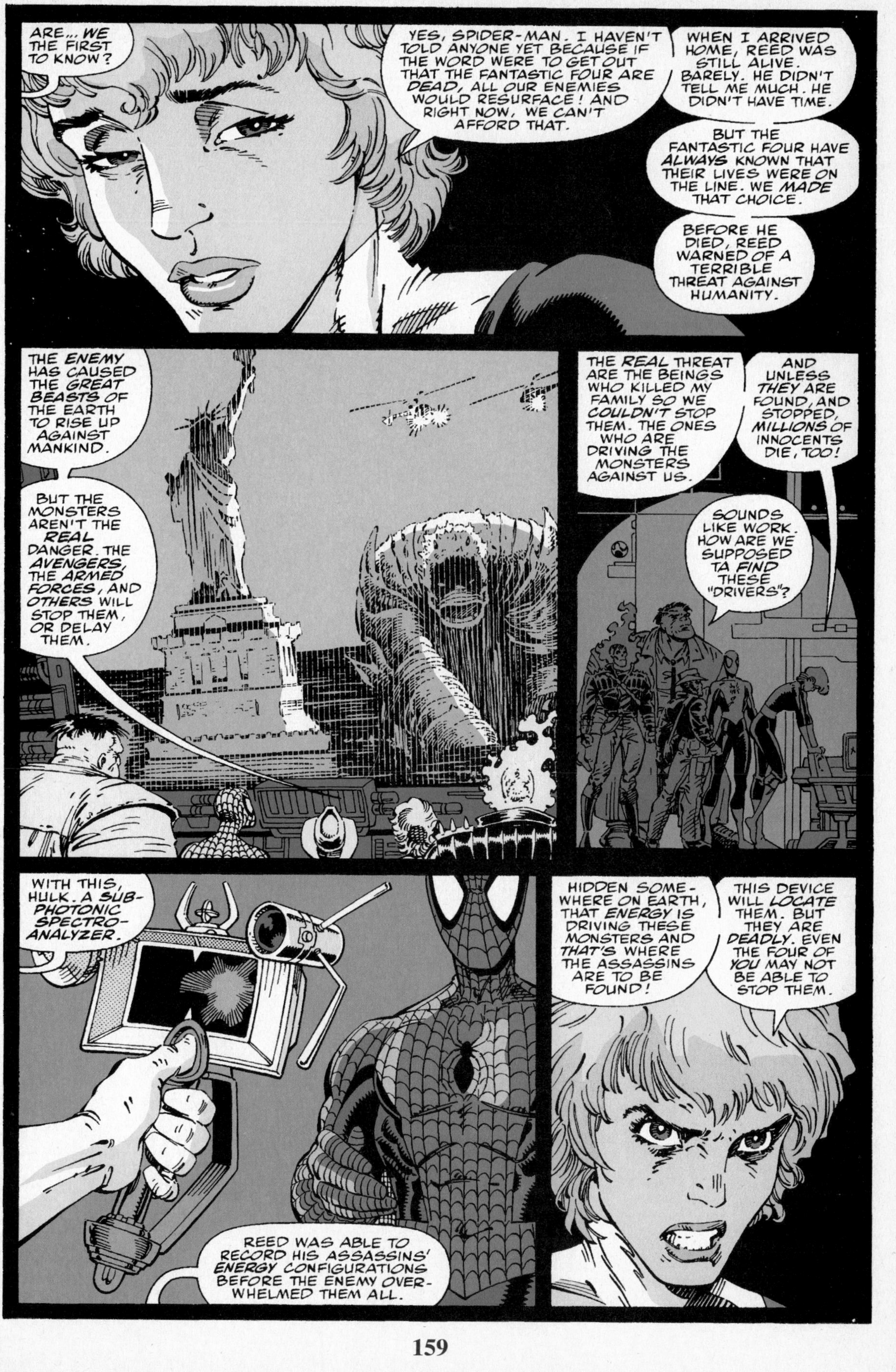
ARE... WE THE FIRST TO KNOW?
YES, SPIDER-MAN. I HAVEN'T TOLD ANYONE YET BECAUSE IF THE WORD WERE TO GET OUT THAT THE FANTASTIC FOUR ARE DEAD, ALL OUR ENEMIES WOULD RESURFACE! AND RIGHT NOW, WE CAN'T AFFORD THAT.
WHEN I ARRIVED HOME, REED WAS STILL ALIVE. BARELY. HE DIDN'T TELL ME MUCH. HE DIDN'T HAVE TIME.
BUT THE FANTASTIC FOUR HAVE ALWAYS KNOWN THAT THEIR LIVES WERE ON THE LINE. WE MADE THAT CHOICE.
BEFORE HE DIED, REED WARNED OF A TERRIBLE THREAT AGAINST HUMANITY.
THE ENEMY HAS CAUSED THE GREAT BEASTS OF THE EARTH TO RISE UP AGAINST MANKIND.
BUT THE MONSTERS AREN'T THE REAL DANGER. THE AVENGERS, THE ARMED FORCES, AND OTHERS WILL STOP THEM, OR DELAY THEM.
THE REAL THREAT ARE THE BEINGS WHO KILLED MY FAMILY SO WE COULDN'T STOP THEM. THE ONES WHO ARE DRIVING THE MONSTERS AGAINST US.
AND UNLESS THEY ARE FOUND, AND STOPPED, MILLIONS OF INNOCENTS DIE, TOO!
SOUNDS LIKE WORK. HOW ARE WE SUPPOSED TA FIND THESE "DRIVERS"?
WITH THIS, HULK. A SUB-PHOTONIC SPECTRO-ANALYZER.
REED WAS ABLE TO RECORD HIS ASSASSINS' ENERGY CONFIGURATIONS BEFORE THE ENEMY OVER-WHELMED THEM ALL.
HIDDEN SOME-WHERE ON EARTH, THAT ENERGY IS DRIVING THESE MONSTERS AND THAT'S WHERE THE ASSASSINS ARE TO BE FOUND!
THIS DEVICE WILL LOCATE THEM. BUT THEY ARE DEADLY. EVEN THE FOUR OF YOU MAY NOT BE ABLE TO STOP THEM.

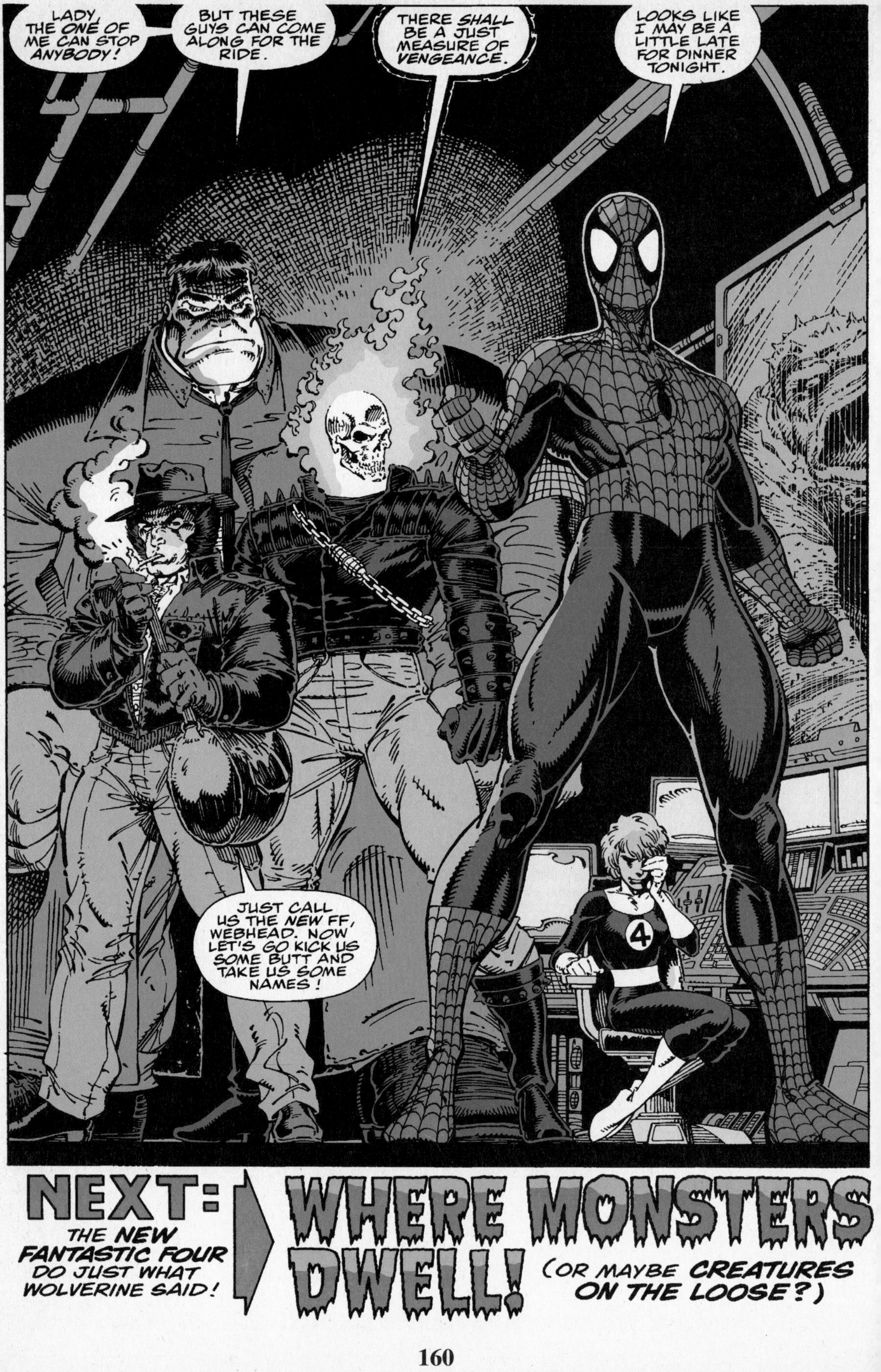
LADY, THE *ONE* OF ME CAN STOP ANYBODY!
BUT THESE GUYS CAN COME ALONG FOR THE RIDE.
THERE *SHALL* BE A JUST MEASURE OF *VENGEANCE*.
LOOKS LIKE I MAY BE A LITTLE LATE FOR DINNER TONIGHT.
JUST CALL US THE *NEW* FF, WEBHEAD. NOW LET'S GO KICK US SOME BUTT AND TAKE US SOME NAMES!

NEXT: THE *NEW* FANTASTIC FOUR DO JUST WHAT WOLVERINE SAID!

WHERE MONSTERS DWELL!

(OR MAYBE *CREATURES ON THE LOOSE?*)

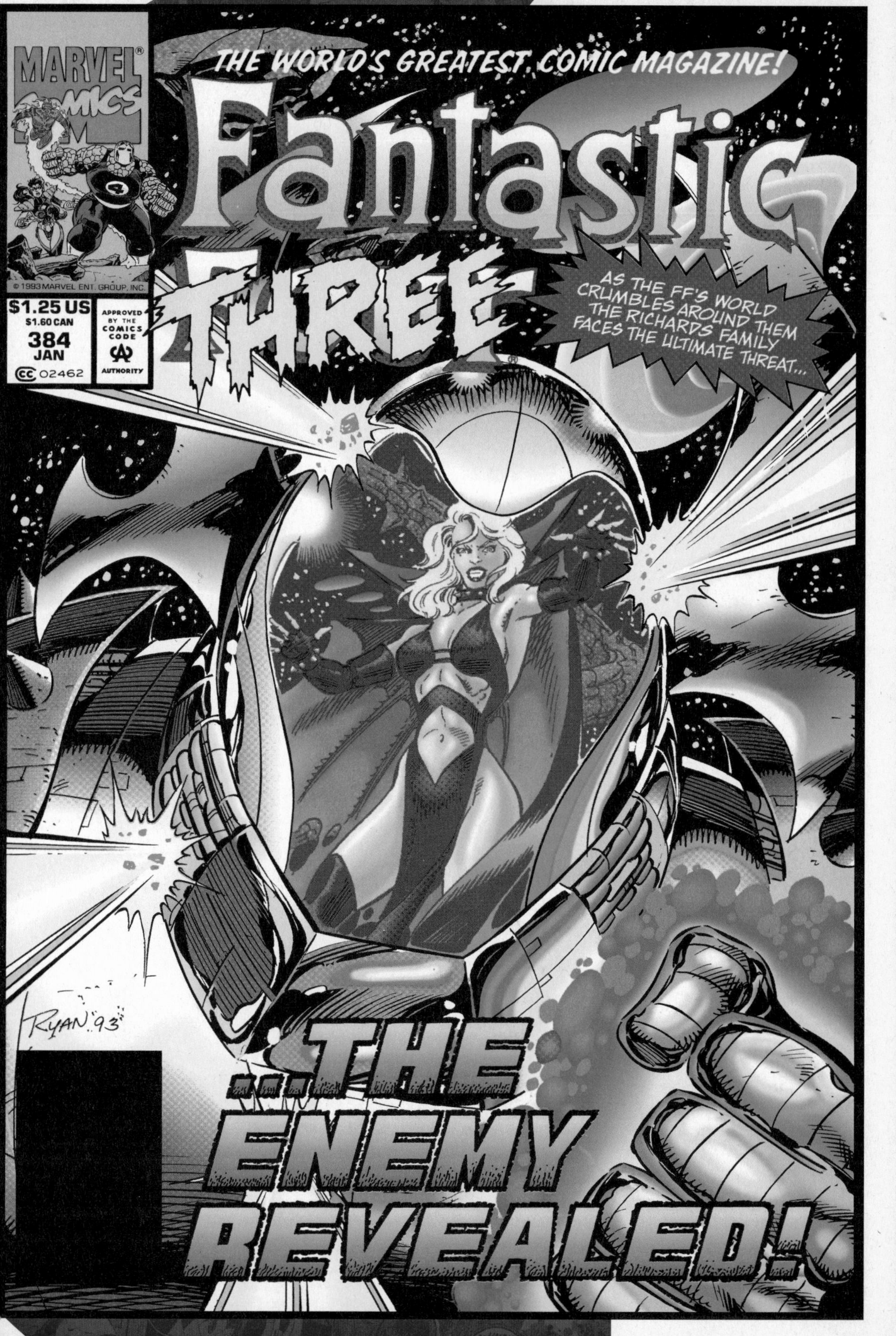
MARVEL® COMICS
© 1993 MARVEL ENT. GROUP, INC.
$1.25 US
$1.60 CAN
384
JAN
02462
APPROVED BY THE COMICS CODE AUTHORITY
THE WORLD'S GREATEST COMIC MAGAZINE!
Fantastic THREE
AS THE FF'S WORLD CRUMBLES AROUND THEM THE RICHARDS FAMILY FACES THE ULTIMATE THREAT...
RYAN '93
...THE ENEMY REVEALED!

REED RICHARDS, MISTER FANTASTIC! BEN GRIMM, THE THING! SUE RICHARDS, INVISIBLE WOMAN! JOHNNY STORM, THE HUMAN TORCH! TRANSFORMED BY AN ACCIDENT IN OUTER SPACE INTO SOMETHING MUCH MORE THAN HUMAN, THEY VOWED TO USE THEIR AWESOME POWERS TO HELP MANKIND CHART THE UNKNOWN. STAN LEE PRESENTS . . .

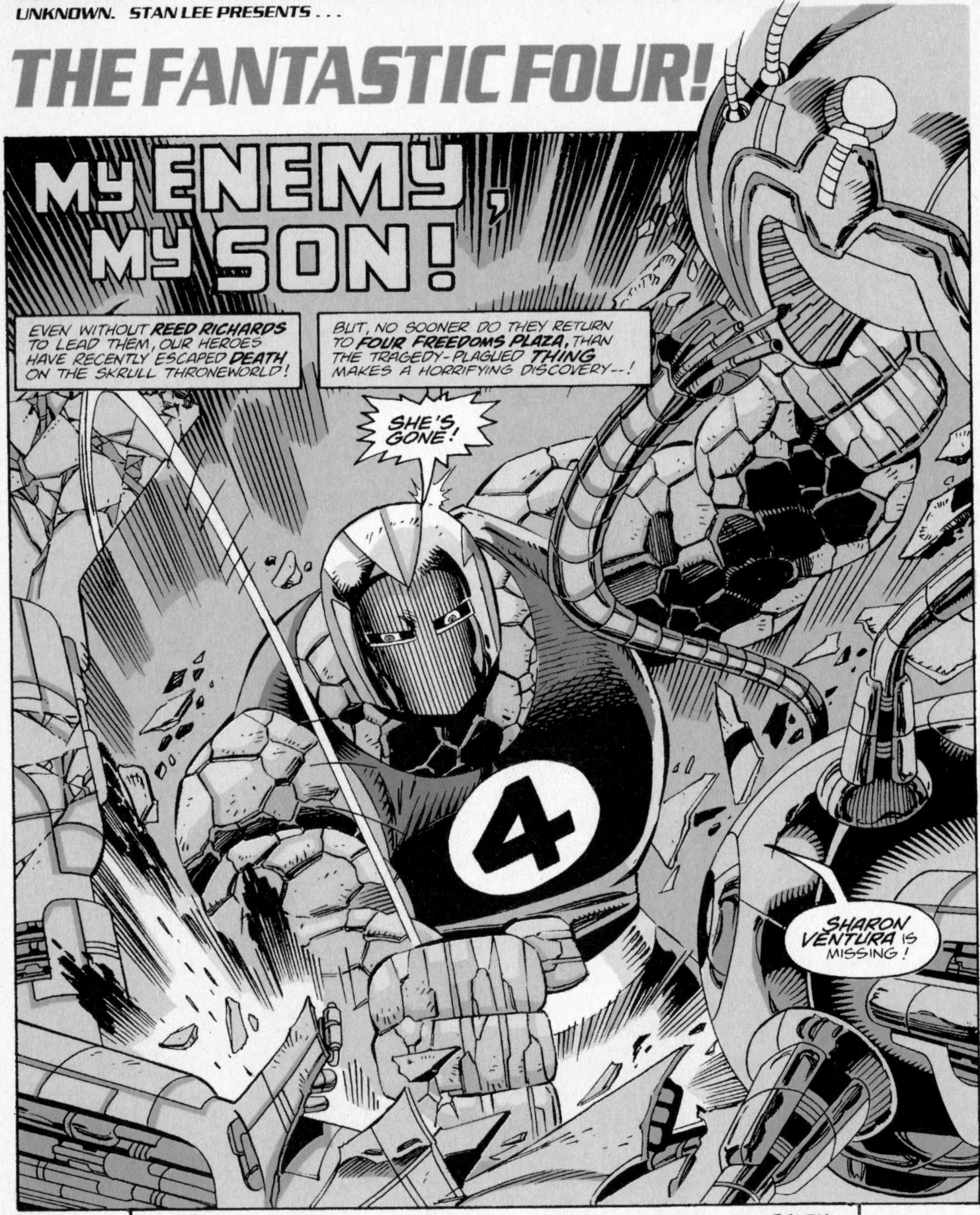
THE FANTASTIC FOUR!
MY ENEMY, MY SON!
EVEN WITHOUT REED RICHARDS TO LEAD THEM, OUR HEROES HAVE RECENTLY ESCAPED DEATH ON THE SKRULL THRONEWORLD!
BUT, NO SOONER DO THEY RETURN TO FOUR FREEDOMS PLAZA, THAN THE TRAGEDY-PLAGUED THING MAKES A HORRIFYING DISCOVERY--!
SHE'S GONE!
SHARON VENTURA IS MISSING!
TOM DEFALCO & PAUL RYAN WORDS, PLOTS & PICTURES
DAN BULANADI INKS
DAVE SHARPE LETTERS
GINA GOING COLORS
RALPH MACCHIO EDITOR

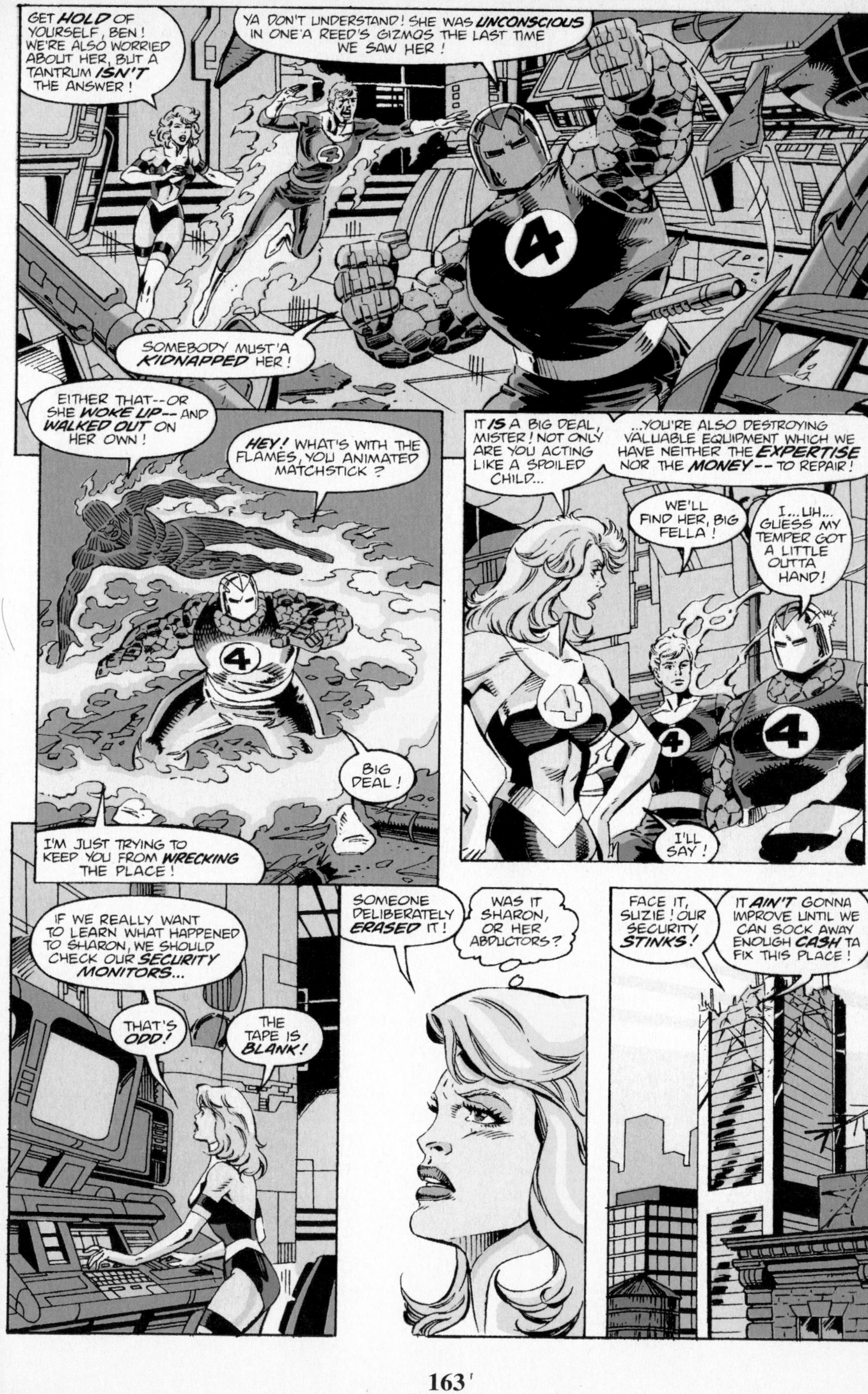

GET HOLD OF YOURSELF, BEN! WE'RE ALSO WORRIED ABOUT HER, BUT A TANTRUM ISN'T THE ANSWER!
YA DON'T UNDERSTAND! SHE WAS UNCONSCIOUS IN ONE'A REED'S GIZMOS THE LAST TIME WE SAW HER!
SOMEBODY MUST'A KIDNAPPED HER!
EITHER THAT--OR SHE WOKE UP--AND WALKED OUT ON HER OWN!
HEY! WHAT'S WITH THE FLAMES, YOU ANIMATED MATCHSTICK?
BIG DEAL!
I'M JUST TRYING TO KEEP YOU FROM WRECKING THE PLACE!
IT IS A BIG DEAL, MISTER! NOT ONLY ARE YOU ACTING LIKE A SPOILED CHILD...
...YOU'RE ALSO DESTROYING VALUABLE EQUIPMENT WHICH WE HAVE NEITHER THE EXPERTISE NOR THE MONEY--TO REPAIR!
WE'LL FIND HER, BIG FELLA!
I...UH... GUESS MY TEMPER GOT A LITTLE OUTTA HAND!
I'LL SAY!
IF WE REALLY WANT TO LEARN WHAT HAPPENED TO SHARON, WE SHOULD CHECK OUR SECURITY MONITORS...
THAT'S ODD!
THE TAPE IS BLANK!
SOMEONE DELIBERATELY ERASED IT!
WAS IT SHARON, OR HER ABDUCTORS?
FACE IT, SUZIE! OUR SECURITY STINKS!
IT AIN'T GONNA IMPROVE UNTIL WE CAN SOCK AWAY ENOUGH CASH TA FIX THIS PLACE!

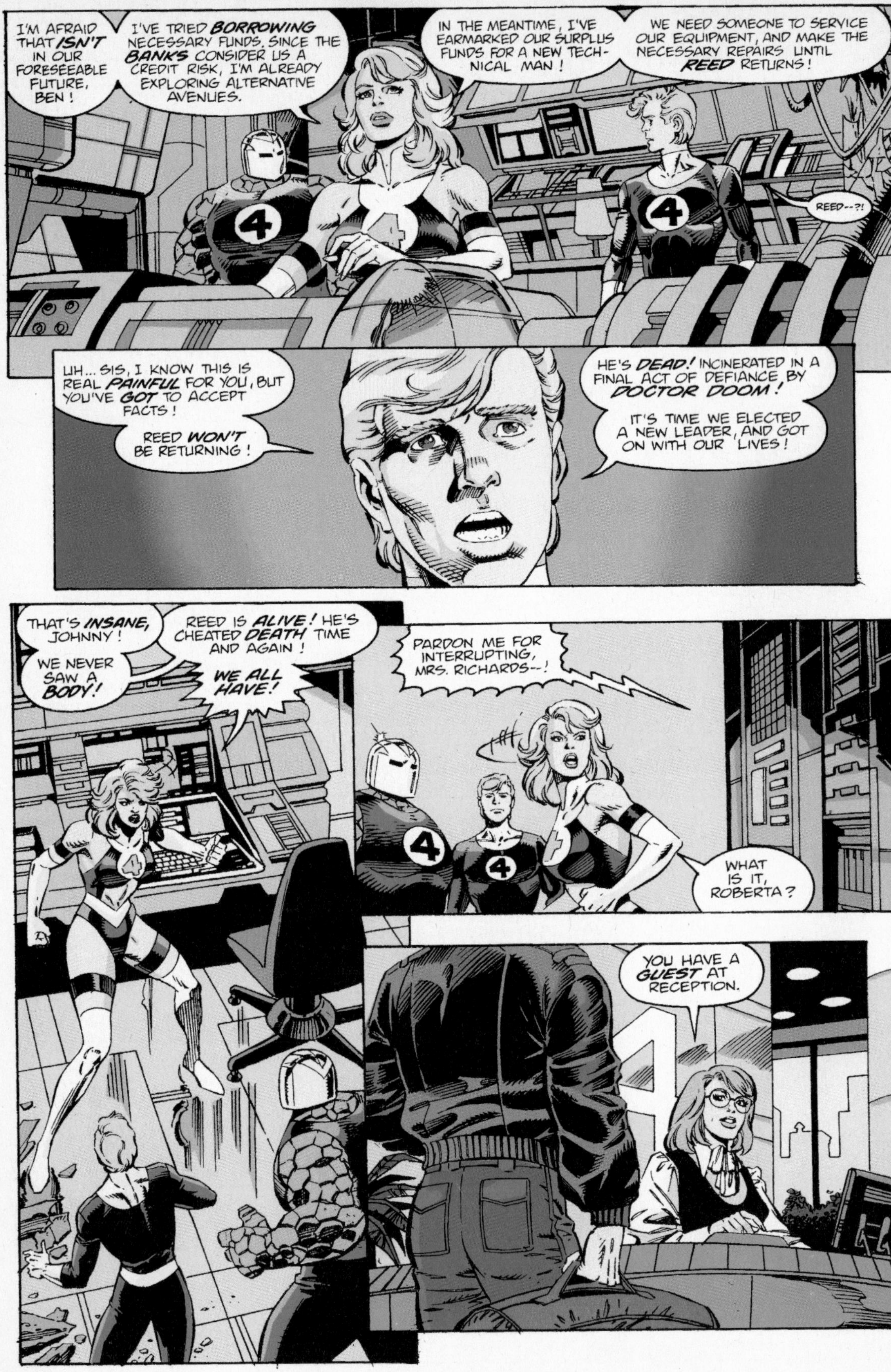
I'M AFRAID THAT ISN'T IN OUR FORESEEABLE FUTURE, BEN!
I'VE TRIED BORROWING NECESSARY FUNDS. SINCE THE BANKS CONSIDER US A CREDIT RISK, I'M ALREADY EXPLORING ALTERNATIVE AVENUES.
IN THE MEANTIME, I'VE EARMARKED OUR SURPLUS FUNDS FOR A NEW TECHNICAL MAN!
WE NEED SOMEONE TO SERVICE OUR EQUIPMENT, AND MAKE THE NECESSARY REPAIRS UNTIL REED RETURNS!
REED--?!
UH... SIS, I KNOW THIS IS REAL PAINFUL FOR YOU, BUT YOU'VE GOT TO ACCEPT FACTS!
REED WON'T BE RETURNING!
HE'S DEAD! INCINERATED IN A FINAL ACT OF DEFIANCE, BY DOCTOR DOOM!
IT'S TIME WE ELECTED A NEW LEADER, AND GOT ON WITH OUR LIVES!
THAT'S INSANE, JOHNNY!
WE NEVER SAW A BODY!
REED IS ALIVE! HE'S CHEATED DEATH TIME AND AGAIN!
WE ALL HAVE!
PARDON ME FOR INTERRUPTING, MRS. RICHARDS--!
WHAT IS IT, ROBERTA?
YOU HAVE A GUEST AT RECEPTION.

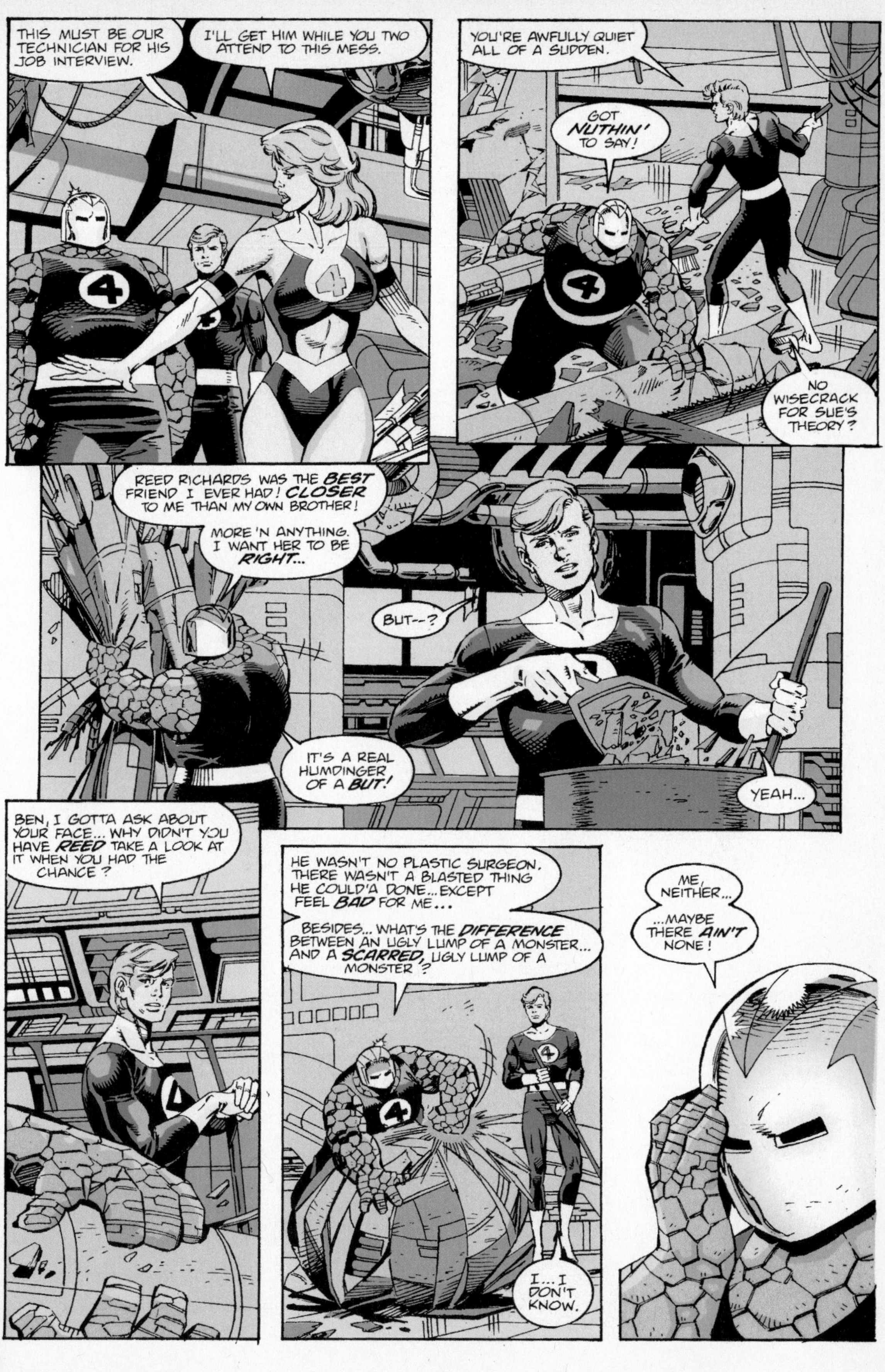
THIS MUST BE OUR TECHNICIAN FOR HIS JOB INTERVIEW.
I'LL GET HIM WHILE YOU TWO ATTEND TO THIS MESS.
YOU'RE AWFULLY QUIET ALL OF A SUDDEN.
GOT NUTHIN' TO SAY!
NO WISECRACK FOR SUE'S THEORY?
REED RICHARDS WAS THE BEST FRIEND I EVER HAD! CLOSER TO ME THAN MY OWN BROTHER!
MORE'N ANYTHING. I WANT HER TO BE RIGHT...
BUT--?
IT'S A REAL HUMDINGER OF A BUT!
YEAH...
BEN, I GOTTA ASK ABOUT YOUR FACE... WHY DIDN'T YOU HAVE REED TAKE A LOOK AT IT WHEN YOU HAD THE CHANCE?
HE WASN'T NO PLASTIC SURGEON. THERE WASN'T A BLASTED THING HE COULD'A DONE... EXCEPT FEEL BAD FOR ME...
BESIDES... WHAT'S THE DIFFERENCE BETWEEN AN UGLY LUMP OF A MONSTER... AND A SCARRED, UGLY LUMP OF A MONSTER?
I... I DON'T KNOW.
ME, NEITHER...
...MAYBE THERE AIN'T NONE!

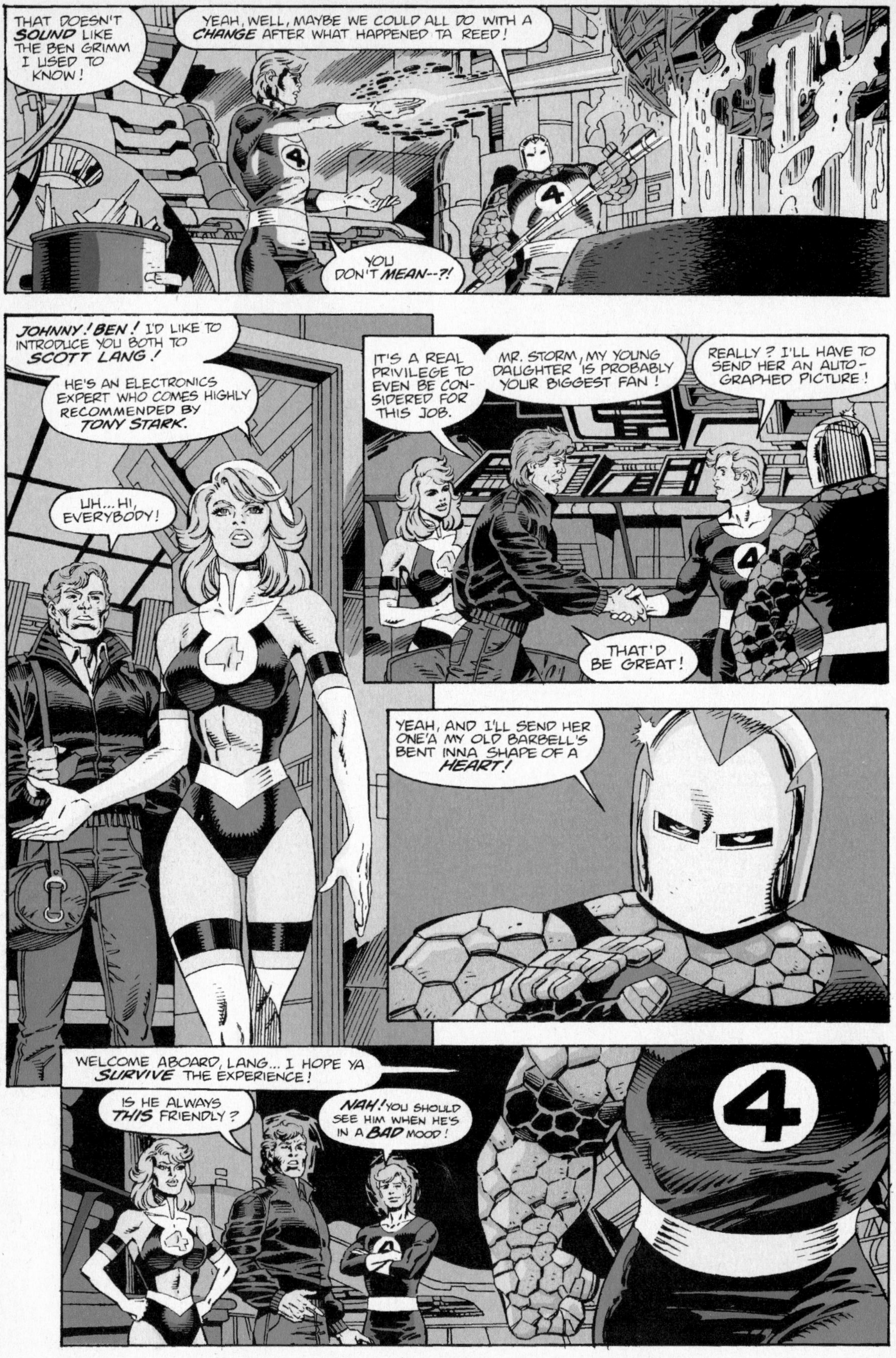
THAT DOESN'T SOUND LIKE THE BEN GRIMM I USED TO KNOW!
YEAH, WELL, MAYBE WE COULD ALL DO WITH A CHANGE AFTER WHAT HAPPENED TA REED!
YOU DON'T MEAN--?!
JOHNNY! BEN! I'D LIKE TO INTRODUCE YOU BOTH TO SCOTT LANG!
HE'S AN ELECTRONICS EXPERT WHO COMES HIGHLY RECOMMENDED BY TONY STARK.
UH... HI, EVERYBODY!
IT'S A REAL PRIVILEGE TO EVEN BE CONSIDERED FOR THIS JOB.
MR. STORM, MY YOUNG DAUGHTER IS PROBABLY YOUR BIGGEST FAN!
REALLY? I'LL HAVE TO SEND HER AN AUTOGRAPHED PICTURE!
THAT'D BE GREAT!
YEAH, AND I'LL SEND HER ONE'A MY OLD BARBELL'S BENT INNA SHAPE OF A HEART!
WELCOME ABOARD, LANG... I HOPE YA SURVIVE THE EXPERIENCE!
IS HE ALWAYS THIS FRIENDLY?
NAH! YOU SHOULD SEE HIM WHEN HE'S IN A BAD MOOD!

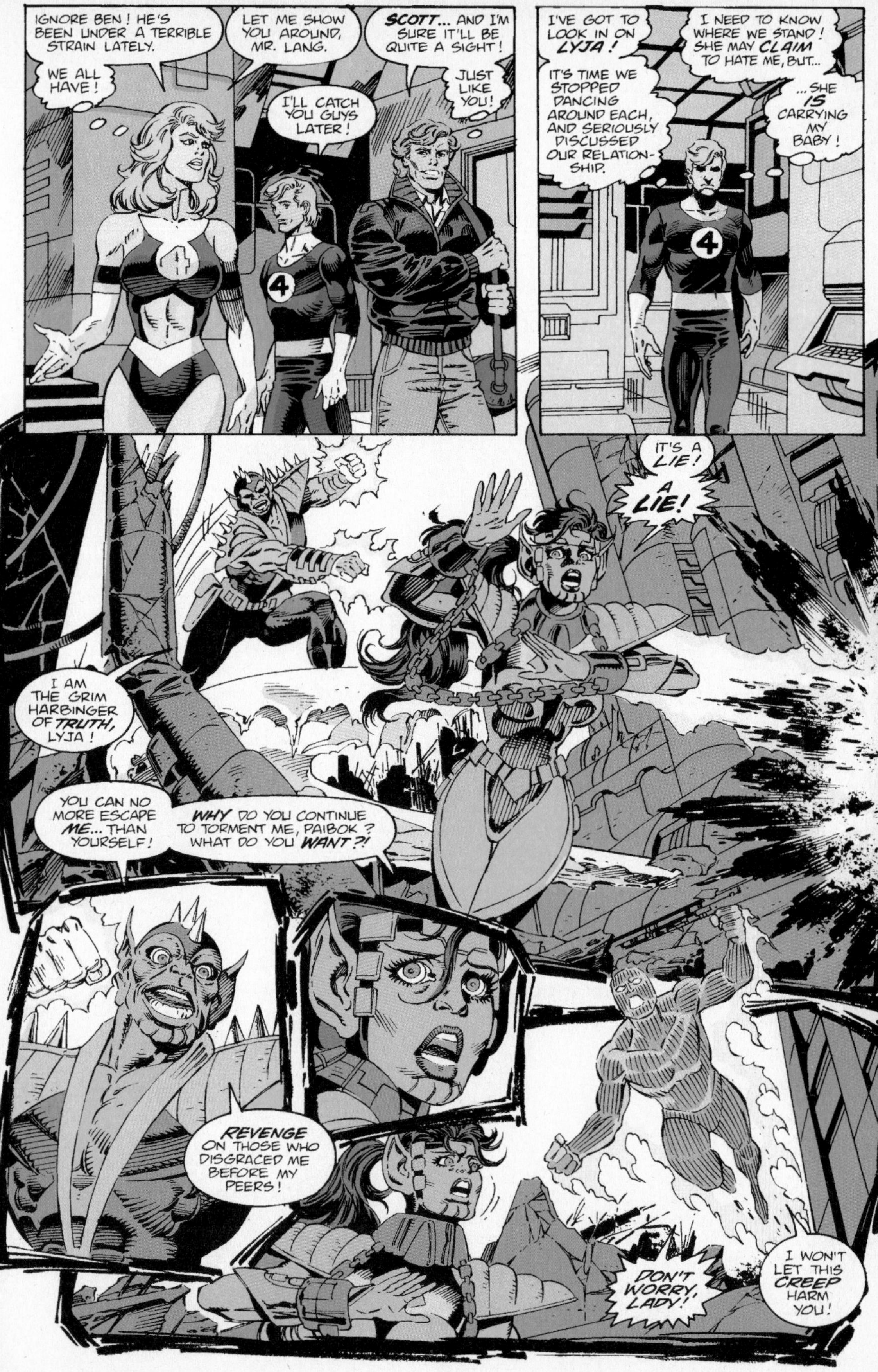

IGNORE BEN! HE'S BEEN UNDER A TERRIBLE STRAIN LATELY.
WE ALL HAVE!
LET ME SHOW YOU AROUND, MR. LANG.
I'LL CATCH YOU GUYS LATER!
SCOTT... AND I'M SURE IT'LL BE QUITE A SIGHT!
JUST LIKE YOU!
I'VE GOT TO LOOK IN ON LYJA!
IT'S TIME WE STOPPED DANCING AROUND EACH, AND SERIOUSLY DISCUSSED OUR RELATIONSHIP.
I NEED TO KNOW WHERE WE STAND! SHE MAY CLAIM TO HATE ME, BUT...
...SHE IS CARRYING MY BABY!
IT'S A LIE!
A LIE!
I AM THE GRIM HARBINGER OF TRUTH, LYJA!
YOU CAN NO MORE ESCAPE ME... THAN YOURSELF!
WHY DO YOU CONTINUE TO TORMENT ME, PAIBOK? WHAT DO YOU WANT?!
REVENGE ON THOSE WHO DISGRACED ME BEFORE MY PEERS!
DON'T WORRY, LADY!
I WON'T LET THIS CREEP HARM YOU!

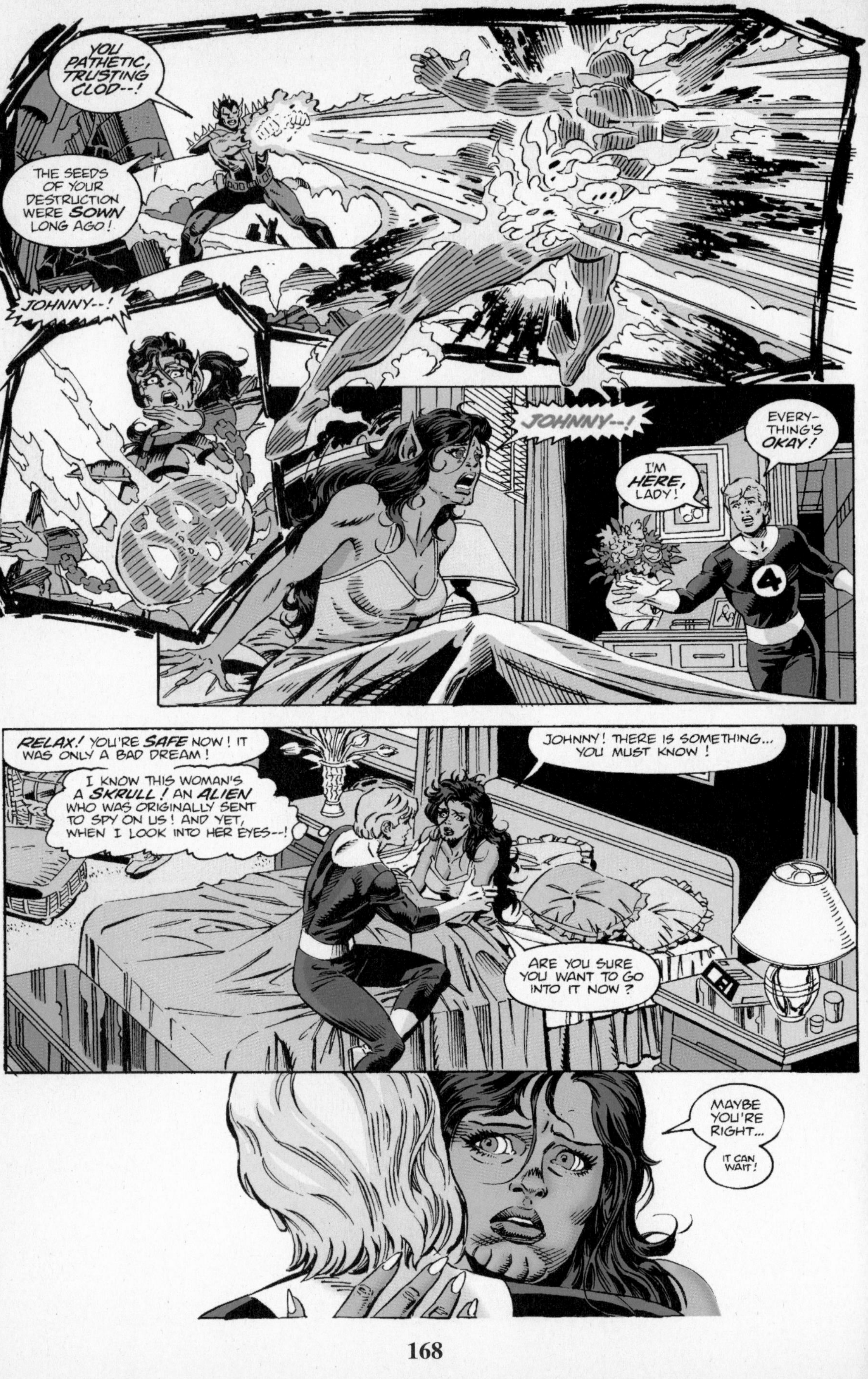
YOU PATHETIC, TRUSTING CLOD--!
THE SEEDS OF YOUR DESTRUCTION WERE SOWN LONG AGO!
JOHNNY--!
JOHNNY--!
I'M HERE, LADY!
EVERY-THING'S OKAY!
RELAX! YOU'RE SAFE NOW! IT WAS ONLY A BAD DREAM!
I KNOW THIS WOMAN'S A SKRULL! AN ALIEN WHO WAS ORIGINALLY SENT TO SPY ON US! AND YET, WHEN I LOOK INTO HER EYES--!
JOHNNY! THERE IS SOMETHING... YOU MUST KNOW!
ARE YOU SURE YOU WANT TO GO INTO IT NOW?
MAYBE YOU'RE RIGHT...
IT CAN WAIT!

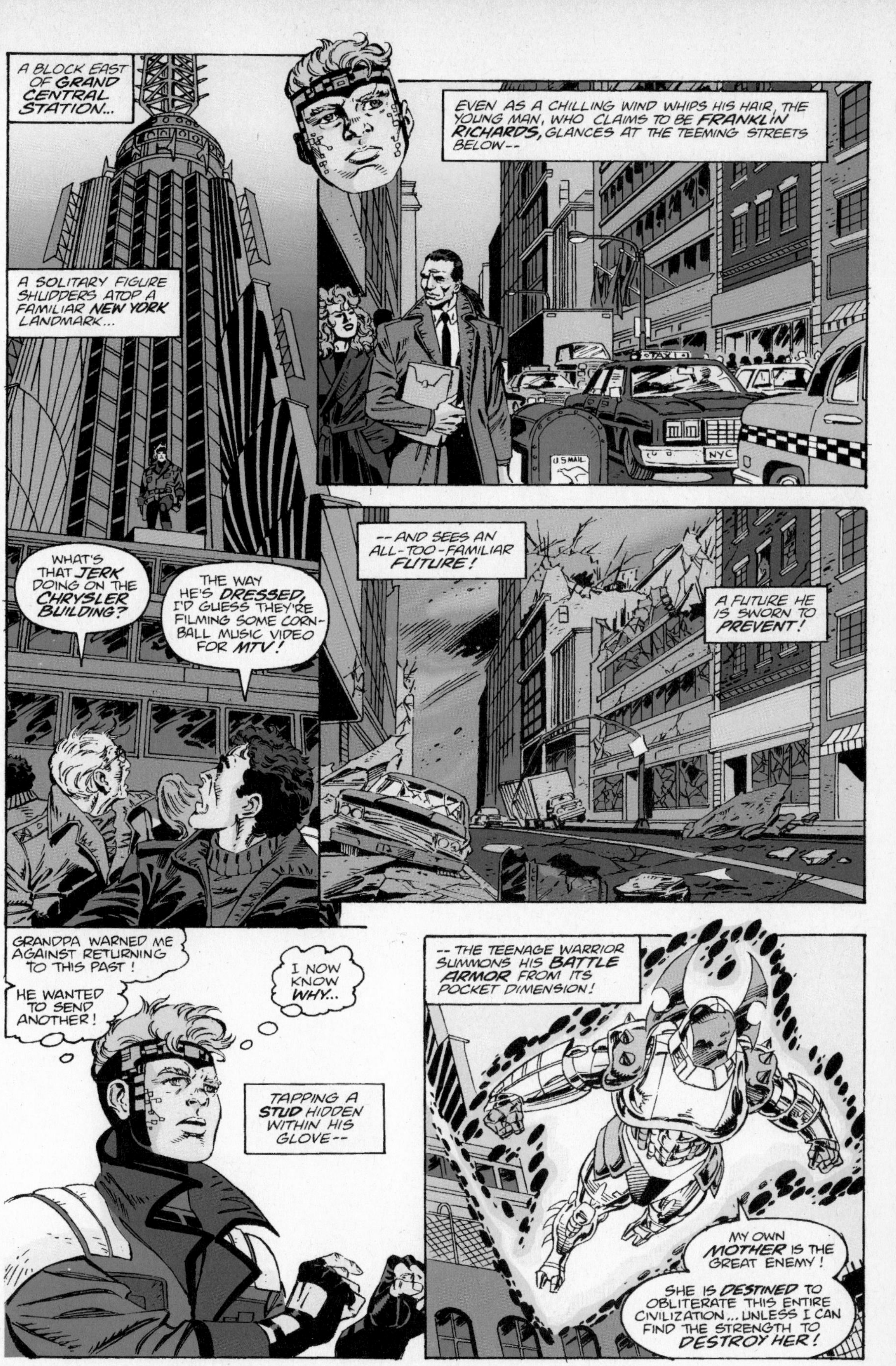
A BLOCK EAST OF GRAND CENTRAL STATION...
EVEN AS A CHILLING WIND WHIPS HIS HAIR, THE YOUNG MAN, WHO CLAIMS TO BE FRANKLIN RICHARDS, GLANCES AT THE TEEMING STREETS BELOW--
A SOLITARY FIGURE SHUDDERS ATOP A FAMILIAR NEW YORK LANDMARK...
U.S. MAIL
NYC
WHAT'S THAT JERK DOING ON THE CHRYSLER BUILDING?
THE WAY HE'S DRESSED, I'D GUESS THEY'RE FILMING SOME CORNBALL MUSIC VIDEO FOR MTV!
--AND SEES AN ALL-TOO-FAMILIAR FUTURE!
A FUTURE HE IS SWORN TO PREVENT!
GRANDPA WARNED ME AGAINST RETURNING TO THIS PAST!
HE WANTED TO SEND ANOTHER!
I NOW KNOW WHY...
TAPPING A STUD HIDDEN WITHIN HIS GLOVE--
-- THE TEENAGE WARRIOR SUMMONS HIS BATTLE ARMOR FROM ITS POCKET DIMENSION!
MY OWN MOTHER IS THE GREAT ENEMY!
SHE IS DESTINED TO OBLITERATE THIS ENTIRE CIVILIZATION... UNLESS I CAN FIND THE STRENGTH TO DESTROY HER!

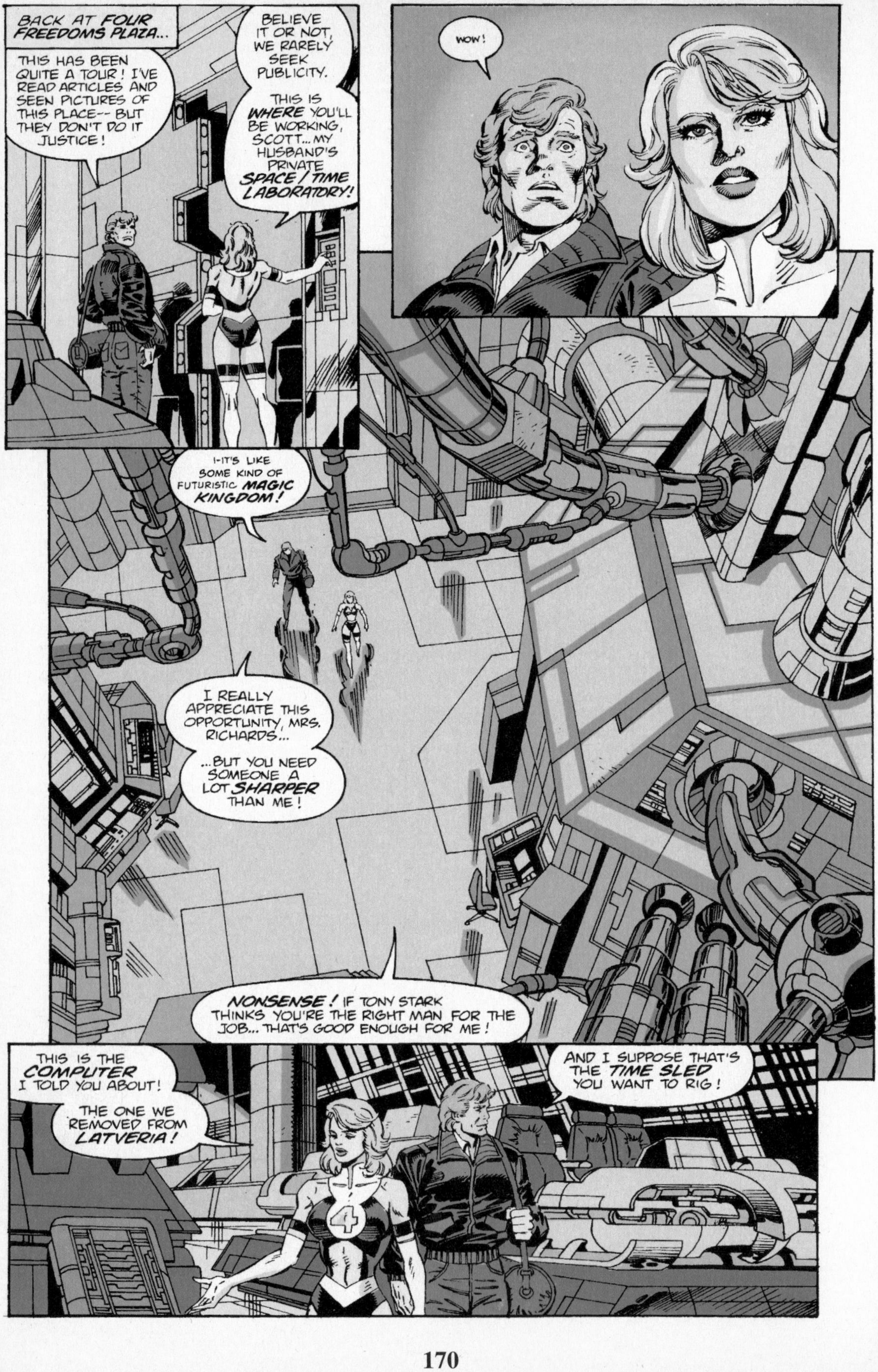
BACK AT FOUR FREEDOMS PLAZA...
THIS HAS BEEN QUITE A TOUR! I'VE READ ARTICLES AND SEEN PICTURES OF THIS PLACE-- BUT THEY DON'T DO IT JUSTICE!
BELIEVE IT OR NOT, WE RARELY SEEK PUBLICITY.
THIS IS WHERE YOU'LL BE WORKING, SCOTT... MY HUSBAND'S PRIVATE SPACE/TIME LABORATORY!
WOW!
I-IT'S LIKE SOME KIND OF FUTURISTIC MAGIC KINGDOM!
I REALLY APPRECIATE THIS OPPORTUNITY, MRS. RICHARDS...
...BUT YOU NEED SOMEONE A LOT SHARPER THAN ME!
NONSENSE! IF TONY STARK THINKS YOU'RE THE RIGHT MAN FOR THE JOB... THAT'S GOOD ENOUGH FOR ME!
THIS IS THE COMPUTER I TOLD YOU ABOUT!
THE ONE WE REMOVED FROM LATVERIA!
AND I SUPPOSE THAT'S THE TIME SLED YOU WANT TO RIG!

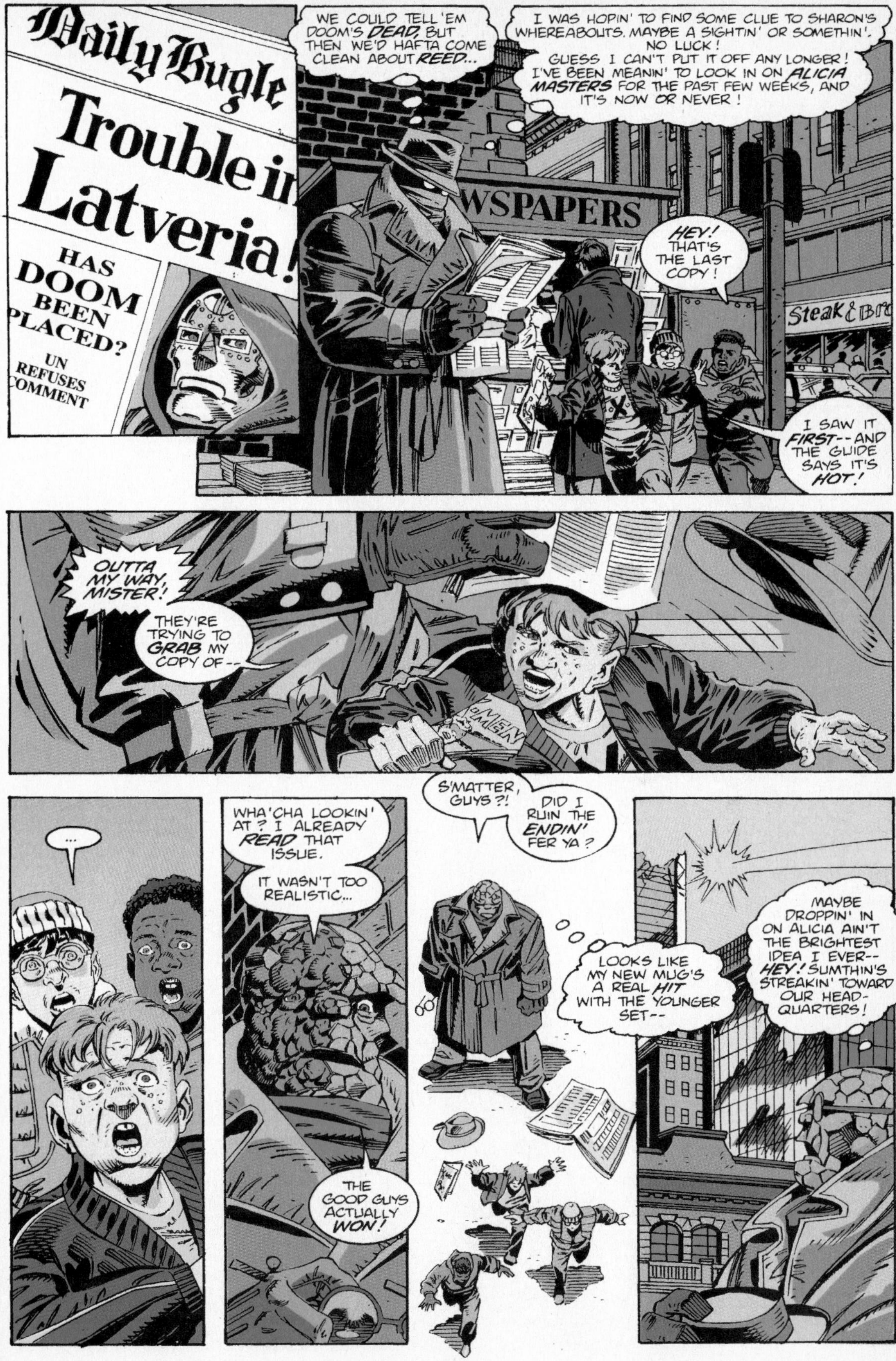
Daily Bugle
Trouble in Latveria!
HAS DOOM BEEN REPLACED?
UN REFUSES COMMENT
WE COULD TELL 'EM DOOM'S DEAD, BUT THEN WE'D HAFTA COME CLEAN ABOUT REED...
I WAS HOPIN' TO FIND SOME CLUE TO SHARON'S WHEREABOUTS. MAYBE A SIGHTIN' OR SOMETHIN'. NO LUCK! GUESS I CAN'T PUT IT OFF ANY LONGER! I'VE BEEN MEANIN' TO LOOK IN ON ALICIA MASTERS FOR THE PAST FEW WEEKS, AND IT'S NOW OR NEVER!
WSPAPERS
HEY! THAT'S THE LAST COPY!
Steak & Bro
I SAW IT FIRST--AND THE GUIDE SAYS IT'S HOT!
OUTTA MY WAY, MISTER!
THEY'RE TRYING TO GRAB MY COPY OF--
...
WHA'CHA LOOKIN' AT? I ALREADY READ THAT ISSUE.
IT WASN'T TOO REALISTIC...
THE GOOD GUYS ACTUALLY WON!
S'MATTER, GUYS?!
DID I RUIN THE ENDIN' FER YA?
LOOKS LIKE MY NEW MUG'S A REAL HIT WITH THE YOUNGER SET--
MAYBE DROPPIN' IN ON ALICIA AIN'T THE BRIGHTEST IDEA I EVER--HEY! SUMTHIN'S STREAKIN' TOWARD OUR HEAD-QUARTERS!

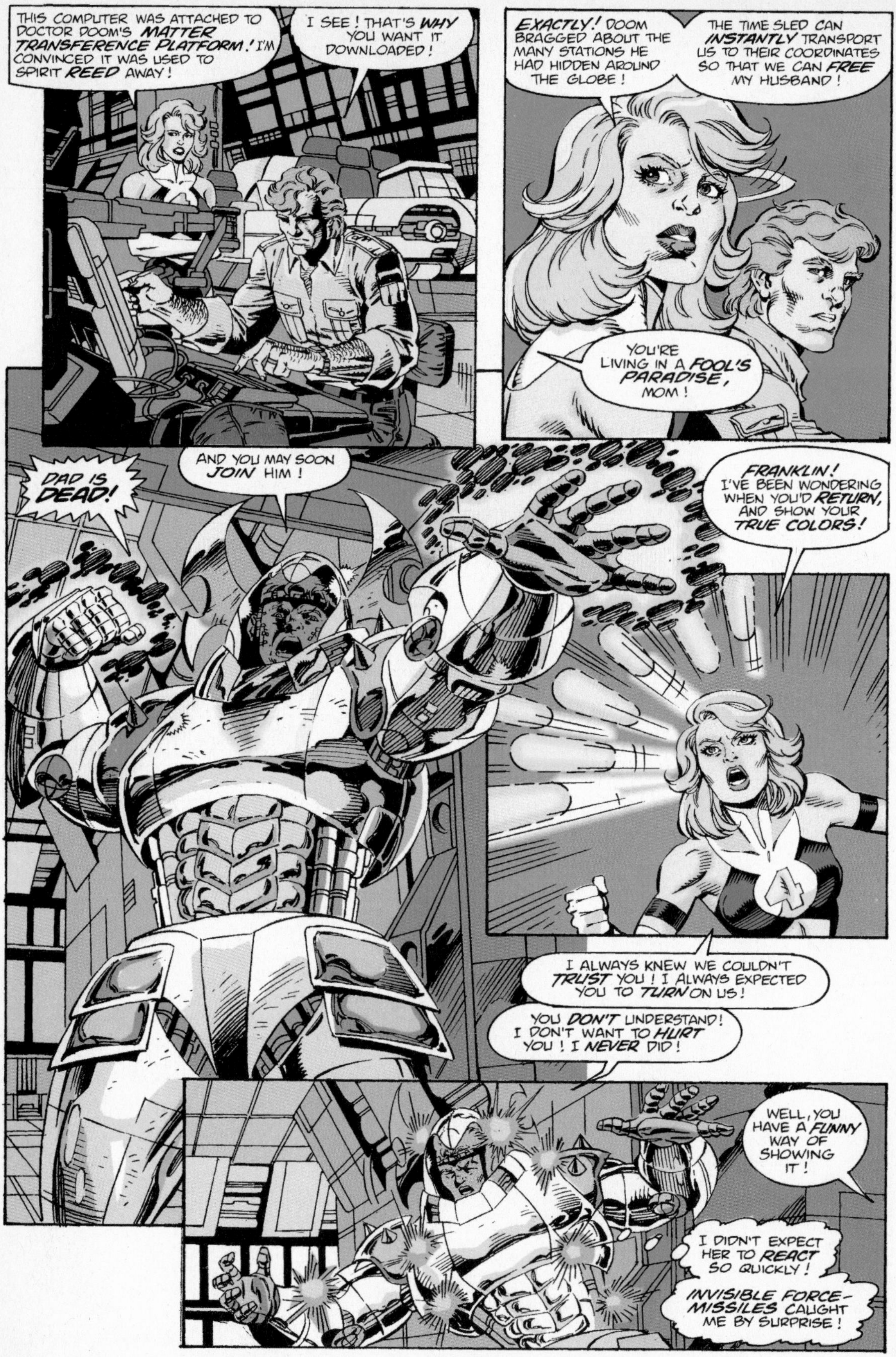
THIS COMPUTER WAS ATTACHED TO DOCTOR DOOM'S MATTER TRANSFERENCE PLATFORM! I'M CONVINCED IT WAS USED TO SPIRIT REED AWAY!
I SEE! THAT'S WHY YOU WANT IT DOWNLOADED!
EXACTLY! DOOM BRAGGED ABOUT THE MANY STATIONS HE HAD HIDDEN AROUND THE GLOBE!
THE TIME SLED CAN INSTANTLY TRANSPORT US TO THEIR COORDINATES SO THAT WE CAN FREE MY HUSBAND!
YOU'RE LIVING IN A FOOL'S PARADISE, MOM!
DAD IS DEAD!
AND YOU MAY SOON JOIN HIM!
FRANKLIN! I'VE BEEN WONDERING WHEN YOU'D RETURN, AND SHOW YOUR TRUE COLORS!
I ALWAYS KNEW WE COULDN'T TRUST YOU! I ALWAYS EXPECTED YOU TO TURN ON US!
YOU DON'T UNDERSTAND! I DON'T WANT TO HURT YOU! I NEVER DID!
WELL, YOU HAVE A FUNNY WAY OF SHOWING IT!
I DIDN'T EXPECT HER TO REACT SO QUICKLY!
INVISIBLE FORCE-MISSILES CAUGHT ME BY SURPRISE!

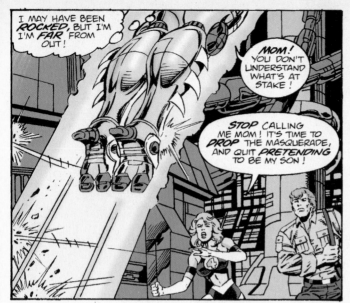

I MAY HAVE BEEN *ROCKED*, BUT I'M I'M *FAR* FROM OUT!

MOM! YOU DON'T UNDERSTAND WHAT'S AT STAKE!

STOP CALLING ME MOM! IT'S TIME TO *DROP* THE MASQUERADE, AND QUIT *PRETENDING* TO BE MY SON!

I *WISH* I WERE PRETENDING!

I AM *FRANKLIN!*

THAT'S WHY THIS IS ALL SO *PAINFUL!*

BARELY ERECTED THAT *FORCE FIELD* IN TIME!

RUN, SCOTT! GET TO SAFETY! THIS DOESN'T CONCERN YOU!

MS. RICHARDS, THERE'S SOMETHING YOU SHOULD *KNOW--!*

SAVE THE PERSONAL REVELATIONS FOR A QUIETER TIME, MISTER! I SAID *GO--*

--AND I *MEANT* IT!

B-BUT I CAN *HELP!* I'M THE-- *YEOW!*

GOOD IDEA, MOM! WE'LL KEEP THIS STRICTLY BE-TWEEN THE TWO OF US!

I'LL TELEKINETICALLY GUARANTEE US *TOTAL PRIVACY!*

SLAM!

173

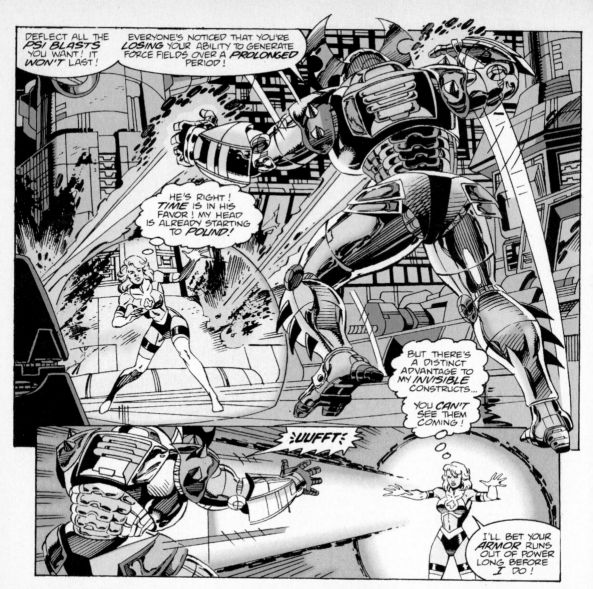

DEFLECT ALL THE *PSI BLASTS* YOU WANT! IT *WON'T* LAST!

EVERYONE'S NOTICED THAT YOU'RE *LOSING* YOUR ABILITY TO GENERATE FORCE FIELDS OVER A *PROLONGED* PERIOD!

HE'S RIGHT! *TIME* IS IN HIS FAVOR! MY HEAD IS ALREADY STARTING TO *POUND!*

BUT THERE'S A DISTINCT ADVANTAGE TO MY *INVISIBLE* CONSTRUCTS...

YOU *CAN'T* SEE THEM COMING!

:UUFFT:

I'LL BET YOUR *ARMOR* RUNS OUT OF POWER LONG BEFORE *I* DO!

YOU'LL *LOSE* THAT BET!

DAD ONCE WARNED YOU THAT I POSSESSED ENOUGH *PSIONIC ENERGY* TO DESTROY ALL LIFE ON EARTH!

HE *WASN'T* EXAGGERATING!

GRANDPA DESIGNED THIS ARMOR TO *DRAIN* MY EXCESS PSI ENERGY AND PREVENT *ME* FROM OVERLOADING!

I AM THE *SOURCE* OF ITS POWER!

I AM *PSI-LORD!*

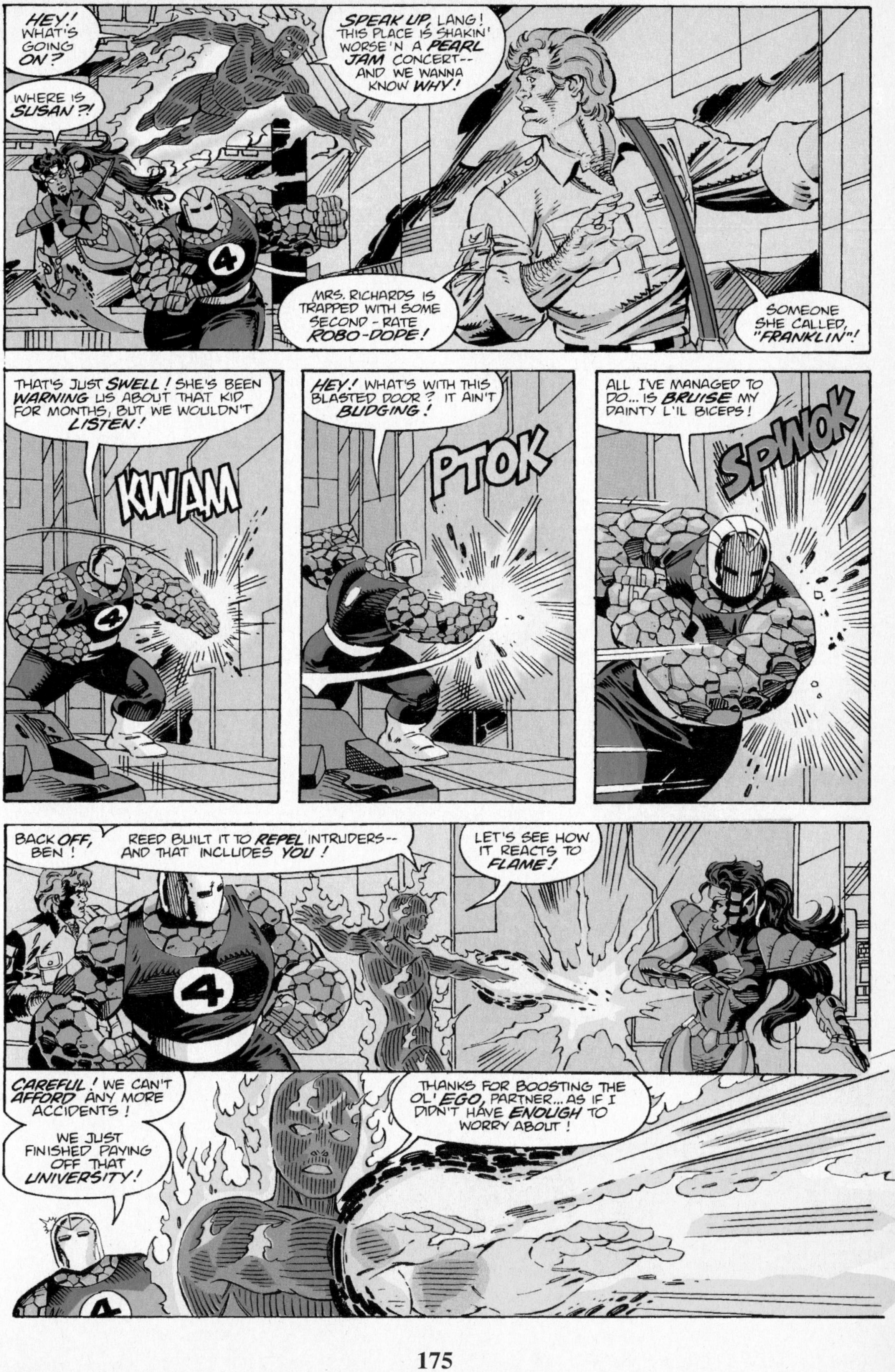
HEY! WHAT'S GOING ON?
WHERE IS SUSAN?!
SPEAK UP, LANG! THIS PLACE IS SHAKIN' WORSE'N A PEARL JAM CONCERT-- AND WE WANNA KNOW WHY!
MRS. RICHARDS IS TRAPPED WITH SOME SECOND-RATE ROBO-DOPE!
SOMEONE SHE CALLED, "FRANKLIN"!
THAT'S JUST SWELL! SHE'S BEEN WARNING US ABOUT THAT KID FOR MONTHS, BUT WE WOULDN'T LISTEN!
KWAM
HEY! WHAT'S WITH THIS BLASTED DOOR? IT AIN'T BUDGING!
PTOK
ALL I'VE MANAGED TO DO... IS BRUISE MY DAINTY L'IL BICEPS!
SPWOK
BACK OFF, BEN!
REED BUILT IT TO REPEL INTRUDERS-- AND THAT INCLUDES YOU!
LET'S SEE HOW IT REACTS TO FLAME!
CAREFUL! WE CAN'T AFFORD ANY MORE ACCIDENTS!
WE JUST FINISHED PAYING OFF THAT UNIVERSITY!
THANKS FOR BOOSTING THE OL' EGO, PARTNER... AS IF I DIDN'T HAVE ENOUGH TO WORRY ABOUT!

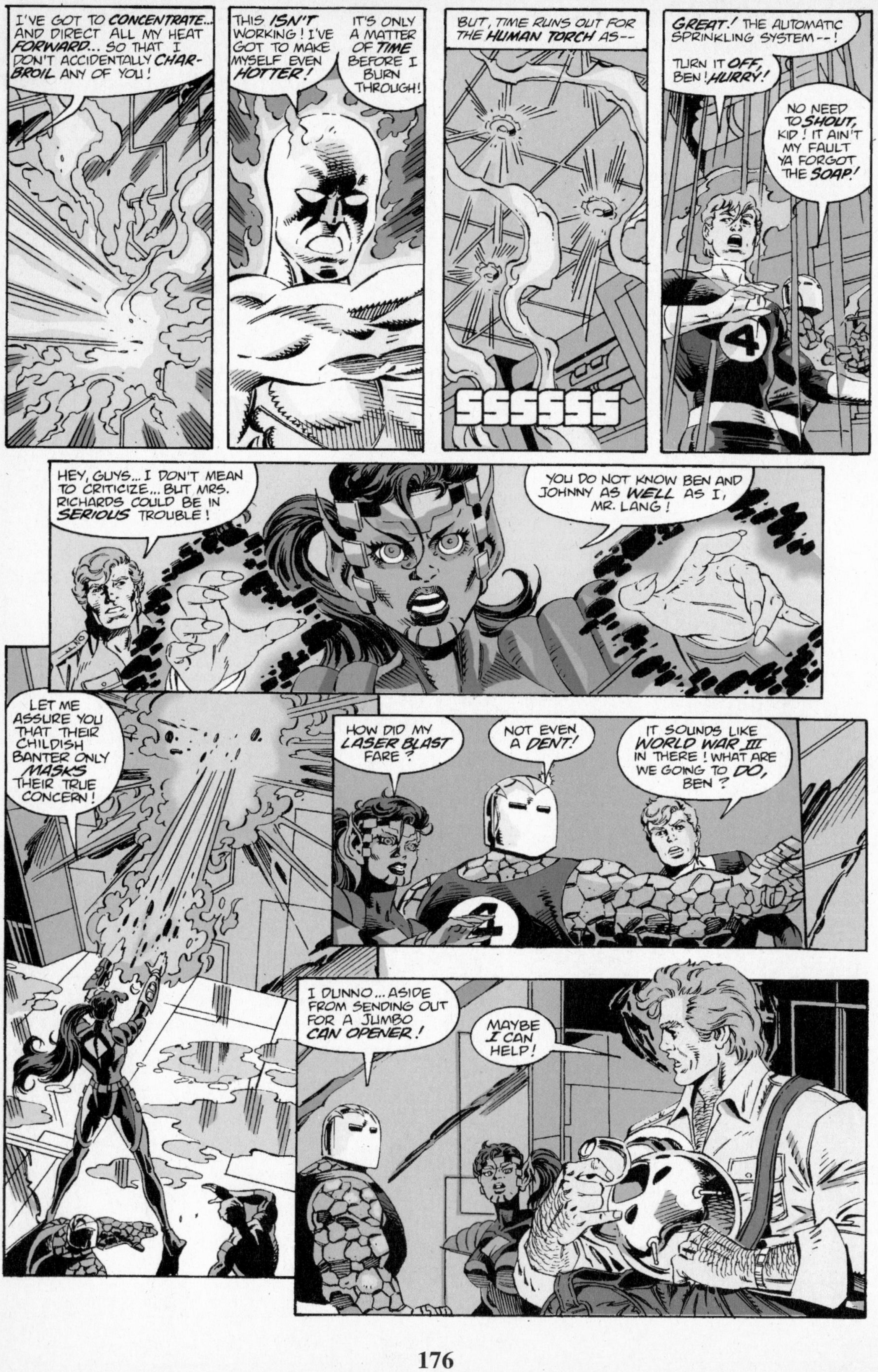
I'VE GOT TO CONCENTRATE... AND DIRECT ALL MY HEAT FORWARD... SO THAT I DON'T ACCIDENTALLY CHAR-BROIL ANY OF YOU!
THIS ISN'T WORKING! I'VE GOT TO MAKE MYSELF EVEN HOTTER!
IT'S ONLY A MATTER OF TIME BEFORE I BURN THROUGH!
BUT, TIME RUNS OUT FOR THE HUMAN TORCH AS--
SSSSSS
GREAT! THE AUTOMATIC SPRINKLING SYSTEM--!
TURN IT OFF, BEN! HURRY!
NO NEED TO SHOUT, KID! IT AIN'T MY FAULT YA FORGOT THE SOAP!
HEY, GUYS... I DON'T MEAN TO CRITICIZE... BUT MRS. RICHARDS COULD BE IN SERIOUS TROUBLE!
YOU DO NOT KNOW BEN AND JOHNNY AS WELL AS I, MR. LANG!
LET ME ASSURE YOU THAT THEIR CHILDISH BANTER ONLY MASKS THEIR TRUE CONCERN!
HOW DID MY LASER BLAST FARE?
NOT EVEN A DENT!
IT SOUNDS LIKE WORLD WAR III IN THERE! WHAT ARE WE GOING TO DO, BEN?
I DUNNO... ASIDE FROM SENDING OUT FOR A JUMBO CAN OPENER!
MAYBE I CAN HELP!

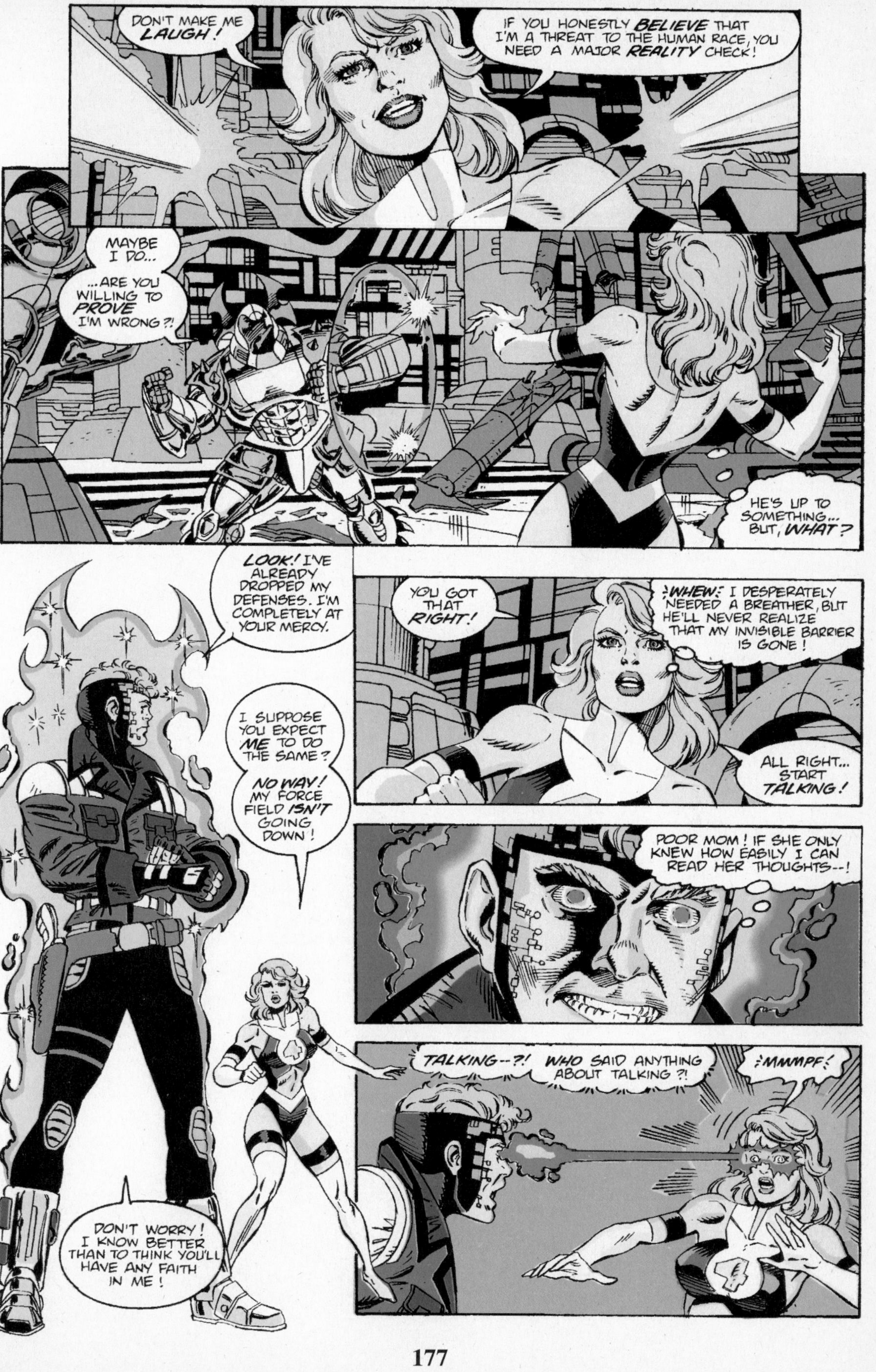

DON'T MAKE ME LAUGH!
IF YOU HONESTLY BELIEVE THAT I'M A THREAT TO THE HUMAN RACE, YOU NEED A MAJOR REALITY CHECK!
MAYBE I DO...
...ARE YOU WILLING TO PROVE I'M WRONG?!
HE'S UP TO SOMETHING... BUT, WHAT?
LOOK! I'VE ALREADY DROPPED MY DEFENSES. I'M COMPLETELY AT YOUR MERCY.
I SUPPOSE YOU EXPECT ME TO DO THE SAME?
NO WAY! MY FORCE FIELD ISN'T GOING DOWN!
DON'T WORRY! I KNOW BETTER THAN TO THINK YOU'LL HAVE ANY FAITH IN ME!
YOU GOT THAT RIGHT!
WHEW! I DESPERATELY NEEDED A BREATHER, BUT HE'LL NEVER REALIZE THAT MY INVISIBLE BARRIER IS GONE!
ALL RIGHT... START TALKING!
POOR MOM! IF SHE ONLY KNEW HOW EASILY I CAN READ HER THOUGHTS--!
TALKING--?! WHO SAID ANYTHING ABOUT TALKING?!
MMMPF!

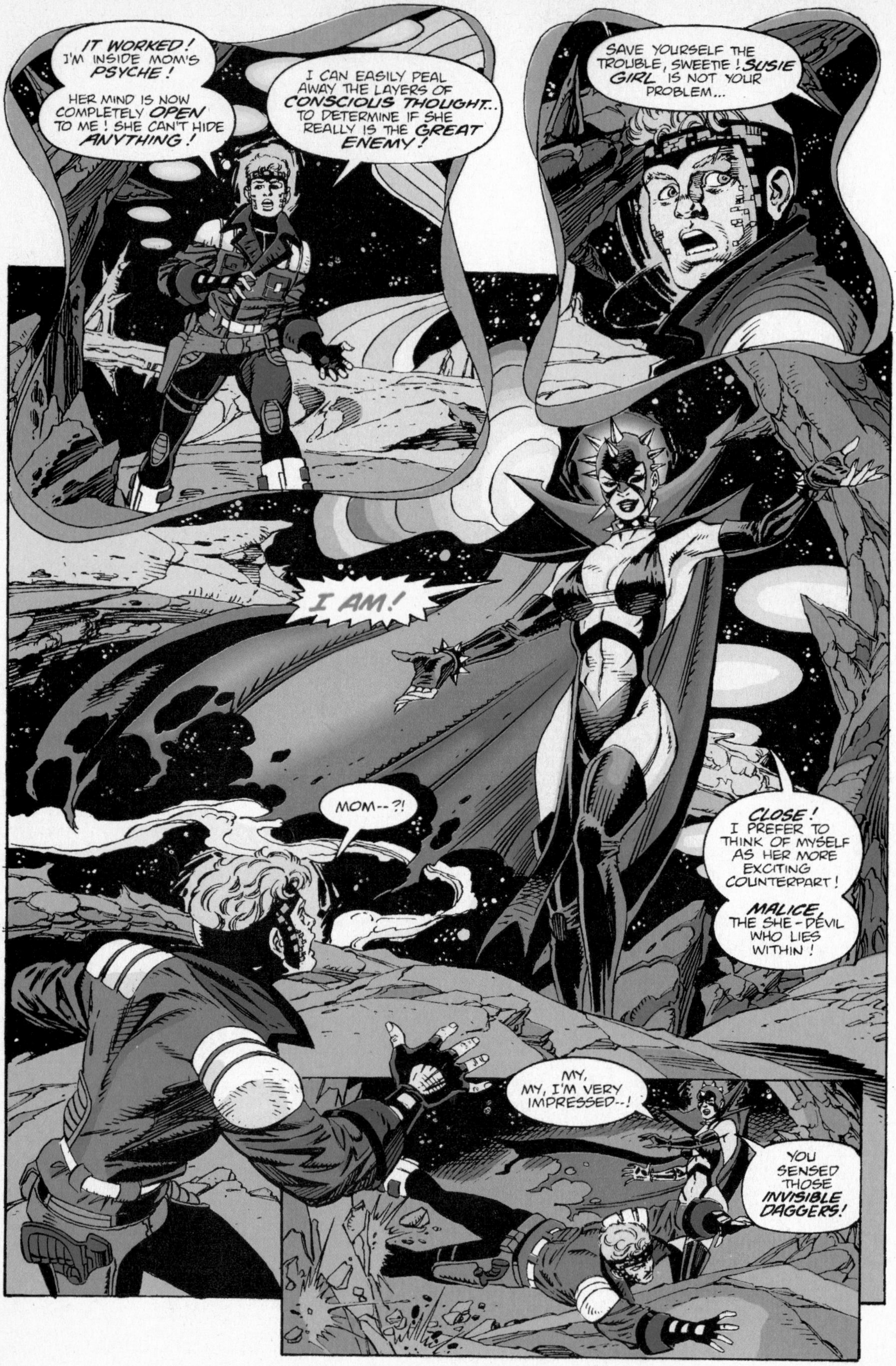
IT WORKED! I'M INSIDE MOM'S PSYCHE!
HER MIND IS NOW COMPLETELY OPEN TO ME! SHE CAN'T HIDE ANYTHING!
I CAN EASILY PEAL AWAY THE LAYERS OF CONSCIOUS THOUGHT... TO DETERMINE IF SHE REALLY IS THE GREAT ENEMY!
SAVE YOURSELF THE TROUBLE, SWEETIE! SUSIE GIRL IS NOT YOUR PROBLEM...
I AM!
MOM--?!
CLOSE! I PREFER TO THINK OF MYSELF AS HER MORE EXCITING COUNTERPART!
MALICE, THE SHE-DEVIL WHO LIES WITHIN!
MY, MY, I'M VERY IMPRESSED--!
YOU SENSED THOSE INVISIBLE DAGGERS!

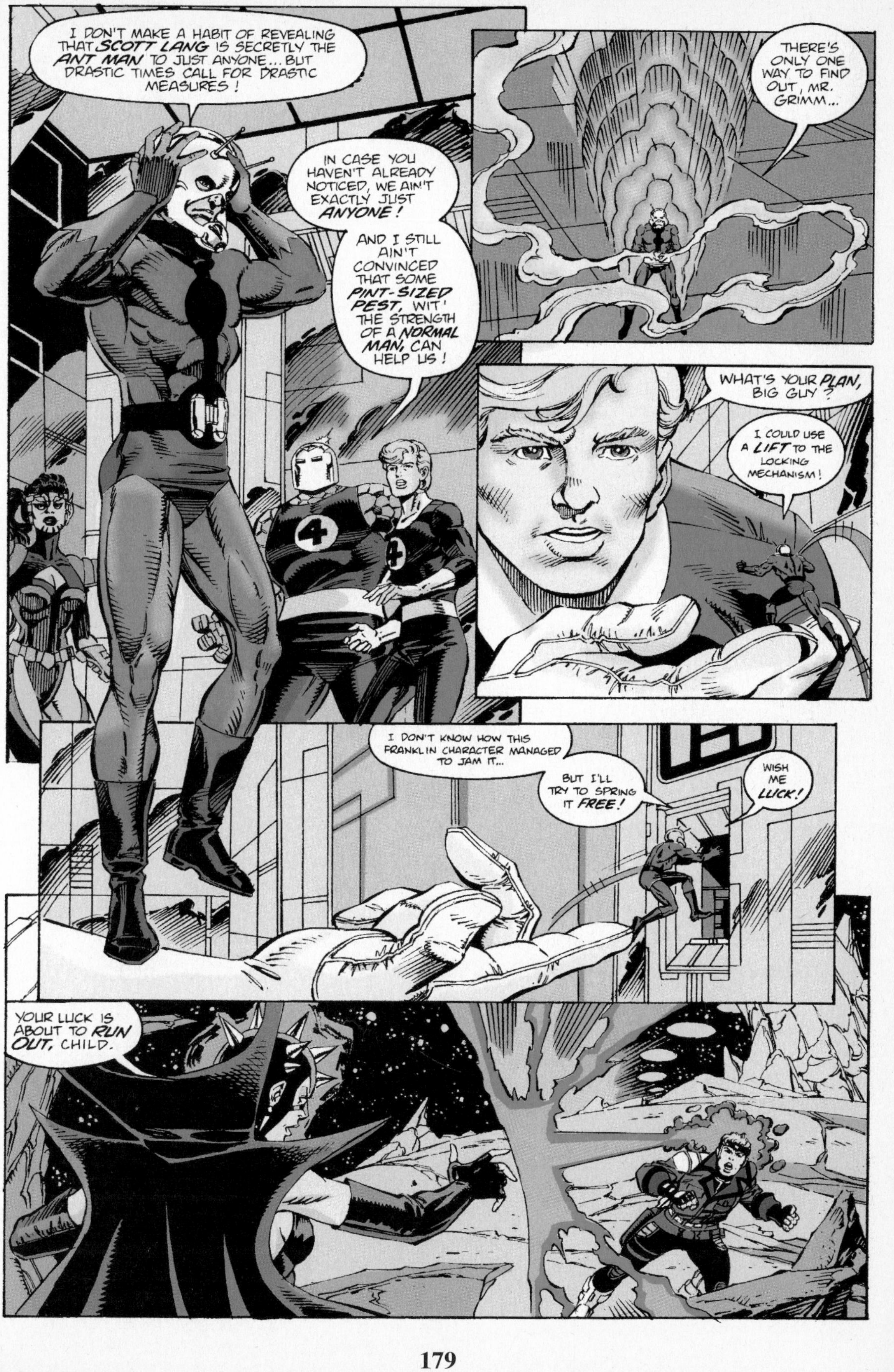

I DON'T MAKE A HABIT OF REVEALING THAT SCOTT LANG IS SECRETLY THE ANT MAN TO JUST ANYONE... BUT DRASTIC TIMES CALL FOR DRASTIC MEASURES!
IN CASE YOU HAVEN'T ALREADY NOTICED, WE AIN'T EXACTLY JUST ANYONE!
AND I STILL AIN'T CONVINCED THAT SOME PINT-SIZED PEST, WIT' THE STRENGTH OF A NORMAL MAN, CAN HELP US!
THERE'S ONLY ONE WAY TO FIND OUT, MR. GRIMM...
WHAT'S YOUR PLAN, BIG GUY?
I COULD USE A LIFT TO THE LOCKING MECHANISM!
I DON'T KNOW HOW THIS FRANKLIN CHARACTER MANAGED TO JAM IT...
BUT I'LL TRY TO SPRING IT FREE!
WISH ME LUCK!
YOUR LUCK IS ABOUT TO RUN OUT, CHILD.

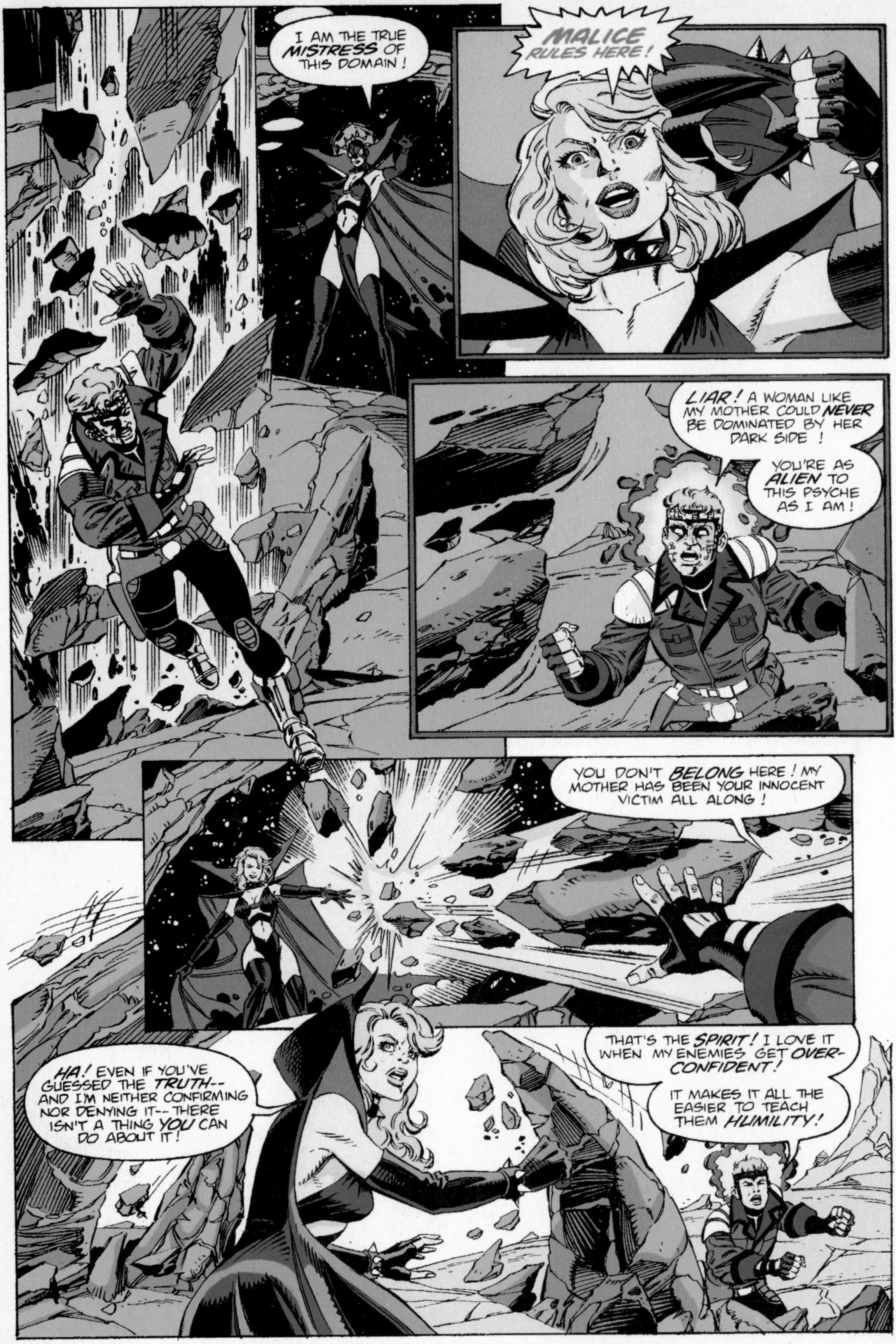
I AM THE TRUE MISTRESS OF THIS DOMAIN!
MALICE RULES HERE!
LIAR! A WOMAN LIKE MY MOTHER COULD NEVER BE DOMINATED BY HER DARK SIDE!
YOU'RE AS ALIEN TO THIS PSYCHE AS I AM!
YOU DON'T BELONG HERE! MY MOTHER HAS BEEN YOUR INNOCENT VICTIM ALL ALONG!
HA! EVEN IF YOU'VE GUESSED THE TRUTH-- AND I'M NEITHER CONFIRMING NOR DENYING IT-- THERE ISN'T A THING YOU CAN DO ABOUT IT!
THAT'S THE SPIRIT! I LOVE IT WHEN MY ENEMIES GET OVER-CONFIDENT!
IT MAKES IT ALL THE EASIER TO TEACH THEM HUMILITY!

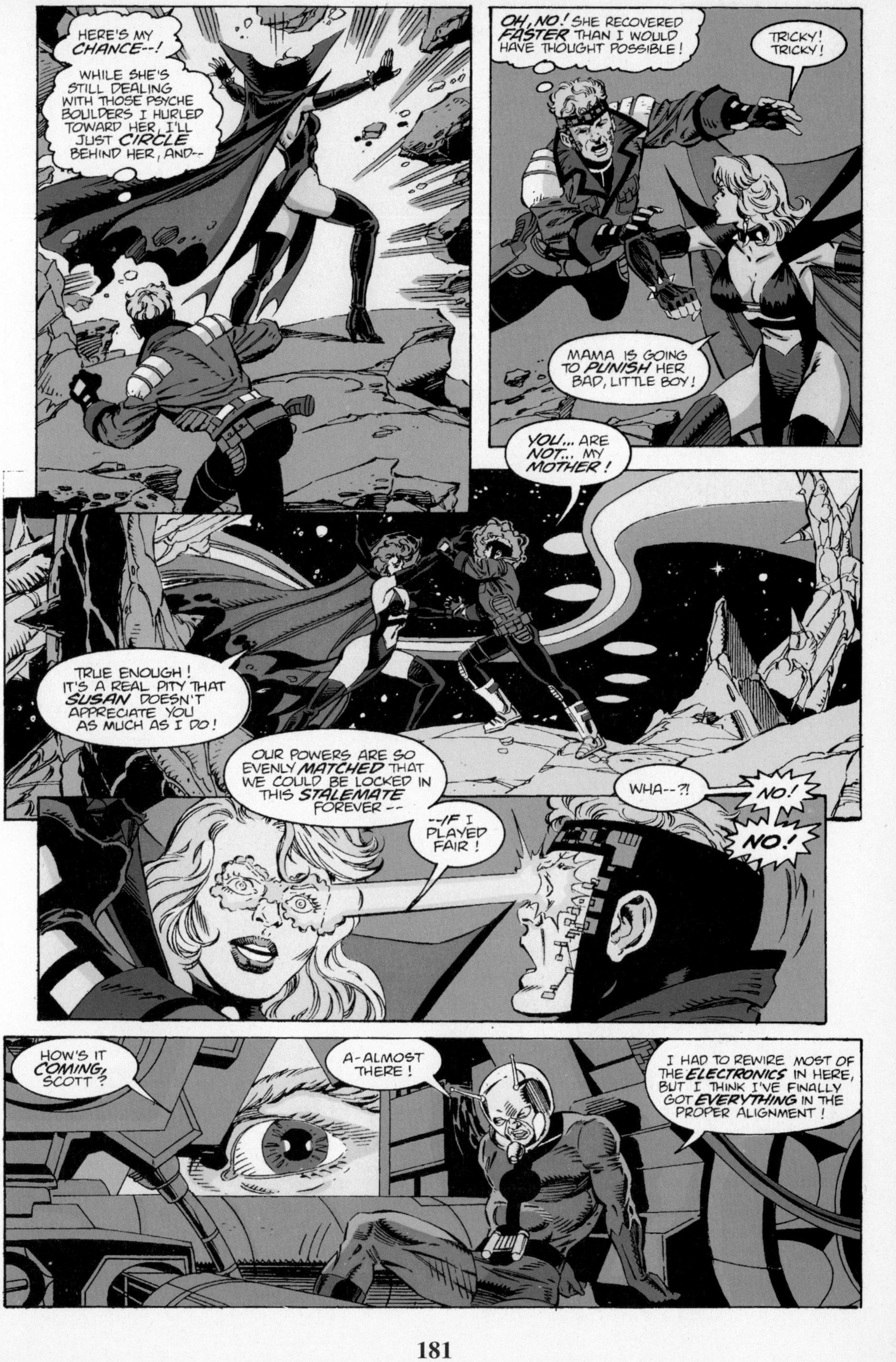
HERE'S MY CHANCE--!
WHILE SHE'S STILL DEALING WITH THOSE PSYCHE BOULDERS I HURLED TOWARD HER, I'LL JUST CIRCLE BEHIND HER, AND--
OH, NO! SHE RECOVERED FASTER THAN I WOULD HAVE THOUGHT POSSIBLE!
TRICKY! TRICKY!
MAMA IS GOING TO PUNISH HER BAD, LITTLE BOY!
YOU... ARE NOT... MY MOTHER!
TRUE ENOUGH! IT'S A REAL PITY THAT SUSAN DOESN'T APPRECIATE YOU AS MUCH AS I DO!
OUR POWERS ARE SO EVENLY MATCHED THAT WE COULD BE LOCKED IN THIS STALEMATE FOREVER--
--IF I PLAYED FAIR!
WHA--?!
NO!
NO!
HOW'S IT COMING, SCOTT?
A-ALMOST THERE!
I HAD TO REWIRE MOST OF THE ELECTRONICS IN HERE, BUT I THINK I'VE FINALLY GOT EVERYTHING IN THE PROPER ALIGNMENT!

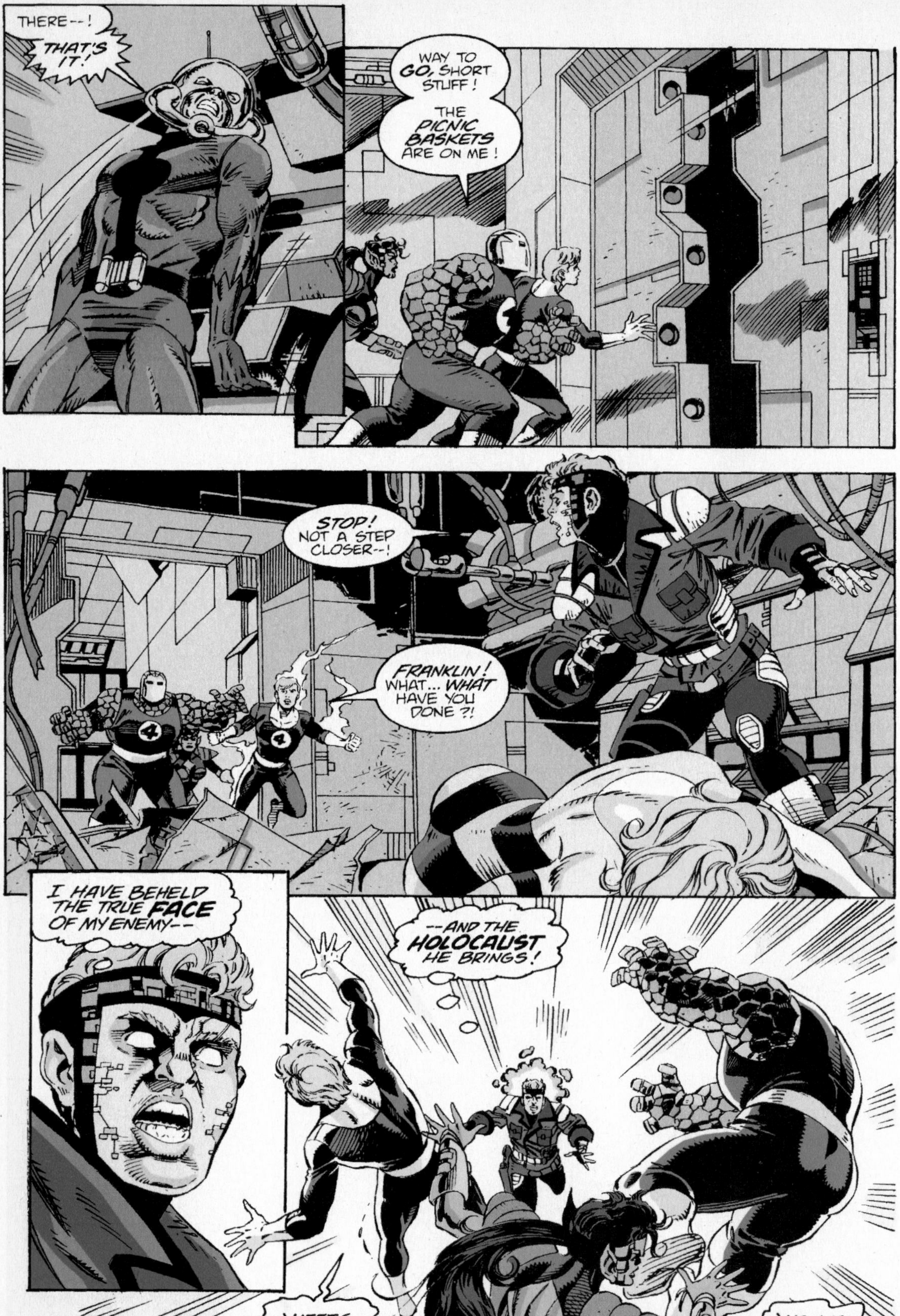
THERE--!
THAT'S IT!
WAY TO GO, SHORT STUFF!
THE PICNIC BASKETS ARE ON ME!
STOP! NOT A STEP CLOSER--!
FRANKLIN! WHAT... WHAT HAVE YOU DONE?!
I HAVE BEHELD THE TRUE FACE OF MY ENEMY--
--AND THE HOLOCAUST HE BRINGS!
UFFT
UGNN

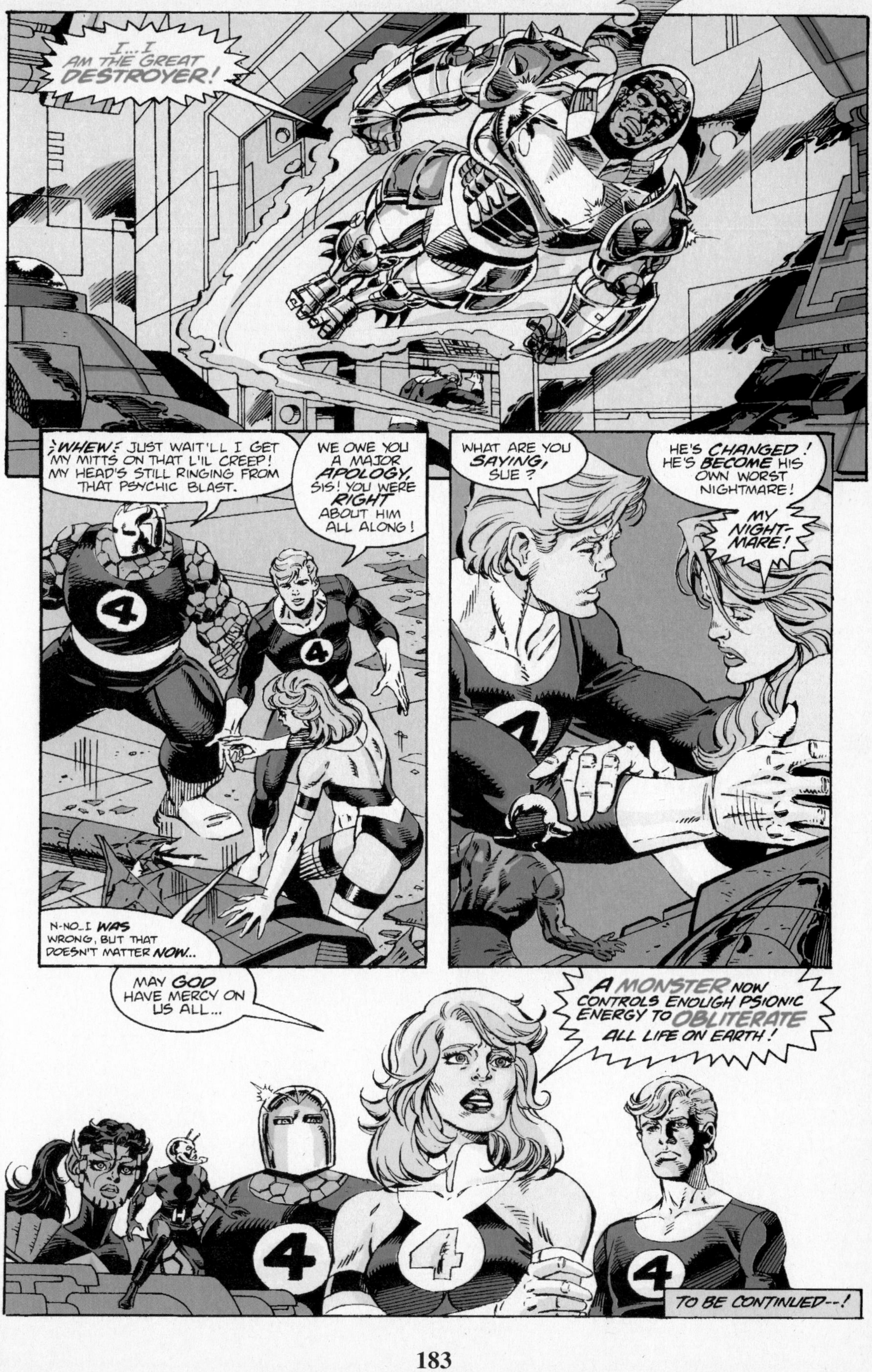
I... I AM THE GREAT DESTROYER!
WHEW! JUST WAIT'LL I GET MY MITTS ON THAT L'IL CREEP! MY HEAD'S STILL RINGING FROM THAT PSYCHIC BLAST.
WE OWE YOU A MAJOR APOLOGY, SIS! YOU WERE RIGHT ABOUT HIM ALL ALONG!
N-NO...I WAS WRONG, BUT THAT DOESN'T MATTER NOW...
WHAT ARE YOU SAYING, SUE?
HE'S CHANGED! HE'S BECOME HIS OWN WORST NIGHTMARE!
MY NIGHT-MARE!
MAY GOD HAVE MERCY ON US ALL...
A MONSTER NOW CONTROLS ENOUGH PSIONIC ENERGY TO OBLITERATE ALL LIFE ON EARTH!
TO BE CONTINUED--!

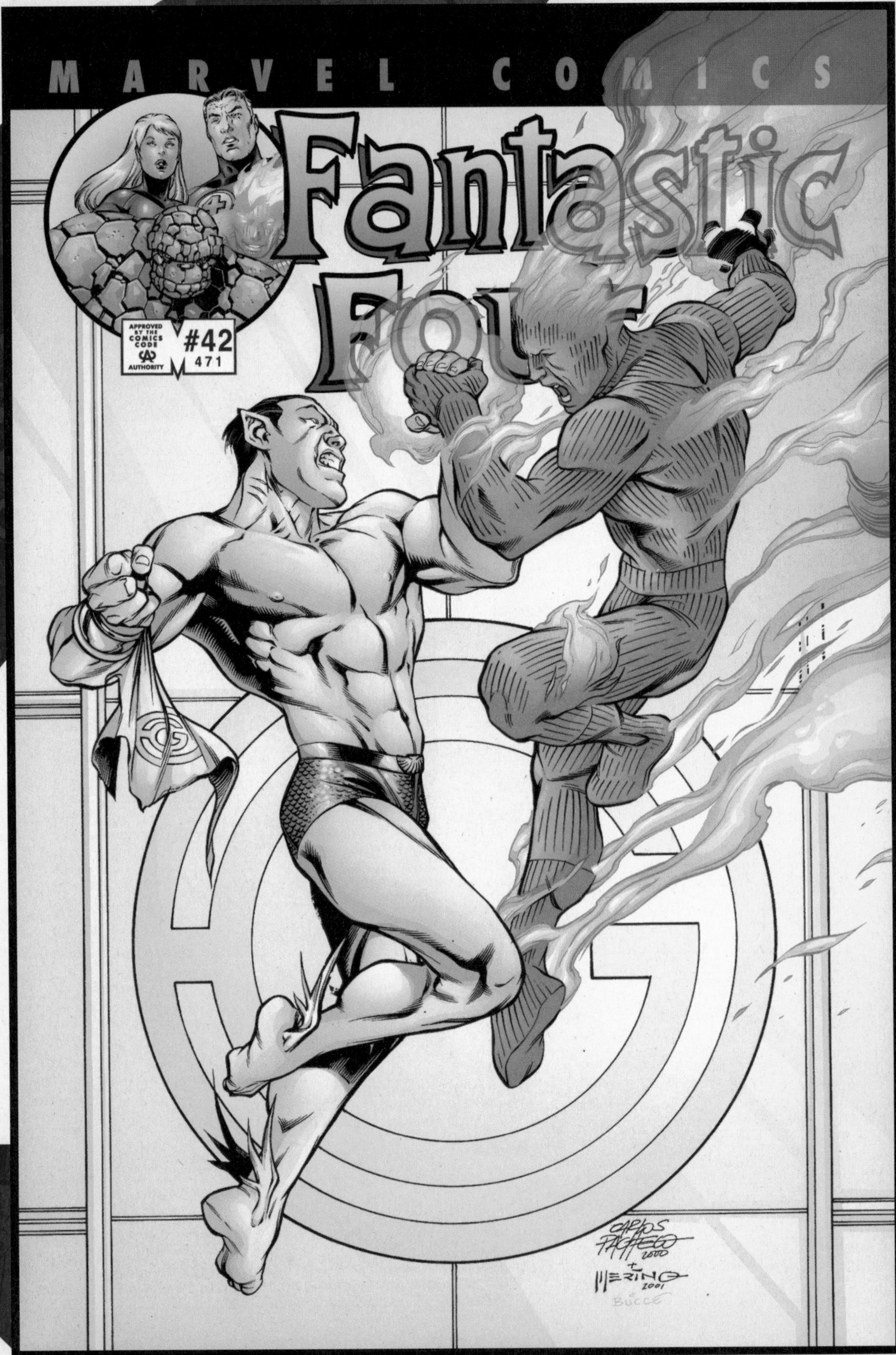
MARVEL COMICS
Fantastic Four
APPROVED BY THE COMICS CODE AUTHORITY
#42
471
CARLOS PACHECO 2000
MERINO 2001

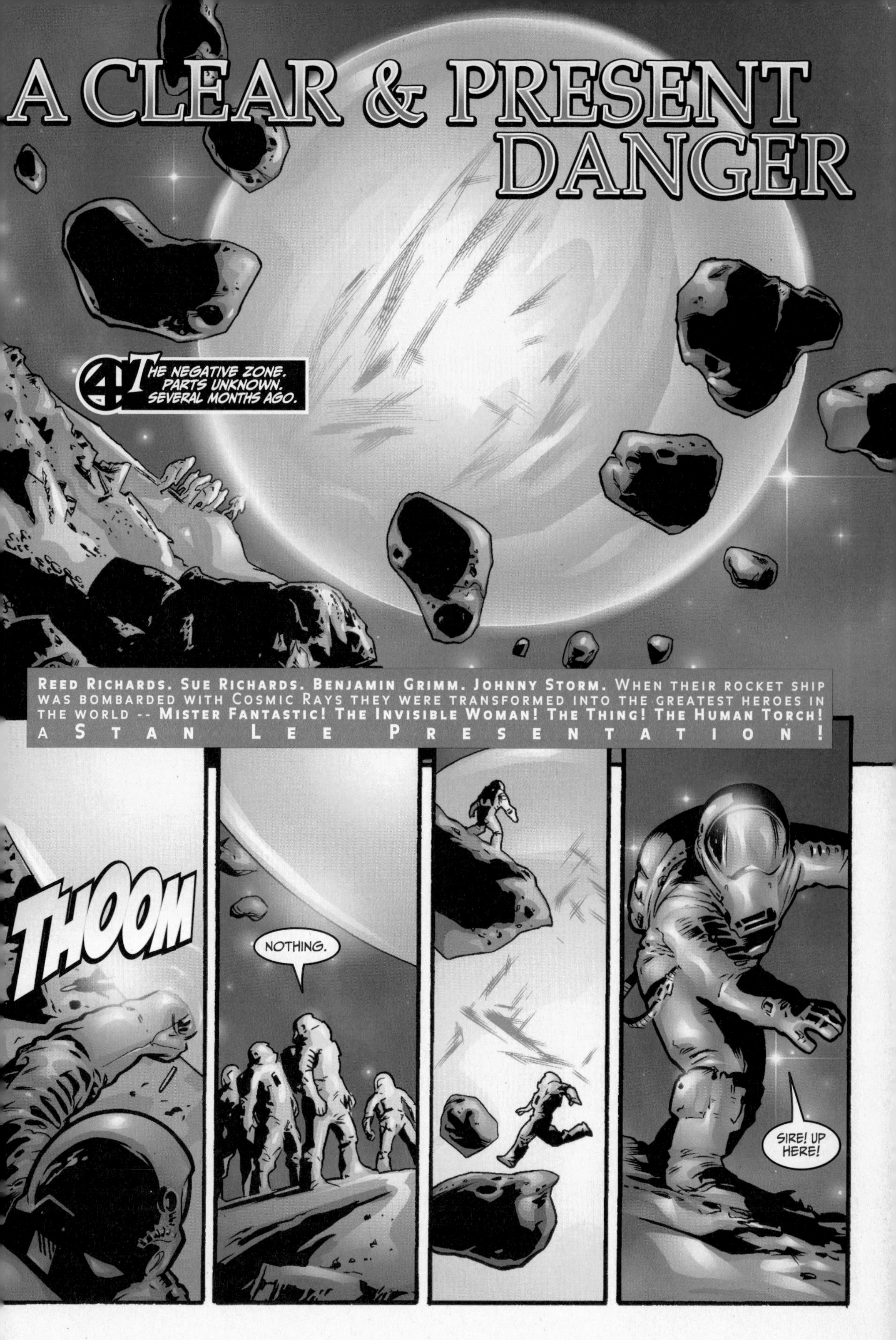
A CLEAR & PRESENT DANGER
THE NEGATIVE ZONE. PARTS UNKNOWN. SEVERAL MONTHS AGO.
REED RICHARDS. SUE RICHARDS. BENJAMIN GRIMM. JOHNNY STORM. WHEN THEIR ROCKET SHIP WAS BOMBARDED WITH COSMIC RAYS THEY WERE TRANSFORMED INTO THE GREATEST HEROES IN THE WORLD -- MISTER FANTASTIC! THE INVISIBLE WOMAN! THE THING! THE HUMAN TORCH!
A STAN LEE PRESENTATION!
THOOM
NOTHING.
SIRE! UP HERE!

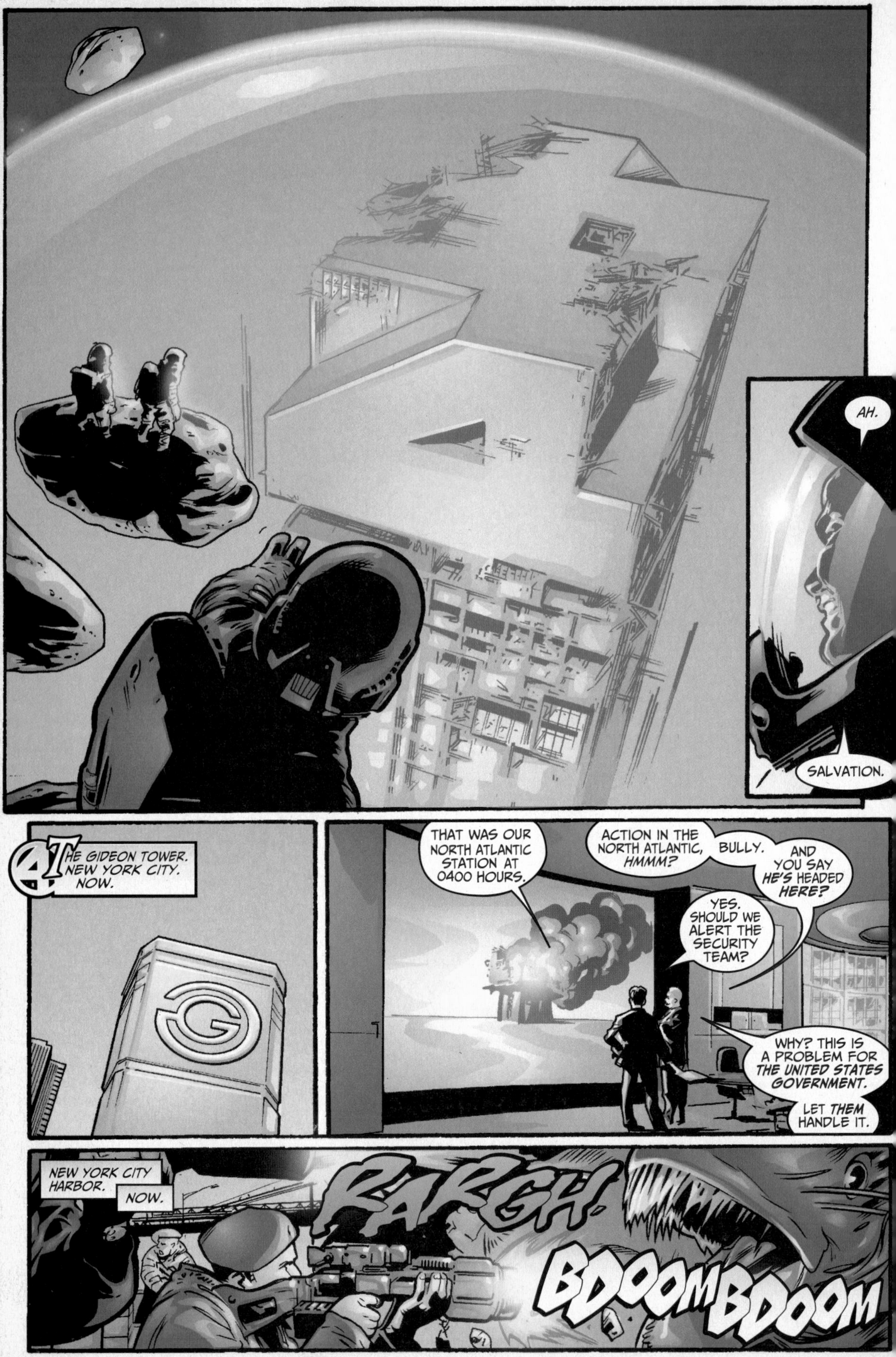
AH.
SALVATION.
THE GIDEON TOWER. NEW YORK CITY. NOW.
THAT WAS OUR NORTH ATLANTIC STATION AT 0400 HOURS.
ACTION IN THE NORTH ATLANTIC, HMMM?
BULLY.
AND YOU SAY HE'S HEADED HERE?
YES. SHOULD WE ALERT THE SECURITY TEAM?
WHY? THIS IS A PROBLEM FOR THE UNITED STATES GOVERNMENT.
LET THEM HANDLE IT.
NEW YORK CITY HARBOR.
NOW.
RARGH!
BDOOM BDOOM

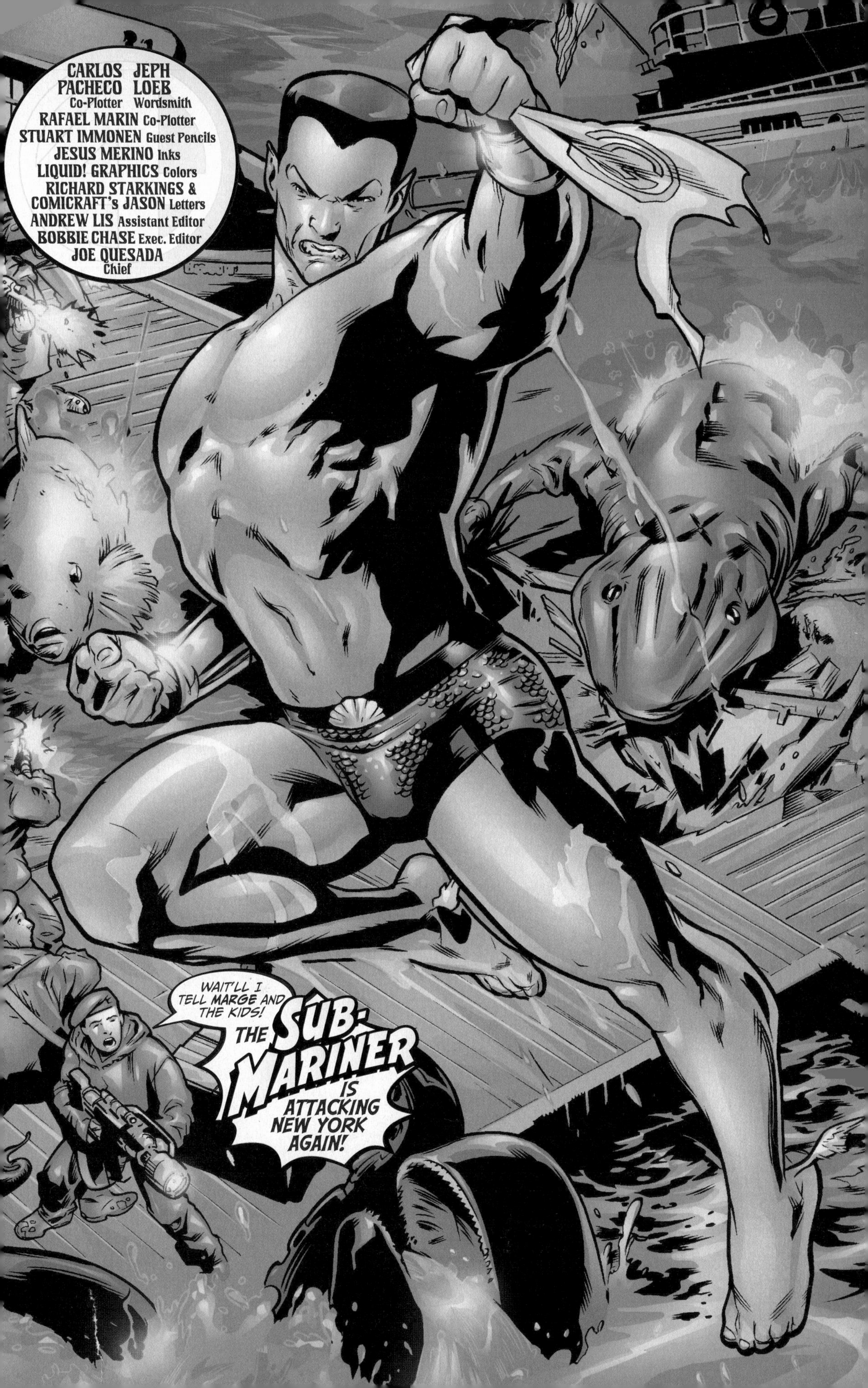
CARLOS PACHECO Co-Plotter
JEPH LOEB Wordsmith
RAFAEL MARIN Co-Plotter
STUART IMMONEN Guest Pencils
JESUS MERINO Inks
LIQUID! GRAPHICS Colors
RICHARD STARKINGS & COMICRAFT's JASON Letters
ANDREW LIS Assistant Editor
BOBBIE CHASE Exec. Editor
JOE QUESADA Chief
WAIT'LL I TELL MARGE AND THE KIDS! THE SUB-MARINER IS ATTACKING NEW YORK AGAIN!

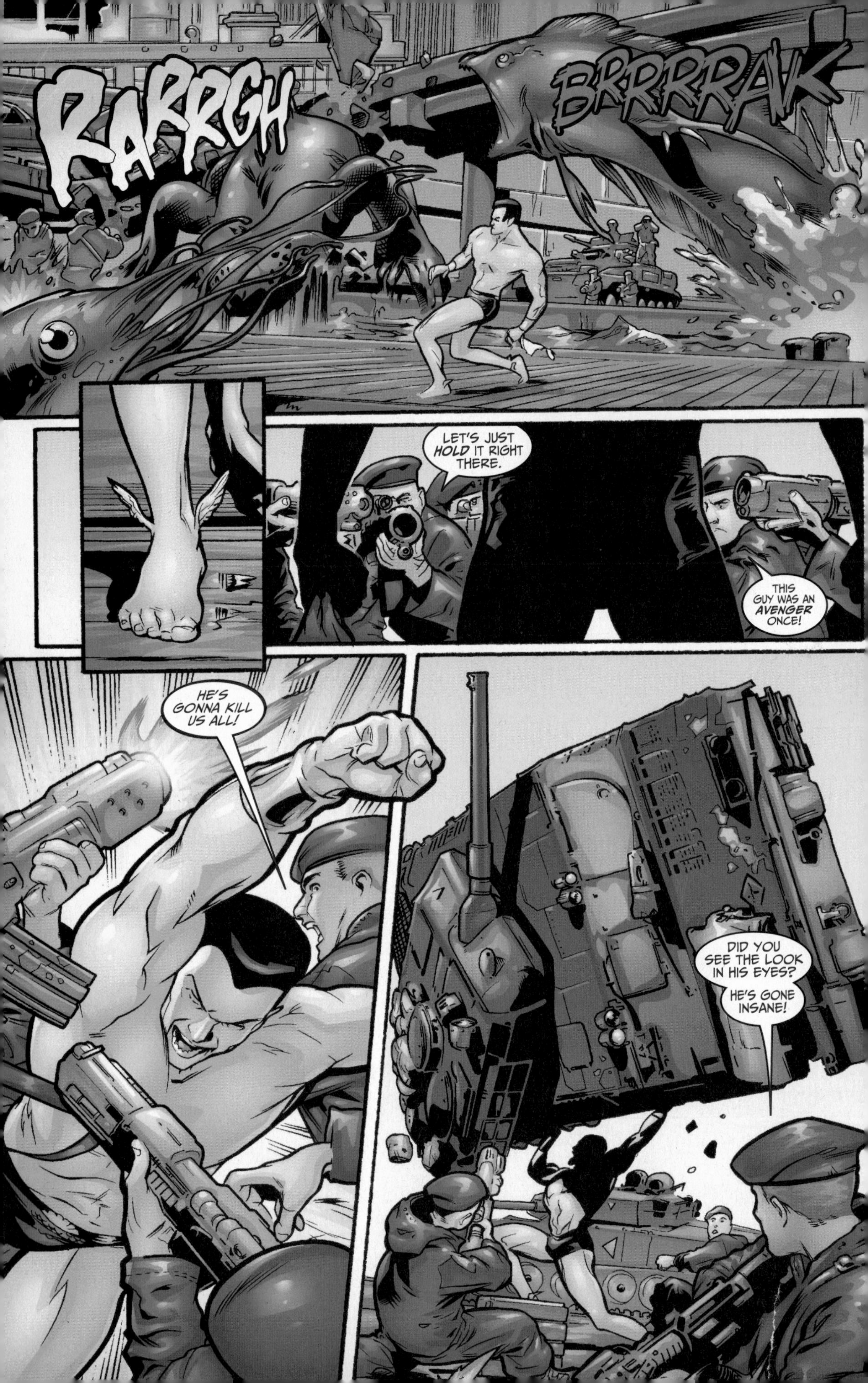
RARRGH
BRRRRAK
LET'S JUST HOLD IT RIGHT THERE.
THIS GUY WAS AN AVENGER ONCE!
HE'S GONNA KILL US ALL!
DID YOU SEE THE LOOK IN HIS EYES?
HE'S GONE INSANE!

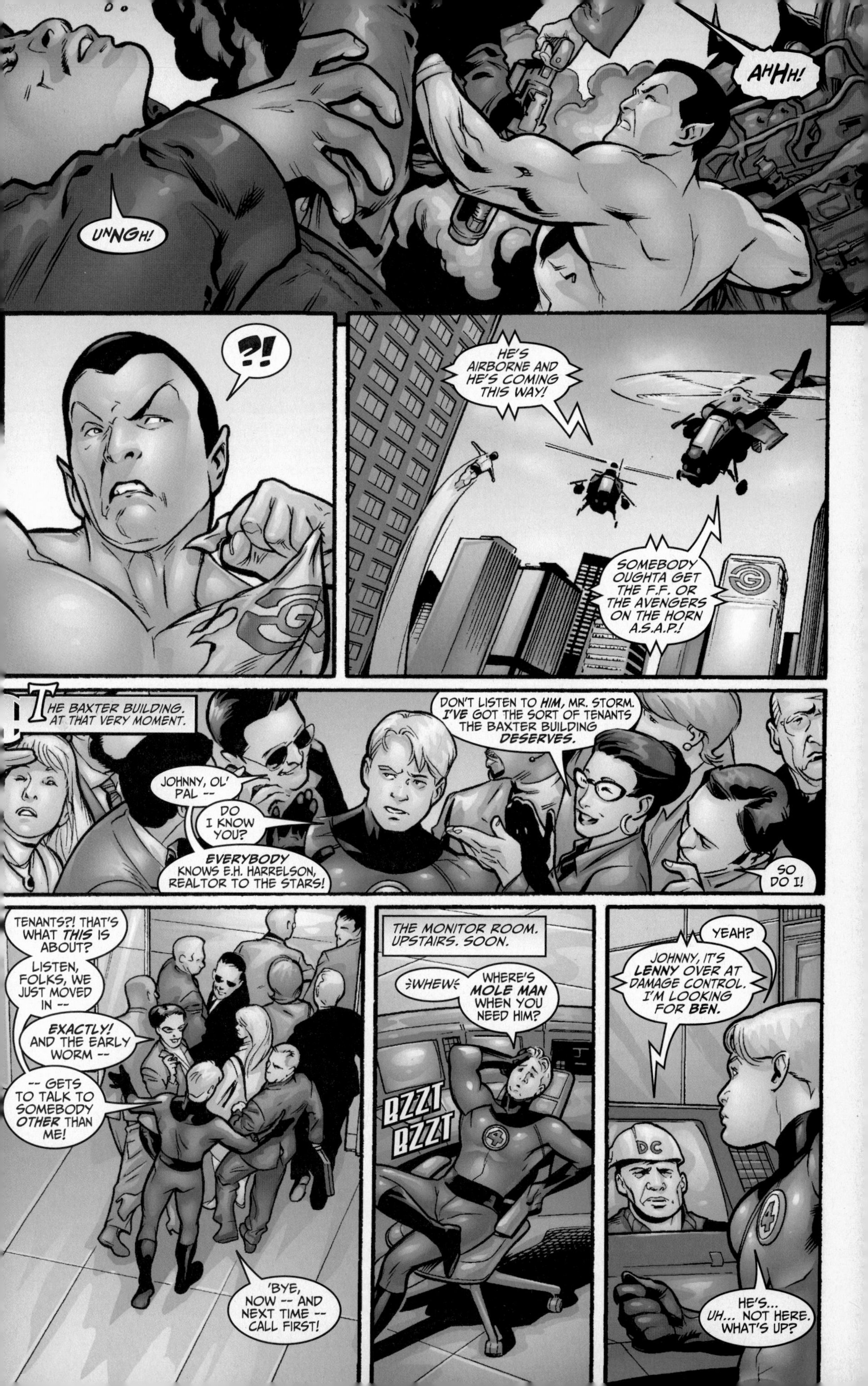
AHHH!
UNNGH!
?!
HE'S AIRBORNE AND HE'S COMING THIS WAY!
SOMEBODY OUGHTA GET THE F.F. OR THE AVENGERS ON THE HORN A.S.A.P.!
THE BAXTER BUILDING. AT THAT VERY MOMENT.
JOHNNY, OL' PAL --
DO I KNOW YOU?
EVERYBODY KNOWS E.H. HARRELSON, REALTOR TO THE STARS!
DON'T LISTEN TO HIM, MR. STORM. I'VE GOT THE SORT OF TENANTS THE BAXTER BUILDING DESERVES.
SO DO I!
TENANTS?! THAT'S WHAT THIS IS ABOUT?
LISTEN, FOLKS, WE JUST MOVED IN --
EXACTLY! AND THE EARLY WORM --
-- GETS TO TALK TO SOMEBODY OTHER THAN ME!
'BYE, NOW -- AND NEXT TIME -- CALL FIRST!
THE MONITOR ROOM. UPSTAIRS. SOON.
WHEW
WHERE'S MOLE MAN WHEN YOU NEED HIM?
BZZT BZZT
YEAH?
JOHNNY, IT'S LENNY OVER AT DAMAGE CONTROL. I'M LOOKING FOR BEN.
DC
HE'S... UH... NOT HERE. WHAT'S UP?

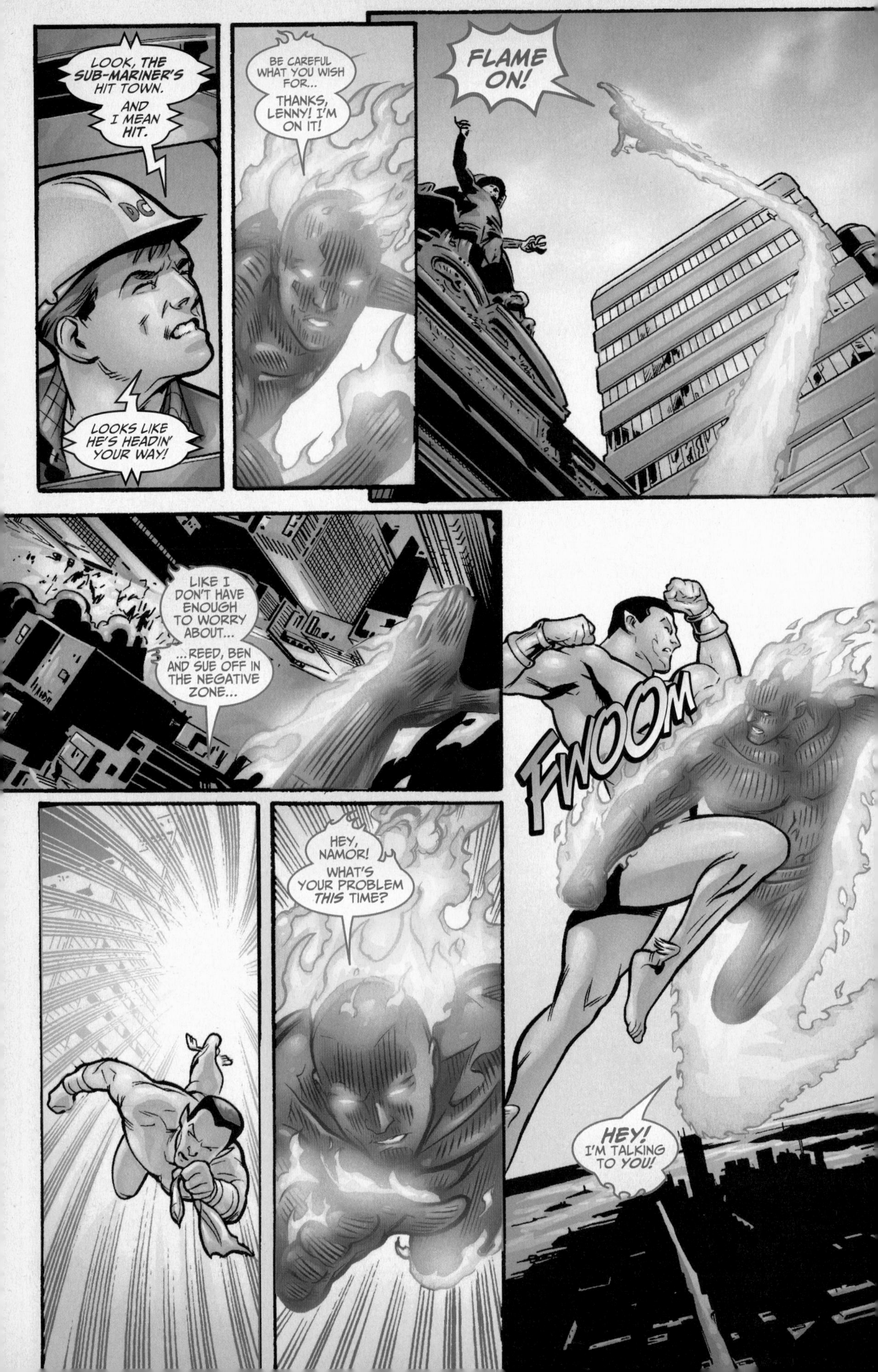
LOOK, THE SUB-MARINER'S HIT TOWN.
AND I MEAN HIT.
LOOKS LIKE HE'S HEADIN' YOUR WAY!
BE CAREFUL WHAT YOU WISH FOR...
THANKS, LENNY! I'M ON IT!
FLAME ON!
LIKE I DON'T HAVE ENOUGH TO WORRY ABOUT...
...REED, BEN AND SUE OFF IN THE NEGATIVE ZONE...
FWOOM
HEY, NAMOR!
WHAT'S YOUR PROBLEM THIS TIME?
HEY! I'M TALKING TO YOU!

YOU CAN'T JUST GO BUSTING --

BAM

4 THE NEGATIVE ZONE. MILES FROM PILGRIM'S ROCK. NOW.

ANYBODY GOT ANY IDEA WHERE WE'RE HEADIN'?

THAT'S NOT AS LUDICROUS A QUESTION AS ONE MIGHT IMAGINE, BEN.

GEE. THANKS.

SOMETHING OR *SOMEONE* IS SEEKING TO BREACH THE WALL BETWEEN *OUR* POSITIVE ION UNIVERSE AND *THIS* NEGAVERSE.

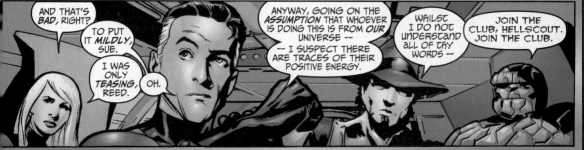

AND THAT'S BAD, RIGHT?

TO PUT IT *MILDLY*, SUE.

I WAS ONLY *TEASING*, REED.

OH.

ANYWAY, GOING ON THE *ASSUMPTION* THAT WHOEVER IS DOING THIS IS FROM *OUR* UNIVERSE --
-- I SUSPECT THERE ARE TRACES OF THEIR POSITIVE ENERGY.

WHILST I DO NOT UNDERSTAND ALL OF THY WORDS --

JOIN THE CLUB, HELLSCOUT. JOIN THE CLUB.

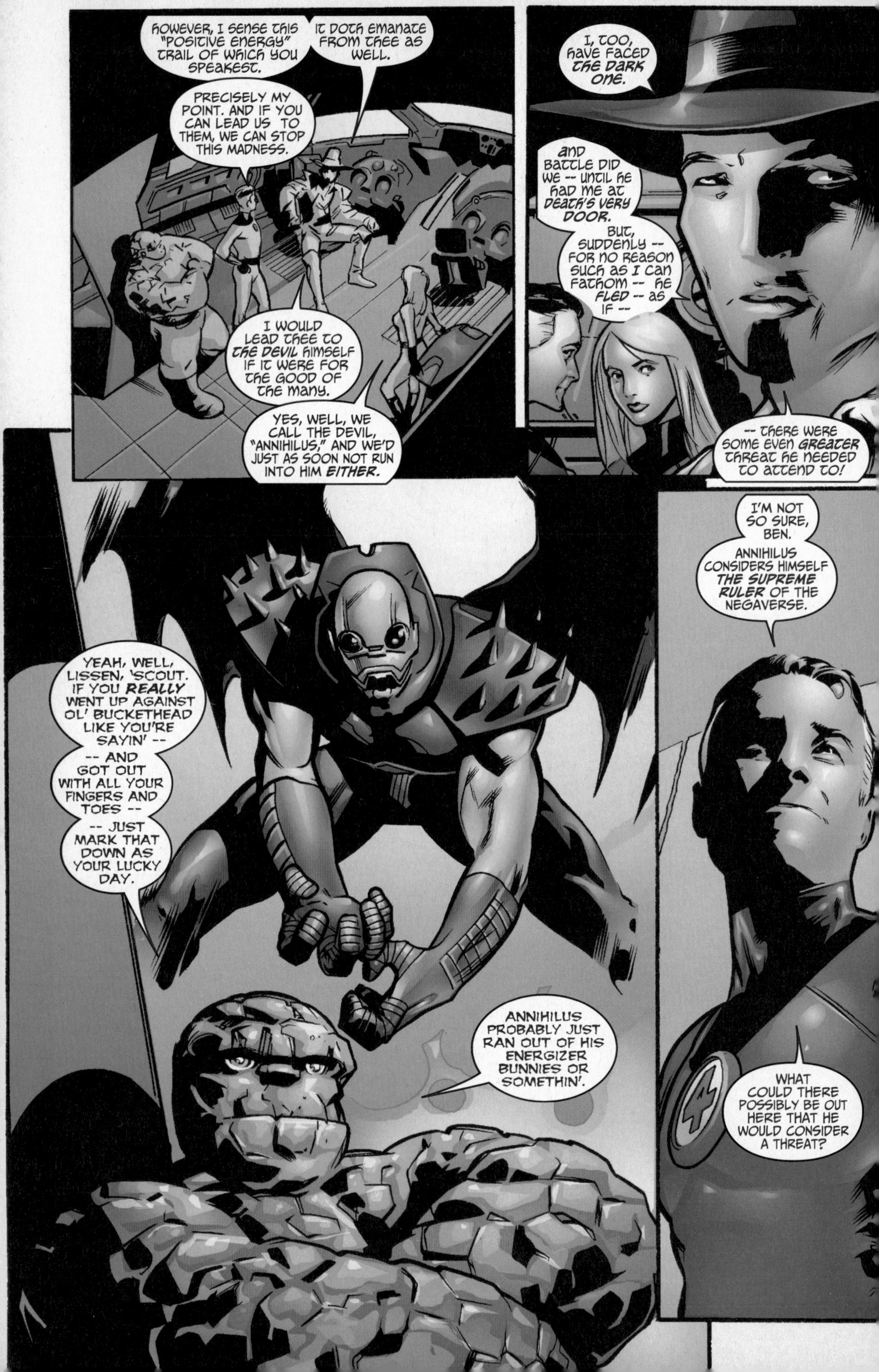
HOWEVER, I SENSE THIS "POSITIVE ENERGY" TRAIL OF WHICH YOU SPEAKEST.
IT DOTH EMANATE FROM THEE AS WELL.
PRECISELY MY POINT. AND IF YOU CAN LEAD US TO THEM, WE CAN STOP THIS MADNESS.
I WOULD LEAD THEE TO THE DEVIL HIMSELF IF IT WERE FOR THE GOOD OF THE MANY.
YES, WELL, WE CALL THE DEVIL, "ANNIHILUS," AND WE'D JUST AS SOON NOT RUN INTO HIM EITHER.
I, TOO, HAVE FACED THE DARK ONE.
AND BATTLE DID WE -- UNTIL HE HAD ME AT DEATH'S VERY DOOR.
BUT, SUDDENLY -- FOR NO REASON SUCH AS I CAN FATHOM -- HE FLED -- AS IF --
-- THERE WERE SOME EVEN GREATER THREAT HE NEEDED TO ATTEND TO!
YEAH, WELL, LISSEN, 'SCOUT. IF YOU REALLY WENT UP AGAINST OL' BUCKETHEAD LIKE YOU'RE SAYIN' --
-- AND GOT OUT WITH ALL YOUR FINGERS AND TOES --
-- JUST MARK THAT DOWN AS YOUR LUCKY DAY.
ANNIHILUS PROBABLY JUST RAN OUT OF HIS ENERGIZER BUNNIES OR SOMETHIN'.
I'M NOT SO SURE, BEN.
ANNIHILUS CONSIDERS HIMSELF THE SUPREME RULER OF THE NEGAVERSE.
WHAT COULD THERE POSSIBLY BE OUT HERE THAT HE WOULD CONSIDER A THREAT?

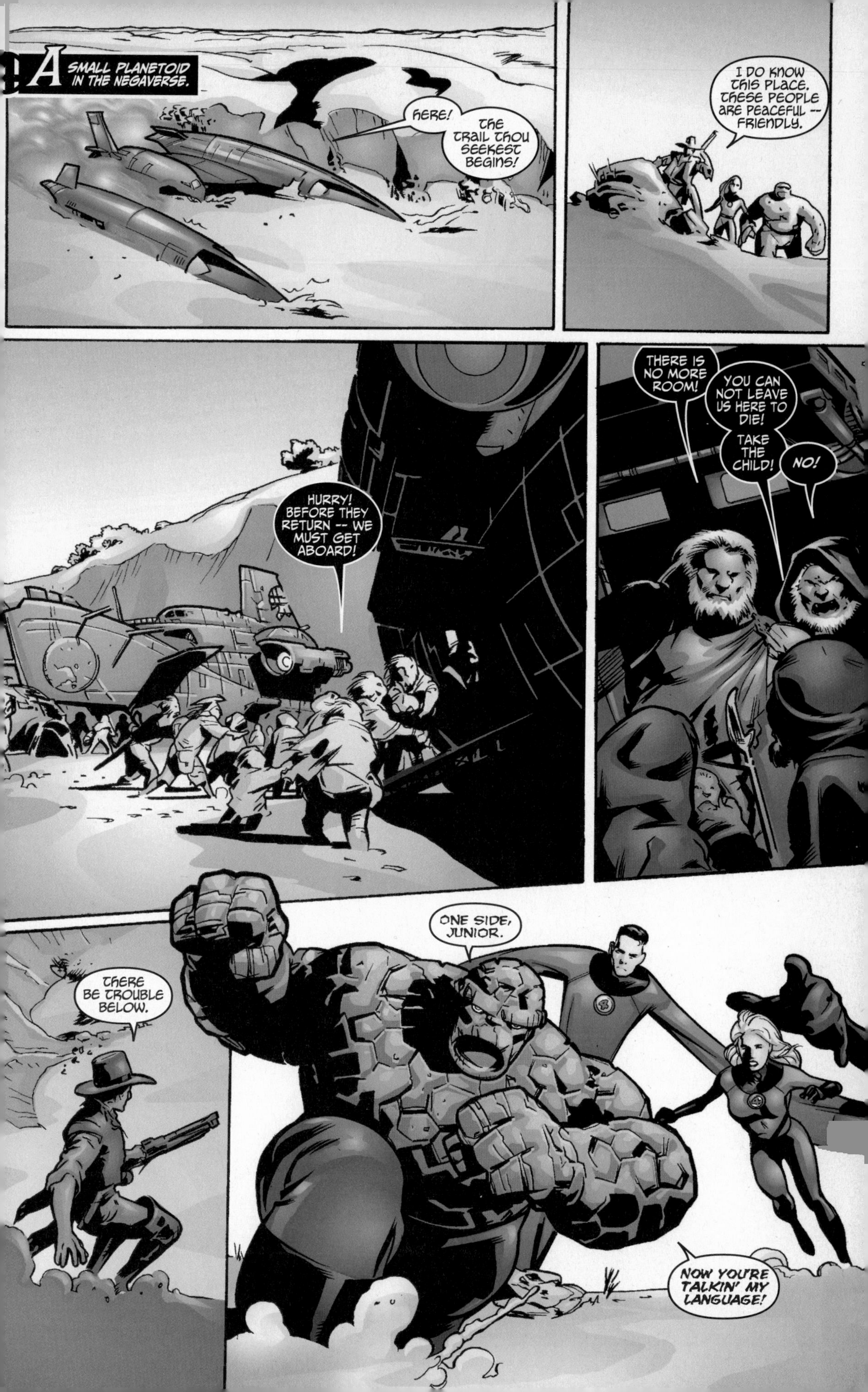
A SMALL PLANETOID IN THE NEGAVERSE.
HERE!
THE TRAIL THOU SEEKEST BEGINS!
I DO KNOW THIS PLACE. THESE PEOPLE ARE PEACEFUL -- FRIENDLY.
HURRY! BEFORE THEY RETURN -- WE MUST GET ABOARD!
THERE IS NO MORE ROOM!
YOU CAN NOT LEAVE US HERE TO DIE!
TAKE THE CHILD!
NO!
THERE BE TROUBLE BELOW.
ONE SIDE, JUNIOR.
NOW YOU'RE TALKIN' MY LANGUAGE!

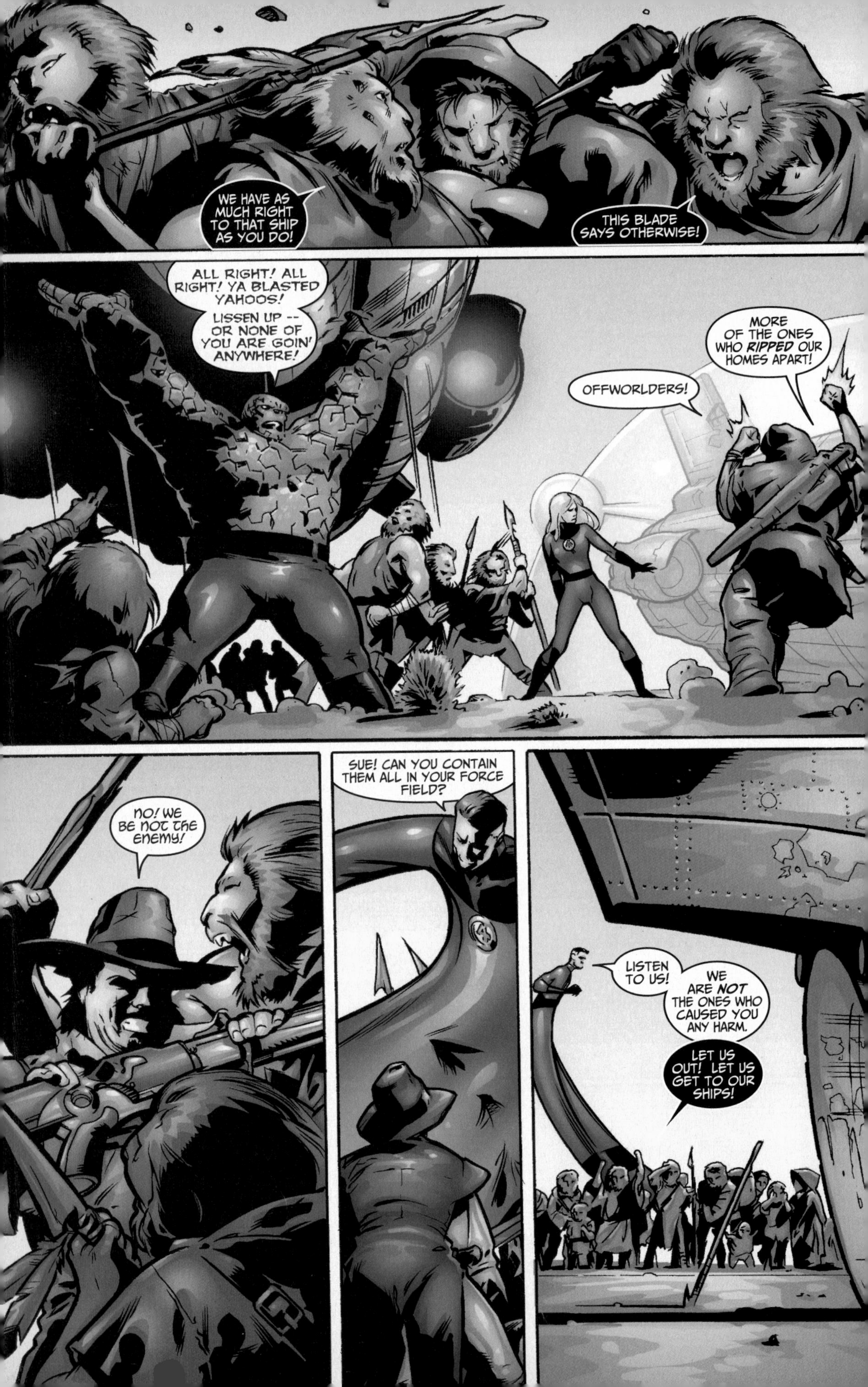
WE HAVE AS MUCH RIGHT TO THAT SHIP AS YOU DO!
THIS BLADE SAYS OTHERWISE!
ALL RIGHT! ALL RIGHT! YA BLASTED YAHOOS!
LISSEN UP -- OR NONE OF YOU ARE GOIN' ANYWHERE!
MORE OF THE ONES WHO RIPPED OUR HOMES APART!
OFFWORLDERS!
NO! WE BE NOT THE ENEMY!
SUE! CAN YOU CONTAIN THEM ALL IN YOUR FORCE FIELD?
LISTEN TO US!
WE ARE NOT THE ONES WHO CAUSED YOU ANY HARM.
LET US OUT! LET US GET TO OUR SHIPS!

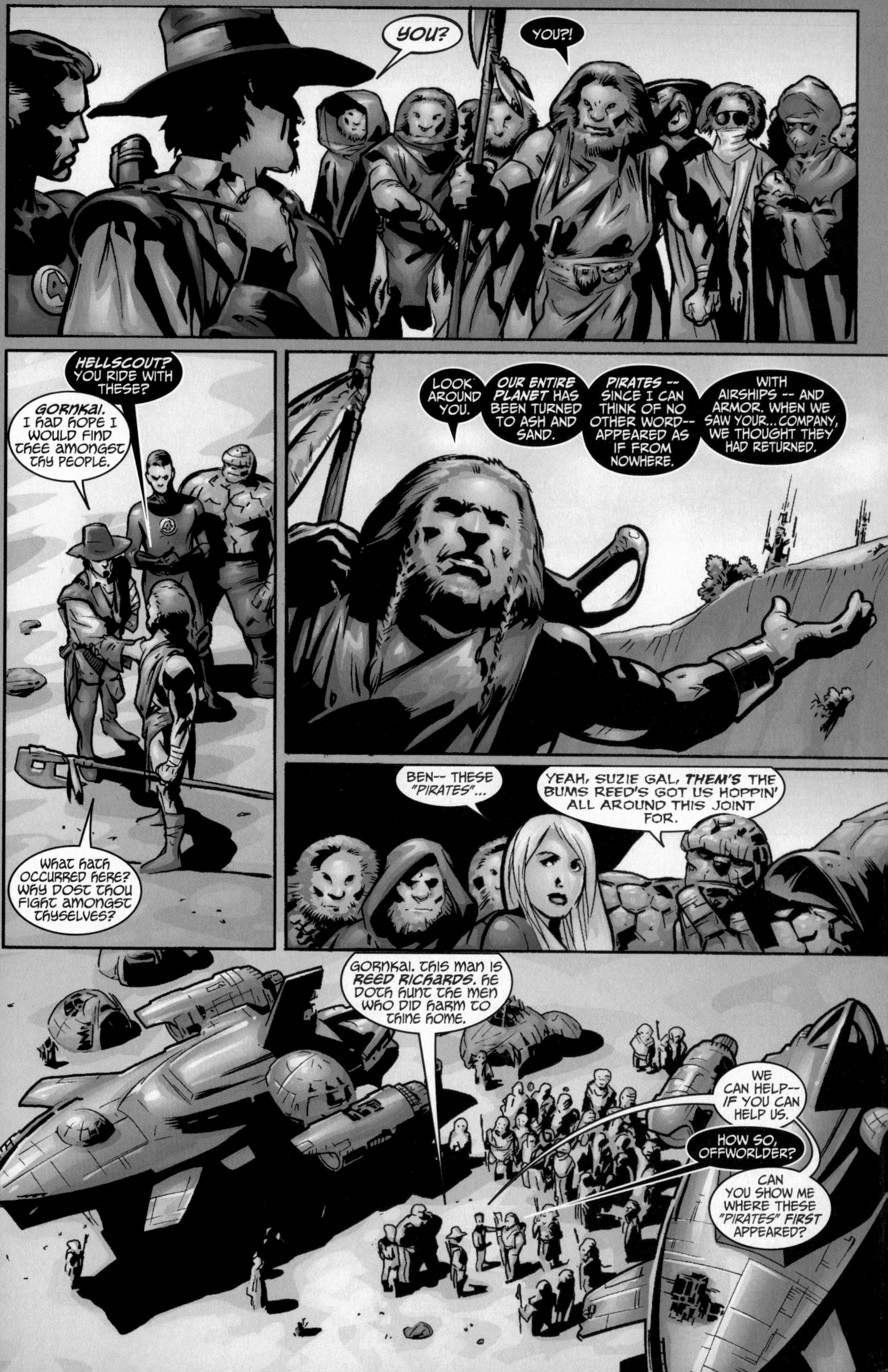
YOU?
YOU?!
HELLSCOUT? YOU RIDE WITH THESE?
GORNKAI. I HAD HOPE I WOULD FIND THEE AMONGST THY PEOPLE.
WHAT HATH OCCURRED HERE? WHY DOST THOU FIGHT AMONGST THYSELVES?
LOOK AROUND YOU.
OUR ENTIRE PLANET HAS BEEN TURNED TO ASH AND SAND.
PIRATES -- SINCE I CAN THINK OF NO OTHER WORD-- APPEARED AS IF FROM NOWHERE.
WITH AIRSHIPS -- AND ARMOR. WHEN WE SAW YOUR...COMPANY, WE THOUGHT THEY HAD RETURNED.
BEN-- THESE "PIRATES"...
YEAH, SUZIE GAL, THEM'S THE BUMS REED'S GOT US HOPPIN' ALL AROUND THIS JOINT FOR.
GORNKAI. THIS MAN IS REED RICHARDS. HE DOTH HUNT THE MEN WHO DID HARM TO THINE HOME.
WE CAN HELP-- IF YOU CAN HELP US.
HOW SO, OFFWORLDER?
CAN YOU SHOW ME WHERE THESE "PIRATES" FIRST APPEARED?

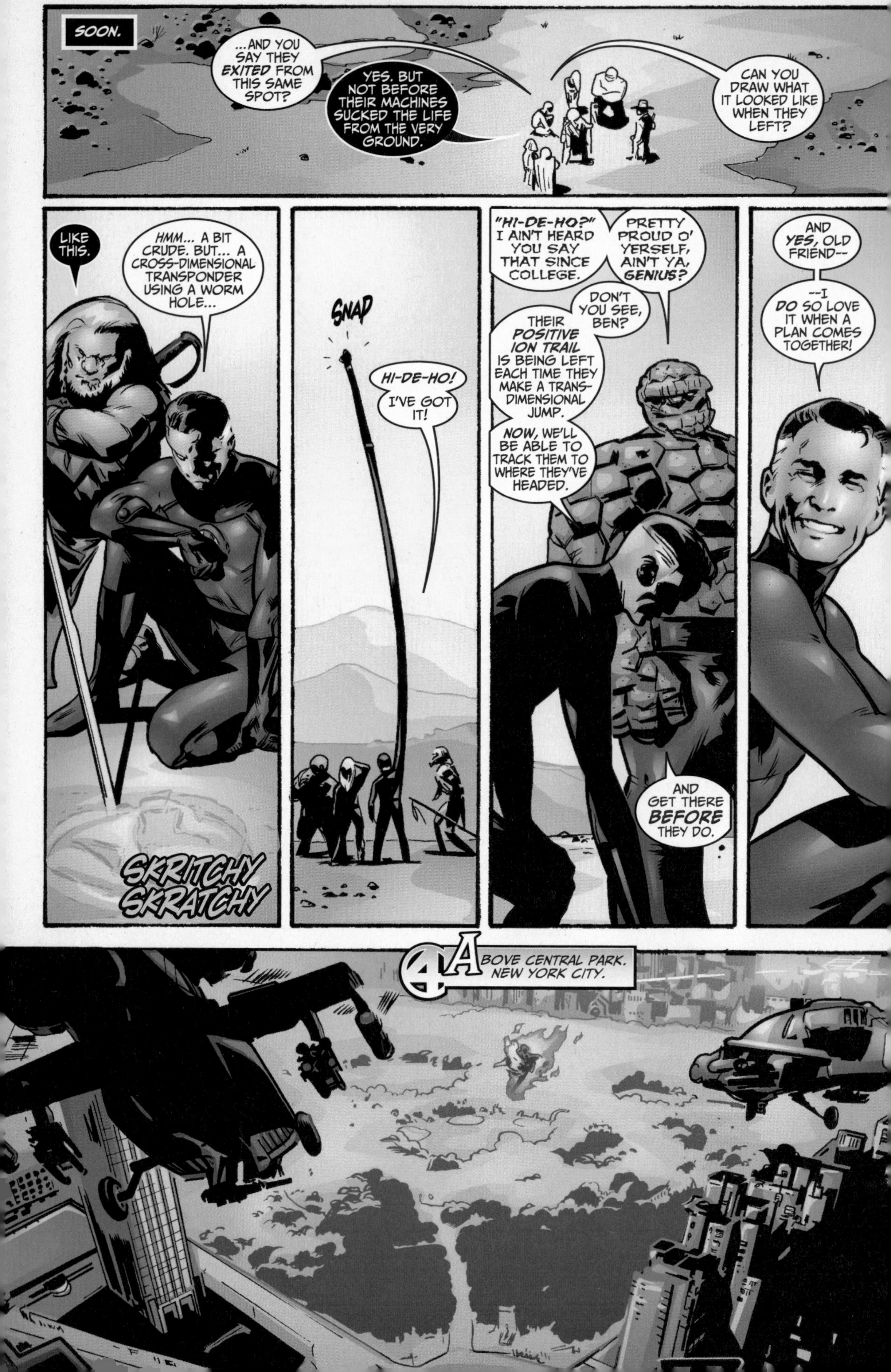
SOON.
...AND YOU SAY THEY EXITED FROM THIS SAME SPOT?
YES. BUT NOT BEFORE THEIR MACHINES SUCKED THE LIFE FROM THE VERY GROUND.
CAN YOU DRAW WHAT IT LOOKED LIKE WHEN THEY LEFT?
LIKE THIS.
HMM... A BIT CRUDE. BUT... A CROSS-DIMENSIONAL TRANSPONDER USING A WORM HOLE...
SKRITCHY SKRATCHY
SNAP
HI-DE-HO!
I'VE GOT IT!
"HI-DE-HO?" I AIN'T HEARD YOU SAY THAT SINCE COLLEGE.
PRETTY PROUD O' YERSELF, AIN'T YA, GENIUS?
DON'T YOU SEE, BEN?
THEIR POSITIVE ION TRAIL IS BEING LEFT EACH TIME THEY MAKE A TRANS-DIMENSIONAL JUMP.
NOW, WE'LL BE ABLE TO TRACK THEM TO WHERE THEY'VE HEADED.
AND GET THERE BEFORE THEY DO.
AND YES, OLD FRIEND--
--I DO SO LOVE IT WHEN A PLAN COMES TOGETHER!
ABOVE CENTRAL PARK. NEW YORK CITY.

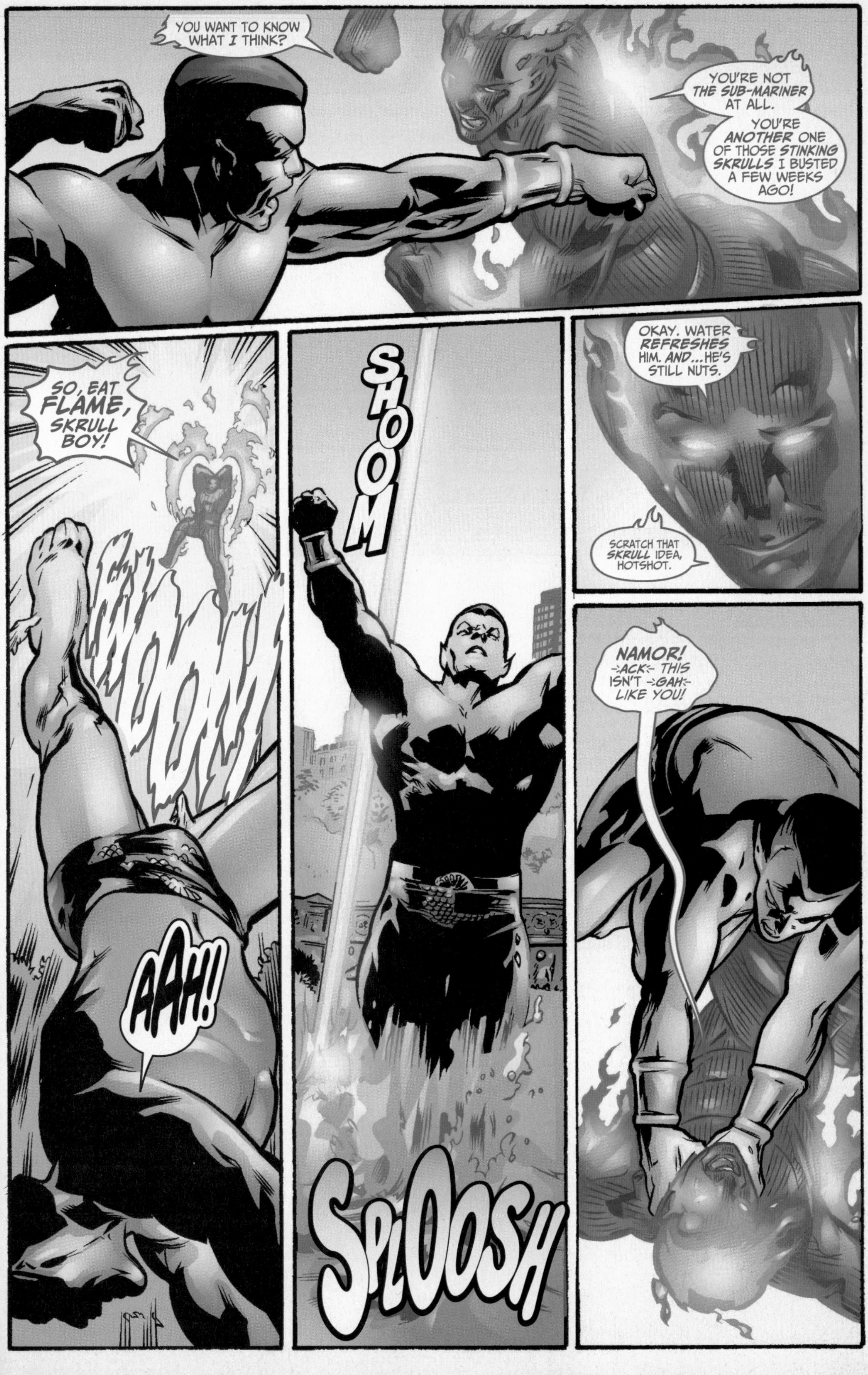
YOU WANT TO KNOW WHAT I THINK?
YOU'RE NOT THE SUB-MARINER AT ALL.
YOU'RE ANOTHER ONE OF THOSE STINKING SKRULLS I BUSTED A FEW WEEKS AGO!
SO, EAT FLAME, SKRULL BOY!
AAH!
SHOOM
SPLOOSH
OKAY. WATER REFRESHES HIM. AND...HE'S STILL NUTS.
SCRATCH THAT SKRULL IDEA, HOTSHOT.
NAMOR! -ACK- THIS ISN'T -GAH- LIKE YOU!

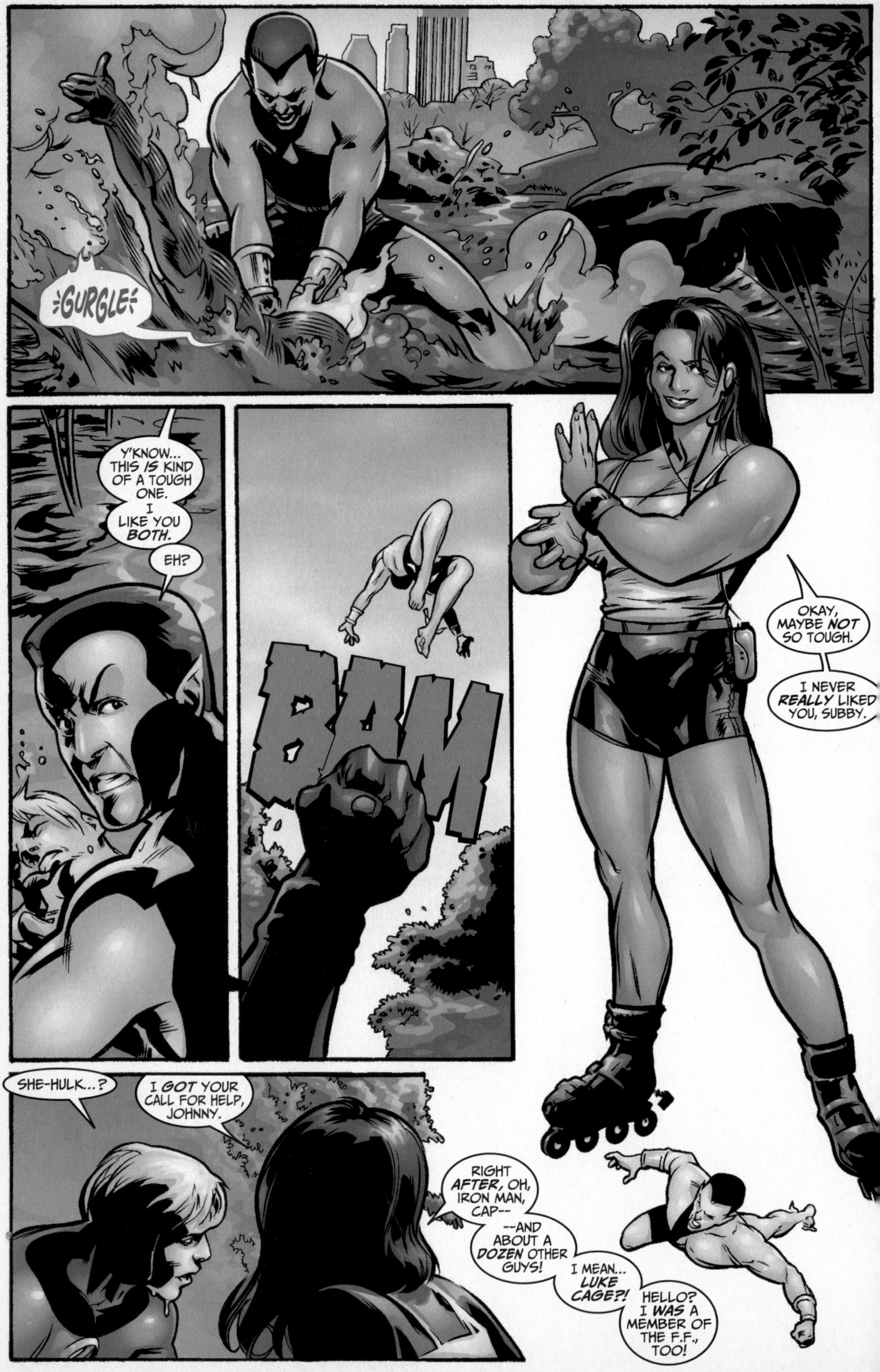
GURGLE
Y'KNOW... THIS IS KIND OF A TOUGH ONE.
I LIKE YOU BOTH.
EH?
BAM
OKAY, MAYBE NOT SO TOUGH.
I NEVER REALLY LIKED YOU, SUBBY.
SHE-HULK...?
I GOT YOUR CALL FOR HELP, JOHNNY.
RIGHT AFTER, OH, IRON MAN, CAP--
--AND ABOUT A DOZEN OTHER GUYS!
I MEAN... LUKE CAGE?!
HELLO? I WAS A MEMBER OF THE F.F., TOO!

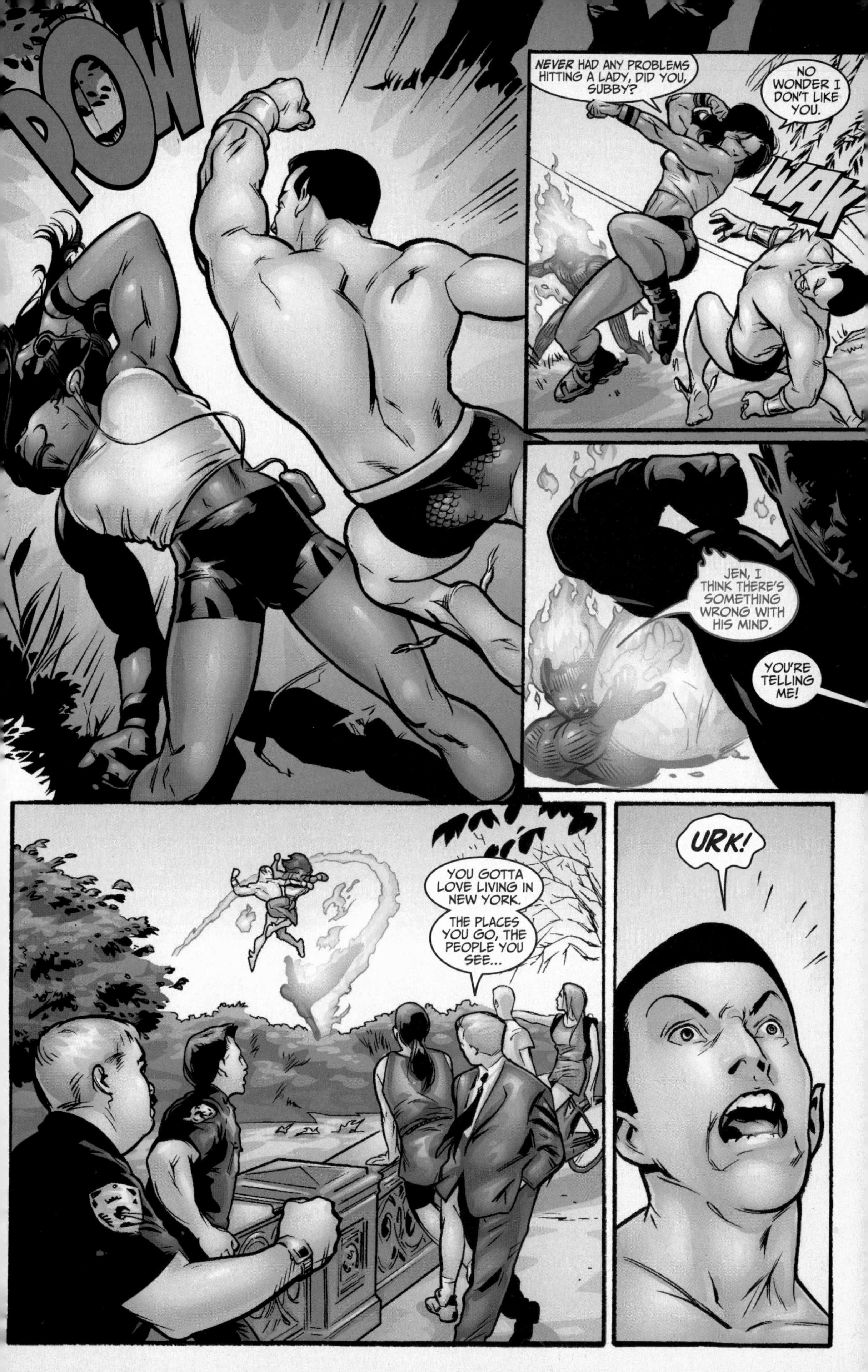
POW
NEVER HAD ANY PROBLEMS HITTING A LADY, DID YOU, SUBBY?
NO WONDER I DON'T LIKE YOU.
WAK
JEN, I THINK THERE'S SOMETHING WRONG WITH HIS MIND.
YOU'RE TELLING ME!
YOU GOTTA LOVE LIVING IN NEW YORK.
THE PLACES YOU GO, THE PEOPLE YOU SEE...
URK!

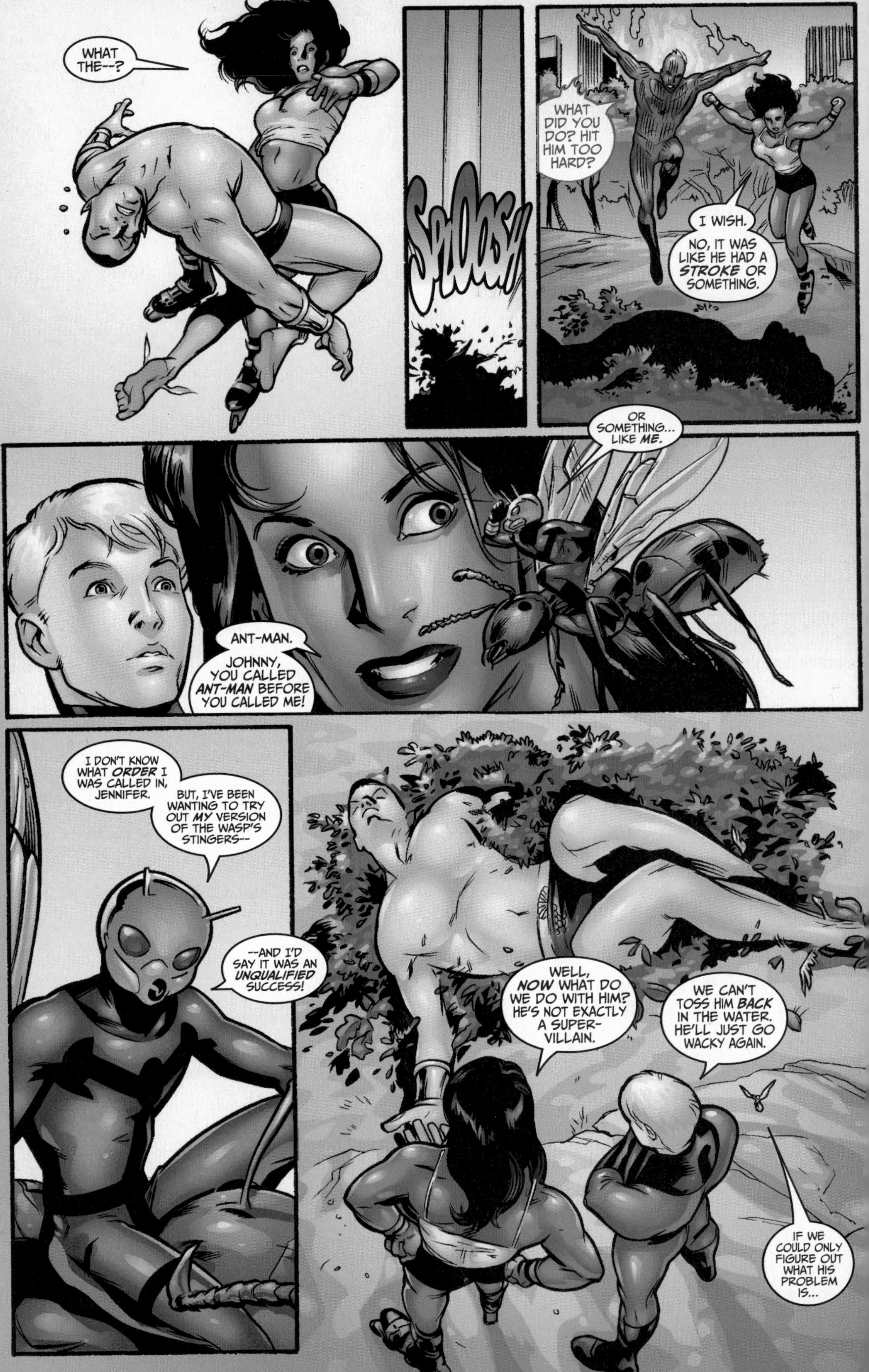
WHAT THE--?
SPLOOSH
WHAT DID YOU DO? HIT HIM TOO HARD?
I WISH.
NO, IT WAS LIKE HE HAD A STROKE OR SOMETHING.
OR SOMETHING... LIKE ME.
ANT-MAN.
JOHNNY, YOU CALLED ANT-MAN BEFORE YOU CALLED ME!
I DON'T KNOW WHAT ORDER I WAS CALLED IN, JENNIFER.
BUT, I'VE BEEN WANTING TO TRY OUT MY VERSION OF THE WASP'S STINGERS--
--AND I'D SAY IT WAS AN UNQUALIFIED SUCCESS!
WELL, NOW WHAT DO WE DO WITH HIM? HE'S NOT EXACTLY A SUPER-VILLAIN.
WE CAN'T TOSS HIM BACK IN THE WATER. HE'LL JUST GO WACKY AGAIN.
IF WE COULD ONLY FIGURE OUT WHAT HIS PROBLEM IS...

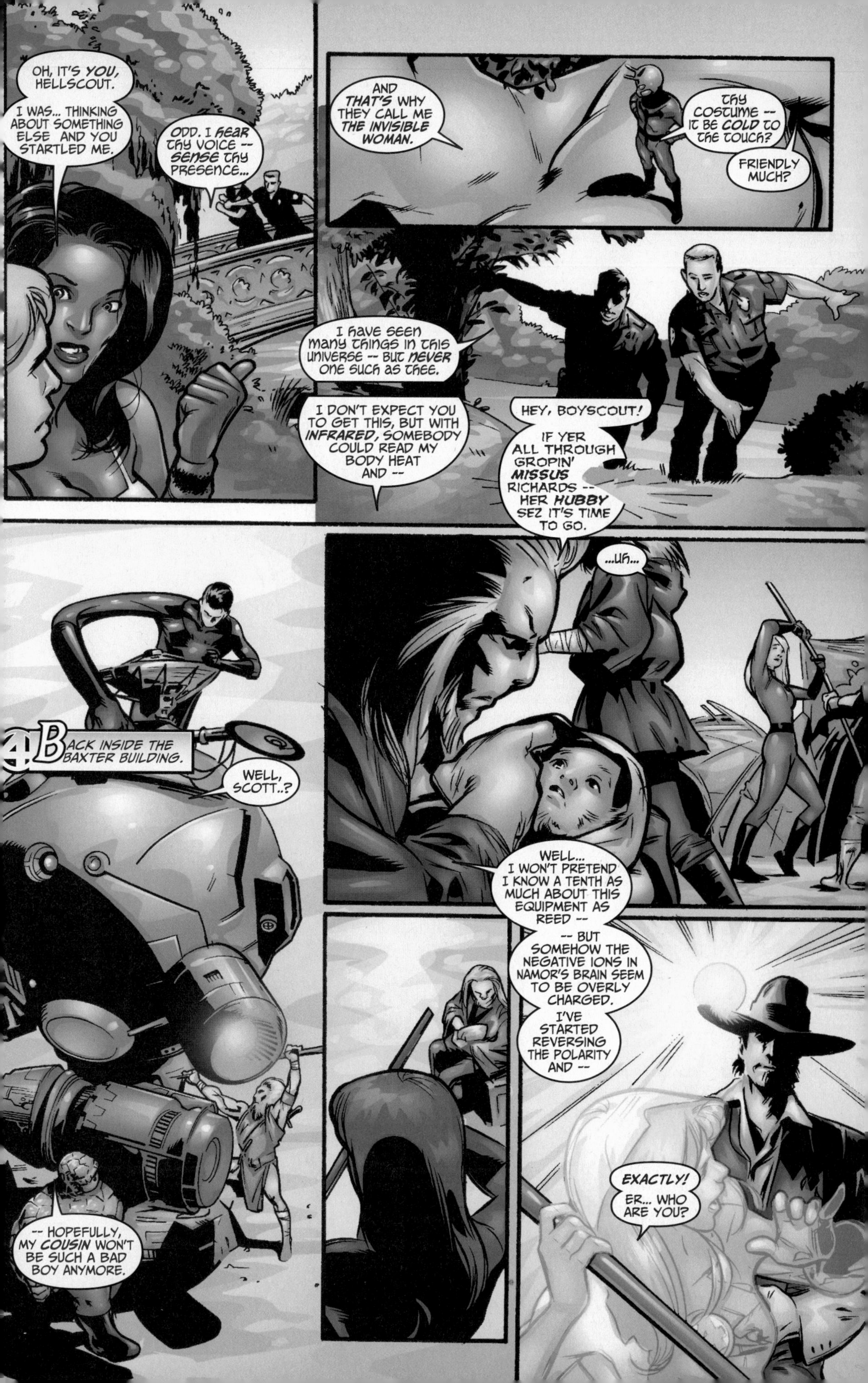
OH, IT'S YOU, HELLSCOUT.
I WAS... THINKING ABOUT SOMETHING ELSE AND YOU STARTLED ME.
ODD. I HEAR THY VOICE -- SENSE THY PRESENCE...
AND THAT'S WHY THEY CALL ME THE INVISIBLE WOMAN.
THY COSTUME -- IT BE COLD TO THE TOUCH?
FRIENDLY MUCH?
I HAVE SEEN MANY THINGS IN THIS UNIVERSE -- BUT NEVER ONE SUCH AS THEE.
I DON'T EXPECT YOU TO GET THIS, BUT WITH INFRARED, SOMEBODY COULD READ MY BODY HEAT AND --
HEY, BOYSCOUT!
IF YER ALL THROUGH GROPIN' MISSUS RICHARDS -- HER HUBBY SEZ IT'S TIME TO GO.
BACK INSIDE THE BAXTER BUILDING.
WELL, SCOTT..?
...UH...
WELL... I WON'T PRETEND I KNOW A TENTH AS MUCH ABOUT THIS EQUIPMENT AS REED --
-- BUT SOMEHOW THE NEGATIVE IONS IN NAMOR'S BRAIN SEEM TO BE OVERLY CHARGED.
I'VE STARTED REVERSING THE POLARITY AND --
-- HOPEFULLY, MY COUSIN WON'T BE SUCH A BAD BOY ANYMORE.
EXACTLY!
ER... WHO ARE YOU?

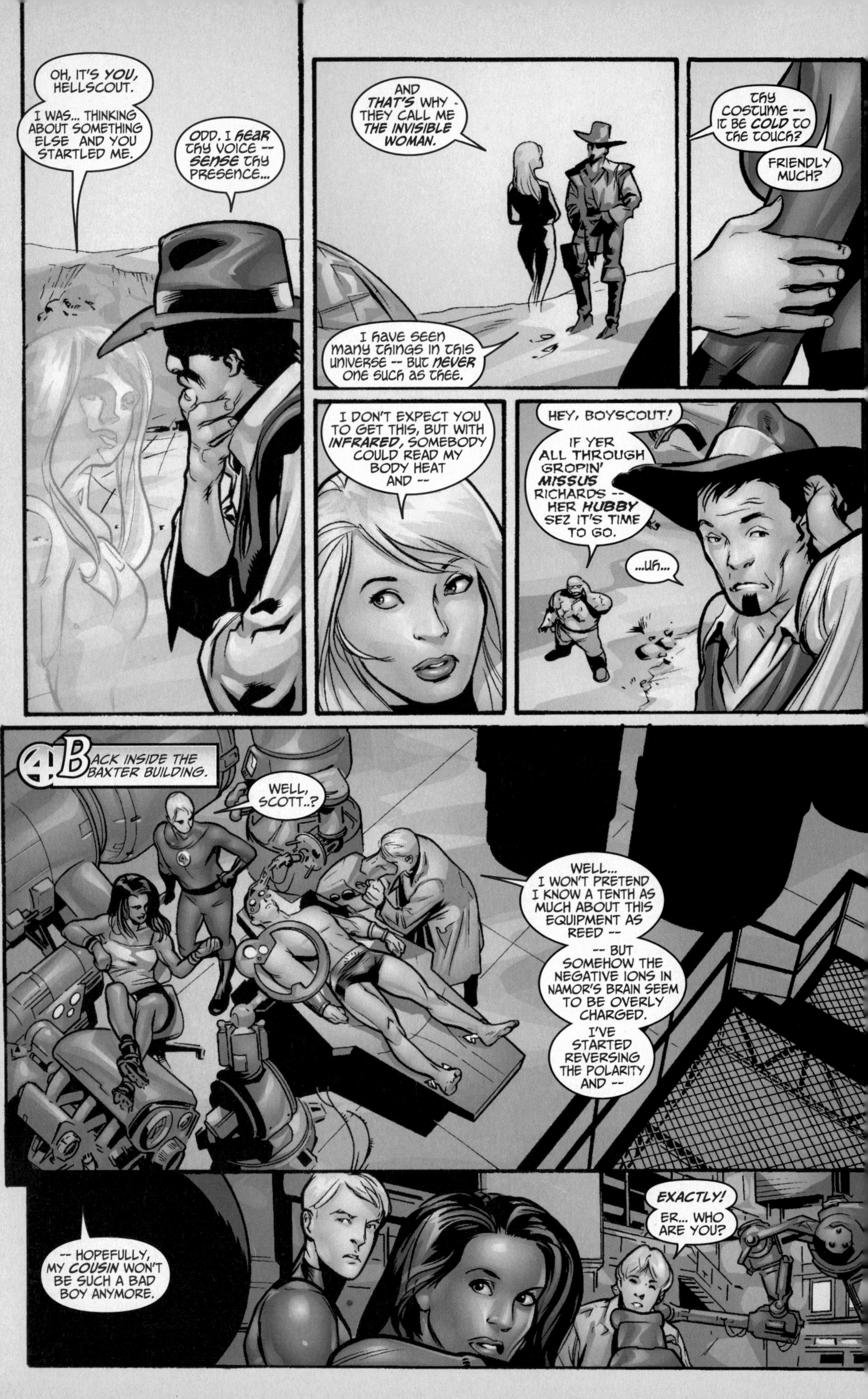
OH, IT'S YOU, HELLSCOUT.
I WAS... THINKING ABOUT SOMETHING ELSE AND YOU STARTLED ME.
ODD. I HEAR THY VOICE -- SENSE THY PRESENCE...
AND THAT'S WHY THEY CALL ME THE INVISIBLE WOMAN.
I HAVE SEEN MANY THINGS IN THIS UNIVERSE -- BUT NEVER ONE SUCH AS THEE.
THY COSTUME -- IT BE COLD TO THE TOUCH?
FRIENDLY MUCH?
I DON'T EXPECT YOU TO GET THIS, BUT WITH INFRARED, SOMEBODY COULD READ MY BODY HEAT AND --
HEY, BOYSCOUT!
IF YER ALL THROUGH GROPIN' MISSUS RICHARDS -- HER HUBBY SEZ IT'S TIME TO GO.
...UH...
BACK INSIDE THE BAXTER BUILDING.
WELL, SCOTT..?
WELL... I WON'T PRETEND I KNOW A TENTH AS MUCH ABOUT THIS EQUIPMENT AS REED --
-- BUT SOMEHOW THE NEGATIVE IONS IN NAMOR'S BRAIN SEEM TO BE OVERLY CHARGED.
I'VE STARTED REVERSING THE POLARITY AND --
-- HOPEFULLY, MY COUSIN WON'T BE SUCH A BAD BOY ANYMORE.
EXACTLY!
ER... WHO ARE YOU?

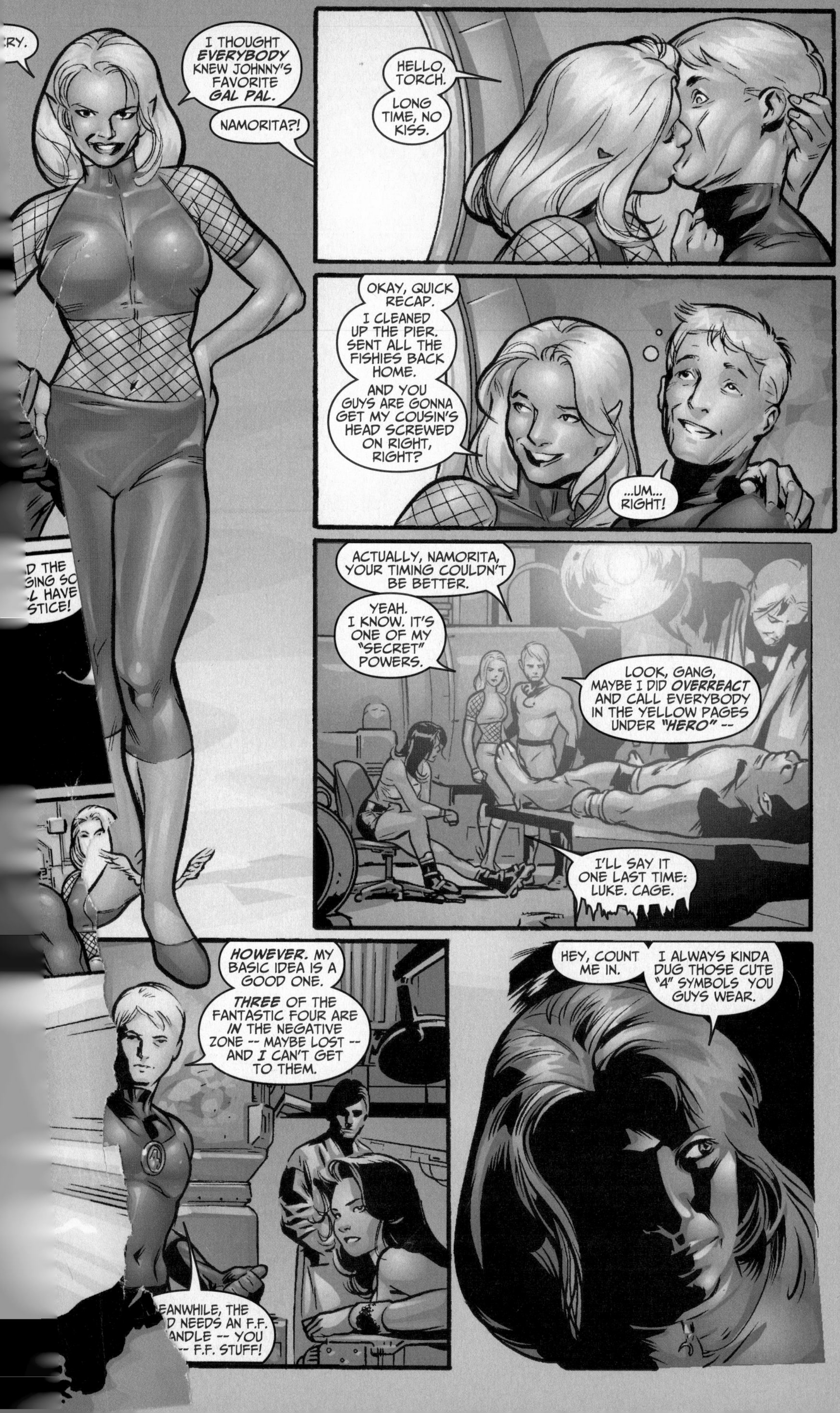

I THOUGHT EVERYBODY KNEW JOHNNY'S FAVORITE GAL PAL.
NAMORITA?!
HELLO, TORCH.
LONG TIME, NO KISS.
OKAY, QUICK RECAP.
I CLEANED UP THE PIER. SENT ALL THE FISHIES BACK HOME.
AND YOU GUYS ARE GONNA GET MY COUSIN'S HEAD SCREWED ON RIGHT, RIGHT?
...UM... RIGHT!
ACTUALLY, NAMORITA, YOUR TIMING COULDN'T BE BETTER.
YEAH. I KNOW. IT'S ONE OF MY "SECRET" POWERS.
LOOK, GANG, MAYBE I DID OVERREACT AND CALL EVERYBODY IN THE YELLOW PAGES UNDER "HERO" --
I'LL SAY IT ONE LAST TIME: LUKE. CAGE.
HOWEVER. MY BASIC IDEA IS A GOOD ONE.
THREE OF THE FANTASTIC FOUR ARE IN THE NEGATIVE ZONE -- MAYBE LOST -- AND I CAN'T GET TO THEM.
HEY, COUNT ME IN.
I ALWAYS KINDA DUG THOSE CUTE "4" SYMBOLS YOU GUYS WEAR.

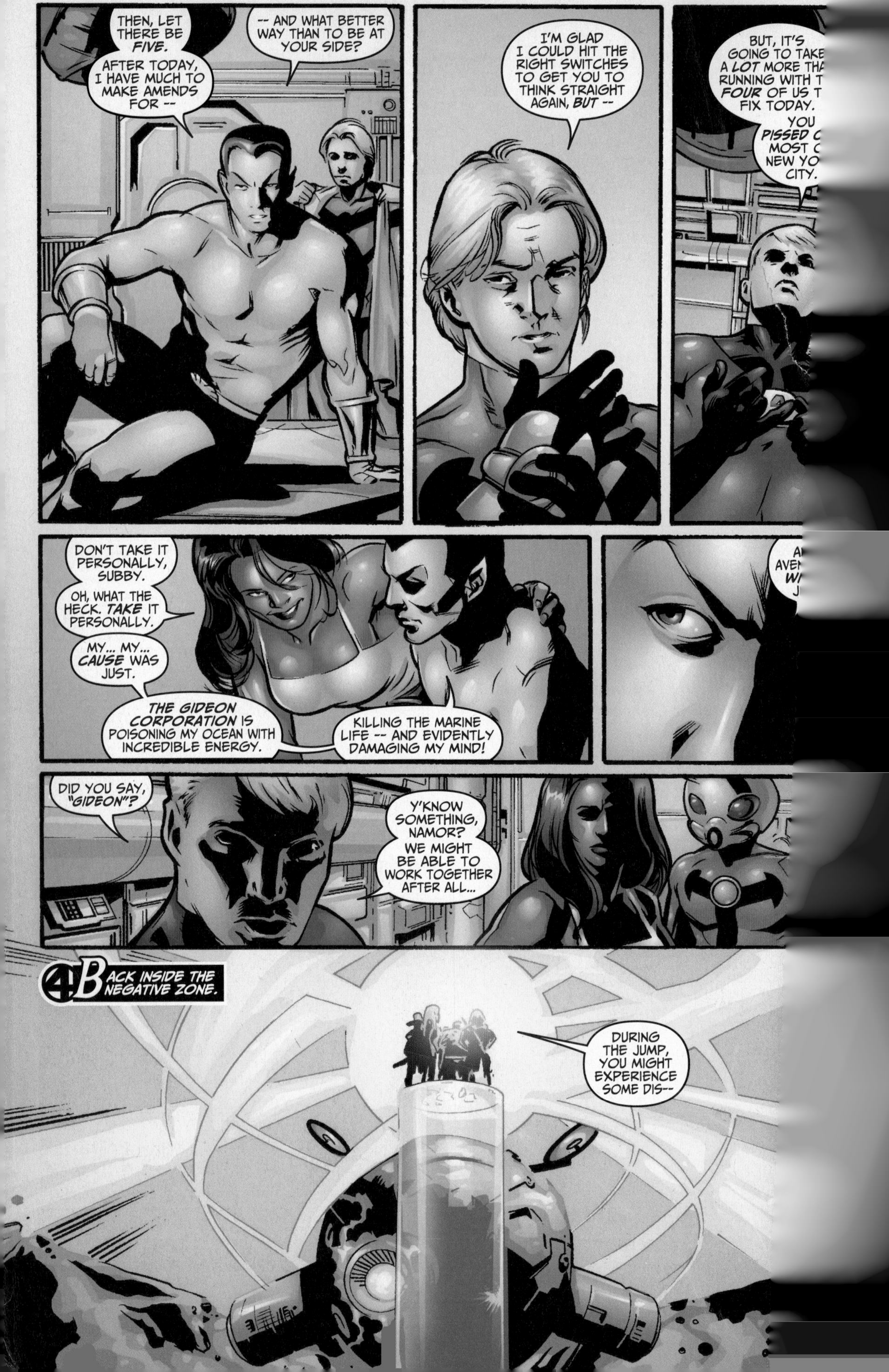
THEN, LET THERE BE FIVE.
AFTER TODAY, I HAVE MUCH TO MAKE AMENDS FOR --
-- AND WHAT BETTER WAY THAN TO BE AT YOUR SIDE?
I'M GLAD I COULD HIT THE RIGHT SWITCHES TO GET YOU TO THINK STRAIGHT AGAIN, BUT --
BUT, IT'S GOING TO
FIX TODAY.
DON'T TAKE IT PERSONALLY, SUBBY.
OH, WHAT THE HECK. TAKE IT PERSONALLY.
MY... MY... CAUSE WAS JUST.
THE GIDEON CORPORATION IS POISONING MY OCEAN WITH INCREDIBLE ENERGY.
KILLING THE MARINE LIFE -- AND EVIDENTLY DAMAGING MY MIND!
DID YOU SAY, "GIDEON"?
Y'KNOW SOMETHING, NAMOR? WE MIGHT BE ABLE TO WORK TOGETHER AFTER ALL...
BACK INSIDE THE NEGATIVE ZONE.
DURING THE JUMP, YOU MIGHT EXPERIENCE SOME DIS--

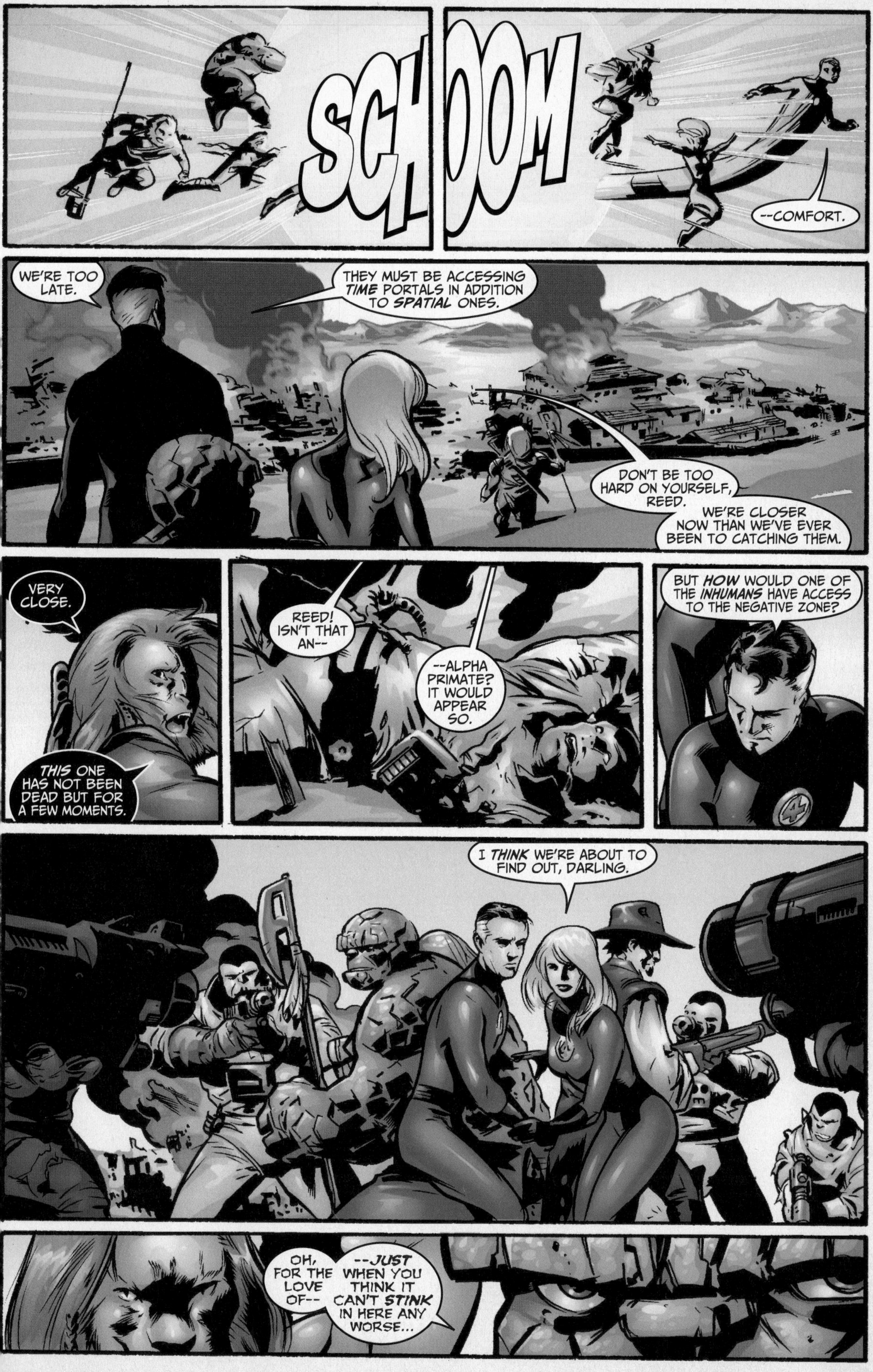
SCHOOM
--COMFORT.
WE'RE TOO LATE.
THEY MUST BE ACCESSING TIME PORTALS IN ADDITION TO SPATIAL ONES.
DON'T BE TOO HARD ON YOURSELF, REED.
WE'RE CLOSER NOW THAN WE'VE EVER BEEN TO CATCHING THEM.
VERY CLOSE.
THIS ONE HAS NOT BEEN DEAD BUT FOR A FEW MOMENTS.
REED! ISN'T THAT AN--
--ALPHA PRIMATE? IT WOULD APPEAR SO.
BUT HOW WOULD ONE OF THE INHUMANS HAVE ACCESS TO THE NEGATIVE ZONE?
I THINK WE'RE ABOUT TO FIND OUT, DARLING.
OH, FOR THE LOVE OF--
--JUST WHEN YOU THINK IT CAN'T STINK IN HERE ANY WORSE...

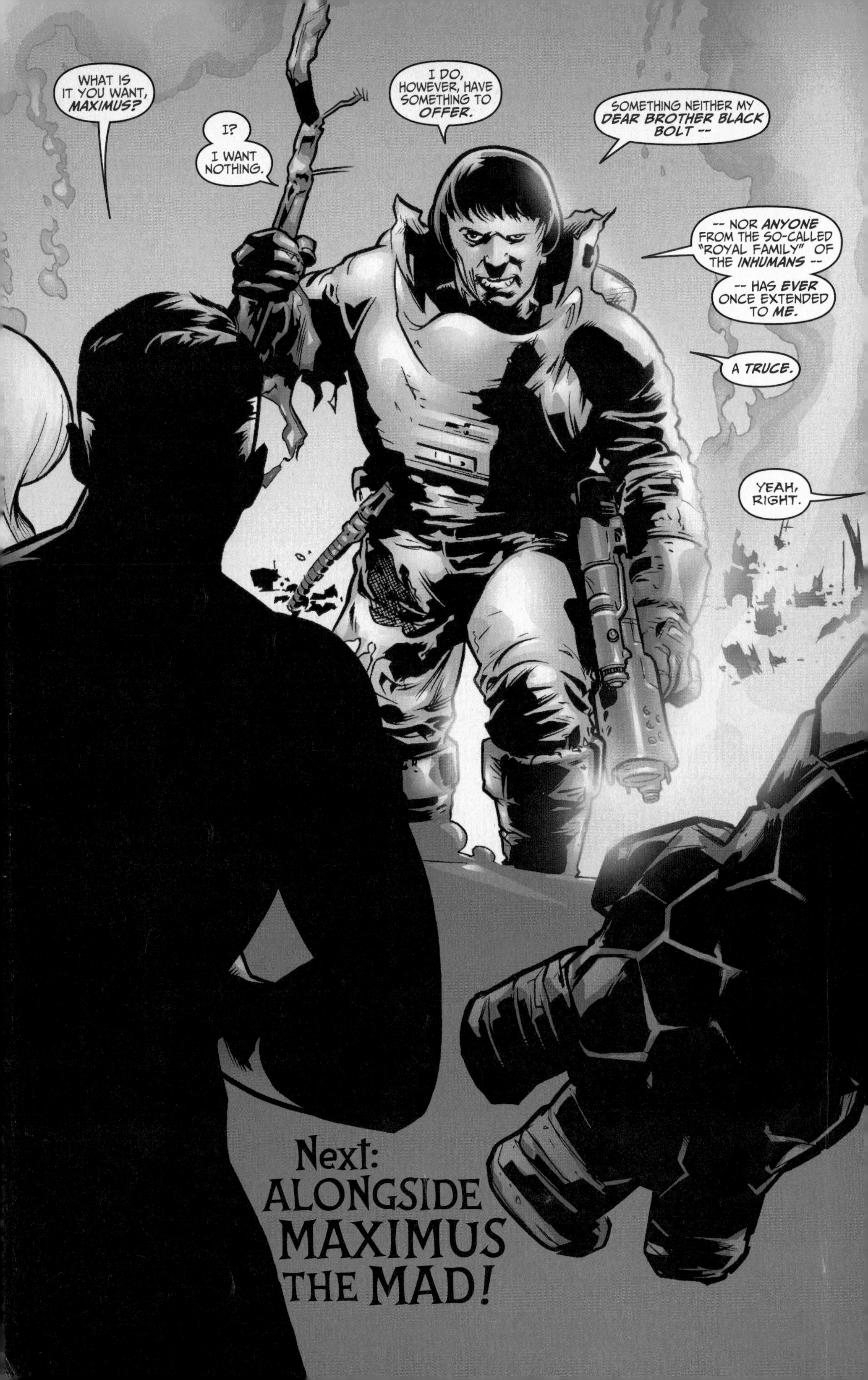
WHAT IS IT YOU WANT, MAXIMUS?
I?
I WANT NOTHING.
I DO, HOWEVER, HAVE SOMETHING TO OFFER.
SOMETHING NEITHER MY DEAR BROTHER BLACK BOLT --
-- NOR ANYONE FROM THE SO-CALLED "ROYAL FAMILY" OF THE INHUMANS --
-- HAS EVER ONCE EXTENDED TO ME.
A TRUCE.
YEAH, RIGHT.
Next: ALONGSIDE MAXIMUS THE MAD!

MARVEL
544
.com
THE INITIATIVE
McDUFFIE
PELLETIER
MAGYAR
THE NEW
Fantastic
Four
MICHAEL TURNER

FINALLY, I HAVE OBTAINED THE CHRYSALIS.

BALANCING THE FORCES WITHIN A NAKED EVENT HORIZON STRAINS EVEN *MY* POWER. BUT THE RISK IS WORTH IT.

WITH BUT THE SUBTLEST OF MANIPULATIONS, I FORCE THE BEING WITHIN TO MATURE TO ITS ULTIMATE FORM. ONLY A MATTER OF MOMENTS UNTIL--

HOLD! SOMETHING APPROACHES.

MY MACHINATIONS CANNOT BE DISCOVERED YET. I MUST HIDE FOR NOW--

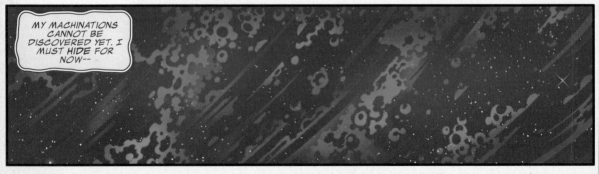

--UNTIL I HAVE GAINED THE STRENGTH TO DIRECTLY CONFRONT MY ENEMY.

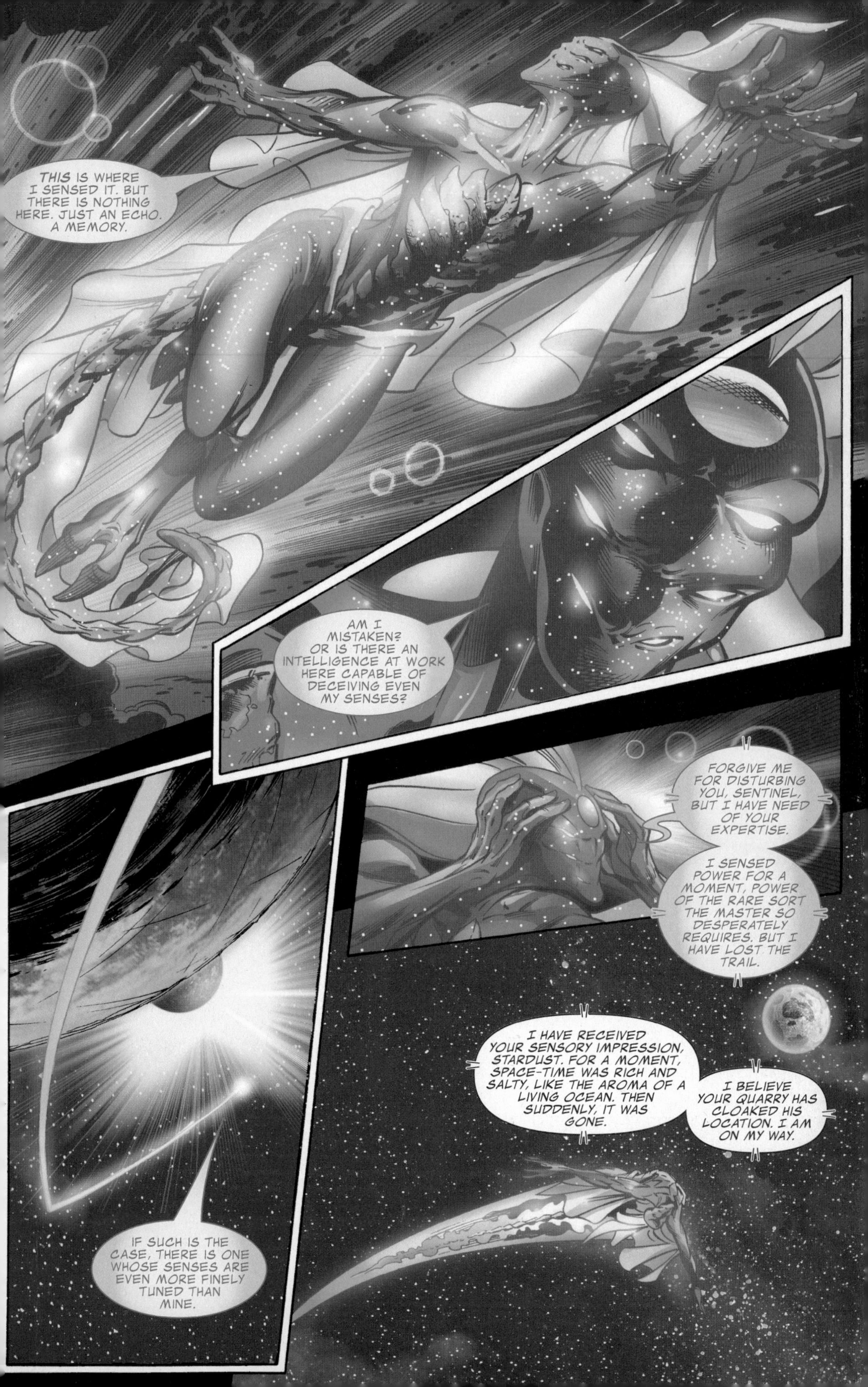
THIS IS WHERE I SENSED IT. BUT THERE IS NOTHING HERE. JUST AN ECHO. A MEMORY.
AM I MISTAKEN? OR IS THERE AN INTELLIGENCE AT WORK HERE CAPABLE OF DECEIVING EVEN MY SENSES?
IF SUCH IS THE CASE, THERE IS ONE WHOSE SENSES ARE EVEN MORE FINELY TUNED THAN MINE.
FORGIVE ME FOR DISTURBING YOU, SENTINEL, BUT I HAVE NEED OF YOUR EXPERTISE.
I SENSED POWER FOR A MOMENT, POWER OF THE RARE SORT THE MASTER SO DESPERATELY REQUIRES. BUT I HAVE LOST THE TRAIL.
I HAVE RECEIVED YOUR SENSORY IMPRESSION, STARDUST. FOR A MOMENT, SPACE-TIME WAS RICH AND SALTY, LIKE THE AROMA OF A LIVING OCEAN. THEN SUDDENLY, IT WAS GONE.
I BELIEVE YOUR QUARRY HAS CLOAKED HIS LOCATION. I AM ON MY WAY.

THE BAXTER BUILDING. HEADQUARTERS OF THE FANTASTIC FOUR.

COULD YOU GO AGAIN? I'M NOT FOLLOWIN' THIS.

REED AND I ARE TAKING SOME TIME OFF.

TO RECONNECT. A SECOND HONEYMOON, OF SORTS.

T'CHALLA AND ORORO WILL BE STAYING HERE FOR A WHILE.

RECONSTRUCTION · CHAPTER ONE
FROM THE RIDICULOUS TO THE SUBLIME*

*BUT NOT NECESSARILY IN THAT ORDER.

DWAYNE McDUFFIE WRITER | PAUL PELLETIER PENCILER | RICK MAGYAR INKERS | PAUL MOUNTS COLORIST | VC'S RUS WOOTON LETTERER | MOLLY LAZER ASST. EDITOR | TOM BREVOORT EDITOR | JOE QUESADA EDITOR IN CHIEF | DAN BUCKLEY PUBLISHER

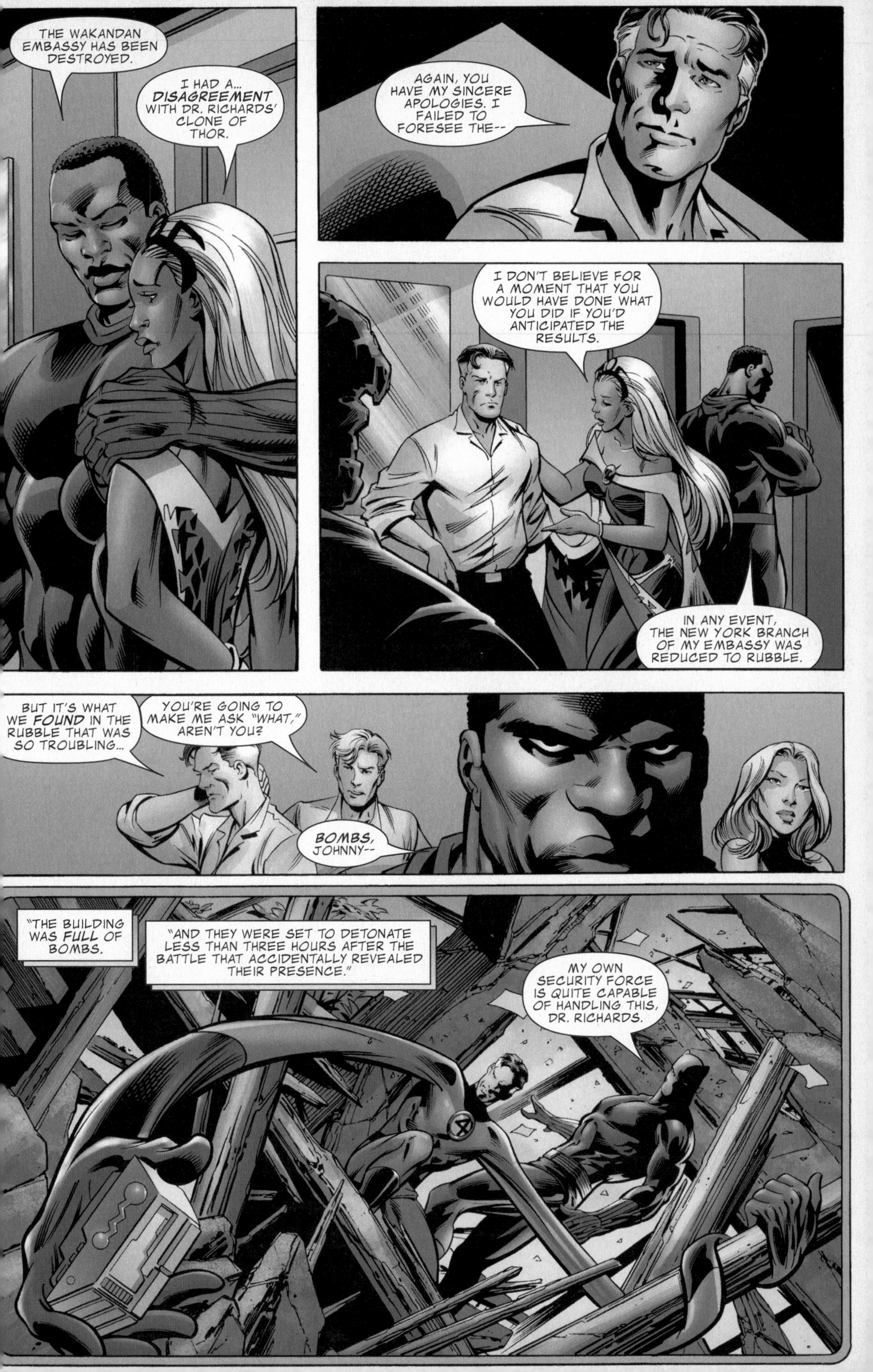
THE WAKANDAN EMBASSY HAS BEEN DESTROYED.
I HAD A... DISAGREEMENT WITH DR. RICHARDS' CLONE OF THOR.
AGAIN, YOU HAVE MY SINCERE APOLOGIES. I FAILED TO FORESEE THE--
I DON'T BELIEVE FOR A MOMENT THAT YOU WOULD HAVE DONE WHAT YOU DID IF YOU'D ANTICIPATED THE RESULTS.
IN ANY EVENT, THE NEW YORK BRANCH OF MY EMBASSY WAS REDUCED TO RUBBLE.
BUT IT'S WHAT WE FOUND IN THE RUBBLE THAT WAS SO TROUBLING...
YOU'RE GOING TO MAKE ME ASK "WHAT," AREN'T YOU?
BOMBS, JOHNNY--
"THE BUILDING WAS FULL OF BOMBS.
"AND THEY WERE SET TO DETONATE LESS THAN THREE HOURS AFTER THE BATTLE THAT ACCIDENTALLY REVEALED THEIR PRESENCE."
MY OWN SECURITY FORCE IS QUITE CAPABLE OF HANDLING THIS, DR. RICHARDS.

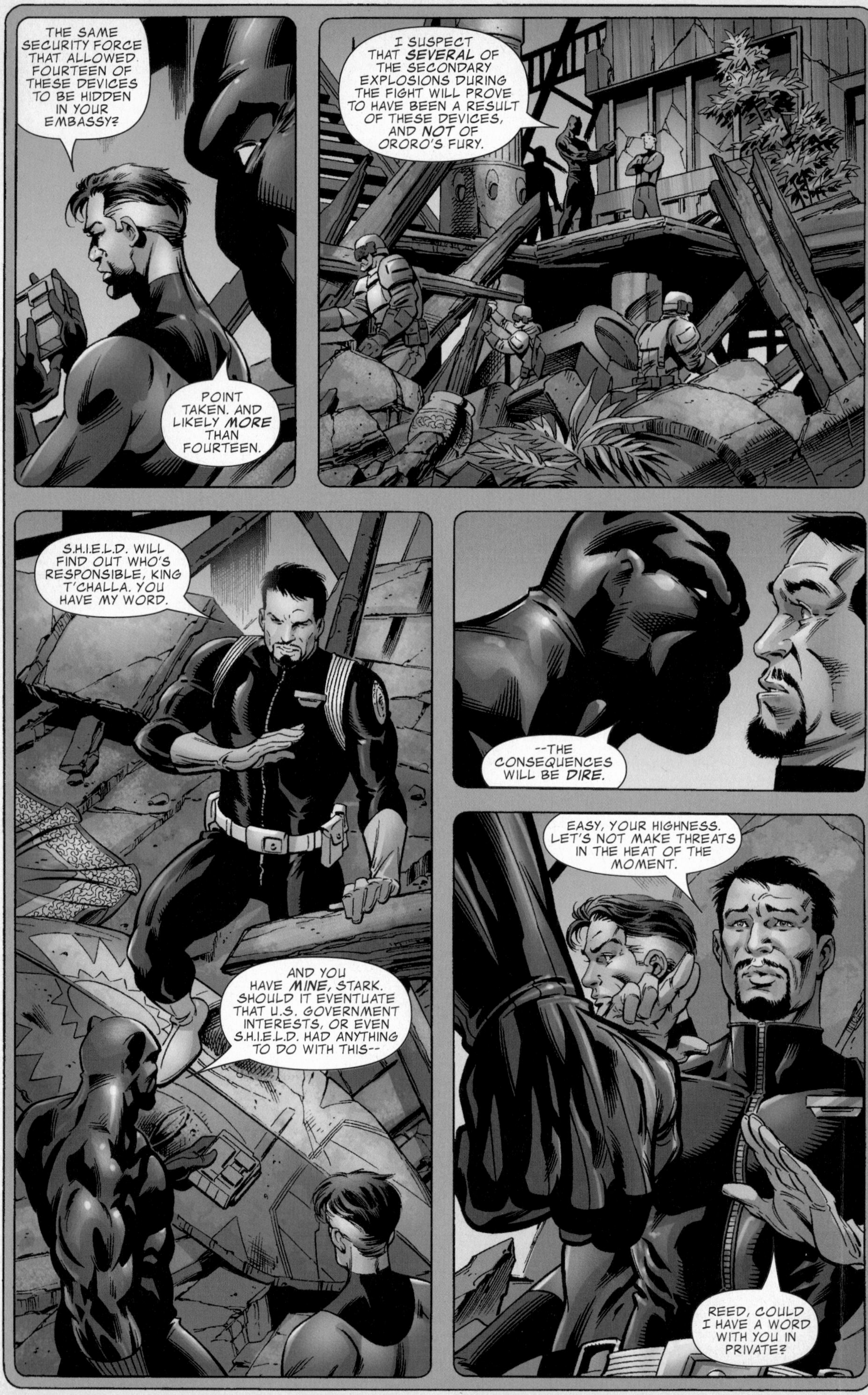
THE SAME SECURITY FORCE THAT ALLOWED FOURTEEN OF THESE DEVICES TO BE HIDDEN IN YOUR EMBASSY?
POINT TAKEN. AND LIKELY MORE THAN FOURTEEN.
I SUSPECT THAT SEVERAL OF THE SECONDARY EXPLOSIONS DURING THE FIGHT WILL PROVE TO HAVE BEEN A RESULT OF THESE DEVICES, AND NOT OF ORORO'S FURY.
S.H.I.E.L.D. WILL FIND OUT WHO'S RESPONSIBLE, KING T'CHALLA. YOU HAVE MY WORD.
AND YOU HAVE MINE, STARK. SHOULD IT EVENTUATE THAT U.S. GOVERNMENT INTERESTS, OR EVEN S.H.I.E.L.D. HAD ANYTHING TO DO WITH THIS--
--THE CONSEQUENCES WILL BE DIRE.
EASY, YOUR HIGHNESS. LET'S NOT MAKE THREATS IN THE HEAT OF THE MOMENT.
REED, COULD I HAVE A WORD WITH YOU IN PRIVATE?

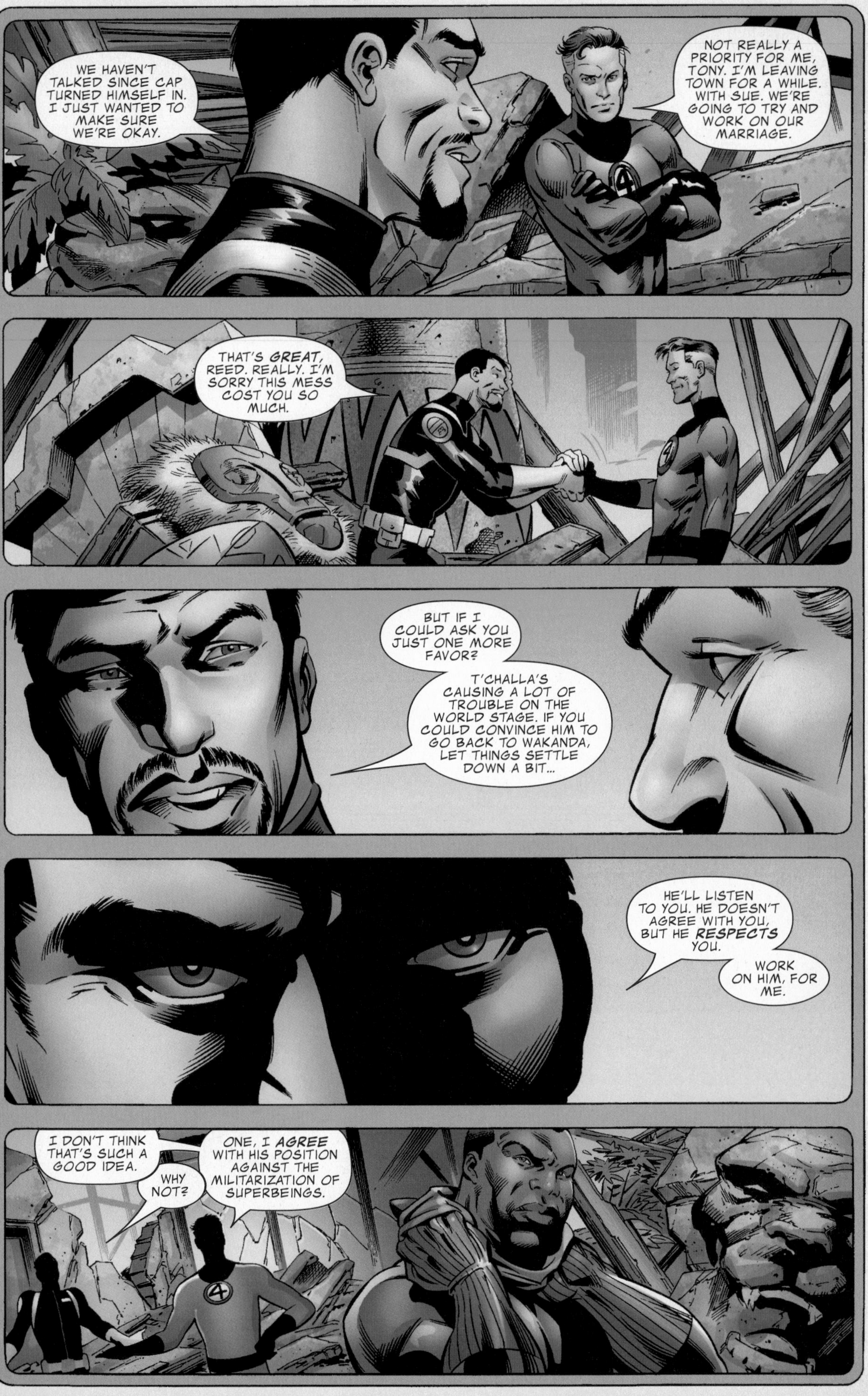
WE HAVEN'T TALKED SINCE CAP TURNED HIMSELF IN. I JUST WANTED TO MAKE SURE WE'RE OKAY.
NOT REALLY A PRIORITY FOR ME, TONY. I'M LEAVING TOWN FOR A WHILE. WITH SUE. WE'RE GOING TO TRY AND WORK ON OUR MARRIAGE.
THAT'S GREAT, REED. REALLY. I'M SORRY THIS MESS COST YOU SO MUCH.
BUT IF I COULD ASK YOU JUST ONE MORE FAVOR?
T'CHALLA'S CAUSING A LOT OF TROUBLE ON THE WORLD STAGE. IF YOU COULD CONVINCE HIM TO GO BACK TO WAKANDA, LET THINGS SETTLE DOWN A BIT...
HE'LL LISTEN TO YOU. HE DOESN'T AGREE WITH YOU, BUT HE RESPECTS YOU.
WORK ON HIM, FOR ME.
I DON'T THINK THAT'S SUCH A GOOD IDEA.
WHY NOT?
ONE, I AGREE WITH HIS POSITION AGAINST THE MILITARIZATION OF SUPERBEINGS.

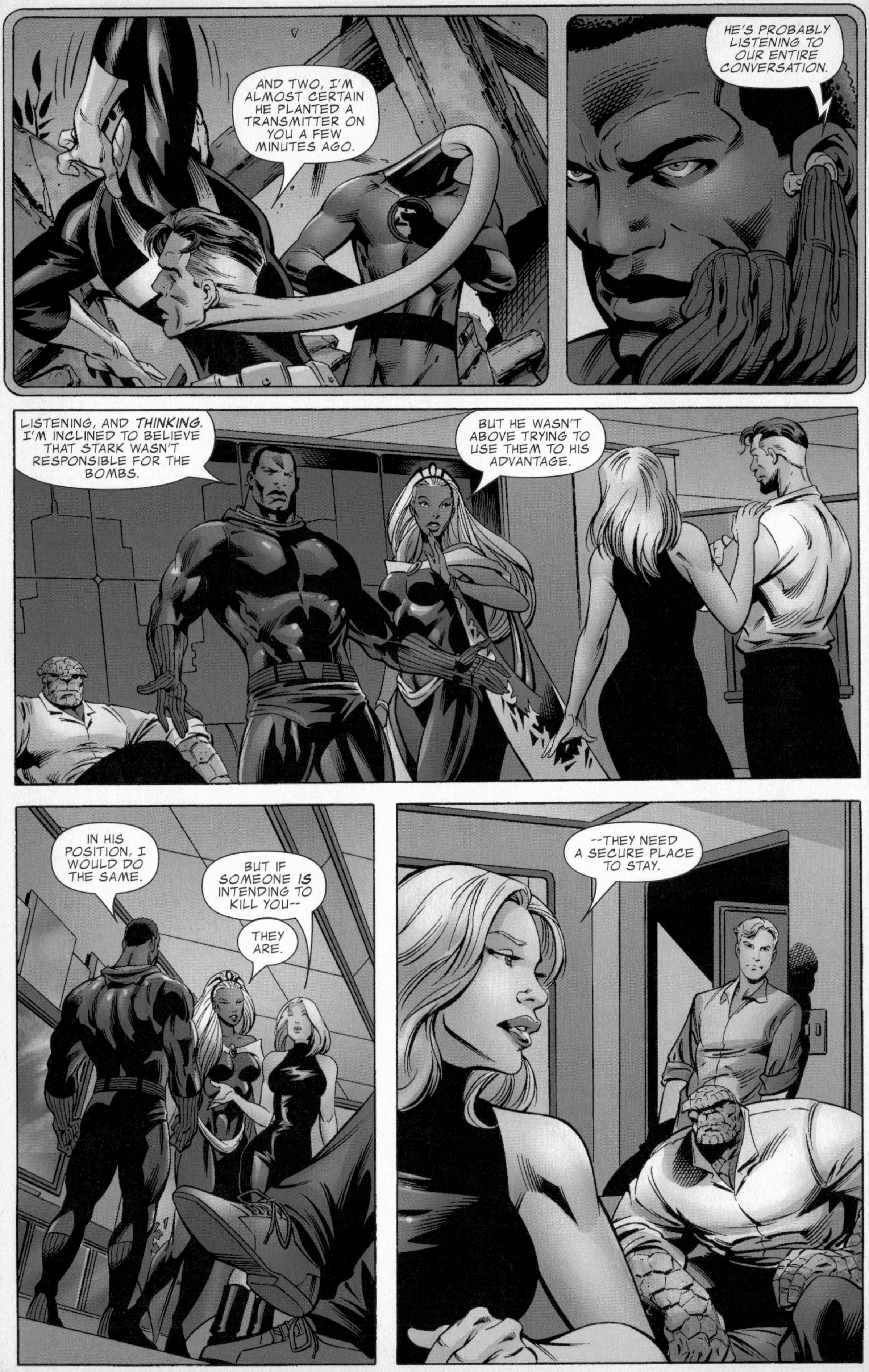
AND TWO, I'M ALMOST CERTAIN HE PLANTED A TRANSMITTER ON YOU A FEW MINUTES AGO.
HE'S PROBABLY LISTENING TO OUR ENTIRE CONVERSATION.
LISTENING, AND THINKING. I'M INCLINED TO BELIEVE THAT STARK WASN'T RESPONSIBLE FOR THE BOMBS.
BUT HE WASN'T ABOVE TRYING TO USE THEM TO HIS ADVANTAGE.
IN HIS POSITION, I WOULD DO THE SAME.
BUT IF SOMEONE IS INTENDING TO KILL YOU--
THEY ARE.
--THEY NEED A SECURE PLACE TO STAY.

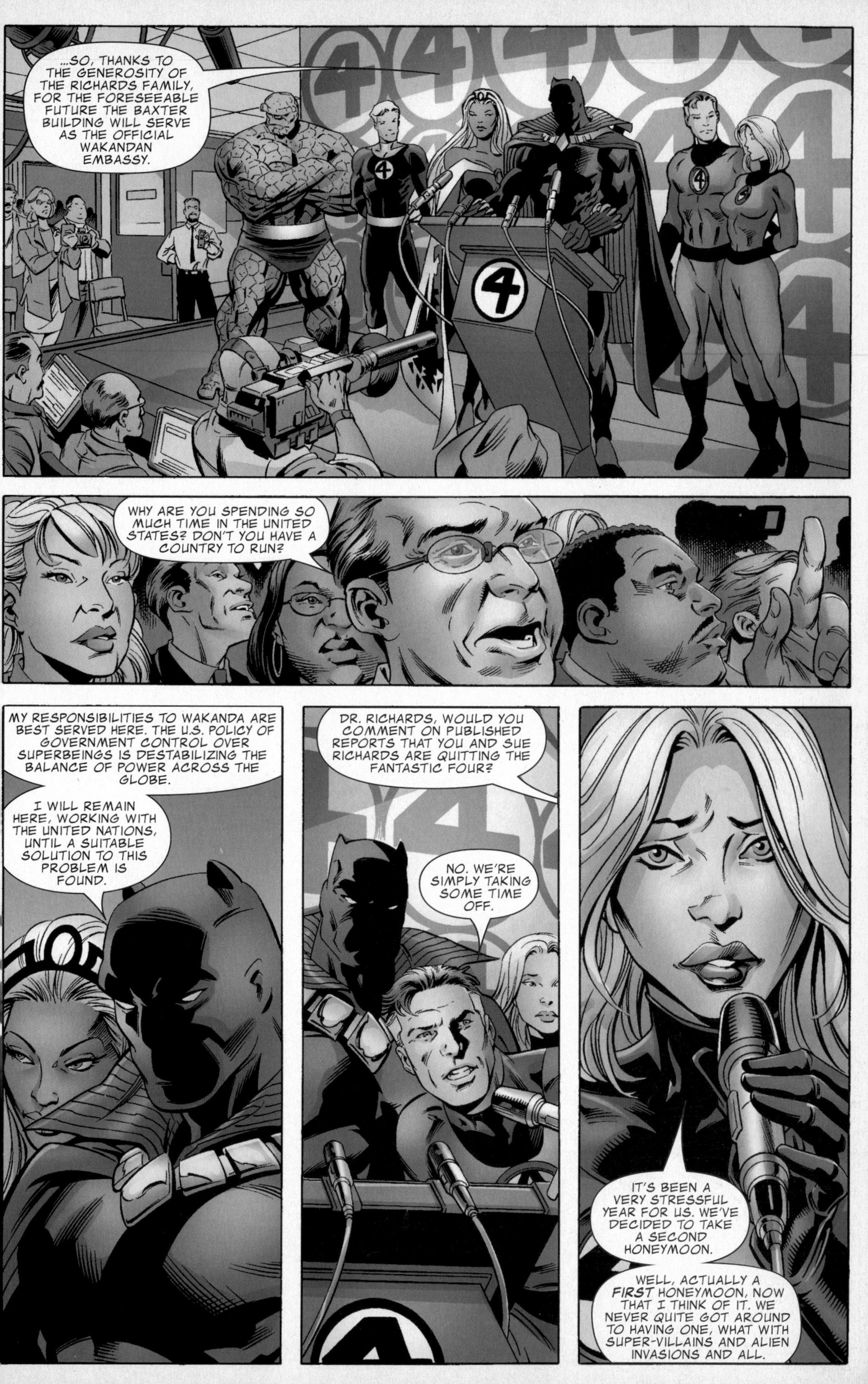
...SO, THANKS TO THE GENEROSITY OF THE RICHARDS FAMILY, FOR THE FORESEEABLE FUTURE THE BAXTER BUILDING WILL SERVE AS THE OFFICIAL WAKANDAN EMBASSY.
WHY ARE YOU SPENDING SO MUCH TIME IN THE UNITED STATES? DON'T YOU HAVE A COUNTRY TO RUN?
MY RESPONSIBILITIES TO WAKANDA ARE BEST SERVED HERE. THE U.S. POLICY OF GOVERNMENT CONTROL OVER SUPERBEINGS IS DESTABILIZING THE BALANCE OF POWER ACROSS THE GLOBE.
I WILL REMAIN HERE, WORKING WITH THE UNITED NATIONS, UNTIL A SUITABLE SOLUTION TO THIS PROBLEM IS FOUND.
DR. RICHARDS, WOULD YOU COMMENT ON PUBLISHED REPORTS THAT YOU AND SUE RICHARDS ARE QUITTING THE FANTASTIC FOUR?
NO. WE'RE SIMPLY TAKING SOME TIME OFF.
IT'S BEEN A VERY STRESSFUL YEAR FOR US. WE'VE DECIDED TO TAKE A SECOND HONEYMOON.
WELL, ACTUALLY A *FIRST* HONEYMOON, NOW THAT I THINK OF IT. WE NEVER QUITE GOT AROUND TO HAVING ONE, WHAT WITH SUPER-VILLAINS AND ALIEN INVASIONS AND ALL.

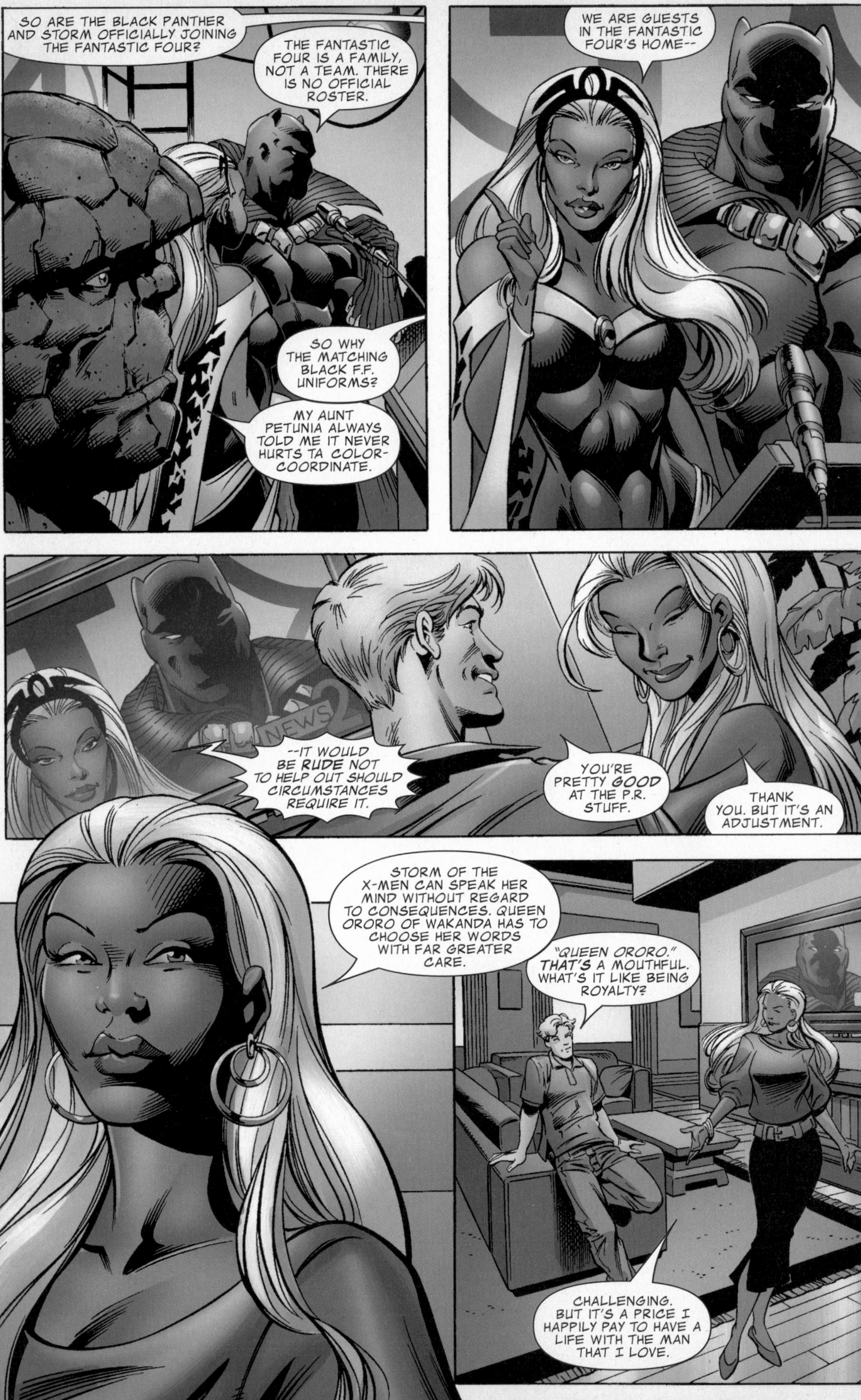
SO ARE THE BLACK PANTHER AND STORM OFFICIALLY JOINING THE FANTASTIC FOUR?
THE FANTASTIC FOUR IS A FAMILY, NOT A TEAM. THERE IS NO OFFICIAL ROSTER.
SO WHY THE MATCHING BLACK F.F. UNIFORMS?
MY AUNT PETUNIA ALWAYS TOLD ME IT NEVER HURTS TA COLOR-COORDINATE.
WE ARE GUESTS IN THE FANTASTIC FOUR'S HOME--
NEWS 2
--IT WOULD BE RUDE NOT TO HELP OUT SHOULD CIRCUMSTANCES REQUIRE IT.
YOU'RE PRETTY GOOD AT THE P.R. STUFF.
THANK YOU. BUT IT'S AN ADJUSTMENT.
STORM OF THE X-MEN CAN SPEAK HER MIND WITHOUT REGARD TO CONSEQUENCES. QUEEN ORORO OF WAKANDA HAS TO CHOOSE HER WORDS WITH FAR GREATER CARE.
"QUEEN ORORO." THAT'S A MOUTHFUL. WHAT'S IT LIKE BEING ROYALTY?
CHALLENGING. BUT IT'S A PRICE I HAPPILY PAY TO HAVE A LIFE WITH THE MAN THAT I LOVE.

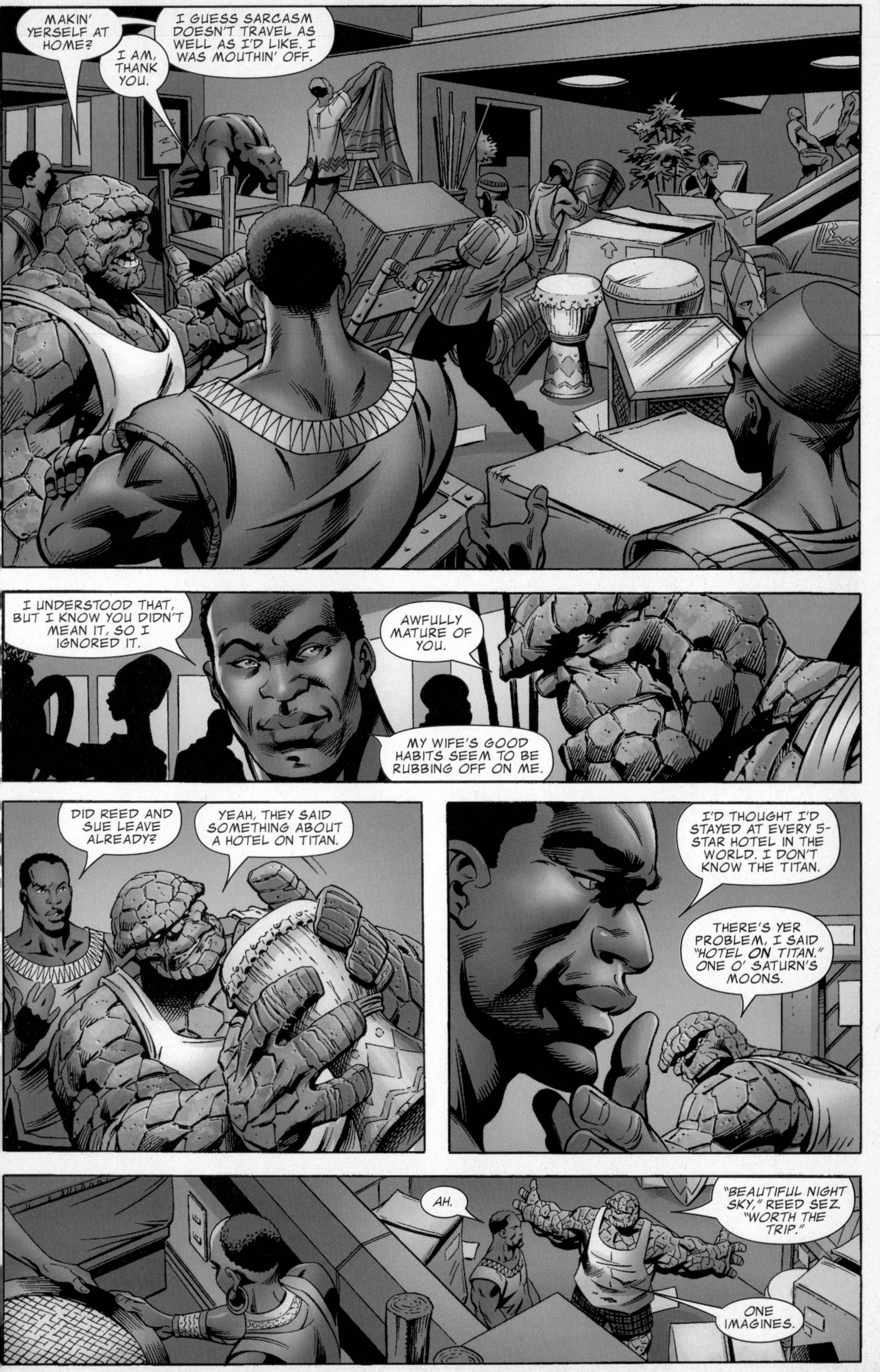
MAKIN' YERSELF AT HOME?
I AM, THANK YOU.
I GUESS SARCASM DOESN'T TRAVEL AS WELL AS I'D LIKE. I WAS MOUTHIN' OFF.
I UNDERSTOOD THAT, BUT I KNOW YOU DIDN'T MEAN IT, SO I IGNORED IT.
AWFULLY MATURE OF YOU.
MY WIFE'S GOOD HABITS SEEM TO BE RUBBING OFF ON ME.
DID REED AND SUE LEAVE ALREADY?
YEAH, THEY SAID SOMETHING ABOUT A HOTEL ON TITAN.
I'D THOUGHT I'D STAYED AT EVERY 5-STAR HOTEL IN THE WORLD. I DON'T KNOW THE TITAN.
THERE'S YER PROBLEM, I SAID "HOTEL ON TITAN." ONE O' SATURN'S MOONS.
AH.
"BEAUTIFUL NIGHT SKY," REED SEZ. "WORTH THE TRIP."
ONE IMAGINES.

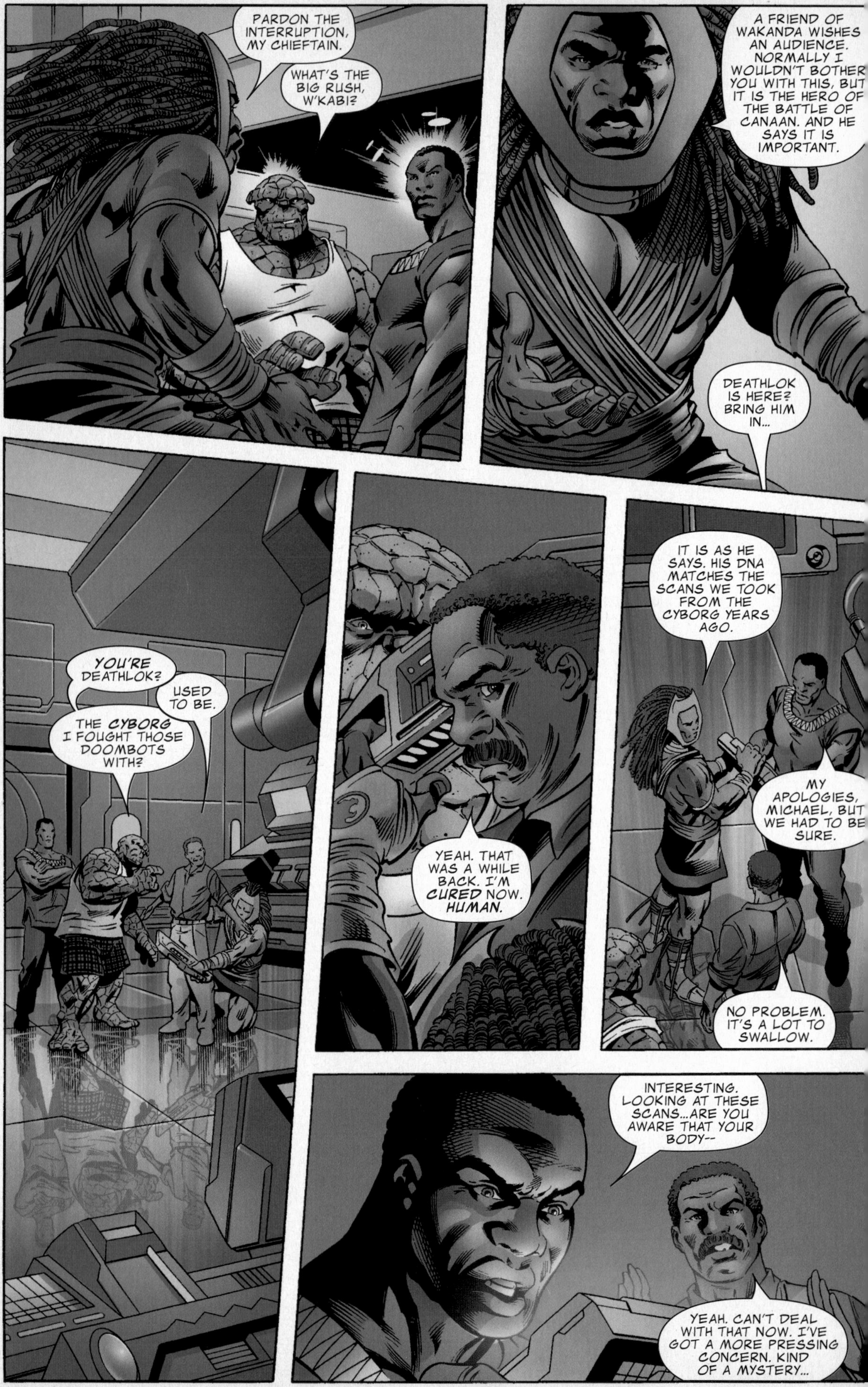
PARDON THE INTERRUPTION, MY CHIEFTAIN.
WHAT'S THE BIG RUSH, W'KABI?
A FRIEND OF WAKANDA WISHES AN AUDIENCE. NORMALLY I WOULDN'T BOTHER YOU WITH THIS, BUT IT IS THE HERO OF THE BATTLE OF CANAAN. AND HE SAYS IT IS IMPORTANT.
DEATHLOK IS HERE? BRING HIM IN...
YOU'RE DEATHLOK?
USED TO BE.
THE CYBORG I FOUGHT THOSE DOOMBOTS WITH?
YEAH. THAT WAS A WHILE BACK. I'M CURED NOW. HUMAN.
IT IS AS HE SAYS. HIS DNA MATCHES THE SCANS WE TOOK FROM THE CYBORG YEARS AGO.
MY APOLOGIES, MICHAEL, BUT WE HAD TO BE SURE.
NO PROBLEM. IT'S A LOT TO SWALLOW.
INTERESTING. LOOKING AT THESE SCANS...ARE YOU AWARE THAT YOUR BODY--
YEAH. CAN'T DEAL WITH THAT NOW. I'VE GOT A MORE PRESSING CONCERN. KIND OF A MYSTERY...

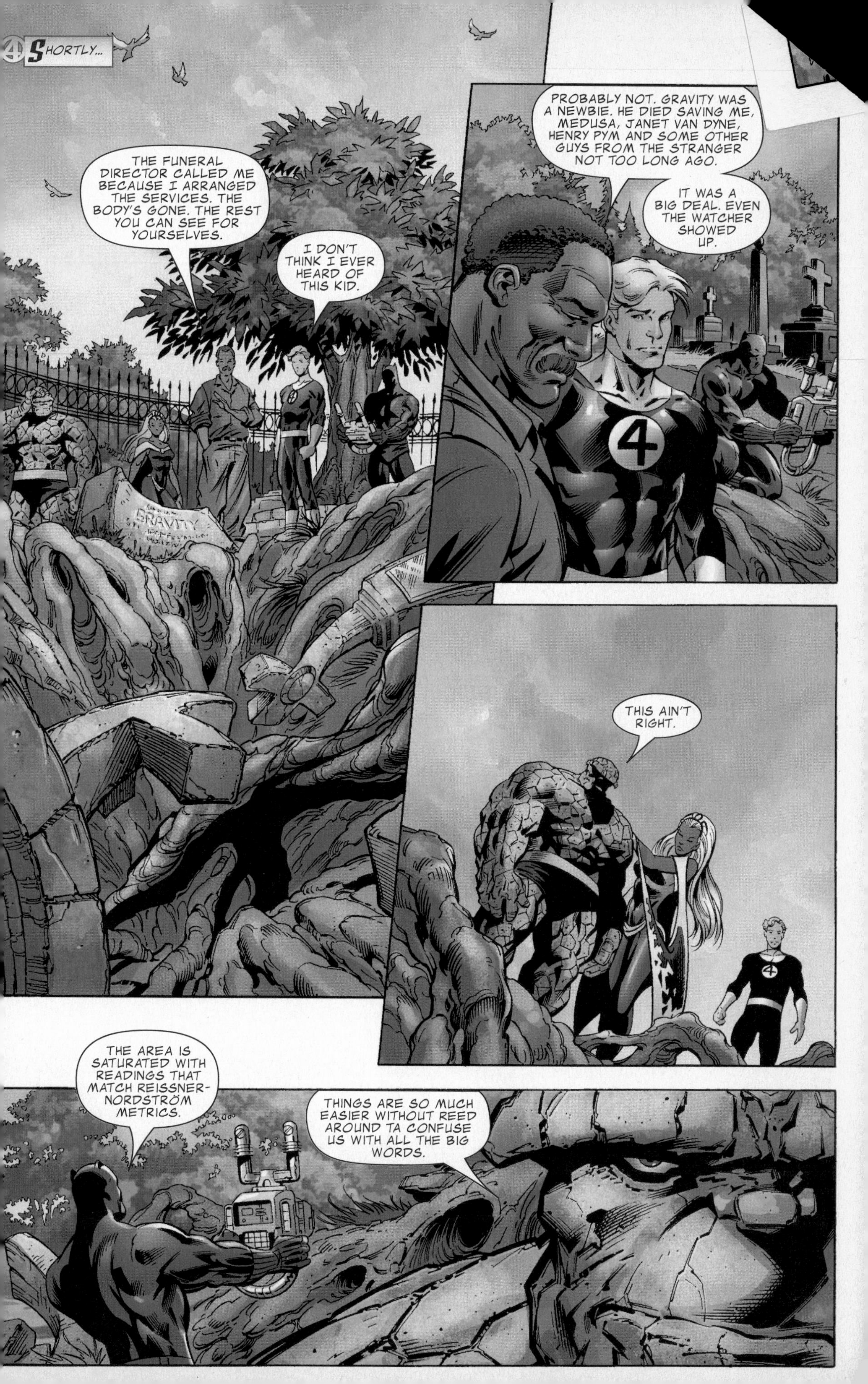
SHORTLY...
THE FUNERAL DIRECTOR CALLED ME BECAUSE I ARRANGED THE SERVICES. THE BODY'S GONE. THE REST YOU CAN SEE FOR YOURSELVES.
I DON'T THINK I EVER HEARD OF THIS KID.
GRAVITY
PROBABLY NOT. GRAVITY WAS A NEWBIE. HE DIED SAVING ME, MEDUSA, JANET VAN DYNE, HENRY PYM AND SOME OTHER GUYS FROM THE STRANGER NOT TOO LONG AGO.
IT WAS A BIG DEAL. EVEN THE WATCHER SHOWED UP.
THIS AIN'T RIGHT.
THE AREA IS SATURATED WITH READINGS THAT MATCH REISSNER-NORDSTRÖM METRICS.
THINGS ARE SO MUCH EASIER WITHOUT REED AROUND TA CONFUSE US WITH ALL THE BIG WORDS.

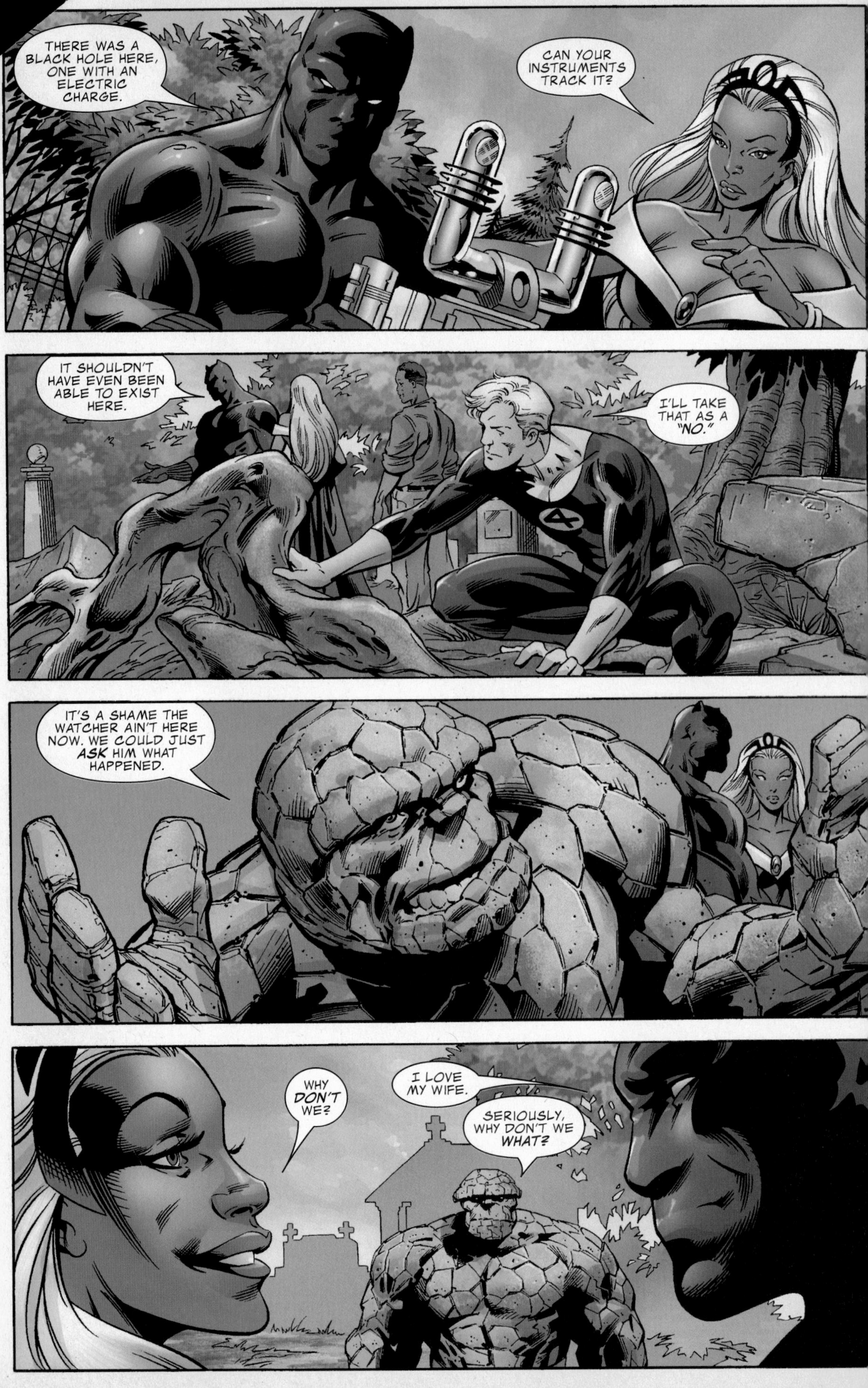
THERE WAS A BLACK HOLE HERE, ONE WITH AN ELECTRIC CHARGE.
CAN YOUR INSTRUMENTS TRACK IT?
IT SHOULDN'T HAVE EVEN BEEN ABLE TO EXIST HERE.
I'LL TAKE THAT AS A "NO."
IT'S A SHAME THE WATCHER AIN'T HERE NOW. WE COULD JUST ASK HIM WHAT HAPPENED.
WHY DON'T WE?
I LOVE MY WIFE.
SERIOUSLY, WHY DON'T WE WHAT?

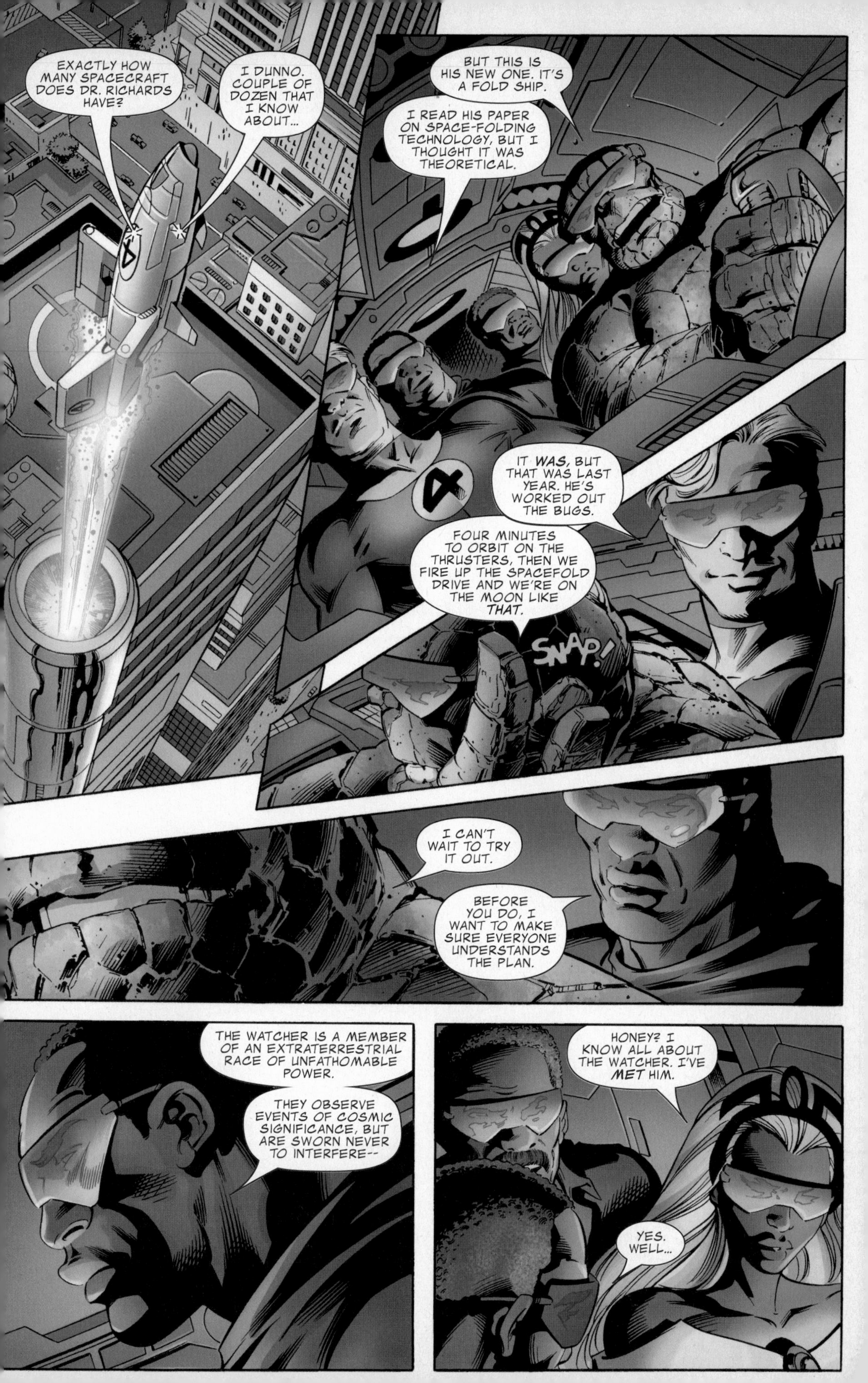
EXACTLY HOW MANY SPACECRAFT DOES DR. RICHARDS HAVE?
I DUNNO. COUPLE OF DOZEN THAT I KNOW ABOUT...
BUT THIS IS HIS NEW ONE. IT'S A FOLD SHIP.
I READ HIS PAPER ON SPACE-FOLDING TECHNOLOGY, BUT I THOUGHT IT WAS THEORETICAL.
IT WAS, BUT THAT WAS LAST YEAR. HE'S WORKED OUT THE BUGS.
FOUR MINUTES TO ORBIT ON THE THRUSTERS, THEN WE FIRE UP THE SPACEFOLD DRIVE AND WE'RE ON THE MOON LIKE THAT.
SNAP!
I CAN'T WAIT TO TRY IT OUT.
BEFORE YOU DO, I WANT TO MAKE SURE EVERYONE UNDERSTANDS THE PLAN.
THE WATCHER IS A MEMBER OF AN EXTRATERRESTRIAL RACE OF UNFATHOMABLE POWER.
THEY OBSERVE EVENTS OF COSMIC SIGNIFICANCE, BUT ARE SWORN NEVER TO INTERFERE--
HONEY? I KNOW ALL ABOUT THE WATCHER. I'VE MET HIM.
YES. WELL...

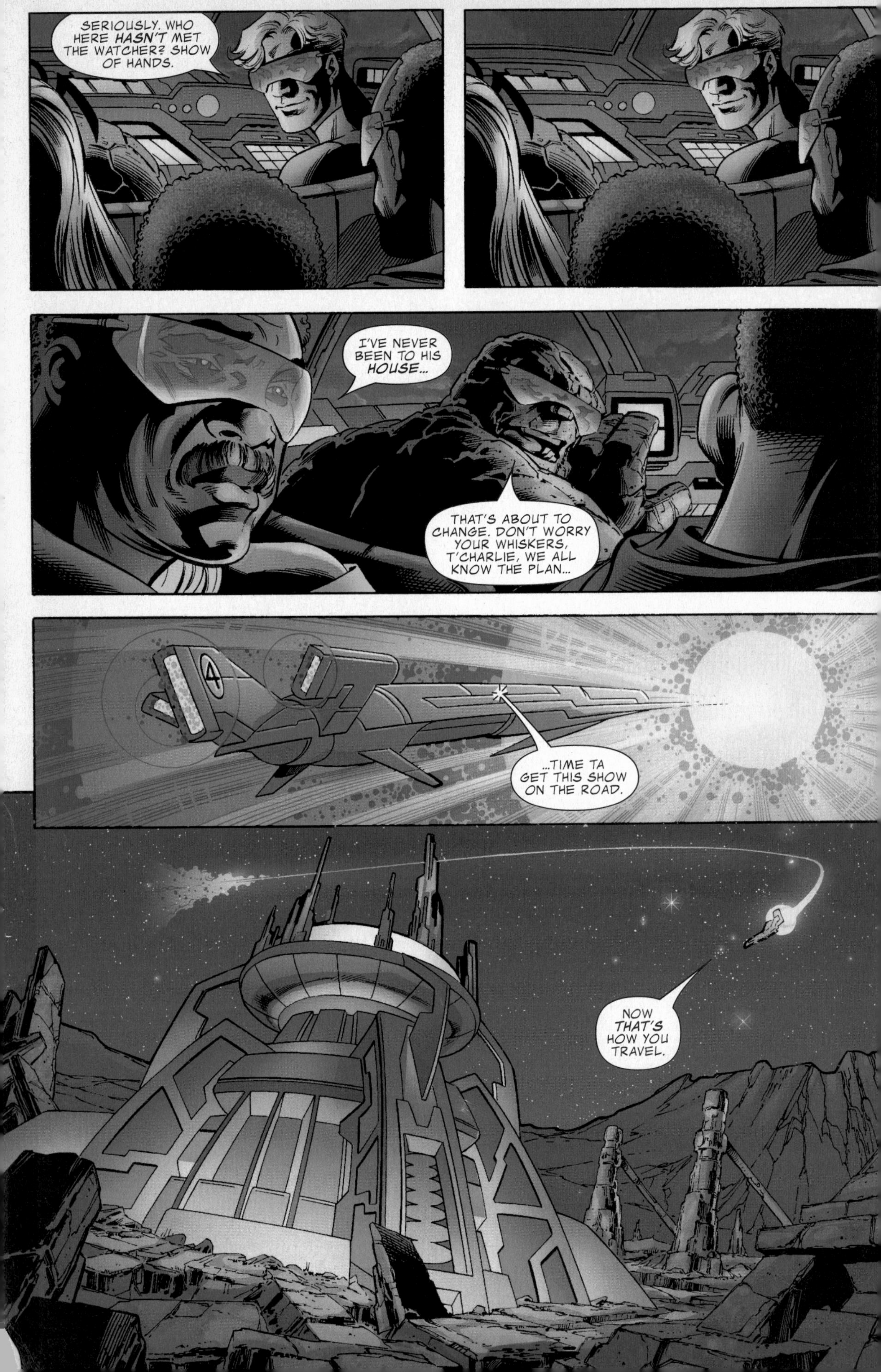

SERIOUSLY. WHO HERE HASN'T MET THE WATCHER? SHOW OF HANDS.
I'VE NEVER BEEN TO HIS HOUSE...
THAT'S ABOUT TO CHANGE. DON'T WORRY YOUR WHISKERS, T'CHARLIE, WE ALL KNOW THE PLAN...
...TIME TA GET THIS SHOW ON THE ROAD.
NOW THAT'S HOW YOU TRAVEL.

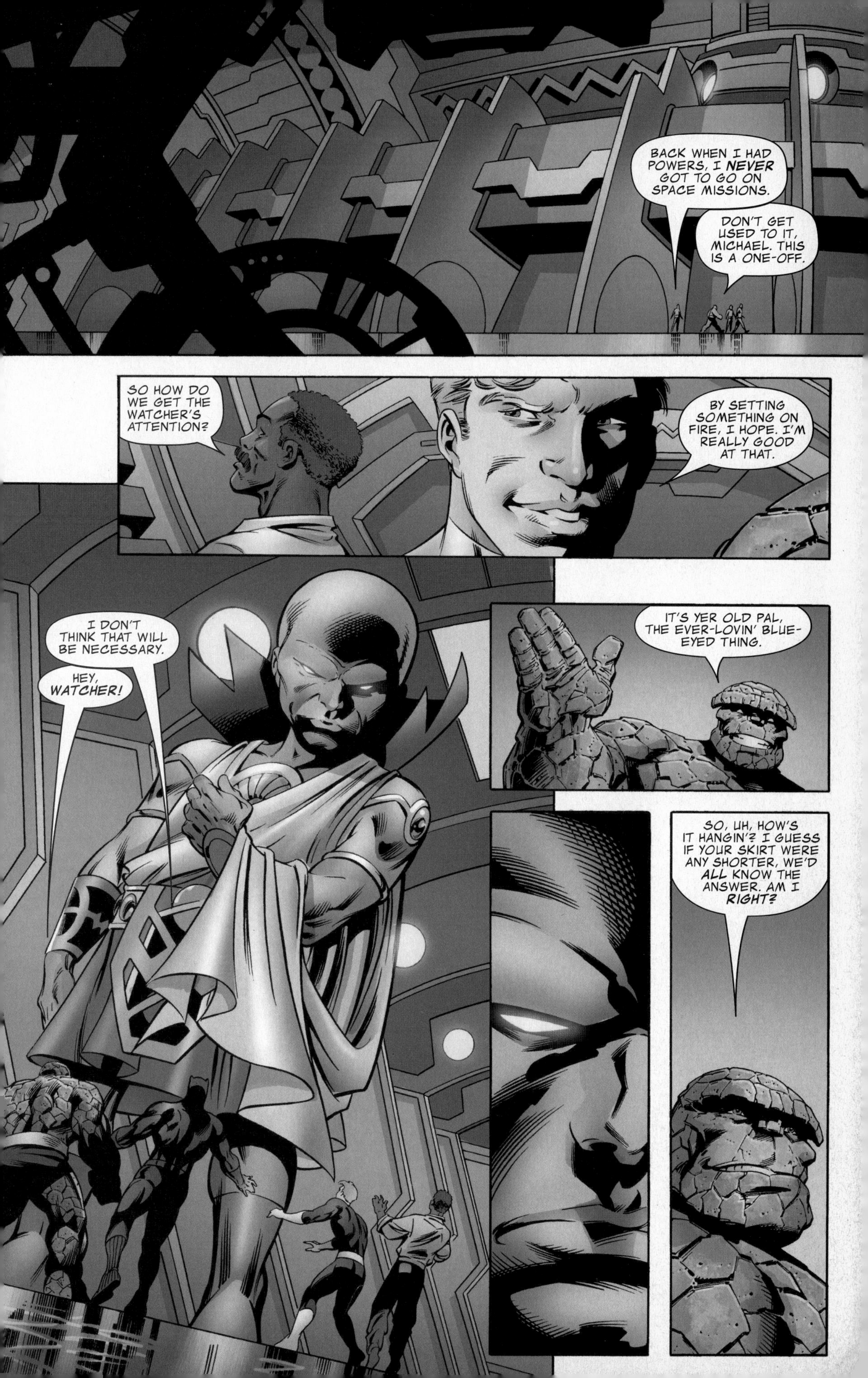
BACK WHEN I HAD POWERS, I NEVER GOT TO GO ON SPACE MISSIONS.
DON'T GET USED TO IT, MICHAEL. THIS IS A ONE-OFF.
SO HOW DO WE GET THE WATCHER'S ATTENTION?
BY SETTING SOMETHING ON FIRE, I HOPE. I'M REALLY GOOD AT THAT.
I DON'T THINK THAT WILL BE NECESSARY.
HEY, WATCHER!
IT'S YER OLD PAL, THE EVER-LOVIN' BLUE-EYED THING.
SO, UH, HOW'S IT HANGIN'? I GUESS IF YOUR SKIRT WERE ANY SHORTER, WE'D ALL KNOW THE ANSWER. AM I RIGHT?

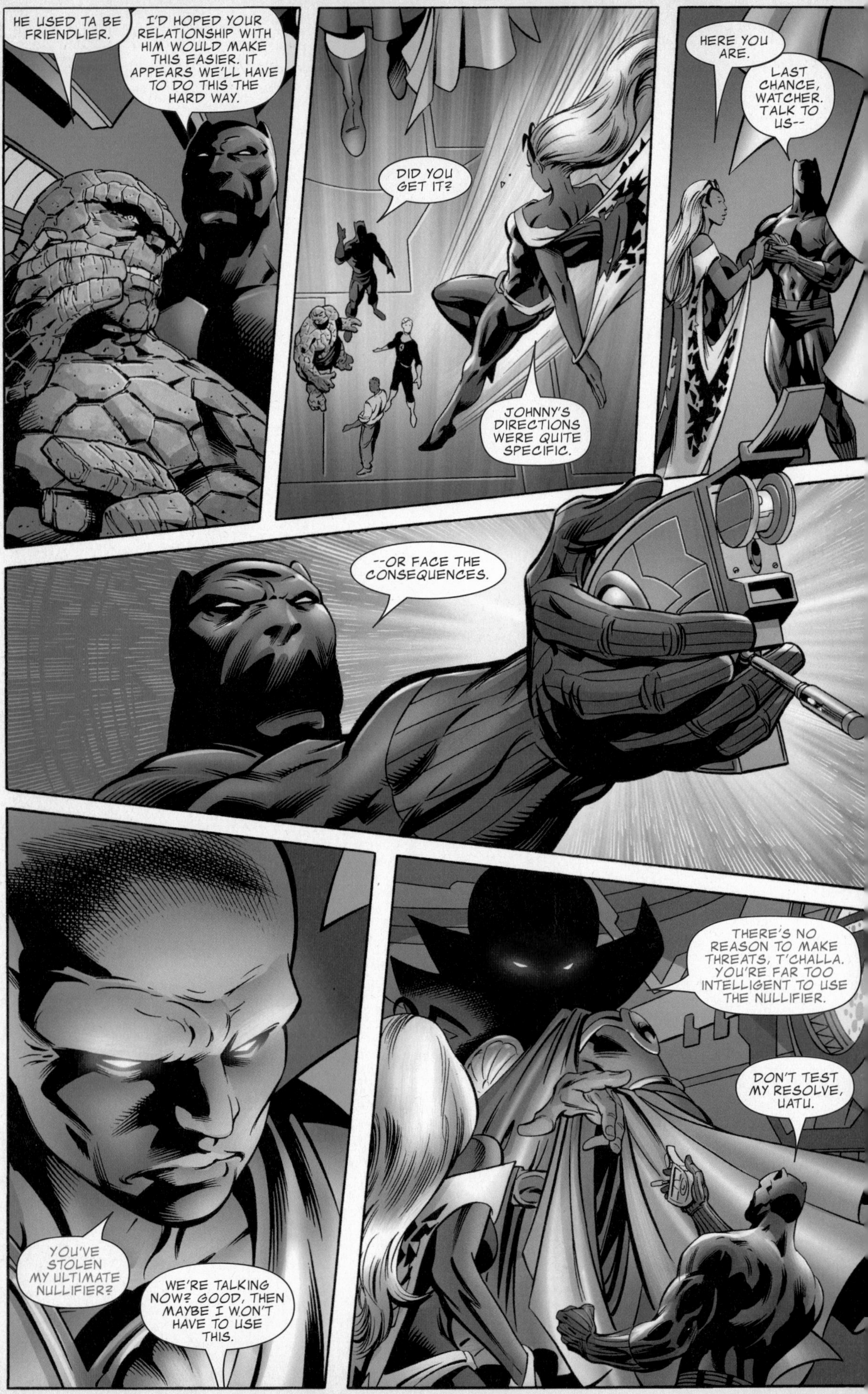
HE USED TA BE FRIENDLIER.
I'D HOPED YOUR RELATIONSHIP WITH HIM WOULD MAKE THIS EASIER. IT APPEARS WE'LL HAVE TO DO THIS THE HARD WAY.
DID YOU GET IT?
JOHNNY'S DIRECTIONS WERE QUITE SPECIFIC.
HERE YOU ARE.
LAST CHANCE, WATCHER. TALK TO US--
--OR FACE THE CONSEQUENCES.
YOU'VE STOLEN MY ULTIMATE NULLIFIER?
WE'RE TALKING NOW? GOOD, THEN MAYBE I WON'T HAVE TO USE THIS.
THERE'S NO REASON TO MAKE THREATS, T'CHALLA. YOU'RE FAR TOO INTELLIGENT TO USE THE NULLIFIER.
DON'T TEST MY RESOLVE, UATU.

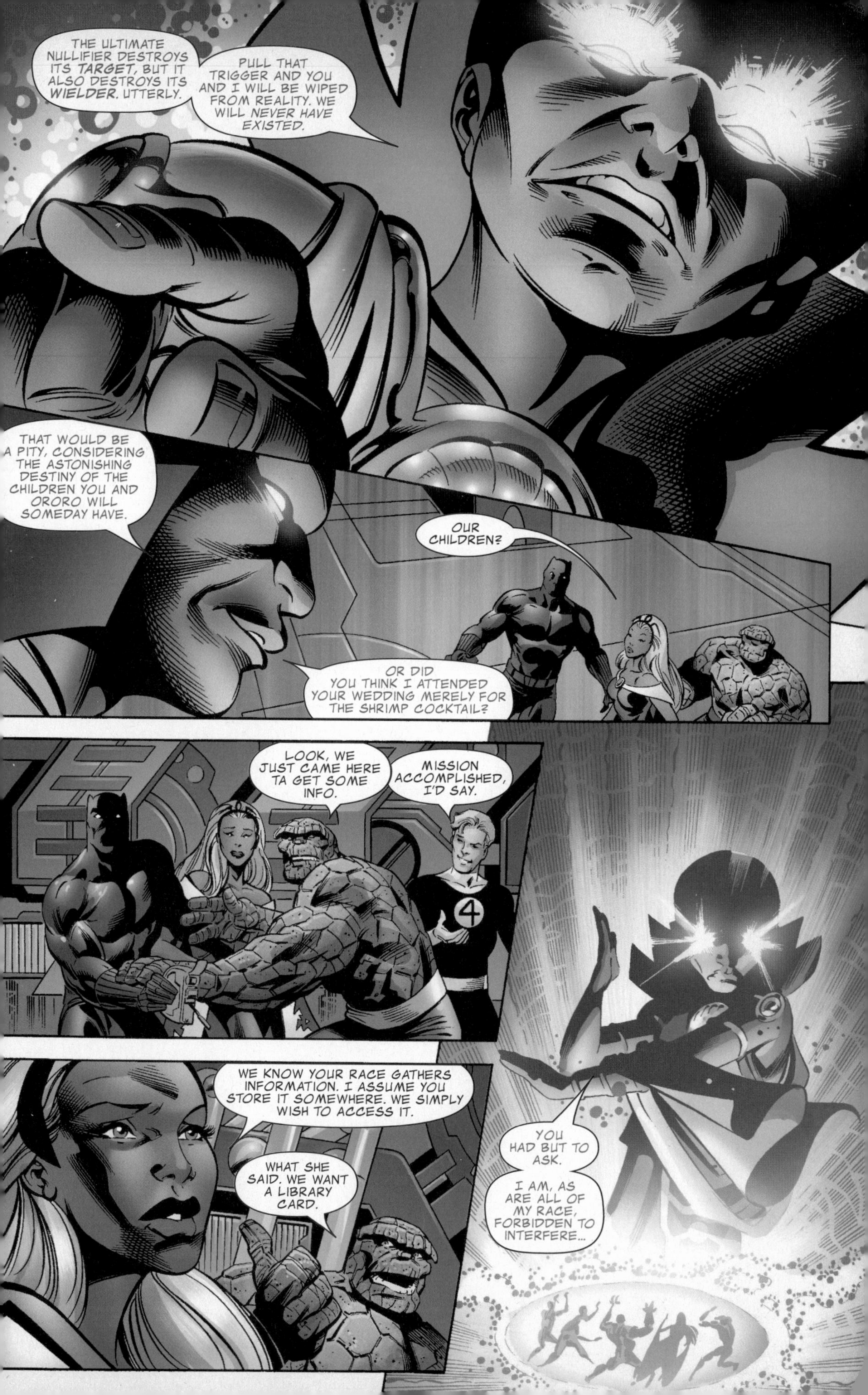
THE ULTIMATE NULLIFIER DESTROYS ITS TARGET, BUT IT ALSO DESTROYS ITS WIELDER. UTTERLY.
PULL THAT TRIGGER AND YOU AND I WILL BE WIPED FROM REALITY. WE WILL NEVER HAVE EXISTED.
THAT WOULD BE A PITY, CONSIDERING THE ASTONISHING DESTINY OF THE CHILDREN YOU AND ORORO WILL SOMEDAY HAVE.
OUR CHILDREN?
OR DID YOU THINK I ATTENDED YOUR WEDDING MERELY FOR THE SHRIMP COCKTAIL?
LOOK, WE JUST CAME HERE TA GET SOME INFO.
MISSION ACCOMPLISHED, I'D SAY.
WE KNOW YOUR RACE GATHERS INFORMATION. I ASSUME YOU STORE IT SOMEWHERE. WE SIMPLY WISH TO ACCESS IT.
WHAT SHE SAID. WE WANT A LIBRARY CARD.
YOU HAD BUT TO ASK.
I AM, AS ARE ALL OF MY RACE, FORBIDDEN TO INTERFERE...

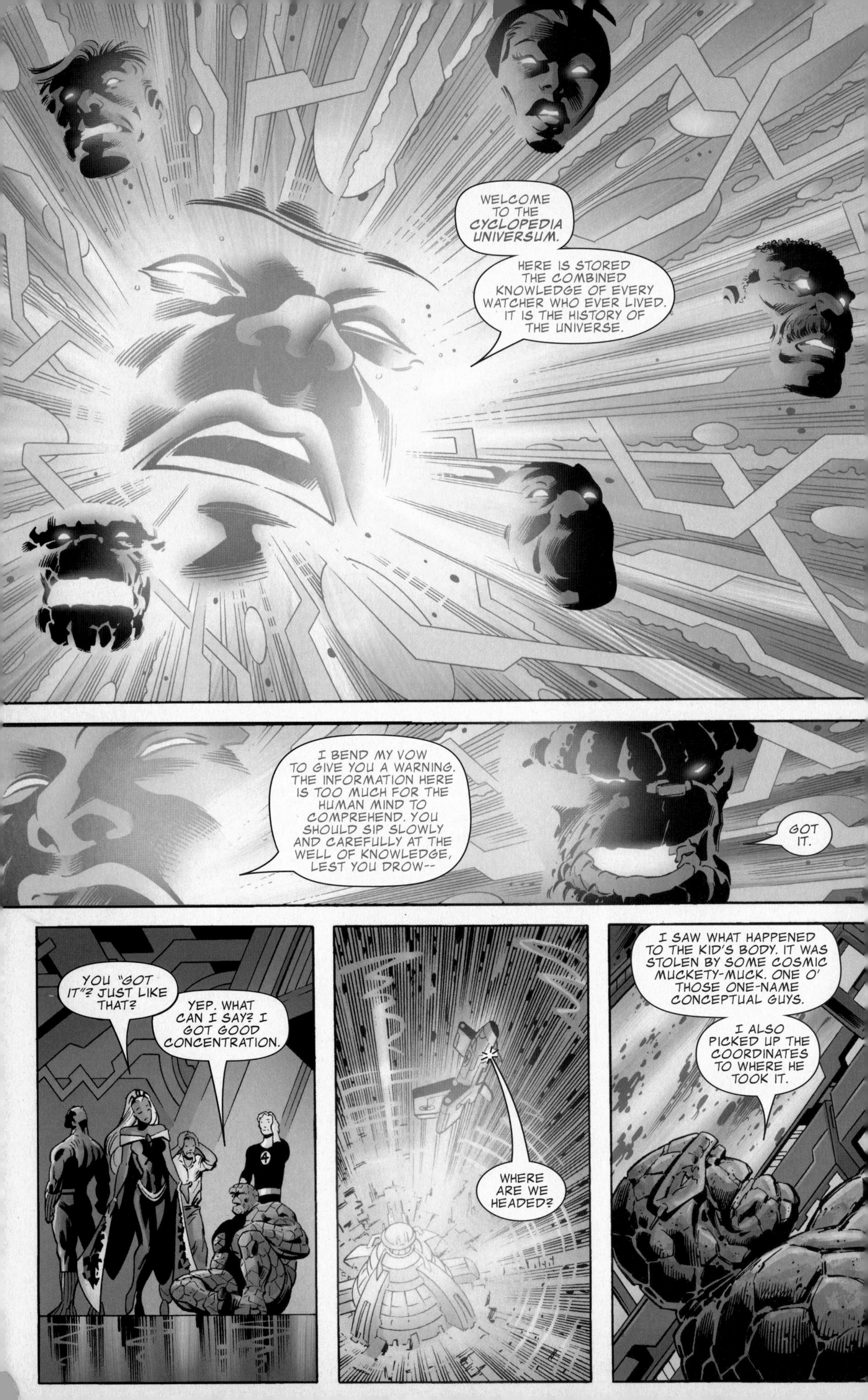
WELCOME TO THE CYCLOPEDIA UNIVERSUM.
HERE IS STORED THE COMBINED KNOWLEDGE OF EVERY WATCHER WHO EVER LIVED. IT IS THE HISTORY OF THE UNIVERSE.
I BEND MY VOW TO GIVE YOU A WARNING. THE INFORMATION HERE IS TOO MUCH FOR THE HUMAN MIND TO COMPREHEND. YOU SHOULD SIP SLOWLY AND CAREFULLY AT THE WELL OF KNOWLEDGE, LEST YOU DROW--
GOT IT.
YOU "GOT IT"? JUST LIKE THAT?
YEP. WHAT CAN I SAY? I GOT GOOD CONCENTRATION.
WHERE ARE WE HEADED?
I SAW WHAT HAPPENED TO THE KID'S BODY. IT WAS STOLEN BY SOME COSMIC MUCKETY-MUCK. ONE O' THOSE ONE-NAME CONCEPTUAL GUYS.
I ALSO PICKED UP THE COORDINATES TO WHERE HE TOOK IT.

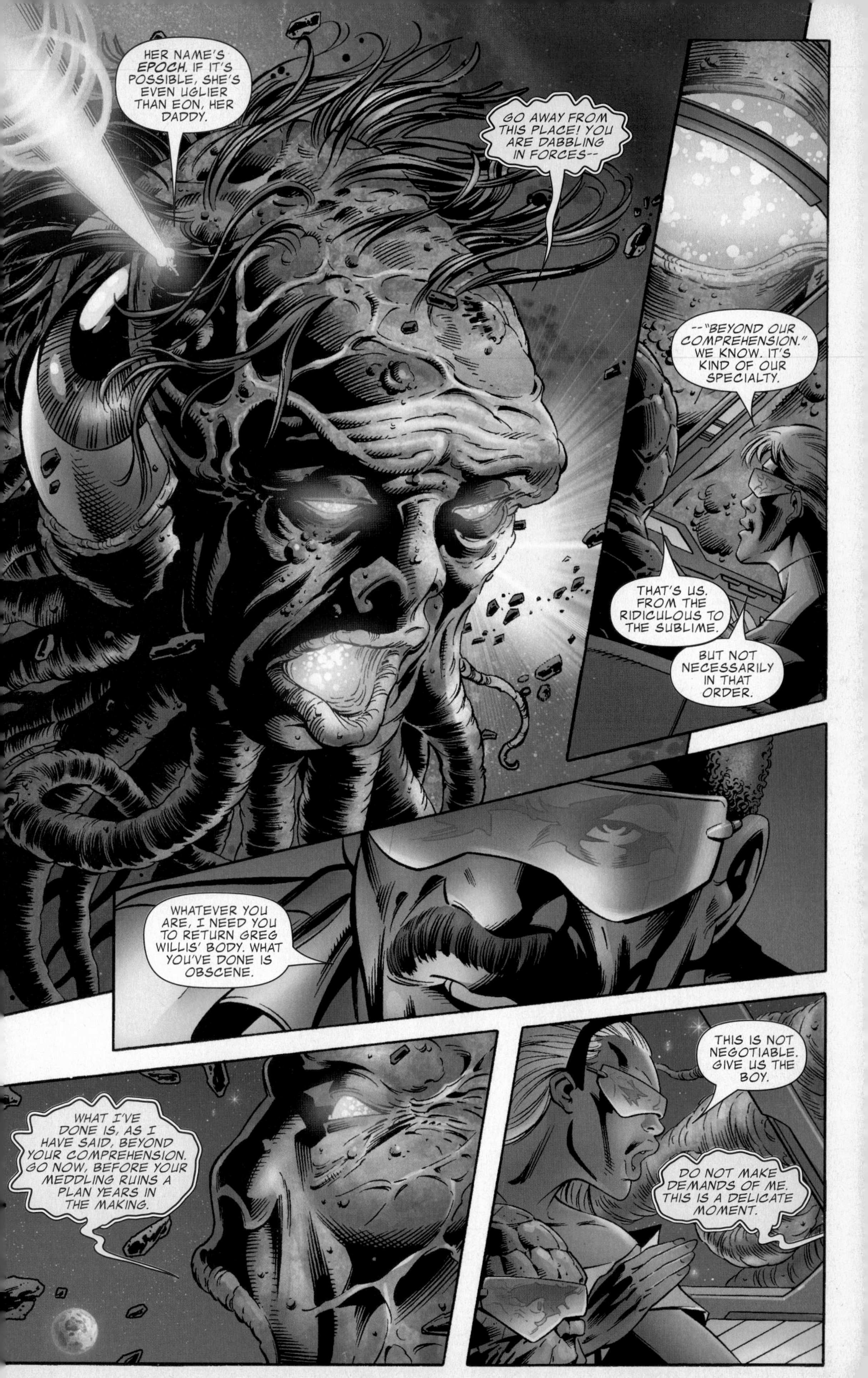
HER NAME'S EPOCH. IF IT'S POSSIBLE, SHE'S EVEN UGLIER THAN EON, HER DADDY.
GO AWAY FROM THIS PLACE! YOU ARE DABBLING IN FORCES--
--"BEYOND OUR COMPREHENSION." WE KNOW. IT'S KIND OF OUR SPECIALTY.
THAT'S US. FROM THE RIDICULOUS TO THE SUBLIME.
BUT NOT NECESSARILY IN THAT ORDER.
WHATEVER YOU ARE, I NEED YOU TO RETURN GREG WILLIS' BODY. WHAT YOU'VE DONE IS OBSCENE.
WHAT I'VE DONE IS, AS I HAVE SAID, BEYOND YOUR COMPREHENSION. GO NOW, BEFORE YOUR MEDDLING RUINS A PLAN YEARS IN THE MAKING.
THIS IS NOT NEGOTIABLE. GIVE US THE BOY.
DO NOT MAKE DEMANDS OF ME. THIS IS A DELICATE MOMENT.

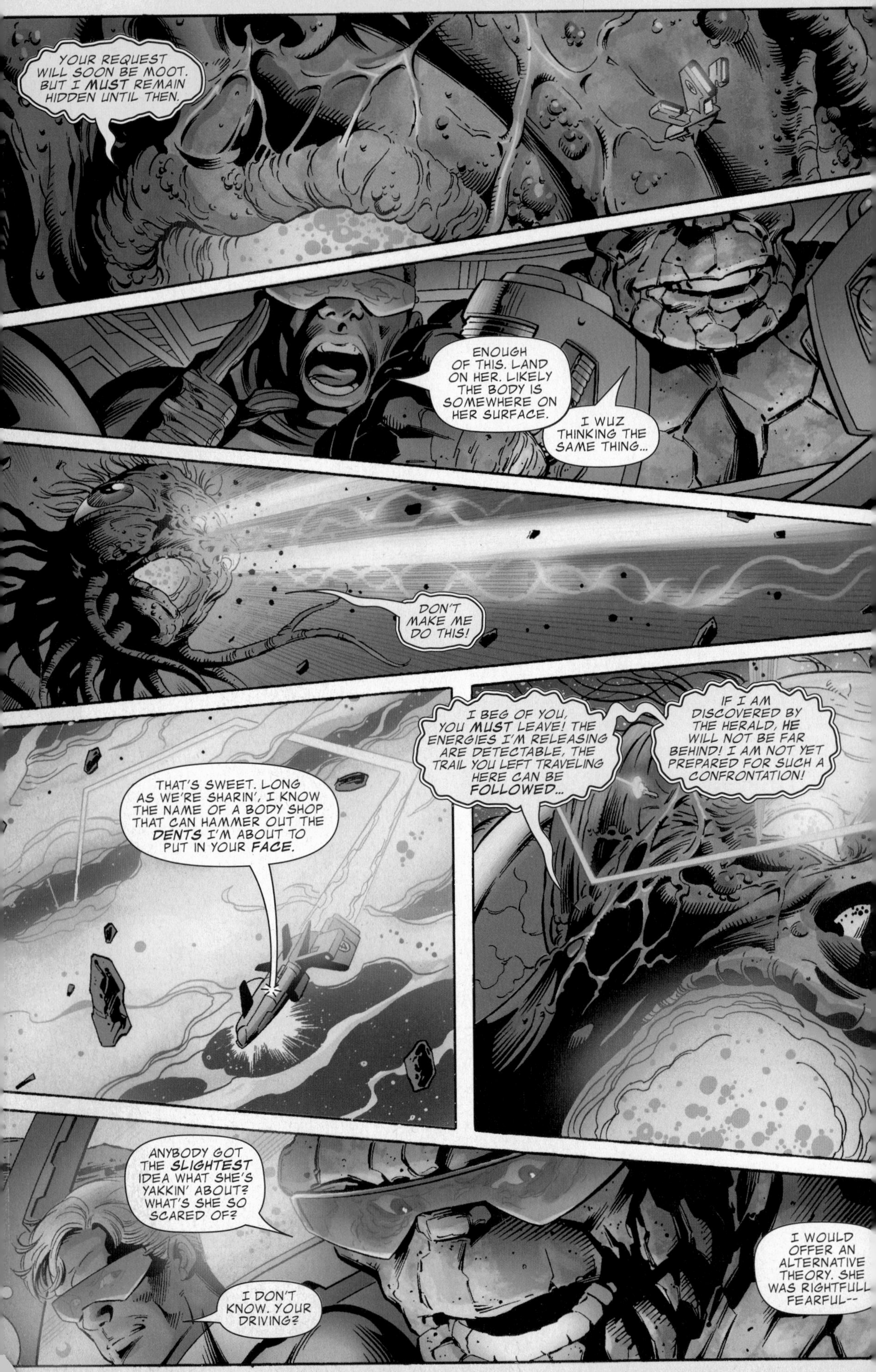
YOUR REQUEST WILL SOON BE MOOT. BUT I MUST REMAIN HIDDEN UNTIL THEN.
ENOUGH OF THIS. LAND ON HER. LIKELY THE BODY IS SOMEWHERE ON HER SURFACE.
I WUZ THINKING THE SAME THING...
DON'T MAKE ME DO THIS!
THAT'S SWEET. LONG AS WE'RE SHARIN', I KNOW THE NAME OF A BODY SHOP THAT CAN HAMMER OUT THE DENTS I'M ABOUT TO PUT IN YOUR FACE.
I BEG OF YOU, YOU MUST LEAVE! THE ENERGIES I'M RELEASING ARE DETECTABLE, THE TRAIL YOU LEFT TRAVELING HERE CAN BE FOLLOWED...
IF I AM DISCOVERED BY THE HERALD, HE WILL NOT BE FAR BEHIND! I AM NOT YET PREPARED FOR SUCH A CONFRONTATION!
ANYBODY GOT THE SLIGHTEST IDEA WHAT SHE'S YAKKIN' ABOUT? WHAT'S SHE SO SCARED OF?
I DON'T KNOW. YOUR DRIVING?
I WOULD OFFER AN ALTERNATIVE THEORY. SHE WAS RIGHTFULL FEARFUL--

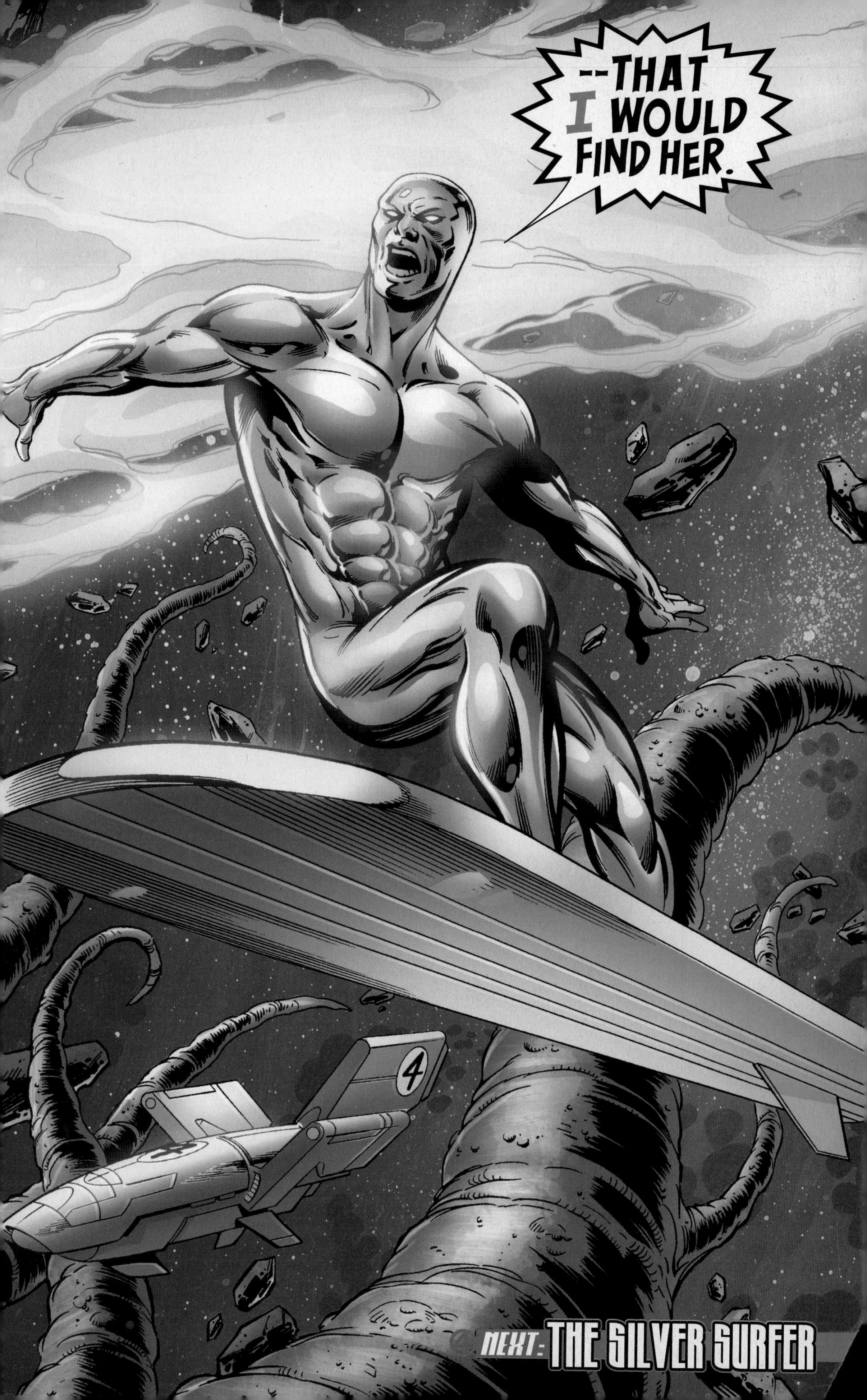
--THAT I WOULD FIND HER.
NEXT: THE SILVER SURFER

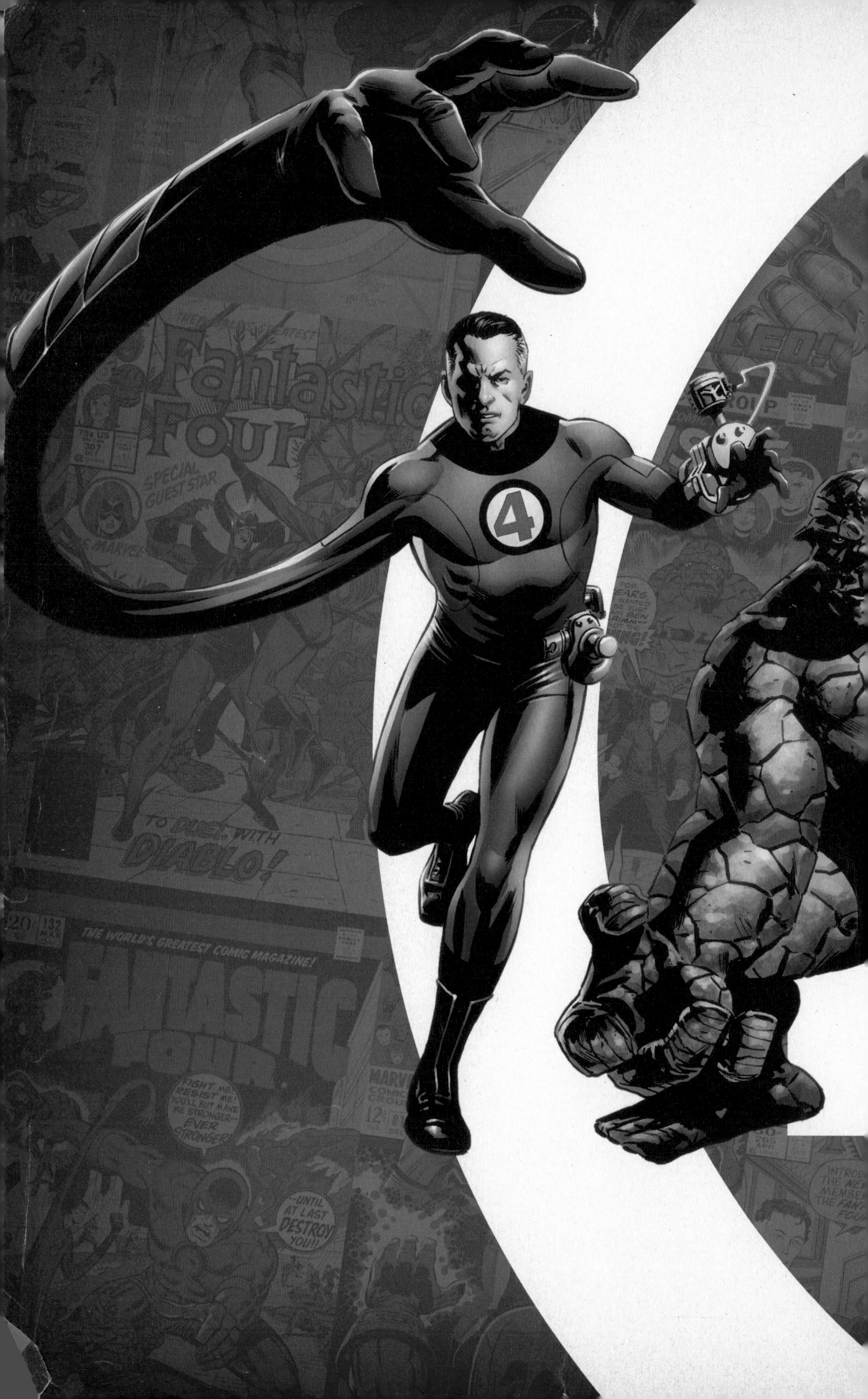

Fantastic Four
SPECIAL GUEST STAR
TO DUEL WITH DIABLO!
THE WORLD'S GREATEST COMIC MAGAZINE!
FIGHT ME! RESIST ME! YOU'LL BUT MAKE ME STRONGER— EVER STRONGER!
—UNTIL AT LAST DESTROY YOU!!

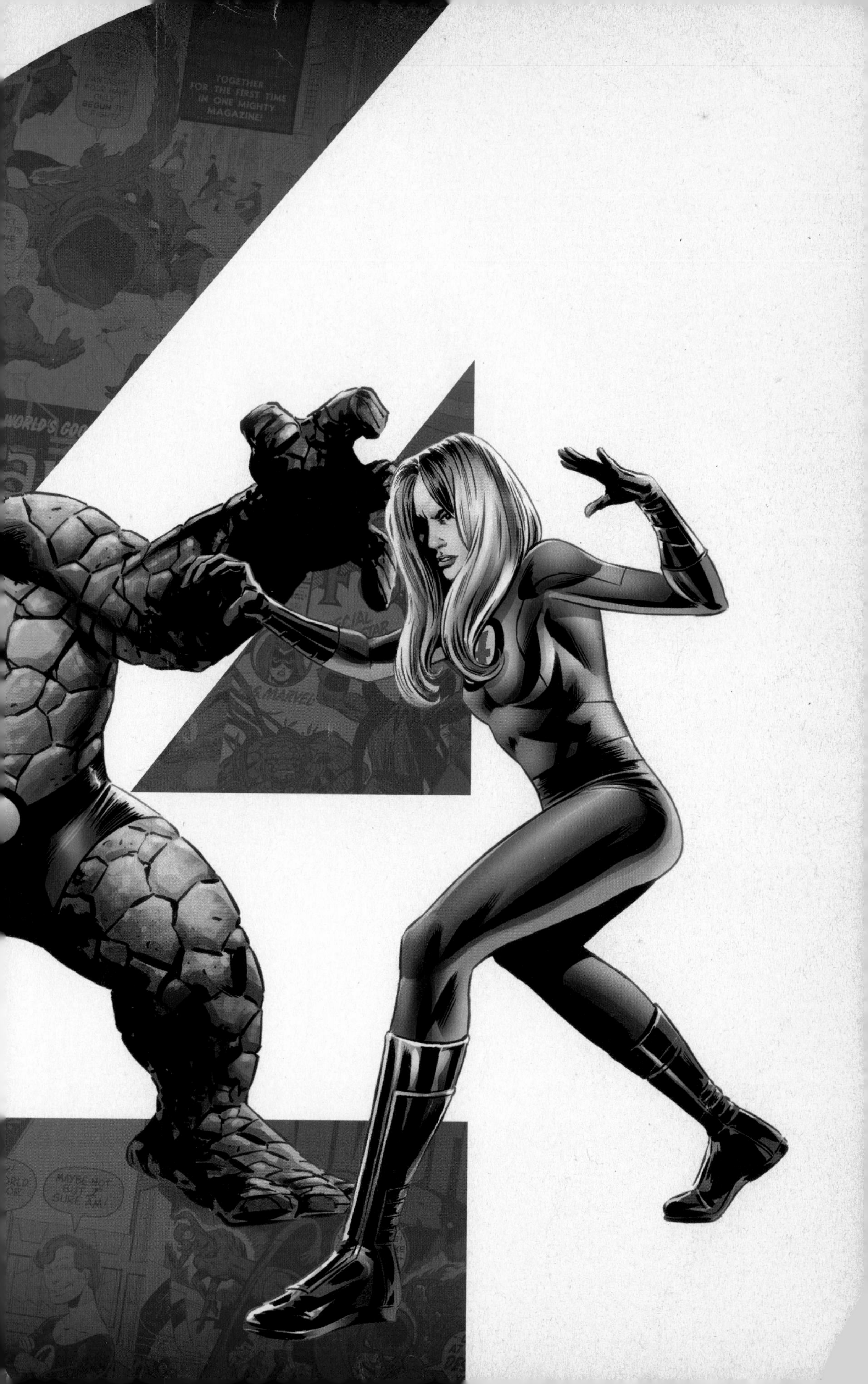
TOGETHER FOR THE FIRST TIME IN ONE MIGHTY MAGAZINE!
WORLD'S GOO
MS. MARVEL
MAYBE NOT-- BUT I SURE AM!

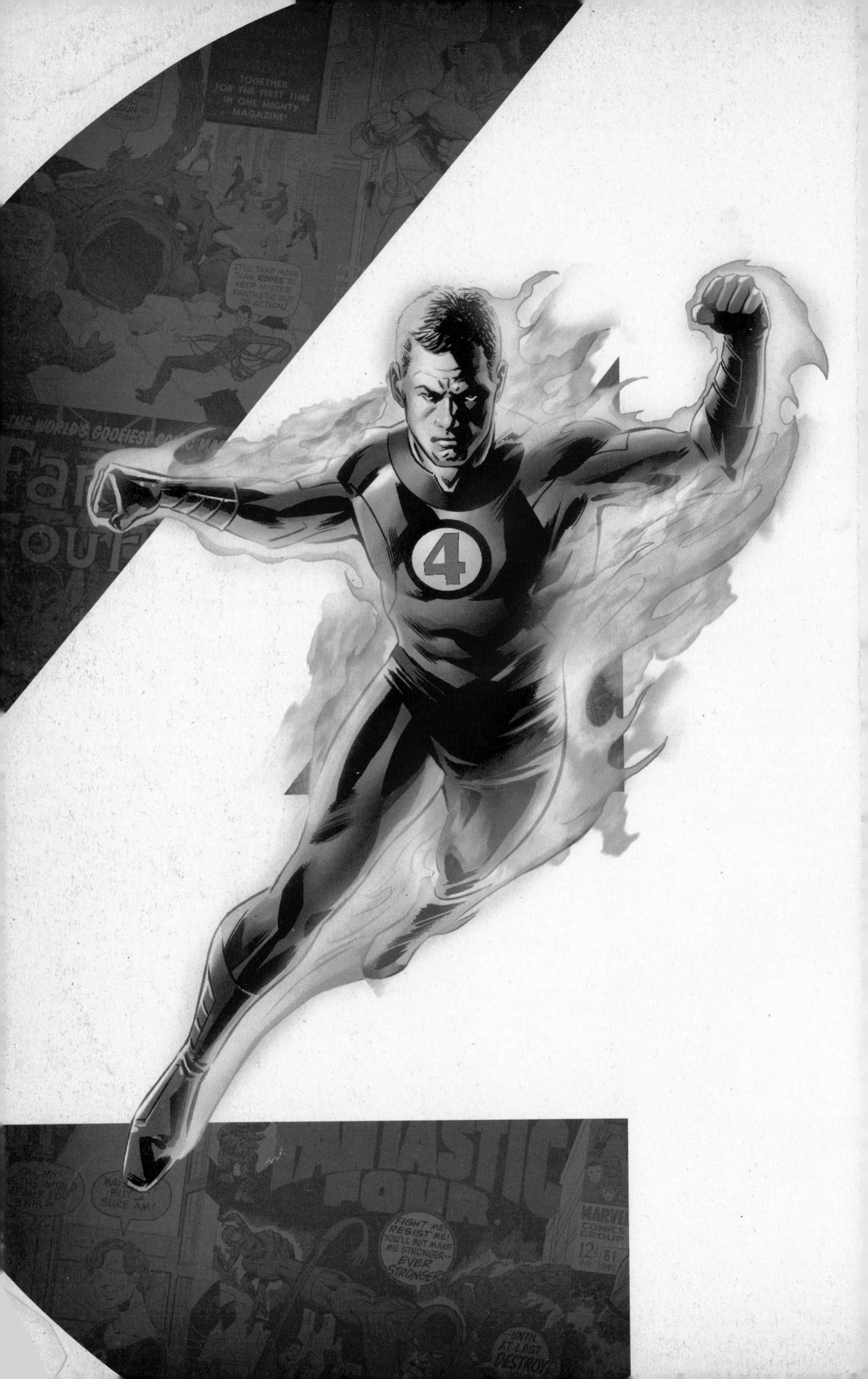
TOGETHER FOR THE FIRST TIME IN ONE MIGHTY MAGAZINE!
IT'LL TAKE MORE THAN ROPES TO KEEP MISTER FANTASTIC OUT OF ACTION!
FOUR
FIGHT ME! RESIST ME! YOU'LL BUT MAKE ME STRONGER-- EVER STRONGER!
MARVEL COMICS GROUP
12¢
--UNTIL AT LAST DESTROY